Westward Dharma

Westward Dharma

Buddhism beyond Asia

Edited by
CHARLES S. PREBISH
MARTIN BAUMANN

UNIVERSITY OF CALIFORNIA PRESS
Berkeley   Los Angeles   London

University of California Press
Berkeley and Los Angeles, California

University of California Press, Ltd.
London, England

Chapter 1 is a revised version of "Night-Stand Buddhists and Other
Creatures," chapter 5 of *American Buddhism,* edited by Duncan Ryūken
Williams and Christopher S. Queen, published by Curzon Press in 1999.

Chapter 21 was adapted from portions of the introduction and chapter 3
of Christopher S. Queen's *Engaged Buddhism in the West.* © Christopher S. Queen 2000. Reprinted with permission of Wisdom Publications, 199 Elm Street, Somerville, MA 02144, U.S.A.

Library of Congress Cataloging-in-Publication Data

    Westward Dharma : Buddhism beyond Asia / edited by Charles S.
Prebish, Martin Baumann.
    p.   cm.
    Includes bibliographical references and index.
    ISBN 0-520-22625-9 (Cloth : alk. paper) —
    ISBN 0-520-23490-1 (Paper : alk. paper)
    1. Buddhism—Missions—History.   2. Buddhism—20th
century—History.   3. Globalization—Religious aspects—
Buddhism.   I. Prebish, Charles S.   II. Baumann, Martin, 1960–

BQ5925 .W47   2002
294.3'09—dc21   2002000717

Manufactured in the United States of America
10 09 08 07 06 05 04 03 02
10 9 8 7 6 5 4 3 2 1

*In loving memory of Rick Fields, whose keen insight,
incredible wit, trailblazing spirit, and delightful prose
encouraged us in wonderful ways.*

*It is his work that nurtured all future studies of
Western Buddhism.*

Contents

Tables

Introduction

Paying Homage to the Buddha
in the West

Martin Baumann and Charles S. Prebish

At the turn of the new millennium, Buddhism undoubtedly has become heard, visible, and experienced in numerous countries outside of Asia. The last decade of the twentieth century saw an unparalleled interest, and at times enthusiasm, for things Buddhist. The media discovered Buddhism as trendy, cool, and exotic, and seemed to have a predilection for related stories about actors and actresses, artists, and high-profile figures, as well as prominent Buddhist leaders, such as the Dalai Lama, Thich Nhat Hanh, and Sulak Sivaraksa. Buddhist groups, centers, and institutions mushroomed across the globe in an unprecedented way. In addition, the decade of the 1990s witnessed an explosion of academic studies researching Buddhism in North and South America, Europe, Australia, and South Africa. However, a concise overview surveying and analyzing the various histories associated with these new and dramatic developments is lacking. We thought it important to bring together leading scholars in this emerging field to provide an overview and evaluation of the rapidly expanding phenomenon of "Buddha in the West."

The first time we met was at the book display of the University of California Press at the annual meeting of the American Academy of Religion, held in Orlando, Florida, in 1998. Although this was our first face-to-face meeting, we had exchanged numerous letters and e-mails for many years. The occasion for this meeting was our participation in a panel entitled "American Buddhism at the Millennium," on which we were joined by Richard Seager, Kenneth Tanaka, Christopher Queen, and Duncan Ryūken Williams. That panel attracted more than 150 attendees, the largest audience for any panel devoted to Buddhism at that year's meeting. Similar results from professional society meetings in Canada and Europe could also be cited. Buoyed by the enthusiasm and exciting questions from the audience, we felt our interests and perspectives made a good match both to fill the research gap and to overcome the apparent continental centrism or parochialism in studying Buddhism outside of Asia. One of us concentrates

1

on "Western Buddhism" (especially in North America) and the other focuses on past and present developments of Buddhism in Europe. We began to hatch a plan to invite the world's foremost scholars of Western Buddhism to contribute to the volume that was rapidly taking shape in our collective imagination. Initial letters of invitation were sent out in July 1999, and we held a second round of face-to-face discussions at the International Association of Buddhist Studies congress in Lausanne in August 1999, this time also including Michelle Spuler, Douglas Padgett, Ajahn Tiradhammo, Lionel Obadia, and Michel Clasquin. By the 1999 annual meeting of the American Academy of Religion, the table of contents was firmly in place, and within a year the volume had become a reality.

BUDDHISM'S WESTERN PRESENCE IN HISTORICAL PERSPECTIVE

In many respects, Buddhism's spread to regions beyond the Asian landmass is historically new. Of particular interest is *how* the teachings and practices of Buddhism found new homes in foreign lands. At the risk of being overly general, a marked feature of the spread of Buddhism in Asia seems to have been its top-down introduction. Kings and rulers adopted Buddhism, invited monks, and established Buddhism as the state religion. The state support of Buddhist monasteries and their residents further centralized power and at the same time introduced a culture that was often valued as superior to the native variety.

As a striking counterexample, however, the informed reader will think of China in the first centuries of the common era. In the first and second centuries, Buddhist monks and scholars were *not* invited and *not* welcomed. Rather, the educated ruling Han elite devalued Buddhist teachings as foreign, and even barbarous, constituting a threat to the ideal of a harmonious political and social order. The monastic way of life seemed incompatible with Chinese ideals of filial piety, this-worldly pragmatism, and the importance of productive work. Certainly the newly emergent Mahāyāna Buddhism with its ideal of the bodhisattva (who could be a lay Buddhist, active in this world) and the evolving blend of Confucian, Daoist, and Buddhist elements soften the critique. Nevertheless, Buddhism remained in a risky state during most of its first half-millennium on Chinese soil.

Compared to the histories of Buddhism's spread, acculturation, and indigenization in the variety of Asian countries, what is new and different about Buddhism in the West? Only a few points can be listed here. The contributors to this volume elaborate on more specific characteristics.

Strikingly, Buddhism has not been established as state religion in any Western country, and nowhere has it experienced the lavish patronage it enjoyed at times in South, Southeast, East, and Central/Inner Asia. Buddhist teachings and practices have not been introduced from the top down, but commenced their diffusion from below, often championed by economically disadvantaged people. Buddhism has spread, and is spreading, as a ferment in the various Western societies. Initial results of this "Awakening of the West," as the British writer Stephen Batchelor titled his important narrative of the encounter of Buddhism and Western culture,[1] are recognizable in the arts, in steadily increasing number of converts and Buddhist institutions, and in the growing recognition of Buddhist groups as participants and partners in the multi-religious composition of Western societies.

Furthermore, Buddhism in Asia reached the so-called ordinary people, the masses, by the absorption of and blending with local cultural features and ritual practices. The diffusion of Buddhist teachings and worldviews to the nonelite, lower strata of society developed through *practice* . . . by way of ritual and performance. It was through its abundant use of folk-religious, shamanic aspects and practices that Buddhism gained a lasting grounding and impact in the larger segment of society. Michael Ames has called this religion of the masses—practices allowed to flourish beneath the official doctrines as exercised in the monasteries and by the virtuosi— the "magical animism . . . solely concerned with well-being in this life."[2] The Western diffusion generally lacks this trajectory of magical or shamanic practices. Most Western Buddhists, with the important exception of Asian Buddhist immigrants, have not engaged in this folk-religious or popular Buddhist aspect. Rather, they praise Buddhism as rational and scientific, grounded on reason and individual experience. No matter how disenchanted and rationalized Western converts might understand and interpret Buddhism, just as in Asia, the dissemination of Buddhist concepts to a broader clientele took place when the practical and this-worldly elements (called the "integration of Buddhism") became emphasized. Although the performance of magical or shamanic rituals may not have been involved, the practice-based features of meditation and liturgy seem to have enabled Buddhism's rapidly increasing diffusion since the 1960s.

Whereas we note here both similarities and differences, we would like to highlight three further characteristics. First, in Asia it generally took many centuries before acculturated, regionalized forms of Buddhism evolved. Thus, indigenous forms of Chinese Buddhist traditions—such as Chinese Pure Land, T'ien-t'ai, Ch'an—evolved no sooner than the Sui and T'ang Dynasties (589–906).

In Japan, it took approximately five hundred years for indigenous schools to develop (in the Kamakura Period). In the West, attempts to create adapted, regionalized forms of Buddhism seem to occur at a much faster pace. During the last three or four decades, in only Buddhism's second century of Western presence, Western Buddhists have proposed vigorous endeavors to form a so-called Western, European, or American Buddhism. Whatever premature or mature state these new shapes have already taken, the proclamation of innovative, non-Asian, derived forms mirrors the self-consciousness and ambitious attempts of Western Buddhists. It is no risk to forecast that, in the twenty-first century, independent, Western forms and schools of Buddhism will develop and prosper on a much larger scale.

Second, the development of Western Buddhist forms is a recent phenomenon. In addition, these new schools and lineages pluralize the spectrum of Buddhist schools and traditions present in Western countries. This plurality and diversity constitutes a marked characteristic of Buddhism in the West. In Asia, a country usually embraces one *yāna* or major tradition, be it Theravāda in South and Southeast Asia, Mahāyāna in China and East Asia, or Vajrayāna in Central and Inner Asia. In the West, however, all these different *yānas* have appeared in *one* country or region, perhaps even in one city, say, Los Angeles, London, Berlin, or Sydney. Traditions previously separated by thousands of miles in Asia have become neighbors in the West. The process of getting to know each other has started. And it seems that cooperation and mutual recognition flow with more ease in Western than Eastern settings. Some Western Buddhists have been quick to speak of a Buddhist *ecumenicism,* a term borrowed from mainly Protestant Christian movements of the twentieth century. In fact, in the days of the term's Christian adoption and use by the early Church Fathers, the Greek notion of *oikouménê* denoted the entire region populated by people to which the gospel of Jesus was to be spread. In a related aspect, the ecumenical movements, councils, and alliances of the nineteenth and twentieth centuries aimed to unite the by-then intensely fragmented Christianity in order to more successfully spread the gospel through shared belief and organizational cooperation. In this respect, the now-global presence of Buddhism, and awareness of common ground despite apparent doctrinal and practice-related heterogeneity, seems to perfectly justify the term's adoption. Emphasis is placed on a unity within the varieties of Buddhism, and endeavors to spread the teachings (as in the Christian case) are generally played down.

Third, the past and present spread of Buddhism to Western regions enables researchers to scrupulously investigate the progress of diffusion; the processes of settlement and growth; and the strategies utilized to adapt to new, socio-culturally foreign contexts. We are now able to rely on a variety of sources and to apply different methodological approaches when we scrutinize the lives of individual Buddhists in Western countries, or when we follow the details of institutionalization, fragmentation, or the dissolution of a specific Buddhist group or school.[3] In contrast, research on Buddhism's spread to new regions and cultures in Asia—at least a millennium ago—often simply lacks this type of detailed information. The Asian material is usually fragmentary, incomplete, and led by specific interests and polemics. At times, it is simply coincidental or even accidental. A detailed account of how Buddhist traditions and their proponents gained a footing in a new, religiously different culture in Asia can often only be sketched for periods ranging from several decades to centuries. In recent years, researchers have examined Buddhist institutions and developments in Western contexts from the perspectives of ethnography and of the sociology of religion.[4] This type of analysis is extremely difficult, if not impossible, to apply to Buddhism's spread through Asia. The long-standing, textual orientation of Buddhist Studies has prevented many scholars from using methods other than philology. Gregory Schopen has called this bias a Protestant presupposition, a methodological narrowing that has been enlarged during the past two decades.[5]

THE WEST AND GLOBALIZATION

Throughout this volume, the reader repeatedly will find the expression "Buddhism in the West." We would like to clarify at the outset that we certainly do not perceive "the West" as a homogeneous whole with similar socio-political, cultural, and legal settings in the countries considered. Quite the contrary. Instead, the chapters in this volume underscore the differences and the apparent heterogeneity. Also, at times it might appear that the contributors or the editors understand the sum of geographic regions outside of Asia collectively as "the West." We do not; such an approach would fall victim to the criticism and insights of Edward W. Said's *Orientalism*,[6] transferred here to "the Occident." Rather, in a pragmatic view— or as some contributors called it, in "a reasonably accurate way"—the notion of *the West* denotes non-Asian industrialized nation states where Buddhist teachings, practices, people, and ideas have become established. In this book, *the West* can be taken as an abbreviation for Canada; the United States of America; Brazil; the various states of Europe; Israel; South Africa; Australia; and New Zealand. It is in these non-Asian countries that we have a strong and sufficient knowledge of Buddhist activities past and present.

Here we can rely on responsible research and resources, and therefore are able to sketch the specific histories and narratives of Buddhism. Although brief accounts exist of Buddhists and Buddhist activities in, for example, Mexico, Peru, the Caribbean, and Ghana, the available data so far is too scarce and occasional. We hope that additional regional histories will be available in the near future, as Buddhism continues to spread and as academic research keeps extending its scope of interest.

Viewed from an Asian perspective, Buddhist people, ideas, and practices have traveled in both directions: to the West and the East. In the nineteenth century, workers from Japan or China came to South and North America. In the second half of the twentieth century, emigrants and refugees from Korea, Hong Kong, and Southeast Asia headed for Canada and the United States.

In the period of globalization, distances appear to be measured only by the amount of jet lag encountered. Numerous scholars, including historian of religion Ninian Smart, have spoken of the "Global Period of world history,"[7] which commenced with the 1960s. Transcontinental travel and the spread of Buddhist concepts, texts, and teachers had occurred a century earlier. However, tremendously improved modes of transportation now enable an intensity of communication previously unknown. Aided by postmodern technology, especially telecommunications and the internet, formerly distant regions have become virtual neighbors. In this global period, the maintenance of close links between the (mainly) Asian home country and the "overseas" centers of a Buddhist tradition takes place with a historically unprecedented scope and speed. Up to now, however, scholars researching Buddhist traditions and organizations have only rarely applied theories of globalization and transnationalism to the worldwide spread of Buddhism. In this introduction, we shall provide only one hint of this important analytical perspective.[8]

An obvious feature of globalization is the geographic spread of Buddhist ideas, practices, and people to new, non-Asian places. This spread continues, with other traditions coming from Asian countries to the West, as witnessed by recently founded orders from Taiwan and Thailand (such as the Fo Kuang Shan order and the Dhammakaya Foundation, respectively). During the last two decades, this diffusion process has been augmented as newly emergent Western Buddhist organizations gain a foothold on a global scale (e.g., the British-founded Friends of the Western Buddhist Order, or the Diamond Sangha, founded by Robert Aitken).

This descriptive level deserves a closer look. The globalization of Buddhism does not refer only to a spread from the center to the periphery, that is, from Asia to Western countries. It also encompasses the emergence of new centers, with regionalized Buddhist interpretations and practices. The creation of consciously labeled Western Buddhist forms is a development within this overall process. In other words, Buddhism spreading globally encounters "local transformation."[9] The global becomes particularized and socio-culturally particular.[10] As a consequence, globalization involves a dissolving of the Asian center(s) as the main or only agent of authority and the emergence of a variety of authority centers. We hold that with the end of the twentieth century we have entered a period in which the globalization of Buddhism has truly begun, because a multi- or polycentric form is emerging, step by step. Buddhist networks and organizations have become comfortable operating on a global scale. Centers of Buddhist authority and legitimacy can be found in Eastern and Western, as well as Southern and Northern, regions of the globe. The study of the impact of globalization and the emergence of "new voices" within the generalized Buddhist tradition deserves further attention and detailed research. In this volume, the contributors can only break some of this ground and provide important snapshots and material related to the ongoing globalization and the "Westernization" of Buddhism.

THE STRUCTURE AND ORGANIZATION OF THE VOLUME

This book is divided into five parts.

Part One, Profiling Global Buddhism: A Description of the Landscape, starts with an outline of the phenomenon under discussion. Thomas A. Tweed scrutinizes "Who Is a Buddhist?" and explores a variety of categories, including individuals who self-identify as Buddhists, "sympathizers," not-just-Buddhists, lukewarm-Buddhists, Dharma-hoppers, and night-stand Buddhists. He amply demonstrates that religious identity in Western Buddhism is a hybrid issue, and one that has perhaps not been satisfactorily resolved. B. Alan Wallace provides an informed portrayal of the spectrum of Buddhist practices, illustrating the wide variety of devotional and meditational forms. His chapter spans the Theravāda, Mahāyāna, and Vajrayāna traditions, as well as their sectarian permutations in South, Southeast, East, and Inner/Central Asia. Martin Baumann suggests a new analytical perspective with which to understand Buddhism in the West via the strands of traditional and modern Buddhism. He looks not only at Western countries but also at past patterns in Asian Buddhism, seeking to learn how religious changes have served as prerequisites for a second and then a third trajectory of transmission. Charles S. Prebish demonstrates how the issues raised in the first three chapters combine with many of the specific applications described in the following chapters to form the basis of a new subdiscipline within the overall discipline of Buddhist Studies. His conclusion is based on data collected from surveys, individual testimonies, and a survey of published literature on the topic.

Part Two, Diffusion: The Histories of Buddhism in Western Countries, concentrates on the histories of Buddhism's diffusion to the West. How did Buddhism come to the various countries outside of Asia, and what dominant shapes are observable in those countries? The chapters portray the past and present of Buddhism in Europe (Martin Baumann), the United States (Richard Hughes Seager), Canada (Bruce Matthews), Australia and New Zealand (Michelle Spuler), South Africa (Michel Clasquin), Brazil (Frank Usarski), and Israel (Lionel Obadia). Each chapter in this section has been prepared by a scholar with an outstanding publication record in the area of inquiry. The encompassing overview of this section underscores both the new global nature of Buddhism and the emergence of regionally formed Buddhist configurations.

From birdseye views, we move to more closely focused considerations in Part Three, Change: Adaptations and Innovations. The contributors concentrate on the adaptation, change, and innovation of Buddhism as it spread and settled in Western countries. Duncan Ryūken Williams amplifies his stirring paper from the 1998 annual meeting of the American Academy of Religion, demonstrating the effect of the internment of Japanese-Americans during World War II on the accelerated Americanization of Shin Buddhism in the United States. Also looking at Asian immigrants in the United States, Douglas M. Padgett examines the Thai Buddhist temple of Tampa (Florida), providing both rich ethnographic description and an insightful application of diaspora theory. Shifting attention from Asian-American Buddhists to sympathizers toward and converts to Buddhism, the next two chapters concentrate on Zen in the West and on scandals in Western Buddhist communities, respectively. David L. McMahan outlines how Zen became "repackaged" for the West, and describes the shape it currently takes in the United States. He demonstrates how Zen in the West has matured in innovative ways since its initial repackaging. He looks at its concern for social engagement, rethinking of authority issues, and emphasis on the role of women, as well as the recognition of American Zen as a primarily lay tradition. Sandra Bell then discusses scandals in Western Buddhism, providing two case studies—at Shambhala International and the San Francisco Zen Center—where teachers left the Buddhist path.

Certainly, as the contributors themselves indirectly suggest, many additional chapters could have been included in this section on adaptations and innovations. The informed reader will think of specific organizations and orders that have gained momentum and popularity in the West. Among these is the *vipassanā* tradition, especially as evidenced by the Insight Meditation Society and by the Friends of the Western Buddhist Order (FWBO), founded in London in the late 1960s. However, two practical reasons suggest *not* having separate chapters on these and other specifically Western orders: (1) the book's already significant length, and (2) recently published accounts of these new Western Buddhist communities, which would have created obvious redundancies.[11]

Part Four, Lifestyle: Being a Buddhist in Western Societies, focuses on the issue of living a Buddhist life in a Western society. Ajahn Tiradhammo, a Canadian-born Buddhist monk in the Thai tradition, presents a selected discussion of the many challenges a Theravāda monk faces in the West, gleaned from his own rich experience living in a variety of Western Buddhist monastic communities. Karma Lekshe Tsomo, an American-born Buddhist nun and a leading figure in Sakyadhita, an international organization of Buddhist women, provides the corollary chapter on Buddhist nuns and their challenges of living in the West.

Yet however important and influential the community of ordained men and women has been in spreading and developing Buddhism in the West, a characteristic of Buddhism outside of Asia has been its heavy reliance and emphasis on non-ordained, lay teachers. Sylvia Wetzel portrays the function and importance of these teachers, and especially of female teachers. She coins for them the name of *full-time practitioners*.

Collectively, these three chapters cogently assess the wholeheartedly committed Buddhist life, as composed by a number of its most visible and articulate proponents on the world stage. The final chapter in this part deals with ethics and moral behavior. With a penetrating perspective, Gil Fronsdal, a well-known *vipassanā* teacher, takes stock of the incorporation of ethics in the Insight Meditation Society, and also provides a provocative insider's look at the history of the movement.

The final section, Part Five, Buddhism Facing New Challenges, examines selected facets of how Buddhism is meeting new challenges in the West. Judith Simmer-Brown gives an overview of women and of women's Dharma in the West. She focuses on women in ethnic Asian communities, Western Buddhist women living in communities (as opposed to practicing individually), and women who have made significant contributions to the development of Western Buddhism. She speculates about the potential to retrieve the roots of the women's tradition in Buddhism. No scholar has been more instrumental in theorizing about and investigating socially engaged Buddhism than Christopher S. Queen. His contribution sketches the current status and development of engaged Buddhism as it has taken shape in Western contexts. Here, for the first time, he includes several exciting accounts of engaged Buddhist practitioners. The encounter of Buddhism and psychology, a topic of particular prominence and interest in North America, is analyzed in a pointed way by Franz Aubrey Metcalf. Metcalf focuses on the increasing mutual influence of Buddhism and Western psychology, and concludes by calling attention to the role that scholars play in this process. Finally, Ian Harris has taken on the task of tracing the mutual influence of Buddhism and the arts in the West, delineating, in his colorful portrayal, periods of faddish fascination, engagement and understanding, or involvement of Western (Buddhist) artists. He demonstrates how Westerners have become involved in almost all aspects of traditional Buddhist forms of creativity, and have gained a more informed understanding of the function of the arts in these contexts.

Again, several other topics and challenges come to mind which deserve a place in this volume. Originally, chapters on Buddhism and the internet and Buddhism as idealized religion were planned. However, practical reasons dictated their omission, and the reader is referred to recently published studies on these topics.[12] The most painful decision for the editors of this volume is the elimination of a complete bibliography on Buddhism in the West. We quickly realized that a thorough bibliography would have been much longer than the volume's longest chapter. Positively turned, this underscores the rapid development of studies of Buddhism in the West. We thus decided to include only a selected bibliography. Both *The Faces of Buddhism in America* (1998) and *Luminous Passage* (1999) have extensive bibliographies on Buddhism in the West,[13] and we have tried to minimize overlap with those volumes. Further, the internet has proved to be both a workable and a practical bibliographical resource. We now have access to online bibliographies for Buddhism in Australia (by Michelle Spuler), in Brazil (by Cristina Moreira Rocha), and in Europe and North America (both by Martin Baumann).[14] We hope the reader will augment this book's traditional, printed bibliography with the online bibliographical work presented in the *Journal of Buddhist Ethics* and the *Journal of Global Buddhism*, each of which can be easily accessed.[15] We hope that this pragmatic and innovative solution compensates for the smaller bibliography and at the same time aligns the prospering study of Buddhism in the West with current technological developments.

Far more people contributed to this volume than can possibly be acknowledged in a short space. Frank Korom, Kenneth Kraft, and Paul Numrich provided valuable input from the very beginning of—and continuing throughout—the entire project. In addition, we are deeply indebted to dozens of Buddhist practitioners and teachers throughout the world who responded to our many questions, offering wise counsel and insightful suggestions. Many Buddhist communities in North and South America, Europe, Australia, and New Zealand compassionately opened their facilities to the researchers involved in this project. Special Buddhist events, such as the twentieth anniversary celebration of Zen Mountain Monastery in Mount Tremper, New York, in June 2000, also provided the occasion for furious brainstorming, involving at various stages Richard Seager, Christopher Queen, Charles Prebish, Robert Thurman, John Daido Loori Rōshi, and even Helen Tworkov (the editor of *Tricycle*). Finally, the editors express their profound thanks to Reed Malcolm of the University of California Press. He brought to this project generous helpings of editorial insight, scholarly acumen, noble encouragement, and stern advice without ever losing his focus or his sense of humor. His contribution far exceeds what one might expect from a traditional editor, and we deeply appreciate his very personal involvement in the entire project.

NOTES

1. Stephen Batchelor, *The Awakening of the West: The Encounter of Buddhism and Western Culture* (Berkeley: Parallax Press, 1994).

2. Michael Ames, "Ideological and Social Change in Ceylon," *Human Organization* 22 (1963), 46.

3. For example, we are thinking of the approximately 130 life portrayals of early German Buddhists painstakingly collected by Hellmuth Hecker, published as *Lebensbilder deutscher Buddhisten: ein bio-bibliographisches Handbuch*, 2nd ed., 2 vols. (Konstanz: University of Konstanz, 1996, 1997). These biographies have been analyzed in sociological context by Martin Baumann, *Deutsche Buddhisten: Geschichte und Gemeinschaften*, 2nd ed. (Marburg, Germany: Diagonal-Verlag, 1995), 233–43. Also, see the detailed research by Thomas A. Tweed, *The American Encounter with Buddhism, 1844–1912: Victorian Culture and the Limits of Dissent* (Bloomington: Indiana University Press, 1992).

4. For example, see Bryan Wilson and Karel Dobbelaere, *A Time to Chant: The Sōka Gakkai Buddhists in Britain* (Oxford: Clarendon Press, 1994); Paul David Numrich, *Old Wisdom in the New World: Americanization in Two Immigrant Theravada Buddhist Temples* (Knoxville: University of Tennessee Press, 1996); and Helen Waterhouse, *Buddhism in Bath: Adaptation and Authority* (Leeds, U.K.: Community Religions Project, University of Leeds, 1997).

5. See Gregory Schopen, "Archaeology and Protestant Presuppositions in the Study of Indian Buddhism," *History of Religions* 31, no. 1 (1991), 19*ff*. Today, quite a number of studies that use philological *and* other methods can be referred

to, among them certainly Schopen's *Bones, Stones, and Buddhist Monks: Collected Papers on the Archaeology, Epigraphy, and Texts of Monastic Buddhism in India* (Honololu: University of Hawaii Press, 1997). Another polymethodological approach to studying Buddhism is presented by Jeffrey F. Hamburger, *Nuns as Artists: The Visual Culture of a Medieval Convent* (Berkeley: University of California Press, 1997).

6. Edward W. Said, *Orientalism: Western Conceptions of the Orient* (London: Routledge and Kegan Paul, 1978).

7. Ninian Smart, "The Importance of Diasporas," in *Gilgut,* edited by S. Shaked, D. Shulman, and G. G. Stroumsa (Leiden: Brill, 1987), 291.

8. For globalization theory, see especially Roland Robertson, *Globalisation: Social Theory and Global Culture* (London: Sage, 1992); Peter Beyer, *Religion and Globalization* (London: Sage, 1994); and Arjun Appadurai, *Modernity at Large: Cultural Dimensions of Globalization* (Minneapolis: University of Minnesota Press, 1996). For transnationalism theory, see Nancy Foner, "What's New about Transnationalism? New York Immigrants Today and at the Turn of the Century," *Diaspora* 6, no. 3 (1997), 355–75, and the issue of *Ethnic and Racial Studies* 22, 2 (1999).

9. Anthony Giddens, *The Consequences of Modernity* (Stanford, California: Stanford University Press, 1990), 64.

10. Roland Robertson, "Globalization, Modernization, and Postmodernization: The Ambigious Position of Religion," in *Religion and Global Order,* edited by Roland Robertson and William R. Garrett (New York: Paragon House, 1991), 283.

11. For the Insight Meditation Society, see Gil Fronsdal, "Insight Meditation in the United States: Life, Liberty, and the Pursuit of Happiness," in *The Faces of Buddhism in America,* edited by Charles S. Prebish and Kenneth K. Tanaka (Berkeley: University of California Press, 1998), 163–80; Charles S. Prebish, *Luminous Passage: The Practice and Study of Buddhism in America* (Berkeley: University of California Press, 1999), 148–58; Richard Hughes Seager, *Buddhism in America* (New York: Columbia University Press, 1999), 146–51. For the FWBO, see Batchelor, *The Awakening of the West,* 323–40; Sandra Bell, "Change and Identity in the Friends of the Western Buddhist Order," *Scottish Journal of Religious Studies* 17, no. 1 (1996), 87–107; and Martin Baumann, "Work as Dharma Practice: Right Livelihood Cooperatives of the FWBO," in *Engaged Buddhism in the West,* edited by Christopher S. Queen (Boston: Wisdom, 2000), 372–93. Also, mention should be made of the by-now mainly German-based order, Arya Maitreya Mandala, founded as early as 1933 by the famous Lama Govinda; see Baumann, *Deutsche Buddhisten,* 146–64, and Martin Baumann, "Buddhism in the West: Phases, Orders and the Creation of an Integrative Buddhism," *Internationales Asienforum* 27, 3–4 (1996), 345–62.

12. On Buddhism and the internet or new technologies, see Prebish, *Luminous Passage,* 203–32, and Richard P. Hayes, "The Internet as Window onto American Buddhism," in *American Buddhism: Methods and Findings in Recent Scholarship,* edited by Duncan Ryūken Williams and Christopher S. Queen (Richmond, U.K.: Curzon Press, 1999), 168–79. For Buddhism as idealized religion, exemplified by the prominent case of Tibet and Tibetan Buddhism, see Peter Bishop, *Dreams of Power: Tibetan Buddhism and the Western Imagination* (London: Athlone Press, 1993); Thierry Dodin and Heinz Räther (eds.), *Mythos Tibet: Wahrnehmungen, Projektionen, Phantasien* (Cologne: Du Mont, 1997); Donald S. Lopez, Jr., *Prisoners of Shangri-La: Tibetan Buddhism and the West* (Chicago: University of Chicago Press, 1998); and Martin Brauen, *Traumwelt Tibet: Westliche Trugbilder* (Bern: Haupt, 2000).

13. See Prebish and Tanaka, *The Faces of Buddhism in America*, 343–47, and Prebish, *Luminous Passage*, 301–10.

14. See Michelle Spuler, "Buddhism in Australia: A Bibliography" (2001), http://www.spuler.org/ms/biblio.htm [8 Dec. 2001]; Cristina Moreira Rocha, "Buddhism in Brazil: A Bibliography" (2000), http://sites.uol.com.br/cmrocha/[8 Dec. 2001]; Martin Baumann, "Buddhism in Europe: An Annotated Bibliography" (2001), http://www.rewi.uni-hannover.de/for4.htm [1 Feb. 2002]; and Martin Baumann, "American Buddhism: A Bibliography on Buddhist Traditions and Schools in the U.S.A. and Canada" (1999), http://www.uni-bremen.de/~religion/baumann/bib-ambu.htm [1 Feb. 2002]. For bibliographical resources compiled with regard to Buddhism in South Africa, consult Michel Clasquin and Jacobus Krüger (eds.), *Buddhism and Africa* (Pretoria: University of South Africa, 1999), 125–30.

15. See the Scholarly Resources section of the *Journal of Buddhist Ethics*, http://jbe.la.psu.edu [1 Feb. 2002], and the Resources section of the *Journal of Global Buddhism*, http://jgb.la.psu.edu [22 Jan. 2002]. Each of these journals will continue to publish online bibliographies as they become available.

I

PROFILING GLOBAL BUDDHISM
A Description of the Landscape

1 Who Is a Buddhist?

Night-Stand Buddhists and Other Creatures

Thomas A. Tweed

An American Catholic bishop once confided to me with dismay that the Vietnamese who attend mass in his archdiocese are "not really Catholic." Initially I was perplexed by this claim. Did he mean that they had not been baptized in their homeland? Something else? "They're still too Buddhist," he explained. He meant that the Buddhist influence was great among Vietnamese Catholics and that they carried that hybrid tradition with them to the United States when they fled after the fall of Saigon in 1975. I thought of that conversation as I read a newspaper article that called attention to hundreds of thousands of Americans who practice Buddhist meditation but do not affiliate with any Buddhist temple or center. What do these examples—Vietnamese Catholics and Buddhist meditators—have in common? They raise central questions in the study of religion. How do we define religious identity? (Who is Catholic? Who is Buddhist?) And how do we view those who have interest in a religion but do not affiliate? In this essay, I focus on the issue of religious identity as it confronts scholars who investigate the history of Buddhism in the West, especially the United States. First, I propose a strategy for establishing religious identity. Second, I suggest that we add another category—*sympathizer*—to those we use to interpret religious life.[1]

ADHERENTS: COMPLICATING RELIGIOUS IDENTITY

Even though many monographs have described peoples with creole practices that have changed in interaction with other traditions—as in the religious histories of Cuba and Haiti, Thailand and China—most Western scholars of religion still have assumed that religious identity is singular and fixed, and that the subjects of studies fall into two categories: adherents and non-adherents. Further, identifying adherents seems straightforward. An adherent can be defined as one who accepts certain defining beliefs and practices, a strategy I call an *essentialist* or *normative approach*. For others, an adherent is one who joins a religious organization or participates in its ritual life. But these three standard strategies for defining religious identity—applying norms, counting members, or observing attendance—introduce conceptual confusions and overlook important characters. The normative approach might suggest, for example, that a Buddhist is one who has formally taken refuge in the Three Jewels (the Dharma, the Buddha, and the Sangha), practiced prescribed rituals at a Buddhist temple (chanting), or affirmed defining beliefs (the Four Noble Truths). But this constructs an essentialized notion of the tradition, imagining the religion as static, isolated, and unified. It fails to acknowledge that traditions change, that they have contacts and exchanges with other traditions, and that hybrid traditions with diverse expressions emerge and claim authenticity. Any normative definition of a religion, therefore, excludes many who might want to count themselves as followers. The other two strategies for establishing religious identity—membership and attendance—invite fewer conceptual difficulties, because they do not imagine a defining core, but they fail to account for those who have little or no relation with a Buddhist institution yet still understand the world in Buddhist terms, engage in Buddhist practices, or (at least) view themselves as Buddhists. In short, the usual ways of deciding who is Buddhist—or Christian, Hindu, or Muslim—fail to take seriously enough the complexity of religious identity.[2]

And, as some studies have shown, religious identity can be complex in several ways. First, as in Japan, religions can be functionally compartmentalized: you might be married in one tradition (Shinto) and memorialized in another (Buddhism). Second, especially in diverse cultural contexts where religious identity does *not* carry harsh political or economic consequences, some religious women and men self-consciously and unapologetically draw on varied practices from multiple traditions. In some periods and regions in China, for instance, men and women have turned to Buddhist bodhisattvas, Confucian sages, and Taoist immortals—along with a host of other human or suprahuman exemplars who have emerged from vernacular religious traditions. In seventeenth-century America, many Massachusetts Puritans combined occult practices, like astrology, with their Protestant piety, just as some who attended Spiritualist séances in the 1850s identified themselves as Episcopalians. Today, some who turn to the healing powers of crystals during the weekday sing hymns at a United Methodist Church on Sunday.[3]

Third, even in cultural contexts where admitting that you incorporate practices or beliefs from multiple traditions can get you sanctioned by religious leaders, relegated to menial labor, or sentenced to prison, religious identity can be multiple or ambivalent. There can be *ism*-crossing—a combining in practice of more than one tradition (often less self-conscious), as in the influence of Santería on Cuban Catholicism or the impact of Shinto on Japanese Buddhism. In fact, these sorts of religious combinations are so common that if we ignore those who affiliate with hybrid traditions, engage in creole practices, or express ambivalent identities, there would be no one left to study. Most of the religions I know emerged in contact and exchange with other traditions, and they continued to change over time—always in interaction. Scholars cannot locate a pristine beginning or pre-contact essence to use as a norm to define orthodoxy or orthopraxis. There is hybridity all the way down. In this sense, religious identity is usually complex. Ambivalence is the norm.[4]

Finally, religious identity also can be complex for converts. Conversion involves a more or less (often less) complete shift of beliefs and practices. The old tradition never fades completely; the new one never shapes exclusively. This was true of Christian converts in colonial Africa, Asia, and North and South America, where indigenous practices colored the religious life of many native "converts." It remains true of self-identified Buddhist converts in modern industrialized nations with legislated religious freedom. Conversion also has its social costs and payments, and these affect the character of religious belief and practice. In some colonized nations in nineteenth-century Africa, for example, conversion to Christianity could slightly raise one's social status. On the other hand, in nineteenth-century Britain, conversion to Vedānta Hinduism might prompt derision. In periods and places where conversion has high social *value*, the number of self-announced converts might multiply, even though their spiritual practice might retain many elements of the denounced tradition. Where conversion has high social *costs*, many of the converted who have found their frameworks of meaning and habits of practice profoundly altered by a realignment with another tradition might do all they can to hide that from public view. Some celebrate conversion; others conceal it. Either way, the converts' self-understanding and everyday practice are complex.[5]

If religious identity is as complex as I have suggested, then this has implications for the study of Buddhist adherents in the West. Those adherents include convert Buddhists; followers of European and African descent who chose the faith for themselves; and several types of so-called cradle Buddhists who were born into the tradition—"oldline" Buddhists who are the descendants of the earliest Asian migrants; immigrants and refugees who have arrived since 1965; and converts' children, who—if Western-convert Buddhism manages to flourish—will be a more visible presence in the next twenty-five years. And as we study these adherents we must note the complexities of religious identity. For example, as we study the recently arrived cradle Buddhists we should be alert to the ways that their religious practice has been hybrid and their religious identity ambivalent—in the homeland, in transit, and in the new land. As we study converts, we should attend carefully to the evidence in language, artifact, and gesture that their religious life reveals influences from multiple sources, including the tradition they rejected when they joined the Buddhist Sangha.[6]

SYMPATHIZERS AND THE STORY OF WESTERN BUDDHISM

So far I have discussed only adherents: cradle Buddhists who inherited the faith and converts who chose it, those followers who might meet the standard criteria for defining Buddhist identity. But placing the focus there excludes a great deal. It overlooks those who have not offered full or formal allegiance to the tradition.

Many in the West fit that profile. Fifteen percent of the French express "an interest" in Buddhism and two million describe it as "the religion they like best," according to one report. Of the six hundred thousand Buddhists in France, less than one hundred thousand are "full-blown Buddhists." But, the report continued, "many millions are said to be influenced by Buddhism." The recent article about meditators that I mentioned at the start of this essay made a similar point about the United States. One scholar quoted in that story suggested—correctly, I think—that we do not know how many Americans use Buddhist meditation practices. But, she estimated, "the number is large, probably in the many hundreds of thousands, possibly more." In that same article, Helen Tworkov, the editor of the popular Buddhist quarterly *Tricycle*, estimated that half of the publication's sixty thousand subscribers do not describe themselves as Buddhists. I call those thirty thousand *Tricycle* subscribers and the hundreds of thousands of unaffiliated meditators *sympathizers*, or, in a flashier but less precise and inclusive phrase, *night-stand Buddhists*.[7]

What, then, is a sympathizer or night-stand Buddhist? It might be useful to clarify first what it is *not*. *Sympathizer* does not refer to men and women who identify with a tradition self-consciously but fail to practice it vigorously or regularly. Lukewarm adherents deserve scholarly attention, but they are not night-stand Buddhists. The term *sympathizer* does not signal the level of commitment among those who self-identify with a tradition.[8]

Rather, it points to those who have some sympathy for a religion but do not embrace it exclusively or fully. When asked, these people would *not* identify themselves as Buddhists. They would say they are Methodist, or

Jewish, or unaffiliated. If we could talk with them long enough—or, better yet, visit their homes and observe their daily routines—we would notice signs of interest in Buddhism. They might practice zazen, subscribe to a Buddhist periodical, or read books about the tradition. They might attend lectures at the local university. They might visit a Buddhist center's web page or participate in an online Buddhist discussion group. They might self-consciously decorate their homes with Buddhist artifacts. Night-stand Buddhists, then, are those who might place a how-to book on Buddhist meditation on the night-stand—say, Philip Kapleau's *The Three Pillars of Zen*—and read it before they fall to sleep, and then rise the next morning to practice, however imperfectly or ambivalently, what they learned the night before. If I am right, these sympathizers have been an important part of the story of Buddhism in North America and the West since the 1880s— from philosopher Paul Carus and businessman Andrew Carnegie to composer John Cage and painter William Wiley and, more important, the many ordinary sympathizers whose names have been lost to us.[9]

These Western sympathizers have encountered Buddhism in different social sites—in other words, several cultural practices have created and sustained their interest in the tradition. Those include reading texts, viewing artifacts, and performing rituals. We could consider artifacts (including domestic furnishings and landscape architecture, as well as paintings and computers) or analyze ritual practices (including meditation, chanting, and the medical uses of mindfulness practice). But consider just one example: contemporary American sympathizers' engagement with Buddhism through reading. In recent decades, the number of books with Buddhist themes has multiplied many times. For example, in 2000, *Books in Print* listed 218 titles that begin with *Zen*. The list includes, by my count, 70 how-to books that apply Zen to one or another aspect of life, from the silly to the sophisticated, including *Zen and Creative Management, Zen and the Art of Kicking Butts: The Ultimate Guide for Quitting Smoking Forever, Zen in the Art of Golf, Zen and the Art of the Internet*, and *Zen and the Art of Changing Diapers*. However we might assess these popular prescriptive texts, which sometimes have little to do with Zen as most scholars and practitioners understand it, they clearly show the breadth of Buddhist sympathy in the culture.[10]

The list of recent titles on Buddhism also includes fine translations of sacred texts, informed advice about practice, and reflections by Western or Asian teachers. Among the latter, Thich Nhat Hanh's *The Miracle of Mindfulness* (1975) is a good example. Beacon Press reports that the book has sold "about 125,000" copies. If we added the publication figures for Nhat Hanh's other English-language books, from Riverhead Press and Parallax

Press, his influence seems indisputable. (For example, his recent text, *Living Buddha, Living Christ*, has sold 80,000 copies for Riverhead Press.) As with all texts, it is impossible to count the proportion of sympathizers included among Nhat Hanh's readers (or to determine how readers interpret the books). It seems clear, however, that many of his readers do not belong to Buddhist groups or identify themselves with Buddhism.[11]

THE MEANING OF *ADHERENT* IN THE SCHOLARSHIP

Some readers might object at this point. They would say, "But we know this. You have built a monument to the obvious. We know that religious identity is hybrid and that there are Buddhist dabblers." And it is true that some of the best writing about Buddhism in North America acknowledges the problem of determining identity. In his important 1979 study, *American Buddhism*, Charles Prebish takes on the issue in a two-page section titled "What Constitutes a Buddhist?" Prebish acknowledges that "it has become difficult to know what constitutes a Buddhist today." He points to the varying ways in which Buddhist institutions count members. Does membership refer to those who donate, attend, or join? Emma McCloy Layman, in *Buddhism in America*, a study published three years earlier, also noticed the problem as she tried to count American Buddhists. "There are several reasons for the difficulty in estimating the number of Buddhists in America," Layman proposed. Among the four she listed were these: that most "nominal Buddhists" had failed to ritually accept the tradition, while other "self-styled Buddhists" had not joined any Buddhist institution.[12]

Other more recent reflections on Asian-immigrant Buddhists acknowledge a related difficulty in defining Buddhists, making the point I emphasize here: religious belief and practice, in the homeland and the new land, have been hybrid. In his study of the Vietnamese in the United States, the anthropologist Paul James Rutledge noticed:

> The religious thought of many Vietnamese has been a *blending* of a number of systems, choosing not to claim one and denounce the others but rather to *mix* the teachings of various faiths in order to meet the particular needs of their community or family. This *syncretistic* practice is deeply rooted in the practice of religion by Vietnamese people. . . . Although most Vietnamese are Buddhist, either by practice or claim, Vietnamese refugees in America also ascribe [to] Confucianism, Taoism, Roman Catholicism and a variety of Eastern religions less known in the West.[13]

Penny Van Esterik, an anthropologist who specializes in Southeast Asia, makes a similar point in *Taking Refuge*, her book-length study of Lao Buddhists in Toronto. She notes that Lao religion combines both "spirit worship" and Theravāda Buddhism. The vernacular tradition of venerating spirits has been strong in Laos, as strong as anywhere in Asia, and for Van Esterik that indigenous tradition has become part of Laotian Buddhism. "Ghosts and spirits," she suggests, "are interacted with as part of the Buddhist world order." For that reason, "understanding Lao religion in the past and the present requires close attention to obeisance owed to the spirit world as well as the system of Theravāda Buddhism. The relation between these two systems provides the unique characteristics of Lao religion." Van Esterik essentializes and isolates the two religious "systems" a bit too much for me—interpreting them as if they were two originally distinct and self-contained cultural forms that then came into contact with each other—but still she recognizes the hybrid character of Buddhist identity.[14]

Other scholars have noticed how cradle and convert Buddhists have had complex and ambivalent relationships with Western cultural and religious values and practices. Even if he offers an interpretation that is not sympathetic enough to Henry Steel Olcott's self-understanding as a Buddhist, Stephen Prothero's sophisticated book, *The White Buddhist*, centers on the issue of religious identity. In an imaginative use of linguistic theory, Prothero argues that Olcott's was a "creole" faith, combining a Buddhist "lexicon," a Theosophical "accent," and a liberal Protestant "grammar." Olcott, according to Prothero, accepted and promoted a Protestantized and Americanized Buddhism. In his study of Americanization in two Theravāda Buddhist temples in Los Angeles and Chicago, Paul Numrich noticed that in Los Angeles temples hold summer camps, and in Chicago monks wear overcoats. In other words, Asian-American Buddhists have accommodated themselves to American culture, as well as resisted it, and complex forms of the tradition have emerged in this cultural context, where Buddhists meet not only Christians, Jews, and Muslims, but a wider variety of Buddhists than anywhere in Asia. Many scholars and Buddhists, and some Buddhist scholars, have considered the problems of adapting this Asian tradition to a Western culture. One scholar, writing for an issue of *Amerasia Journal*, exhorted Asians not to be afraid of "religious symbiosis" as the younger generations seek to revitalize "Asian American religious identities." Some Buddhist leaders in the United States have made similar suggestions, while others have held a more traditional line. Either way, observers have noticed cultural exchanges and new forms of Buddhism as practitioners make their way in America, as they meditate in chairs, sing Buddhist hymns, bite into burgers, and gather on Sundays.[15]

If some scholars have acknowledged the hybrid character of Buddhist identity, others have not; but even those who note its complexity have not usually explored that fully in their writings. Let's return to one of the first and best books on the subject, Prebish's *American Buddhism*. Prebish acknowledges the problem of defining Buddhist identity in two pages, as I have noted. He then writes as if that were not very complicated, as he surveys the Buddhist scene in the 1970s. He considers in turn, the various Buddhist traditions and groups: Buddhist Churches of America, San Francisco Zen Center, Buddhist Vihara Society, Tibetan Nyingma Meditation Center, and so on. Rick Fields, in his lively and important historical narrative of Buddhism in the United States, also shows that he knows that Buddhism has been creole, assuming varied forms in Asian cultures and encountering great diversity in America. He repeats, for example, the common wisdom about Chinese religious blending in China and America: "The Chinese temples reflected popular Chinese religion, which was a *mixture* of Taoism, Confucianism, and Buddhism." Still, most of his story overlooks or underemphasizes the hybrid character of Buddhism in the United States, especially among Asian immigrants. My point here—and I want to be clear—is not that these writers, and the rest of us, too, have failed to notice the complexity of Buddhist identity. Most of us have. Rather, we have not taken that insight seriously enough. Those of us working in this subfield have not always systematically or fully applied our best insights about the hybrid character of Buddhist identity in our studies.[16]

To shift the focus slightly—and approach the center of my interest in this topic—I think that part of the problem in the study of Western Buddhism, and in religious studies more broadly, is that we continue to draw on essentialist-normative definitions of religious identity, those that construct a core or essence of right practice or belief and measure all historical expressions against it. Fields, for instance, suggests that "Buddhist history is the record of lineage—of who gave what to whom. . . ." To apply this standard means that those who have teachers and who affiliate with institutions are authentic Buddhists; others are suspect, and (mostly) excluded from our stories about Western Buddhist history. In order to avoid the theoretical problems of essentialist definitions and allow more characters into our historical narratives, I suggest that we use self-identification as one helpful standard for identifying Buddhists. Of course, we will use other standards too, and we want to know who takes the precepts, who studies with a teacher, and who chants at a temple. That information tells us important things. But we cannot exclude from our analysis those who don't meet the traditional standards but still claim Buddhist identity for themselves. For our purposes as scholars, Buddhists are those who say they are.[17]

Some readers might object that this position is too uncritical, that it allows a flood of Buddhist pretenders through the scholarly gates. That concerns Philip C. Almond, the author of a fine study of Buddhism in Britain, and he worries most about occult Buddhists, those connected with the Theosophical Society. His solution: ignore them, even though esoteric Buddhists far outnumbered all other self-identified Caucasian Buddhists in Europe and America during the late nineteenth century. He explains his stance in a footnote: "I have not dealt with the Esoteric Buddhism of Madame Blavatsky and her English disciple, Alfred Sinnett. Esoteric, it may have been. Buddhism it certainly was not. . . ." Fields never responds directly to this issue, but he, too, implicitly rejects self-identification as a standard when he emphasizes the importance of lineages and institutions. In his *American Buddhism*, Prebish follows Holmes Welch, the accomplished scholar of Chinese Buddhism, in arguing that "it is insufficient to simply ask 'Are you a Buddhist?'" Because of the interpenetration of religious traditions, in China, and the concomitant overlapping of religious identities, the respondent might say that, yes, he is a Buddhist. In the next minute, however, he might also admit to being a Taoist or a Confucian. Prebish proposes another strategy for settling Buddhist identity: "A more appropriate question might be (as Professor Welch suggests): 'Have you taken the Three Refuges?' Further, 'Do you practice the five layman's vows?'" Prebish then complicates the issue further by pointing out that he has ignored "a consideration of the *quality* of membership and *commitment* to the tradition." And here enters a misleading essentialist-normative definition of Buddhist identity. In this view, which I think remains common among scholars and almost universal among practitioners, a Buddhist is someone who meets certain standards of orthodoxy or orthopraxis. She is a Buddhist if she takes refuge in the Three Jewels, accepts the doctrine of no-self, or chants regularly. But Prebish worried that some readers might misinterpret him: "It might be inferred my sympathies rest with the older, traditional forms of Buddhism; that I assume the only valid form of a religious tradition is its pristine expression. Each claim, however, would simply be ungrounded." Still, though Prebish tried to clear a middle path by acknowledging the need for accommodation to the host culture, there are limits on what he (and most scholars and practitioners) will accept as Buddhist: "Of course there is no *Ur*-Buddhism, but we must ask at what point the 'aloha-amigo' amalgam becomes so strange and fantastic that it ceases to be *Buddhist, American,* or a *meaningful combination of the two.*" I see his point, of course: some claims to Buddhist identity seem very odd when measured against the history of the tradition in Asia, or even the

West. Still, I stand by my proposal—that attending carefully to self-identification can be very useful.[18]

Let me support that claim with two U.S. examples, one from the turn of the twentieth century and the other from the contemporary period. F. Graeme Davis, a self-proclaimed Buddhist from Vermillion, South Dakota, is one of the characters in the story of Buddhism in America whom we might exclude if we use the usual standards for settling religious identity. Graeme, one of the most memorable figures in the Victorian American encounter with Buddhism, saw himself as a Buddhist. He subscribed to a Buddhist magazine, *The Light of Dharma*, and even corresponded with the Japanese priests at the Jōdo Shinshū Buddhist mission in San Francisco. "My sympathies are altogether with you and your work," Graeme wrote to the Reverend Nishijima in San Francisco in 1901, "[and] it is my hope that I may sometime be able and worthy to aid in working for the same cause, for I believe Buddhism to be the religion of humanity." But I have been unable to find evidence that he ever joined, or even attended, a Buddhist institution or ritually proclaimed his allegiance by taking refuge in the Buddha, Dharma, and Sangha. He tried his best to live the Buddha's teachings. He even organized a group, with three other students at the University of South Dakota, which met every Friday evening "for the purpose of studying Buddhism." Not enough historical evidence survives to offer a textured interpretation of the meaning of Buddhism for Graeme and his three friends—wouldn't you love to sit in that dorm room in 1901 and hear his study group's conversations about Buddhism?—but he is an important character in the story of American Buddhism, even if essentialist or institution-focused standards for deciding religious identity would lead us to ignore him.[19]

A second example of a self-proclaimed Buddhist who might be excluded if we use other criteria for deciding identity, is, I hope, familiar to you. Margaret—let's give her a pseudonym to protect her—is a middle-aged woman from a suburb just outside a major northern city. When we inquire about her life, we find that she practices zazen intermittently, dangles a crystal from her rearview mirror, watches television programs on yoga, and reads books on Zen and Tibetan Buddhism. At home she is (mostly) vegetarian and, on the mornings when she can find the time, she practices t'ai ch'i. On some Saturday afternoons, after she finishes with the soccer carpool and before preparing dinner, Margaret visits the local bookstore, lingering around the "New Age" section, and usually leaves with a book on past lives or healthy relationships. On most Sundays, she attends St. Mark's Episcopal Church. Margaret has never attended or joined a Buddhist group. She has not taken refuge in the Three Jewels. Nor does she seem to meet most formal criteria for Buddhist identity. Still, when we ask her, Margaret insists that she is a Buddhist. Now, why would we want to take her claim seriously? In short, because of what it reveals about her and the culture. It helps us attend to someone—and a wider cultural pattern—that we otherwise might have missed. It is important to know that in American culture at this particular moment, or at least in that middle-class (mostly white) suburban subculture, some folks want to claim Buddhist identity. Then we can begin to ask a series of questions, beginning with the most basic: why does she say she is Buddhist? We might learn that it is fashionable in her circle to be Buddhist or that she wants to signal, to anyone who will listen, her dissent from the Christian church she visits on Sunday, a church she attends mostly because she feels compelled to raise her children in some faith and the local Buddhist center has no religious education (and joining there would invite too much ridicule from her extended family). There are other reasons she identifies with Buddhism, ones that we cannot fully or confidently recover. In any case, my point is that a normative definition of Buddhism excludes Margaret, and Graeme, from the historical narrative, and thereby overlooks important characters and significant trends.

These examples, and many others, indicate that there might be reasons to widen our definition of *Buddhist* to include these self-identified followers. I realize that some readers still might have other grounds for rejecting the strategy I propose, since personal religious commitments and role-specific obligations can shape our responses on this issue. For practitioners, and especially for religious leaders, it might make sense to draw boundaries, to set limits on acceptable belief and practice. In one sense, religious leaders have a role-specific obligation to disallow certain practices and contest certain beliefs. Some followers might insist, for example, that *authentic* Buddhists do not condone violence or affirm theism. Yet scholars, and practitioners who are working as scholars, do not have the same obligations to establish right practice or right belief. Scholars' duty, I suggest, is to understand as much as possible about religion and culture. For that reason, self-identification is a useful standard for defining religious identity, and not only because it avoids the theoretical problems of essentialist approaches and includes the greatest range of characters. It also uncovers much about the status and meaning of the religion at a given historical moment and in a given cultural setting.

THE SIGNIFICANCE OF SYMPATHIZERS

Whether or not scholars have used self-identification as one important standard for locating Buddhists (and most have not), some have acknowledged the hybrid character of religious identity, even if they have not always emphasized this awareness in their work. Fewer interpreters, however, have taken seriously the many Westerners who have had sympathy for Buddhism but have not self-identified with the tradition.[20]

Among those who have written about Western Buddhism, Emma Layman did seriously consider sympathizers. She called them, alternately, *inquirers* or *Dharma-hoppers,* and discussed each briefly. By *inquirers,* she meant those "who are transients at the temple or meditation center, as well as non-Buddhist scholars and Christian clergymen who may be on several Buddhist mailing lists." *Dharma-hoppers,* in her usage, are "shopping around for a magic key to happiness and peace of mind, then dropping out." "Many have tried several Buddhist sects," Layman continues, "some have tried several Christian denominations before becoming Buddhists, and some played around with Yoga, Krishna Murti, or Sufi [*sic*]". It is not clear that Layman's Dharma-hoppers are actually sympathizers in my terminology, since some (or many) might identify themselves as Buddhists at some point along their religious journey. Still, Layman recognizes that among non-Asians there have been many seekers who have been interested in Buddhism, and have had some ambivalent entanglement with the tradition, even if these "hoppers" never self-identify or formally affiliate.[21]

But *sympathizer* is not an interpretive category for most scholars of religion, or students of Western Buddhism in particular, and so these so-called inquirers and Dharma-hoppers are not among the characters in our narratives about the history of Buddhism in the West.

CONCLUSION: INCLUDING DIVERSE CHARACTERS IN THE STORY

I have argued, first, that religious identity is hybrid (which scholars have sometimes acknowledged but rarely emphasized) and that using self-identification to locate Buddhists helps us account for this religious hybridity. Second, I have argued that scholars have attended even less carefully to those who have sympathy for Buddhism but do not fully or formally embrace it, and that these sympathizers enrich the narrative of Buddhist history, revealing a great deal about the beliefs and practices of Western cultures.

A wide assortment of characters have played their roles in the story of Buddhism in the West, and we should find a place in the scholarly narratives for them all. Of course, we need to consider both *cradle Buddhists,* those born into the faith, and *convert Buddhists,* those who choose it, as we highlight the creole character of their religious life—for example, Asian immigrants who unself-consciously blend Laotian spirit-religion with Theravādin practices, or Euro-American converts who unwittingly combine Protestant principles and Vajrayāna values. But there are also *not-just-Buddhists,* who (if asked) might acknowledge dual or multiple religious identities: the Vietnamese refugee who says she is Confucian and Buddhist, the Zen convert who claims to be both a practicing Buddhist and a religious Jew. We also should remember *lukewarm Buddhists,* who practice more at some times of the year than others, or, even though they join a temple or center, practice less vigorously than most religious leaders would prescribe. *Dharma-hoppers,* to use Emma Layman's term, move from one group to another in their spiritual journey, and some claim Buddhist identity while others, distancing themselves from all institutional piety, prefer the *seeker* label. Some other non-Buddhists, whom I have not discussed here, also play an important role in the story: *Buddhist opponents,* such as evangelical Protestants who dismiss Buddhism as a dangerous "cult" or try to convert followers in Asia; and *Buddhist interpreters,* journalists, filmmakers, scholars, poets, painters, and novelists who represent the tradition for Western audiences. And, as I have tried to suggest, we should remember the many *night-stand Buddhists,* who have found themselves drawn to Buddhism, even if they never have gone farther in their practice than sitting almost cross-legged on two folded pillows, imitating an illustration in Kapleau's *The Three Pillars of Zen,* silently facing a bedroom wall.[22]

NOTES

1. This essay is a revised version of Thomas A. Tweed, "Night-Stand Buddhists and Other Creatures: Sympathizers, Adherents, and the Study of Religion," in *American Buddhism: Methods and Findings in Recent Scholarship,* edited by Duncan Ryūken Williams and Christopher S. Queen (Richmond, U.K.: Curzon Press, 1999), 71–90. The initial comments come from a personal interview with The Most Reverend Agustín A. Román, 9 June 1994, Archdiocese of Miami Pastoral Center, Miami Springs, Florida. See also Ira Rifkin, "The Accidental Buddhist," *News and Observer* (Raleigh), 7 February 1997, 1E, 4E. For a review of literature on Buddhism in the West see Martin Baumann, "The Dharma Has Come West: A Survey of Recent Studies and Sources," *Journal of Buddhist Ethics* 4 (1997), 194–211, http://jbe.la.psu.edu/4/baum2.html [1 Feb. 2002]. For a hard copy of that review, see *Critical Review of Books in Religion* 10 (1997), 1–14. See also Peter N. Gregory, "Describing the Elephant: Buddhism in America," *Religion in American Culture* 11, no. 2 (Summer 2001), 233–63, and Martin Baumann, "American Buddhism: A Bibliography on Buddhist Traditions and Schools in the U.S.A. and Canada," www-user.uni-bremen.de/~religion/baumann/bib-ambu.htm [1 Feb. 2002].

2. Most students of Buddhist history know well that religion is hybrid. It is not only classic studies of Chinese or Thai religion that teach us that; see, for instance,

Erik Zürcher's *The Buddhist Conquest of China* (Leiden: Brill, 1959) and Stanley J. Tambiah's *Buddhism and the Spirit Cults in Northeast Thailand* (Cambridge: Cambridge University Press, 1970). Throughout Asia, Buddhist religious belief and practice changed as they encountered new cultures and other traditions—for example, Buddhist ideas combined with vernacular spirit religions, blended with Confucianism, mixed with Shinto, and incorporated Taoism. In a similar way, students of Christian history have emphasized the Hellenization, and later Germanization, of Christianity as it moved throughout the Mediterranean and Europe. On the latter see, for example, James C. Russell, *The Germanization of Early Medieval Christianity* (New York: Oxford University Press, 1994). Contact and exchange among indigenous, African, and European religions is especially clear in the Caribbean and Latin America. Consider, for example, the studies of religious life in Cuba and Haiti in Leslie G. Desmangles, *The Faces of the Gods: Vodou and Roman Catholicism in Haiti* (Chapel Hill: University of North Carolina Press, 1992), and George Brandon, *Santeria from Africa to the New World: The Dead Sell Memories* (Bloomington: Indiana University Press, 1993). See also Anthony M. Stevens-Arroyo and Andres I. Pérez y Mena (eds.), *Enigmatic Powers: Syncretism with African and Indigenous Peoples' Religions among Latinos*, Program for the Analysis of Religion among Latinos Series, no. 3 (New York: Bildner Center for Western Hemisphere Studies, 1994). Many other historical and ethnographic monographs document religious hybridity, while many theorists in cultural studies have emphasized hybridity in other areas of culture. For example, Homi K. Bhabha takes "the cultural and historical hybridity of the postcolonial world" as his "point of departure" in *The Location of Culture* (London: Routledge, 1994), 21.

3. Howard Kerr and Charles L. Crow (eds.), *The Occult in America: New Historical Perspectives* (Urbana: University of Illinois Press, 1983); David D. Hall, *Worlds of Wonder, Days of Judgment: Popular Religious Belief in Early New England* (Cambridge: Harvard University Press, 1990); R. Laurence Moore, *In Search of White Crows: Spiritualism, Parapsychology, and American Culture* (New York: Oxford University Press, 1977); James R. Lewis and J. Gordon Melton (eds.), *Perspectives on the New Age* (Albany: State University of New York Press, 1992).

4. I have made a similar point in my analysis of Cuban religion in "Identity and Authority at a Cuban Shrine in Miami: Santería, Catholicism, and Struggles for Religious Identity," *Journal of Hispanic/Latino Theology* 4 (August 1996), 27–48, and in *Our Lady of the Exile: Diasporic Religion at a Cuban Catholic Shrine in Miami* (New York: Oxford University Press, 1997), 43–55.

5. My view of religious transformation is shaped by many studies in the sociology of conversion, including David Snow and Richard Machalek, "The Convert as a Social Type," in *Sociological Theory*, edited by R. Collins (San Francisco: Jossey-Bass, 1983); David Snow and Richard Machalek, "The Sociology of Conversion," *Annual Review of Sociology* 10 (1984), 167–90; Clifford L. Staples and Armand L. Mauss, "Conversion or Commitment? A Reassessment of the Snow and Machalek Approach to the Study of Conversion," *Journal for the Scientific Study of Religion* 26 (1987), 133–47; John Lofland, "'Becoming a World-Saver' Revisited," *American Behavioral Scientist* 20 (July/August 1977), 805–18; and Lorne Dawson, "Self-Affirmation, Freedom, and Rationality: Theoretically Elaborating 'Active' Conversions," *Journal for the Scientific Study of Religion* 29 (June 1990), 141–63. The anthropological literature on conversion is helpful, too, because it is even more sensitive to the wielding of power and the persistence of hybridity. For example, see John L. Comaroff and Jean Comaroff, *Of Revelation and Revolution: Christianity, Colonialism, and Coercion in South Africa* (Chicago: University of Chicago Press, 1991); Elizabeth Colson, "Converts and Tradition: The Impact of

Christianity on Valley Tonga Religion," *Southwestern Journal of Anthropology* 26 (1970), 143–56; Cornelia Kammerer, "Customs and Christian Conversion among Akha Highlanders of Burma," *American Ethnologist* 17 (1990), 277–91.

6. *Oldline Buddhists* is Richard Hughes Seager's term, from *Buddhism in America* (New York: Columbia University Press, 1999), 10. Other scholars have considered the types of Buddhists in the West, especially the United States. See Charles S. Prebish, "Two Buddhisms Reconsidered," *Buddhist Studies Review* 10 (1993), 187–206; bell hooks, "Waking Up to Racism," *Tricycle: The Buddhist Review*, no. 13 (Fall 1994), 42–5; Jan Nattier, "Buddhism Comes to Main Street," *Wilson Quarterly* 21 (Spring 1997), 72–80; Jan Nattier, "Who Is a Buddhist? Charting the Landscape of Buddhist America," in *The Faces of Buddhism in America*, edited by Charles S. Prebish and Kenneth K. Tanaka (Berkeley: University of California Press, 1998), 183–95; and Gregory, "Describing the Elephant: Buddhism in America."

7. "Buddhist Revival French-Style," *Religion Watch* 12 (December 1996), 7. This piece originally appeared in the *National Catholic Register* for November 1996, 17–23. See also Rifkin, "The Accidental Buddhist," 1E, 4E. I used the term *sympathizers* in *The American Encounter with Buddhism, 1844–1912: Victorian Culture and the Limits of Dissent*, rev. ed. (Chapel Hill: University of North Carolina Press, 2000; original publication, 1992). I introduced the phrase *nightstand Buddhists* in "Asian Religions in America: Reflections on an Emerging Subfield," in *Religious Diversity and American Religious History: Studies in Traditions and Cultures*, edited by Walter Conser and Sumner Twiss (Athens: University of Georgia Press, 1998).

8. For a Christian example, see David Hall's discussion of "horse-shed Christians" in Hall, *Worlds of Wonder*, 15. Hall borrowed the term *horse-shed Christians* from the psychologist G. Stanley Hall, who used it to describe his own male relatives in his memoirs, *Life and Confessions of a Psychologist* (New York: D. Appleton, 1923), 58.

9. Rōshi Philip Kapleau, *The Three Pillars of Zen: Teaching, Practice, and Enlightenment, Twenty-Fifth Anniversary Edition* (New York: Anchor, 1989). This book, which originally appeared in 1965, has been popular. It had four hardcover printings by Weatherhill (the first publisher) and Harper and Row (the second publisher), as well as fourteen printings in paperback by Beacon Press. In 1989, Anchor Books issued a twenty-fifth-anniversary paperback edition. In the contemporary period, other media—videocassette and computer—can function in similar ways for sympathizers. For example, Zen Mountain Monastery in Mount Tremper, New York, under the leadership of Abbot John Daido Loori, has distributed a how-to video on zazen, *Introduction to Zen Meditation*, produced by John Daido Loori and Dharma Communications (54 min., 1991, videocassette). That Buddhist community also has an elaborate web page, sells recordings of Dharma discourses, and maintains an online Zen-practice training advisor via electronic mail, called *cybermonk* (cybermonk@mhv.net), where would-be meditators or longtime practitioners can get advice. Paul Carus wrote many works on Buddhism, even if he never embraced the tradition exclusively or fully, but he expressed his personal religious views (and sympathy for Buddhism) most clearly in his voluminous correspondence in the Open Court Publishing Company Papers, Morris Library, Southern Illinois University, Carbondale, Illinois. On Andrew Carnegie's affection for Buddhism, and Edwin Arnold's poetic life of the Buddha in particular, see Andrew Carnegie, *Autobiography of Andrew Carnegie* (Boston: Houghton Mifflin, 1920), 207. I offer overviews of Carus's and Carnegie's sympathy for Buddhism in *The American Encounter with Buddhism*, 65–7 (Carus) and 44–5 (Carnegie). For

evidence of Buddhism's influence on Cage's work, see John Cage, *Silence: Lectures and Writings* (Middletown, Connecticut: Wesleyan University Press, 1973). For a helpful autobiographical fragment concerning his relation to Buddhism, see "Where I'm Now," in *Beneath a Single Moon: Buddhism and Contemporary American Poetry*, edited by Kent Johnson and Craig Paulenich (Boston: Shambhala, 1991), 43–4. An exhibition catalog helpfully discusses the painter William Wiley's sympathy for Buddhism, and the tradition's influence on his art. It is Gail Gelburd and Geri De Paoli, *The Transparent Thread: Asian Philosophy in Recent American Art* (Philadelphia: University of Pennsylvania Press, 1990), 112–15.

10. *Books in Print, 1999–2000: Subjects* (New Providence, New Jersey: R.R. Bowker, 2000); Albert Low, *Zen and the Art of Creative Management* (Rutland, Vermont: Charles E. Tuttle, 1993); Dennis G. Marthaler, *Zen and the Art of Kicking Butts: The Ultimate Guide for Quitting Smoking Forever* (Duluth, Minnesota: Dennis G. Marthaler, 1995); Joseph D. McLaughlin, *Zen in the Art of Golf* (Atlanta: Humanics Trade, 1997); Brendan P. Kehoe, *Zen and the Art of the Internet: A Beginner's Guide* (Englewood Cliffs, New Jersey: Prentice-Hall, 1993); Sarah Arsone, *Zen and the Art of Changing Diapers* (Ventura, California: Printwheel, 1991). Of course, the number of books on Zen is much larger still. On 3 September 2000, the online catalog of the Library of Congress listed 4,208 books under the keyword *Zen*. Of those, 1,472 were in English.

11. Thich Nhat Hanh, *The Miracle of Mindfulness: A Manual on Meditation*, translated by Mobi Ho, rev. ed. (Boston: Beacon Press, 1987). The sales figures for *Miracle of Mindfulness* and *Living Buddha* were provided by Beacon Press in communication with the author, by Susan G. Worst, editor, Beacon Press, electronic mail, 14 March 1997.

12. Charles S. Prebish, *American Buddhism* (North Scituate, Massachusetts: Duxbury Press, 1979), 42–3; Emma McCloy Layman, *Buddhism in America* (Chicago: Nelson-Hall, 1976), xiv–xv. Although he does not emphasize hybridity or sympathy, Richard Seager also raises the question, "Who are American Buddhists?" See Seager, *Buddhism in America*, 9–10.

13. Paul James Rutledge, *The Vietnamese Experience in America* (Bloomington: Indiana University Press, 1992), 47. Italics mine.

14. Penny Van Esterik, *Taking Refuge: Lao Buddhists in North America* (Tempe, Arizona: Program for Southeast Asian Studies, Arizona State University, 1992), 41.

15. Stephen Prothero, *The White Buddhist: The Asian Odyssey of Henry Steel Olcott* (Bloomington: Indiana University Press, 1996); Paul David Numrich, *Old Wisdom in the New World: Americanization in Two Immigrant Theravada Buddhist Temples* (Knoxville: University of Tennessee Press, 1996); Rudy V. Busto, "Response: Asian American Religious Identities, Building Spiritual Homes on Gold Mountain," *Amerasia Journal* 22, no. 1 (1996), 189.

16. Rick Fields, *How the Swans Came to the Lake: A Narrative History of Buddhism in America*, 2nd ed. (Boston: Shambhala, 1986), 74.

17. Fields, *How the Swans Came to the Lake*, xiii. The position I argue here on religious identity, and the role of self-identification, has been revised somewhat. I am grateful to those who read my work and discussed these issues with me at the Workshop in Buddhist Studies at Princeton University on 3 March 2000 — especially Jacqueline Stone, R. Marie Griffith, and Stephen F. Teiser, of Princeton, and Donald Swearer of Swarthmore. I have softened my insistence on self-identification as the sole criterion, though I continue to hold that we should attend closely to those who claim Buddhist identity, whether or not they meet long-established standards for determining affiliation among Buddhists.

18. Philip C. Almond, *The British Discovery of Buddhism* (Cambridge: Cambridge University Press, 1988), 147, n. 10, and Prebish, *American Buddhism*, 43–4. Although Richard Seager does not highlight the issue, he seems to presuppose self-identification as the primary criterion for determining Buddhist identity when he addresses the diversity of Western Buddhists: "At the outset, it should be assumed that there are many different kinds of Americans who, in one way or another, identify themselves as Buddhist" (Seager, *Buddhism in America*, 9).

19. F. Graeme Davis to Rev. Nishijima, 27 April 1901, reprinted in *Light of Dharma* 1 (June 1901), 28–9. On F. Graeme Davis, see Tweed, *American Encounter with Buddhism*, 44.

20. Prebish's *American Buddhism* did not consider those who did not affiliate formally with Buddhism. Only a handful of sympathizers find their way into Fields's long narrative, *How the Swans Came to the Lake*, 153–4, 164. In his *Buddhism in America*, Seager mentions only a few figures I would identify as sympathizers as he discusses the 1960s history of U.S. Buddhism (34–44).

21. Layman, *Buddhism in America*, xiv, 203. For an analysis of one Dharma-hopper—or, in my terms, religious seeker—who actually did ritually align herself with Buddhism in a public ceremony, only to later practice Baha'i and Vedānta Hinduism, see Thomas A. Tweed, "Inclusivism and the Spiritual Journey of Marie de Souza Canavarro (1849–1933)," *Religion* 24 (1994), 43–58.

22. For a contemporary evangelical Protestant interpretation of Buddhism as a dangerous or misguided "cult," see Walter Martin, *Kingdom of the Cults* (Minneapolis, Minnesota: Bethany House Publishers, 1985), 261–9. Other evangelical handbooks and pamphlets do not classify Buddhism as a cult but still dismiss it, refuting its major claims and challenging its practices, often as a means of preparing Christians to evangelize. For example, see Fritz Ridenour, *So What's the Difference?* (Ventura, California: Regal Books, 1979), 83–92. That evangelical description and assessment of the world's religions has been popular among conservative Christians: more than 615,000 copies of the first edition were in print when the second edition appeared in 1979. The publisher now claims "more than 800,000" copies have been sold. Buddhist opponents, then, are an important part of the story. Our imaginary meditator might consult chapter 9 of Kapleau's *Three Pillars of Zen*, called "Postures," which includes fifteen drawings of meditators in various positions, from the full lotus to the Burmese posture, on zafus, benches, and chairs (327–53).

2 The Spectrum of Buddhist Practice in the West

B. Alan Wallace

INTRODUCTION

As Buddhism was propagated for its first twenty-five hundred years in diverse societies throughout Asia, a wide range of practices came to be followed both by "professional" Buddhists—namely, priests, monks, nuns, contemplatives, and scholars—and the laity. Differences in practices were especially salient in the training of professionals, ranging from the austere monastic training of forest monks in northern Thailand to the pastoral training of Jōdo Shinshū priests in Japan and the highly philosophical and scholastic training of *lamas* in the monastic universities of Tibet. In the twentieth century, Buddhist practitioners, both professional and lay, emigrated throughout the world to an unprecedented degree. Buddhist immigrants to the West—referring to Europe and all lands colonized by Europeans—have left Asia primarily for two reasons: they came seeking greater economic opportunities or they were fleeing from the oppression of communism. They brought their Buddhist heritages with them.

In addition to the expansion of Buddhism due to the migrations of Asian Buddhists, the latter half of the twentieth century witnessed an unprecedented growth of interest in Buddhism by non-Asians. In the literature on this subject, Westerners who practice Buddhism are commonly referred to as *converts*, and the purely religious nature of Buddhism is rarely called into question.[1] But the reality is far more complex and interesting. Drawing from a typology suggested by Stark and Bainbridge,[2] three groups of Western practitioners of Buddhism can be identified: (1) members of an audience for Buddhist teachings, who may participate occasionally in Buddhist meditation retreats, initiations, or other group practices; (2) those who enter into a student relationship with a Buddhist teacher; and (3) those who have a self-conscious sense of converting to Buddhism and who thereafter refer to themselves not simply as having an interest in Buddhism or as studying Buddhism, but as being Buddhist. Members of the first two groups include, for example, devout Roman Catholics, Jews, clinical psychologists, and a wide range of other religious and nonreligious people. This points to a high degree of eclecticism in Western Buddhist practice by people who combine selected Buddhist ideas and practices with those of their own religious heritage, New Age movements, or simply their personal beliefs and preferences.

This raises the complex and fascinating question as to whether Buddhism should be regarded straightforwardly as a religion, either in Asian cultures—which did not until recently develop the discrete disciplines of religion, science, and philosophy as we define them today—or in the West.[3] Clifford Geertz argues that those who adhere to a religion characteristically accept divine authority as a basis for escaping from adversity through the use of ritual and belief in the supernatural.[4] While this may generally be true of Asian Buddhists, it is not the attitude of many Buddhist audiences and students or even of many self-avowed Western Buddhist converts. Buddhism in the West frequently is not practiced as a religion; many Westerners who engage in Buddhist practices do not regard themselves as Buddhists; and, to make any study of Buddhist practice all the more intriguing, many of the religious, or quasi-religious, practices of Asian Buddhists, such as fortune-telling, palm-reading, funerary rites, and propitiation of mundane gods and spirits, cannot be deemed truly *Buddhist* in any canonical sense of the term.

For all the diversity of Buddhist practices in the West, general trends in the recent transformations of Buddhist practice, which will be illustrated throughout this essay, can be identified. These include an erosion of the distinction between professional and lay Buddhists; a decentralization of doctrinal authority; a diminished role for Buddhist monastics; an increasing spirit of egalitarianism; greater leadership roles for women; greater social activism; and, in many cases, an increasing emphasis on the psychological, as opposed to the purely religious, nature of practice.

The structure of this presentation of Buddhist practices in the West will be based upon the traditional Buddhist triadic classification of practice as (1) a way of viewing the world, (2) a matrix of meditations, or ways of cultivating the mind, and (3) a way of life. It is important to recognize that in Buddhism the views one holds are not regarded as mere "theories," as opposed to "practices." Rather, engaging with the world by way of Buddhist views is an essential element of Buddhist practice, as indicated from the beginning by the inclusion of *right view* as one element of the Eightfold Noble Path. Second, while the English term *meditation* often has the narrow connotation of sitting quietly while calming the mind, the Buddhist Sanskrit term *bhāvanā* has the much broader meaning of *cultivation*, as in methods for cultivating the mind. Thus in this essay I shall include under the rubric of *meditation* all formal practices of focused concentration, mindfulness, prayer, chanting, and other ritual activities that are performed as means of cultivating one's heart and mind or expressing one's faith. Finally, the way one views the world and applies oneself to formal practice manifests in the type of life one leads, so this is the third and often most public aspect of Buddhist practice.

In an essay of this brevity, it is not possible to do justice to the whole range of practices of immigrant Buddhists from Central, East, and Southeast Asia, as well as the Buddhist practices of Western Buddhists and non-Buddhists. For simplicity's sake, I shall focus on just five representative schools, most of them comprised of both Asian and Western members. These are: (1) Theravāda Buddhism and the *vipassanā* movement, (2) Zen Buddhism, (3) Nichiren Shōshū Buddhism and Sōka Gakkai International, (4) Jōdo Shinshū and Pure Land Buddhism, and (5) Tibetan Buddhism. Although these five traditions have established themselves in distinct ways in different Western societies, these differences in practice, too, cannot be explored within such a brief essay, so I shall focus on elements of practice that are common throughout the West, with no special emphasis on any one continent.

THERAVĀDA BUDDHISM AND THE *VIPASSANĀ* MOVEMENT

The Theravāda Buddhist worldview is originally based on the Pāli Buddhist canon, as interpreted by the great fifth-century commentator Buddhaghosa and later Buddhist scholars and contemplatives. For the immigrant Theravāda Buddhist laity, the central feature of this worldview is the affirmation of the reality of reincarnation and karma. The possibility of achieving *nirvāṇa* is primarily a concern for Buddhist monastics, while the laity are more concerned with avoiding karma that would propel them to a miserable rebirth, and with accumulating meritorious karma that will lead to a favorable rebirth and, in the long run, to ultimate liberation.

The principal Theravāda Buddhist meditative practices of meditative quiescence (Pāli: *samatha*) and contemplative insight (Pāli: *vipassanā*) are rarely practiced by the immigrant laity, for these are generally thought to require a monastic way of life and rigorous training that are not feasible for the householder. On the other hand, the laity as well as monastics do commonly engage in the practice of individual and group chanting, which primarily entails paying homage to and taking refuge in the Buddha, Dharma, and Sangha. As part of the regular services in the temple, ritual offerings are made to the Buddha, as well as to mundane gods, most of whom are intimately associated with particular locales in Asia. In the West, such propitiation of mundane gods seems to be on the decline, due at least in part to the separation from the regions with which those gods are affiliated.

Over the course of daily life, lay Theravāda Buddhists may occasionally take the eight precepts for a period ranging from one day to a week, during which time they may stay in a temple and devote themselves to religious practices, including meditation and chanting. The eight precepts include the more common five lay precepts of refraining from (1) killing, (2) stealing, (3) false speech, (4) sexual misconduct, and (5) the use of intoxicants, in addition to the three precepts of refraining from (6) eating after midday, (7) enjoying worldly amusements, and (8) indulging in luxurious sleeping arrangements and sexual intercourse. As a direct result of their belief in the efficacy of karma, Theravāda lay Buddhists commonly make offerings of food, goods, and money to the ordained Sangha. Such meritorious conduct is thought to lead to a better rebirth either for themselves or for their deceased loved ones, depending on how the merit is dedicated by the person who performs this service. Around the world, immigrant Theravāda Buddhists from various southeast Asian countries have also established after-school programs, Buddhist summer camps, and Sunday Dharma schools, all centered around their temples, which are commonly run by ordained monks and nuns.

The formal meditation practices of quiescence and insight meditation, traditionally practiced primarily by monks and nuns, have been appropriated by the modern *vipassanā*, or insight meditation, movement, which began to spread during the latter half of the twentieth century throughout South Asia and the West. Asian and Western monastic *vipassanā* teachers generally promote the traditional views of Theravāda Buddhism, as well as the monastic ideals of detachment and renunciation. Many Western lay teachers, in contrast, draw freely from other schools of Buddhism, non-Buddhist contemplative teachings, and humanistic psychotherapy, in which the spirit of renunciation plays a moderate role at best. Moreover, in this lay movement, which attracts a high proportion of non-Buddhists, belief in reincarnation, karma, and *nirvāṇa* are commonly de-emphasized, if not outright rejected, by both teachers and students. This is certainly not to imply that the meditative practices taught in this movement lack an underlying worldview, but rather that the views of *vipassanā* meditators are very diverse and that many of them are incompatible with those of Theravāda Buddhism.

In the lay-oriented *vipassanā* centers throughout the West, meditation is taught in a way that is largely divorced from the monastic and lay elements of the Theravāda tradition, together with its vocabulary, history, and literature. For these reasons, the *vipassanā* movement presents arguably the most decontextualized, or rather diversely recontextualized, form of

Buddhist practice in the West. Rather than a religion, *vipassanā* is presented as the cultivation of mindfulness as a means of psychological healing and spiritual awakening. Silent meditation retreats, involving sitting and walking meditation, are commonly held for periods ranging from three days to three months, with intermittent times for work and listening to Dharma talks by the leader of the retreat.

The various forms of *vipassanā* meditation are based on, or at least inspired by, the meditation techniques preserved in the Pāli writings of Theravāda Buddhism.[5] The primary Pāli source for these methods is the *Satipaṭṭhāna-sutta*, or the Buddha's *Discourse on the Applications of Mindfulness*, which is correctly regarded as the primary treatise on insight meditation in early Buddhism. The first stage of this meditative training in insight is cultivating mindfulness of the respiration. According to a commentary on this *sutta*, composed in the fifth century by Buddhaghosa, before *applying* one's mindfulness to inquire into the nature of reality, one first *cultivates* mindfulness by attending steadily and vividly to the respiration. By following the gradual steps of this preliminary training, one progressively achieves the first, second, third, and fourth stages of meditative stabilization (Pāli: *jhāna*).[6] Upon reaching the fourth stabilization, according to Buddhaghosa, one experiences a "purity of mindfulness due to equanimity,"[7] in which one's whole being is pervaded with a pure and lucid mind. While dwelling in this state of equipoise, says a late master of the Theravāda tradition, the meditator is "intensely conscious and mindful of the object whereon his mind is concentrated, free from all mental disturbances, having eliminated every kind of activity, both bodily and mental."[8] Buddhaghosa adds that once one has achieved this state of mental purification, one can remain in such a state of uninterrupted, unsullied meditative absorption for a whole day.[9]

As a foundation for the cultivation of insight, one is encouraged in the Theravāda tradition to achieve the fourth stabilization, although such a high degree of meditative concentration is not considered to be imperative. This tradition does maintain, though, that one must achieve at least the first of the four stabilizations, which is an extraordinary state of sustained meditative equipoise in itself.[10] To achieve *any* of the four stabilizations is a formidable task, generally requiring years of intensive, sustained meditation, usually pursued in the context of a monastic, or cloistered, way of life. This is obviously not very inviting to or feasible for Westerners, who generally have time for at most an hour or two of meditation each day, fitted into a busy, highly non-monastic way of life. The modern *vipassanā* tradition accommodates the modern way of life by de-emphasizing the detachment and austerities of monasticism and the rigorous training in meditative stabilization. Moreover, some recent advocates of *vipassanā* meditation have proposed that the only degree of meditative concentration, or *samādhi*, needed as a prerequisite for insight practice is momentary stabilization (Pāli: *khaṇika-samādhi*). As I have explained elsewhere, this proposal is based on a misinterpretation of authoritative Pāli treatises, and does not represent the Theravāda tradition as a whole.[11]

A complementary practice also often taught and practiced in the *vipassanā* tradition is the meditative cultivation of loving-kindness.[12] In this practice, one cultivates thoughts of loving-kindness first for oneself, then for one's friends, then for strangers, and finally for one's enemies. The aim of such meditation is to break down all barriers to loving-kindness, so that one can embrace all sentient beings in a spirit of affection and friendliness. This meditation is the first of four cultivations of the heart known as the *divine abidings* in immeasurable loving-kindness, compassion, empathetic joy, and equanimity.[13]

The dominant theme for practice throughout each day is to maintain mindfulness in all one's activities, distinguishing between (1) the phenomena presented to one's perceptual awareness and (2) the mind's emotional and conceptual superimpositions upon perceived phenomena. *Bare attention* is cultivated in place of the mind's compulsive associations and conceptual wanderings throughout the day.[14] As mentioned previously, many *vipassanā* meditators do not regard themselves as Buddhist converts at all, and in this movement there is a general de-emphasis on ritualism and the celebration of the traditional ceremonial cycle of Buddhist holidays, the foremost being Vesak, which commemorates the Buddha's birth, enlightenment, and final passing in *nirvāṇa*. Moreover, for obvious reasons, there is little emphasis in this movement on accumulating merit, either by serving the ordained Sangha or by other virtuous deeds. On the other hand, *vipassanā* meditators have been very active in altruistically introducing mindfulness practices into non-Buddhist venues such as stress-reduction clinics, prisons, hospices, psychology clinics, and sports clinics. Such activism is pursued as a good in its own right, without consideration for any personal benefits in future lives, and this attitude is widely seen by its advocates as an improvement upon the more traditional Buddhist attitude of accruing merit for oneself.

ZEN BUDDHISM

Zen is the specific form of Buddhism which the "Bodhidharma lineage" assumed in Japan, especially during the post-Heian period. Closely related schools of East Asian Buddhism include Ch'an in China, Sŏn in Korea, and Thien Buddhism in Vietnam. In the West over the past century, all of these have interacted with each other and with the Theravāda and Tibetan traditions as they never did when they were confined to their host countries. The views of traditional Zen Buddhism are based on the teachings on emptiness in such Buddhist scriptures as the *Perfection of Wisdom Sūtras* and the *Diamond Cutter Sūtra,* and on the Buddha-nature as expounded in other Mahāyāna *sūtras* and commentaries. They also rely heavily on the writings of the great Zen masters of the past, none being more important than the thirteenth-century Japanese contemplative Dōgen.

The two main schools of Zen are Sōtō and Rinzai. In the Sōtō Zen tradition, the primary practice is zazen, or "just sitting" in a full-lotus posture, mindfully attending to one's respiration, often while counting breaths to help maintain the attention. The eyes are kept open but cast down and lightly focused, often while facing a blank wall. In such practice there may be no object at all on which one meditates, for the aim is simply to be aware of the mind's incessant activity without being drawn into it and identifying with it. The underlying principle here is that the mind by its own nature is pure, indeed it is none other than the enlightened awareness of a Buddha. So the meditator's chief task is to "get out of the way," so that this innate Buddha-mind can manifest.

The Rinzai school is known for its emphasis on the meditative use of *kōans,* which range from stories or remarks made by earlier Zen masters in conveying the spirit of the Zen tradition, to paradoxical questions designed to transcend one's ordinary dualistic way of thinking. These pithy, often paradoxical, stories and questions are to be contemplated while in meditative equipoise, and are designed to break through one's habitual structuring of experience in terms of such dualities as subject and object, good and bad, "I" and "not I." When the mind is simply quieted, such conceptual structuring may merely go dormant, without bringing about any deep breakthrough to a conceptually unmediated realization of one's Buddha-nature. So these questions are designed to arouse the habitual conceptual structuring of experience, shatter it, and thereby achieve *kenshō,* in which one realizes one's own Buddha-mind. In both the Sōtō and Rinzai traditions, walking meditation, done either slowly or quickly, is also practiced in Zen centers and monasteries between periods of formal sitting. In addition, it is the custom for student and teacher to meet privately, especially during retreats, so that the teacher can offer personal guidance to individual meditators.

While the Sōtō and Rinzai schools were traditionally followed separately in Japan, in the recent past they have increasingly been combined both in Japan and in the West.[15] Zen masters who have emigrated to the West commonly teach the theory and practice of Zen in close accordance with their own Japanese traditions, but many of their non-Asian disciples who have become teachers in their own right have de-emphasized the more theological, philosophical, and ritualistic elements of this tradition. As Zen is increasingly practiced under the guidance of Western *rōshis*, the focus has shifted more toward meditation practice alone.

In terms of their way of life, many traditional Zen Buddhists take the sixteen precepts taught in the Sōtō tradition: taking refuge in the (1) Buddha, (2) Dharma, and (3) Sangha; following the three pure precepts of (4) doing no evil, (5) doing good, and (6) doing good for others; and following the ten grave precepts of (7) not killing, (8) not stealing, (9) not engaging in sexual misconduct, (10) not lying, (11) not becoming intoxicated, (12) not speaking of others' faults, (13) not elevating oneself while demeaning others, (14) being generous to others, (15) not being angry, and (16) not slandering the Buddha, Dharma, or Sangha. While such precepts set the ethical constraints on one's day-to-day life, the general spirit of Zen is to maintain a mindful spontaneity that is brought to such diverse activities as the practice of archery, calligraphy, flower arranging, gardening, martial arts, and poetry.

Like the worldwide *vipassanā* movement, Zen Buddhist meditation in the West has been removed from its monastic milieu in Japan and other East Asian countries and introduced into lay life, with the demands of the workplace and family obligations. Another similarity between *vipassanā* and Zen in the West is their assimilation of views from other Buddhist and non-Buddhist traditions, especially those of humanistic psychotherapy. Since the vast majority of Western Zen practitioners are laypeople, in addition to daily meditation sessions, intensive practice is condensed into retreats to fit their schedules. Such silent retreats, called *sesshins* (meaning "collecting the heart-mind"), usually last from three to seven days, or for as long as three months, and are held at regular intervals throughout the year.

As Zen has been assimilated into the West, the traditional ceremonial life of the Japanese temple, together with its linguistic and social customs, has gradually become marginalized. Few Western Zen followers have chosen to make the commitment of entering full-blown Zen monastic practice by taking monastic ordination, or *tokudo*. On the other hand, this movement in the West has been socially active in founding the Buddhist Peace Fellowship and other organizations committed to providing employment for the needy, homeless, and unskilled, and to establishing facilities for the homeless, for childcare, and for job training. The parallels with the modern *vipassanā* school are obvious: both are shifting away from monasticism, traditional beliefs, and customs, and both are emphasizing private and group meditation, combined with service to the community and the environment.

NICHIREN SHŌSHŪ BUDDHISM
AND SŌKA GAKKAI INTERNATIONAL

The school of Buddhism founded by the thirteenth-century Japanese reformer Nichiren is one of many East Asian Buddhist sects that are centered on the *Lotus Sūtra*. The organization of this movement, known as the Nichiren Shōshū Temple (NST), is strongly sectarian and committed to converting the world to what it deems to be the one "true Buddhism." Here is a purely religious approach to Buddhism, in which enlightenment can be achieved only through reliance upon the Nichiren priesthood, specifically the lineage of the high priest at Taisekiji, which is the basis for the authority of this school.

The central meditative practice of Nichiren Buddhism consists of chanting the *daimoku*, "Nam-Myōhō-Renge-Kyō," meaning "Homage to the *Sublime Dharma Lotus Sūtra*." This is chanted by a group in unison, sometimes with the accompaniment of drums, for between fifteen and twenty minutes, while facing the *gohonzon*, a small paper scroll that is a consecrated replica of scrolls originally inscribed by Nichiren. The *gohonzon* is enshrined in an altar and thought to embody the Dharma and Nichiren himself, who is regarded as an incarnation of the Buddha. The power of the *gohonzon* is believed to flow from the camphor-wood original carved by Nichiren himself, which is housed in the temple at Taisekiji. Following the chanting of the *daimoku*, Nichiren Buddhists may then recite selected passages from the *Lotus Sūtra* for as long as two hours a day. This highly devotional mode of practice is aimed at achieving material benefits, such as financial prosperity and good health, as well as spiritual insights. Its overall purpose on a very practical level is to help people take responsibility for their own lives, learning how to transform adversities into benefits.

Apart from the formal meditative practices of chanting and recitation, Nichiren Buddhism very strongly emphasizes the importance of *shakubuku*, a form of evangelizing and preaching, designed to convert others to this sect, relieve poverty and disease, and eventually realize a utopian vision of world peace and harmony. In line with these ideals, this school is known for the high value it places on progressive education, political activism, and the development of Buddhist family life. Another important element of Nichiren Buddhist practice is making the pilgrimage to Taisekiji, the head Nichiren Shōshū temple near Mount Fuji.

Until 1991, the Nichiren Shōshū Temple worked in collaboration with the lay branch of this movement, known as Sōka Gakkai (Value Creation Society), which has established national organizations on every continent. Like the NST, the Sōka Gakkai is a form of evangelical Buddhism, largely comprised of non-Japanese, with more converts from African and Hispanic racial backgrounds than any other school of Buddhism, due in part to its successful efforts in evangelizing in cities. But tension mounted as the lay-centered Sōka Gakkai rebelled against what it deemed the overly authoritarian nature of the priest-centered NST, resulting, in 1991, in the excommunication of the Sōka Gakkai by the NST. Following this formal schism, the Sōka Gakkai took on the name Sōka Gakkai International (SGI), and this is the organization that most non-Japanese followers of Nichiren adhere to today.

The worldview of the SGI is very similar to that of the NST, with the exception that it rejects the NST's insistence that the Sangha consists solely of the priesthood, which must be relied upon to achieve enlightenment. Abandoning this hierarchy, the SGI focuses more on the equality of all people due to their common Buddha-nature. Unlike the *vipassanā* and Zen movements in the West, the SGI is a purely lay organization, so it does not have to contend with the tension between the monastic and lay ways of life. Formal practice according to the SGI consists of the same chanting and rituals as taught by Nichiren, and they are performed in order to achieve the psychological benefits of mental focus and clarity, the pragmatic benefits of material success and prosperity, and finally the spiritual goal of realizing one's Buddha-nature. Although street solicitation and evangelizing have decreased in recent years, this well-organized, home-based movement maintains a stance of social activism and encourages religious dialogue both among Buddhists and with members of other faiths.

JŌDO SHINSHŪ AND PURE LAND BUDDHISM

Based upon such Indian Mahāyāna Buddhist scriptures as the *Sukhāvatīvyūha-sūtras*,[16] Pure Land schools originated in China and later spread in different forms into Japan and other East Asian countries and now to the West. Jōdo Shinshū, or "True Pure Land School," founded in the thirteenth century by the Japanese master Shinran, is one of those sects, and most of its followers in the West are Japanese, some of them second-

and third-generation immigrants. The central belief of Jōdo Shinshū, or Shin Buddhism, is in the existence of the Pure Land of Sukhāvatī, a heavenly environment in which one may be reborn and achieve enlightenment. This Pure Land was created eons ago by the bodhisattva Dharmākara, who dedicated the merit of his practice to the creation of this ideal realm for all who sincerely and joyfully entrusted themselves to the Buddha he was to become, namely, Amida, or Amitābha, meaning "Infinite Light." Amida is regarded by Shin Buddhists as the source of all love and compassion, and the possibility of achieving rebirth in his Pure Land stems from his power, not that of the individual practitioner. Unlike all the preceding Buddhist traditions discussed here, this school believes that all practices that rely upon one's own powers—of meditation and so forth—are fruitless.

Outwardly, the central practice of Shin Buddhism is the recitation of the *nembutsu*, pronounced *Namu Amida Butsu*, meaning "Homage to Buddha Amitābha." This is chanted not as a means to gain rebirth in the Pure Land, but as an expression of joyful gratitude to Amida for having already granted this desire. Psychologically, chanting this phrase is a way of entrusting oneself to Amida, who is believed to support one through the adversities and vicissitudes of life. Inwardly, followers of this tradition seek to sustain their faith in Amida, which leads to insight into the Mahāyāna doctrines of interdependence of all things in the universe and the oneness of all sentient beings.

In addition, Shin Buddhists commonly perform specific ritual practices associated with the principal holy days of their Buddhist calendar. Worldwide, followers of various sects of Pure Land Buddhism also express their faith by engaging in altruistic social action, such as charity and disaster-relief work, ritual release of captive animals, and following a vegetarian diet.

TIBETAN BUDDHISM

Among all the schools of Buddhism presently being propagated in the West, Tibetan Buddhism is internally the most diverse, in terms of its views, meditative practices, and lifestyles. More so than other schools of Buddhism, Tibetan Buddhism has a long-standing tradition of non-monastic contemplatives and religious leaders. This fact inspires many Western lay followers of Tibetan Buddhism to believe that they may achieve states of spiritual realization comparable to those of such great lay contemplatives as the eleventh-century householder adept Marpa; his renowned lay contemplative disciple Milarepa; and the late head of the Nyingma order of Tibetan Buddhism, Dudjom Rinpoche. The worldview in support of such effective non-monastic practice is found in the teachings of Vajrayāna, or Buddhist Tantra, which promotes the ideal of sublimating sensual desire, rather than the Buddhist monastic ideal of simply eliminating all such desires. But Tibetan Buddhism is not simply Vajrayāna, for it also incorporates the monastic ideals of early Buddhism, as well as the bodhisattva ideals of Indian Mahāyāna Buddhism.

The meditations taught and practiced in Tibetan Buddhism are difficult to synopsize within an essay of this brevity, for they are extremely diverse.[17] To begin with, while meditation in the Zen and *vipassanā* traditions is mostly non-conceptual in nature, in Tibetan Buddhism, meditation includes not only the cultivation of non-conceptual concentration and mindfulness, but a wide range of conceptually discursive practices. Tibetan Buddhist meditative practice usually begins with reflecting on such topics as "the four thoughts that turn the mind," namely: (1) the significance of having a human life of leisure and spiritual opportunity, (2) death and impermanence, (3) the unsatisfactory nature of the cycle of existence, and (4) the laws of karma. In addition, this tradition is known for its strong emphasis on ritual chanting of prayers, mantras, and long liturgies, all of which are conceptually discursive in nature.

Tibetan Buddhist practice includes extensive and diverse methods for the cultivation of meditative quiescence (Skt. *śamatha*) and contemplative insight (Skt. *vipaśyanā*). Unlike the range of quiescence techniques taught in the Zen and Theravāda traditions, Tibetan Buddhism strongly emphasizes the practice of visualization as a means for developing attentional stability and vividness.[18] When it comes to the cultivation of insight, some meditations are highly analytical, drawing from the syllogistic modes of inquiry set forth in the Madhyamaka philosophy of Nāgārjuna and Candrakīrti. These are aimed at experientially ascertaining the absence of inherent existence, or the emptiness, of all phenomena, including oneself.[19] More widely taught and practiced in the West, however, are the meditations set forth in the Mahāmudrā and Dzogchen, or Atiyoga, traditions of Tibetan Buddhism. These are far less discursive and analytical, and, like Zen meditation, are aimed at recognizing the nature of one's own primordial awareness, unstructured by any concepts or other conditioning. Indeed, the practices of Mahāmudrā and Dzogchen are at least on the surface so similar to Zen and the contemporary *vipassanā* tradition that a growing number of Western Buddhist teachers and students are combining techniques from these historically separate traditions.

In Tibetan Buddhism, a prominent genre of teaching given for day-to-day living is the practice of *lojong* (Tib. *blo sbyong*), or "mind-training."

The most widely taught and practiced *lojong* is the "Seven-Point Mind-Training" initially taught in Tibet in the eleventh century by the Indian Buddhist teacher Atīśa.[20] One of the central features of this type of training is the transformation of all the vicissitudes of life, including adversity and felicity, into spiritual maturation. Such practice may be combined with the specific Vajrayāna techniques of cultivating a sense of "divine pride," identifying oneself with an archetypal embodiment of one's own Buddha-nature, and cultivating a "pure perception" of reality. In the latter, one seeks to view all external things and events as displays of embodiments of enlightened awareness, all sounds as enlightened speech, and all mental events as displays of one's own Buddha-mind. In marked contrast to the "bare attention" emphasized in the *vipassanā* tradition, both the mind-training tradition and the practice of Vajrayāna powerfully employ one's intellectual and imaginative faculties in daily life.

CONCLUSION

As the light of multiple Asian Buddhist traditions is refracted through the many facets of the prism of modern Western civilization, a broad spectrum of ways of viewing the world, meditative practices, and lifestyles is cast upon the contemporary cultural landscape. Judging by the trends noted in the above traditions of Buddhist practice in the West, it would appear that a kind of Buddhist protestant reformation is in the making. In this reformation, as in the Christian Protestant Reformation, the role of monks, nuns, priests, and professional contemplatives is on the decline; there is an erosion of the very distinction between laity and clerics; and the importance of the laity, very much including women, is on the rise. These changes are induced by multiple and diverse influences, including individualism and nonconformism, democracy and egalitarianism, humanistic psychotherapy, feminism, the disenchantment of the natural world as viewed by modern science, and, of course, Christianity and Judaism.

The nature of these influences is varied and complex. For instance, many Westerners practicing Buddhism reject the Buddhist assertion of rebirth in miserable states of existence, such as hells, as a result of sinful behavior. The basis of their objection to this Buddhist belief is that it is *too compatible* with Christianity. On the other hand, some Westerners who practice Buddhism and who may even regard themselves as Buddhist discard the Buddhist assertions of the continuity of consciousness following death and the efficacy of karma from one life to the next, on the grounds that they are *too incompatible* with modern science. This is an interesting position to take in light of the fact that current scientific understanding of the nature of consciousness is scant at best. In the words of two of America's most prominent philosophers of mind, "Consciousness stands alone today as a topic that often leaves even the most sophisticated thinkers tongue-tied and confused,"[21] and "where the mind is concerned we are characteristically confused and in disagreement."[22] But perhaps ongoing dialogues and increased collaboration between Christians, Jews, Buddhists, and cognitive scientists will shed clearer light on such problems.[23]

Buddhism makes many extraordinary claims about the capacity of human consciousness for achieving dramatic and irreversible kinds of transformation. These include the complete elimination of all mental afflictions (Skt. *kleśa*); freedom from the cycle of rebirth; boundless love and compassion; a vast expansion of awareness, both in terms of ultimate truth and various modes of extrasensory perception (Skt. *abhijñā*) of the phenomenal world; and a wide variety of paranormal abilities (Skt. *siddhi*). Such assertions are the "currency" of the faith of traditional Buddhists, who have been encouraged to accept the validity of these claims on the basis of the gold standard of experiences of generation upon generation of accomplished Buddhist contemplatives and saints, beginning with the Buddha himself.

As the role of professional contemplatives declines in the present reformation of global Buddhism, it remains to be seen whether this alleged gold standard will be maintained. A process of declension and laicization has obviously been taking place within the past two generations, during which there has been a rapid dilution of Buddhist views and practices in the West, as well as a high degree of assimilation of non-Buddhist ideas and techniques. With the disappearance of professional contemplatives and their alleged accomplishments, some Western Buddhist teachers, apparently disillusioned by the inability of contemporary meditators to corroborate the truth-claims of earlier Buddhist adepts, have already begun to claim that many traditional accounts of Buddhist insights and transformations are counterfeit, or misleading.[24]

In all schools of Buddhism, worldviews, meditative practices, and lifestyles are profoundly interrelated, making it impossible to understand Buddhist practice without taking into account this entire triad. Moreover, given the inextricable relationships among these three facets of practice, it is infeasible to alter or discard Buddhist worldviews without this having a powerful influence on one's meditative practice and way of life. If the way one views the world is out of accord with traditional Buddhist worldviews, there is no way that one's meditation and lifestyle can be

Buddhist in any manner that accords with traditional Asian forms of Buddhism.

Certainly some Western Buddhists, following the lead of their Asian teachers, are committed to maintaining the "purity" of their own traditions, without influence either from other Buddhist schools or from any non-Buddhist elements. As a general trend, it appears that the more religiously oriented Buddhists are, the less they tend to be eclectic in this sense of drawing from different Buddhist and non-Buddhist traditions, and the more they emphasize the practice of viewing the world by way of Buddhist beliefs. More secular Buddhists, on the other hand, seem less concerned with the intact preservation of ancient traditions and more pragmatically concerned simply with exploring what ideas and meditation techniques help them in their daily lives. The tension between these two trends—of tradition versus modernity, of preservation versus innovation, and of continuity versus adaptation—is a prominent feature of Western Buddhism today.

Never in its long history has Buddhism gone through such a dramatic and swift array of changes, while it was violently suppressed during the twentieth century by Communists throughout much of Asia, and its traditions were subsequently carried throughout the rest of the world, often intermingling with each other in unprecedented ways. Buddhism has always emphasized the ubiquitous reality of impermanence and change, and it is now passing through a period of such profound and swift change—and in turn having such a significant impact on its host societies—that the future course of these transitions is hard to foresee. While the status of Buddhism as a religion is being seriously challenged by many of its own followers, its impact on the West goes far beyond the simple conversion of a small minority of the population to the Buddhist faith. The full nature and extent of this impact on Western ideas, values, and ways of life can hardly be anticipated this early in the story of Buddhism's unprecedented globalization.

NOTES

1. See, for example, the excellent overview of Buddhism in America in Richard Hughes Seager, *Buddhism in America* (New York: Columbia University Press, 1999).

2. Rodney Stark and William Sims Bainbridge, *The Future of Religion* (Berkeley: University of California Press, 1985), chapter 2.

3. For a more detailed analysis of the status of Buddhism within the Western framework of religion, philosophy, and science, see the section called "Tsongkhapa's Methodology" in B. Alan Wallace, *The Bridge of Quiescence: Experiencing Tibetan Buddhist Meditation* (Chicago: Open Court, 1998).

4. Clifford Geertz, *The Interpretation of Cultures* (New York: Basic Books, 1973), 104.

5. See Nyānaponika Thera, *The Heart of Buddhist Meditation: A Handbook of Mental Training Based on the Buddha's Way of Mindfulness* (New York: Samuel Weiser, 1973). For a modern overview of the teachings of Theravāda Buddhism, see Walpola Rahula, *What the Buddha Taught*, rev. ed. (New York: Grove, 1974).

6. See Soma Thera, *The Way of Mindfulness* (Kandy, Sri Lanka: Buddhist Publication Society, 1975), 71.

7. Buddhaghosa, *The Path of Purification*, translated by Bhikkhu Ñānamoli (Kandy, Sri Lanka: Buddhist Publication Society, 1979), II.IV.183.

8. Paravahera Vajirañāna, *Buddhist Meditation in Theory and Practice* (Kuala Lumpur, Malaysia: Buddhist Missionary Society, 1975), 41.

9. Buddhaghosa, *The Path of Purification*, II.IV.125.

10. On a technical point, while the commentary and subcommentary to the text maintain that one must achieve the first actual stabilization (Pāli: *appanā-samādhi*), Nyānaponika Thera, *The Heart of Buddhist Meditation*, suggests on page 103 that the first liminal stabilization (Pāli: *upacāra-samādhi*) is a sufficient basis for the successful cultivation of insight in Theravāda Buddhist practice. Buddhologist Winston L. King, in *Theravāda Meditation: The Buddhist Transformation of Yoga* (University Park: Pennsylvania University Press, 1980), concurs with Nyānaponika Thera on this point.

11. See Wallace, *The Bridge of Quiescence*, 258–61.

12. See Sharon Salzberg and Jon Kabat-Zinn, *Lovingkindness: The Revolutionary Art of Happiness* (Boston: Shambhala, 1997).

13. See B. Alan Wallace, *Boundless Heart: The Four Immeasurables* (Ithaca, New York: Snow Lion, 1999).

14. For a popular, well-written account of this practice, see Joseph Goldstein and Jack Kornfield, *Seeking the Heart of Wisdom: The Path of Insight Meditation* (Boston: Shambhala, 1987).

15. See D.T. Suzuki, Erich Fromm, and Richard De Martino, *Zen Buddhism and Psychoanalysis* (New York: Harper, 1970); Shunryu Suzuki, *Zen Mind, Beginner's Mind* (New York: Weatherhill, 1988); Rōshi Philip Kapleau, *The Three Pillars of Zen: Teaching, Practice, and Enlightenment* (Garden City, New York: Anchor, 1989); and Thich Nhat Hanh, *The Miracle of Mindfulness: A Manual on Meditation*, translated by Mobi Ho (Boston: Beacon Press, 1996).

16. See Luis O. Gómez, *The Land of Bliss: The Paradise of the Buddha of Measureless Light* (Honolulu: University of Hawaii Press, 1996).

17. For an overview of Tibetan Buddhist meditative practice, see B. Alan Wallace, *Tibetan Buddhism from the Ground Up* (Boston: Wisdom, 1993).

18. See Gen Lamrimpa, *Calming the Mind: Tibetan Buddhist Teachings on the Cultivation of Meditative Quiescence*, translated by B. Alan Wallace (Ithaca, New York: Snow Lion, 1995).

19. See Gen Lamrimpa, *Realizing Emptiness: The Madhyamaka Cultivation of Insight*, translated by B. Alan Wallace (Ithaca, New York: Snow Lion, 1999).

20. See Dilgo Khyentse Rinpoche, *Enlightened Courage: An Explanation of Atisha's Seven Point Mind Training*, translated by the Padmakara Translation Group (Ithaca, New York: Snow Lion, 1993), and B. Alan Wallace, *Buddhism with an Attitude: Tibet's Seven Point Mind-Training* (Ithaca, New York: Snow Lion, 2001).

21. Daniel Dennett, *Consciousness Explained* (Boston: Little, Brown 1991), 21–2.

22. John R. Searle, *The Rediscovery of the Mind* (Cambridge: Massachusetts Institute of Technology Press, 1994), 247.

23. See James H. Austin, *Zen and the Brain: Toward an Understanding of Meditation and Consciousness* (Cambridge: Massachusetts Institute of Technology

Press, 1998); Christopher de Charms, *Two Views of the Mind: Abhidharma and Brain Science* (Ithaca, New York: Snow Lion, 1997); Thich Nhat Hanh, *Living Buddha, Living Christ* (New York: Riverhead, 1995); Rodger Kamenetz, *The Jew in the Lotus: A Poet's Rediscovery of Jewish Identity in Buddhist India* (San Francisco: HarperSanFrancisco, 1994); H.H. Dalai Lama, *The Good Heart: A Buddhist Perspective on the Teachings of Jesus* (Boston: Wisdom, 1996); and Zara Houshmand, Robert B. Livingston, and B. Alan Wallace (eds.), *Consciousness at the Crossroads: Conversations with the Dalai Lama on Brainscience and Buddhism* (Ithaca, New York: Snow Lion, 1999).

24. To cite just two examples, see Stephen Batchelor, *Buddhism without Beliefs: A Contemporary Guide to Awakening* (New York: Riverhead, 1997), and Jack Kornfield, "No Enlightened Retirement," *Inquiring Mind* 16, no. 2 (Spring 2000), 20–1, 49.

3 Protective Amulets and Awareness Techniques, or How to Make Sense of Buddhism in the West

Martin Baumann

INTRODUCTION

The past decades have seen a double growth regarding things Buddhist. In institutional terms, Buddhism has become firmly established in Western countries, with a bewildering multitude of schools, lineages, and traditions. Local groups and centers, as well as national and international organizations, continue to be founded. In many countries, the peak of proliferation has not been reached yet. Historian of American religion Richard Seager is convinced "that for many years to come, Buddhists in a number of schools and traditions will look back on the years between 1960 and 2000 as an era in which the foundations were laid for their sanghas."[1] In academic terms, the past decade was exceptionally fertile in producing a substantial collection of empirical studies and interpretive analyses of Buddhism's spread and settlement outside of Asia. These take stock of past and present developments in a country, set up analytical categories, and apply theoretical frameworks. At the beginning of the twenty-first century, scholars and observers of the field can look back on a multitude of sophisticated publications. It is increasingly difficult to remain up-to-date.[2]

Buddhism's spread and settlement outside of Asia have been scrutinized in general analytical perspectives, too. How did Buddhism "come over"? In other words, what trajectories can we distinguish for the way Buddhist ideas and practices came from Asia to the—broadly perceived—"West"? And what dominant patterns of Buddhist presence in a country are observable, due both to the transplantation processes and to developments in the receiving and sending countries?

This article shall focus on the second question. The first question—how a "foreign" religion (in this case, Buddhism) has been transferred to a new socio-cultural context—shall be summarized in rough terms, differentiating three main trajectories. First, the religion might reach the new shores by way of migrating people who, after having settled, strive to preserve and continue their traditions. Second, the religion might be sent by intention, with a missionary zeal to win converts. In the case of Buddhism, often expressly depicted as "passive" and non-missionary, two examples of this sort come to mind. Twentieth-century reformist Theravāda Buddhists founded societies explicitly to spread the Dharma (teaching) in the West. Convinced that Buddhism was the most appropriate religion for modern times, monks traveled to Europe and North America. Whereas these missionary efforts so far have not matched the high expectations of the senders, the second example, that of the Sōka Gakkai, is more impressive in several ways. Founded in Japan in 1930 and spread to all continents since the 1960s, this group's particular emphasis on chanting practice enjoys a growing interest and membership in many parts of the world. Finally, the "foreign" religion might have deliberately been fetched from abroad by sympathizers and initial converts. In the case of Buddhism, texts in Asian languages were translated and published, Buddhist ideas and practices were adopted, and Asian teachers were invited to lecture.[3]

Turning to the second question—that of detecting dominant patterns of Buddhism in the West—this article shall rest on two main arguments. First, I hold that in order to understand Buddhism's Western presence better, it is not sufficient to look only at past and present developments of Buddhism in these countries. Rather, the view has to turn to Asia and past religious changes *there*, because developments in Asia have been a prerequisite for activities and efforts located within the second and third trajectories of transmission. Second, my considerations shall be based on the heuristic "two Buddhisms" typology proposed by Charles S. Prebish and later adopted by others.[4] My focus will be a different one, however. The notions of *immigrant* or *ethnic* on the one hand and *convert* or *white* Buddhist on the other, developed by others from Prebish's early dichotomy, suggest that the main line of difference between these two Buddhist strands is one of people and ethnic ancestry. I shall rather argue that the *religious concepts held* and *practices followed* take prime importance in shaping the predominant strands of Buddhism in the West. I suggest that attention needs to be drawn to a contrast between traditionalist and modernist Buddhism, prevalent in non-Asian as well as in Asian settings.

THE PARADIGM OF IMMIGRANT AND CONVERT BUDDHISM RECONSIDERED

The classification of immigrant versus convert Buddhism originates with Prebish's 1979 observation "that there have always been two distinct lines of development for Buddhism in America."[5] As Prebish elaborates, "one form of Buddhism places primary emphasis on sound, basic doctrines, shared by all Buddhists, and on solid religious practice."[6] The second line of development, to quote at length, "includes those groups that seem to emerge shortly after radical social movements (such as the Beat Generation or the Drug Culture). . . . Stressing less the basic doctrine and painstaking practice, they usually base their attraction on the promise of something new, frequently centered on the personal charisma of a flamboyant leader. . . . By nature flashy, opaquely exotic, and 'hip,' these movements gain much attention in the press but are inherently unstable."[7] Prebish's differentiation did *not* use the terminology of *immigrant* and *convert* Buddhism, and the characteristics listed, especially of the second type, clearly reflected the unresolved, fluid state of Buddhist affairs in the 1970s.

In the 1990s, after a decade's long silence, the classification came into wide use in the study of Buddhism in North America. The brief and vaguely outlined differentiation articulated by Prebish proved to have hit a nerve in describing Buddhism's development in the United States. On the one hand, that part of Buddhism's presence constituted by Asian-American Buddhists had started to strive for greater recognition and for a say as to who would represent Buddhism in North America. On the other hand, those who encountered Buddhist ideas and practices in the 1960s demonstrate that they had not been "inherently unstable," but had established an enduring presence. Prebish "reconsidered" the proposed typology and now specified one type as constituted by "ethnic Asian-American Buddhist groups," and the second form as including "mostly members of European-derived ancestry."[8] Again, he did not use the notions of *immigrant* and *convert* Buddhism, terms that subsequent studies, in particular those by Paul Numrich, Rick Fields, and Richard Seager, brought into play and that Prebish has employed in his latest consideration on the topic.[9]

The success of the binary differentiation stems from its wide applicability, and indeed it holds true for many cases, both in North America and elsewhere. It orders the apparently diffuse and disparate field of inquiry (Buddhism's past and present in a country) and brings forth focused research approaches. Nevertheless, the notions become blurred when faced with empirical data. Certainly, Buddhists from Asia who left their ancestral country and migrated to a non-Asian region can be called *immigrants*. However, does this label also apply to their children and grandchildren? And what about the fourth and fifth generations? In most cases, members of the second and third generations had become citizens of the state, regarding themselves not as immigrants but as a part of the nation's citizenry.

Indeed, more often than not they considered *immigrant* to be a term of social and political exclusion. Such a generational run has taken place with Japanese and Chinese Buddhists in the Americas, and it will become true for Vietnamese, Cambodian, and Laotian refugees, as well as other recent migrants from Asian countries in the next decades, whether they live in Australia, Europe, or North America. Although emigration from Asia continues, in a historical perspective the category of *immigrant* is too transitory and in the long run a misnomer.[10] In the same way, should children and grandchildren of convert Buddhists, if raised as Buddhists, be qualified as convert Buddhists without conversion? This strand of Buddhist followers will need to be renamed, as the number of children grown into Buddhism will outnumber the actual converts. Without going into detail, again, the category appears ambiguous. It certainly carries heuristic explanatory value for the generation whose members actually converted. As it turns out, the labels *immigrant* and *convert* differentiate and qualify the first generation of each strand. Those labels become increasingly meaningless when applied to consecutive generations and a longer span of time.

I have questioned the immigrant and convert labels as being too transitory and, for reasons given below, I do not subscribe to a model consisting of the three categories of *elite, evangelical,* and *ethnic* Buddhism proposed by Jan Nattier.[11] My suggestion for a system with hopefully explanatory value shall be introduced with a somewhat passing remark made by Seager. He holds, "The most prominent feature of American Buddhism for the last three or so decades has been the gulf between immigrants and converts, created by a range of deep cultural, linguistic, and social difference. A less obvious but extremely important dimension of this gulf is more strictly religious; here the contrast between tradition and innovation often appears in particularly high relief."[12] This "less obvious but extremely important dimension," the "more strictly religious," shall constitute my criterion.

CLASSIFICATION RENAMED: TRADITIONALIST AND MODERNIST BUDDHISM

The so-called more strictly religious or, as Prebish called it with regard to the first of his two types, the "sound, basic doctrines, shared by all Buddhists, and . . . solid religious practice,"[13] does not constitute an unchangeable, static entity. Rather, Buddhist doctrines and practices have been subject to a wide variety of interpretations, and have blended and combined with local cultures. Indeed, fierce debates have taken place over what is "shared by all Buddhists." The millennia-long history of Buddhism's development in doctrinal and praxis-related terms provides ample examples. Furthermore, as Buddhism has started to settle outside of Asia, other examples of new interpretations, blending, and innovations are created and brought forward.

Buddhologists have striven to systematize the history and the religious developments of the "cumulative religious tradition" of Buddhism into different periods.[14] Due to space, such a division into periods shall be sketched for Southern or Theravāda Buddhism only. The outline illustrates the ongoing change of the syncretic "cumulative tradition" and provides both the background and the terms for my ensuing classificatory proposal.

Scholars like Heinz Bechert, Stanley J. Tambiah, George D. Bond, and Richard Gombrich and Gananath Obeyesekere have divided the history of Buddhism in South Asia into three periods: (1) canonical or early Buddhism, (2) traditional or historical Buddhism, and (3) reformist, protestant, or modern Buddhism. The first period is the Buddhism reflected in the Pāli Canon and may be taken to refer to the form of Buddhist tradition developing until the time of Aśoka (third century B.C.E.). Traditional or historical Buddhism started with the reign of Aśoka and lasted until the beginning of revival or reformist Buddhism in the late nineteenth century. During this period the gradual path of purification developed in formal terms, especially so as the soteriological goal of attaining arhantship (becoming an *arhant,* an enlightened person) in this life is increasingly perceived to be attainable only after an immensely long, gradual path of purifying oneself from imperfections. Buddhists came to perceive *nibbāna* (Pāli) or *nirvāṇa* (Skt.) "a thousand lives away," as Winston King's classic phrase resonates in wonderful tune.[15] During this period, merit-making rituals, *deva,* and spirit cults became integral to Buddhism, both in the course of Buddhism's geographical spread across Asia and by laypeople entering the long-range problem of rebirth and immediate needs of this life. The third period, revival or modern Buddhism, commenced when Buddhist monks and leaders responded to the challenges posed by the impact of colonialism, missionary Christianity, and the disestablishment of the Sangha in the nineteenth century. Main features of this reformist Buddhism included an emphasis on rationalist elements in Buddhist teachings accompanied by a tacit elimination of traditional cosmology; a heightened recognition and use of texts; a renewed emphasis on meditational practice; and a stress on social reform and universalism.[16]

The form of Buddhism which evolved during the period of traditional Buddhism did not end with the emergence of revival or modern Buddhism. Both forms coexisted in suspense and reformist Buddhists strongly criticized traditional Buddhist ritual practices and views. It should be noted, and this applies to the early as well as the late twentieth century, that the two strands have been and are internally multifold and diverse. They shall be understood as Weberian ideal types. Also, for convenience and to pointedly relate to the specific Buddhist form in question, I shall refer to the second form as *traditionalist* and to the third form as *modernist* Buddhism. This nomological specification intends to avoid possible terminological confusion and aims to standardize the varied designations chosen by the above-named Buddhologists.

Returning from Asia and looking at Theravāda Buddhism as lived, taught, and practiced in twentieth-century Western countries, a striking observation comes to the fore. As is well documented, Theravāda Buddhism had already caught the interest of intellectuals in the West a century ago. However, it was not the traditionalist form of Buddhism that was taken up, the form that places emphasis on ritual and devotional acts of merit-making and holds specific cosmological worldviews. Rather, converts from the 1880s onward adopted a form that was refashioned by Western orientalists and South Asian modernists alike. This modernist Buddhism, which characteristically departed from hitherto traditionalist Buddhism, emphasized rational, scientific, and scriptural elements in Theravāda Buddhism. In contrast, so-called popular or traditionalist Buddhism was devalued as being incompatible with modern times.

This cognitive, modernist strand of Theravāda Buddhism has remained rather small in Western countries. Pioneering examples of its proponents may be Paul Carus (1852–1919) in the United States, Paul Dahlke (1865–1928) and Georg Grimm (1868–1945) in Germany, and Charles F. Knight (1890–1975) and Natasha Jackson (1902–90) in Australia. The highly intellectualized and anti-ritualistic strand does continue to these days, although it has rarely captured a widespread audience.[17]

However, a related modernist Theravāda strand, one that emphasizes meditation, has gained a growing popularity in the West during the past three decades. Western teachers instructing the meditational practices of *vipassanā* (penetrative seeing), *samatha* (self-cultivating meditation), or *satipaṭṭhāna* (application of mindfulness) have founded numerous groups and organizations. These teachers—including, for example, Jack Kornfield, Joseph Goldstein, Sharon Salzberg, Ruth Denison, John Colemann, Fred von Almen, and Christopher Titmuss—have been disciples of Burmese meditation masters Sayagyi U Ba Khin (1899–1971), Mahāsi Sayādaw (1904–82), or Satya Narayan Goenka (born 1924 and a disciple of U Ba Khin). Best known among the institutions founded by these Western lay teachers is the Insight Meditation Society, established in 1975 in Barre, Massachusetts.[18]

It has to be kept in mind that this distinct emphasis on meditational practice is a recent phenomenon, characteristic of revival Buddhism in South Asia. Although Buddhists have practiced meditation since the tradition's start twenty-five hundred years ago, generally speaking meditation was not considered a practice for lay Buddhists. It was reserved for the ordained. In the course of the revival of Theravāda Buddhism, however, meditational practices were also taken up by lay Buddhists on the basis of texts or were taught by monks to laypeople. Meditation centers, quite different from monasteries, became established in rapidly increasing numbers. Such often lay-led institutions were unknown in pre-modern, traditionalist Buddhism. Since the 1960s, lay teachers like U Ba Khin and Goenka were increasingly visited by young Americans and Europeans, in addition to many Burmese practitioners. Since the 1970s, these Western disciples have spread the modernist forms and approaches, attracting a growing number of Western converts. Not only lay men, but also lay women, taught. And, as best exemplified by the Insight Meditation Society, the meditational practice was not presented as a training rooted in a religious system, but rather as an awareness technique and an approach for psychological healing.[19]

In contrast to this strand of modernist Theravāda Buddhism, with its emphasis on cognitive or meditational elements, the strand of traditionalist Theravāda Buddhism has a very different focus and form. In Western countries, this strand can be found in many "ethnic" temples and its carriers are Asian migrants, immigrants, and their descendants. Emphasis is placed on the monk lay hierarchy, in which the monk embodies the ideal of a pious Buddhist life and aspiration. Lay Theravāda Buddhists are engaged in various forms of acquiring merit (Pāli: *puñña*) in order to gather good "deeds" or "actions" to achieve better circumstances in both this and subsequent existences. They donate to the Sangha by giving *dāna*, take part in ritualized chanting and *pūjas* (worship), and at times participate in meditation. However, "[m]editation is not a major component of temple-centered religious activities for the immigrant congregations of these temples," as Numrich observed in his study of two Theravāda temples in the United States.[20] Furthermore, a variety of so-called folk-religious practices are requested from the monks, including palm-reading, fortune-telling, countering evil spells, and preparing protective amulets. These practices and the belief in their right-working, usefulness, and benefit are rooted in specific cosmological and ontological views that are taken for granted.[21]

The contrast between traditionalist Buddhism and modernist interpretations becomes most apparent with regard to the underlying religious assumptions and premises. As the cosmological views and religious goals are very different, so the pursued practices are held to be effective. The findings can be summarized in a polarized, idealized way: traditionalist Buddhism, with its emphasis on devotion, ritual, and specific cosmological concepts, stands in contrast to modernist Buddhism, with its emphasis on meditation, text reading, and rationalist understanding. Whereas traditionalist Buddhists strive to acquire "merit" and aim for good conditions in this life and the next, most Western modernist Buddhists have abandoned the idea of rebirth. They do not aim to accrue "merit," but rather they endeavor to reach "enlightenment" or "awakening" in this life. Western convert Buddhists have already started to shape a "Buddhism without beliefs," as a recent book by Stephen Batchelor is titled. Concepts such as karma and reincarnation are held to be beliefs that need to be checked critically against a Buddhist, existential agnosticism.[22]

This chapter has sketched the "two Buddhisms" for the Theravāda tradition(s) only. Similar contrasts and departing practices are observable in other Buddhist traditions that are also prevalent in non-Asian countries. The characteristic contrast between Zen traditionalist temples, visited mainly by Japanese immigrants and their descendants, and Zen modernist centers, visited mainly by Western Buddhists, recently has been worked out in detail for the United States by Senryo Asai and Duncan Ryūken Williams. The authors' data "strongly suggests a kind of parallel world between Asian American Buddhism and primarily Euro-American Buddhism, with the former focusing on cultural rites and the latter on meditation."[23] Again, it is paramount to bear in mind that Zen Buddhism in Japan has been substantially reinterpreted by Japanese Buddhist philosophers and modernizers such as Nishida Kitaro (1870–1945) and Daisetz T. Suzuki in the early twentieth century. As Robert Sharf underscored, the reformist, or modernist, "laicized styles of Zen . . . strive to rationalize Zen practice through minimizing the importance of the pietistic, ritualistic, and sacramental dimensions of practice in favor of an instrumental or goal-directed approach."[24] Zen Buddhism was purged of so-called degenerate accretions of tradition and culture. Instead, notions of "inner" or "universal experience," to be achieved through meditational training, were stressed. Again, as in the case of revival Buddhism in South Asia, only a minority took over this modernized Buddhism. However, it was this 5 to 10 percent that elite and Western observers perceived to be representative of the Buddhist traditions practiced in South Asia and Japan.[25]

Applying the suggested analytical perspective to other Buddhist traditions, it becomes obvious that convert Buddhists primarily take up modernized interpretations of Buddhism. This applies to the Korean Kwan Um School of Zen, founded in 1983; to the Zen meditational practice spread by the Vietnamese monk Thich Nhat Hanh; to many others; and, last but not least, to the numerically strong Sōka Gakkai. Perceiving the Sōka Gakkai primarily as a modernized version of Japanese Nichiren Buddhism would make it possible to subsume the second element of Nattier's three-fold categorization, that of missionary, or evangelical, Buddhism, under the broad strand of modernist Buddhism. In contrast to Nattier, I suggest that differentiation is not primarily a question of transmission (or how a particular strand arrived in the West) but of what religious concepts and practices are favored.

However, an exception to the rule might be suggested. Is it not true that Western followers of Tibetan Buddhist traditions hold in high regard such traditionalist elements as devotional practices (e.g., prostrations, Tib.: *ngöndro*), liturgical *pūjas*, and the supremacy of the teacher? One may argue that it is the exoticism and the motive to re-enchant the world, perceived as cold, rational, and (in Max Weber's words) deprived of all mystique,[26] that attract Westerners. True, converts focus on the charisma of the *lama*, but they seek his guidance for meditative purposes and for understanding texts. Most Tibetans, in contrast, emphasize donation and devotion. And undoubtedly Tibetan Buddhism has been strongly adapted to Western cultural settings, acquiring modernized forms in the interpretations shaped by Chögyam Trungpa Rinpoche, Tarthang Tulku, Lama Surya Das (Jeffrey Miller), Sogyal Rinpoche, Ole Nydahl, and Robert Thurman.[27]

CONCLUSION

This essay has questioned the classificatory terms of *immigrant* and *convert* Buddhism, seeing them as transitory misnomers in the generational run. Although the terms carry explanatory value for each first generation of the current two main strands of Buddhism's Western presence, and possibly for the second generation, they have started to become blurred and questionable. What is gained, however, if the terms are replaced by the designations of *traditionalist* and *modernist* Buddhism? First, this change would de-emphasize the current concentration on ethnic ancestry, skin-color difference, and citizenship. It would be better to pay attention to the actual religious concepts and cosmological views that underlie the practices. In mutual contrastive comparison, these new terms bring to the fore the apparent differences between the two strands in religious matters. Numrich has shown for the Theravāda case that these two strands do not stay apart all the time, but sometimes meet under the same temple roof. Similar "parallel congregations," as Numrich calls the fact of "intersection without interaction,"[28] can be found in other traditions: at Japanese Zen temples, Vietnamese pagodas, or a few Tibetan Buddhist temples. Instead of focusing on "ethnic parallelism,"[29] the terminological change would direct attention to the religious parallelism taking place in a common space. An analysis which begins from this perspective could more viably explain the differences between the congregations and give reasons for their mutual distance and non-interaction.

Second, these parallel congregations do not always coexist in harmony. For example, as Cristina Moreira Rocha observed at the Zen temple Busshinji in São Paulo, Brazil, the parallel congregations of Japanese Brazilians and non-Japanese Brazilians existed for only a short time. Ongoing rivalry and tensions between the strands brought about a conflict that ended with the dismissal of the abbot and the walk-out of the meditationally based group of non-Japanese Brazilians. The juxtaposition of traditionalist and modernist Buddhism produces tension in both religious and representational terms, a fact apparent in Asia as well.[30]

Third, speaking of traditionalist and modernist Buddhism relates the interpretations and practices back to the periods and places of formation in Asia. It underlines that each "authentic" or "traditional" form has been shaped by long-term developments and influences. Looking at the Asian past from a distance, a view of the Western presence enables one to clearly delineate changes, adaptations, and innovations. It is useful to state where the cumulative tradition of Buddhism has engendered new interpretations of Buddhist practice and teachings. In this regard, certainly some modernist Buddhist interpretations that have been reshaped and appropriated in the West during the past three or so decades deserve to be called a *post-modernist* form of Buddhism. The approach of the Insight Meditation Society—to portray the meditational practice as an awareness technique that promotes psychological healing and awakening—certainly would deserve to be listed here. Also, Chögyam Trungpa's Shambhala Training, designed as a secular path for the cultivation of a contemplative life, might be described as a jump from traditionalist to post-modernist Buddhism. If modernist Buddhists have de-mythologized and rationalized traditionalist Buddhism, one may say that post-modernist Buddhist practitioners secularize and psychologize modernist Buddhism.

Fourth, and moving one step back from post-modern forms of Buddhism, it seems easily understandable that modernist Buddhist interpretations carry a high degree of compatibility with Western assumptions, views, and ethos. Modernist interpretations of Buddhist teachings emphasize the rational and scientific foundations of the Dharma. They praise Buddhism as pragmatic, optimistic, and socially engaged. Whether these interpretations tell us more about the interpreters than about Buddhism is a subject well worth discussing.[31]

Of similar interest is how traditionalist Buddhism faces modern (and, in our case, Western) legally secular and predominantly rationalized contexts. To state a concrete and specific example: the aim of a Western traditionalist temple is to provide a home-away-from-home for its members and visitors of Asian origin. It has been set up to serve the religious and cultural needs of the transplanted community. In the diasporic, non-Asian context, a number of the cultural or folk-religious customs (such as palm-reading for fortune-telling, amulet-blessing, god-worship, and acts of protection against malevolent spirits) are questioned by monks and temple visitors. These people start to look down upon these practices as "ceremonial" or "popular Buddhism."[32] It is most interesting to observe to what extent these ritual activities have been or will be set aside, being disregarded and considered inappropriate in a temple set up in a Western society. In Asia, similar criticisms and the so-called purifying or purging of Buddhist practices constituted an important element of the reinterpretation and modernization of Buddhism. In the same way, we could study the processes of Westernization and modernization of traditionalist Buddhism in a small-scale locale outside of Asia. Or, to the contrary and taking into account the attributed conservative nature of traditionalist temples, we might study the strength and potential to withstand and oppose demythologization and modernization.

Finally, changes have occurred and will occur in the conceptual field of traditionalist Buddhism. Traditionalist Buddhism in the West, formerly conceived by the grandparents and parents as an encompassing way of life, becomes for the children and grandchildren a chosen pursuit, a "compartment of sense" parallel with other compartments. The tenets of faith become reconceptualized, and the lived and experienced religious and cultural tradition develops into a believed, considered, and systematized religion. It is exactly this development which Kenneth Tanaka notices in his research on Japanese-American Buddhists in the United States. At the close of Jōdo Shinshū Buddhism's first hundred years on the North American continent and in view of ongoing processes of "Americanization," Tanaka observed a call to shape and assert one's religious identity: "This push toward Dharma-centered temples is partially due to an increased desire to understand Buddhist teachings on the part of a growing number of members, including newer converts. The younger generation is better educated and less ethnically isolated and lives in a religiously pluralistic world. . . . They feel a need to better understand their religion for themselves and to explain their teaching in an intelligent manner to those of other faiths."[33] At stake is, as Tanaka holds, whether Jōdo Shinshū Buddhism in its organized form as the Buddhist Churches of America (BCA) will "make the effective transition from being traditionally ethnic-centered to becoming more Dharma-centered."[34] In fact, according to him, "the time has now arrived for the BCA to undertake a concerted effort in 'Shinshū-ology' in the rapidly changing American social and religious milieu."[35]

This conclusion has concentrated on discussing changes and developments regarding traditionalist Buddhism in the West, neglecting, for the time being, trends within modernist Buddhism. However, in both strands the problem is balance between appropriate adaptations to Western contexts on the one hand and the maintenance of religious identity on the other.[36] At stake is the simultaneous endeavor (1) to keep the integrity of Buddhist practice and teachings and (2) to indigenize the thus-far "foreign" religion of Buddhism. The strands of traditionalist and modernist Buddhism apply different "strategies of adaptation"[37] to resolve this tension. It seems most likely that communities within traditionalist Buddhism in the West sooner or later will make moves toward a modernist Buddhism, a step held unavoidable to reach the youth and next generation. At the same time, modernist Buddhism in the West is changing toward forms I have tentatively called *post-modernist Buddhism*. Although the binary dichotomy of "two Buddhisms" proposed here will hold true for the next decade or so, it, too, will need to be reconsidered before long.

NOTES

1. Richard Hughes Seager, *Buddhism in America* (New York: Columbia University Press, 1999), 236.

2. An overview of studies up to 1997 is provided by Martin Baumann, "The Dharma Has Come West: A Survey of Recent Studies and Sources," *Journal of Buddhist Ethics* 4 (1997), 194–211; reprinted in *Critical Review of Books in Religion* 10 (1997), 1–14. See also the review sections of the online *Journal of Buddhist Ethics* (http://jbe.la.psu.edu [1 Feb. 2002]) and *Journal of Global Buddhism* (http://jgb.la.psu.edu [22 Jan. 2002]).

3. For the migrant religion trajectory, see Janet McLellan, *Many Petals of the Lotus: Five Asian Buddhist Communities in Toronto* (Toronto: University of

Toronto Press, 1999), and Harold Coward, John R. Hinnells, and Raymond B. Williams (eds.), *The South Asian Religious Diaspora in Britain, Canada, and the United States* (New York: State University of New York Press, 2000). For the missionary-driven transmission, with regard to the Sōka Gakkai, see Phillip Hammond and David Machacek, *Sōka Gakkai in America: Accommodation and Conversion* (Oxford: Oxford University Press, 1999), 89–172. For the demand-driven transmission, see Mark R. Mullins, "The Transplantation of Religion in Comparative Sociological Perspective," *Japanese Religion* 16, no. 2 (1990), 43–62, and Martin Baumann, "The Transplantation of Buddhism to Germany: Processive Modes and Strategies of Adaptation," *Method and Theory in the Study of Religion* 6, no. 1 (1994), 35–61.

4. See three works by Charles S. Prebish: *American Buddhism* (North Scituate, Massachusetts: Duxbury Press, 1979), 51; "Two Buddhisms Reconsidered," *Buddhist Studies Review* 10, no. 2 (1993), 187–206; and *Luminous Passage: The Practice and Study of Buddhism in America* (Berkeley: University of California Press, 1999), 57–63.

5. Prebish, *American Buddhism*, 51.

6. Ibid.

7. Ibid.

8. Prebish, "Two Buddhisms Reconsidered," 189.

9. Paul David Numrich, *Old Wisdom in the New World: Americanization in Two Immigrant Theravada Buddhist Temples* (Knoxville: University of Tennessee Press, 1996), xxii, 63–4; Paul David Numrich, "How the Swans Came to Lake Michigan: The Social Organization of Buddhist Chicago," *Journal for the Scientific Study of Religion* 39, no. 2 (2000), 189–203; Rick Fields, "Divided Dharma: White Buddhists, Ethnic Buddhists and Racism," in *The Faces of Buddhism in America*, edited by Charles S. Prebish and Kenneth K. Tanaka (Berkeley: University of California Press, 1998), 196–206; and Seager, *Buddhism in America*, 232–48. Also see Prebish, *Luminous Passage*, 58. Prebish provides a concise discussion of the topic on pages 57–63. The important issue of sympathizers of Buddhism, or *nightstand Buddhists* as Thomas A. Tweed calls them, cannot be considered here for the time being; see Tweed's chapter in this volume.

10. Fields also points to this fact and suggests the term *ethnic Buddhism*, a disputed notion as well, as Fields admits; see Fields, "Divided Dharma," 197, 202–6. An insightful discussion of this issue is provided by Kenneth Tanaka, who elaborates on the century-long history of (formerly Japanese) Jōdo Shinshū Buddhists in the United States; see Tanaka, "Issues of Ethnicity in the Buddhist Churches of America," in *American Buddhism: Methods and Findings in Recent Scholarship*, edited by Duncan Ryūken Williams and Christopher S. Queen (Richmond, U.K.: Curzon Press, 1999), 3–19.

11. See three works by Jan Nattier: "Visible and Invisible: The Politics of Representation in Buddhist America," *Tricycle: The Buddhist Review* 5, no. 1 (1995), 42–9; "Buddhism Comes to Main Street," *Wilson Quarterly* 21 (Spring 1997), 72–80; and "Who Is a Buddhist? Charting the Landscape of Buddhist America," in *The Faces of Buddhism in America*, edited by Charles S. Prebish and Kenneth K. Tanaka (Berkeley: University of California Press, 1998), 183–95. A close presentation of Nattier's proposal would double existent discussions; see Prebish, *Luminous Passage*, 60–1, and Tanaka, "Issues of Ethnicity," 4 and 14–5. See also Numrich, "How the Swans Came to Lake Michigan," 197.

12. Seager, *Buddhism in America*, 233.

13. Prebish, *American Buddhism*, 51; similarly Prebish, "Two Buddhisms Reconsidered," 187.

14. George D. Bond, *The Buddhist Revival in Sri Lanka: Religious Tradition, Reinterpretation and Response* (Columbia: University of South Carolina Press, 1988), 22.

15. Winston King, *A Thousand Lives Away: Buddhism in Contemporary Burma* (Cambridge: Harvard University Press, 1964).

16. Heinz Bechert, *Buddhismus, Staat und Gesellschaft in den Ländern des Theravāda-Buddhismus*, vol. 1 (Frankfurt am Main, Germany: Schriften des Instituts für Asienkunde, 1966); Heinz Bechert, "Sangha, State, Society, 'Nation': Persistence of Traditions in 'Post-Traditional' Buddhist Societies," *Daedalus* 102, no. 1 (1973), 85–95; Bond, *The Buddhist Revival*, 22–40; Stanley J. Tambiah, "The Persistence and Transformation of Tradition in Southeast Asia, with Special Reference to Thailand," *Daedalus* 102, no. 1 (1973), 55–84; and Richard Gombrich and Gananath Obeyesekere, *Buddhism Transformed: Religious Change in Sri Lanka* (Princeton: Princeton University Press, 1988), 15–29, 202–40. See now also H. L. Seneviratne, *The Work of Kings: The New Buddhism in Sri Lanka* (Chicago: University of Chicago Press, 1999) on the role of the Sangha in ethno-religious nationalism.

17. On Carus, see Thomas A. Tweed, *The American Encounter with Buddhism, 1844–1912: Victorian Culture and the Limits of Dissent* (Bloomington: Indiana University Press, 1992), 60–8, and Martin J. Verhoeven, "Americanizing the Buddha: Paul Carus and the Transformation of Asian Thought," in *The Faces of Buddhism in America*, 207–27. On early modernist Buddhists in Germany, see Martin Baumann, "Culture Contact and Valuation: Early German Buddhists and the Creation of a 'Buddhism in Protestant Shape,'" *Numen* 44, no. 3 (1997), 270–95. On Knight and Jackson, see Paul Croucher, *Buddhism in Australia: 1848–1988* (Kensington: New South Wales University Press, 1989), 37–84, especially 54–5.

18. For these and further Asian Theravāda meditation teachers, see Jack Kornfield, *Living Buddhist Masters* (Kandy, Sri Lanka: Buddhist Publication Society, 1993). The Asian teachers themselves had been disciples of earlier Buddhist reformers, especially Ledi Sayādaw (1846–1923), Phra Mun Bhuridatta (1870–1949), and U Nārada (1868–1955). Certainly, Anagārika Dharmapāla deserves to be listed here as well. For the Western *vipassanā* Sangha, see Andrew Rawlinson, *The Book of Enlightened Masters: Western Teachers in Eastern Traditions* (Chicago: Open Court, 1997), 586–96.

19. For the changes and developments in Burma, see the classic by King, *A Thousand Lives Away*. For Ceylon, see in detail Bond, *The Buddhist Revival*, 130–240. Further relevant literature is provided in Robert H. Sharf, "Buddhist Modernism and the Rhetoric of Meditative Experience," *Numen* 42 (1995), 228–83, especially notes 18–22 and 31–50. Mention certainly needs to be made of the German-born *bhikkhu* Nyānaponika (1901–94), disciple and successor of Nyānatiloka and the author of a bestseller, *The Heart of Buddhist Meditation* (1953); see *Nyānaponika: A Farewell Tribute*, edited by Bhikkhu Bodhi (Kandy, Sri Lanka: Buddhist Publication Society, 1995).

20. Numrich, *Old Wisdom in the New World*, 82.

21. On these practices as conducted in Thai and Laotian temples in the U.S., see Numrich, *Old Wisdom in the New World*, 84. See in more detail the chapter by B. Alan Wallace in this volume. For South Asia, see, among many resources, Bechert, "Sangha, State, Society," and Bond, *The Buddhist Revival*. Certainly it is a simplification to portray traditionalist Buddhism with these few characteristics. Like modernist Buddhism, traditionalist Buddhism also changes and is neither static nor monolithic.

22. Stephen Batchelor, *Buddhism without Beliefs: A Contemporary Guide to Awakening* (New York: Riverhead, 1997). See also Richard P. Hayes, *Land of No Buddha: Reflections of a Sceptical Buddhist* (Birmingham, U.K.: Windhorse, 1998), 59–61.

23. See Senryo Asai and Duncan Ryūken Williams, "Japanese American Zen Temples: Cultural Identity and Economics," in *American Buddhism: Methods and Findings in Recent Scholarship*, 20–35, quote 30.

24. Sharf, "Buddhist Modernism," 250. See also the chapter by David L. McMahan in this volume.

25. Instead of providing a long list of relevant literature, I refer the reader to Sharf, "Buddhist Modernism."

26. Max Weber, *Die protestantische Ethik I: eine Aufsatzsammlung*, 1920 (Tübingen: Mohr, 7th ed. Gütersloh: Mohn, 1984), 123, 367.

27. I am indebted to Frank Korom for pointing out the difference to me. Donald S. Lopez, Jr., alludes to this difference in *Prisoners of Shangri-La: Tibetan Buddhism and the West* (Chicago: University of Chicago Press, 1998), 191, 198. For modernist Tibetan Buddhist approaches see, among others, Frank J. Korom (ed.), *Constructing Tibetan Culture: Contemporary Perspectives* (Québec: World Heritage Press, 1997); Seager, *Buddhism in America*, 132–5; and Lionel Obadia, *Bouddhisme et Occident: la diffusion du bouddhisme tibétain en France* (Paris: L'Harmattan, 1999).

28. Numrich, *Old Wisdom in the New World*, 67.

29. Ibid., 63.

30. Cristina Moreira Rocha, "Zen Buddhism in Brazil: Japanese or Brazilian?" *Journal of Global Buddhism* 1 (2000), 31–55, especially 40–2. The mutual impact and influence of the two strands on each other has been sketched by Numrich in four scenarios; see Numrich, *Old Wisdom in the New World*, 76–8.

31. See Tweed, *The American Encounter with Buddhism*, 133–56; Baumann, "Culture Contact and Valuation," 286–7 and, although only partly convincing, Joseph B. Tamney, *American Society in the Buddhist Mirror* (New York: Garland, 1992).

32. See Numrich, *Old Wisdom in the New World*, 61, 85.

33. Tanaka, "Issues of Ethnicity," 13–4.

34. Ibid., 14.

35. Ibid. Such developments "to move the Dharma more to center stage" (15) have been referred to by others as processes of protestantization of Buddhist tradition in Western contexts. See Numrich, *Old Wisdom in the New World*, 142, or Baumann, "Culture Contact and Valuation," 284.

36. Michelle Spuler, "The Adaptation of Buddhism to the West: Diamond Sangha Zen Buddhist Groups in Australia" (Ph.D. diss., University of Queensland, Australia, 1999), 164–72, published as *Facets of the Diamond: Developments in Australian Buddhism* (Richmond, U.K.: Curzon Press, 2002).

37. Baumann, "The Transplantation of Buddhism." See also the discussion in Eva K. Neumaier-Dargyay, "Is Buddhism Like a Tomato? Thoughts about the Transplantation of Buddhism to Germany: A Response to Martin Baumann," *Method and Theory in the Study of Religion* 7, no. 2 (1995), 185–94, and Martin Baumann, "Methodological Smugness and the Transplantation of Symbolic Systems: A Reply to Eva K. Neumaier-Dargyay," *Method and Theory in the Study of Religion* 8, no. 4 (1996), 367–72.

*The Emergence of Western Buddhism as a
New Subdiscipline within Buddhist Studies*

Charles S. Prebish

INTRODUCTION

In 1975, when I taught my first academic course devoted solely to Buddhism in the United States, it was an incredibly challenging and frustrating enterprise. Even a casual perusal of the most popular books used as texts in introductory courses on Buddhism at that time reveals that Western Buddhism was not included in the discipline called *Buddhist Studies*. As Jan Nattier aptly points out in "Who Is a Buddhist? Charting the Landscape of Buddhist America," neither the first edition of Richard Robinson's *The Buddhist Religion* nor Edward Conze's *Essence and Development of Buddhism* has much to say about Western Buddhism, and Sangharakshita's *A Survey of Buddhism* does not even mention it in the first five editions of the volume.[1] The first textbook to actually consider Western Buddhism as a separate topic was the edited volume *Buddhism: A Modern Perspective* (1975), in which five pages of text by Roger Corless and four pages of listings of Buddhist groups in the United States (compiled by Corless and myself) were devoted to the topic. Finding bibliographic materials on Western Buddhism was equally hopeless. In the extensive bibliography that accompanied *Buddhism: A Modern Perspective*, only Louise Hunter's *Buddhism in Hawaii* comprehensively addressed Buddhism in a Western environment. Four years later, when my book *American Buddhism* was published, the situation was not much better, prompting me to remark in the preface: "Nevertheless, the few books that do address the question of Buddhism in an American setting directly are either too restrictive (such as Louise Hunter's *Buddhism in Hawaii*), too outdated (such as Van Meter Ames's *Zen and American Thought*), or both."[2] Had I included Christmas Humphreys's three books—*The Development of Buddhism in England*, published in 1937; *Zen Comes West: The Present and Future of Zen*

Buddhism in Britain, published in 1960; and *Sixty Years of Buddhism in England (1907–1967),* published in 1968, the circumstance really wouldn't have been improved much. Nonetheless, by the century's close, the study of and teaching about American Buddhism had changed dramatically, as we shall see.

STATE OF THE DISCIPLINE

In the Winter 1991 issue of the *Journal of the American Academy of Religion,* former editor Ray L. Hart was afforded 112 pages to present the results of a survey entitled "Religious and Theological Studies in American Higher Education: A Pilot Study."[3] Thirty-five of these pages presented statistical evidence gleaned from a questionnaire distributed to 678 faculty members at eleven types of institutions; the rest of the space contained Hart's interpretive narrative. Hart's useful findings have already been widely utilized in the discipline, clearly reflecting the perceived importance of self-definition and self-recognition within the broad profession of Religious Studies.

Curiously, Hart's findings were nearly coincident with a five-year administrative review of the Buddhism Section of the American Academy of Religion, arguably the largest academic arena for Buddhologists in North America (if not the entire world). AAR's external evaluator for the review, Professor Malcolm David Eckel of Boston University, noted in his 1991 report: "The most important achievement of the Buddhism Group and Section at the AAR in the last 10 years has been to create a safe and reliable forum for Buddhist scholars who represent a wide variety of approaches, disciplines, and geographical orientations to exchange views and build bonds of cooperation and understanding that create an active and imaginative scholarly community."[4] In a later article, Eckel reveals that in the five years between 1986 and 1991, attendance at the Buddhism Section's annual business meeting grew from 60 to 140, and the mailing list expanded from 106 to 600![5]

Almost twenty years ago, I titled a review article on recent Buddhist literature "Buddhist Studies American Style: A Shot in the Dark," explaining at the outset that the conjured image of Inspector Clouseau "falling through banisters, walking into walls, crashing out of windows, and somehow miraculously getting the job done with the assistance of his loyal Oriental servant,"[6] was not an accidental choice on my part: Buddhist Studies in America was just as erratic as poor Clouseau. Less than a decade ago, in October 1992, my interest piqued by the data in Hart's report and the suppositions inherent in Eckel's, I set out to gather data from the North American community of Buddhologists that would afford this academic community the opportunity to conduct a new level of self-reflection.

It was clear from the outset that the six-hundred-member mailing list mentioned above contained, in addition to so-called Buddhologists, a large number of scholars of other Asian religions, many non-specialist comparativists, and a profusion of "others." After careful sorting and synthesis, I came up with 125 scholars whose primary teaching and research work fell within the discipline of Buddhist Studies. I sent these individuals requests for both data and narrative statements about the discipline. Following two additional requests, and with a rather surprising response rate of 69.6 percent (Hart received 64 percent), I collated the material. The preliminary results were presented in a paper at the 1993 AAR annual meeting in Washington, D.C., and published in the fledgling electronic journal *Gassho*, with the full results appearing slightly later in *Religion*,[7] jointly published in England and the United States.

A second survey was conducted beginning in fall 1995. In the intervening years, the list of scholars was updated, revised, and refined, reflecting the arrival of new scholars into the Buddhological community, the deaths of others, and shifting interests. The new survey involved 140 requests and received 106 responses (75.7 percent). On an individual level, the results provide an ample look at the demographics of Buddhist Studies in America. With regard to individual training, I was able to document the gender, educational background, language facility, and the like for those polled. Institutionally, I tracked the academic ranks of the respondents, the types of universities in which they teach, and the specific departments that employ them. I collected data on memberships in professional organizations, editorships held, geographical area(s) of specialization, grants and fellowships received, professional papers presented, honors awarded, and categories of publications (including books, refereed articles, and book reviews). From the narratives included with many of the responses, I was able to determine a sense of the sample's collective perception of issues deemed critical to the continuing development and advancement of the discipline. It was also possible to compile information on universities with extensive resources for the study of Buddhism. Much of the data from these two surveys was ultimately published in *Luminous Passage: The Practice and Study of Buddhism in America* (chapter 4, "The Silent Sangha: Buddhism in the Academy").[8]

Around the same time as I began my surveys, Buddhist Studies throughout the world began to engage in the useful process of self-reflection, and the results of that inquiry are fruitful and inspiring. Following David Sey-fort Ruegg's insightful "Some Observations on the Present and Future of Buddhist Studies,"[9] the *Journal of the International Association of Buddhist Studies* devoted an entire issue (Winter 1995) to the topic, entitled "On Method," in which scholars reflected on various aspects of the discipline. Part of the problem in understanding just where studies in Western Buddhism fit into the overall discipline is captured by Luis Gómez's remark that "Buddhist Studies continues to be a Western enterprise about a non-Western cultural product."[10] There is little doubt, I think, that Gómez's statement accurately reflected the majority opinion of scholars at that time. Books from the 1970s, like *Buddhism in the Modern World* (edited by Heinrich Dumoulin and John Maraldo), and the 1980s, like *The World of Buddhism* (edited by Heinz Bechert and Richard Gombrich) barely noticed Buddhism outside of Asia. In other words, as recently as 1995, Buddhism was perceived to be an exclusively non-Western product. I contend that now—barely a half-decade later—that is no longer the case. I would certainly not disagree with José Cabezón when he summarizes the critical question for Buddhist Studies:

> Although the academic study of Buddhism is much older than the International Association of Buddhist Studies and the journal to which it gave rise, the founding of the latter, which represents a significant— perhaps pivotal—step in the institutionalization of the field, is something that occurred less than twenty years ago. Nonetheless, whether a true discipline or not—whether or not Buddhist Studies has already achieved disciplinary status, whether it is proto-disciplinary or superdisciplinary—there is an apparent integrity to Buddhist Studies that at the very least calls for an analysis of the field in holistic terms.[11]

Rather, I would simply argue that any inquiry into the disciplinary status of Buddhist Studies must now include the subdiscipline of Western Buddhism as part of that self-reflection.

THE STUDY OF WESTERN BUDDHISM

Generally speaking, the subdisciplines of Buddhist Studies have traditionally been defined by geographic area, and most often include South Asia, Southeast Asia, East Asia, and Inner/Central Asia. Of course the entire spectrum of methodological approaches utilized in the study of religious traditions are regularly employed in these studies, singly or in combination, thus providing a healthy cross-fertilization between discipline and method.[12] While the area-study approach mentioned above was in place prior to the current generation of Buddhological scholars, it is not clear if those delineations were based on programmatic, pedagogic, intellectual, scholarly, or political grounds, or on some other basis altogether. That having been said, how, then, is subdisciplinary status determined, and then verified, for Buddhist Studies? What criteria should be applied to Western Buddhism, or "socially engaged Buddhism," or any potentially new subdiscipline? What combination of

1. scholarly literature on the topic, including bibliographic materials,
2. scholarly and popular journals devoted to the topic,
3. conferences focusing on the topic, and papers at scholarly meetings,
4. courses taught in colleges and universities,
5. scholars with professional training in the topic, and
6. other criteria

are necessary, and in what baseline quantities, before we can ascribe subdisciplinary status to a topic of inquiry in Buddhist Studies?

As noted above, there was little primary or secondary literature available when I undertook my initial research on American Buddhism. Nor did much appear until the mid-1980s. There were virtually no journal articles, and no more than a handful of scholarly volumes. The first general, introductory book to make a serious, well-informed effort to discuss Western Buddhism as an independent topic was Peter Harvey's *An Introduction to Buddhism* (1990). Ross Reat's *Buddhism: A History* (1994) also devoted considerable space to Western Buddhism, and the fourth edition of *The Buddhist Religion* by Robinson and Johnson (1997) offered valuable insights about the growth of Western Buddhism. Newer books routinely include sections and bibliographic resources on Western Buddhism. Research articles have begun to appear regularly in scholarly journals devoted to the study of Buddhism, and, beginning with the publication of Thomas Tweed's *The American Encounter with Buddhism, 1844–1912: Victorian Culture and the Limits of Dissent* (1992), a rich and diverse series of scholarly monographs and edited volumes have begun to appear. These include general volumes such as *Deutsche Buddhisten: Geschichte und Gemeinshaften* (by Martin Baumann), *Many Petals of the Lotus: Five Asian Buddhist Communities in Toronto* (by Janet McLellan), *Buddhism and Africa* (edited by Michel Clasquin and Jacobus Krüger), *The Faces of Buddhism in America* (edited by Charles Prebish and Kenneth Tanaka), *Luminous Passage: The Practice and Study of Buddhism in America* (by Charles Prebish), *American Buddhism: Methods and Findings in Recent Scholarship* (edited by Duncan Ryūken Williams and Christopher Queen), and *Buddhism in America* (by Richard Seager). They also include tradition-specific volumes, like *A Time to Chant: The Sōka Gakkai Buddhists in Britain* (by Bryan Wilson and Karel Dobbelaere), *Soka Gakkai in America: Accommodation and Conversion* (by Philip Hammond and David Machacek), *The Lotus and the Maple Leaf: The Sōka Gakkai Buddhist Movement in Canada* (by Daniel Metraux), *Old Wisdom in the New World: Americanization in Two Immigrant Theravada Buddhist Temples* (by Paul Numrich), and *The Adaptation of Buddhism to the West: Diamond Sangha Buddhist Groups in Australia* (by Michelle Spuler). We now also have topical volumes, including *Buddhism through American Women's Eyes* (edited by Karma Lekshe Tsomo) and *Engaged Buddhism in the West* (edited by Christopher Queen).

Comprehensive bibliographies for specific countries and areas are also increasingly available. Martin Baumann's "Buddhism in Europe: An Annotated Bibliography" and "American Buddhism: A Bibliography on Buddhist Traditions and Schools in the U.S.A. and Canada," Michelle Spuler's "Buddhism in Australia," and Cristina Moreira Rocha's "Buddhism in Brazil" are all available on the website of the *Journal of Global Buddhism* (http://www.globalbuddhism.org/res.html [19 June 2002]).

Until 2000, there was not a single scholarly journal devoted solely to the topic of Western Buddhism. This should hardly be surprising, considering the dearth of scholarly journals worldwide that are exclusively devoted to the study of Buddhism: only the *Journal of the International Association of Buddhist Studies*, *The Eastern Buddhist*, *Pacific World*, and *Journal of Buddhist Ethics*. Only the first three ranked in the top eighteen journals identified as publication vehicles by scholars in my 1995 survey.[13] In January 2000, the online *Journal of Global Buddhism* was launched with a mission almost exclusively committed to the investigation of Western Buddhism, as can be seen from a quick glance at the nine subject classifications it considers for publication:

Historical Studies—Major historical investigations of Buddhist development with a focus on Western countries; developments within individual Buddhist traditions concentrating on historical trends in Western Buddhism.

Transnational Studies—Comparative studies in the development of Western Buddhism; area studies and their interconnectedness; concerns for de-territorialization of locality.

Issues in the Development of Buddhist Traditions—Investigation of
membership determination; ethnicity; Buddhist practice(s); democratization; adaptation and acculturation; ecumenical movements; future
trends.

Case Studies and Biographical Studies—Investigations of individual
Buddhist groups(s); multiple studies of Buddhist communities within
Buddhist traditions and sectarian divisions; studies of leading figures
in modern Buddhism, reflecting both Asian immigrant and Western
convert communities; studies of leading figures in modern Buddhism,
reflecting both Asian immigrant and Western convert communities.

Survey Results and Their Interpretation—Empirical findings resulting from individual investigations; results from journal-sponsored
surveys.

Research Bibliographies—Inclusive, broadly based, comprehensive bibliographies; case-specific tradition-based bibliographies; country-
specific bibliographies; issue-oriented bibliographies.

Human Rights Issues and Socially Engaged Buddhism—Concerns for
all areas of human rights; issues of equality; justice; freedom; privacy;
women's rights; international codes; peace issues; ecological issues;
animal rights; prison reform; social activism.

Interfaith Dialogue—Similarities and differences between modern
Buddhist traditions and other world religions; cross-cultural hermeneutics.

Theoretical and Methodological Studies—Transcultural transplantation
of Buddhist traditions: models and systematizations; images, projections, and idealizations of Buddhism; politics of representation; the
impact of globalization; examination of approaches to the study of
global Buddhism, such as diaspora studies.

The investigation of Western Buddhism also benefits from a series of semi-
scholarly journals sponsored by various Western Buddhist communities,
such as *Mountain Record*, published by Zen Mountain Monastery; *Journal
of the Order of Buddhist Contemplatives*, published by the students of the
now-deceased Jiyu Kennett; and the *Western Buddhist Review*, published
by the Friends of the Western Buddhist Order (FWBO). These semi-
scholarly journals often contain articles by well-known scholars and
scholar-practitioners (see below), as do a number of popular, but literate,
Buddhist periodicals like *Tricycle* and *Shambhala Sun*. Moreover, much research material that is clearly journal-quality can be found on the World
Wide Web. The best entry portals for this material can be found through

DharmaNet International and the "Global Resources" link of the *Journal of Buddhist Ethics*.[14]

Before 1994, only two conferences in North America were devoted to the topic of American Buddhism, and neither was scholarly. In 1977, Syracuse University sponsored a conference ambitiously titled "The Flowering of Buddhism in America." In 1987, the Zen Lotus Society in Ann Arbor, Michigan, sponsored the "Conference on World Buddhism in North America." The first genuinely scholarly conference focusing on American Buddhism was held in 1994, at the Institute of Buddhist Studies in Berkeley, with sponsorship through the Numata Lecture Series. Almost weekly through the fall of 1994, a noted scholarly authority on American Buddhism offered a lecture, and the collected papers were eventually published in 1998 as *The Faces of Buddhism in America*. This initial conference was followed by another, three years later (in May 1997), entitled "Buddhism in America: Methods and Findings in Recent Scholarship," sponsored by the Harvard Buddhist Studies Forum. Harvard professor Diana Eck, in her foreword to the edited volume in which the papers were collected and published, observed that

> [t]he conference that gave rise to this volume was a landmark in Buddhist studies and in American studies, bringing together scholars from both fields of study to focus on new research in American Buddhism. . . . As the field of Buddhist studies begins to take the reality of American Buddhist communities seriously, and as scholars of American religion begin to wrestle with the presence and the significance of old and new Buddhist communities, the dialogue of disciplines represented by this volume will become increasingly necessary, and increasingly fruitful.[15]

In his preface, Duncan Ryūken Williams, one of the conveners of the conference, echoed Diana Eck: "In addition to the presentation of original research, the conference also served as a forum to discuss methodological issues in the emerging field of studies on American Buddhism."[16] This is one of the earliest references to Western Buddhism as an emergent discipline.

Because conferences are expensive to stage and difficult to arrange, the most usual arenas for the presentation of research in Buddhist Studies are the annual or semiannual meetings of professional societies. For North American scholars, the regular home for Buddhist Studies scholars is the Buddhism Section of the American Academy of Religion. Begun in 1981 as a "group" by George Bond and Charles Prebish, this AAR unit provides five yearly panels devoted to Buddhist Studies. Until the mid-1990s, there were virtually no papers on any aspect of Western Buddhism to be found.

By 1998, a panel on "American Buddhism at the Millennium" was attended by more than 150 scholars, representing that year's largest attendance of any Buddhism Section presentation. The following year, the presentation of the film *Becoming a Buddha in L.A.*, also sponsored by the Buddhism section, was enormously successful. Unquestionably, the flagship professional society for Buddhist Studies scholars is the International Association of Buddhist Studies, founded in 1976 under the direction of A. K. Narain. Although the society sponsors worldwide conferences every other year, until 1999 not a single paper on Western Buddhism had been presented. At the XIIth Congress, held in Lausanne in August 1999 and attended by slightly more than three hundred scholars, the "Buddhism in the West" panel was attended by approximately seventy-five scholars, despite being one of seven panels scheduled at the same time. It is worth reporting, too, that in 1997, the Society for the Scientific Study of Religion / Religious Research Association sponsored a panel entitled "Problems of Sex and Power in American Buddhism" at its annual meeting in San Diego. If these examples represent the current level of interest in Western Buddhism in professional societies, there can be little doubt that Western Buddhism is becoming important to Buddhist Studies scholars worldwide.

CURRENT DATA

Over the last five years, I have collected a significant amount of anecdotal information about courses in Western Buddhism. In 2000, in an attempt to formalize and document that information, I posted two inquiries on the "budschol" list created by Charles Muller in Japan. At that time, the list had nearly three hundred members, all of whom established credentials in Buddhist Studies as a condition of being allowed to join the list. As such, it reflected the primary constituency, worldwide, that I was seeking to contact. I received almost thirty responses, which I considered both good and bad. It was good in the sense that I learned of some courses being taught that I had not imagined, and disappointing in the sense that some individuals who taught courses in Western Buddhism did not bother to respond. Some individuals did not teach complete courses on the topic, but devoted a major section of a more general course to the topic. The courses mentioned immediately above were taught in North America, Europe, South America, Australia, and New Zealand. Not all who responded taught courses on the topic, but responded to additional queries about publication or the presentation of papers at scholarly meetings. Nonetheless, the almost unanimous sentiment collected from the responses was excitement and enthusiasm over the success of each course on the part of the faculty member and a forward-looking approach with regard to repeating the course. Enrollment in the courses reported ranged from a low of fifteen students to a high of fifty.

In my "budschol" request, I invited those surveyed to offer narrative comments regarding the status and role of Western Buddhism in the general discipline of Buddhist Studies. The most revealing comments, on the positive side, were these:

> (1) My sense is that it is a field that is growing in importance and respectability among Buddhist Studies scholars. In the past, I think many would have looked askance at my intention to put down my Pāli, Sanskrit, and Buddhist Hybrid Sanskrit dictionaries for a while and concentrate on American Buddhism—like I was copping out and studying "Buddhism Lite." While some would still no doubt feel this way, I think some of the recent scholarship on the subject has convinced many in the Buddhist Studies community that this is an important subject and that we are probably witnessing the next major development in the history of Buddhism.
>
> (2) The level of interest in courses on Western Buddhism has been unusually high both times I taught it. . . . I have detected an increasing interest among graduate students in doing theses on some aspect of American Buddhism. . . . I would strongly encourage students to work in this area if they felt so inclined. This is a radical change since 1990, when I strongly discouraged students from exploring Western Buddhism, on the grounds that specializing in such an area would marginalize them in the academic world and limit their opportunities for academic employment. (Obviously, I am better at history than prophecy.)
>
> (3) The study of Western Buddhism has, since about 1997, at last begun to come out into the open, as scholars have acknowledged they can learn from issues raised by the changes occurring in Western Buddhism, issues that throw light on and even affect Buddhism in history and in Asia.

On the negative side, there was only one response offered:

> I specifically forbid my students from writing research papers on Western Buddhism. Since my experience is that American undergraduates are extremely self-absorbed, I simply use the course as an example of a non-Western religious and cultural form.

Nonetheless, at least one well-known Buddhist Studies professor has suggested that no resources whatsoever ought to be committed to the study of Western Buddhism, because such a gesture subtracts valuable, needed resources from "real Buddhist Studies." Other, anecdotal reports suggest that this is not a solitary opinion.

Table 4.1. Buddhist Studies, Areas of Specialization, 1995

Area	Number of Respondents	Percent
Japan/East Asia	39	36.8
India/South Asia	37	34.9
Tibet/Inner Asia	22	20.8
China/East Asia	16	15.1
Korea/East Asia	2	1.9
Other areas	3	2.8

Above, I referred to two surveys I conducted about the discipline of Buddhist Studies. Of primary concern was the subdisciplinary area of specialization of those responding. However, in terms of specialization, comparison between the two samples would be incongruous. For the 1993 sample, only one primary specialization was recorded, while in the 1995 sample it became clear that in many cases multiple specializations were emphasized. As such, in 1993, 37.0 percent of the sample reported specializing in Japan/East Asia, while 29.6 percent reported India/South Asia, 23.5 percent Tibet/Inner Asia, 6.2 percent China/East Asia, 2.5 percent Korea/East Asia, and 1.2 percent indicated other choices. The results of the 1995 survey are shown in table 4.1. Because multiple listings were allowed in the 1995 sample, the survey yielded a total in excess of 100 percent.

In neither 1993 nor 1995 did a single individual list Western Buddhism as an area of specialization. By 1999, when Duncan Ryūken Williams published his two appendixes on "Dissertations and Theses on American Buddhism" and "North American Dissertations and Theses on Topics Related to Buddhism," the circumstances had changed dramatically—at least with regard to the period from 1990 to 1997 (the final year for which Williams offers data). Of the total number of Ph.D. dissertations devoted to Buddhist-related topics recorded between 1990 and 1997, 5.9 percent focused on aspects of American Buddhism.[17] Unfortunately, it is difficult to draw overly specific conclusions regarding the discipline, because many dissertations cut across subdisciplines, reflecting a cross-cultural approach to topics such as ethics, Madhyamaka philosophy, or bodhisattva practice. My suspicion is that, as new and updated data become available, the numbers of dissertations focusing on Western Buddhism will rise dramatically.

Previously many, if not most, Buddhist Studies scholars have not listed their area of specialization on their curriculum vitae. Their scholarly interest was usually discernable from language proficiency and publication data, or, in the case of newly minted Ph.D.s, from their coursework and dissertation topic. In fact, of the 106 files submitted to me in 1995, only a few directly stated an area of specialization. As the World Wide Web expands, profoundly influencing the way in which departments and programs in Religious Studies advertise themselves, it is increasingly common for scholars included in the "faculty" link of a departmental web page to offer more complete descriptions of themselves and their work. Individuals interested in doing a quick survey of their own would be well advised to utilize Gene Thursby's remarkably useful guide to these programs. It is clearly most complete for North America (http://www.clas.ufl.edu/gthursby/rel/depts-na.htm [23 Jan. 2002]), but it also surveys Great Britain, continental Europe, and Australia/New Zealand. A quick perusal finds such specialization descriptions as "Asian Religions in America" (Thomas Tweed), "Asian Religious Traditions in the U.S." (Stephen Prothero), "Buddhism in the West" (Michelle Spuler; Martin Baumann), and "Western Buddhism" (Charles Prebish), and the list is growing.

At the 1997 Harvard Buddhist Studies Forum mentioned above, following Diana Eck's opening presentation, Duncan Ryūken Williams remarked that as we approached the turn of the millennium, it was impossible to earn a degree in Buddhist Studies without paying proper attention to its newest subdiscipline, American Buddhism. Williams's remark, and my continued emphasis of the same point, has implications that go beyond this new subdiscipline. Ken Kraft, for example, says "Charles Prebish and others go so far as to argue that a doctoral degree in Buddhist Studies should now include 'proper attention' to American Buddhism. If American Buddhist Studies and engaged Buddhist Studies continue to develop, the two fields will have areas that overlap." [18] It is also interesting to note that in 2000 Professor John Crossley, director of the School of Religion at the University of Southern California, said in a *Los Angeles Times* article that USC was "desperately hoping to hire a Buddhologist knowledgeable about Buddhism in America." Moreover, the description for the Hershey Chair of Buddhist Studies at Harvard University required that

> [t]he first permanent incumbent of this chair will be a specialist with appropriate linguistic competence in at least one area of the Buddhist tradition and able to guide students in the exploration of its classical texts, historical developments and social contexts. The scholar should also be knowledgeable about the thought, practice, and values of contemporary

Buddhism both in Asia and the West and should be able to take a broad approach to the tradition as a whole in his or her teaching and advising.[19]

It would appear that job descriptions are now beginning to reflect recognition of the importance of the study of Western Buddhism in the Religious Studies curricula of colleges and universities.

ADDITIONAL CONSIDERATIONS

At the outset of chapter 4 of *Luminous Passage: The Practice and Study of Buddhism in America,* I related a story from 1967 in which I discovered, in rather theatrical fashion, that some Buddhist Studies scholars also considered themselves Buddhist practitioners. This was my first exposure to a plausible resolution to the dichotomy that seemingly existed between Buddhist scholarship and Buddhist practice.

Stories reflecting this dichotomy between study and practice abound in both the primary and the secondary literature on the subject. Walpola Rahula's *History of Buddhism in Ceylon* provides a good summary of the issue.[20] During the first century B.C.E. in the midst of potential foreign invasion and a severe famine, Sri Lankan monks feared that the Buddhist *Tipiṭaka,* preserved only in oral tradition, might be lost. Thus the scriptures were committed to writing for the first time. Nonetheless, in the aftermath of the entire dilemma, a new question arose: what is the basis of the "teaching" (i.e., *Sāsana*)—learning or practice? A clear difference of opinion resulted in the development of two groups: the Dhammakathikas, who claimed that learning was the basis of the *Sāsana,* and the Paṃsukūlikas, who argued for practice as the basis. The Dhammakathikas apparently won out, as attested to by several statements quoted by Rahula.[21] The two vocations described above came to be known as *gantha-dhura,* or the "vocation of books," and *vipassanā-dhura,* or the "vocation of meditation," with the *former* being regarded as the superior training (because surely meditation would not be possible if the teachings were lost). Moreover, not the least characteristic of these two divisions was that the *vipassanā-dhura* monks began to live in the forest, where they could best pursue their vocation undisturbed, while the *gantha-dhura* monks began to dwell in villages and towns. As such, the *gantha-dhura* monks began to play a significant role in Buddhist education, and Rahula says as much.[22] In view of the above, it would probably not be going too far to refer to the *gantha-dhura* monks as *scholar-monks.* These so-called scholar-monks would largely fulfill the role of *settled monastic renunciant* in Reginald Ray's creative three-tiered model for Buddhist practitioners (contrasted with the *forest renunciant* and *layperson*).[23]

Why is this distinction so important? It is significant for at least two reasons. First, and most obviously, it reveals why the tradition of study in Buddhism, so long minimized in popular and scholarly investigations of the American Buddhist tradition, has such an impact on that same tradition, and has resulted in the rapid development of American Buddhist schools and institutes of higher learning in the latter quarter of the twentieth century. Second, it explains why the American Buddhist movement has encouraged a high level of "Buddhist literacy" among its practitioners. It also highlights the fact that the American Buddhist movement has been almost exclusively a *lay* movement. While many leaders of American Buddhist groups may have had formal monastic training (whether or not they continue to lead monastic lifestyles), the vast majority of their disciples have not. Thus the educational model on which American Buddhists pattern their behavior differs from the traditional Asian Buddhist archetype. It is, in fact, the *converse* of the traditional model. As such, at least with regard to Buddhist study and education, there is a leadership gap in the American Buddhist community, one largely not filled by an American Sangha of so-called scholar-monks.

Above, it was noted that in Asia the monastic renunciants were almost exclusively responsible for the religious education of the lay Sangha. On the other hand, virtually everyone who writes on American Buddhism sees it almost exclusively as a lay movement, devoid of a *significant* monastic component. Emma Layman, one of the earliest researchers in the field, said as much: "In general, American Buddhists are expected to lead their lives within the lay community rather than in a monastic setting. . . ."[24] Later, Rick Fields echoed the same sentiment: "Generalization of any kind seems to dissolve in the face of such cultural and religious diversity. And yet it does seem safe to suggest that lay practice is the real heart and koan of American Buddhism."[25] In the absence of the traditional scholar-monks so prevalent in Asia, it may well be that the scholar-practitioners of today's American Buddhism will fulfill the role of quasi-monastics, or at least treasure-troves of Buddhist literacy and information, functioning as guides through whom one's understanding of the Dharma may be sharpened. In this way, individual practice might once again be balanced with individual study so that Buddhist study deepens one's practice, while Buddhist practice informs one's study. Obviously, such a suggestion spawns two further questions: (1) are there sufficient scholar-practitioners currently active in American Buddhism to make such an impact? and (2) are they actually making that impact?

With regard to the former question, much of the information reported above is necessarily anecdotal. By simply making mental notes at conferences attended by American Buddhologists, based on discussions of individual practice, one can develop a roster of scholar-practitioners who are openly Buddhist. While such a roster is certainly not publishable, the number is quite clearly *at least* half of all those with credentials sufficient to gain membership on "budschol." My suspicion is that the list on a worldwide basis would present an equal percentage of scholars who are Buddhist. What remains to be seen—and is currently impossible to estimate—is how many of the scholar-practitioners of Western Buddhism have already focused, or will begin to focus, on Western Buddhism as a research topic.

NOTES

1. Jan Nattier, "Who Is a Buddhist? Charting the Landscape of Buddhist America," in *The Faces of Buddhism in America*, edited by Charles S. Prebish and Kenneth K. Tanaka (Berkeley: University of California Press, 1998), 319.

2. Charles S. Prebish, *American Buddhism* (North Scituate, Massachusetts: Duxbury Press, 1979), viii.

3. See Ray L. Hart, "Religious and Theological Studies in American Higher Education: A Pilot Study," *Journal of the American Academy of Religion* 59, no. 4 (Winter 1991), 715–827.

4. Malcolm David Eckel, "Review and Evaluation of the Buddhism Section of the American Academy of Religion," December 1991, 2.

5. Malcolm David Eckel, "The Ghost at the Table: On the Study of Buddhism and the Study of Religion," *Journal of the American Academy of Religion* 62, no. 4 (Winter 1994), 1088.

6. See Charles S. Prebish, "Buddhist Studies American Style: A Shot in the Dark," *Religious Studies Review* 9, no. 4 (October 1983), 323–30.

7. "The Academic Study of Buddhism in America: A Current Analysis," *Gassho* 1, no. 2 (January/February 1994); "The Academic Study of Buddhism in the United States: A Current Analysis," *Religion* 24 (1994), 271–8.

8. Pages 185–96.

9. In *Journal of the International Association of Buddhist Studies* 15, no. 1 (Summer 1992), 104–17.

10. Luis Gómez, "Unspoken Paradigms: Meanderings through the Metaphors of a Field," *Journal of the International Association of Buddhist Studies* 18, no. 2 (Winter 1995), 190.

11. José Cabezón, "Buddhist Studies as a Discipline and the Role of Theory," *Journal of the International Association of Buddhist Studies* 18, no. 2 (Winter 1995), 236.

12. So as to avoid confusion, and to circumvent the debate about terms such as *discipline* and *field* that went on during the 1970s and beyond, I have chosen to utilize the nomenclature of *discipline* for Buddhist Studies and *methodology* for the regimens employed to investigate them. This practice is also consistent with the terminology employed by most scholars in writing about Buddhist Studies.

13. It should be noted that in 1995, the *Journal of Buddhist Literature* did not yet exist and the *Journal of Buddhist Ethics* was less than one year old.

14. See http://www.dharmanet.org [1 Feb. 2002] and http://jbe.la.psu.edu [1 Feb. 2002], respectively.

15. See Duncan Ryūken Williams and Christopher S. Queen (eds.), *American Buddhism: Methods and Findings in Recent Scholarship* (Richmond, U.K.: Curzon Press, 1999), xi.

16. Ibid., xii.

17. Ibid., 262–311.

18. Kenneth Kraft, "New Voices in Engaged Buddhist Studies," in *Engaged Buddhism in the West,* edited by Christopher S. Queen (Boston: Wisdom, 2000), 488.

19. See *The Chronicle of Higher Education* online at http://chronicle.com/che-data/jobads.dir/ads-by-search-000331/all/144528.html [20 Apr. 2000].

20. See Walpola Rahula, *History of Buddhism in Ceylon,* 2nd ed. (Colombo, Sri Lanka: M. D. Gunasena, 1966), 157–63.

21. Ibid. 158–9: "Even if there be a hundred thousand bhikkhus practicing *vipassanā* (meditation), there will be no realization of the Noble Path if there is no learning (doctrine, *pariyatti*)" (from the Commentary on the *Aṅguttara Nikāya*). Commentaries from the *Dīgha Nikāya, Majjhima Nikāya,* and *Vibhaṅga* echo the same sentiment.

22. Ibid., 287.

23. See Reginald Ray, *Buddhist Saints in India: A Study in Buddhist Values and Orientations* (New York: Oxford University Press, 1994), 433–47.

24. Emma McCloy Layman, *Buddhism in America* (Chicago: Nelson-Hall, 1976), 18.

25. Rick Fields, *How the Swans Came to the Lake: A Narrative History of Buddhism in America,* 3rd revised and updated ed. (Boston: Shambhala, 1992), 371.

II

DIFFUSION
The Histories of Buddhism in Western Countries

Buddhism in Europe
Past, Present, Prospects

Martin Baumann

INTRODUCTION

Interest in Buddhism has grown exponentially in Europe since the early 1990s. In television newscasts, talk shows, and newspaper reports, Buddhism has been featured widely. Around the turn of the twenty-first century, Buddhism is "in" in many European countries. A magazine even declared Buddhism as the "trend religion 2000." Suddenly, film stars and starlets, soccer players, and many other public people profess to be followers of Buddhism, a religion held to be fashionable, modern, and deep in content. This euphoric interest in Buddhism and its positive recognition throughout the media contrasts a conversation I had in 1990, during which I plainly had to justify my Ph.D. research on Buddhism in Germany. "Buddhism? Are there any Buddhists in Germany?" a university colleague asked, partly puzzled, partly amused.

Times have changed. Today such a question would turn the concern back to the questioner. It has become public knowledge that Buddhism is not confined to Thailand or Japan, and that a growing number of Buddhists live in Europe. Few know, however, that the history of Buddhism in Europe dates back more than 150 years. This chapter shall outline the historic developments, from incipient interest in intellectual circles during the mid-nineteenth century, to the founding of first societies around 1900, up to the explosive institutional growth since the mid-1970s. Buddhism in Europe is characterized by a diversity and plurality of traditions, schools, orders, and lineages. Far from the regions that experience homogeneity in legal, social, and cultural terms, country-related specificities have made a lasting impact on the spread and institutionalization of these traditions and lineages. The final section will address the prospects of Buddhism in Europe, stretching current developments within the two strands of convert and immigrant Buddhism into the future.

HISTORICAL DEVELOPMENTS: BUDDHIST IDEAS COME TO EUROPE

The first century of encounter between Buddhism and Europe was clearly dominated by the intellectual and ethical interests of Westerners who took up Buddhism as their new life orientation. In contrast to North and South America, Asian immigrants with a Buddhist background did not arrive until the second half of the twentieth century. Buddhist migrant communities started to form no earlier than the 1960s and 1970s.

The beginning of the encounter can be dated to the mid-nineteenth century, although fragmentary and distorted information about Buddhist customs and concepts had trickled into Europe since the seventeenth century. Around 1800, as texts and descriptions about Indian religions became known in literate and academic circles in Europe, a glorifying enthusiasm for the East took hold. In particular, the Romantic movement with its rejection of the pre-eminence of rationalism, and the Oriental Renaissance, a movement first named by the German Sanskritist Friedrich Schlegel (1772–1829) in 1803, discovered the Asian world and its religious and philosophical traditions. Like many fellow Romantics, Schlegel was determined to trace the supposedly lost, genuine spirituality in India and in Sanskrit texts.[1]

During this time, Buddhism was not understood as a religious tradition of its own. Rather, European intellectuals conceived Buddhist ideas as forming part of the beliefs of the "Hindoos." The academic work of the French philologist Eugène Burnouf (1801–52) served to mark the boundaries and differences between the religions. In his *L'introduction à l'histoire du bouddhisme indien*, Burnouf presented a scientific survey of Buddhist history and doctrines for the first time. He imposed a rational order on ideas hitherto perceived as unrelated, thus creating the "prototype of the European concept of Buddhism."[2] Since the 1850s, Europe has witnessed a boom of translations, studies, and portrayals. These paved the way for an enhanced knowledge of and interest in Buddha as a historic person and in his doctrines. The writings of Arthur Schopenhauer (1788–1860) stirred up a particular interest in Buddhist philosophy and ethics among artists, academics, and intellectuals. Buddhism was not exported from abroad by Asian emissaries; it was imported from within by European orientalists. The discovery of the Asian religion was, however, essentially treated as a textual object, being located in books, oriental libraries, and institutes of the West. Buddhism as a lived tradition was of no interest.[3]

France, England, and Germany had been the countries foremost in studying and textualizing Buddhism. In 1860, Jules Barthélemy-Saint-Hilaire published one of the most popular works on Buddhism of the time, *Le Bouddha et sa religion*. Like his fellow clergymen, he intended, however, to discredit the Buddhist tradition and to restore the superiority of Christianity. Up to the 1870s, scholars relied mainly on accidentally collected

Mahāyāna Buddhist texts, be they Nepalese, Tibetan, or Chinese manuscripts. Based on these, the American Henry Steel Olcott (1832–1907) and the flamboyant Madame Helena Petrovna Blavatsky (1831–91) founded the Theosophical Society in New York in 1875, strongly increasing the interest in Eastern religions in the United States and Europe.[4]

Around 1880, a decisive shift toward the texts of the Pāli Canon is observable. The British scholar Thomas W. Rhys Davids (1843–1922) established the Pāli Text Society in 1881. The society's aims were (and still are) the study of Buddhist texts preserved in the Pāli language and the distribution of those texts in scholarly editions and translations. Within the German-speaking area, the Pāli-based study *Buddha: His Life, His Doctrine, His Order*, by Hermann Oldenberg (1854–1920), popularized Buddhism more than any other work of the time. The Pāli Canon was held to represent the authentic, "original," and "pure" Buddhist teachings, devoid of the interpretations and changes of later times. Parallel to the academic studies, first treatises appeared that glorified the Buddha and his teachings. Sir Edwin Arnold's poem *The Light of Asia* (1879) aroused a strong interest among bourgeois, educated members of the upper and middle classes. "The sale of the book exceeded a million copies in Europe and America, its circulation being wider than that of any other book on Buddhism," as William Peiris noted a century later.[5] Likewise, the *Buddhist Catechism* of Olcott, published in 1881 and with a strong theosophical bias, enjoyed many reprints and reached a widespread audience. The shift toward Pāli texts by no means included a shift toward paying attention to the living Theravāda tradition in South Asia. Interest was solely oriented toward ethical and philosophical concepts as they could be extracted from the texts.

THE TURN OF THE CENTURY: EUROPE AND SOUTH ASIA MEET

The glorification of Buddhism in publications and treatises persuaded a few learned men to take up Buddhism. By way of reading and intellectual examination, these "self-converted followers of the teaching" became Buddhists in the early 1880s. To lead a "proper" Buddhist life was thought of, however, in terms of becoming a monk in South Asia. The first to do this was Gordon Douglas, ordained as Aśoka in Colombo in 1899. The Scottish chemist and former Golden Dawn occultist Allan Bennett McGregor (1872–1923) became more famous than Douglas. He was ordained as a monk, a *bhikkhu* (Pāli), under the name Ananda Metteyya in 1902. Having returned to England, he founded the Buddhist Society of Great Britain and Ireland in London in 1907. The second prominent *bhikkhu* at that time was the German musician Anton W. F. Gueth (1878–1957), ordained as Nyānatiloka in 1904. In the years to come, Nyānatiloka became well known for his Pāli translations and Buddhist lectures and for the founding of the Island Hermitage in Ceylon in 1911. This hermitage became the focus of European Buddhist activity in South Asia.[6]

Becoming a *bhikkhu* and wearing the monastic robe remained the rare exception, however. The ethical and intellectual interests in the teachings of Theravāda Buddhism gained organizational momentum with the founding of Buddhist societies. Indologist Karl Seidenstücker (1876–1936) formed the Society for the Buddhist Mission in Leipzig, Germany, in 1903. In lectures, pamphlets, and books, the first professed Buddhists tried to win members from the educated middle and upper social strata. This and other, often short-lived, societies praised Buddhism as the "religion of reason," the religion that rested on insight and knowledge alone. In a similar orientation, the society formed in Great Britain in 1907 published a quarterly journal, *The Buddhist Review*, that stressed a rational interpretation of Buddhism.[7]

The incipient Buddhist movement in Europe has to be put into proper light by considering Buddhism's changes in Asia in the late nineteenth century and the beginning of its global spread. The close interaction between Europe and—mainly—South Asia is of prime importance. Confronted by colonialism, Western ideas, and missionary Christianity, monks and spokesmen in Asia had started to reinterpret Buddhist teachings to fit modernity and Western challenges. In Ceylon, the focal point of South Asian Buddhist revival, urban, educated Buddhists emphasized the rational and scientific aspects of the Buddhist teachings. In collaboration with nineteenth-century European scholarship and its historic-critical approach, Buddhists worked to unearth a thus-conceived "original" Buddhism, as could be found in the texts of the Pāli Canon. Ceylonese modernist Buddhists, deriving from the new social strata that came into existence in colonial times, portrayed Buddhism as pragmatic, rational, universal, and socially active.[8]

Foremost among these Buddhist modernizers was the Ceylonese Anagārika Dharmapāla (1864–1933). In 1891, Dharmapāla set up the Mahā Bodhi Society, the first lay-led Theravāda organization, and strove to resuscitate Buddhism in India. Dharmapāla's well-received speech at the World's Parliament of Religions in Chicago in 1893 established him as the spokesman for the Buddhist revival in South Asia. During the following four decades, until his death in 1933, Dharmapāla untiringly toured the globe, visiting England four times, the United States six times, China, Japan, and Thailand, as well as France, Italy, and Germany. Overseas branches of the Mahā Bodhi Society were formed in the United States (1897), Germany (1911), and Great Britain (1926). Undoubtedly, Dharmapāla can be called the first global Buddhist missionary or propagandist and the Mahā Bodhi Society the first inter- or transnational Buddhist organization.[9]

Dharmapāla had a far-reaching impact in invigorating the incipient Buddhist activities in Europe and the United States. As a lay Buddhist, an *anagārika* (non-householder), he was not restricted to the many rules of a *bhikkhu*. During this early phase, lay Buddhists were more influential than Theravāda *bhikkhus*, regardless of whether the monks were Ceylonese or European converts. This was in marked contrast to conditions at the same time in South Asia. Although monks were praised as honorary examples and shining models, their role and status seemed too exotic and unfamiliar in Europe right into the 1970s.

THE 1920S AND 1930S: NEW ACTIVITIES

Efforts to spread and establish Buddhism in Europe were thus taken up and continued by lay followers. After the disaster of World War I, Buddhists began to practice the teachings. Although in some of the small circles members continued to play aesthetically with Buddhist ideas, in other, newly founded societies or "parishes" religious practices (such as worship, spiritual exercises, and devotional acts) caught on.

In Germany, Georg Grimm (1868–1945) joined Karl Seidenstücker in founding the Buddhist Parish for Germany in Munich in 1921. The parish saw itself expressly as a religious community of Buddhist lay followers. Its members had resorted to the Three Jewels, that is, to the Buddha, Dhamma, and Sangha, and followed the five ethical precepts of a lay Buddhist. Lectures by Grimm were attended by about five hundred, occasionally a thousand, listeners. During the same time, the Berlin Buddhist Paul Dahlke (1865–1928) started to publish his Buddhist treatises and, in 1924, built the now-famous Buddhist House. In this house, which was half residence and half temple, Dahlke led the same kind of ascetic and religious life as a South Asian Buddhist monk. The specific interpretations of the Pāli Canon and Theravāda Buddhism by Grimm and Dahlke led to the formation of two independent schools. A kind of schism arose within the German Buddhist movement, despite its small numbers, as the two honored teachers fought a fierce and polemic dispute on the interpretation of the teaching of *anatta* (no-self). Both schools continued their work during the Nazi regime, albeit restricted to small, private circles, at times under political control. In 1934, books by Grimm were burned and later leading Buddhists were temporarily arrested. Buddhists were regarded by the Nazis as pacifists and eccentrics. With the exception of those who had abandoned their Jewish faith and become Buddhists, no official or open persecution of Buddhism took place.[10]

In Great Britain, Christmas Humphreys (1901–83) formed the Buddhist Lodge of the Theosophical Society in London in 1924. As the society's name indicates, British Buddhists were more eclectic than their German co-followers and did not, as German Buddhists did, distance themselves from Theosophists. The society opened a Buddhist shrine room in 1925 and regularly celebrated Buddhist festival days. As a result of Dharmapāla's missionary efforts in Britain during the mid-1920s, a branch of the Mahā Bodhi Society opened in 1926 and a Buddhist *vihāra* (monastery) with three resident *bhikkhus* was established in London (1928–40, re-opened 1954). It was the first time that several Theravāda monks stayed for a long period outside of Asia and lived according to the *Vinaya* (monastic rules) in that unfamiliar place.[11]

Until the mid-twentieth century, Buddhist activities in Europe were strongest in Germany, followed by Great Britain. In other European countries, only a few organizational developments had occurred. Buddhist activities relied almost exclusively on one leading person who was able to gather more, but often got less, people. In France, the wealthy, American-born Grace Constant Lounsbery (1876–1964) founded the society called Les amis du Bouddhisme in 1929. The Paris-based group remained small, but succeeded in publishing its own journal, *La pensée bouddhique*. In Switzerland, Max Ladner (1889–1963) inspired some Buddhist activities during the 1940s and 1950s; between twelve and fifteen people met once a month in his house. The Zürich-based group published the Buddhist journal *Die Einsicht*, which appeared until 1961; the group itself ended in the same year. Although there had been a few scattered individual Buddhists in Austria, Hungary, and Italy (the famous Giuseppe Tucci), no further Buddhist organizations came into being until the late 1940s or early 1950s.[12]

Clearly, people who had taken up Buddhism as their new orientation in life dominated the small Buddhist scene. Except for Buddhist activists like Anagārika Dharmapāla or a few Japanese Zen Buddhists (Zenkai Omori, D. T. Suzuki) on academic visiting tours, no Asian Buddhist migrants had come to Europe so far. There are two exceptions to this pattern, however. Both relate to Russian Kalmyk Buddhists, who migrated from the Volga region to new places. In the early twentieth century, people from Kalmykia and from Southeast Siberian Buryatia had established sizable communities in Saint Petersburg, the tsarist Russian capital until 1917. Buddhism in a

Mongolian form, dominated by the Tibetan Gelug school, was the established religion of these people and the regions in which they lived. In Saint Petersburg, Kalmyk and Buryat people built a Gelugpa temple and monastery in 1909–15. The first Buddhist monastery on European soil thus was established not by Western European convert Buddhists, but by the Buryat-Mongol *lama* Agvan Dorzhev. During the Communist Revolution in 1917, however, the temple was desecrated. Following the comparative calm of the 1920s, Buddhists and scholars were persecuted and murdered under Stalin's dictatorship (1930s to 1953). Not until the 1980s did Buddhists see conditions improve in Russia.[13]

Kalmyk people also stayed temporarily in Belgrade (Yugoslavia) from the late 1920s to the mid-1940s. Fleeing the aftermath of the Russian Revolution, and following a brief sojourn in Turkey, a few hundred Kalmyks settled in the outskirts of Belgrade and established a Buddhist community. The refugees built a temple with a typical tower, consecrated in 1929 according to the traditional rituals. Buddhist festivals and regular ceremonies were scrupulously observed, marriages were conducted, and a Kalmyk Sunday school was set up. At the end of World War II, the Kalmyk community came to an end because its members, having fought on the German side, had to flee Belgrade and retreated to Germany.[14]

POST-WAR RENEWAL AND THE PLURALIZATION OF BUDDHISM

Since the 1880s, the texts of the Pāli Canon and the Theravāda monk as ideal and model had dominated the European adoption of Buddhism. Philosophical, ethical, and cognitive interests stood out clearly. The norm of a Buddhist in Europe was conceived of as a rational, detached person who intellectually purifies himself (seldom herself) from the root defilements of ignorance, hatred, and lustfulness. From the 1950s onward, this norm had to give way successively to a plurality of Buddhist traditions.

World War II had ended most Buddhist activities in Europe. However, after 1945, before the war's ruins had been cleared away, Buddhists reconstructed former Theravāda groups or founded new ones. The agony of the war led fair numbers of people to look for non-Christian, alternative life orientations. Buddhist lectures were well attended and Buddhist books and journals were well received. From the 1950s on, new Buddhist traditions were brought to Europe. Japanese Jōdo Shinshū (True Pure Land Teachings) came to Britain (1952) and to Germany (1956). Zen Buddhism became known through the writings of Daisetz T. Suzuki and Eugen Herrigel.

Before Zen became popular in Europe, Nichiren Buddhism traveled with Japanese businessmen and students to Britain, France, Italy, Germany, and elsewhere. During the 1970s and 1980s, a multitude of local Sōka Gakkai groups were founded and European convert members by far outnumbered the Japanese members. Until the mid-1990s, the Sōka Gakkai had been exclusive and formed no bonds or forms of cooperation with other Buddhist traditions. The Sōka Gakkai appears to be one of the numerically strongest Buddhist organizations in contemporary Europe.[15]

From the 1960s on, a multitude of new groups, societies, and institutions were founded in Austria, Belgium, France, Italy, Switzerland, Denmark, Norway, Finland, and Sweden. Buddhism spread widely as attractive books and translations became readily available. Simultaneously, Asian teachers started visiting the incipient groups, lecturing and conducting courses on a regular basis.[16]

During the 1960s, a considerable change occurred in the way that members and interested people wanted to experience Buddhism both spiritually and physically. Meditation became very popular. Courses in Zen and *vipassanā* meditation were booked up well in advance. Zen seminars took place in increasing numbers, with teachers coming from Japan to guide the newly formed Zen groups. In addition, increasing numbers of young Europeans started to travel to India or Burma in search of "Indian spirituality" and religious guidance. The romantic yearning for wholeness and originality was sought—again—in the East.

The Zen boom of the 1960s and 1970s was followed by a sharp rise of interest in Tibetan Buddhism. Tibetan teachers (the *lamas*) had first come to England, France, and Switzerland in the late 1960s, and had established small centers. From the mid-1970s on, however, as further high-ranking *lamas* conducted preaching tours in Europe, Tibetan Buddhism took off. Many members of the protest movements and the counterculture of the late 1960s became fascinated by Tibetan Buddhist rituals, symbols, and the lives of the *lamas*. In addition to the personal charisma of the numerous Tibetan teachers, the outstanding appearances of the 14th Dalai Lama inspired the Western followers. Since his first journey to Europe in 1973, the Dalai Lama has repeatedly visited centers all over Europe. For many, the Gelugpa monk is a living symbol and embodiment of deep spirituality, social engagement, and altruism. Within only two decades, converts to Tibetan Buddhism were able to found a multitude of centers and groups, at times outnumbering all other traditions in a country.[17]

This rapid increase, accompanied by an expansion of existing institutions, led to a considerable rise in the number of Buddhist groups and centers. In Britain, for example, the number of groups and centers quintupled in twenty years, from seventy-four to four hundred (1979–2000). In Germany, interest in Buddhism resulted in an increase from some forty groups to more than five hundred meditation circles, groups, centers, and societies (1975–99).[18] Comparable explosive growth rates occurred in other European countries, such as Italy, Austria, Switzerland, France, the Netherlands, and Denmark. Also, Eastern European countries witnessed a growing interest in Buddhism following the political changes since 1989. Numerous Buddhist groups, Tibetan and Zen groups in particular, have been founded in Poland, the Czech Republic, Hungary, and the western parts of the Russian Federation. Visits by European and North American Buddhist teachers, as well as a longing for spiritual alternatives to the established Roman Catholic and Orthodox Churches, brought about a steady growth of Buddhism in Eastern Europe.[19]

In addition to the strand of Western convert Buddhists, since the 1960s many Buddhists from Asian countries have come to Western Europe. In France, particularly numerous communities of refugees from Vietnam, Laos, and Cambodia have emerged. Paris has become the central place for Southeast Asian Buddhist migrants.[20] Although Vietnamese Buddhists in France aim to build a huge pagoda near Paris, so far the biggest pagoda in Europe has been built by Vietnamese Buddhists in Hannover (Germany). In Great Britain, the Netherlands, and other Western European nation-states, refugees, migrants and businessmen from Asian countries have found asylum or a working place. In the process of settling down, they founded religious and cultural institutions to preserve their religious-cultural identity and heritage. By visiting pagodas and temples, performing customary acts of devotional worship, and jointly celebrating Buddhist festivals, the Asian Buddhists regain an *esprit de clocher*,[21] a home away from home. More often than not, Asian migrant communities have turned out to be markedly conservative, presenting a primarily stable and familiar environment for their members in the socio-culturally foreign, often discriminatory, environment. Changes are inevitable, however, as the second generation grows up and aims to combine its religious-cultural heritage with Western ideas, aspirations, and ideals.

PRESENCE: DIVERSITY AND UNITY

Looking back over the first century of Buddhism's presence in institutionalized form in Europe, changes in the adoption and the availability of Buddhist traditions become obvious. From 1900 to 1950, Theravāda so-

Table 5.1. Categorization of Buddhism According to Tradition in
Selected European Countries

Tradition	Great Britain (%)	France (%)	Germany (%)	Switzer- land (%)	Nether- lands (%)
Theravāda	18.5	6.5	15.2	21	14
Mahāyāna (Zen)	18.1	53	35.6	29	44
Tibetan	36.9	36.8	42.2	48	37
Non-aligned	26.5	3.7	7	2	5

SOURCES: Great Britain in 1999 according to the *Buddhist Directory*, edited by The Buddhist Society, 8th ed. (London: Buddhist Society, 2000; 1st ed. 1979); France in 1997 according to Philippe Ronce, *Guide des centres bouddhistes en France* (Paris: Noesis, 1998); Germany in 1999 according to Baumann, *Buddhism-Buddhismus* (Hannover: Lutherisches Verlagshaus, 1999), 7; Switzerland in 1997 according to Martin Baumann, "Buddhism in Switzerland," *Journal of Global Buddhism* 1 (2000), 154–9, also at http://jgb.la.psu.edu/1/ [22 Jan. 2000]; the Netherlands in 1996 according to Boeddistische Unie Nederland, "Boeddhisten in Nederland" (Amsterdam: Boeddistische Unie Nederland, 1996), 21. The directories and guides are far from being accurate and complete, as some include the Sōka Gakkai or the New Kadampa Tradition, and others exclude these.

cieties and parishes predominated. During the 1950s and 1960s, the first Mahāyāna groups, with an emphasis on Zen meditational groups, came into existence. The 1970s saw an increase in Zen circles and groups, superseded by a boom in Tibetan Buddhist centers and institutions since the 1980s. During recent decades, groups and organizations with no alignment to a specific tradition have also been founded. Most prominent among these are the Friends of the Western Buddhist Order (FWBO), founded by the British Sangharakshita in 1967, with an especially strong presence in Great Britain. As a result of these rapid developments, a plurality of Buddhist schools and traditions has evolved in many European countries. The monolithic resonating notion of "Buddhism in Europe" conceals the internal diversity and far-ranging heterogeneity. Theravāda, Mahāyāna, and Tibetan Buddhist traditions, along with non-aligned groups or centers, can be found in a single country, often even in one major city, with thirty or forty different Buddhist groups in one place. The percentage of groups affiliated with a particular tradition shall be singled out for a few selected countries (table 5.1).

These figures can provide only a very rough idea of the breakdown of Buddhism's presence in a country. The results are based on the institutionalized form of Buddhism and in no way enable direct references to the absolute numbers or percentage figures of Buddhists in a country. The main point of table 5.1 is to direct attention to the strong impact of Zen and Tibetan Buddhism in Europe, which these traditions have acquired within the last quarter of the twentieth century.

Zen or Tibetan Buddhist groups and centers have mainly been initiated by convert Buddhists. This refers to *samatha* and *vipassanā* meditational and non-aligned Buddhist institutions too. Sociologically speaking, the newly assumed religious orientation of the converts "crystallized" into organizational frameworks, and resources were mobilized to establish firm and lasting bases (groups, centers, retreat houses).[22]

In contrast, Asian or immigrant Buddhists established only a few institutions, compared to their absolute numbers. A main reason is that the pattern and structure of religious life and practice differ considerably from those of convert Buddhists. A regular visit to a center or meeting place, as many convert Buddhists do once or twice a week, is uncommon. Rather, a Thai, Chinese, Vietnamese, or Cambodian Buddhist might go to a monastery or local temple to carry out devotional acts in order to acquire "merit," to listen to a discourse of a monk or nun, to attend a festival, or to have a life-cycle ritual performed. Regularity is neither required nor intended.[23] Thus, for example, in Switzerland the splendidly built Wat Srinagarindravaram in the Solothurn canton attends to the religious and cultural needs of the eight thousand to nine thousand Thai Buddhists. Only a few other local Thai Buddhist places exist. We can observe the same pattern in Great Britain, where the spectacular Buddhapadipa Temple, inaugurated in London in 1982, caters to the Thai population. In Germany, the approximately sixty thousand Vietnamese Buddhists have established a main pagoda in Hannover, plus six temples and some twenty-three local lay Buddhist societies. The thirty institutional places thus numerically equal, for example, the about thirty Zen groups and *dōjōs* (sitting halls) of the Zen Union Germany, comprising about five hundred members.[24] In straightforward terms, the dynamic of institutional rise is related to convert Buddhist activities, but the overall sum of Buddhists is mainly due to immigrants.

Table 5.2 specifies the number of Buddhists in selected European countries. Stating such figures constitutes a risky undertaking, due to methodological uncertainties. Altogether, Asian or immigrant Buddhists might be estimated to be 600,000 to 700,000 people. Of Europe's estimated 900,000 to 1,000,000 Buddhists, they thus comprise two-thirds of the whole and often outnumber convert Buddhists by two or three times in a country. Table 5.2 underscores this proportional relation.

Table 5.2. Buddhists and Buddhist Groups in European Countries in the Late 1990s

Country	Buddhists	Buddhists from Asia	Groups and Centers	Approximate Total Population (Millions)	Percentage of Total Population That Were Buddhists
France	~350,000	~300,000	~280	58	0.6
Britain	180,000	130,000	400	58	0.3
Germany	170,000	120,000	530	82	0.2
Italy	70,000	~25,000	~50	57	0.1
Netherlands	33,000	20,000	60	15	0.2
Switzerland	25,000	20,000	100	7	0.3
Austria	16,000	5,000	50	8	0.2
Denmark	~10,000	~5,000	~32	5	0.1
Hungary	7,000	1,000	~12	10	0.1
Poland	~5,000	500	30	39	0.02

NOTE: ~ denotes very rough estimate

In contrast to the geographic expanses of Canada, the United States, South Africa, and Australia, in Europe as a region Buddhism faces an unusually wide variety of social, cultural, and legal contexts. These differences at times have a lasting impact on the (1) spread, (2) institutionalization, (3) form of organization, (4) doctrinal standardization, and (5) representational issues of Buddhism in a country. Let us take a brief look at these factors.

1. *Spread:*   Although Buddhist schools and traditions now generally face few difficulties in settling in a European country, a century ago Buddhism was less welcome in religious and cultural terms. Around the beginning of the twentieth century, Christian theologians outspokenly criticized Buddhism as "devastating nihilism" and "wretched pessimism."[25] Although the attacks softened due to more accurate knowledge about the Buddhist teachings, polemics and stigmatizations have nevertheless continued until today.[26] In socio-cultural terms, Buddhism was also negatively portrayed at times. For example, in the 1890s the German Emperor Wilhelm II designed a picture with the legend, "People of Europe, defend your holiest possessions." The huge picture depicts allegorical figures of the civilized nations of Europe ready for battle with the onrushing legions of the Antichrist who, shrouded in dark clouds and the smoke of burning cities,

takes the shape of the Buddha. As a consequence of such negative press, early German Buddhists decided against establishing a monastery in the German Empire and shifted their attempt to Switzerland. Certainly, a century later suspicion of and distance toward the "foreign" religion of Buddhism has softened, although it is not absent, despite the current positive press and reception.[27]

2. *Institutionalization:* As a consequence of spread, the founding of institutions might follow. Legal restrictions can interfere here, however. For example, Tibetan refugees in Switzerland intended to establish a monastery after their arrival in the 1960s. However, a Swiss law enacted in 1874 prohibited this. Although the law in Protestant Switzerland had been directed against the Jesuit order, it now posed problems for the Tibetans. As a result, no official monastery was built. Instead, a Monastic Tibetan Institute building, inaugurated in 1968 in Rikon near Zürich, serves as a religious and academic institution and accommodates a monastic community of seven to nine people.[28] A somewhat different legal case surrounding institutionalization occurred in Greece during the mid-1990s. A convert Tibetan Buddhist was arrested by the police and found guilty of "operating a house of prayer without government permission." The Kagyupa practitioner, Mrs. Hara Kalomiri, operated a small retreat center. When the case was taken to the European Court, the court ruled that Greece violated the Treaty of Rome in its religious legislation. It will take time before the laws can be changed and a spread of religions not related to the Orthodox Church will be possible.[29]

3. *Form of organization:* In an institutionalized form, *European Buddhism* is most often arranged as a society or association. Some societies are officially registered, some are not. This form already departs from established models in Asia. However, if Buddhists wish to be entitled to certain rights in a country—such as access to the media, financial support, legal standing and recognition equal to those of Christian churches, or the right to teach in school—specific requirements have to be met. Complying with these state requirements usually involves setting up specific organizational structures. Two examples shall be given. Since the mid-1970s, Buddhist spokesmen in Austria had worked for recognition of Buddhism by the state. To achieve this end, they set up a unifying Austrian Buddhist Association, headed by a democratically elected committee, and fulfilled many other specific requirements, In 1983, the Austrian state officially recognized Buddhism as a religion entitled to special rights (e.g., to teach Buddhist religion in school, and access to broadcast time on TV and radio). The association thus is the acknowledged representative of Buddhism in Austria.

In 1998, eleven traditions, orders, and centers had been members of this umbrella organization. However, some fifteen traditions and schools had *not* been affiliated with the association.[30] The successful state recognition in Austria served as a shining example for other national Buddhist unions in their aim to gain state recognition. In quite a few countries, Buddhists felt that they were on the move. Official acknowledgment of Buddhism would help them secure a place and standing in each country and—importantly—would ensure that Buddhist groups were not considered "sects" or "cults." In West Germany, Buddhists also strove for public recognition. To achieve this end, a new association with certain structures had to be set up, parallel to the existing umbrella organization of Buddhist groups (the German Buddhist Union). Even though the Buddhists fulfilled this legal prerequisite and adopted a commonly accepted "Buddhist Confession" (a self-designation), state recognition was not granted. According to the state, the financial backing and the number of members were not sufficient to warrant the status.[31]

4. *Doctrinal standardization.*   Complying with legal requirements also involved the naming and fixing of Buddhist doctrines. What do Buddhists jointly believe and teach? Despite the far-ranging differences among Buddhist traditions in doctrinal terms and views, common denominators had to be agreed upon. The process of defining shared views brought together Buddhists of different traditions within a country. It served as a catalyst for the flourishing of a Buddhist "ecumenical" cooperation (again, a self-designation) and it strengthened an intra-Buddhist dialogue. The adopted shared doctrines standardized confessional contents, a point most obviously reached with the "Buddhist Confession" agreed upon by German Buddhists of many different traditions. Similar processes of self-definition and standardization took place earlier in Austria, and, quite recently, have occurred in Portugal and Italy, where Buddhism achieved state recognition in 1998 and 2000, respectively.[32] It needs to be mentioned, however, that quite a number of Buddhist groups and centers deliberately do not join national umbrella organizations due to the existence of doctrinal standardization.

5. *Representation:*   As it appears to me, Buddhism in Europe is unusual in its high number of intra-Buddhist organizations and platforms. In many European countries, national umbrella organizations bring together spokesmen and spokeswomen of different traditions and schools. These unions exist in Germany (since 1955), Austria (1976), Switzerland (1976), the Netherlands (1979), Italy (1985), France (1986), Belgium (1997), and Portugal (1997). In Great Britain, the Network of Buddhist Organizations,

formed in 1994, fulfills similar functions. On a broader European scale, Buddhists formed the European Buddhist Union in 1975. The union, currently with forty-five members (national unions, larger centers, internationally spread orders and lineages) from fifteen countries, fosters intra-Buddhist communication. It organizes conferences every few years, attended by about fifteen hundred people. Both the European union and the national organizations emphasize Buddhism's "unity in diversity."[33] This diversity and alleged unity, however, consist primarily of convert Buddhist groups, centers, and organizations. The absence of immigrant Buddhists at the conferences and national conventions is conspicuous. Very few institutions founded by immigrant Buddhists are members of national unions. Despite the absolute numbers of migrant Buddhists, they do not represent Buddhism in public. Overwhelmingly, the public sees convert Buddhists and their well-organized institutions, their eloquent speakers, and their well-written and widely distributed publications.

So far, who represents Buddhism has not been an issue between immigrant and convert Buddhists. During the past decade, as Buddhism has attracted the interest of the media, however, the question of who speaks for Buddhism has become a matter of dispute within the strand of convert Buddhists. Not every teacher and not every lineage or center of convert Buddhists is held to be representative of Buddhism. Controversies and heated discussions sparked off, for example, with regard to the Danish teacher Ole Nydahl and his Diamond Way organization or with regard to the exclusive stance of Geshe Kelsang Gyatso's New Kadampa Tradition. In view of their attitudes toward other Buddhist schools, should they be accepted as members in a national umbrella organization or should they be banned? In Britain, for example, the Network of Buddhist Organizations faced a large-scale departure of other affiliates as the New Kadampa Tradition became a member. The disputes point to the fragility of the alleged "unity in diversity."

PROSPECTS

These and other controversies have rarely left the subcultural discourse of Buddhists (mainly that of the convert strand). So far, public interest in Buddhist meditation and teachings has been too enthusiastic to focus on these and other internal tensions. Also, some recent public criticism of leading Buddhists or organizations, such as the disparagement of the Sōka Gakkai or allegations against Sangharakshita and the FWBO voiced in one of Britain's leading national newspapers, *The Guardian*,[34] have not changed the positive public opinion to a critical or negative attitude. Buddhists do not exceed 0.5 percent of the population in any European country (presumably excepting France). Subtracting the silent majority of Asian Buddhists, who rarely appear as Buddhism's spokespeople, the figure would dwindle to an even smaller visible percentage. However, Buddhism's religious impact and the general interest in its practices and teachings seem far beyond this minute figure. How can we explain this? An answer certainly has to take into account that among the convert Buddhist strand, the vast majority are well educated, urban, and economically well-off. Furthermore, many of these have professions as teachers, doctors, journalists, lawyers, publishers, employers, translators, artists, and the like. Many are thus accustomed to organizational work and articulate speech, to being present in public, and to holding a role which sets a tone. The multiplicatory function of these convert Buddhists compensates for their small numbers. The professional basis of many convert Buddhists certainly points to good prospects for Buddhism in various European countries. These chances are certainly aided by the media's interest in public figures like the Dalai Lama, Thich Nhat Hanh, and other "model" Buddhists.

In addition to these supportive contextual factors, aspects of Buddhism's internal development also point to prospering prospects. During the last decade, the public appearance of Buddhism has become more professional. Former low-budget journals have become proficient magazines; a multitude of Buddhist publishers have come into existence; former in-group meetings have changed to polished, sometimes costly, public conventions. An increasing number of Western Buddhists have taken on professional roles, that is, they have become priests, nuns, monks, or full-time lay teachers. A second generation of Western teachers is maturing—those who have been students of Western, not Asian, teachers.[35] In addition, since the 1960s a growing number of South Asian *bhikkhus*, Japanese *rōshis*, and Tibetan *lamas* have taken up permanent residence in Europe. The presence of Asian monastic instructors has had a catalytic effect on Buddhism's growth in Europe. Finally, during the 1990s prominent teachers from the United States—such as Richard Baker Rōshi, Jack Kornfield, the late Prabhasa Dharma Rōshi, and many more—visited Europe for lecture tours. Often branch centers developed from there. European teachers—such as Stephen Batchelor, Sangharakshita, Ajahn Sumedho, Ole Nydahl, and many more—have also exported their particular interpretations of Buddhist teachings and practices. In addition, other Japanese, Korean, Taiwanese, Vietnamese, Tibetan, and South Asian monks, nuns, and teachers tour the globe and establish transcontinental networks and organizations.[36]

These positive prospects mainly refer to the strand of convert Buddhism. They only partly apply to the strand of immigrant Buddhism. As in other Western geographic areas, Buddhism in Europe is made up of "two completely distinct lines of development."[37] These two strands rarely meet, and often a disinterest and nonrecognition prevails on both sides. Having passed the initial phase of establishing institutions to preserve their religious-cultural heritage, the immigrant communities face new challenges as the second generation grows up. In the new, non-Asian context, Buddhism no longer is "caught," but needs to be taught. How will the traditions be passed on to the children? What language will be used in Buddhist meetings and rituals—the language of the host country, in which the children are fluent, or the Asian language, of which many children have only a rudimentary knowledge? In which ways will traditional forms of worship and ritual have to change in order to respond more to the experiences and aspirations of a generation grown up in a socio-cultural context characterized by time pressure, rationality, and individualism? To what extent will folk or popular Buddhist practices, such as palm-reading or protective acts against malevolent spirits, be questioned and declared inappropriate in a modern, secular context? In addition to many other issues and problems, the question of leadership is a peculiar one. Up to now, most immigrant communities have recruited monks, nuns, and priests from Asian countries. To a growing extent, Western-educated youth feel uncomfortable with the traditional views and attitudes of many Asian teachers. Will a new leadership be able to step up among the second generation, and how will they mediate between traditional and modernized forms and interpretations? Or will Western convert Buddhists be invited to replace the Asian personnel? The parallel presence of a highly organized and well-trained convert strand, to which second- and third-generation Buddhists might turn for instruction, seems to be a peculiarity among transplanted Asian religions in Western contexts. The mutual impact has rarely been studied so far for the European case. Also, scholarly attention has strongly focused on convert Buddhists. Little research has been done with regard to the strand of immigrant Buddhists. Also, theoretical approaches have not been applied to produce a better understanding of current developments and changes. Up to now, no studies have related, for example, the concepts of *compartmentalization* and *diaspora* to immigrant Buddhist communities. In the study of Muslim, Hindu, Sikh, and Jain immigrant communities, these analytical perspectives have proven to be highly useful and valuable.[38]

The prospects for both Buddhist strands seem to be good, despite internal tensions and the need for adaptive changes and reformulations. Notwithstanding the increased interest in things Buddhist, Buddhism will certainly remain a minority religion in Europe during the twenty-first century. Buddhists hope, however, that being a Buddhist in Europe is less regarded as a trendy affair, an expression of romantic exoticism, or a clinging to Asian roots. Rather, Buddhism, in whatever shape, should become a nonsensational, normal, and accepted part of Europe's landscape of religions.

NOTES

1. For the early encounter, see: Raymond Schwab, *La renaissance orientale* (Paris: Payot, 1950), translated into English as *The Oriental Renaissance: Europe's Rediscovery of India and the East, 1680–1880* (New York: Columbia University Press, 1984); and Wilhelm Halbfass, *India and Europe: An Essay in Understanding* (Albany: State University of New York Press, 1988). Also, detailed information can be obtained from Rick Fields, *How the Swans Came to the Lake: A Narrative History of Buddhism in America*, revised and updated 3rd ed. (Boston: Shambhala, 1992), 31–53, and Stephen Batchelor, *The Awakening of the West: The Encounter of Buddhism and Western Culture* (Berkeley: Parallax Press, 1994), 227–71.

2. Burnouf's *L'introduction à l'histoire du bouddhisme indien* (Paris: Imprimerie Royale, 1844). The quote is from Batchelor, *The Awakening of the West,* 239.

3. Philip Almond traced this development for Great Britain; see Philip C. Almond, *The British Discovery of Buddhism* (Cambridge: Cambridge University Press, 1988). See also Douglas Brear, "Early Assumptions in Western Buddhist Studies," *Religion* 7 (1977), 136–59.

4. See, among many, Fields, *How the Swans Came to the Lake,* 83–118. Branches of the Theosophical Society were established in numerous countries, for example in Germany in 1884 and in Austria in 1894.

5. Oldenberg's book was published in German in 1881 and in an English translation in 1882. William Peiris wrote his comment on Arnold's book in *The Western Contribution to Buddhism* (Delhi: Motilal Banarsidass, 1973), xxiv.

6. The entrance of these pioneering Europeans into the Buddhist monastic order, the Sangha, and their subsequent work is well documented. For Ananda Metteyya, see Christmas Humphreys, *Sixty Years of Buddhism in England, 1907–1967: A History and a Survey* (London: Buddhist Society, 1968), 2–11, and Ian Oliver, *Buddhism in Britain* (London: Rider, 1979), 43–5. For Nyānatiloka, see Hellmuth Hecker, *Der erste deutsche Bhikkhu: Das bewegte Leben des Ehrwürdigen Nyānatiloka (1878–1957) und seine Schüler* (Konstanz: University of Konstanz, 1995), and Michael B. Carrithers, *The Forest Monks of Sri Lanka: An Anthropological and Historical Sketch* (Oxford: Oxford University Press, 1983), 26–45.

7. For details see Lance S. Cousins, "Theravāda Buddhism in England," in *Buddhism into the Year 2000: International Conference Proceedings,* edited by the Dhammakaya Foundation (Bangkok: Dhammakaya Foundation, 1994), 141–50, and Martin Baumann, *Deutsche Buddhisten: Geschichte und Gemeinschaften,* 2nd enlarged ed. (Marburg, Germany: Diagonal-Verlag, 1995), 49–59. For a general outline, see Heinz Bechert, "Buddhist Revival in East and West," in *The World of Buddhism,* edited by Heinz Bechert and Richard Gombrich (London: Thames and Hudson, 1984), 273–85, and Martin Baumann, "Creating a European Path to Nirvana: Historical and Contemporary Developments of Buddhism in Europe," *Journal of Contemporary Religion* 10, no. 1 (1995), 55–70.

8. For the Buddhist revival in Ceylon, see, among many, Heinz Bechert, *Buddhismus, Staat und Gesellschaft in den Ländern des Theravāda-Buddhismus*, vol. 1 (Frankfurt am Main, Germany: Schriften des Instituts für Asienkunde, 1966); George Doherty Bond, The *Buddhist Revival in Sri Lanka: Religious Tradition, Reinterpretation and Response* (Columbia: University of South Carolina Press, 1988); and Richard Gombrich and Gananath Obeyesekere, *Buddhism Transformed: Religious Change in Sri Lanka* (Princeton: Princeton University Press, 1988). For an overview of Buddhism's revival and changes in various other Asian countries, see Heinrich Dumoulin and John C. Maraldo (eds.), *Buddhism in the Modern World* (New York: Collier Macmillan, 1976), and Ian Harris (ed.), *Buddhism and Politics in Twentieth-Century Asia* (London: Pinter, 1999).

9. For Dharmapāla, apart from a detailed mentioning in the studies listed in the previous note, see also B. C. Gokhale, "Anagārika Dharmapāla: Toward Modernity through Tradition in Ceylon," in *Tradition and Change in Theravāda Buddhism*, edited by Bardwell L. Smith (Leiden: Brill, 1973), 30–9.

10. For details on the specific Buddhist interpretations, see Klaus-Josef Notz, *Der Buddhismus in Deutschland in seinen Selbstdarstellungen: eine religionswissenschaftliche Untersuchung zur religiösen Akkulturationsproblematik* (Frankfurt am Main, Germany: Peter Lang, 1984), 58–67; Baumann, *Deutsche Buddhisten*, 59–67; and Hellmuth Hecker, *Lebensbilder deutscher Buddhisten: ein biobibliographisches Handbuch*, vol. 1, *The Founders*, 2nd enlarged ed. (Konstanz: University of Konstanz, 1996).

11. For details, see Humphreys, *Sixty Years of Buddhism in England*, 20–45; Oliver, *Buddhism in Britain*, 50–3, 66–7; Jeffrey Somers, "Theravāda Buddhism in Great Britain," *Religion Today* 7, no. 1 (1991), 4–7; and instructively Cousins, "Theravāda Buddhism in England," 146–7. The Buddhist Lodge became the Buddhist Society (London) in 1943, and still exists (http://www.thebuddhistsociety.org.uk [1 Feb. 2002]).

12. Scattered articles provide more information on the rare Buddhist activities during this interwar time; see the country-wise organized listing in Martin Baumann, "Buddhism in Europe: An Annotated Bibliography on Its Historical Developments and Contemporary State of Affairs" (1998), 2nd updated version, http://www.rewi.uni-hannover.de/for4.htm [1 Feb. 2002].

13. See Batchelor, *The Awakening of the West*, 283–302.

14. See Mile Pekic, "Kalmyk Buddhist Temple in Belgrade, 1929–1944: An Exhibition" (2000), http://members.tripod.com/kakono/ [8 Dec. 2001]. Years later, a temple was opened in Munich (Germany) in 1966. A resident Tibetan *lama* cared for the little Kalmyk community until the temple's closure, due to onward migration of the Kalmyks to the United States or France; see Helmut Klar, "Kalmuecken und ihr Tempel in Belgrad und Muenchen," *Bodhi Baum* 5, no. 1 (1980), 29–30.

15. References to and studies of the Sōka Gakkai in Europe include Batchelor, *The Awakening of the West*, 150–6; Bryan Wilson and Karel Dobbelaere, *A Time to Chant: The Sōka Gakkai Buddhists in Britain* (Oxford: Clarendon Press, 1994); Baumann, *Deutsche Buddhisten*, 99–100; Helen Waterhouse, *Buddhism in Bath: Adaptation and Authority* (Leeds, U.K.: Community Religions Project, University of Leeds, 1997), 91–134; and Louis Hourmant, "La Sōka Gakkai: un bouddhisme 'paria' en France?" in *Sectes et Démocratie*, edited by Françoise Champion and Martine Cohen (Paris: Le Seuil, 1999), 182–204. Sōka Gakkai groups do exist in many countries of Europe; an especially strong branch evolved in Italy (twenty-two thousand members). The success is partly due to the famous soccer player Roberto Baggio and to Sabina Guzzanti, both members of the Sōka Gakkai; see

Karel Dobbelaere, *La Sōka Gakkai: Un movimento di laici diventa una religione* (Torino: Elle Di Ci, Leumann, 1998).

16. The Swiss Buddhist Max Ladner provides an interesting assessment of Buddhism's diffusion in Europe in the late 1950s; see Ladner, "Buddhistische Mission in Europa," *Zeitschrift für Missionswissenschaft und Religionswissenschaft* 10 (1958), 317–33. A narrative account of the situation in the mid-1960s is given by Kosho Yamamoto, *Buddhism in Europe* (Ube City, Japan: Karinbunko, 1967).

17. For details of the rapid development and of the Asian and Western teachers involved, see Batchelor, *The Awakening of the West*, 119–23, 205–23, and Baumann, "Creating a European Path," 59–63.

18. Numbers for Great Britain are based on *The Buddhist Directory*, edited by The Buddhist Society, 8th ed. (London: Buddhist Society, 2000; 1st ed., 1979), and Waterhouse, *Buddhism in Bath*, 13–9. For Germany, see Baumann, *Deutsche Buddhisten*, 218–23, and Martin Baumann, *Buddhism-Buddhismus* (Hannover, Germany: Lutherisches Verlagshaus, 1999), 7, 25. The numbers primarily substantialize the trend of growth. It has to be borne in mind that the size, activities, and membership regulations of the groups and organizations vary considerably.

19. Relevant studies are listed in the online bibliography, Baumann, "Buddhism in Europe." In Russia, a new law on religion, passed in 1997, severely blocks the establishment of new and further Buddhist traditions. The law, strongly inspired by the Russian Church, places restrictions on any religious organizations that have not been established in Russia for fifteen years; see *Dharma Life* 2, no. 6 (1997), 6.

20. See Catherine Choron-Baix, *Bouddhisme et migration: la reconstitution d'une paroisse bouddhiste Lao en banlieue parisienne* (Paris: Ministère de la culture, Conseil du patrimoine ethnologique, 1986), and Milada Kalab, "Cambodian Buddhist Monasteries in Paris: Continuing Tradition and Changing Patterns," in *Cambodian Culture since 1975: Homeland and Exile*, edited by May M. Ebihara, Carol A. Mortland, and Judy Ledgerwood (Ithaca, New York: Cornell University Press, 1994), 57–71.

21. Catherine Choron-Baix, "De forêts en banlieues: la transplantation du bouddhisme Lao en France," *Archives de sciences sociales des religions* 36, no. 73 (1991), 17–33, quote 22.

22. Eisenstadt employs the notion of *crystallization* in a Weberian sense; see Samuel N. Eisenstadt, "Introduction," in Max Weber, *On Charisma and Institution Building: Selected Papers*, edited by Samuel N. Eisenstadt (Chicago: University of Chicago Press, 1968), xxxix.

23. For details, see the chapter by B. Alan Wallace in this volume.

24. See *Thai-Swiss News* 1 (1998), 30–1; Loc Ho, *Vietnamesischer Buddhismus in Deutschland* (Hannover, Germany: Pagoda Vien Giac, 1999); and Martin Baumann, *Migration, Religion, Integration: Buddhistische Vietnamesen und Hinduistische Tamilen in Deutschland* (Marburg, Germany: Diagonal-Verlag. 2000), 68–91.

25. See, among others, Robert Falke, *Der Buddhismus in unserem modernen deutschen Geistesleben* (Halle an der Saale, Germany: Innere Mission, 1903), 70, and Hermann Römer, "Die Propaganda für asiatische Religionen im Abendland," *Baseler Missions-Studien* 36 (1910), 162 (translated by the author).

26. For example, see the portrayal of Buddhist teachings by Pope John Paul II in *Crossing the Threshold of Hope* (New York: Knopf, 1994).

27. In the 1980s and early 1990s, some Buddhist organizations were accused of constituting "cults" or "sects." In Belgium and France in particular, the Sōka Gakkai and certain branches of the Kagyu tradition were strongly attacked and labeled "dangerous sects."

28. See Peter Lindegger, *20 Jahre Klösterliches Tibet-Institut Rikon/Zürich: eine Bestandesaufnahme* (Rikon, Switzerland: Monastic Tibetan Institute, 1988). For the consecration rituals during the building process, see Mary Van Dyke, "Grids and Serpents: A Tibetan Foundation Ritual in Switzerland," in *Constructing Tibetan Culture: Contemporary Perspectives,* edited by Frank J. Korom (Montréal: World Heritage Press, 1997), 178–227.

29. Reports in *Dharma Life* 1, no. 2 (1996), 9, and *Lotusblätter* 10, no. 4 (1996), 63, and 13, no. 2 (1999), 63. Certainly the changed law on religion in Russia could also be referred to here; see note 19.

30. See Franz Ritter, "Austro-Buddhismus: eine kleine Geschichte des Buddhismus in Österreich," *Bodhi Baum* 18, no. 2 (1993), 4–10, and the extra supplement of the journal of the Austrian Buddhist Association, *Ursache und Wirkung* (Autumn 1998).

31. The two organizations were merged in 1988; see *Lotusblätter* 2, no. 3 (1988), and 9, no. 3 (1995). See also Baumann, *Deutsche Buddhisten,* 193–202, 252–58.

32. See the home page of the União Budhista Portuguesa at http://www.uniaobudista.com/ [1 Feb. 2002].

33. This was the title of the conference held in Berlin in 1992; see the proceedings, *Einheit in der Vielfalt-Buddhismus in Europa,* edited by the German Buddhist Union (Munich: German Buddhist Union, 1994); a brief report and analysis in English is given in Baumann, "Creating a European Path," 65–6.

34. *The Guardian,* October 1997, supplement, 27. A reply to the accusations is given in "The FWBO Files: A Response" (Birmingham, U.K.: FWBO, 1998), also at http://www.fwbo.org/communications/[1 Feb. 2002], and through articles in *Dharma Life,* 3, no. 7 (1998).

35. See the chapters by Ajahn Tiradhammo, Karma Lekshe Tsomo, and Sylvia Wetzel in this volume.

36. Names of relevant teachers and organizations are given in Stephen Batchelor, "Buddhism and European Culture in Europe," in *Religion in Europe: Contemporary Perspectives,* edited by Sean Gill, Gavin D'Costa, and Ursula King (Kampen, Netherlands: Pharos, 1994), 86–104, especially 93–8; Batchelor, *The Awakening of Buddhism;* and Baumann, "Creating a European Path," 59–66.

37. Charles S. Prebish, "Two Buddhisms Reconsidered," *Buddhist Studies Review* 10, no. 2 (1993), 187–206, quote 187.

38. John R. Hinnells, "Comparative Reflections on South Asian Religion in International Migration," in *A New Handbook of Living Religions,* edited by John R. Hinnells (Cambridge, Massachusetts: Blackwell, 1997), 819–47; Steven Vertovec, "Three Meanings of 'Diaspora,' Exemplified among South Asian Religions," *Diaspora: A Journal of Transnational Studies* 6, no. 3 (1997), 277–99; and Harold Coward, John R. Hinnells, and Raymond B. Williams (eds.), *The South Asian Religious Diaspora in Britain, Canada, and the United States* (Albany: State University of New York Press, 2000). See also the chapter by Douglas Padgett in this volume.

6 American Buddhism in the Making

Richard Hughes Seager

INTRODUCTION

In the late 1980s and early 1990s, as a first generation of native-born Buddhist teachers came of age in the United States, the idea that a typically American Buddhism had been born entered into wide currency. The idea was part of a broader debate that touched on a number of issues. Who counts as being a Buddhist? What is American Buddhism and what ought it to be? Who speaks for the American Buddhist community? The course of the debate and some of its major texts have been reviewed elsewhere and need not be repeated here.[1] One outcome is that there now appears to be a general consensus among many informed observers that there is not one American Buddhism but three, although commentators parse them somewhat differently.

One kind of American Buddhism is often seen among *old-line Asian-American ethnic groups,* primarily Chinese and Japanese, but most specifically in the Jōdo Shinshū Buddhist Churches of America (BCA), an organization founded in the nineteenth century. A second form is frequently referred to as *Euro-American Buddhism,* although this term masks the diverse ethnic and racial makeup of the community. Some prefer the term *convert,* to emphasize that these Buddhists turned to the Dharma in substantial numbers only since the 1960s, but *convert Buddhism* creates its own anomalies: a child born of converts is by definition no longer a member of a convert community. A third kind, sometimes referred to as *ethnic Buddhism,* is said to be found among newer immigrants, exiles, and refugees who have come to the United States in the past thirty years from South, Southeast, Central, and East Asian countries.

The notion that there are three American Buddhisms is rooted to a degree in social reality and reflects the fact that there tends to be little communication among the different groups, particularly among rank-and-file members. The historical experience of the groups can also be quite different—World War II internment camps for the first; revolutionary 1960s-era idealism for the second; and upheavals involved in recent transplantation to a new culture for the third. There are also highly generalized but discernible differences in existential uses of the Dharma in the communities. Japanese-Americans in the BCA may view the temple as a source of religious faith, heritage maintenance, and ethnic identity. Many converts approach the Dharma from secular backgrounds and some are self-consciously adapting it to psychotherapy. For most immigrants, exiles, and refugees, Buddhism remains richly informed by traditional cosmic worldviews and Asian cultural and social norms, which are in the process being adapted to contemporary American mores.

The three-Buddhism schema used to interpret the landscape of the Dharma in the United States has, in short, a definite utility and seems to have attained some legitimacy in the American Buddhist community. I employ it here for the sake of convenience but, by way of conclusion, I question its continued value as an interpretive device and I therefore attempt to place the current interest in it into a broader perspective.

OLD-LINE ASIAN-AMERICAN BUDDHISM

The Dharma was first practiced in the United States by Chinese who arrived on the West Coast, drawn by the gold rush of 1848. The social organizations they formed were based on kinship and linguistic groups and on mutual aid societies. These voluntary associations, later consolidated into merchant organizations called the Six (or Seven) Companies, became influential institutions when anti-Chinese violence flared in the post–Civil War decades. By 1875, there were eight temples in San Francisco, although a great many more, small and often informally constituted, existed up and down the West Coast. The religion practiced in these temples was a mixture of Confucian ancestor veneration, popular Taoism, and Pure Land Buddhism. Chinese immigration was drastically curtailed in the late nineteenth century and, as a result, the number of Chinese dipped as low as 150,000 in 1950. As a result, most Chinese Buddhist organizations in the United States today are of a more recent vintage.

The Japanese Jōdo Shinshū of the BCA is the oldest major institutional form of Buddhism in the United States.[2] Its formal history dates from 1899, when Shuye Sonoda and Kakuryo Nishijima, the first permanent Jōdo Shinshū missionaries, established the Buddhist Mission of North America (BMNA) to serve Japanese immigrants, who had begun to arrive in this country shortly after the Chinese. The following decades were marked by institution building. Young Men's Buddhist Associations and later temples were founded along the West Coast from Seattle to San Diego. The Fujinkai, or Buddhist Women's Association, was established and would subsequently play an important role in development of American Jōdo Shinshū. In 1907, Japanese immigration was restricted, which both limited the growth of the community and fostered the emergence of stable, family-centered religious and social communities.

The twentieth century was marked by a long, often highly traumatic, march by these Japanese Buddhists from the margins of a nation dominated by Anglo-Protestantism to mainstream, middle-class status in a religiously plural, multi-ethnic, post-Christian society. Anti-Asian sentiments and legislation were one major force at work in shaping the BMNA, which increasingly took on a dual role of providing both cultural and religious continuity with Japan and a safe haven for Americanization. The Oriental Exclusion Act of 1924 included a provision that no Japanese not already citizens or born in the United States could gain citizenship. This injustice worked to strengthen Buddhist identity within the community, increased interest in Japanese culture and language, and fostered an inward turn. But at the same time, temples increasingly functioned as centers of community life in ways they had not in Japan. They began to sponsor rotating credit systems, baseball leagues, Boy Scout troops, and American-style dances, as well as funerals, weddings, and memorial ceremonies.

A second major force at work was the emergence of second-generation issues as a rift widened between Issei, a first generation still largely identified with Japan, and Nisei, a native-born generation thoroughly accustomed to U.S. norms. Beginning in the 1920s, this encouraged a gradual process of Anglicization of Jōdo Shinshū religious life, which had until then been conducted exclusively in Japanese. In the short term, Anglicization posed a threat of unintended Christianization as ideas about God, heaven, and church began to shade Pure Land doctrine. In the long term, however, it helped to create a fluid vocabulary, part Japanese, part English, that continues today to give a distinct ethnic and religious character to the Jōdo Shinshū community.

The community was thrown into an acute crisis in 1942 when President Franklin Roosevelt signed Executive Order 9066, designating the West Coast a military district from which all people of Japanese ancestry were to be removed. Well over one hundred thousand Japanese—Buddhist, Catholic, and Protestant—were interned in about a dozen camps located in a variety of states across the nation. Of these, over sixty thousand were Buddhist, the majority Jōdo Shinshū. The internment camps accelerated

Anglicization and Americanization and fostered the emergence of the Nisei as leaders of the community. The camps also played a decisive role in reshaping Jōdo Shinshū institutions. In 1944, an assembly of ministers voted to change the name of the BMNA to Buddhist Churches of America, repudiate all ties to Japan, redefine their relation to its headquarters in Kyoto, and recreate the office of *sōchō* or bishop as an elective position. They also redesigned the BCA's organizational structure to shift more power to the Nisei.

During the postwar years, the BCA began to emerge as a small, ethnically distinct form of American Buddhism. It also began to face challenges similar to those encountered by other immigrant religions when they attain mainstream status, such as declining membership, the loss of ethnic and religious identity, and a high rate of out-marriage. Largely due to its small size and collective sense of decorum, the BCA is often overlooked in current debates about immigrants, converts, and the future of Buddhism in the United States. It has, however, established what many other Buddhists in this country are still attempting to create—a stable, institutionalized form of the Dharma that is thoroughly integrated into American culture but retains the spirit and many forms that reflect the depth and nuance of its Asian heritage.

EURO-AMERICAN OR CONVERT BUDDHISM

Over the last four decades, convert Buddhists attained a high degree of visibility for a variety of reasons. The community's rate of growth has been astonishing. Don Morreale, in his *The Complete Guide to Buddhist America*, lists as of 1997 more than one thousand meditation centers, most associated with converts, a dramatic increase from the twenty-one centers founded between 1900 and the early 1960s.[3] The community also supports a range of successful publishing concerns, including the popular book publisher Shambhala Publications and the journals *Inquiring Mind, Shambhala Sun,* and *Tricycle,* which appeal to general readers. From the "Zen boom" of the 1950s to the Tibet-related media campaigns of the 1990s, it has been moreover converts, not old-line ethnics or new Buddhist immigrants, who have claimed the attention of the mainstream press. The persistent popular vogue for Buddhism in America during the last half of the twentieth century was a phenomenon in its own right. Thomas A. Tweed has called attention to how Zen-inspired literature has proliferated in recent decades; in 1997, he counted nearly two hundred *Zen in . . . , Zen and . . . ,* and *The Zen of . . .* titles in *Books in Print.*[4]

But even a cursory examination of convert Buddhism in the States reveals that it is composed of at least four distinct practice communities. Three of the four—Zen, Tibetan Buddhism, and the Theravāda-inspired Insight Meditation Movement—are often seen as related, due to their close association with the 1960s counterculture and a shared emphasis on sitting meditation. First published in 1981, Rick Fields's influential chronicle of American Buddhism, *How the Swans Came to the Lake*, created for this cohort a common sense of an American prehistory in such disparate figures as Henry David Thoreau, Walt Whitman, and Helena Petrovna Blavatsky, the co-founder of Theosophy.[5] The fourth, Sōka Gakkai International (SGI-USA), is seen as standing apart from these three for a variety of reasons—it has a more complex ethnic and racial composition; it is less identified with the 1960s; and its primary practice is chanting, not sitting.

All four communities have quite distinct origins and seem to be following their own unique developmental trajectories. Zen is the oldest convert tradition and has the most layered and varied bibliography devoted to its history.[6] The origins of American Zen date from the appearance of Shaku Sōen, a Rinzai monk, at Chicago's World Parliament of Religions of 1893. In the early twentieth century, his colleagues, Sokei-an and Nyōgen Senzaki, followed in his footsteps to become the first to teach Zen practice to Americans. One of Sōen's lay students, D. T. Suzuki, became a leading exponent of a popularized form of Zen philosophy and was a major figure, along with the Beat poets, in the Zen boom of the 1950s. Sōen's students and the Beat poets shared an approach to Zen which emphasized individualism, spontaneity, and intuition, qualities that appealed to counterculturists who were largely responsible for the explosive growth of Buddhism in the 1960s.

Suzuki and the Beats remain important models for enthusiasts, but a more disciplined, practice-oriented approach to Zen in America is largely an outgrowth of the work of a generation of American and Japanese teachers who came to prominence in and around the 1960s. Two Americans, Robert Aitken, founder of Hawaii's Diamond Sangha, and Philip Kapleau, who established Rochester Zen Center in central New York, played early and important roles in popularizing practice-oriented Zen. Important Japanese teachers include Joshu Sasaki and Eidō Tai Shimano, two Rinzai monks, and Shunryu Suzuki and Taizan Maezumi, Sōtō teachers who established influential practice communities at the San Francisco Zen Center and the Zen Center of Los Angeles, respectively. Harada Yasutani, an innovative teacher who drew upon both Rinzai and Sōtō, is often cited as a figure who helped define the character of American Zen as laicized monastic practice based on a hybrid of the two traditions. His reputation, however, has been clouded by the revelation of his wartime nationalism and anti-Semitism.[7]

The center of American Zen is currently defined by the native-born successors to Suzuki and Maezumi, among whom the Americanization of a Japanese heritage is proceeding in a variety of ways. Since the 1960s, Suzuki's San Francisco Zen Center has been at the cutting edge of developments in American Zen and retains a high degree of influence through its many affiliated centers, mostly located on the West Coast. The White Plum Sangha, a loose affiliation of Maezumi's students nationwide, includes teachers who represent the spectrum of styles to be found to American Zen—socially engaged Buddhism, family practice, Zen and the arts, secularized Zen, and progressive traditionalism. The current influence of Zen, however, rests on more than these Japanese-inspired institutions. Thich Nhat Hanh, the Vietnamese monk and leading exponent of socially engaged Buddhism, is a major force in American Buddhism, and the Zen community includes Seung Sahn Sunim's Kwan Um School of Zen, a Korean-American synthesis. These and other movements all share the formidable task of creating institutions that can, over the long term, sustain and perpetuate the kind of monastic-inspired lay practice that is at the heart of the American Zen community.

The development of Tibetan Buddhism in America has a distinct history, largely driven by the Chinese invasion of Tibet and the subsequent creation of a Tibetan diaspora community.[8] Geshe Wangal, a Gelugpa monk who founded the first Tibetan monastery in the United States, settled in New Jersey in 1955, but the Tibetan Dharma became a significant factor in American Buddhism only in the 1970s. At about that time, a number of *lamas* in exile, such as Tarthang Tulku, Kalu Rinpoche, and Chögyam Trungpa Rinpoche, established teaching and practice centers, first in temporary locations and only later in permanent facilities. The uniquely rich mythological and practice traditions of Tibet soon became prominent elements in the counterculture, and *lamas* from all four Tibetan schools and numerous teaching lineages soon became attractive, often charismatic, figures, whose Himalayan origins lent them a distinct, if sometimes highly romanticized, spiritual authority. Chögyam Trungpa Rinpoche, a one-time Kagyu monk and exponent of a "crazy wisdom" well suited to the ethos of the time, played a unique role as arbiter between the Tibetan tradition and the counterculture throughout the 1970s and into the 1980s. During this period of intense activity, Trungpa also laid foundations for a range of educational, arts, and practice institutions, among them Naropa Institute in Boulder, Colorado, a city that became for a time the epicenter of countercultural interest in Tibet. After a period of strife following Trungpa's death in 1987, his teachings were incorporated into Shambhala International, headquartered in Halifax, Nova Scotia, in which a blend of tradition and innovation has been further developed under the direction of Trungpa's son, Mipham Rinpoche, known in the movement as Sakyong, or "earth-protector."

With the waning of the counterculture, the tenor of Tibet-related movements shifted as Tibetan cultural and political issues gained public prominence, and a highly differentiated community began to follow its own unique developmental trajectory. Scholarly work on the Tibetan Dharma has been a concern since Deshung Rinpoche arrived at Seattle's University of Washington in 1961. By 1990, efforts to study, preserve, and disseminate Tibetan traditions gained a range of expressions from Jeffrey Hopkins's work at the University of Virginia to the Asian Classic Input Project directed by Geshe Michael Roach, a Gelugpa monk and the first American to receive the *geshe* degree. Tarthang Tulku's Dharma Publishing, Snow Lion Publications (associated with the Gelugpa tradition), and Tibet House (a New York public education concern funded in part by Richard Gere) brought Tibetan traditions, placed in peril by the Chinese occupation, before the public. At the same time, the Free Tibet movement gained momentum through high-profile media campaigns radiating from Hollywood, the concerted efforts of numerous Tibet-support groups working at the grassroots, and the diligent efforts of Tenzin Gyatso, the 14th Dalai Lama. Numerous centers, led by a new generation of *lamas* in exile and a first generation of American teachers, continue to form the core of a practice community quite distinct from Zen, due to its grounding in the uniquely rich traditions of Tibet.

Insight Meditation, the third convert movement devoted to sitting meditation, has its origins in meditation retreat centers in South and Southeast Asia. The most prominent teachers in the movement are lay Americans who traveled to Asia in the 1960s, where they trained with a variety of Theravāda teachers, some monks, others laity. Upon returning to the United States, they began to teach one or another form of *vipassanā* or "insight" meditation, more or less divorcing it from traditional monastic and lay devotional elements central to the religious life of Asian Theravāda communities, and many undertook training as psychotherapists. Early teachers Ruth Denison, who founded Dhamma Dena in the high desert of California in 1977, and Sharon Salzberg, Jack Kornfield, and Joseph Goldstein, co-founders of the Insight Meditation Society in Barre, Massachusetts, in 1975, soon developed eclectic styles of teaching. For over a decade, IMS was the flagship of the movement until 1988, when Kornfield helped to found its West Coast counterpart in Marin County at Spirit Rock, which soon became an integral part of the San Francisco Buddhist community.

The eclecticism of early Insight Meditation teachers continues to be a hallmark of the movement, which by the 1990s enabled it to grow into one of the most popular and overtly Americanized forms of American Buddhism. Like Zen, Insight Meditation is a movement of laity engaged in meditative practices traditionally associated with monasticism. But in contrast to Zen, the movement is less identified with the vocabulary and literature of one particular Asian tradition and draws freely upon several schools of Buddhism as well as humanistic psychotherapy. Much of the movement literature has moreover an appealing devotional and inspirational tone. These factors have enabled its teachers to create readily accessible forms of practice that fit comfortably with liberal, often secular, American norms. Taken as a whole, Buddhism taught as Insight Meditation is usually not presented as a religion but as a set of awareness techniques that foster awakening and psychological healing. It is often associated with other forms of practice that have been self-consciously integrated with psychotherapy, such as that developed by Jon Kabat-Zinn at the Stress Reduction Clinic he founded in 1979 at the University of Massachusetts Medical Center.

SGI-USA, while neither an old-line ethnic Buddhist group nor a new immigrant Buddhist community, fits awkwardly in the convert camp and follows its own unique developmental trajectory. SGI-USA is an American branch of Sōka Gakkai Japan, a large and dynamic lay group associated for most of its seventy-year history with Nichiren Shōshū, a *Lotus Sūtra*–based sect to which it remains indebted for much of its philosophy and practice. It was introduced to this country by Japanese immigrants in the 1950s, but gained much of its membership during 1960s-era social upheavals, when its collective energy was devoted to *shakubuku*, an active form of recruitment. During this time, the movement also developed a membership that includes substantial numbers of African-Americans and Latinos, giving it the reputation of being the most multi-ethnic of American convert Buddhist groups.

The history of SGI-USA has been largely shaped by tensions in Japan between the lay movement, which became increasingly progressive under the leadership of its third president, Daisaku Ikeda, and the conservative priestly leadership of Nichiren Shōshū. In 1991, these tensions erupted in a schism between the two groups. Since that time, SGI-USA, along with affiliates in numerous countries, has developed a form of Buddhist humanism under Ikeda's direction, which is a synthesis of the teachings of Nichiren, a thirteenth-century Japanese reformer, and those of Tsunesaburo

Makaguchi, a liberal educator who founded Sōka Gakkai in 1928. Today SGI-USA resembles other convert Buddhisms insofar as it shares a tendency to support liberal social reforms, such as feminism, environmental concerns, multiculturalism, and world peace. Unlike them, however, there are few lingering questions about how to reconcile its lay orientation with practice styles developed in Asian ecclesiastical settings. SGI-USA is now wholly lay in spirit and membership. Sacramental roles once played by Nichiren Shōshū priests have been taken up by volunteers in nonpaying ministerial offices that are filled on a rotating basis.

NEW IMMIGRANT OR ETHNIC BUDDHISM

A general reform of United States immigration law in 1965 and special exceptions designed for people displaced during the Vietnam War opened up a new era in the history of migration to the United States. By the mid-1980s, it was apparent that these new policies had also inaugurated a new era in American Buddhism, as the Theravāda traditions of South and Southeast Asia and the Mahāyāna traditions of Central Asia, Indochina, and the Far East began to flourish in new immigrant communities. The growth of immigrant or ethnic Buddhist communities is a nationwide phenomenon, but of particular importance in New York, California, Texas, and Illinois, states that have absorbed most of the Asian immigration.

Many commentators have been slow to grasp the importance of this immigration for the development of the Dharma in this country, and a strong tendency remains to over-identify American Buddhism with the convert community. But demographic figures on American Buddhists, while rough and highly variable, suggest that one-half to two-thirds of Buddhists in the United States may be found in immigrant communities.[9] Immigration has been one of the most important forces behind religious change in the United States, classic cases being Jews and Catholics who between 1840 and 1920 wholly reshaped a predominately Anglo-Protestant national landscape. The process of adapting immigrant religion to American norms and mores is driven by a number of forces, such as institution-building, Anglicization, and heritage maintenance. These forces are well understood by historians but operate intergenerationally and are thus difficult to assess in the short term. If older trends in immigration history persist, the current wave of immigrant Buddhists can be expected to contribute new and important variables into a perennial American preoccupation with religion, ethnicity, and personal and group identity and will forge enduring religious, cultural, and political links to their Asian homelands.

There is to date only one book-length study of these new immigrants, Paul Numrich's comparison of the Americanization process in two Theravāda temples, one in Los Angeles, the other in Chicago.[10] Numrich estimates that there were between one-half and three-quarters of a million Theravāda immigrants at the time of the 1990 census. In 1996, he confirmed the existence of about 150 organizations functioning as temples, some formally recognized, others operating on a more ad hoc basis. Many were first established in apartments, homes, or storefront rentals. Fully articulated temples only came later, when communities achieved economic stability, at which time new construction required that traditional architectural and religious forms be adapted to comply with zoning regulations. Numrich's account vividly portrays the unfolding of important issues, the resolution of which will shape American Theravāda for decades. Some are specific to a tradition led by monastics, such as tensions between laity and monks over the management of temples and the continuing need for Asian clergy due to the reluctance of young Asian-American men to enter orders. Others issues—the negotiation of inter-ethnic relations, the creation of Dharma schools and summer camps, and the retailoring of norms to suit new American lifestyles—confront all Buddhist immigrants and are essentially generic.

A great deal of national variety exists among the new immigrant Buddhists—Chinese, Korean, Vietnamese, Cambodian, Laotian, Thai, and Sri Lankan, among others. There is also a wide variety of regional and sectarian traditions within these communities that make it difficult to generalize about how immigrants practice or in what ways these practices are being reshaped through Americanization. But, by and large, most immigrant Buddhists engage in one or another form of lay practice, which includes such things as *Sanghika-dāna* (the offering of gifts to the Sangha), temporary ordinations in the Theravāda tradition, chanting the *sūtras*, the observance of major Buddhist holidays, fire *pūjas*, and the release of captive animals. Class variables are also at work within communities. Some temples are rapidly mainstreaming as they serve the religious needs of educated professionals in the computer industries in suburban Los Angeles and San Francisco, while others primarily address the lingering emotional scars of refugees from the war in Southeast Asia in low-rent, inner-city communities in Chicago or in Long Beach, California.

To understand different communities requires examination on a case-by-case basis, but important long-term developments are emerging that suggest the cumulative effect immigrants may eventually have on American Buddhism. For example, different traditions of Buddhism that may have developed for centuries in isolation are now found in the same neighborhood and in ecumenical organizations. Among these are the American Buddhist Congress, an umbrella organization of loosely affiliated immigrant and convert groups nationwide, and the College of Buddhist Studies in Los Angeles, which fosters the study of Buddhist traditions from a nonsectarian point of view. A number of immigrant leaders have developed constituencies outside immigrant communities, such as Korean immigrants Seung Sahn and Samu Sunim and Henepola Gunaratana, a Sri Lankan monk who leads the Bhavana Society in West Virginia. Some Theravāda temples have also developed what Numrich calls *parallel congregations*, a two-tier organization within a temple, one designed to address the needs of immigrants, the other to provide instruction for Euro-Americans.

The current wave of Buddhist immigration, which seems to show few signs of abating, is certain to have an important impact on the religious and political landscape of the United States over the long term. To date, however, no cadre of high-profile leaders has emerged to project the influence of these communities into the American mainstream. The funding controversy involving the Democratic National Committee and the Hsi Lai Temple, the head temple in the United States of the Taiwan-based Fo Kuang Buddhist movement, has raised the specter of anti-Asian political sentiments and, as such, may discourage such funding efforts throughout the immigrant Buddhist community.[11] Whatever the case, the vast majority of literature about the Dharma in America continues to be published about and within convert communities. As a result, the contributions of immigrants to the formation of American Buddhism remains difficult to assess and is, I think, greatly underrated.

THREE BUDDHISMS REVISITED

The idea that there are three Buddhisms in the United States is convenient because it provides a kind of shorthand for general descriptions of the current landscape. It has a good deal of explanatory power and its simplicity is likely to give it a long life, particularly if the current tendency for little communication among these groups persists. But given the complex picture of American Buddhism that has emerged in the recent crop of scholarly works,[12] it is apparent that this view, if taken too literally, distorts the historical record and may do a disservice to the ongoing development of American Buddhism.

First, the appeal to three Buddhisms masks a critical aspect of the history of the last forty or so years. Convert Buddhists, despite the great significance of the emergence of a generation or two of native-born teachers, owe an immense debt to Asian-immigrant teachers. Even though convert Buddhists may make appeals today to Henry David Thoreau or Erich Fromm, the communities stand—as Buddhist communities—on links forged between Asian traditions and the American experience established by long-term, face-to-face relationships among American students and Asian teachers, the history of which is hardly recorded and remains little understood by scholarly interpreters. In this regard, David Chadwick's *Crooked Cucumber: The Life and Zen Teachings of Shunryu Suzuki* is a refreshing and insightful addition to the new literature on American Buddhism.[13] Equal parts history, biography, Dharma rap, and hagiography, *Crooked Cucumber* lacks the critical distance associated with scholarly work. But it is an apparently trustworthy, interpretive account of American students and their teacher interacting over the course of tumultuous yet formative years in one Zen community. Historically minded interpreters need comparable works on a range of other crucial episodes centered on Taizan Maezumi, Thich Nhat Hanh, Seung Sahn Sunim, Chögyam Trungpa, and a wide range of other figures whose teaching laid the foundations for American convert Buddhism.

The parsing out of the landscape into three broadly construed American Buddhisms also disguises the fact that distinct historical circumstances, issues, and developmental trajectories have been and are at work in different communities. However much Euro-American and other converts may share with native-born Buddhists, different forces have helped to shape different communities. D. T. Suzuki, the Beats, and the philosophical and literary heritage of the 1950s boom were and are influential in Zen; the Chinese occupation of Tibet continues to shape American Tibetan Buddhism; therapeutic values are of particular importance in the Insight Meditation movement; and the momentum generated by the schism between Nichiren Shōshū and Sōka Gakkai Japan continues to inform the progressivism of the SGI-USA community. The emotional, social, and financial forces at work are also different among new immigrants, exiles, and refugees, and BCA Buddhists and other old-line Asian-Americans wrestle with both the blessing and the curse of having a secure position in the middle-class American mainstream. As useful as the tripartite schema may be, the more nuanced differences that can readily be discerned and are amenable to historical and social interpretation remain important and are, to my mind, far more interesting.

The view I attempted to develop in *Buddhism in America*—one that reflects my interests as an Americanist and historian, but not a Buddhologist or practitioner—is that under close examination there are so many forms of Buddhism and so many different modes of Americanization that it is premature to settle on any schematic typology. In this light, I think that the discovery of three distinct Buddhisms might best be considered an important moment in the development of American Buddhist self-consciousness as it began to emerge out of the chaotic flux of a founding era. It marked a dawning awareness on the part of commentators, most of them Euro-Americans with experience in or around the counterculture, that there were a variety of powerful forces, some well beyond the much publicized florescence of Buddhism among converts, at work in the creation of an indigenous American Dharma. In as much as the main outlines of the schema are grounded in typically American ethnic and racial preoccupations, it may also be taken as indirect evidence of the ongoing process of Americanization. But at this juncture the schema may well hamper the further development of genuinely indigenous American Dharma. Its genesis reflects in part a lack of understanding and communication among American Buddhist communities over the last forty years. To raise the idea of three Buddhisms above the level of conventional wisdom to a sustained social analysis may only exacerbate the situation at a time when American ideals tend to privilege multiculturalism, religious pluralism, and dialogue among the many different groups that give the United States its vibrant complexity.

Historical precedents in Asia suggest that there is no question that an indigenous American form of the Dharma will emerge, but that it is likely to take more than a generation to do so. It is my own view that the idea that there are three American Buddhisms can be shelved, only to be brought out from time to time to gauge how issues articulated in a founding era are progressing. To my mind, the real question is which of the many forms of the Dharma flourishing in the United States today will survive a winnowing process that is likely to occur over the next twenty or so years as a large-scale, generational shift in all the Buddhist communities re-shuffles the issues in unanticipated ways. Then questions about the Americanization of the Dharma will be in the hands of Americans, old-line ethnics, converts, and new immigrant groups who inherited communities that positioned themselves to be viable over the long term. For the time being, a genuinely indigenous American Buddhism remains in the making.

NOTES

1. Charles S. Prebish, *Luminous Passage: The Practice and Study of Buddhism in America* (Berkeley: University of California Press, 1999), 51–93; Peter N. Gregory, "Describing the Elephant: Buddhism in America," *Religion and American Culture: A Journal of Interpretation* 11, no. 2 (Summer 2001), 233–63.

2. Tetsuden Kashima, *Buddhism in America: The Social Organization of an Ethnic Religious Institution* (Westport, Connecticut: Greenwood Press, 1977).

3. Don Morreale (ed.), *The Complete Guide to Buddhist America* (Boston: Shambhala, 1998), xvi.

4. Thomas A. Tweed, "Night-Stand Buddhists and Other Creatures: Sympathizers, Adherents, and the Study of Religion," in *American Buddhism: Methods and Findings in Recent Scholarship*, edited by Duncan Ryūken Williams and Christopher S. Queen (Richmond, U.K.: Curzon Press, 1999), 76.

5. Rick Fields, *How the Swans Came to the Lake: A Narrative History of Buddhism in America*, 3rd revised and updated ed. (Boston: Shambhala, 1992).

6. Layered interpretations of a single aspect of American Buddhism are hard to marshall. Studies of American Zen include Louis Nordstrom (ed.), *Namu Dai Bosa: A Transmission of Zen Buddhism to America* (New York: The Zen Studies Society, 1976); David L. Preston, *The Social Organization of Zen Practice: Constructing Transcultural Reality* (Cambridge: Cambridge University Press, 1988); Helen Tworkov, *Zen in America: Five Teachers and the Search for an American Buddhism* (New York: Kodansha International, 1989); G. Victor Sōgen Hori, "Japanese Zen in America: Americanizing the Face in the Mirror," in *The Faces of Buddhism in America*, edited by Charles S. Prebish and Kenneth K. Tanaka (Berkeley: University of California Press, 1998), 49–78; Senryo Asai and Duncan Ryūken Williams, "Japanese American Zen Temples: Cultural Identity and Economics," in *American Buddhism: Methods and Findings*.

7. See, for example, "Yasutani Roshi: The Hardest Koan," in *Tricycle: The Buddhist Review* 9, no. 1 (Fall 1999), 60–75.

8. Amy Lavine, "Tibetan Buddhism in America: The Development of American Vajrayāna," in *The Faces of Buddhism in America*, 99–115.

9. Martin Baumann, "The Dharma Has Come West: A Survey of Recent Studies and Sources," *Journal of Buddhist Ethics* 4 (1997), 194–211, and http://jbe.la.psu.edu/ [3 Nov. 2000].

10. Paul David Numrich, *Old Wisdom in the New World: Americanization in Two Immigrant Theravada Buddhist Temples* (Knoxville: University of Tennessee Press, 1996).

11. See, for example, Richard Hughes Seager, *Buddhism in America* (New York: Columbia University Press, 1999), 164.

12. These include Prebish, *Luminous Passage;* Prebish and Tanaka, *The Faces of Buddhism in America;* Williams and Queen, *American Buddhism: Methods and Findings;* Thomas A. Tweed and Stephen Prothero (eds.), *Asian Religions in America: A Documentary History* (New York: Oxford University Press, 1999); Richard Hughes Seager, *Buddhism in America*.

13. David Chadwick's *Crooked Cucumber: The Life and Zen Teachings of Shunryu Suzuki* (New York: Broadway Books, 1999). Chadwick can be profitably read against the more personalized memoir of the early years of the San Francisco Zen Center in Erik Fraser Storlie, *Nothing on My Mind: Berkeley, LSD, Two Zen Masters, and a Life on the Dharma Trail* (Boston: Shambhala, 1996).

7 Buddhism in Canada

Bruce Matthews

INTRODUCTION

Buddhism in Canada has had an interesting and distinguished history since the late nineteenth century, though it has only emerged as a major religious force in the mid-1960s. Its *vihāras*, pagodas, and organizations have become a visible part of Canada's urban landscape. Canada's burgeoning multicultural world reveals many hundreds of thousands of people of Asian extraction. Many are linked in some way to Buddhism. A recent survey of country-wide Buddhist institutions discovered nearly seven hundred Buddhist temples, centers, libraries, and meditation groups in Canada's ten provinces and two territories.[1] It is possible to assume that there are at least about three hundred thousand devotees of one kind or another out of a total national population of thirty million.[2] The demographic question is complicated, however, by the whole issue of determining just who *is* a Buddhist. Much has recently been written about this issue in the North American context, notably by Charles S. Prebish, Kenneth K. Tanaka, and others.[3] Canada, like the United States, contains an astonishing variety of ethnic Buddhist denominations, as well as a complex array of what might be called Euro-Canadian Buddhist associations. As Jan Nattier has rightly noted, "At first glance this colorful assortment of Buddhists seems virtually impossible to characterize in any meaningful way. Yet characterize them we must, for simply to list them all will tell us next to nothing."[4]

This chapter analyses Buddhism in Canada largely from historical, communal, and denominational perspectives. The so-called ethnic Buddhism of immigrant Asian peoples is by far the most important aspect of the faith in Canada, but the analysis aims as well to show how Buddhism has made an impact on a large, growing, non-Asian constituency. By way of method, I first review the quiet beginnings of the faith on Canada's West Coast. Then I turn to the exponential growth of Buddhism since the late 1960s due to widening immigration patterns and the acceptance of large numbers of Southeast Asian refugees. I include reflections on the sorts of strain that confront Canadian-born generations of ethnic Buddhists. Finally, I turn to the phenomenon of Euro-Canadian or non-Asian Buddhist interest and practice, and to a collateral issue of Buddhist Studies in Canada. I show how Buddhism has long been an important subject in the academy, initially gaining momentum and reputation through the work of non-Asian, non-Buddhist scholars. I draw conclusions that suggest why, for a number of reasons, a "Canadianized" form of Buddhism emerges only very slowly. Buddhism will likely remain compartmentalized in an ethnic denominational structure for a long time. It will not be a religion that speaks with a single voice to the non-Buddhist Canadian public. But this will be to its benefit, providing a flexible, nonaggressive, largely accommodating renown. It will have ways of presenting itself to the Western convert that still recall the Asian birthplace of the Dharma—yet remain in a specifically North American context.

ETHNIC CANADIAN BUDDHISM

When Buddhism first appeared on Canada's West Coast, it just "came along," so to speak, to minister to specific Chinese and Japanese immigrant communities.[5] Chinese miners arrived in British Columbia's Fraser Valley as early as 1858, and by 1891 statistics indicate over nine thousand Chinese in Canada.[6] The Chinese population steadily increased despite discrimination by both provincial and federal legislation; the Chinese were disenfranchised by British Columbia in 1875 and by the Chinese Immigration (Exclusion) Act in 1923. Then the immigrants slowly began to shift toward central and eastern Canada. For those who did not convert to Christianity, the religion of choice was generally syncretistic, a blend of Buddhist, Confucian, Taoist, and Little Tradition devotion. Less eclectic was the Buddhism of the Japanese, largely the Jōdo Shinshū or Pure Land tradition. Japanese immigrants began to appear in British Columbia and Alberta from 1889. This particularly important part of the Buddhist legacy in Canada deserves some consideration. By 1904, the community requested ministerial help from the Honpa Honganji Temple in Kyoto, thus beginning a long relationship with the mother temple. As largely menial jobs became available in southern Alberta (mostly sugar-beet farming), increasing numbers of Japanese moved to the border region south of Lethbridge. When World War II resulted in the expulsion or internment of most of British Columbia's Japanese and the closure of their sixteen temples because of putative security concerns, about three thousand shifted to southern Alberta, augmenting its established Jōdo Shinshū presence.[7]

Not unexpectedly for the time, Jōdo Shinshū had no wider proselytizing outreach to Euro-Canadians. Racial stigma and religious prejudice on the part of the largely Europeanized Christian Canadian majority would have seen to that. In addition, the Japanese immigrants were reluctant to abandon their strong cultural loyalty to a traditional way of identifying with the Dharma in order to appeal to Western sensibilities. Yet, ironically, one response to Canadian condescension and indifference was for Buddhists to eventually make their houses of worship and even some of their ritual practices conform to what one might have found in a Christian church (Sunday services, pews, hymns, organ music, and so forth). In time this included more use of English in services, a feature which led eventually to increased interest in Pure Land by non-Asian Canadians. But the shift was also welcomed by many Japanese themselves, since English became their everyday language of choice.[8] This, along with a rapidly accelerating rate of intermarriage with non-Japanese partners, made Jōdo Shinshū a moderately popular form of Buddhism beyond the strictly Japanese community. Many temples in southern Alberta, for example, claim 25 percent non-Asian participation, and the denomination readily ordains non-Asians into its ministry. Further, although Jōdo Shinshū was well organized as a unified national religious body by 1955 (as the Buddhist Churches of Canada), the very place of Pure Land devotion in public and private life was challenged by a widening generation gap, as first-generation Issei gave way to second- and third-generation Nisei and Sansei.[9] According to Gordon Hirabayashi, this has led to two different modes of adaptation to mainstream Canadian life: the *integrative assimilative mode*, whereby the ethnic Pure Land believers do not use faith or ethnicity to set themselves apart (the hyphenated Japanese-Canadians), and the *pluralistic mode*, those who "integrate structurally into the Canadian social fabric, but with an effort to do so on the springboard of their Japanese heritage."[10] This essential dichotomy persists not only with Pure Land but with other ethnic Buddhist communities and congregations. Adaptation to so-called Canadian ways is essential if these denominations wish to attract non-Asian members. But not all Buddhist communities are interested in this mission. Some see themselves as spiritual and cultural centers for what Louis-Jacques Dorais has tellingly called "exiles in a cold land."[11]

Second, from a historical perspective, Buddhism in Canada changed utterly in 1962, when modified Canadian immigration law permitted a huge influx of Asians, many with a Buddhist allegiance of some kind.[12] Canada's 1962 Immigration Act replaced selection by race with selection by education and ability. Between 1963 and 1968, there was a seven-fold increase of

Hong Kong Chinese immigrants, usually well educated and with a reasonable knowledge of English.[13] The reunification of families (spouses, children, grandparents) represented just under half the immigrants, and the subsequent balancing of the sex ratio provided a new dynamic to the Chinese community. Several waves of Hong Kong immigration followed, particularly after Tiananmen Square (13 June 1989). With the further introduction of Entrepreneur and Investor Class programs for immigrants, up to 60,000 Hong Kong Chinese per annum emigrated to Canada during the 1990s. This brought the Chinese population from 118,815 in 1971 to over 600,000 by 2000, many of them with loyalties to Buddhism. Among this number were immigrants from Taiwan and a few from the People's Republic of China. Most of these preferred to settle in Vancouver. Toronto, however, has the largest population of Chinese (over 400,000), with an impressive outreach of their own forms of communion, communications networks, and religio-cultural services.

Another demographic feature important for the transmission of Buddhism to Canada was the massive advent of Indochinese refugees as a result of the war in Vietnam. In this regard, McLellan reminds us that, historically and sociologically, there is an important distinction between *immigrant Buddhist* and *refugee Buddhist*, and the kinds of Buddhism these groups are likely to espouse express their different needs.[14] The refugee (for example, Vietnamese, Cambodian, Tibetan) has often come to Canada with a traumatized background. There is a distinct and obvious necessity for the healing balm of whatever faith the refugee might have, to recover and to accept karmic fate (though some Indochinese have felt the abandonment of hope occasioned by failure of divine assistance to come to their rescue in the hour of peril). The political refugee in particular might also be slower than the immigrant in acculturating to the new, disorienting Canadian milieu.

Between 1975 and 1978, Canada received over 9,000 Indochinese refugees. Only in 1976 did the government fundamentally broaden the definition of *refugee* to admit a wider category of persecuted people (the 1976 Immigration Act, proclaimed into legislation in April 1978).[15] But at the Geneva Conference in 1979, Canada announced acceptance of up to 60,000 Indochinese refugees (mostly Vietnamese and Sino-Vietnamese "boat people," but including Laotians and Cambodians) for resettlement.[16] This, combined with the Orderly Departure Program (for families left behind), brought to Canada about 130,000 Indochinese/Vietnamese (though official statistics do not always give a reliable picture).[17] It has been argued that this refugee community had (and continues to have) very different religious needs than, for example, the immigrant Chinese diaspora. Although precise statistics on the matter are elusive, a frequently proffered estimate is that 60 percent of the Indochinese were (and are) Buddhists or in some way associated with the faith.[18] The importance of the temple, or *vihāra*, and Sangha as a place of spiritual and cultural restoration remains very significant. As Louis-Jacques Dorais has pointed out, this is particularly the case with the Theravāda, which has an urgent requirement for a temple-based faith.[19] Oddly, this does not necessarily translate into participation in daily or weekly temple devotions. (Much guesswork confronts the inquirer on this matter. The monk at the Semple Street Cambodian temple in Calgary, for example, claimed over 90 percent of the six hundred Cambodians in his city came regularly to services. His lay advisors quietly suggested 35 percent. On the other hand, Van Esterik estimates that only 15 percent of Lao refugees in Toronto attend regular Buddhist services.)[20] The temple and traditional duties surrounding care of the Sangha are still regarded as the most appropriate "field of merit" (*puñña*), and the only repository of Theravāda cultural values. The presence of ordained monks is especially valued, and many Theravāda communities have gone to extraordinary lengths to bring clergy from the motherland, an expensive proposition often involving significant bureaucratic hurdles. In this regard, one cannot help but be impressed by the immense devotion that lies behind the efforts of small and not particularly affluent expatriate communities to bring over a monk. Their temples are often no more than an apartment or small suburban residence. The monk is not permitted to drive, and unless near public transport he is forced to be housebound or completely dependent on his parishioners to get about. (This also makes learning English or French difficult, an issue which will become increasingly urgent if the Buddhism of the parent generation is to appeal to their children, as well as subsequent generations.) Sri Lankan, Thai, and Burmese immigrants (only a few Sinhalese were refugees in the late 1980s) comprise another element of ethnic Theravāda Buddhist presence in Canada. Thai and Burmese temples are found in most major cities and in some smaller locations. The first Sri Lankan temple was the Toronto Mahavihara Buddhist Centre (1978). There and elsewhere (notably Calgary and Vancouver), English-speaking monks continue to provide some outreach to non-Asians interested in *vipassanā* and *Abhidharma*, though their ministry is first centered on Sinhala-speaking devotees. The Sir Lankan temples are nonetheless well ahead in the matter of adaptation to a new cultural environment, with "Sunday schools" and classes for a wide variety of interested people. Sri Lankan and Burmese temples and organizations are largely confined to

Canada's biggest cities, and their identity is not unexpectedly at times fused with a sense of Asian home nationalism. If they do have non-Asian devotees, these groups often meet as separate congregations.[21] Some Theravāda centers are not so much *vihāras* for the expatriate community as they are meditation facilities available to anyone interested in the techniques of, for example, Mahāsi Sayādaw or S. N. Goenka, with appeal particularly to non-Asian participants.

It is sometimes claimed that those from a Mahāyāna background place less emphasis on temple embodiment for the faith, but among the Vietnamese and Chinese community loyalty to the temple as the focus of key rituals is still strong (for example, memorials for the deceased, Tet, and Buddha's birthday). Because Vietnamese refugees initially came in large numbers to Québec (thirty thousand) and Ontario (sixty thousand), it is appropriate to look briefly at Vietnamese Buddhism in this context. The first Vietnamese temple (*la congregation-mère*, Liên-Hoa in Brossard, near Montréal) was established only in 1975 to accommodate the several waves of refugees of the time. Thich Tam Chan from France was the spiritual leader. Thich Thien Nghi looked after congregational affairs until he left in 1980, to establish Tam Bao as well as the Union of Vietnamese Buddhist Churches in Canada, one of the largest Vietnamese temple communities in the country (of the thirty-six Vietnamese temples accounted for in Canada in July 2000, nine are associated with this group). One reason for this outward fragmentation was Vietnamese regionalism, with the lay founders of Liên-Hoa deriving from the north and Thich Thien Nghi deriving from the center of Vietnam. Several other congregations arose as a result of new waves of immigration or association with a particular political perspective (Quan Am, 1983; Tu Quang, 1985; Thuyên Tôn, 1987). Different political affiliations have also caused pronounced divisions in the Vietnamese diaspora in Toronto and elsewhere. Though there is inter-temple communication and both an Overseas Buddhist Association and a Vietnam Buddhist Association of Canada, McLellan notes the continuance of "economic, regional, political, and class divisions (based on previous status in Vietnam and new status identities in Canada), and disparate migratory experiences. . . ."[22] There is as well the "engaged Buddhism" of Tiep Hien associated with Thich Nhat Hanh, with its unique interpretation of key Buddhist doctrines (and with a significant appeal to non-Asians who appreciate such things as Tiep Hien's ecological sensitivity, family and "hugging" meditation, relaxation, and "joy"). This shows that Vietnamese Buddhism is receptive to non-Vietnamese participation and adaptation to Canadian society. Indeed, English is periodically used in most temples, though unlike in the United States there are as yet in Canada no non-Asians ordained to the Vietnamese Sangha.

Chinese forms of Buddhism are expectedly numerous, given the relatively large expatriate and Canadian-born Chinese population. These include traditional schools such as Ch'an, Pure Land, Tien-t'ai, and Vajrayāna. There are as well guru-driven sects: Master Sheng-Yen Lu's esoteric True Buddha School (highly eclectic temples, such as Pai Yuan in Calgary, with Hindu as well as Chinese and Nepalese iconography), Master Hsing Yun's Fo Kuang Shan Buddhist Order and Buddha's Light International Association (which claims interest in reinterpreting Buddhism in terms of contemporary needs and has four million followers worldwide), and Master Hsüan Hua's Dharma Realm Buddhist Association (associated with The City of Ten Thousand Buddhas, Talmage, California).[23] Canada's three largest cities (Toronto, Montréal, and Vancouver) have extensive Chinese populations, often concentrated in certain sections or suburbs. Even medium-sized cities like Calgary, Edmonton, and Winnipeg have a substantial Chinese presence, and Chinese Buddhist temples are a common sight. Some, like north Toronto's Cham Shan (founded in 1979) are huge, visited by thousands. McLellan notes, however, that a central aim of these temples is to "perpetuate a Chinese ethnic institution," and that accordingly there are "few mechanisms to welcome non-Chinese to their temples and associations."[24]

Tibetan Vajrayāna, on the other hand, has through Chögyam Trungpa Rinpoche made a substantial outreach to non-Asians. With its international headquarters in Halifax, Vajradhatu (with its collateral Nalanda Foundation and Shambhala training centers) has a presence in every province of Canada. Although its subscribing membership is a modest seventeen hundred, very many more participate in Shambhala programs. In some ways Shambhala is an anomaly: its constituency is non-Tibetan, but its spiritual leadership is still associated with the Kagyupa and Nyingmapa lineages (the current head, the Sawang Ösel Rangdröl Mukpo, son of Shambhala's founder, resides in Halifax, and Shambhala programs often involve prominent Tibetan monks).[25] Other Tibetan groups associated with Tibetan masters are found throughout Canada, including Nunavut and the Yukon, but for the most part they, too, are aimed at non-Tibetans. The actual Tibetan ethnic diaspora in Canada is small and, as McLellan notes, rarely do ethnic Tibetans share religious practices with the non-Tibetan Vajrayāna community.[26] Arriving in 1959, ethnic Tibetans were among the first religious refugees in Canada, but, like other Asian refugees, with the third and following generations, cultural uniqueness and language are threatened by assimilation. It can be argued that, whether Theravāda,

Mahāyāna, or Vajrayāna, refugees reach out to the faith to help them survive the passage from one culture and society to another of very different character and geography. Canda and Phaobtong have rightly pointed out that religiously based indigenous healers and helpers are important sources of support for many Southeast Asian refugees. Monks provide a wide range of counseling services, including help in bereavement, meditation instruction, and even exorcism.[27]

To sum up, the history of ethnic Buddhism in Canada indicates several distinct periods of settlement and development, beginning in the mid-nineteenth century and meeting a point of maximum acceleration in the last two decades of the twentieth century. Immigrant and refugee communities face different challenges as they acclimatize to Canadian society and cultures. Nonetheless, certain shared concerns which confront ethnic Buddhism in contemporary Canada can be identified. Some have already been touched upon. These all focus on the issue of how ethnic Buddhism might transform or adapt itself to the social, political, and economic situation it experiences as a minority religion among a Euro-Canadian, largely Judeo-Christian demographic majority. Among the most important are adjustment of the ethnic culture to a geographically variable and strange setting; intermarriage with non-Asians and a less traditional role for women in religious life and witness; widening generation gaps; survival under the hegemony of a dominant Christian culture; and problems in Buddhist interdenominational relations due to ethnic identities. This last point is indirectly related to multiculturalism, a federal government initiative in Canada that encourages protection and development of specific cultural identities yet is under critical review because it leads to implosive communalism and social fragmentation.

We must now turn to challenges that unavoidably confront ethnic Buddhism, which must seek to preserve and enhance its integrity by appropriate adjustment of its spiritual ethos and cosmology without transforming itself in the new land.

First, no form of ethnic Buddhism in Canada is entirely without a Little Tradition. This is the domain of the guardian spirits and their complex association with a faith that traditionally eschews superstition. The spirit cult is closely associated with sacred geography, the realm of the homeland thousands of kilometers away. Much of the Little Tradition, like Buddhism itself, depends on a different understanding of time. In traditional Indochinese Buddhist societies, for example, time is perceived as a *quality* (auspicious, inauspicious) determined, as Van Esterik points out, by the intersecting of astronomical and agricultural cycles.[28] Buddhism and its attendant Little Tradition are never separate from everyday secular life. In the North American setting, however, this close relationship is often compromised. Ritual acts associated with these moments often have to be severely condensed, for example, from three days to one day or even half a day.[29] Buddhist spirituality and the conduct of life preclude, functionally and theoretically, any distinction between the sacred and the secular.

Second, except for the Chinese community (which is large enough to have a sufficient cohort of marriageable partners), ethnic Buddhism must confront serious conflict emerging from interracial marriage, something Jōdo Shinshū congregations, for example, have been accommodating for decades. The Toronto Buddhist Church is one of the few places where one finds non-Asians, or *hakujin*, in attendance, usually spouses of Japanese, but in time other ethnic Buddhist temples will have to adapt to this phenomenon. Gender issues have surfaced in some ethnic Buddhist communities as women, with educational gains, take on more religious ritual, administrative, and counseling roles.

Third, a generation gap widens as the initial immigrant and refugee settlers give way to their progeny's children, who in turn may have different spiritual expectations, possibly less reliance on a traditional culture and worldview to meet those expectations, and a desire to be part of the Canadian mainstream of culture, business, and the professions. Divorce from the home culture as the generations evolve is not inevitable. Indeed, in studying the socio-linguistic adaptation among the Vietnamese community in Québec, Louis-Jacques Dorais has identified a period of installation (one to three years), integration (three to six years), and finally identification, where "Vietnamese identity is reinforced after a successful period of integration."[30] But how to ensure that there is opportunity to move successfully into the greater matrix of Canadian society without abandonment of key aspects of ethnic communal identity and social control (familial and institutional) is often problematic. A major concern is that ethnic children be taught Buddhism, and that instruction is a traditional responsibility of temple and monk.[31] But well-trained, educated monks are hard to come by, and as yet there is no strong indigenous order of an ethnic Buddhist Sangha anywhere in Canada. Want of a temple and its monk is not the only problem. In some instances, Canadian-born ethnic Buddhists display a palpable lack of interest in the rituals, theology, and religious hierarchical status quo of their parents and ancestors. Recent academic literature attests to the widespread nature of this circumstance (that is, young people find teachings and services boring and resent being treated like children in the traditional environment).[32] This is, of course, an issue shared with virtually all mainline religions in the West, where youth interest in religion tends to be low. But there is some repudiation here as well, as overseas-born ethnic Buddhists are replaced by Canadian-born Buddhists. The continuing necessity to express the principles and rituals of Buddhism in English (or, where appropriate, French) is something an older generation is sometimes reluctant to do. Ethnic Buddhist spokespersons often agree that the faith needs to modify itself to Canada, just as it has done throughout the long history of its transmission in Asia.

A fourth issue is the question of the insularity and exclusivist particularism of ethnic Buddhist communities. This is understandable, given the natural human tendency to look to and enjoy first one's ethnic roots. Kenneth Tanaka is likely right when he claims that there is no serious conflict here, no intention to exclude, but just "a natural tendency to gravitate to those with shared background and interests."[33] This tendency results, nonetheless, in a paucity of theological communication and sharing of ritual between the denominations. From time to time, there is an effort to bring ethnic Buddhist communities together. Buddhists in most major cities, for example, have on occasion joined together for Vesak and other important Buddhist days, producing something that is rare indeed—clergy from a large spectrum of Buddhist allegiances on the same stage, cultural performances, shared ethnic foods, and the like. There is no single, unifying Buddhist body in Canada, no national alliance that coordinates such things. (Despite its name, the 1955 Buddhist Churches of Canada represented only Jōdo Shinshū.) Suwanda Sugunasiri notes that this should hardly be surprising, "given the traditional Buddhist aversion to organization." In 1980, he and others in Toronto brought together Chinese, Japanese, Korean, Sri Lankan, Ambedkar, and Tibetan Buddhists, an initiative which led to the Buddhist Federation of Toronto and, in 1983, to the Buddhist Council of Canada. The latter was essentially an ambitious misnomer, born of the necessity to have a formal "national identity" to meet requirements for a broadcasting opportunity. Despite efforts to invigorate this body, it remains associated only with Toronto.[34] Elsewhere, others have brought Buddhist groups together in specific locations, such as Leslie Kawamura's International Buddhist Foundation of Canada and Steven Aung's International Buddhist Friends Association. Despite their bold names, these efforts are almost entirely confined to the cities of Calgary and Edmonton, respectively, where they continue to do excellent work in bringing Buddhists closer to each other, sponsoring visits by famous monks, helping with temple building, and making outreach efforts to non-Asian Buddhists. In most locations, however, there is little continuing close contact between particularist ethnic Buddhist temples and groups. This may seem strange for non-Buddhists and even for some immigrant Buddhists, given the pronounced cultural pluralism most Canadian cities now exhibit and the fact that ethnic Buddhist temples are often located near each other. How different this pluralist environment is from the places of origin of most of these denominations. Often, each of these Buddhist expressions is the majority religion in the originating country. Often the different regional forms of Buddhism in Asia barely tolerate each other. Van Esterik warns that it is easy to make too much of this, to overstress the self-chosen isolation of, for example, Lao Buddhism in the context of Southeast Asian history. But in Toronto today, not to put too fine or important a point on it, apart from the sacred language of Pāli, which Lao Theravāda shares with some other denominations, and the common challenge of trying to maintain their version of Buddhism in a largely Judeo-Christian city, "they have no other basis for cooperation." [35]

It could be argued that a major factor that feeds this fragmentation is the federal public policy of multiculturalism. Multiculturalism was established by Pierre Trudeau (prime minister from 1968–79 and 1980–84) as part of a strategy whereby immigrants and refugees would be "integrated" but not "assimilated" into Canadian society. Trudeau's Multicultural Directorate in the Department of the Secretary of State and the subsequent 1988 Multiculturalism Act were designed "to assist in the preservation of culture and language, to reduce discrimination, to enhance cultural awareness and understanding, and to promote culturally sensitive institutional change." [36] This was reinforced by the *Canadian Charter of Rights and Freedoms*, Part 1 of the Constitution Act of 1982 (Item 27, on the preservation and enhancement of the multicultural heritage of Canadians and "the new salience of citizenship").[37] Since 1993, a new ministry, the Heritage Department, has underwritten many multicultural endeavors, but only as cultural, not religious, projects. Many Buddhist groups have learned to live with this, sometimes calling their places of worship "cultural centers" rather than temples in order to get around the obstructing rubric. The main point here is that when multiculturalism was officially promulgated, it represented a sea-change for Buddhist organizations, which suddenly obtained "the same legal status and political rights as Christian churches." [38] Not all Asian immigrants welcome the multicultural policy, however. Neil Bissoondath, for example, argues that the Canadian government's encouragement of ethnic differences leads immigrants to adopt a psychology of separation from the mainstream culture, "that people, coming here from elsewhere, wish to remain what they have been; that personalities and ways of doing things, ways of looking at the world, can be frozen in time, that Canadian cultural influences pale before the exoticism of the foreign." Further, although "culture becomes folklore, lightened and simplified, stripped of the weight of the past," it also isolates ethnic communities, setting one against another in a competition for power and resources.[39]

A fifth aspect of ethnic Buddhist transformation derives situationally from the mere fact of living in the presence of institutional Christianity, still a major cultural and religious force in Canadian society despite its diminished stature. Refugee Buddhists often came out of years of hardship in holding camps, where the record shows their religion was sometimes seriously compromised by active Christian missionary interference and the lure of sponsorship by well-meaning but narrow-minded Christian evangelical groups. Given the fact that 10 to 15 percent of the Indochinese population, for example, is Roman Catholic, and that there is a long tradition of eclecticism, not unexpectedly there is some crossover between religions, with joint acknowledgment of cultural festivals and sometimes even religious services. For example, Van Esterik reports that "the Lao argue there should be no conflict between Christianity and Buddhism. In fact, many of them attend Buddhist merit-making services on Saturday and Christian services on Sunday." Despite a "common ethics," this masks "incredible differences in logic and beliefs," and if a Lao chooses to actually join a Christian church (rather than just attend), that individual would be expected to "break with Buddhist practice."[40] For most ethnic Buddhists, however, there is little intercourse with other mainline religions in Canada, and no particular interest in interfaith dialogue. Mainstream Canadian attitudes toward Asian immigrants have also changed in the last two decades, partly as a result of official multiculturalism and partly because the traditional Christian dominance has gradually (and in some cases, like Québec, greatly) diminished. If there was any public fear twenty years ago when Buddhism became such a visible feature in Canada, it has completely evaporated. In general, public attitudes in the West have changed dramatically. Even non-Asian Buddhists are not perceived to be peculiar. This has perforce given ethnic Buddhism the fortuitous chance to flourish under social conditions far different from what someone like Yutetsu Kawamura (one of the first missionaries, or *kai kyoshi*, from Japan) would have experienced in Alberta during the Depression years.

CANADIAN CONVERT BUDDHISM

I turn now to a brief examination of the non-Asian Buddhist phenomenon. It is valuable to point out that for over seventy years Buddhist scholarship in Canada has been a feature of university research, much of it of a very high order indeed, and largely associated with non-Asian contributors (many of whom were and are not Buddhists). Canadian universities were quick to include courses that reflected the surge of interest in Eastern cultures and religions, partly as a result of the Vietnam War. Although Canada was not involved in Vietnam militarily, the *angst* associated with that conflict flowed over into its society nonetheless—especially among younger people. The war precipitated a wave of immigration of some of America's "best and brightest" to Canada. They brought to their immigration homesteading, handicrafts and skills of all kinds, artistic talent, and strong spiritual and religious needs. Indeed, some had already "turned East," like the Beatles had in Britain. It was a kind of "underground railway" whose *animus* was not merely an antiwar phenomenon but spiritual seeking. The tragic military struggles in Asia gave the 1960s and early '70s their special nuance. Students wanted courses on Asian religions as part of a way of identifying with "the other side." Some wanted the intellectual engagement and the factual information such studies would bring. Others were in search of spiritual values or sentiments they felt lacking or even unobtainable in their own Judeo-Christian tradition. The universities obliged where they could, particularly the newly founded ones, which were often given *carte blanche* on what they could offer. Thus thirty years ago, Buddhism became a common piece of the curriculum in most larger Canadian universities, and even many smaller colleges. This has had a lasting impact on the phenomenon of non-Asian interest and participation in Buddhism. Not unexpectedly, there were exponents of a philosophical, non-ritualized Buddhism, one that emphasizes the tradition's rational and esoteric (but not superstitious) hallmarks. Indeed, a number of Buddhist thinkers themselves have championed this cool, logical, "sapiential" or philosophical model of Buddhism as the appropriate one for our age (for example, K. N. Jayatilleke). Less desirable was the amount of cannibalization of the faith in the West by any number of New Age or quasi-Buddhist groups, seizing upon techniques like *vipassanā* meditation and taking key Buddhist teachings and practices out of cultural and institutional context, as if acquired on a shopping spree.[41]

But for the most part, non-Asian Buddhism in Canada was, and continues to be, closely associated with the three great vehicles (*yānas*), and has so far not seriously aimed to seek an independent, nonsectarian way of identifying itself apart from the traditional roots. A review of George Klima's compendium of Buddhist associations in Canada suggests that most, if not all, have some generic connection with an Asian school.[42] Some (like White Wind Zen Monastery, Ottawa) have Western clergy or staff, and some appeal specifically to a non-Asian constituency. Among the latter, the most successful is Shambhala International, mentioned above, which represents Tibetan Buddhism adapted for Western use—spotlessly antiseptic temples, with virtually no Asian presence except for presiding officials and visiting ethnic *lamas, tulkus,* and teachers.

Because of their proficiency in the English language in particular, it is likely that non-Asian Buddhists will continue to dominate the field of Buddhist interpretation and studies. Except for the Chinese Buddhists in Toronto and Vancouver, the ethnic Buddhist communities are generally not wealthy and most cannot afford to publish English tracts, books, and mission material that might be of interest or use beyond their limited groups. Many ethnic Buddhists also frankly know little about the great philosophical and theological achievements of Buddhism and are uninterested in its profusion of texts, its scholarly interpretation, or its general dissemination. Non-Asian Buddhists will continue to be called upon to provide analysis and explanation for what the Dharma means in its newfound home. There is, of course, a paradox here. Most non-Asian Buddhists become participants in the faith by joining temples or Buddhist societies that have an Asian connection. Prebish asks whether this "cultural translocation" of Buddhism has inhibited "meaningful progress" for the religion in its Western context.[43] In other words, how important is it for the future of Buddhism in the West to eventually assume a specifically Western identity, to take root in a Western worldview and environment, with only the loosest of historical, traditional, and theological connections with Asia? It is not entirely clear whether Buddhism, if it aims to become anything more than an exotic variety of religion in Canada (which suggests superficiality), need take on a unique identity, one that distances it from the Asian continent. All of the strongest sects in non-Asian or Western Buddhism have at least some acknowledged and treasured link with Asia. Ironically, however, even though almost all non-Asian Buddhist churches and organizations derive from one of Buddhism's classical three *yānas,* there is very little dialogue with the other side of Buddhism in the West, the ethnic Buddhists. It is an odd situation: ethnic Buddhists in the West are not particularly keen to make more than token contact with non-Asian Buddhists. Further, with some important exceptions (like Jōdo Shinshū), there is little suggestion that ethnic Buddhist organizations do anything ministerial except to their own specified ethnic community, attending to its rites of passage and other cultural demands as much as to the spiritual needs of its devotees. There is no question at all of maturation into a comprehensive Buddhist denomination, one that might be energized by the overcoming of fragmentation and empowered with a larger voice in Canadian society. Only if this were to be accomplished could we discover whether there are distinctively Buddhist answers to Canadian or Western problems, however defined.

CONCLUSION

Buddhism in Canada does not really have its ecumenical "act" together. It does not seem to find this an important goal. By way of example, some years ago the Swiss theologian Hans Küng was in Toronto to lecture on religious diversity and the need for dialogue. The host, Trinity College professor Willard Oxtoby, called upon a distinguished Japanese-Canadian scholar to represent Buddhism. When it came time for this individual to reflect on the possible significance of what interreligious dialogue purports for the future, he remarked that the search for dialogue appeared to be a Christian "problem." He was attending the session only out of compassion! This is not an unusual incident. The Buddhist Council of Canada, a loose umbrella group of various ethnic Buddhist congregations, refused to add a clause to its agenda promoting dialogue, citing the fact that they had nothing to be sorry for (as if dialogue is in large part apology) and didn't feel particularly threatened (as if dialogue is an instrument of self-interested protection). Of all the challenges that confront the future of Buddhism in Canada, the matter of dialogue strikes me as the most important.

Non-Asian Buddhism in Canada reveals an amorphous scene. There is on the one hand a distinguished scholarly record that is in large part attributable to Euro-Canadian scholars, all of whom respect the subject enormously, though few are practicing Buddhists. On the other hand, there are some *bona fide* tradition-based Buddhist temples and schools, presided over by non-Asian monks or teachers, as well as guru-based organizations with largely (though not completely) Asian Buddhist teachers. But Buddhism has a far wider impact on non-Asian Canadian awareness than its temple-based presence. Media attention given to the Dalai Lama and Thich Nhat Hanh; numerous films and endorsements, of certain Buddhist lifestyle features by renowned figures and entertainment stars; consciousness about the tragedy of Tibet—these and similar phenomena have helped Buddhism attain a place in public consciousness unimaginable a generation ago. How different all of this is from ethnic Buddhism. Yet clearly, taken together these all in some sense represent Buddhism in Canada.

To conclude, I offer four points for consideration. First, over twenty years ago, Yutetsu Kawamura wrote that "unless the teachings of Buddhism extend beyond the ethnic boundaries of the Japanese there will be no future for Buddhism."[44] Perhaps he had in mind the conversion of non-Asians. If so, then that future would still be in doubt, for although a few thousand must have fully crossed over to the Buddha Dharma from the Judeo-Christian tradition, it is not enough to put a Buddhist church for a non-Asian congregation in every Canadian city, much less our towns. But if, on the other hand, Kawamura meant other modalities of ethnic Buddhism, then the faith is alive and prospers among hundreds of thousands of immigrant and refugee Asians in Canada. Second, even if the communalistic roots of ethnic Buddhism are to a degree intensified by Canada's policy of multiculturalism, Canadian-Asian Buddhists continue to retain their ethnic identities with certainty and pride, finding security in cultural and spiritual roots in an adopted country that is not in the least antagonistic to their religion. Technological globalization has also made voice and other forms of rapid communication with distant homelands so much easier that they function in effect as taproots, sending up the juices of spiritual life. Though there may not be much formal contact, Buddhism in Canada is clearly "embedded within a global transnational network."[45] Admittedly, such contacts with Asia may in one sense retard Canadianized forms of Buddhism based on fusion and syntheses of ethnic and non-Asian Buddhism. There is less need for acculturation of the Dharma to a specifically Canadian pattern.

Finally, although Buddhism in Canada does not have a unified presence, single prelate, or spokesperson, it still bears certain identifying features, whether Asian or non-Asian. Most, if not all, of these are entirely inoffensive in Canadian society. Buddhism is not a religion burdened with dogmatic fundamentalism, different dress codes, unusual diet, or special demands for educational needs beyond what the state can provide. The Dharma has found a good place to settle in all of its grand diversity and complexity. It must be worldly, universal in scope, tolerant, informed, and ethical. Only thus can Buddhism truly reach out to others and, in the words of scripture, invite them to "come and see" (*ehi passika*).

NOTES

1. Located at http://www.buddhismcanada.com [1 Feb. 2002]. This valuable list is prepared and regularly updated by George Klima, K'un Li Shih, and Chris Ng. Some Buddhist groups are fleeting, and new ones regularly come forward. Ontario has the largest concentration of Buddhist groups (124), followed by British Columbia (84) and Québec (53). Most of these citations refer to major temples and organizations of ethnic Buddhists (e.g., Cham Shan and Tam Bao), but a remarkable number are evidently aimed at a non-Asian, Euro-Canadian constituency (e.g., Shambhala and university meditation centers).

2. Statistics Canada lists 163, 415 Buddhists in the last enumeration (1991), but this number has doubled in the last decade. For an internet reference, see the data at http://www.statcan.ca/english/Pgdb/People/Population/demo32.htm. [1 Feb. 2002].

3. See Jan Nattier, "Who Is a Buddhist? Charting the Landscape of Buddhist America," in *The Faces of Buddhism in America*, edited by Charles S. Prebish and Kenneth K. Tanaka (Berkeley: University of California Press, 1998), 183.

4. Ibid., 188.

5. Harold Coward and Leslie Kawamura (eds.), *Religion and Ethnicity* (Waterloo, Ontario: Wilfrid Laurier University Press, 1978), 42.

6. Didier Hia, "The Chinese Community in Montréal: A Case Study of Socio-Economic Integration" (M.A. thesis, Université Rouen, France, 1993).

7. An interesting account of early Japanese-Canadian experience is Toyo Takata, *Nikkei Legacy: The Story of Japanese Canadians from Settlement to Today* (Toronto: NC Press, 1983). Reverend Yutetsu Kawamura, a Jōdo Shinshū minister who came to Raymond, Alberta, in 1934, is still active in 2000. He is a much-appreciated source of information about the half-century of his ministry. See Leslie Kawamura (ed.), *The Dharma Survives with the People* (1997) and *Chronicles of True Pure Land Buddhism in Canada, 1933–1985* (1999), both published by the Religious Studies Department at the University of Calgary, Alberta.

8. The *Seiten: Book of Worship* published by the British Columbia Buddhist League in 1967 and still in use in Pure Land temples has many evangelical hymns in English, such as "In Lumbini's Garden" and "Nirvana's Bliss."

9. In 2000, there are an estimated fifty-five thousand Japanese-Canadians.

10. Gordon Hirabayashi, "Japanese Heritage: Canadian Experience," in *Religion and Ethnicity*, edited by Harold Coward and Leslie Kawamura, 66.

11. Louis-Jacques Dorais, Lise Pilon-Lê, and Nguyên Huy, *Exile in a Cold Land: A Vietnamese Community in Canada* (New Haven: Yale Center for International and Area Studies, 1987).

12. Alan Cairns, et al. (eds.), *Citizenship, Diversity and Pluralism: Canadian and Comparative Perspectives* (Montréal: McGill-Queen's University Press, 1999), 34.

13. Vivien Lai, *The Assimilation of Chinese Immigrants in Toronto* (M.A. thesis, York University, Toronto, 1970), 9.

14. Janet McLellan, *Many Petals of the Lotus: Five Asian Buddhist Communities in Toronto* (Toronto: University of Toronto Press, 1999), 20.

15. Elliot Tepper (ed.), *Southeast Asian Exodus: From Tradition to Resettlement: Understanding Refugees from Laos, Kampuchea and Vietnam in Canada* (Ottawa: Canadian Asian Studies Association, 1980), 138.

16. Sixty-six percent of the Sino-Vietnamese settled initially in Montréal (about half had some knowledge of French).

17. McLellan, *Many Petals of the Lotus*, 106.

18. Louis-Jacques Dorais remarks on the eclectic nature of this religious allegiance: "la majorité de ces Canadiens d'origine vietnamienne ou sino-vietnamienne se rattache à la tradition du *tam giao* (les trois enseignements), une synthèse de cosmologie taoiste, de morale confucéenne et de foi bouddhique . . . les adeptes de cette tradition formaient 64% des réfugiés du Vietnam." From "Vie religieuse et adaptation: les Vietnamiens de Montréal," *Culture* 13, no. 1 (1993), 4.

19. Louis-Jacques Dorais, in *Uprooting, Loss and Adaptation: The Resettlement of Indochinese Refugees in Canada*, edited by K.B. Chan and D.M. Indra (Ottawa: Canadian Public Health Association, 1987), 39.

20. Penny Van Esterik, *Taking Refuge: Lao Buddhists in North America* (Toronto: York Lanes Press, 1992; also published, Tempe: Program for Southeast Asian Studies, Arizona State University 1992), 63. Interview with Venerable Lok Hin, Calgary, 23 May 2000.

21. This is more evident in Toronto, where the Sinhalese are greatly outnumbered by the expatriate Ceylon Tamil refugee community, now consisting of about 130,000 in that city alone. Sri Lanka's civil war has long involved commentary by the powerful Sangha (e.g., the Eksath Bhikkhu Peramuna of the 1950s and 1960s, as well as several current *deshapremi* or "patriotic" organizations, for example, Hela Urumaya).

22. McLellan, *Many Petals of the Lotus*, 108.

23. Temples for the True Buddha and Dharma Realm schools enshrine images of their founders, Lu Sheng-yen and Hsüan Hua, on the same altars as images of Śākyamuni or the cosmic Buddhas.

24. McLellan, *Many Petals of the Lotus*, 181.

25. Shambhala has widened the understanding of Sangha to include its membership, but in addition nine senior teachers, all non-Asians, are selected as *acharyas* to assume greater responsibilities in both teaching and administration. Women are included, notably the famous non-ethnic nun, Pema Chödrön.

26. McLellan, *Many Petals of the Lotus*, 85.

27. Edward Canda and Thitiya Phaobtong, "Buddhism as a Support System for Southeast Asian Refugees," *Social Work* 37, no. 1 (1992), 64.

28. Van Esterik, *Taking Refuge*, 114.

29. Morton Beiser notes that Asian cultures are usually described as holding to a more integrated view of time than North Americans, emphasizing the past more and preoccupied with the future less, but "the current data suggest that time splitting is adapted by people under adversity." This is certainly an identifiable feature among some ethnic Buddhist groups in Canada. See "Changing Time Perspective and Mental Health among Southeast Asian Refugees," *Culture, Medicine and Psychiatry* 11, no. 4 (1987), 455.

30. Louis-Jacques Dorais, in *Uprooting, Loss and Adaptation*, 61.

31. See Louis-Jacques Dorais and Lise Pilon-Lê, "L'affirmation ethnique: la transmission de la langue, valeurs familiales et éducation," in *Les Communautés Cambodgienne et Laotienne de Québec*, Documents de Recherche 5 (Québec: Faculté des sciences sociales, Université Laval).

32. Kawamura, *The Dharma Survives with the People*, 48; Dorais, et al., *Exile in a Cold Land*, 154.

33. Kenneth K. Tanaka, "Epilogue," in *The Faces of Buddhism in America*, 288.

34. Suwanda Sugunasiri, "Buddhist Organizational Unity in Canada," *Karuna: A Journal of Buddhist Meditation* (Vancouver), no issue identification (1985), n.p.

35. Van Esterik, *Taking Refuge*, 91.

36. Marc Leman, *Canadian Multiculturalism* (Ottawa: Library of Parliament 933-6E, January 1997). For Trudeau's 1971 formulation of what a multicultural society within a bilingual framework would be like, see J. W. Berry and J. A. Laponce, *Ethnicity and Culture in Canada: The Research Landscape* (Toronto: University of Toronto Press, 1994), 103.

37. Alan Cairns and Douglas Williams, *Reconfigurations: Canadian Citizenship and Constitutional Change* (Toronto: McLelland Stewart, 1995), 158.

38. McLellan, *Many Petals of the Lotus*, 195.

39. Neil Bissoondath, *Selling Illusions: The Cult of Multiculturalism in Canada* (Toronto: Penguin, 1994), 43, 89.

40. Van Esterik, *Taking Refuge*, 51, 115.

41. Ibid.

42. See note 1.

43. Charles S. Prebish, *American Buddhism* (North Scituate, Massachusetts: Duxbury Press, 1979), xviii.

44. Kawamura, *Chronicles of True Pure Land Buddhism in Canada, 1993–1985*, 49.

45. McLellan, *Many Petals of the Lotus*, 7.

8 The Development of Buddhism in Australia and New Zealand

Michelle Spuler

INTRODUCTION

Buddhism has recently undergone substantial growth in both Australia and New Zealand, as it has in many Western countries. The geographical and cultural proximity of these two countries often causes similarities between them to be assumed; however, this paper examines the development of Buddhism in each separately, as a means of demonstrating how differences between these two cultures are reflected in slightly differing histories and Buddhist demographics. The socio-cultural factors that have enabled this expansion are focused on, as a means of illustrating how the developing forms of Buddhism reflect the cultures in which they are now situated. In its early days in the West, Buddhism was considered an alien religion; however, contemporary Buddhist practice in Australia and New Zealand is becoming more and more mainstream.

According to the 1996 Australian Bureau of Statistics census, 1.1 percent of the population, or 199,812 people, identified themselves as Buddhist. This represented an increase of 42.9 percent from the 1991 census. In 1996, 0.8 percent of the New Zealand population, or 28,131 people, identified themselves as Buddhists in the Statistics New Zealand census, an enormous 120-percent increase over the 1991 census figure.

HISTORY

There are few historical accounts exploring the reasons behind the current state of affairs. Croucher provides an excellent historical narrative on Buddhism in Australia, but other Australian sources are scarce.[1] However, Australian sources are a font of information when compared to the published material on the history of Buddhism in New Zealand. Ajahn Viradhammo has a chapter on Buddhism in *Religions of New Zealanders* that includes several pages of history (in addition to the routine explanations of Buddhist doctrines and practices); this currently comprises the authoritative (that is, only) published work in the area.[2]

Buddhism came to both countries through immigration in the mid-1800s. Buddhism probably first reached Australia in 1848 and New Zealand in 1863, when Chinese immigrants arrived to work in the gold fields. In both countries, this early influence was slight. The first organizations did not form until some time later. The first Buddhist organization in Australia was the Little Circle of Dharma, founded in Melbourne in 1925; the second was the Buddhist Study Group in 1938. The first Buddhist organization in New Zealand is hard to identify, due to the lack of information; the Buddhist Society of New Zealand, founded in 1956, was certainly one of the earliest. While early versions of Buddhism in both countries followed the Western pattern of being secular in orientation, focusing on Buddhist texts or philosophy, this slowly changed as more and more teachers from various traditions visited. The first teacher to visit Australia was Sister Dhammadinna in 1952. Teachers from other traditions followed, such as U Thittila, a Burmese Theravāda monk (in 1954), and Daisaku Ikeda, president of Sōka Gakkai International (in 1964). In New Zealand, monks and lay teachers from various traditions came in the 1970s, including Karma Tenzin Dorje Namgyal Rinpoche of the Karma Kagyu lineage in 1973; Zen master Joshu Sasaki Rōshi, founder and abbot of Rinzai-ji, in 1974; and Lama Thubten Yeshe and Lama Thubten Zopa, of the Foundation for the Preservation of the Mahāyāna Tradition, in 1975. At the same time, interest in meditation was rising in both countries and many more groups were forming in a variety of traditions.

Due to the increasing interest, residential teachers and monasteries began to appear. In 1971, the Venerable Somaloka, a Sri Lankan monk, moved to Australia, and in 1973 he established the Australian Buddhist Vihāra as the first Australian Buddhist monastery, in Katoomba, New South Wales. In 1974, an English-born, Thai-trained monk, Khantipalo Thera, established a second Theravāda monastery, Wat Buddharangsee, in Stanmore, New South Wales. Australia is now home to the largest Buddhist temple in the Southern Hemisphere. Located in Wollongong, New South Wales, the Nan Tien Temple is part of the Fo Kuang Shan school of Buddhism. The temple complex was built between 1990 and 1996; most of its AUD $50 million construction cost was donated by Fo Kuang Shan members in Taiwan. The complex includes an eight-story pagoda, Pilgrim Lodge (with one hundred rooms of three- to four-star-rated accommodations), conference hall, museum, café, bookshop, teahouse, and multiple gardens. The temple is becoming so well known that in 1999 it was a finalist in the "significant regional attraction" category of the New South Wales Tourism Awards.

Exact information is again not available for New Zealand. However, early residential teachers included, Dharmachari Achala, an Englishman living in New Zealand who was ordained in the World Buddhist Order in New Zealand in 1975, and the Venerable Lama Karma Samten Gyatso, who has been the resident teacher of the New Zealand Karma Kagyu Trust center since 1981. The Venerable Lama Samten and the Venerable Lama Karma Shedrup Senge were ordered in 1979 by the 16th Gyalwa Karmapa to begin teaching in New Zealand, and have since established two centers. One of the earliest monasteries established was Bodhinyanarama, a Thai Forest Tradition monastery established near Wellington in 1986.

While many of the early Buddhist groups were convert in orientation,[3] increased Asian immigration changed the scene. With the ending of the Vietnam War in 1974–75, large numbers of refugees from Laos, Cambodia, and Vietnam arrived in Australia. Immigration to New Zealand from Southeast Asian countries grew in the early 1980s. With the plethora of traditions and lineages now present in both countries, ecumenical Buddhist societies also increased. A major ecumenical body, the Buddhist Federation of Australia, had formed in 1958, but a number of other ecumenical bodies formed in Australia in the 1980s, such as the Buddhist Council of Brisbane in 1982 and the Buddhist Council of New South Wales in 1985. In New Zealand, the Wellington Buddhist Association formed in 1981, although there may have been earlier incarnations that have not been documented. Another organization, the Pan Buddhist Association, was started in 1990. Australian ecumenical groups have achieved far more than their New Zealand counterparts, probably due to the greater number of Buddhist groups in Australia. For example, the Buddhist Council of New South Wales provides assistance on matters ranging from immigration and local government matters to religious instruction for Buddhist students in state schools. It is the Department of School Education's recognized accrediting body for teachers of Buddhism. In 1994, the Buddhist Council of New South Wales was accepted as a regional center of the World Fellowship of Buddhists.[4]

Buddhism's development has undergone similar periods in both Australia and New Zealand, although many major events occurred approximately ten years later in New Zealand than in Australia. However, this is to be expected from a country that has one-fifth of Australia's population and is even more geographically isolated. The latest stage of historical

Table 8.1. Traditions Represented by Buddhist Groups in
Australia and New Zealand in 2000

	Australia (%)	New Zealand (%)
Theravāda	25	29
Mahāyāna	34	40
Vajrayāna	27	24
Triyāna (Western Buddhist)	–	5
Nonsectarian	14	2

development has been the continuing diversification and growth of Buddhist groups in each country. In June 2000, BuddhaNet provided a listing of 315 Australian Buddhist groups, compared to approximately 60 in New Zealand in 2000.[5] These figures are almost equal in statistical terms when compared to the countries' populations. The two countries have similar breakdowns of the major Buddhist traditions and lineages present, as demonstrated by table 8.1.

BuddhaNet does not use the Triyāna classification; however, my own summary of groups in 1998 identified 2 percent of Australia's Buddhist groups as part of this category.[6] There is a large difference in the number of nonsectarian groups in both countries; it is probable that nonsectarian organizations such as hospices, social action groups, libraries, bookstores, and journals are not large enough to be independent groups in New Zealand and are consequently classified as part of the lineage or tradition to which they have some connection.

DEVELOPMENTAL FACTORS

There are a number of factors affecting Buddhism's development in Australia and New Zealand. Examination of the ethnicity of Buddhists shows that immigration has been a key contributor. Direct comparison of the ethnicity of Buddhists in New Zealand and Australia is slightly difficult, because the available data on Australian Buddhists' ethnicity classifies by birthplace, while New Zealand census data classifies by ethnicity. Nevertheless, comparison of this data provides a useful starting point, and is contained in table 8.2.

Table 8.2. Comparison of the Birthplaces of Australian Buddhists with the Ethnicities of New Zealand Buddhists

Australian Category by Birthplace[a]	Australian Buddhist Population (%)	New Zealand Category by Ethnicity[b]	New Zealand Buddhist Population (%)
Australia	19.7	NZ European	9.3
		NZ Maori	2.3
		European	4.2
Vietnam	31.0	Vietnamese	4.9
Indonesia	2.2	Indonesian	0.2
Malaysia	7.5	Malaysian	1.9
Sri Lanka	5.2	Sri Lankan	5.8
Thailand	6.2	Thai	7.0
Cambodia	6.8	Cambodian	10.7
Laos	3.4	Lao	3.7
China	4.6	Chinese	39.7
Taiwan	2.5	Taiwanese	not stated
Japan	not stated >2.2	Japanese	4.9
Korea	not stated >2.2	Korean	2.4
Other	10.9	Other	3.0

[a] Philip J. Hughes, *Religion in Australia: Facts and Figures* (Kew, Victoria: Christian Research Association, 1997), 17.

[b] Statistics New Zealand, "6.4 Religion and Ethnicity," *1996 Census of Population and Dwellings: Ethnic Groups* (Wellington, New Zealand: Statistics New Zealand, 1997), 106–14.

Since the vast majority of Buddhists in Australia and New Zealand were either born in or identify ethnically with an Asian country, these figures indicate that ethnic Buddhists far outweigh convert Buddhists. Exact figures are not known; ethnic Buddhists in Australia have been estimated at 85 percent and the New Zealand percentage is probably similar. However, the census only identifies those people who classify themselves as Buddhists. Other studies demonstrate that many more people in Western countries practice Buddhism to varying degrees than identify themselves as Buddhists.[7] For example, Fronsdal notes that many Americans of European descent practicing *vipassanā* do not refer to themselves as students of Buddhism.[8] Similarly Hughes, Black, and Kaldor present evidence that 11.5 percent of the Australian population had practiced some form of

Table 8.3. Adherents of Major Religions in Australia and
New Zealand in 1996

	Australia[a] (%)	New Zealand[b] (%)
Christianity	70.3	60.5
Buddhism	1.1	0.8
Hinduism	0.4	0.7
Islam	1.1	0.4

[a]Hughes, *Religion in Australia.*
[b]Statistics New Zealand, "6.4 Religion and Ethnicity,"
106–14.

Eastern meditation (although not necessarily Buddhist) in the previous
twelve months.[9]

Another major factor affecting the development of Buddhism in these
two countries has been the socio-cultural context in which both converts
and immigrants practice Buddhism. Both Australia and New Zealand are
considered multicultural, religiously plural, and predominantly secular.
The 1989 National Agenda on Multiculturalism affirmed the right of all
Australians to express and share their religion "within carefully defined
limits."[10] New Zealand claimed multiculturalism in the 1980s, although
contemporary government publications now also emphasize biculturalism
in recognition of the status of the indigenous Maori population. Multiculturalism has meant that Buddhism has a fertile ground in which to grow,
as have other world religions of recent importation. While the number of
Buddhists in Australia increased by 43 percent between 1991 and 1996, the
number of Hindus increased by 54 percent and the Muslims increased by
36 percent. In New Zealand, while Buddhists increased 120 percent from
the 1991 figure, Hinduism increased dramatically from 0.2 percent to 0.7
percent and Islam grew by 50 percent. (Percentages of each religion in the
1996 populations of the two countries are presented in table 8.3.)

There are other reasons for the religious plurality in both countries.
Neither Australia nor New Zealand has had a state religion dominating the
scene and, as in many other Western countries, mainstream religions are
on the decline. Bouma provides some other reasons, noting that Australia
has a lack of overlap between ethnic and religious differences, depoliticiza-
tion of religious differences, and a long history of nonviolent religious and
ethnic conflict.[11]

These socio-cultural conditions have also resulted in the rise of many New Religious Movements (NRMs) in both countries. New Age spirituality has been another growth area. In 1985, based on analysis of New Zealand census data, Hill and Bowman concluded: "While there has been a marked decline in both membership and participation in church-type religious groups there has also been a rapid increase in sectarian and cultic groups."[12] NRMs and New Age spirituality are often considered to deviate from the norm, and thus attract members of society who are not satisfied by mainstream religion. However, it is now being argued that many of these organizations succeed because they incorporate elements of mainstream society that the dominant religions do not. To some degree, these alternative religions are now more mainstream than established religions. For example, Hill argues that New Age spirituality has arisen out of contemporary society, and is not a reaction to it: "There is a great deal of resonance too between cultic groups of this kind and the urban social environment of contemporary New Zealand: for this reason it makes sense to treat them *not* as deviant responses of opposition to the dominant culture, but as groups which articulate the experience of a substantial part of the population."[13]

While these arguments are usually applied to NRMs and New Age spirituality, they can also be used to explain the growth of Buddhism in the West. While scholars studying NRMs often include Buddhism in their classification, and a few Buddhist scholars employ this classification themselves, many Buddhist scholars disagree with this categorization. It is argued that Buddhism is not a NRM in the West because, although it may be new in Western countries, Western groups descend directly from long-established Asian traditions. However, the factors identified as responsible for the rise and success of NRMs can also be identified for Buddhist groups in the West, and for convert Buddhism in particular.

The argument that many NRMs and New Age spirituality now reflect mainstream culture more than they deviate from it may be useful to understanding the rise of convert Buddhism. Recent studies examining the development of Buddhism in countries such as the United States of America, Germany, South Africa, and Australia have identified common trends in adaptation.[14] Queen's identification of the features of the emerging American Buddhism classifies these characteristics as *democratization*, *pragmatism*, and *engagement;* these are similar to those identified elsewhere.[15] *Democratization* refers to the emphasis on lay practice and feminization; *pragmatism* incorporates the emphasis on ritual practices (particularly meditation, chanting, devotional, and ethical activities); and *engagement* refers to the broadening of spiritual practice to include both family and community and the social and environmental concerns of the broader world.

With the exception of some ritual practices, these characteristics all seem to fit with Western cultural values, assisting Buddhism's integration into Western culture. Baumann has demonstrated that some German Buddhists have interpreted Buddhism in a way that conforms with German cultural values and attitudes;[16] it seems probable that this is the case in each Western country. In a similar vein, a number of scholars have examined Buddhism in the West and concluded that this is "Protestant Buddhism"— that some Buddhist groups have a liberal Protestant outlook, and their Buddhism affirms these values.[17] Indeed, the Auckland Shambhala Center in New Zealand writes: "A unique quality of the Buddhist teachings is that they can be expressed through existing cultural norms, making use of them rather than destroying or replacing them. This allows many westerners to practice Buddhism today without renouncing their cultural heritage or radically changing their lifestyles."[18] Similar to some other Western Buddhist groups (particularly some *vipassanā* groups), the Auckland Shambhala Center offers meditation within a secular setting (Shambhala Training), in addition to Buddhist practices.

Buddhist groups in Australia and New Zealand show some conformity to the characteristics described by Queen. My own study of the characteristics of Buddhism in Australia concluded that examples of each of these characteristics are evident; however, further research must be undertaken before it can be concluded that these are more than isolated cases.[19] In the case of New Zealand, no research has been done. However, like the Australian situation, examples can certainly be found. My own analysis of the development of Buddhism in New Zealand indicates that the situation is similar to that in Australia; a few characteristics can be seen in obvious patterns, but most cannot.

An example of adaptation to the socio-cultural context is the Maitai Zendo, the main center for the Diamond Sangha (the Zen Buddhist network founded by Robert Aitken) in New Zealand. The Maitai Zendo is innovative in many areas. The group's teacher, Mary Jaksch Sensei, is the first female Zen master in New Zealand, and only the third female Zen master in the Diamond Sangha lineage. As part of the broadening of practice to include wider concerns (one the characteristics of Western Buddhist groups), Buddhist teachings and practices are often synthesized with other disciplines. An emphasis on health and healing, particularly in cooperation with psychology, produces a common amalgamation. The Maitai Zendo runs a healing group led by the teacher and practicing psychotherapist, Mary Jaksch, which is integrated with Zen practice. One practitioner describes some of the practices: "We move into the silence of Zazen. Directly experiencing the breath of life. Then on to the other healing part—the laying on of hands. It sounded so audacious to me, however the instructions were quite simple; hands in *gasshō*, feel the warmth generated between the hands, and slowly lower them to another body." [20] The Maitai Zendo is also experimenting with new ways of teaching, and since 1999 has offered a Zen Distance Training program to students who would like to practice Zen but are prevented by distance or circumstance from working with a Zen teacher. Much of the communication between student and teacher is carried out via e-mail, although students are also expected to attend at least one retreat with the teacher each year in person. In addition to traditional Zen practices, students are encouraged to take up areas such as bodywork, creative skills, and compassionate action. This last category of ethical action incorporates activities such as helping at local youth centers, joining Amnesty International, or becoming involved with environmental protection, which is another common characteristic of Western Buddhist groups.

An Australian Buddhist center of note for its innovative ideas for upholding and spreading the Dharma is BuddhaNet, an internet site founded by Australia's e-monk, the Venerable Pannyavaro:

> BuddhaNet is the result of a vision to link up with the growing world-wide culture of people committed to the Buddha's teachings and lifestyle, as an on-line cyber sangha. In this way, an ancient tradition and the information superhighway will come together to create an electronic meeting place of shared concern and interests. . . . BuddhaNet is a non-sectarian organization, offering its services to all Buddhist traditions. It aims to facilitate a significant Buddhist presence in the ever-expanding realm of computer communications technology, applying this technology to helping make the Buddha's teachings freely available to all. [21]

BuddhaNet provides a host of useful resources, ranging from the "Australia Buddhist Directory" (used to supply the statistics above) to a Buddhist magazine (*BuddhaZine*, replete with comic strip) to a "What's On" section that lists national events and notices. BuddhaNet is affiliated with the Buddha Dharma Education Association, Inc., a *vipassanā* meditation center in Sydney that is led by the Venerable Pannyavaro.

While the practices of many Australian and New Zealand Buddhist groups seem to reflect their socio-cultural contexts, there are also many examples of traditional practices that have been maintained despite their seeming discord with Australian and New Zealand society. Maintenance of tradition is also vital for ensuring the efficacy and legitimacy of Buddhism in the West. For example, monks at a Thai Forest Tradition monastery in New Zealand, Bodhinyanarama, have continued the practice of going on alms rounds in the surrounding community. Bell provides an excellent analysis of how this practice legitimizes the Thai Forest Tradition in England through emphasis on tradition; a similar case could be argued in New Zealand.[22] Bodhinyanarama upholds tradition in various other ways. Because it is primarily a monastic residence, it maintains many of the practices of its Thai monastic forefathers. Since the establishment of the monastery in 1985, with two monks from the United Kingdom, the monastery has grown to its current resident community of six *bhikkhus*, one *sāmaṇera*, and three *anagārikas*.

However, in some areas Bodhinyanarama exhibits considerable adaptation to the New Zealand environment, reflecting some of the characteristics identified by Queen. For example, democratization is demonstrated in the existence of a Women's Meditation Group, which meets weekly. The Women's Meditation Group has recently hosted weekend retreats with visiting teachers, including Anja Tactor, a resident lay teacher at Wat Buddha Dhamma in Australia. While Wat Buddha Dhamma is a Theravāda Buddhist center, it is not part of the Thai Forest Tradition lineage, demonstrating a willingness to engage in dialogue with other lineages that is commonly seen in some Western Buddhist groups. A degree of engagement in relation to the environmental concerns of the broader world can be seen in Bodhinyanarama's forest management strategy. The monastery's property is considered to be important ecologically, due to its wide diversity of indigenous plant species and the habitat that it provides for native birds. Because of this, the Wellington Theravāda Buddhist Association, the charitable trust supporting and administering the monastery, has designated the monastery as a Native Reserve in order to protect, enhance, and restore the land.

While Queen's characteristics are more commonly identified in groups that are open to adaptation to the new host culture, particularly convert groups, other interesting examples can also be found. Karma Choeling, the first Karma Kagyu Trust monastery in New Zealand, has strong links to its parent center that have resulted in an emphasis on the maintenance of tradition. But emphasis on characteristics such as engagement can be identified here and there in unusual ways. In one center newsletter, a student of the Venerable Lama Samten recounts an amusing and illustrative tale. In 1993, New Zealand's hydroelectric supply was low, a cause of great concern to a country highly dependent on this form of electricity. At this time, the Venerable Lama Karma Samten asked if he could visit Lake Tekapo, a key area of hydroelectric generation:

> What was unusual about this request was that he said he might be able to do something towards ending the electricity crisis! . . . He told me he wanted to do practices to placate the spirits that lived in that area, in particular nagas. . . . He thought the natural balance of the MacKenzie Basin had been upset and these beings weren't very happy. In the weeks leading up to our arrival, Lama said he had established contact with these spirits and they were expecting us.[23]

The *lama* identified the land behind the Church of the Good Shepherd as the ideal site for the required fire *pūja*, but the local vicar vehemently denied his request to use the site. However, the local police constable granted permission and the *pūja* was performed. A week later, the lake had reached a comfortable level and the hydroelectric problems were over.

Analysis of the development of Buddhism in Australia and New Zealand indicates many similarities between the two countries. A variety of Buddhist groups exist. Some maintain strong connections with the traditions from which they have developed, while others demonstrate significant adaptation to the local culture. While both Australia and New Zealand ostensibly support religious diversity, the need for imported religions to fit their new surroundings has seen many adaptations that reflect Western values and beliefs. Buddhism may have initially been attractive to some people because of its otherness; however, adaptation to Western cultural values is making it more and more acceptable to the mainstream.

NOTES

1. Paul Croucher, *Buddhism in Australia, 1848–1988* (Kensington: New South Wales University Press, 1989). Other publications include Michelle Spuler, "Characteristics of Buddhism in Australia," *Journal of Contemporary Religion* 15, no. 1 (2000), 29–44; Enid Adam and Philip J. Hughes, *The Buddhists in Australia* (Canberra: Australian Government Publishing Service, 1996); Enid L. Adam, *Buddhism in Western Australia* (Perth: the author, 1995); Roderick S. Bucknell, "The Buddhist Experience in Australia," in *Religion and Multiculturalism in Australia: Essays in Honour of Victor Hayes,* edited by Norman Habel (Adelaide: Australian Association for the Study of Religions, 1992), 214–24; Robert Humphreys and Rowland Ward, "Buddhism," in *Religious Bodies in Australia,* 3rd ed. (Melbourne: the authors, 1995), 203–12; and Terrance McDonnell and Rod Bucknell, "Buddhists," in *Many Faiths, One Nation: A Guide to the Major Faiths and Denominations in Australia,* edited by Ian Gillman (Sydney: Collins, 1988), 318–31.

2. Ajahn Viradhammo, "Buddhism," in *Religions of New Zealanders,* edited by Peter Donovan (Palmerston North, N. Z.: Dunmore, 1990), 33–4 and 43–5.

3. Prebish provides an excellent discussion of the use of the terms *convert* and *ethnic* in Charles S. Prebish, *Luminous Passage: The Practice and Study of Buddhism in America* (Berkeley: University of California Press, 1999), 57–63.

4. "Buddhist Council of New South Wales: Its Past, Present and Future" (n.d.), http://www.buddhistcouncil.org/bcgrnd.htm [20 September 2000].

5. Dean Jones, "Statistics on Australian Buddhist Organizations" (2000), www.buddhanet.net/badstats.htm [17 July 2000]. A more detailed breakdown of the traditions and lineages present in Australia in 1998 is available in Spuler, "Characteristics of Buddhism in Australia," 31.

6. Spuler, "Characteristics of Buddhism in Australia," 32.

7. Tweed examines difficulties in defining Buddhists in Western countries in Thomas A. Tweed, "Night-Stand Buddhists and Other Creatures: Sympathizers, Adherents, and the Study of Religion," in *American Buddhism: Methods and Findings in Recent Scholarship*, edited by Duncan Ryūken Williams and Christopher S. Queen (Richmond, U.K.: Curzon Press, 1999), 71–90.

8. Gil Fronsdal, "Insight Meditation in the United States: Life, Liberty, and the Pursuit of Happiness," in *The Faces of Buddhism in America*, edited by Charles S. Prebish and Kenneth K. Tanaka (Berkeley: University of California Press, 1998), 164.

9. Philip Hughes, Alan Black, and Peter Kaldor, "Responses to the Multiplicity of Faiths in Australia," *South Pacific Journal of Mission Studies* 23 (April 2000), 17. The 11.5 percent total was provided privately by Philip Hughes.

10. Quoted in National Multicultural Advisory Council, *Multicultural Australia: The Next Steps Towards and Beyond 2000*, vol. 1 (Canberra: Australian Government Publishing Service, 1995), 2.

11. Gary D. Bouma, "The Emergence of Religious Plurality in Australia: A Multicultural Society," *Sociology of Religion* 56, no. 3 (1995), 297.

12. Michael Hill and Richard Bowman, "Religious Adherence and Religious Practice in Contemporary New Zealand: Census and Survey Evidence," *Archives de Sciences Sociales des Religions* 50, no. 1 (1985), 109.

13. Michael Hill, "Religion and Society: Cement or Ferment?" in *Religion in New Zealand*, edited by Christopher Nichol and James Veitch, 2nd ed. (Wellington: Tertiary Christian Studies Programme of the Combined Chaplaincies and the Religious Studies Department, Victoria University, 1983), 276.

14. For information on the United States of America, refer to Prebish, *Luminous Passage*; Williams and Queen, *American Buddhism*; and Prebish and Tanaka, *The Faces of Buddhism in America*. For Europe, refer to Martin Baumann, "Creating a European Path to Nirvana: Historical and Contemporary Developments of Buddhism in Europe," *Journal of Contemporary Religion* 10, no. 1 (1995), 55–70; and Detlef Kantowsky, "Buddhist Modernism in the West/Germany," in *Buddhism and Christianity: Interactions between East and West*, edited by Ulrich Everding (Colombo, Sri Lanka: Goethe-Institut, 1995), 101–15. For South Africa, see Michel Clasquin and J.S. Kruger (eds.), *Buddhism and Africa* (Pretoria: University of South Africa Press, 1999). And for Australia, see Spuler, "Characteristics of Buddhism in Australia."

15. Christopher S. Queen, "Introduction," in Williams and Queen, *American Buddhism*, xix.

16. Martin Baumann, "Culture Contact and Valuation: Early German Buddhists and the Creation of a 'Buddhism in Protestant Shape,'" *Numen* 44, no. 3 (1997), 287.

17. A good overview is provided in Martin Baumann, "Adapting a Religion in a Foreign Culture: Rationalistic Interpretation of Buddhism in Germany," in Everding, *Buddhism and Christianity*, 72–100.

18. Auckland Shambhala Study Group, "The Buddhist Path of Practice and Study" (n.d.), http://msnhomepages.talkcity.com/dharmadr/dlugose/dharma dhatu.htm [1 Feb. 2002].

19. Spuler, "Characteristics of Buddhism in Australia," 41.

20. "Healing Group," *Maitai Zendo News* 3, no. 1 (1998), 4.

21. "BuddhaNet," http://www.buddhanet.net/about_bn.htm [18 Sept. 2000]. The full site can be accessed at www.buddhanet.net [1 Feb. 2002].

22. Sandra Bell, "Being Creative with Tradition: Rooting Theravāda Buddhism in Britain," *Journal of Global Buddhism* 1 (2000), 1–30. See also http://jgb.la.psu.edu/contents.html [21 July 2000].

23. Refer to John Herrett, "Ven. Lama Karma Samten's Visit to Lake Tekapo, Winter '93," http://www.kagyu.org.nz/content/ktc-laketekapo.html [1 Feb. 2002].

9 Buddhism in South Africa

Michel Clasquin

INTRODUCTION

Buddhism in South Africa is largely a late twentieth-century phenomenon. Nevertheless, it has not only a history but also a prehistory of sorts. Whether it will have a future will depend largely on its ability to relate to indigenous African thought.[1] The story of South African Buddhism goes back to 1686. In that year, the Portuguese ship *Nossa Senhora dos Milagros* was shipwrecked off the west coast of South Africa. The area at that time had been settled by Dutch expeditions and was known as the Cape Colony, named for the Cape of Good Hope. Among the newly stranded passengers were three Thai *bhikkhus* on their way to Europe as emissaries of the Siamese king. For four months, until a passing ship enabled them to continue their journey, they were quartered in the house of a free burgher.[2] This was the first Buddhist presence ever in South Africa, but the moment passed without leaving a trace. There may have been other Buddhists at the Cape during the seventeenth and eighteenth centuries, but there are few records and they left little evidence. For the citizens of the Cape Colony, the only information on Buddhism came from travel writings, often wildly fanciful ones like those by George Psalmanaazaar. By the nineteenth century, however, continuing Western explorations in Asia were producing far more reliable information on Buddhism, and literature produced at the Cape described Buddhism more or less accurately. But accurate description does not imply unbiased evaluation. Thus, a curious debate raged at the Cape that tried to place the historical Buddha in Africa rather than India. This debate seems to have started with the English orientalist William Jones, and was later echoed in the writings of Gutzlaff. Even when the theory was completely discredited elsewhere, a subliminal racism seems to have kept it alive in South Africa as late as the mid-twentieth century: "Delegates at a congress of the Suid-Afrikaanse Buro vir Rasse-Aangeleenthede in 1956 learned from the ethnologist J. P. Bruwer that 'The black Buddha of India originated in the physical image of the Negroid.'"[3]

If the Buddha himself was not an African, a new question was posed: perhaps there had been Buddhists in Africa? In 1911, James McKay noted artistic similarities between Chinese paintings and the rock paintings of the San (Bushmen) and suggested that the San must therefore be descended from a mixed Chinese/Egyptian people living in East Africa who would have been Buddhists![4] We can surmise that these attempts to conflate African and Asian otherness, many of which were promoted by missionaries, served primarily to accentuate the uniqueness and importance of the Christian message.

Despite this, positive evaluations of Buddhism started to appear in South Africa by the late nineteenth and early twentieth centuries, mostly from Unitarians and Theosophists. From the first countrywide census in 1911 onward, Buddhists start to appear in the official records of the Union of South Africa. These official statistics have long been regarded with suspicion, mostly due to the persistent appearance of a few thousand black Buddhists whom no one has actually been able to find. It seems that statistical manipulations of data have skewed the picture fatally. Today, informal estimates of the number of Buddhists in South Africa vary from six thousand to as many as thirty thousand.[5]

EARLY DEVELOPMENTS

The first South African Buddhists came from areas where Buddhism was an established religion. There had been a large Chinese community in the Cape from the eighteenth century on,[6] but it consisted mostly of transient sailors. Lasting settlement of Chinese in South Africa did not commence until the early twentieth century. Among these later settlers, conversion to Christianity was frequent and Buddhist practice slowly faded away. Until 1992, when the Nan Hua Temple near Bronkhorstspruit was established (Fo Kuang Shan school), there was no clearly defined Chinese Buddhist presence in South Africa.

Another interesting development was the conversion to Buddhism of low-caste Hindus in Kwazulu-Natal province in the 1920s and 1930s. Strictly speaking, this is not an "ethnic" Buddhism—these people's ancestors were not Buddhists—but one factor that caused them to adopt Buddhism as an alternative to Hinduism was that, unlike Christianity or Islam, Buddhism was at least of Indian origin. Calling their religion an "ethnic Buddhism" is therefore not too far off the mark.

This process started in 1917 with the establishment of the Overport Buddhist Sakya Society by Rajaram Dass. There may by then already have been Buddhists among Indian immigrants—the 1911 census report shows 394 Buddhists of Asian origin. However, immigration from India was halted by the South African authorities around the time of World War I, and the apparent escalation of the Asian Buddhist presence to 12,487 ten years later[7] was not due to a sudden influx from the east, but to South African low-caste Hindus attempting to escape from their social position by rejecting the religious context in which that position was embedded. This process ran parallel to the revival of Buddhism in India itself, but it is unclear if there were any links between the Indian revival that would later culminate in the Ambedkarian mass conversions and the South African equivalent. Theirs was not a transcendental faith: only 25 percent of those interviewed by Van Loon regarded *nirvāṇa* as the goal of religious practice, while most gave pride of place to the improvement of one's quality of life. Out of all Van Loon's respondents, not one "could conceive of karma operating without an inner 'self' through which alone it could become motivated and effective."[8] Only much prompting by the interviewer produced an answer closer to Buddhist orthodoxy.

From its apex in the 1920s and 1930s, the Indian Buddhist community steadily declined. Many reasons have been suggested for this: perhaps most significantly, the importance of caste itself declined steadily in South African Hindu society. The Indian Buddhist community in Kwazulu-Natal never achieved the kind of critical mass that might have enabled them to go on. Nor, given their low-caste origins, could they compensate for low numbers by having access to social and financial resources. When Van Loon studied this group in the late 1970s, only about forty families still called themselves Buddhist. By that time, however, a new form of Buddhism was emerging. It was found almost exclusively among the urbanized middle class, which meant that it was almost entirely restricted to white South Africans.

THE 1970S

Little is known about the position of white South African Buddhists prior to 1970. Most likely they were solitary practitioners, gaining some support from correspondence with institutions like the Buddhist Society in London. Others may have found their spiritual homes within Theosophical lodges. It is known, however, that literary figures such as Olive Schreiner and C. Louis Leipoldt were at least highly sympathetic to Buddhism. Later in the twentieth century, the poet, painter, and activist Breyten Breytenbach continued this tradition of artistic involvement in Buddhism by expressing his identity as a Zen Buddhist.

From about 1970 on, small Buddhist groups started to spring up in the main metropolitan centers of South Africa. Each was generally associated with one or two founder members. Although many of these groups were associated with the main streams of Western Buddhism, at this stage they tended to be open to practicing Buddhists and sympathizers of all persuasions.

The range of sectarian divisions on offer to South African Buddhists did not differ much from those available elsewhere in Western Buddhism: they included Theravāda, Tibetan Buddhism, Nichiren, and Zen. "Engaged Buddhism" has yet to make an impact here. Individual South African Buddhists may involve themselves in social and environmental projects, but one can hardly speak of a movement.

In the 1970s and early 1980s, the main focus was on a nondenominational Buddhism, best exemplified by the *vipassanā* teachings of Joseph Goldstein and Jack Kornfield. Although largely based on Theravāda teachings, this practice discarded most of the monastic ritual and became the basis for typical South African Buddhist groups of the early 1970s to the middle 1980s. In these groups, it was almost impossible to tell if one was attending a nominally Tibetan, Zen, or Theravāda meeting.

Even today, this is still the dominant form of Buddhism one can find at the Buddhist Retreat Centre (BRC) near Ixopo.[9] The BRC started operating in 1979 and was formally inaugurated in 1980. It has survived the political turmoil of the transition to democracy to become the closest thing South African Buddhism has to a central point. Buddhists who started out at the BRC but who have since moved into more doctrinally delineated groups affectionately refer to it as the "kindergarten." Nominally Theravāda in orientation, the BRC has expanded its vision considerably since its founding and also presents retreats in which meditative practice is combined with artistic expression, nature awareness, and work on interpersonal relationships.

Indeed, although Theravāda was one of the major forms of Buddhism available in South Africa during the formative stages, and the BRC was visited by many Theravādin monks, only in 1997 was orthodox Theravāda formally established on South African soil, with the founding of a center in Pietermaritzburg for the small Burmese community.[10] Although most of the monks are involved only with the religious requirements of Burmese immigrants, the Venerable Dhammarakkhita has made great progress in uniting the Buddhist communities in Kwazulu-Natal province.

Other Theravāda-based groups, including many local groups affiliated to the BRC, in fact support the Westernized *vipassanā* approach. This nonsectarian Theravāda-type practice remains a mainstay of South African Buddhism.

THE 1980S

In the late 1980s, South African Buddhist organizations entered a new phase. From a close linkage to liberal Western culture, the emphasis changed to a positioning back toward the Asian homeland, or a recoupment. Links with overseas organizations were established or strengthened. The ritual and monastic, or at least quasi-monastic, elements of Buddhist practice were reintroduced. The Dharma Centre in Somerset West, for example, had hosted teachers and adherents from various traditions since its inception in 1982. Although Heila Downey, one of the founders, was a student of Philip Kapleau Rōshi, the center had never become a formal subsidiary of the Zen Center in Rochester, New York. Around 1987, the group did slowly start to incorporate more specifically Zen-inspired ritual, based on that followed in Rochester, but this was kept to a minimum.

In 1989, however, the Dharma Centre became an integral part of the Kwan Um school, an international Korean Zen organization headed by Zen master Seung Sahn. Within a year or two, robes had become an accepted part of practice, prostrations and chanting increased in number and duration, and a semi-monastic discipline was more clearly implemented. Chants that were formerly performed in English were now done in Korean.

There are other Zen groups in South Africa, notably in Johannesburg, but the Dharma Centre, now headquartered in the town of Robertson, is clearly the leading Zen-based organization. The institutional support it receives from the Kwan Um organization means that it is able to import teachers with relative ease. However, it should be noted that in a suburban satellite center in Cape Town, the Dharma Centre has been forced by popular demand to reinstitute a weekly meditation session shorn of all ritual, much as things were before 1989.

A similar process has occurred among South Africa's Vajrayāna Buddhists. Both the Kagyupa and Gelugpa schools are represented. Of these, the Kagyupa have had the longest presence, dating back to the founding of a Tibetan Friendship Group in 1969. Kagyu groups were established in most of the main cities over the next ten years, but at this early stage they maintained close links with the Theravāda- and Zen-oriented organizations, and both membership and hosting of teachers were widely shared. As in those other groups, meditation rather than ritual was stressed. By

1982, the organization was strong enough to set up a meditation center in the hamlet of Nieu Bethesda. At this stage, it also hosted teachers from other traditions, but by the mid-1980s precedence was slowly being given to Tibetan, and particularly Kagyupa, teachings. When Rob Nairn, one of the founding figures of Vajrayāna Buddhism in South Africa, left in 1988 to do a four-year retreat in Scotland, the center slowly fell into disuse. When he returned, the Nieu Bethesda center was sold and the Kagyu Buddhists started to concentrate on strengthening their urban structures. The Kagyu establishment is mainly under the direction of Akong Rinpoche, is directly linked to the Samyê Ling Temple in Scotland, and is regularly visited by Tibetan monks from that source. In 1992, the Kagyu establishment was joined by a Johannesburg Gelugpa center under the direction of Geshe Damcho, who visits it regularly.

The Fo Kuang Shan school occupies a strange position in South African Buddhism. In its traditional Chinese practice of Buddhism, it paradoxically presents to Africa the most radical presentation of Buddhism yet. The Nan Hua temple complex near Bronkhorstspruit serves two main purposes: it ministers to the needs of the Chinese Buddhist community in South Africa and it has established the African Buddhist Seminary, where young African men can train to be Buddhist monks in the Fo Kuang Shan order. While the seminary is open to South Africans, it actively recruits novices in Tanzania, Congo, and elsewhere. It is unique in South African Buddhism in that it was actively brought here in a missionary spirit. All other forms of Buddhism in the country were fetched from elsewhere. Small satellite centers have been established across the country.

At the Nan Hua Temple, practice is uncompromisingly Chinese. Novices are required to learn the Chinese language, participate in Chinese rituals, practice Chinese martial arts, and so on. Although the founder of the local temple, the Venerable Hui Li, has acknowledged that a compromise with African traditions will eventually be required, he believes that this will best be done by Africans, and that the Chinese monks and nuns here would do best to teach what they know.[11] The reasoning may be sound, but in my work with these students over the last three years it has become clear that learning a new religion and a new culture at the same time may just be too much of a stumbling block. Nevertheless, the Fo Kuang Shan school is to be commended for at least one thing: the vast majority of the students are black. This is the first real attempt to transplant Buddhism in South Africa beyond the boundaries of the white community, even if most of the students come from Tanzania, the Congo, and other countries beyond the borders of South Africa.

This is not to say that there are no black South African Buddhists at all, but their numbers are extremely small. The Kagyu Buddhists, in particular, have occasionally associated with African traditional healers, and they report a number of black members in their Zimbabwean branch. In South Africa, however, the only group to have attracted significant numbers of black members has been Sōka Gakkai International (SGI).

In keeping with the international situation, the SGI has few ties with the rest of the South African Buddhist community, and little is known about them beyond the information on their web site [12] and what can be gleaned from Darrell Wratten's doctoral research. According to Wratten, the establishment of the SGI in South Africa can be traced to 1983. By 1994, there were about a hundred members divided among nine groups.[13]

The 1980s, then, saw considerable growth for South African Buddhism, both in absolute numbers and in the diversity of groups. However, it was also the period when the apartheid regime was in its final, most paranoid stages, and infiltration of Buddhist groups by security force members was not unknown:

> [A]n exciting new religious dimension came into being with the birth of the new, democratic South Africa. Gone are the days when the fledgling Buddhist movement was being suspected of being a subversive communist cell on the assumption that because Chinese restaurants tended to display fat "Laughing Buddhas," and because the Chinese were communists, therefore people who called themselves Buddhists were communists in disguise. This may now sound comical but the early meditation retreats held at the Buddhist Retreat Centre (it insisted on being multiracial from its inception) were in fact regularly infiltrated by undercover government agents—who, incidentally, stood out like sore thumbs—in an effort to uncover communist spooks. . . . Those were the days too when South Africa witnessed the spectacle of a Buddhist nun belonging to a Japanese Pure Land sect undertaking a long protest march and hunger strike lasting 40 days outside St George's Cathedral in Cape Town, calling for the release of children held in political detention. Or when a Buddhist couple, Lama Anâgārika and Li Gotami Govinda, both world-renowned authors and artists, ran the risk of imprisonment when they visited the country in 1974 because of the Immorality Act, he being German and she a Parsi by birth. Or when a young Buddhist, on the grounds of conscience and religious conviction, objected to serving in the South African army. Initially denied exemption because Buddhism, being non-theistic, could not be considered a "godsdiens" or a "true religion" as then legally defined, he had his case heard in the Supreme Court in Bloemfontein where a review of the case acknowledged that although Buddhists do not necessarily believe in a personal or creator

God, it was undeniable that their faith was as much a religion as Christianity, Judaism, Islam or Hinduism. We have come a long way since then. . . .[14]

THE 1990S

The 1990s saw the arrival of permanent teachers. The BRC obtained the services of two Theravādin ex-monastics, Kittisāro and Thanissara, who committed themselves to spending at least half the year in Ixopo. At the Dharma Centre, Heila Downey was given the title *Poep sa Nim* and was thereby allowed to teach as an instructor of the Kwan Um school. Among the Tibetan Buddhists, there are officially no homegrown teachers yet, but Rob Nairn has occupied the role of homegrown teacher de facto since his return from Scotland, and Tibetan monks now visit South Africa more regularly and for longer periods than in the past. Added to this has been the arrival of Chinese monks at the Bronkhorstspruit temple and of Burmese *bhikkhus* at the monastery in Pietermaritzburg. Although we cannot say that Buddhism in South Africa has become an established religion, the above items are important first steps in that direction.

Informal observation suggests that, as elsewhere in Western Buddhism, the South African form is characterized not only by a small number of committed Buddhists, but also by a much larger group of sympathizers, or what Tweed calls *night-stand Buddhists.*[15]

Another important development in white South African Buddhism that has taken place in the last ten years or so is the increasing isolation of the Vajrayāna Buddhist establishment. While the Zen and Theravāda organizations in South Africa have worked out modi vivendi that allow each to maintain its organizational integrity while they share teachers and venues, the Kagyupa and, to a lesser extent, the Gelugpa traditions have increasingly abandoned the free and easy association of South African Buddhism as it once was. This may well be a harbinger of future developments. A gap is opening up within South African Buddhism, an "us" and "them" division that threatens in the long run to create two separate camps whose members are largely unaware of each other (as both are already largely unaware of the presence of the SGI).

AN ASSESSMENT OF SOUTH AFRICAN BUDDHISM

Martin Baumann has suggested that there are six main themes in the creation of a Western Buddhism.[16] With Indian Buddhism in South Africa moribund and the traditional Chinese form at Bronkhorstspruit an experiment in a very early stage, it remains for us to see to what extent the white South African Buddhism falls into this general pattern:

1. *An emphasis on lay practice and participation.* Given that there are true monastics only in the Pietermaritzburg monastery and the Bronkhorstspruit temple, lay participation is clearly a key factor in South African Buddhism. Many leading figures do lead a semi-monastic lifestyle, but remain lay members who hold down full-time jobs. The South African Buddhist scene in 1999 has two main loci: the meditation or retreat center, often a permanent establishment in the countryside but sometimes an urban school or church property rented for the weekend; and the small group of lay meditators meeting in a prominent member's house for an evening meditation session.

2. *A critical evaluation of women's roles.* There have been retreats where the issue of women's roles has been hotly debated, but more generally one cannot say that this is a matter of primary concern to South African Buddhists. However, among the permanent teachers who emerged in the 1990s (as mentioned above), two are women, and there have been visiting female teachers, such as Ayya Khema, in the past. It could be argued that Buddhist women, most of whom are white and middle-class, are in fact less oppressed by patriarchal structures than their sisters elsewhere in the country. But this does not negate the fact that a lot of introspection still needs to be done on this issue within South African Buddhist circles.

3. *The application of democratic and egalitarian principles.* Although this aspect is less visible in South African Buddhism than in other places, it can be observed in the Western-style committees that run most of the groups. In some cases, of course, this may disguise the real power relations within the group, where actual authority is exercised by a few founding members who may or may not serve on the committees. But the opportunity for ordinary members to make their voices heard does exist.

4. *A close linkage to Western psychological concepts.* This is evident, but the observation needs qualification. The Western psychological concepts to which South African Buddhists relate well are by no means those of mainstream psychiatry, but unorthodox trends such as transpersonal psychology. The author Ken Wilber seems to be a particular favorite.

5. *The conceptualization of a socially engaged Buddhism.* As we have seen, South African Buddhism lags behind Western (especially North American) Buddhism in this regard.

6. *The creation of an ecumenical, nonsectarian tradition.* This was one of the earliest accomplishments of South African Buddhism back in the

1970s. While it persists in many groups, it has since been overtaken in many cases by a movement toward a more traditional style of Buddhist practice.

It should be clear that South African (white) Buddhism is a form of the emergent Western Buddhism as defined by Baumann in terms both of its origins and of its subsequent development. Local conditions have retarded the development of some of the factors Baumann mentions and speeded up others, but the overall picture does not differ much from his general view.

South African Buddhism is precariously balanced between the need to adapt Buddhist teachings to local needs (currently the needs of the mainly white, middle-class people who practice Buddhism) and the desire to stick as closely as possible to various original Asian models.

Buddhism in South Africa is imperfectly contextualized: it concentrates on the needs and conceptual problems of the current South African Buddhist population, which is by and large white and middle-class. Apart from the Indian, Burmese, and Chinese "ethnic Buddhist" populations, what we find in this country is an overwhelmingly Western Buddhism. This immediately raises the question: can there ever be a specifically Southern (that is, African) Buddhism? The most important aspect of this question is whether or not Buddhism can come to grips with its existence in an African context and with indigenous African religion. In particular, the local concept of *ubuntu*, of a communally expressed humaneness, is a promising avenue for encounter between African religion and Buddhism. *Ubuntu* is an issue that I have tentatively raised elsewhere,[17] and which one can expect to be the most pressing issue in the future development of South African Buddhism.

NOTES

1. This essay is a much abbreviated extract from my doctoral dissertation.

2. Darrell Wratten, "Buddhism in South Africa: From Textual Imagination to Contextual Innovation" (Ph.D. diss., University of Cape Town, Cape Town, South Africa, 1995), 32–35.

3. Darrell Wratten, "The Buddha of Suburbia: A Nineteenth-Century South African Imagining," in *Buddhism and Africa*, edited by Michel Clasquin and J. S. Krüger (Pretoria: University of South Africa Press, 1999), 21. Suid-Afrikaanse Buro vir Rasse-Aangeleenthede (SABRA, or South African Bureau for Racial Affairs) was a government-aligned think tank during the apartheid era.

4. Wratten, "The Buddha of Suburbia," 22.

5. Louis H. Van Loon, "Buddhism in South Africa: Its Past History, Present Status and Likely Future," in Clasquin and Krüger, *Buddhism and Africa*, 40; the lower estimate is my own.

6. Wratten, "Buddhism in South Africa," 179.

7. This figure from the 1921 census is highly suspect. The 1936 census found only 1,771 Asian Buddhists. See Louis H. Van Loon, "The Indian Buddhist Community in South Africa: Its Historical Origins and Socio-Religious Attitudes and Practices," unpublished research paper, 1979, 18. A shortened version was published in *Religion in Southern Africa* 1, no. 1 (July 1980), 3–18.

8. Van Loon, "The Indian Buddhist Community," unpublished version, 46.

9. See http://www.websol.co.za/brc/brc.html or http://users.lia.net/vanloon/ [5 Sept. 2001].

10. See http://users.iafrica.com/m/mb/mbasa/home.htm [5 Sept. 2001].

11. Venerable Master Hui Li, "Fo Kuang Shan in Africa: Heritage and Future Plans," in Clasquin and Krüger, *Buddhism and Africa*, 59.

12. See http://www.pvas.co.za/sgi/sa.html [5 Sept. 2001] or http://members. aol.com/abayaa/africa/letter.htm [5 Sept. 2001].

13. Wratten, "Buddhism in South Africa," 231–35.

14. Van Loon, "Buddhism in South Africa," 41.

15. Thomas A. Tweed, "Night-Stand Buddhists and Other Creatures: Sympathizers, Adherents, and the Study of Religion," in *America Buddhism: Methods and Findings in Recent Scholarship*, edited by Duncan Ryūken Williams and Christopher S. Queen (Richmond, U.K.: Curzon Press, 1999).

16. Martin Baumann, "Does Buddhism in Modernity Take a Post-Modern Shape? Considerations Pertaining to the Historical Development of Buddhist Traditions Outside of Asia" (paper read at the Harvard Buddhist Studies Forum, 16 Nov. 1998), 4.

17. Michel Clasquin, "Ubuntu Dharma—Buddhism and African Thought," in Clasquin and Krüger, *Buddhism and Africa*.

10 Buddhism in Brazil and Its Impact on the Larger Brazilian Society

Frank Usarski

INTRODUCTION

On 18 February 2001, the *Folha da São Paulo*, one of Brazil's most widely read newspapers, reported that 1,000,000 Brazilians were Buddhists.[1] In March 1999, the weekly magazine *Isto é* had referred to the same number.[2] In June 1988, however, the magazine *Elle* claimed that only about 500,000 Brazilians could be considered Buddhists.[3] Moreover, compared with the latest reliable data reported by the Brazilian Institute of Geography and Statistics (IBGE), even the lower figure appears unlikely, since in 1991 only 236,408 Buddhists were officially counted.[4] It does not seem plausible that in only ten years the number of Brazilian Buddhists could have almost doubled, much less quadrupled.

It is true that in the last ten years, as has happened in other Western countries, Buddhism in Brazil has evolved into a trendy religion. There is a growing amount of corresponding literature[5] and Buddhism is supported by a number of public figures.[6] It is established in the alternative-health sector[7] and even in the business community,[8] and is promoted by Asian monks on trips to Brazil, including the Dalai Lama, who visited the country for the second time in 1999. However, as far as declared membership is concerned, there are no significant indicators of a dramatic increase. Rather, as for traditional Japanese Buddhist groups who represent the numerically most relevant sector of Brazilian Buddhism, a stagnation or even decline is apparent. Furthermore, in spite of vivid interest from the press, all Tibetan Buddhist groups together have not attracted more than three thousand Brazilian members, or at least committed practitioners.[9] The growth of the national branch of Sōka Gakkai is considerable but not dramatic. Therefore one can confidently state that in 2001 there are in fact less than three hundred thousand Buddhists in the country, not one million. At the same time, Brazil is known for its religious syncretism, and one can presume that in many cases an affiliation with Buddhism is not exclusive, but only one among other expressions of a multireligious attitude.[10]

Perhaps a more recent count, focusing on organized Buddhist groups, can provide a more realistic assessment of the current situation.[11] This list contains about 160 institutions, different in orientation, size, and level of organization, ranging from small circles (such as the Casa de Dharma in São Paulo, one of only three Theravāda groups in Brazil) to highly frequented Amida temples (such as the Higashi Honganji, also in São Paulo, with dozens of affiliated centers all over the country, especially in those states in which the Japanese influence is strong).

THREE-FOLD TYPOLOGY OF CONTEMPORARY BRAZILIAN BUDDHISM

As in other Western countries, Buddhism in Brazil does not present itself as a homogeneous field, but rather in the form of three different currents. The branch of Buddhism with the longest history in Brazil is rooted in Asian, especially Japanese, ethnic contexts. As an individual or family practice, it can be traced back to 1810, when Chinese workers entered Brazil on short-term labor contracts.[12] While the first current came from outside the country, the second had its starting point in Brazil. It is characterized by the academic intellectuality of its representatives, whose passion for Buddhism is an expression of a universalistic philosophical interest. The third branch took shape in the 1970s, when Zen monks and Tibetan *lamas* arrived in Latin American countries, later than in the United States and Europe.

Ethnically Rooted Buddhism

As a result of Asian immigration, about 1.26 million Brazilian inhabitants are of Japanese origin,[13] about 200,000 are of Chinese origin,[14] and about 80,000 are of Korean origin.[15] By no means are all of these individuals Buddhists. For example, the 1991 national census revealed that of a total of 236,408 Buddhists, only 89,971 were of Asian origin. Within this category, Japanese Buddhists were dominant.

In addition, Japanese Buddhism merits particular attention, because it is institutionally and historically far more accentuated in Brazil than Chinese and Korean Buddhism. While most Chinese temples and the only Korean Buddhist institution appeared beginning in the 1980s, several Japanese Buddhist temples were founded in the 1950s.[16] The wave of Japanese temple foundation was stimulated by a fundamental change of mentality, stemming from Japan's defeat in World War II. Initially intending to stay only as long as necessary to acquire wealth, the immigrants suffered a profound identity crisis, which in turn led to the decision to settle permanently in Brazil. By 1952, the Otani school of Jōdo Shinshū had constructed its first temple. In 1958, the Federaçao das Seitas Budistas no Brasil established itself as an umbrella organization of previously established branches.[17] Today, the Japanese Buddhist field contains temples and centers of almost every type, including various so-called neo-Buddhist groups.[18] However, the traditional Honpa branch of Jōdo Shinshū is considered numerically predominant.

The first, and for about thirty years the only, official Chinese Buddhist institution in Brazil, the Mo Ti Temple in São Paulo, was inaugurated in 1962. Promoted by the Buddhist lay organization Associação de Budismo da China, the construction was actively supported by Chi Ming, a Buddhist master, who had already come to Brazil at the beginning of the 1960s. Later he assumed the leadership of the temple, and remained in this position until his death in 1992. Today, Chi Ming's Chinese disciples are responsible for the Mi To.[19]

The inauguration of the second Chinese temple was held in 1992 in the São Paulo neighborhood of Santo Amaro. It belongs to the Fo Kuang Shan order and its international lay organization, Buddha's Light (BLIA). Later BLIA also opened a small facility in the very center of the city. Today, Fo Kuang Shan and BLIA also run institutions in Cotia, Rio de Janeiro, Recife, Foz do Iguaçu, and Londrina.[20] In 1993, the Tzong Kuang was initiated in São Paulo. It is under the spiritual guidance of the Taiwanese Master Pu Chien, who visits the temple only occasionally, but stays for a number of weeks when he does. Since then, Kuan Yin Temple in the peripheral neighborhood of Santo Amaro also opened a smaller center in the more accessible neighborhood of Liberdade. As for traditional Korean Buddhism, there is only the Jin Kak Temple in the city of São Paulo, inaugurated in 1988 and belonging to the line of Chogye Buddhism.[21]

The Social Impact of Ethnically Rooted Buddhism in Brazil. Due to its high degree of cultural specificity in doctrine, practice, and institutional representation, Japanese Buddhism is not very successful in attracting adherents from outside the Japanese context. This is due especially to the fusion of Buddhism with ancestor worship and the emphasis on devotion and recitation in the tradition of Amida Buddhism as an integral part of family life, characteristics that do not fit the interests of a Western audience generally seeking an idealized "pure" Buddhism based on an individual meditation practice.[22] That explains the strikingly high percentage of people of Japanese origin within the current membership of even the bigger temples. The Nambei Honganji in São Paulo, for example, has at the moment eight thousand families of Japanese origin and only two hundred non-Japanese families.

Nothing indicates that there will be a change in the near future. Instead, the focus is still on the long-standing adherents, who see *their* temple not only as a place of collective worship, but also as a locus for social activities. Therefore, the temple has the character of a cultural center, with a varied program that ranges from karaoke for the younger generation to folkdance groups for the elders.

Attempts to become more open to the larger Brazilian society are still rare and selective. But they do exist. One example is an experiment undertaken in the Honpa Hongwanji Temple in Brasília in which, apart from the traditional Jōdo Shinshū services, a meditation was offered to a non-Japanese public. Meditation, although normally foreign to Pure Land Buddhism, was authorized by the Japanese headquarters as a suitable mission strategy. Even in this case, the number of practitioners remained relatively small. While about 130 immigrant families were associated with the temple, only sixty non-Japanese Brazilians were initiated, and of those only twenty regularly attended meetings.[23]

Generally speaking, compared to traditional Amida Buddhist institutions, Japanese Buddhist groups that offer some kind of meditation are at least slightly better at attracting a larger audience. This is also true for Chinese Buddhist institutions. For example, at the Tzong Kuan Temple in São Paulo, with its combination of Pure Land and Zen, about twenty non-Chinese individuals gather weekly for meditation. In contrast, Chinese come with their families and are more committed to recitations and traditional ceremonies.

Furthermore, it seems that whenever ethnically rooted Buddhist institutions in Brazil open their doors to a larger public, a division arises, with a tradition-fixed majority on the one side and newcomers on the other, each with particular religious expectations, interests, and styles, and even with separate temple schedules. Whether this situation turns overtly tense or not is often a political question, depending on the original community's approval of the monk or nun who supports the innovation. In this context, Rocha recently gave an interesting example referring to developments at the Busshinji Temple of São Paulo. There, Moriyama Rōshi, officially sent to Brazil by his school, attempted to appeal to younger Brazilians outside the ethnic milieu. The new participants provoked uneasy feelings among the elders of the traditional community, until the Sōtō Zenshū headquarters interfered by substituting the nun Cláudia Coên for Moriyama. A native Brazilian, but trained in Japan, Coên managed to overcome the situation by convincing the majority of the authenticity of her approach.[24]

There is also a generational problem within ethnically rooted groups, and these difficulties also contribute to their marginal social position. That became evident at the end of the 1950s, the decade in which the largest number of Japanese Buddhist institutions was founded in Brazil. Between 1908 and 1941, not more than 1.5 percent of all Japanese immigrants were Christians.[25] All the others were considered Buddhists. However, according to a study conducted by the University of Tokyo, the situation had changed dramatically by 1958. According to this study, only 44.5 percent of Japanese living in Brazil still felt committed to their traditional religion. This change was more intense in urban surroundings, where 50.3 percent already had converted to Catholicism. The corresponding percentage in rural areas was 36.5 percent. Even more crucial were the differences between the generations. Of immigrants born in Japan, 70.6 percent still declared themselves in 1958 to be Buddhists. The percentage had dropped to 29.9 percent among the next generation, born in Brazil, and to only 19 percent in the third generation.[26]

For traditional Japanese Buddhist groups, the growing incidence of deconversion is alarming, not only because of the loss of Japanese cultural heritage, but also because of the exit of members who, due to their education, linguistic competence, and social status, are best prepared to play the role of cultural mediator. How seriously this problem is taken within Jōdo Shinshū circles is indicated by the following statement:

> The starting point of an efficient missionary work on Brazilian territory should be . . . a clear-sighted translation of the basic religious texts of this school into Portuguese. It is essential to undertake this task with a certain urgency, because Japanese immigration ended some time ago, the old immigrants who understood Japanese are dead, and most of their descendants are not familiar with the language of their ancestors. . . . If, in this respect, nothing is done quickly, the mission could be forced to put an end to its activities at the moment the last Japanese immigrant to Brazil leaves this world.[27]

The relatively few Japanese descendants trained as Buddhist monks are not capable of counteracting this overall trend in a satisfactory manner. On the other hand, it is they who have played a role in introducing internal reforms. There is, for example, Eduardo Ryoho Sasaki, a geologist trained at the University of São Paulo and now a monk at the Jōdo Shinshū Nippakuji

Temple in Maringá.[28] He is the son of Yomei Sasaki, superior of the Bet-suin Nippakuji in São Paulo and superintendent of the Latin American community of Jōdo Shinshū Buddhism. Another example is Reverend Pedro Inaba, who broke with the religion of his family, which turned to Catholicism while still in Japan, and who is now a missionary monk at the Nippakuji Temple in São Paulo.[29] There is also Eko Ishimoto, a third-generation Japanese descendant, a systems analyst, and reverend of the Comunidade Budista Nitirenshu. He emphasizes, "There are many, both within and outside the Japanese community who think: Buddhism is only for older people, monks fulfill their function only in terms of funeral rites. Generally, monks from Japan come with the pretension to teach Buddhism here as a philosophy or as a Japanese ideology. But I do not think that this works. This is a land of Samba, of beaches, of Carnival. This is not Japan. The philosophy might come from there, but we have to adapt it to the local conditions."[30]

Universalistic Philosophical Buddhism

The second current of Brazilian Buddhism is difficult to identify by its outward expressions. What unites its membership is a cognitive style in dealing with Buddhism, which can be characterized, to use a rather ornate formulation, as a "freethinking intellectualism," with a touch of romanticism.[31] In this sense it should be remembered that as early as the nineteenth century a romanticizing interest in the Orient was at work among Brazilian intellectuals and novelists. These individuals had never traveled to Asia. But, based on secondhand information about a continent full of mystery, peaceful people, and wisdom, authors like Fagundes Varela (1841–75), Machado de Assis (1839–1908), and Raimundo Correia (1859–1911) expressed their vague imaginings in colorful words.[32] As Asian people arrived in Brazil, these stereotypes gave way to more concrete images. Nonetheless, an idealized conception of the East persisted even in the midst of growing resentment against Asian immigrants.[33] It served as a platform on which a positive approach to Japan's spiritual heritage could be built by a Brazilian intellectual minority. These ideological conditions have to be kept in mind when one reflects upon the second current of Brazilian Buddhism.

The most outstanding representatives of this line are certainly Murillo Nunes de Azevedo and Ricardo Mário Gonçalves. Both turned seriously to Buddhism in the early postwar years. Each lived an academic life. Azevedo was trained as an engineer and ended up working for the federal transportation ministry. Gonçalves is a historian and was a professor at the University of São Paulo.

In an autobiographical outline, Murillo Nunes de Azevedo admits that, due to his academic background, he felt completely alienated from any religious sentiment. However, from 1950 on, he came more and more under the influence of the Theosophist Lourenço Borges. In 1923, Borges and other members of the Theosophical Lodge in Rio de Janeiro had founded the first Buddhist association in Brazil, the Sociedade Budista do Brasil. This society closed after a few months, but was revived in 1955. Azevedo's approach was obviously close to that of his friend's holistic perspective, since his reading was oriented by the "universal idea of a great unity which includes everything." [34] Azevedo has remained loyal to this principle, both as a Buddhist and as a member of the Theosophical Society. Similar to Azevedo, but more from the standpoint of a Freemason,[35] Gonçalves stands for a universalist philosophical approach to Buddhism, which he associates with the category of *Sophia Perennis*.[36]

For Azevedo and Gonçalves, the common starting point of their careers as Buddhists was the visit of Rosen Takashina, patriarch of Sōtō Zen, who lived in São Paulo and Rio de Janeiro in 1964, attracting with his talks and retreats a circle of Brazilian intellectuals. For Azevedo, the practice of Zen finally led to his ordination as a Sōtō missionary for Brazil. However, in 1967, due to increasing doubts about whether the Brazilian mentality was compatible with the Samurai spirit of Zen, and inspired by a visit by the Japanese nun Yamamoto to São Paulo, Gonçalves and Azevedo started to become more and more interested in Shingon Buddhism. In 1971, Gonçalves and Azevedo were invited to visit the Kōyasan Temple in Japan. However, Azevedo's impression that the Brazilian mind, predisposed to religious syncretism, is averse to this kind of esoteric Buddhism, was reinforced while teaching this doctrine. At the same time, Gonçalves was invited to give lectures several times by officials of the Higashi Honganji temple in São Paulo. All these factors influenced Azevedo's and Gonçalves's final turn toward Amida Buddhism. In 1981, in Kyoto, Gonçalves was ordained as a monk in the Otani branch of Jōdo Shinshū. Continuing to the present, he plays an important role within the leadership of the Higashi Honganji Temple in São Paulo. In 1982, also in Japan, Azevedo was ordained according to the rules of the Nishi school of Jōdo Shinshū. Due to his work for the federal transportation ministry beginning in 1977, he became active in the Amida Buddhist community in Brasília.

Universalistic philosophical Buddhism associated itself first with Zen and Shingon before being linked to traditional Japanese Buddhist entities. Hence, the social impact of this second line of Brazilian Buddhism is not restricted to its direct effects on the larger society. Rather, due to their activities within certain ethnically dominated temples, Gonçalves and Azevedo have also contributed to changes from within these groups, which in turn led to a greater institutional flexibility in dealing with the general public.

As for the overall social impact, both Gonçalves and Azevedo have contributed as translators, compilers, and authors of books and articles, compensating for the considerable lack of Buddhist literature in Portuguese for a more intellectual audience. Due to their knowledge of the Japanese language, both Gonçalves and Azevedo were also invited by Jōdo Shinshū officials to contribute to the translation of Pure Land literature and missionary material into Portuguese.

Murillo Nunes de Azevedo played an outstanding role in the Honpa Hongwanji in Brasília, especially between 1982 and 1989. He opened the temple to the general public. With time a more committed, but smaller, group of non-Japanese adherents emerged. One of his Brazilian disciples was Marçelo Guiaqueto de Mello, born in 1962 and raised as a Catholic. He began to frequent the community in 1992. He remembered, "Whenever I passed the temple, I wanted to enter, but I said to myself: 'Do not enter, this is a Japanese thing.' However, after I had decided to enter, I was surprised with what I saw: a Brazilian monk, speaking in Portuguese to a Brazilian audience. This gave me a sense of relief and touched me."[37] For Mello, the temple became a spiritual home. After Azevedo returned to Rio de Janeiro, the progressive minister Kyoha Imae followed in his footsteps in Brasília. However, after Imae's transfer to São Paulo the atmosphere changed, due to the entrance of a more conservative minister, Nakabayashi, who came directly from Japan without speaking a word of Portuguese. In the end, Mello left the temple, which demonstrated in retrospect how significant Azevedo's work had been for the unity of the community.

In other cases, however, the ambitions of non-Japanese Brazilians to follow the example of Azevedo and engage themselves in traditional Buddhist communities did not end in disappointment. This is true for at least three students of the Department of Philosophy at the Pontifical Catholic University of Rio de Janeiro. There, Azevedo lectured on Oriental thought for three years in the second half of the 1960s. Much later these courses gave fruit, as Roberto Stein, Airton de Mendonço, and Gustavo Pinto became ministers in the tradition of Jōdo Shinshū. According to Azevedo, Roberto Stein "is doing a great job in spreading Pure Land Buddhism within large national and international companies," while Airton de Mendonço became a minister "in order to create a Buddhism adjusted to Brazil and Japanese descendants."[38] Gustavo Pinto is today responsible for the Honpa Hongwanji

Temple in São Paulo. Azevedo credits Pinto with the construction of the Manshinji Temple in Rio de Janeiro, which has an all-glass exterior as a symbol of its spiritual openness. The main hall does not contain Japanese floor cushions, but simply chairs. This is for practical reasons and suggests the targeted audience, because, according to Pinto, sitting on the ground with their legs crossed "is very painful for Brazilians."[39]

"Globalized" Buddhist Groups in Brazil

The third current has been in evidence since the 1970s and is not restricted to an ethnic context. Its greater racial diversity is accompanied by a greater geographical dispersion. Compared to the first and second currents, the third also differs in terms of its greater doctrinal heterogeneity. Tibetan Buddhist groups are particularly prominent. Furthermore, the third current of Brazilian Buddhism is international in character.[40] In many cases, Brazilian groups are integrated into a global network of institutions not only in terms of common organizational standards, strategies, schedules, and materials, but also in terms of religious substance, adjusted to the intellectual and practical needs of a Western audience.

It would be useful to distinguish between three subcategories that comprise the third current. First, there are a number of Zen institutions that are not inserted within an ethnic context.[41] Second, there is a strong Brazilian branch of the international neo-Buddhist lay organization Sōka Gakkai.[42] Third, there are numerous Tibetan Buddhist groups.

For Zen Buddhism, Ryotan Tokuda especially comes to mind. Tokuda is arguably one of the most important initiators of a Brazilian Zen movement outside an ethnic context. Sent by his headquarters to Brazil in 1968, the Japanese master began working at the Busshinji Temple in São Paulo. In the first half of the 1970s, he broke with the institutional restrictions of that traditional entity, and oriented his teachings toward the general Brazilian public. As Tokuda's work in Brazil gained its own dynamic in the 1980s, the monk began to develop Zen activities in Europe.

Moriyama Rōshi also started his spiritual work in Brazil at the Busshinji Temple. One source of his problems with the hierarchy of this community was the fact that he did not go to Brazil directly from Japan. Rather, he came from San Francisco, where he had been engaged in spreading Zen since the 1960s. Today, Moriyama, who visits Brazil only sporadically, has disciples all over the world, not only in the United States, Canada, and Europe, but also in Argentina and Uruguay.

Recently a circle of Rinzai Zen practitioners constituted itself in association with the Vietnamese master Thich Nhat Hanh. In mid-2000, Thich

Nhat Hanh, whose international Order of Interbeing is based in southern France, stayed in Brazil for several weeks to orient retreats.

When Sōka Gakkai was formally established in 1960, the association had fewer than 150 members, all of them of Japanese origin. In recent decades, the Associação Brazil Sōka Gakkai International has evolved into a Buddhist group with centers in almost every region of Brazil. According to official information from the Sōka Gakkai International headquarters, there are currently 140,000 Brazilian adherents. Pereira estimates that 90 percent of these individuals are of non-Japanese origin.[43] However, Sōka Gakkai is highly standardized, in terms of both doctrine and organizational structure. In this sense, it is clearly an expression of a "globalized" movement, which fits the overall character of the third current of Buddhism in Brazil.

The movement led by Tarthang Tulku started the first Tibetan Buddhist center in Brazil. Preparatory activities by representatives of the headquarters in Berkeley, California, were undertaken in the second half of the 1980s. But the inauguration of the Tarthang Tulku Nyingma Center in São Paulo only took place in 1988. Shortly thereafter, the Centro de Dharma Shi De Choe Tsog, guided by the Gelugpa *lama* Gangchen, was also established in São Paulo. Today, Lama Gangchen leads an international movement. There are local groups in various parts of the world, including Argentina and Chile. In Brazil, this is certainly the group that attracts the most attention from the media. This is due to Michel Lenz Cesar Calmanowitz, alias Lama Michel, now living in the Tibetan Buddhist monastic community of Sera Me, in southern India, and considered a reincarnation of a high Tibetan master.[44]

Three more institutions were inaugurated in 1993, when the Thubten Dargye Ling, the Centro Budista Mahabodhi, and the Ödsal Ling were founded in São Paulo. The first is committed to Geshe Lobsang Tenpa, while the second belongs to the internationally known New Kadampa Tradition. The third was inspired by the Nyingma master Chagdud Tulku, who in 1996 moved from his headquarters at Rigdzin Ling, in northern California, to Três Coroas, in the Brazilian state of Rio Grande do Sul. He had already founded the Chagdud Gonpa Brazil by 1995. The Chagdud Gonpa Brazil functions today as Chagdud Tulku's national umbrella organization, which currently also has centers in Belo Horizonte, Florianopolis, Rio de Janeiro, Salvador, and Goiânia. In addition, during the 1990s a Sakya group in Rio de Janeiro, founded by Sakya Trizin, and two Kagyu groups, both associated with Kalu Rinpoche, emerged. One of the Kagyu groups is located in Brasília. Its history can be traced back to the 1980s and confirms that the third branch of Brazilian Buddhism is in many cases internationally predisposed. In those years, Kalu Rinpoche used to travel to Europe. A number of Brazilians studying in France attended a retreat guided by the Tibetan master. One of these participants had been initiated into Buddhism in Paris. When he returned to Brazil in 1987, he founded the Kagyu center in Brasília, which was officially inaugurated in 1991.

One of the most interesting inaugurations of recent years was that of the Gelugpa Centro Je Tsongkhapa in Porto Alegre in April 2000. Despite its insignificant membership, the institution merits attention because of its founder, Lama Segyu Rinpoche. A native Brazilian, he was a Umbanda medium in Rio de Janeiro until he was officially recognized as a reincarnated *lama* healer. Today, Lama Segyu is not only the abbot of the Tibetan monastery Sed Gyued Datsang, in Nepal, but also the director of the Healing Buddha Foundation, Segyu Gaden Dhargye Ling, in Sebastopol, California.[45]

As a whole, the third current is, by a substantial margin, the most varied and, especially because of Sōka Gakkai, the most successful current in attracting members who are not socialized into Buddhism as children, as are many descendants of Japanese immigrants. For various reasons, it is probable that it will continue to increase its social influence. Five of these reasons are listed below.

First, there is the absence of linguistic obstacles, an important problem for ethnically rooted groups. Second, due to the variety of channels of communication, exchange both among Buddhists and between Buddhists and non-Buddhists is more probable. There is, for example, the Buddhist publishing house Ediçoes Nalanda, specializing in Buddhist monographs, written either by Brazilians or by foreign authors and translated into Portuguese. There are Buddhist magazines, such as *Bodigaya*, spreading Buddhist doctrine and offering information about Brazilian Buddhist groups. There is also the growing importance of the internet. Currently, there are at least three online Buddhist discussion groups in Portuguese. The idea of designing an electronic course on Buddhism has even been discussed. Third, ambitious projects have been mounted to develop a more engaged Buddhism, stressing the social potential of a religion sometimes considered unworldly. For example, the Zen monastery Morro da Vargem, in Ibiraçu, launched an ecological program with the goal of protecting the tropical forest. The project annually attracts thousands of students who attend lessons on ecology. That they also learn something about Buddhism is more than an unintended side effect. Fourth, the final current of Brazilian Buddhism is highly dynamic in terms of organizing and advertising

Buddhist events. There is not a week in which a retreat, talk, ceremony, festival, inauguration, dance performance, or art exhibition in the spirit of Buddhism does not takes place. Fifth, in a religiously predisposed society like Brazil's, one must not forget the attraction exerted by the considerable number of Asian Buddhist leaders who annually visit the country. In 1999, the Dalai Lama visited Brazil for the second time. He was continuously accompanied by journalists and TV cameras, and packed auditoriums in both Curitiba and Brasília.

CONCLUSION

At the end of a roundtable discussion between representatives of local Buddhist groups at the Pontifical Catholic University of São Paulo, the participants concluded that Buddhism in Brazil will never be a mass religion, but will remain restricted to certain segments of society. As has been shown, the first and second currents of Brazilian Buddhism suffer from an ethnic restriction on their growth. Regarding the third branch, it appears that its membership is largely restricted to highly educated academics. However, we still lack empirical data to support this assertion, a situation that has to be overcome by further studies.

NOTES

The author wishes to thank Gabriel Ondetti for his editorial assistance in preparing the final version of this chapter.

1. "Ato multireligioso celebra 80 anos da Folha," *Folha de São Paulo*, 18 Feb. 2001, A17.

2. See "O Brasil dos Budas," *Isto é*, no. 1432 (12 Mar. 1997), 62–70.

3. See "Onda Zen," *Elle Brazil* (June 1998), 91–3.

4. See http://www.ibge.net [15 May 2000].

5. Léa Maria Aarão Reis, "Budismo," *Jornal do Brasil*, 12 Aug. 2000, no page number.

6. One example is Soninha Francine, host of a show on MTV in Brazil. See José Tadeu Arantes, "Meditação: a ginástica do espírito," *Galileu* 88 (November 1998), also at http://galileu.globo.com/edic/88/comportamento1.htm [15 May 2001].

7. See "Uma força contra a crise," *Isto é*, no. 1510 (9 Sept. 1998), 88–94; Arantes, "Meditação: a ginástica do espírito"; Daniela Falcão, "Ofertas zen atraem aluno ioiô e sedentários," *Folha de São Paulo*, Monday health supplement, 7 Sept. 2000, 8–11.

8. "O Brasil dos Budas," 70.

9. See "Reforma nos corações," *Isto é*, no. 1541 (14 Apr. 1999), 70–75, especially 75.

10. See Murillo Nunes de Azevedo, "Contribuições do Budismo para o Brasil," in *Federação das Seitas Budistas do Brasil, Simpósio e Conferência Brasil-Japão de*

Budismo: A Contribuição do Budismo para a Ordem e o progresso do Brasil (São Paulo: Federação das Seitas Budistas do Brasil, 1995), 21–28, especially 26.

11. Cristina Moreira Rocha, "Zen Buddhism in Brazil: Japanese or Brazilian?" *Journal of Global Buddhism* 1 (2000), 31–55, also at http://jgp.la.psu.edu/1/darocha001.pdf [15 May 2000].

12. Maria José Elias, "Introdução ao Estudo da Imigração Chinesa," *Anais do Museu Paulista* 24 (1970), 55–100; Eric Vanden Bussche, "A Dimensão Histórica das Relações Sino-Brasileiras (Séc.: XVI-1943)," *Revista Tempo Brasileira* 137 (Apr.-June 1999), 85–98, especially 8 *ff.*; José Roberto Teixeira Leite, *A China no Brasil* (Campinas, Brazil: Unicamp, 1999).

13. Koryu Nakamura, "Mensagem," in *Federação das Seitas Budistas do Brasil*, 8.

14. *Japoneses, judeus, chineses, coreanos, gregos, latino-americanos e europeus orientais: projecto caixa populi, segunda etapa* (São Paulo: Caixa Exonômica Federal, 2000), 14.

15. See Gilmar Masiero, "Relações Políticas e Econômicas entre o Brasil e a Coréia do Sul," *Carta Asiática*, edited by Gilson Schwartz, published by the Center of Research in International Relations (Núcleo de Pesquisa em Relações Internacionais), University of São Paulo, online publication accessed as a subsite of http://www.usp.br/ [13 May 2000].

16. The Kōmyōji in Cafelândia was founded in 1932. It was the very first Japanese Buddhist temple in Brazil. See Ricardo Mário Gonçalves and Yvonete Silva Gonçalves, "As Religiões dos Imigrantes Japoneses no Brasil," *Imigrações e História da Igreja no Brasil*, edited by Martin N. Dreher (Santuário: Aparacida, 1993), 167–82, especially 174.

17. See Yomei Sasaki, "Palavras de Abertura," in *Federação das Seitas Budistas do Brasil*, 7.

18. See André Mazao Ozaki, *As Religiões Japonesas no Brasil* (São Paulo: Loyola, 1990), 20; Peter Clarkc, "Japanese New Religious Movements in Brazil: From Ethnic to 'Universal' Religions," in *New Religious Movements: Challenge and Response*, edited by Bryan Wilson and Jamie Cresswell (London: Routledge, 1999), 192–210. See also the list compiled by Ronan Alves Pereira in *Cultura japonesa: São Paulo, Rio de Janeiro, Curitiba* (São Paulo: Aliança Cultural Brasil-Japão, n.d.), 440–6.

19. Chung Yuan Alexander Yang, "O Budismo entre os Chineses no Brasil," *China em Estudo* 2, no. 2 (1995), 49–57.

20. Rafael Shoji, "Estratégicas de Adaptação do Budismo Mahayana no Brasil: Brasileiros e Chineses no Fo Kuang Shan," in *Budismo no Brasil: Uma religião entre tradição e adaptação*, edited by Frank Usarski (São Paulo: Verbo Humano, forthcoming 2002).

21. Joa Choi Keum, "Além do Arco-Íris: A Imigração Coreana no Brasil" (master's thesis, University of São Paulo, 1991), 175 *ff*.

22. Janet McLellan, "Buddhist Identities in Toronto: The Interplay of Local, National and Global Contexts," *Social Compass* 45, no. 2 (1998), 227–45.

23. Regina Yoshie Matsue, *O Paraíso de Amida: Três Escolas Budistas em Brasília*, (master's thesis, University of Brasília, 1998), 47.

24. Cristina Moreira Rocha, "Zen Buddhism in Brazil."

25. Yukio Fujii and T. Lynn Smith, *The Acculturation of the Japanese Immigrants in Brazil* (Gainesville, Florida: University of Florida Press, 1959), 14.

26. Takashi Maeyama, "Religião, parentesco e as classes médias dos japoneses no Brasil urbano," in *Assimilação e Integração dos Japoneses no Brasil*, edited by Hiroshi Saito and Takashi Maeyama (Petrópolis: Vozes, 1973), 240–72, especially 248.

27. Ricardo Mário Gonçalves, "Considerações sobre o trabalho de tradução de textos budistas," *Revisto de Instituto Budista de Estudos Missionários* 1 (1995), 9–20, especially 9.

28. See "Monges vão à escola," *Estado de São Paulo*, 25 July 1996, no page number.

29. See Gisele Camargo Regetão, "A flor de sabedoria," *Guia dos alunos*, edited by Cremilda Medina (São Paulo: USP/ECA and CJE, 1993), 151–9, especially 151 and 153.

30. "Transcrição do Simpósio," *Federação das Seitas Budistas do Brasil*, 42.

31. Thomas A. Tweed, *The American Encounter with Buddhism, 1844–1912: Victorian Culture and the Limits of Dissent* (Bloomington: Indiana University Press, 1992).

32. See "Orientalismo na literatura brasileira," *Dicionário de literatura* (Porto, Portugal: Figueirinhas, 1981), 772.

33. John Sasaki, *Japanese Emigrants in Brazil: A Study of the Integration of the Japanese People* (Rio de Janeiro: Sesi, 1957), 8 ff.; Thales de Azevedo, *Cultura é Situação Racial no Brasil.* (Rio de Janeiro: Civilização Brasileira, 1996), 104ff.

34. Matsue, *O Paraíso de Amida*, 103.

35. Ricardo Mário Gonçalves (ed.), *Quintínio Bacaiúva, No. 10: Trajetória de uma Loja Maçônica* (São Paulo: Imprensa Oficial, 1998).

36. Ricardo Mário Gonçalves, "A Trajetória de um Budista Brasileiro," in Usarski, *Budismo no Brasil*.

37. Matsue, *O Paraíso de Amida*, 111.

38. Murillo Nunes de Azevedo, *O Caminho de Cada Um: O Budismo da Terra Pura* (Rio de Janeiro: Bertrand Russell, 1996), 25 ff.

39. "Transcrição do Simpósio," *Federação das Seitas Budistas do Brasil*, 47.

40. See Hirochika Nakamaki, "Religiões Japonesas no Brasil: estratégias multinacionais," *Comunicações do ISER* 5, no. 18 (March 1986), 16–23.

41. Cristina Moreira Rocha, "Zen Buddhism in Brazil."

42. Ronan Alves Pereira, "O Budismo leigo da Sōka Gakkai: Do Japão para o mundo, dos imigrantes para os brasileiros," in *Budismo no Brasil*.

43. Ibid.

44. See Frank Usarski, "Religious Adaptation through Reincarnation? The Role of Lama Michel, the 'Little Buddha' of São Paulo, within the Globalized Tibetan Buddhist Movement of Lama Gangchen" (1999), http://www.cesnur.org/testi/lama_michel.htm [11 May 2001].

45. See Maria Simões, "Entrevista: Segyu Choepel Rinpoche, Psicologia budista no ambiente empresarial," *Revista T&D, Desenvolvendo Pessoas* 87, 8th year (March 2000), 8–11.

Buddha in the Promised Land
Outlines of the Buddhist
Settlement in Israel
Lionel Obadia

INTRODUCTION

In recent studies of Buddhist traditions outside Asia, scholars have focused primarily upon Europe, North America, and Australia, areas which Stephen Batchelor includes in his definition of *Western culture*.[1] Consequently, Buddhist expansion is seen as concerning mainly Western and secularized Christian societies. Nevertheless, Buddhism has recently reached new soil outside this "Western" area, and has recently appeared in Israel, the only Middle Eastern nation, and the only country under political-religious rule, to welcome Buddhism.

The rooting of Asian traditions in Israel raises the issue of the relationships between Judaism and Buddhism, in diaspora as well as in the Jewish nation itself. This chapter examines the history of Jews and Buddhism and attempts to portray the emergence of Buddhism in the Israeli landscape. Israel and its Buddhist communities provide a new and emerging terrain of study, allowing for re-evaluation of the phenomenon of Buddhist expansion in the West.

THE ENCOUNTER BETWEEN JUDAISM AND BUDDHISM

Two best-selling books, Rodger Kamenetz's *The Jew in the Lotus* (1994) and Sylvia Boorstein's *That's Funny, You Don't Look Buddhist* (1997), and the Bill Chayes and Isaac Solotaroff film *Jews and Buddhism* (1999) have given a high degree of visibility to the Buddhist-Jewish encounter in North America.[2] In the last decade, joint programs and interfaith classes and conferences have also been initiated in *zendōs*, in ashrams, and even in Jewish communities throughout the United States.

There are two possible explanations for the sudden interest in the conjunction between Jews and Buddhism. The first, quite simply, is that the encounter itself is of recent date. The second is that any trace of earlier contact has not yet received the attention it deserves. Indeed, historical accounts of the encounter between Buddhism and the West usually focus upon Christianity, and in particular on the following contexts: the discovery of Asian religions by Christian travelers and missionaries in the Middle Ages, the literary study of Buddhism in nineteenth-century European circles in which Buddhism was defined in Christian terms, and the conversion of Christian-born Westerners to Buddhism in the twentieth century. With the exception of ancient localized and sporadic contacts between East and West,[3] Judaism is virtually missing from general and historical accounts of the history of Buddhism in the West before the twentieth century.

The Appeal of Buddhism among Jews

It has been suggested that strong affinities exist between Judaism and Buddhism. According to Charles Prebish, "the Buddhist movement has been especially attractive to individuals from Jewish backgrounds."[4] Richard Seager notes that Jews played an "important role . . . in the introduction and adaptation of the Buddha's teachings to America."[5] In the same vein, Rothberg points out that Jews have been and still are very active in the shaping of an American Buddhism, and especially in the emergent movement of socially engaged Buddhism.[6] Yet, one might ask, to what extent does the relationship between Jews and Buddhism differ significantly from that of Christians and Buddhism? If we consider the phenomenon from a historical and sociological perspective, we find that the attraction for Buddhism among Jews needs to be somewhat qualified.

Throughout the nineteenth century, the appeal of Buddhism was purely intellectual. Buddhism was likely to attract intellectuals and scholars of Christian as well as Jewish origin. Moreover, historically speaking, the active involvement of Jews in Buddhist practices follows closely that of other Western groups. Jewish commitment to Buddhism began with Charles Strauss's conversion to Buddhism during the World Parliament of Religions (Chicago, 1893), and continued notably with Allen Ginsberg's Beat-styled discovery of Eastern philosophies in the 1960s. The late twentieth century saw the emergence of a generation of Jewish-born Western Buddhist masters, such as Joseph Goldstein and Jack Kornfield, co-founders of the Insight Meditation Society in America.

Rodger Kamenetz maintains that the number of Jewish-born Western practitioners of Buddhism in the United States is higher than one might expect.[7] Likewise, Judith Linzer stated in 1996 that more or less "30% of non-Buddhist born American Buddhists were of Jewish origin, and that

30–50 percent of Buddhist scholars in Buddhist Studies departments throughout the United States were of Jewish origin."[8] These statistics can be misleading. Martin Baumann, for instance, found evidence of large numbers of Jewish-born Buddhists in Germany in the early period of the Buddhist settlement in Europe (i.e., the first half of the twentieth century).[9] Statistical rates published in recent sociological inquiries are only up to 5 or 6 percent of Jewish-born American converts either to traditional forms of Buddhism (Zen, Tibetan, and Theravāda)[10] or to modern movements (such as Sōka Gakkai).[11]

From a sociological perspective, Buddhism's resonance among Jews can be interpreted in several ways. Rodger Kamenetz emphasizes similarities in the mystical and meditative traditions of Buddhism and Judaism. This interpretation, however, is based upon an essentialist conception of religion that does not take into account the operative contextual factors. The major impetus of the Jewish-Buddhist encounter historically originates during the 1960s and 1970s, when many American Jews were fascinated by Eastern religions and were engaged in a spiritual odyssey alongside Christians in discovering Buddhism, Hinduism, and other Asian-inspired religious movements.

The reasons for the appeal of Buddhism to both Jews and Christians are important here. Two primary explanations are the failure of Judeo-Christian traditions to respond to social and ideological change, and the subsequent turning to more appealing religious practices and doctrines. The rejection of institutional and traditional forms of the Judeo-Christian faith has also been suggested by Rick Fields for Buddhism in general and by Jane Hurst for Nichiren Shōshū in particular.[12] Judith Linzer, author of the detailed study *Torah and Dharma: Seekers in Eastern Religions*, describes this as a "phobic avoidance" of the Jewish heritage.[13] According to Kenneth Tanaka, the predicament of Western religions may not be considered as the only reason that Jews and Christians have been turning to Buddhism: the emphasis on more concrete and accessible practices is also highly attractive for Jewish and Christian apostates.[14] These hypotheses are confirmed by the fact that Jewish converts to Buddhism are primarily middle-class intellectuals, that is, the secularized and assimilated wing of the diaspora.

Nevertheless, Judaism remains an important basis for the cultural or ethnic self-definition of Western Jewish-born converts to Buddhism. Their commitment to Buddhism is the result of a discomfort with the coercive aspects of Jewish tradition, but does not entail the complete rejection of their cultural heritage and often leads to the rediscovery of their Jewish backgrounds.[15] Mixed identities and assorted practices are thus emerging from the engagement of Jews in Buddhism. On the one hand, a new type of practitioner has recently emerged, described as the *JUBU* by Rodger Kamenetz and by Charles Prebish as *Buddhish*. These people are "passionate Buddhist[s] and faithful Jew[s]" at once, according to Sylvia Boorstein's expression. On the other hand, the practice of Buddhism is also combined with traditional forms of Judaism. For instance, Bernard Glassman Rōshi, the founder of the Zen Peacemaker Order and a famous promoter of engaged Buddhism, has organized a series of "Bearing Witness" sessions, conducted in the concentration camp of Auschwitz. These interfaith commemorations of the Shoah (World War II's holocaust) include the participation of rabbis and the performance of Jewish ceremonials (such as the *Kaddish,* or prayer for the dead) along with Japanese-style *sesshins.*

BUDDHISM AND BUDDHISTS IN ISRAEL

While Buddhism is highly appealing to the American Jewish diaspora community, the arrival of practical forms of Buddhism in Israel has its own history. The appeal of Asian spiritualities and philosophies can be traced back to the pioneer founders of Israel in the mid-twentieth century, and especially David Ben-Gurion, who is said to have been fascinated by Indian philosophy. Nevertheless, the settlement of Buddhist traditions and the existential engagement of Israelis in Buddhism only start in the 1990s.

The Cultural Contacts Hypothesis

Nathan Katz explains the contemporary affinities between Judaism and Buddhism—especially the Tibetan variety—as the consequences of long-standing cultural contacts between Asian civilizations (mainly India) and ancient Israel. Katz recently discussed a series of subtle elements he considers as "evidences" of a cross-cultural fertilization between Buddhism and Judaism in ancient times: analogies in Buddhist and Jewish religious history, the presence of Sanskrit and Hebrew words in respective sacred scriptures (*Jātakas* and *Talmud*), the translation of Buddhist literature by Jewish scholars from the eleventh century on, historically identified contacts with India (Jewish travelers on trade routes to Asia in medieval times), and migrations (Jewish colonies in India, Kashmir, China, and on the Silk Road).[16] It is, however, difficult to determine whether or not these contacts between Israel and South Asia contributed significantly to what Katz sees as affinities between Judaism and Buddhism. The cross-cultural contact continues today, although in a different form, because India and Nepal remain two favorite destinations of young Israeli travelers.

The Settlement of Buddhism in Israel

In North America, Western Europe, and Australia, Buddhism is represented today by a wide variety of schools and lineages. In Israel, on the other hand, specific features dominate. Buddhism's arrival in Israel did not follow the pattern of Asian migration, Asian exportation (or evangelical spread), and Western importation that Jan Nattier describes.[17] Israel is traditionally a country of immigrants, and has mainly welcomed Jewish emigrants from postwar Europe and later from other parts of the world, including Africa and Russia. This history has produced the stratification of Israeli society, which is determined by religiously based conceptions of Zionism and by the definition of *Jewishness* with reference to the *Torah* and the rule of *Halakhah* (or the standard and Biblical definition of *Jewishness*). From the foundation of the Israeli state in 1948 to the present, Jewishness remains an imperative condition for migration *(olah)*, Israeli citizenship, and residence according to the Law of Return *(alya)* for Jews in diaspora. Asian people come to Israel primarily as temporary workers. Because of this, they have not established enduring communities or a noticeable contingent of ethnic or Asian Buddhists. Buddhism was carried into Israel by Asian and Western masters and is mainly practiced by converts.

First Attempts

The settlement of Buddhism in Israel dates to the late 1990s. However, an isolated and unsuccessful attempt to settle Buddhism in Israel before that decade has been noted by Zen master Masumi Shibata. Shibata reported in 1972 that a Zen center existed in Israel (the center probably was founded in the 1960s).[18] Zen master Sōen Nakagawa, head of a temple in Los Angeles, established this center, which he named Kibutsu-ji.[19] Nakagawa sought to legitimize his missionary undertaking by the discovery of a linguistic similarity between the Japanese designation of the center (*ki*, basis; *butsu*, Buddha) and the Hebrew word *kibbutz* (pioneer community form of Jewish settlement). Likewise, Nagakawa's efforts in translating the Zen doctrine to a Jewish audience were facilitated by the phonetic resemblances between Hebrew and Japanese. He even translated Japanese poetry into

Hebrew for his Jewish followers based on a similarity between the Hebrew term *mut* (die) and the Japanese *mu* (emptiness).

Buddhist Groups in the Israeli Landscape

The situation changed in the 1990s with new Buddhist masters' tours and lectures, and the foundation of a series of communities on Israeli soil. The Western Buddhist landscape is a complex one, with Buddhist organizations and movements ranging from more traditional monastic groups (such as Tibetan Buddhism) to lay-oriented modernist organizations (such as the Japanese-based Sōka Gakkai), attended by both Western converts and Asian-native adherents. In contrast, Buddhism in Israel is primarily composed of reformed or newly founded branches within traditional schools.[20]

Tibetans: Unity. A 1989 meeting of American rabbis and the Dalai Lama in the United States initiated the dialogue between Tibetan Buddhism and Judaism. The central point of the discussion with the leading figure of Tibetan Buddhism turned out to be the issue of exile and cultural continuity through the preservation of religious practices and beliefs. The next year, eight rabbis and Jewish scholars went to Dharamsala, India, in order to pursue the dialogue and to explore the parallels between the Jewish and Tibetan nations. Since then, some Israelis have discovered in Tibetan values and ethics a nonviolent alternative to the present situation of war between Israel and its Arab neighbors.

The Dalai Lama is the first Buddhist master whose visits to Israel (since 1994) have been official. Some organizations, such as the Israeli Inter-Religious Coordinating Council and the Jubillennium organization, supported his journey in late 2000. He was welcomed by the IFTIP (Israeli Friends of the Tibetan People),[21] which is pursuing the Jewish-Tibetan dialogue initiated by American rabbis and Jewish scholars. However, the Gelugpa school of Tibetan Buddhism, which is the Dalai Lama's tradition, has not yet been established in Israel. The Diamond Way organization, a Western-style, lay-oriented branch of the Tibetan Kagyu school of Buddhism founded in 1972 in Copenhagen by Ole Nydahl, is prominently represented in Israel.

Ole Nydahl was first invited by American and Israeli Reiki practitioners during the summer of 1999, and gave lectures attended by between fifty and one hundred people in three large cities (Jerusalem, Haifa, and Tel Aviv). A Tel Aviv Tibetan center was founded in December 1999, soon after the departure of the Danish-born Western Buddhist master.[22] By 2000, the Karma Kagyu Israeli network encompassed three more Sanghas, located in Beer Sheva, Haifa, and Jerusalem.

Zen Diversity. Unlike Tibetan Buddhism, several branches of Zen Buddhism have settled in Israel: the Vietnamese modern Zen of Thich Nhat Hanh, the Korean Kwan Um school, and the Japanese Rinzai and Sōtō lineages. The presence of Zen Buddhism in Israel proceeds simultaneously through exportation by American-born Jewish Buddhists or sympathizers and importation by Israeli-born scholar-practitioners.

Thich Nhat Hanh first visited Israel to give public lectures in 1997, having been invited by the American-born sympathizer Michael Rosenbush, who intended to convey a lay-oriented and modern Buddhist's message of peace to the Israeli people. Thich Nhat Hanh conducted short retreats and gave public lectures in Tel Aviv, Haifa, and Jerusalem.[23] The unofficial visit of the Vietnamese master brought about the founding of the Community of Mindfulness of Israel, an umbrella community that unites nine Sanghas in Israel and maintains strong ties with Plum Village, Thich Nhat Hanh's headquarters in France. The leading White Cloud Sangha in Jerusalem serves as a focal point for other Sanghas located in Karmiel, Rosh Pina, Haifa, Tel Aviv, Tivon, E'in E'iron, Beit Hashita, and Naharya. The Naharya group, the atypical Western Galilee Sangha, is headed by Paul Shalom Treat, who promotes an ecumenical and syncretistic approach to religion.[24]

The Tel Aviv Zen Center is the only Sangha affiliated with the Kwan Um Korean School of Zen, headed by Master Seung Sahn, the 78th Patriarch of the Korean Chogye order and founder of the Kwan Um Sangha in 1972. The Kwan Um School is now established worldwide. Fifty-two centers are affiliated with the Providence (Rhode Island) headquarters in the United States. The Tel Aviv Zen Center (TAZC) is the only one established in the Middle East. Its founders began practicing Shiatsu around 1993. In the mid-1990s, Seung Sahn visited Israel to teach in alternative health centers. Revital Dan, currently heading the TAZC, followed the master to Korea and trained in the monastic style of retreat. Back in Israel with her Dharma-teacher degree, she founded a Zen group. The opening ceremony of the TAZC took place in January 1999.[25] The activities of the Kwan Um school have received widespread media coverage and the number of attendees is increasing.

Israeli followers of the Japanese master Masugama Reiho have settled the Zen Sōtō lineage in Israel, led by Danny Waxman (who trained in Japan and is a *sensei* in the Dōgen tradition) and by Ofer Cohen (a Bujinkan

Ninjutsu practitioner and Zen teacher). Each of these people established a Dōgen-Sōtō Zen Dōjō in Ramat-Gan, near Tel Aviv. Cohen's emphasizes "Zen-judo" teaching, a combination of martial arts and meditative practices.[26]

Like anywhere else, the Israeli scholarly milieu has also represented the grassroots in the adoption of Buddhist practices. Books on Buddhism written in Hebrew by local researchers (such as Lydia Aran's *Buddhism*, edited in 1993) add now to the translated classics of Alan Watts and other famous writers in Israeli libraries. One of those Israeli Buddhologists, Professor Jacob Raz—an eminent specialist in Japanese culture—was the founder of a lay and unaffiliated Zen meditation group in the mid-1990s. The group is called Sand Sangha because it gathers on a beach in Tel Aviv. The Sangha is attended by students of Jacob Raz and by sympathizers. Its activities focus upon non-institutionalized practices of Zen in the Rinzai tradition and combine zazen and t'ai ch'i. Although he emphasizes practice rather than textual instruction, Jacob Raz has edited several books on Japan and on Buddhist practices (especially *kōans*) that are available in Hebrew for a large audience.[27]

Vipassanā and Other Groups. The third great tradition to have settled in the West, alongside Tibetan and Zen Buddhism, is Theravāda. This ancient school is represented by the modern approach of the Indian-born Burmese master Satya Narayan Goenka, who has spread *vipassanā* meditation around the world since the early 1970s. The followers of the *vipassanā* tradition of Goenka are united in the Israel Insight Society (ISIS)—also known as Amutat Tovana—an umbrella organization with nine affiliate Sanghas.[28]

It is difficult to count and identify Israeli Sanghas because some local Buddhist networks do not appear in any directories. Some unaffiliated groups appear in internet listings; an example is the People-Who-Meditate-Once-A-Week Group of Jerusalem, a Vajrayāna-oriented Sangha. Others do not; an example is the Tibetan group in Jerusalem founded by American-Jewish—born Buddhist master Thubten Chodron.[29]

The Practice of Buddhism in Israel

Attendance at Israeli Sanghas is around ten to twenty-five persons per session, although the Sanghas reach larger audiences for great masters' visits. The Israeli Buddhist milieu remains very tiny in comparison to the demographics (of the approximately six million inhabitants in Israel, 82 percent are Jewish). The success of Buddhism in Israel is surprising, since monotheistic religions such as Judaism (as well as Christianity and Islam) suppose an exclusive adherence and traditionally prohibit the incorporation of elements from other traditions; this is especially true in Judaism. The filtering of Eastern influences has been allowed by tensions between orthodox or conservative movements and the liberal and progressive wings of Judaism, in diaspora and in Israel as well.

Israeli Buddhist followers come from the secularized and liberal strata of the population. Their approach to Buddhism is mainly characterized by rejection of the institutionalized forms of Judaism, not by withdrawal from their Jewishness. The incorporation of practices and beliefs is not considered as a threat to their identity since they gave up the praxis of orthodox Judaism for a new definition of Jewishness. The recent attempts for a laicization of the Israeli citizenship and Jewish identity are connected to the diversification of the Israeli religious landscape: a series of reform movements promoting pluralism and diversity of religious expression arose in Israel and in the United States in opposition to traditional or conservative trends in the 1960s. While reform movements gradually realigned to Zionist ideals, their lasting influence is apparent in lay and progressive ideologies that have become more prominent in Israel in the last decades.

Another factor of religious pluralism is the settlement of a multitude of religious movements in Israel, including Judeo-Christian–inspired foreign groups and doomsday cults, such as the Raelians.[30] The development of non-Jewish religious groups and cults is restricted by the governmental support of Jewish institutions (2 percent of the funding for local religions is offered to Muslim and Christian institutions) and by the 1977 anti-proselytizing law. Non-Jewish evangelical groups suffered harassment and the low Israeli religious tolerance has been denounced by CESNUR (the Center for Studies on New Religions), an organization opposed to religious intolerance around the world. Such condemnations of Israeli religious intolerance are however refuted by the proliferation in recent decades of New Age movements, Asian organizations (such as ISKCON, the International Society for Krishna Consciousness, based in Tel Aviv), Eastern-inspired religious movements (such as the Sahaja Yoga), and, of course, the recent arrival of Buddhist schools in the Israeli landscape.

Prospects

The structural features of Buddhism in Israel include two interrelated sets of networks: (1) transnational networks (connected with France, the United States, and Korea), concerned with training within tradition-oriented movements, and (2) an Israeli nationwide network. Within the Israeli network, individual groups are somewhat interconnected and also are connected to a larger spiritual milieu, including alternative groups practicing psychology, yoga, and New Age alternative therapies. The transplantation of Buddhist institutions may slowly lead to the dissociation of Buddhism from New Age movements. Although many groups still incorporate practices from various non-Buddhist traditions, this orthodox trend is observable in the Kwan Um Zen group, where the training is firmly aligned with the teachings of the Zen school.

While the transposition of institutions has been successful, the settlement of material forms of Buddhist groups is more problematic because of the lack of religious toleration and freedom in Israel. Governmental laws on religion, for instance, restrict the foundation of Buddhist temples. The Israeli administration only recognizes five religious categories (Judaism, Islam, Christianity, Druze religion, and "other"). With the exception of TAZC, the majority of Buddhist groups have no proper *zendō*, or place of worship. Israeli Buddhist organizations acquire the visibility they lack in the social and material world by means of the internet: an Israeli Internet Network and a Zen-oriented web site, both in Hebrew, are already available.[31]

CONCLUSION

The settlement of Buddhism in Israel is very recent, but has undergone rapid expansion and continues to develop. This phenomenon shows that the diffusion of Buddhism outside Asia is related to factors other than simply the decline of Christian hegemony upon Western societies. It is true, however, that the sociological consequences of secularization, such as religious pluralism and the spiritual quest, play key roles in the success of Buddhism, but that success also depends upon the specific ideological resonance of Buddhism in each particular context. The progress of Buddhism depends as well upon its ability to adapt to new environments. The future of Buddhism in Israel is concerned with such issues as transplantation,[32] institutionalization, and acculturation. Can we expect the emergence of an Israeli-styled Buddhism? Although it is too soon to answer with certainty, this locally acculturated Buddhism may be characterized by its strong political and ethical resonance (due to the Israeli context) and by the joining of Buddhist "wings" on Jewish "roots" (a common feature with the American Jewish diaspora).

NOTES

This chapter provides information on a current fieldwork research project. Consequently, the author cannot lay claim to any exhaustive empirical data. Statements and theoretical assertions must therefore be considered as preliminary reflections.

1. Stephen Batchelor, *The Awakening of the West: The Encounter of Buddhism and Western Culture* (Berkeley: Parallax Press, 1994).

2. Rodger Kamenetz, *The Jew in the Lotus* (San Francisco: HarperCollins, 1994); Sylvia Boorstein, *That's Funny, You Don't Look Buddhist: On Being a Faithful Jew and a Passionate Buddhist* (New York: HarperCollins, 1997); and Bill Chayes and Isaac Solotaroff, *Jews and Buddhism: Belief Amended, Faith Revealed*, video, 41 min., Chayes Productions, Petaluma, California, 1999.

3. Boorstein, *That's Funny, You Don't Look Buddhist*, 27.

4. Charles S. Prebish, "Introduction," in *The Faces of Buddhism in America*, edited by Charles S. Prebish and Kenneth K. Tanaka (Berkeley: University of California Press, 1998), 1–10.

5. Richard Hughes Seager, *Buddhism in America* (New York: Columbia University Press, 1999), 225 ff.

6. Donald Rothberg, "Responding to the Cries of the World: Socially Engaged Buddhism in North America," in Prebish and Tanaka, *The Faces of Buddhism in America*, 283.

7. Kamenetz, *The Jew in the Lotus*, 7–12.

8. Judith Linzer, *Torah and Dharma: Jewish Seekers in Eastern Religions* (Northvale, New Jersey: Jason Aronson, 1996), xxii.

9. Martin Baumann, *Deutsche Buddhisten: Geschichte und Gemeinschaften* (Marburg, Germany: Diagonal-Verlag, 1995), 66–7, 238–43.

10. James W. Coleman, "The New Buddhism: Some Empirical Findings," in *American Buddhism: Methods and Findings in Recent Scholarship*, edited by Duncan Ryūken Williams and Christopher S. Queen (Richmond, U.K.: Curzon Press, 1999), 91–9.

11. Phillip E. Hammond and David W. Machacek, *Sōka Gakkai in America: Accommodation and Conversion* (New York: Oxford University Press, 1999), 45.

12. Rick Fields, "Divided Dharma: White Buddhists, Ethnic Buddhists and Racism," in Prebish and Tanaka, *The Faces of Buddhism in America*, 205; and Jane Hurst, "Nichiren Shōshū and Sōka Gakkai in America: The Pioneer Spirit," in Prebish and Tanaka, *The Faces of Buddhism in America*, 80–97.

13. Linzer, *Torah and Dharma*, 19.

14. Kenneth K. Tanaka, "Epilogue: The Colors and Contours of American Buddhism," in Prebish and Tanaka, *The Faces of Buddhism in America*, 291.

15. See Linzer, *Torah and Dharma*.

16. See Nathan Katz, "Contacts between Jewish and Indo-Tibetan Civilizations through the Ages: Some Explorations," *The Tibet Journal* 16, no. 4 (Winter 1991), 90–109, and "From Legend to History: India and Israel in the Ancient World," *SHOFAR* 17, no. 3 (Spring 1999), 8–22.

17. Jan Nattier, "Who Is a Buddhist? Charting the Landscape of Buddhist America," in Prebish and Tanaka, *The Faces of Buddhism in America*, 183–95.

18. I would like to thank Eric Rommeluere at the UBE (European Buddhist University, Paris) for having pointed out this fact to me, for providing the book reference of Shibata in note 19, and for helping me with the Japanese words. Unfortunately, Shibata did not divulge any dates. An approximation can be derived from the events that have occurred in Zen master Sōen Nakagawa's life.

19. Masumi Shibata, *Dans les monastères zen* (Paris: Hachette, 1972), 120–2.

20. For Tibetan Buddhism, Karma Kagyu lineage, see http://www.diamondway-buddhism.org/centers/z-isr.htm [4 Feb. 2002]; for Zen Buddhism, see http://www.iijnet.or.jp/iriz/index_e.html [4 Feb. 2002].

21. See http://www.tibet.org.il/tibet/index.html [5 Sept. 2000].

22. Interview with Yoel Nessim, at the Tel Aviv Kagyu Center, May 2000.

23. Interview with Michael Rosenbush, Paris, July 2000.

24. At http://pi.co.il/sangha/list.html [4 Feb. 2002]; and e-mail communication with Paul Shalom Treat, April 2000.

25. Interview with Revital Dan, May 2000.

26. See http://www.zenki.com/ [4 Feb. 2002].

27. Interview with Eric Cohen, from the Sand Sangha, Tel Aviv, May 2000.

28. See http://www.geocities.com/Athens/Agora/2304 [4 Feb. 2002].

29. Listed in http://www.dharmanet.org/Dir/World/ctr_il.html [4 Feb. 2002].

30. The Raelians, whom the author met in the streets of Tel Aviv in May 2000, plan to settle a godlike extraterrestrial embassy (Elohim) in Israel. See http://www.theraelian.com [5 Sept. 2000].

31. See http://buddhism.id.co.il/ [5 Sept. 2000] and http://www.zen.org.il/ [4 Feb. 2002].

32. Martin Baumann, "The Transplantation of Buddhism to Germany: Processive Modes and Strategies of Adaptation," in *Theory in the Study of Religion* 6, no. 1 (1994), 35–61.

III

CHANGE
Adaptations and Innovations

12   Camp Dharma

Japanese-American Buddhist
Identity and the Internment
Experience of World War II

Duncan Ryūken Williams

February 18, 1942, early morning, still in our nightclothes and
huddled by the heater, we listened grimly to the news over the
radio. There was a loud rapping on the back door. Three men stood
there. They were the FBI. "We came to arrest Rev. Matsuura," said
one, as they came through the door. . . . I was instructed to pack a
change of clothing for my husband. Hurriedly, I put his underwear
and toiletries in a bag. Separately, I wrapped his koromo and kesa,
seiten and Kanmuryojukyo sutra.

Shinobu Matsuura [1]

INTRODUCTION: TARGETING BUDDHISTS

Buddhist priests, classified by the Federal Bureau of Investigation (FBI) as
the most potentially dangerous of Japanese aliens, were among the first
people arrested by government officials beginning in December 1941, following the bombing of Pearl Harbor. [2] Shinobu Matsuura's husband, Reverend Issei Matsuura, was one of the first Buddhist priests taken by the FBI,
in the early hours of the morning, not knowing whether he would ever see
his family again. Sent to the U.S. Justice Department's "alien enemy"
camps, such as those in Santa Fe, New Mexico, and Crystal City, Texas, Japanese-American Buddhist priests of all denominations, along with Shinto
priests, were targeted by the government. Unlike Japanese-American
Christian priests and ministers, U.S. government officials closely associated Buddhists with Japan and thus with potentially subversive activity.
As Bob Kumamoto has noted, "The 'peculiarity' of Eastern languages, religions, customs, and physical appearance had always separated the Japanese from the mainstream of American society. Once considered inferior
and insignificant, these ethnic distinctions were now considered by the
government as anti-American, potentially subversive and somehow
threatening to American security." This perception that Buddhists, in con-

trast to Christians, were more "Japanese" than "American" was held not only by the FBI and the Wartime Relocation Authority (WRA), but also by the public at large and by some members of the Japanese-American community. The history of Buddhism in the internment camps, as well as the subsequent development of Japanese-American Buddhism, centers around this question of identity, both ethnic and religious.

The first Japanese Buddhist priests arrived in Hawaii and the United States mainland in the 1890s to minister to the first-generation immigrants, most of whom were Buddhist, who initially moved to Hawaii to work on the plantations and to the mainland as contract laborers for railroad, lumber, mining, and cannery companies, as well as on farms. By 1900, the Japanese immigrant population within the United States and Hawaii had risen to 24,326 people. Most of these were transient men. However, by 1930 the Japanese-American population had grown to 138,834, and consisted largely of families with stable jobs and even small businesses.[3] By the eve of World War II, Buddhist temples functioned simultaneously as religious and community centers in all areas where there was a high concentration of Japanese-Americans, especially in California. Buddhist priests of the Jōdo, Jōdo Shin, Nichiren, Shingon, and Sōtō Zen sects were sent by their respective headquarters temples in Japan to serve as missionaries in the United States.

That the FBI targeted these Buddhist priests as potential subversives had little to do with the fact that Buddhist temples, especially those of the Jōdo Shin tradition, had participated in fund-raising campaigns for the Japanese Imperial Army in Manchuria.[4] Japanese-American Buddhist ties to the Japanese military or intelligence agencies, according to FBI surveillance records, were fairly tenuous. Alan Hynd's 1943 "exposé" of the Japanese-German spy network in the years immediately preceding the war, titled *Betrayal from the East: The Inside Story of Japanese Spies in America*, could only cite one incident.[5] The FBI apparently suspected that the Los Angeles Kōyasan Buddhist Temple held spy meetings involving members of the Japanese consulate, Sachiko Furusawa (an advisor to the temple's women's society and the wife of a doctor who apparently had ties to German spies), and other unidentified figures. At one particular meeting, the FBI suspected that these people discussed detonation devices to be placed on the American naval fleet. In reality, the FBI only had unsupported notions that Buddhist priests were more "pro-Japan" than other members of the Japanese-American community. Nevertheless, the FBI classified priests as "known dangerous Group A suspects," along with members of the Japanese consulate, fishermen, and influential businessmen.[6] An assortment of factors must have been at play in the FBI's decision to target Buddhist priests, but probably the biggest factor was the pervasive, racially motivated perception among Euro-Americans that Japanese-Americans were likely to be disloyal and unassimilable because of their "Japanese-ness," especially their being Buddhist. Newspaper editors and congressmen accused all Japanese, as well as their Japanese-American children, of being loyal to the Japanese government and called for their removal from the West Coast. When their priests were taken away to so-called enemy-alien camps, the remaining members of the Buddhist temples tried their best to continue both religious services and community affairs by appointing priests' wives and non-ordained temple leaders to perform the priests' work. Despite this, the communities felt that this would only be a stopgap measure to serve their spiritual and social cohesion.[7]

Indeed, by February 1942, the United States government had set in motion the large-scale incarceration of the broader Japanese-American community. In the months following President Roosevelt's Executive Order No. 9066, issued on 19 February 1942, which ultimately led to the designation of restricted military zones on the West Coast and the removal of all persons of Japanese ancestry from those areas, the atmosphere in the community was one of anxiety, uncertainty, and fear. Immediately following the bombing of Pearl Harbor, the Buddhist Mission of North America (the predecessor of the Jōdo Shin Buddhist Churches of America) sent out the following notice to its members:

> Sirs, REGISTER FOR CIVILIAN DEFENSE—Buddhists! Your loyalty and devotion to the cause of the United States of America in her war against aggressor nations of the Axis, must be translated into action. Do your part unflinchingly in the defense of the STARS AND STRIPES. Acquaint yourself with Air Raid Rules! Mobilize your energies to facilitate America's purpose! Pledge your services unreservedly to the officials and authorities of our country, the UNITED STATES OF AMERICA. With the blessings of Buddha, Rev. K. Kumata (Buddhist Mission of North America).[8]

The major Buddhist organizations tried to provide leadership and convey a strong sense of loyalty to the United States. They urged Japanese-Americans to cooperate with the authorities when rumors circulated about forcible removal from the West Coast: "Buddhists with citizenship in America: Remember the spirit of loyalty to your country and filial piety which you have learned through the teachings of the Buddha. . . . Young Buddhists in Prohibited Areas: Cooperate with your local JACL Chapter in all problems pertaining to the evacuation. With the Blessings of the

Buddha, Rev. Kumata (Buddhist Mission of America)."[9] However, during this period of war hysteria, some Buddhists converted to Christianity.[10] Others burned Japanese-language books and other Japanese cultural artifacts to literally and symbolically destroy their "Japanese-ness" and demonstrate their "American-ness."[11] The Buddhist leadership tried to stem the rumors circulating within the community that those who were Buddhists would be treated more harshly than Christians by sending out the following letter to its membership:

> And contrary to all rumors, those in official positions have assured us that unreasonable persecution shall never be brought against Buddhism or Buddhists. It is with great sorrow then that there have been noted several cases of inferiority complexes, brought about by false tales, wherein Buddhist religious organizations have been disbanded and Buddhists have destroyed or hidden family altars while others have withdrawn from church membership. . . . Buddhists! With true Faith in the Buddha, let us serve our country, the United States of America, in silence. With the Blessings of the Buddha, Rev. Kumata (Buddhist Churches of America).[12]

A community conflicted within itself about identity and loyalty soon had to face the reality that its members were going to be uprooted from their communities and would be allowed to take with them only what they could carry. After they were issued numbers at one of the sixty-four Civil Control stations, Japanese-Americans in the restricted zones had between a week and ten days to sell or store their property, because they could only take what they could carry by hand to the camps. Ultimately, without due process of law, more than 110,000 Japanese-Americans were herded first to "assembly centers" and then imprisoned at one of ten so-called permanent relocation centers. Finding that they had to sell their businesses, land, and other property at vastly reduced prices, many Buddhists stored their possessions at their local temple. While Buddhist temples proved to be relatively secure storage sites, could Buddhism provide a similar sense of refuge inside the camps?

CAMP DHARMA

Arise, Arise, all Buddha's soldiers true, and take your stand upon
   the rock of Truth!
The Holy Law by Lord Buddha taught everyone endure
And all who journey by its Light shall reach Nirvana's shore

In love we stand, by Truth set free, Brothers of Him who found
  true liberty.

  Gathas and Services, Poston 1 Buddhist Church[13]

Enduring the harsh journey to the internment camps and the realities of
the desert heat and the fact that they were prisoners in their own land,
Japanese-American Buddhists faced crises of identity and of faith. Within
the camps, surrounded by barbed wire and armed guards, the question
arose of what it meant to be simultaneously American and Buddhist. What
constituted an American Buddhist?

Buddhist life in the camps revolved around the barracks "churches"
(some were in mess halls or recreation buildings) that held religious services and education, especially on Sundays. According to Reverend Arthur
Takemoto, who was a young man during the internment period, Buddhist
teachings (such as those on suffering) helped alleviate the pain and confusion that many faced. He said, "Understanding the basic tenets of Buddhism orients people to understand the reality of life, that things don't go
the way we want them to go. This becomes *duḥkha*, suffering and pain. To
be able to accept a situation as it is means we could tolerate it more." [14]

The WRA forced Buddhist sects to cooperate with each other, which
meant that doctrinal differences were often ignored in favor of a more common, trans-sectarian Buddhism. At times, this involved finding common
ground in such areas as chanting *Namu Butsu* (Homage to the Buddha) instead of the various sects' unique chants: *Namu Amida Butsu* (Jōdo Shin),
Namu Daishi Henjō Kongō (Shingon), and *Namu Myōhō Renge Kyō*
(Nichiren).[15]

The Buddhist church in the camps held annual festivals and services for
events like as Obon, Higan, and the Buddha's birthday, as well as funerals,
memorial services, and weddings for Buddhist families. The traditional ritual life of Japanese Buddhism was thus continued in the camp despite the
harsh conditions. Having left behind their family altars *(butsudan)* that enshrined their ancestors, Buddhists resorted to collecting odd pieces of wood
in the desert to make altars.[16] The lack of priests to carry out funerary and
memorial services forced Buddhist priests, regardless of sect, to maintain
family necrologies *(kakochō)* for other camp residents and to bestow posthumous names *(kaimyō, given to the dead at the funeral)*—both crucial aspects of honoring ancestors in traditional Japanese Buddhism. For example,
the following is an entry of the posthumous name in the necrology of the
Tayama family, a Sōtō Zen Buddhist family in the Manzanar Camp, whose

deceased father's funeral was conducted by a Jōdo Shin priest, Nagatomi Shinjō:

Date 1942, Dec. 24 (deceased)
    Dharma Name: SHAKU Saishō'in Hōden; Given Name: Tayama Saki; Age at death: 61
    Present address: Death Valley CC; Former address: Los Angeles; Place of death: Manzanar
    Japanese Place of Origin: Yamaguchi Pref.
    Officiant: Nagatomi Shinjō; Head Mourner: Tayama Suguru; Notes: Zenshū (Sōtōshu) believer.[17]

The importance of maintaining Japanese customs of ancestral veneration was so strong that sectarian concerns for each family, while normally crucial for the proper performance of the traditional funeral and the selection of the posthumous name, were set aside in this time of crisis. Providing any funerary rites at all was considered sufficient. In these ways, Buddhism both provided a spiritual refuge for internees during these hard years and also served the social function of maintaining family and community through ancestral and life-cycle rituals and traditional Japanese festivals and ceremonies.

While Buddhism was, in this sense, a repository of Japanese traditions, it also was forced to operate in the context of an "Americanization" program promoted by the WRA to assimilate the Japanese and to demonstrate their loyalty to the United States.[18] The Americanization process, of course, began early, both on the mainland and in Hawaii. Especially in Hawaii, the work of Bishop Yemyo Imamura exemplified a movement within Japanese-American Buddhism to distance itself from the Japanese Buddhist establishment. The goal was to create a more independent movement in the United States, both organizationally and in terms of teaching.[19] According to the 1943 *Investigation of Un-American Propaganda Activities in the United States* (prepared by the Subcommittee of the Special Committee on Un-American Activities, House of Representatives), recreational activities such as baseball and basketball, as well as joining such groups as the Boy and Girl Scouts and the YMCA/YWCA, were to be advocated by camp administrators.[20] Obviously, being Buddhist was not listed as a method of demonstrating loyalty, but Buddhist groups made their own attempts at Americanization.

The camp experience in part accelerated the assimilation process that had begun before the war. During May 1944 at Topaz Camp, the name of the largest Buddhist organization was changed from the Buddhist Mission of North America to the Buddhist Churches of America (BCA)—a more

Christian-sounding name.[21] The Buddhist symbol of the swastika, often used on Buddhist temple stationery or on temple equipment, disappeared and was replaced almost universally by the Dharma wheel. English was used more frequently at the barracks churches. In addition, Euro-American supporters outside the camps, like Julius Goldwater, assisted with the preparation of new "hymnals" that gave a more Christian (and thus American) feel to Buddhist services. The most widely used of these was *A Book of Ceremonies for Use of Buddhists at Gatherings.* By singing *gathas* as hymns, including Dorothy Hunt's "Onward Buddhist Soldiers" (a section of which was quoted above), Buddhists within the camp created a new medium for Americanizing Buddhism. However, they did so in ways that honored their Buddhist traditions while demonstrating loyalty to America. The young members of the community, having studied the Buddhist "Junior Catechism," for example, used a Christian medium to maintain Buddhist identity.

Buddhist barracks churches also sponsored basketball teams (the Rohwer Camp "Bussei" team won tournaments in the spring of 1944, for example) and organized youth social dances. Most important, the Young Buddhist Association (YBA) supported the All-Nisei 100th/422nd Combat Regiment, fighting in Europe to demonstrate their loyalty to America.[22] This Americanization process was, thus, particularly pronounced among the second-generation Japanese-American, the Nisei, who, as David Yoo has suggested, "embraced the very markers of racial and religious difference used against them. The faith of their mothers and fathers enabled the second generation to affirm their ancestry and at the same time, lay claim to their status as Americans. No single definition emerged, but religion offered Nisei Buddhists (also known as Bussei) valuable space to become ethnic Americans."[23]

However, many Japanese-American soldiers had a hard time with the issue of identity as they had to recall the irony of fighting for freedom on behalf of a country that deprived their parents and siblings of this very freedom. One such Buddhist soldier wrote to his parents in broken Japanese on the night before leaving boot camp for the European front:

> Dear Mama and Papa. It's me. Tonight, I'm finally being sent to the front. Thank you for loving me all these years. Mama, and Papa too, there's no need to worry. I'll be back soon. I'll rush back to where you are just as soon as I get back. Both of you stay in good health till then, alright. Since everything's set to go, I've not got nothing else left to say except good-bye. Take care, Mama and Papa. Good-bye, good-bye. Oh wait, I'd forgotten, there is something else Mama. That story, you know,

the one you used to tell me all the time when I was a kid. The story about the Buddha. I remember that really well so you can put your mind at ease. The Buddha will always be with me, even when I'm sent to the front. I'm not sad at all because the Buddha will protect me. Mama and Papa, don't worry about me because I remember that story really well. Well, I've got to be off so you two take care of yourselves. Good-bye.[24]

This letter, given by the parents to a Buddhist priest for safekeeping, reassured the soldier's family that he remembered his Buddhist roots and the power of the Buddha to protect believers. The power of the Buddha thus extended ever eastward, across the Pacific from Japan to America, and now east again across the Atlantic from America to Europe.

CONCLUDING REMARKS

When the war ended and the internees began the process of re-integration into American society, Buddhist temples continued the work of the Dharma by serving as hostels for those who could not immediately find housing and jobs. While another essay would be necessary to recount the postwar history of Japanese-American Buddhism, it would undoubtedly have to account for the so-called Camp Dharma, which had the paradoxical task during the war of simultaneously serving as a repository for Japanese cultural traditions and as a vehicle for becoming more American. It was in the crucible of war that many Japanese-Americans took on the conflicted identity of being Japanese-American-Buddhists.

NOTES

I am indebted to a number of scholars who have undertaken research on the topic of Buddhism in the internment camps. Recent scholarship includes: Susan Davis, "Mountains of Compassion: Dharma in American Internment Camps," *Tricycle: The Buddhist Review* 2, no. 4 (Summer 1993), 46–51; Tara Ogden, "*Gamarimaschō!* Religion among the Japanese in America during World War II" (M.A. thesis, University of California, Santa Barbara, 1995); and Kenneth Tanaka, "BCA: The Lotus that Bloomed behind Barbed Wire," *Turning Wheel* (no issue no.), Spring 1993, 41–2. The research presented here was undertaken with funding from the Yokohama Zenkōji Buddhist Studies Fellowship. Special thanks go to the Buddhist Churches of America (BCA) Archives, Ken Kaji, Kenneth Tanaka, David Riggs, Shinoda Sataye, and the UCLA Library for their advice and assistance in procuring previously unpublished letters and manuscripts for this project.

1. Shinobu Matsuura, *Higan: Compassionate Vow, Selected Writings of Shinobu Matsuura* (Berkeley: Matsuura Family, 1986), 63.

2. Both Buddhist and Shinto priests were classified in the A, or the most potentially subversive, "known dangerous," category of the FBI's so-called ABC list of aliens targeted for arrest in case of war. See Peter Irons, *Justice at War* (New York: Oxford University Press, 1983), 22.

3. For more on the demographics of the early immigrants, see Paul R. Speckard, *Japanese Americans: The Formation and Transformation of an Ethnic Group* (New York: Prentice Hall, 1996), 33.

4. The Buddhist Churches of America (BCA) Archives include letters regarding, and receipts for donations collected by, Japanese-American temples for the Japanese Imperial Army. See BCA Archives, O-Series: Correspondence.

5. Alan Hynd, *Betrayal from the East: The Inside Story of Japanese Spies in America* (New York: Robert M. McBride, 1943), 21, 130–6.

6. For more on FBI classification lists, see Bob Kumamoto, "The Search for Spies: American Counterintelligence and the Japanese American Community, 1931–1942," *Amerasia Journal* 6, no. 2 (1979), 58.

7. On deputation of Buddhist ministers' wives and others to serve as officiants, see Deborah Malone, "Documents from BCA Archives Vital for Redress Case," *Wheel of Dharma* (no issue no.), May 1997, 3.

8. BCA Archives, Box 1B, Letters, "Register for Civilian Defense," 12 Dec. 1941.

9. BCA Archives, Box 1B, Letters, "Evacuation of Aliens," 9 Feb. 1942.

10. On the conversion to Christianity, see Stephan Fujita and David O'Brien, *The Japanese American Experience* (Bloomington: Indiana University Press, 1991), 79.

11. Ibid., 64.

12. BCA Archives, Box 1B, Letters, "Serve in Silence," 5 Mar. 1942.

13. Young Buddhist Association of Butte Camp (ed.), *Gathas and Services* (Rivers, Arizona: Young Buddhist Association, 1944), 9–10.

14. Quoted in Davis, "Mountains of Compassion," 49.

15. Bunyū Fujimura, *Though I Be Crushed* (Los Angeles: The Nembutsu Press, 1995), 95. One exception to this nonsectarian Buddhism occurred in the Manzanar Camp, where the main Buddhist Church was led by a Jōdo Shin priest, but a separate Nichiren Buddhist Church also existed.

16. On collecting wood in the desert to make Buddhist altars, see Akemi Kimumura, *Through Harsh Winters: The Life of a Japanese Immigrant Woman* (Novato, California: Chandler and Sharp, 1981), 53. Susan Davis has also noted: "And in response to the lack of Buddhist articles in some camps, people carved Buddha statues and shrines from scrap wood and sagebrush found in the desert. At the North Dakota camp, Arthur Yamabe, who later became a minister, once carved a figure of a baby Buddha from a carrot." See Davis, "Mountains of Compassion," 49.

17. This necrology is held at Zenshūji Temple in Los Angeles.

18. On the "Americanization" program and religion, see Gary Okihiro, "Religion and Resistance in America's Concentration Camps," *Phylon* 45, no. 3 (1981), 220–33.

19. For more on Bishop Imamura, see Tomoe Moriya, *Yemyo Imamura: Pioneer American Buddhist* (Honolulu: Buddhist Study Center, 2000).

20. For a glimpse into the government's thinking on Americanization, see *Investigation of Un-American Propaganda Activities in the United States* (Washington, D.C.: Subcommittee of the Special Committee on Un-American Activities, House of Representatives, 78th Congress, 1st Session on H. Res. 282, 1943), 21.

21. By July 1944, in addition to the new name, a new constitution was adopted by the BCA in a Salt Lake City conference that adopted English as the organization's primary language. See Tanaka, "The Lotus that Bloomed behind Barbed Wire," 41.

22. For the Buddhist basketball team and YBA activities, see articles from the Rohwer Camp's Buddhist newsletter, "Basketball Title at Hand" and "YBA Girls Help Red Cross," *Sangha News* 1, no. 2 (13 Feb. 1944), 1; and "Bussei Hostesses Serve Local USO," *Sangha News* 1, no. 4 (12 Mar. 1944), 1.

23. David Yoo, "Enlightened Identities: Buddhism and Japanese Americans of California, 1924–1941," *Western Historical Quarterly 27* (1996), 281. For more on the ethnic and religious identities of second-generation Japanese-American Buddhists and Christians, see David Yoo, *Growing Up Nisei: Race, Generation, and Culture among Japanese Americans of California, 1924–49* (Urbana: University of Illinois Press, 2000), 38–67.

24. Kihara Jōin, *Arashi no nakade: kaisen to spai yōgi* (Kyōto: Nagata bunshōdo, 1985).

13 The Translating Temple
Diasporic Buddhism in Florida

Douglas M. Padgett

INTRODUCTION

Wat Mongkolratanaram, a Buddhist temple in Florida, stands a few miles to the east of Tampa's most famous immigrant quarter, Ybor City, on the south bank of the Palm River, an estuary of Tampa Bay. The Palm River neighborhood, an old area formerly populated by farmers and fishers, is in transition, exhibiting evident contradictions as it changes. Capacious pieces of real estate encircle small cinder-block and wood-frame houses, while new gated communities, apartment complexes, and strip malls bloom nearby. The temple itself sits back from the road, across the street from the steepled sanctuary of a Baptist church. On the temple grounds, the former homes of suburban families are now ornamented with Buddhist images and posters of Thailand. And through the temple gates, the world seems to turn again. Most, though not all, of the temple signs are in Thai. Live oaks and cabbage palms grow thick along the river, reaching out to surround the two low, Florida-style ranch houses close to the road. A dirt parking lot and an old basketball goal, where saffron-robed monks have been known to play pick-up ball, cover the territory between the houses. Behind a small worship hall, a Thai spirit house—an altar to the gods and spirits of the place—is hung with incense and offerings. On the riverbank, just a few yards away, looms a yellow aluminum communal hall, as big as a high-school gymnasium.

The arrival and growth of Asian religions in North America over the last century or more has added new twists to the knotty definitional riddles of religion, ethnicity, and adaptation. To speak of Buddhists and Buddhist places in the West is not simple. Observers are being asked to understand a constellation of Buddhist groups—of various national, linguistic, class, and sectarian orientations—that seem hardly to acknowledge one another.[1] Scholars are challenged to examine not only the intricacies of belief and behavior, in unfamiliar and unstable contexts, but to make definitive pronouncements.

In attempting to make sense of Buddhism in the West, we have drawn on a number of different models, sometimes taking our cues from the study of older immigrant religious communities.[2] Thus, we refer to *ethnic Buddhists, culture Buddhists, convert Buddhists,* or, perhaps most clumsily, as I propose here, *transnational diasporic Buddhists.*[3] Such typologies are necessary, useful, and reasonably accurate. And they serve a purpose—to guide us through the maze of identity that is the modern world. Certainly, here, Wat Mongkolratanaram has a readily apparent ethnic and cultural identity and function, a Thai face and a Buddhist form. Still, as we enter into particular temples, specific local universes, we can see how far astray our guides can lead us if we are not careful. The very readiness of that Thai Buddhist identity has the potential to divert our attention from the temple community's labile and often confrontational unfolding. Wat Mongkolratanaram is not simply an ethnic Thai temple, because there is nothing simple about ethnicity and, unfortunately, there is much that confuses.[4]

While always a forum for distinctly Thai cultural practices, the temple's character is in motion, unresolved. The everyday lives of its members are complex and contradictory, linked with a global network of Buddhists, friends, family members, and business partners. Thus, their sense of themselves (collectively and individually) as Thai or Buddhist or American is similarly formed in ongoing relationships with local and national governments, communities and corporations, and a diversity of imagined places—homes and new homes. In coming to terms with how people change, disintegrate, and re-form themselves, all aspects of religion—practice, belief, and, perhaps most especially, modes of religious self-identity—are implicated. The task, in the mercurial world of immigrant religion, is, as Hannerz writes, to "grasp the flux" of practice, belief, and identity as they pass by.[5]

This essay is not an attempt to completely unravel any of these knots. It is both too preliminary and too brief. On the contrary, I hope that, by discussing a few of the particularities of life at this one immigrant Buddhist place, I may further complicate our understanding of the relationship between identity and Buddhism in the West. In so doing, I also hope to place the study of Buddhism in America in conversation with other, complementary fields. Reflection on the field of Asian-American studies and on the work being conducted under the rubric of *diaspora studies* has much to offer those concerned with Buddhism in America.

WORKING THROUGH DIASPORIC RELIGION

The recent conceptual focus on globalization and transnational diasporas presents one way by which we might reconfigure our understanding of immigrant and Asian-American Buddhist institutions and their members.[6] The idea of diaspora itself is unsettled. But if, as Ulf Hannerz suggests, "to deal with globalization is to deal with diversity under increasing interconnectedness," dealing with the notion of diaspora can be no different.[7] The *diasporic* here concerns a diverse, interconnected people who are linked, by affiliation or birth, with a commonly acknowledged place of reference; who share cultural and social traits, with a conscious sense of mutual attachment; and who act on that sense of attachment through transnational organization.[8] Another writer has noted that the notion of diasporic phenomena has been closely coupled with the now decades-old "wider attack on a bounded and static understanding of culture and society."[9] Thus, Nancy Abelmann and John Lie write, of Koreans in Los Angeles, that the notion of a "transnational Korean diaspora alerts us to the enormous diversity of people essentialized into the easy receptacle of 'Koreans' or 'Korean Americans.'"[10] Diaspora studies, then, is yet another, and, for the moment at least, reasonably effective way to talk about communication, change, and diversity.

Diasporic religion, finally, can refer to a broad collection of phenomena: the religion of immigrants, of converts, and of the descendants of immigrants, long after their departure. It can also include a broad collection of conditions. Paula Richman reminds us of the "necessity of viewing religious performances through the analytic categories of class, gender, race and colonialism."[11] Even in more mundane events and activities, scholars should be cognizant of the necessity to see Buddhism in the West as a part of a complicated political and social whole. Steven Vertovec, who also researches South Asian diasporic religion, has written critically of the ways in which scholars have used the language of diaspora to discuss South Asian religions in Great Britain and Europe. Following his lead, I would like to explore two aspects of the transnational diasporic Buddhist experience: first, as such an experience leads to the production of particular cultural forms and practices, and, second, in the sense that it leads to the production of a particular type of consciousness or sense of identity.[12]

In the first sense, the *diasporic* refers to the changes that people undergo after migration—the diversification of the community; new organizational structures and local social life; practices that evolve, fade away, or take on new meanings. In the second sense, the diasporic Buddhist experience can be seen as a particular mode of "cultural production." Through discussions of globalization and localization, we see the condition of diaspora as a particular way in which social and cultural phenomena emerge through transnational processes, through acts of governments and economies, as well as through human ingenuity.[13] The focus here is on the *flows* of globalization, the accelerating transference of goods, ideas, persons, and practices across cultural and political boundaries. The experience of migration as transnational diaspora, then, situates a migrant people such as the Tampa Thai in a "historically deep and geographically wide displacement" in relation to other Thais, other Buddhists, and other diasporas.[14]

Second, diasporic Buddhism, like globalized culture generally, exhibits a *dual or paradoxical nature,* a consciousness highlighted by tensions—between past and future, between home of origin and home of settlement, between experiences of discrimination and opportunity.[15] In religious contexts, Tweed has referred to such a specific sort of diasporic religious consciousness among the Cuban exiles of Miami as *transtemporal* and *translocal*—living, in a sense, in two places and two times at once. Diasporic religion unites the devotee not only vertically with the transcendent or superhuman, but horizontally with others on this plane in a common "imagined moral community." In this way diasporic religion serves to generate "feelings of nostalgia, hopefulness, and commonality," and, I would add, despair, loss, and desire.[16] Diasporic religion also then acts to maintain an emotional, conceptual, or even, in the case of the Tampa temple, organizational bridge across national boundaries. And these exact same sentiments, of course, also act to build new barriers, setting the new diasporic community apart from other local or migrant peoples.

Ultimately these two aspects of the diasporic are mutually generating, reproducing one another in the crucible of new locality and old, new time and past. The diasporic religious consciousness and the diasporic practices it both elicits and depends upon are conjoined and inextricable. The process by which they are formed is dialogic and competitive and it is difficult to speak of the one without identifying the other. A number of factors all combine to produce both a new sense of what it means to be Buddhist and new ways of being Buddhist: the innovation and creativity of the people of the temple; the relative sparseness of their religious options as compared to what was available in Thailand; the exigencies of contemporary American life; and the conservative pulls of the Sangha and the founder. After reviewing the temple's background and constituency, I will discuss some of these points, considering basic issues of organization as well as the manner in which the practices of the temple give rise to a contested but evident diasporic consciousness. Finally, I will discuss some alternative ways we might see this temple as a locus not only of communal cohesion but also of a transcultural "free space."[17]

THE TEMPLE

Wat Mongkolratanaram is the creation of a varied population dispersed throughout a broadly immigrant city. In some ways, the temple's development conforms to a familiar stereotype of Asian religions in the United States: it is an immigrant institution, formed in the cast-off housing of a small semirural neighborhood on the social and geographic edges of a large, coastal, urban area. The Thai community in Tampa, as in many other areas of the country, began to form in the 1970s around Thai women arriving in the United States as the wives of American Air Force servicemen.[18] Thai immigration through most of the 1970s was overwhelmingly female. The ratio of women to men did not equalize until the late 1980s.[19] MacDill Air Force Base was the primary draw for settlement to Tampa, but many families chose to remain after retirement and many Thai relatives joined them. Over the years, family members—siblings and parents, beneficiaries of the post-1965 immigration reforms—began to join their sisters and daughters. Tampa was also a significant point of secondary migration, drawing established Thai professionals—doctors, businessmen, shopkeepers, and nurses—from within the United States. By 1990, at least five thousand Thai resided in Florida. A plurality of them were spread throughout the Tampa Bay area, with most of the rest living around the air force bases of South Florida and Fort Walton Beach.

In the late 1970s, the young community came to the attention of a high-ranking member of the Thai Sangha, the eponymous Venerable Mongkolthepmolin. Venerable Mongkolthepmolin has been active in American Thai communities for nearly two decades, having been one of the founding members of Wat Thai of L.A., the oldest American Thai temple, and having for a time resided in a temple of his own (also called Wat Mongkolratanaram) in Berkeley, California. Over the last two decades, he has made several trips every year to the United States from Bangkok to tour the temples he has helped to found (five at last count). He was and is an incessant fund-raiser.

According to current temple members, the Tampa and Fort Walton Beach Thai communities (and especially the local women) were starved for religious life and in particular for the contact with monks necessary for the most efficacious sorts of merit-making, giving to the Sangha. Members of the community organized a variety of money-raising ceremonial and social events at which Venerable Mongkolthepmolin or other monks would preside. Through these visits, the Florida community raised enough money to prove their readiness to support their own monks. By 1981, two monks were in residence in Tampa. A year later, the community purchased the ranch house on the Palm River. In early 1983, the community began the construction of the worship hall, or *bot*, and renovations on the house, which was to serve as a dormitory and office for the local Sangha. A second house on adjoining property was later bought for use as a school and cultural center. Construction plans have been developed for a controversial, expensive dormitory for monks and guests, though the project was put on hold until a number of organizational and financial issues could be worked out.

Despite its undeniable relationship to Thai people, language, and culture, the temple's representation extends beyond the Tampa Thai. For major festivals and rites, Wat Mongkolratanaram draws devotees from either end of Florida and from four other states. Not all the Tampa Thai patronize Wat Mongkolratanaram, and only about three-quarters of the regular Sunday attendees are Thai immigrants or descendants of Thai immigrants.[20] The temple's constituency also encompasses friends, family, and interested seekers. Non-Thai husbands; children of mixed families; family members whose primary religious affiliations are not Buddhist, but Catholic or Baptist; students; and local Lao, Cambodian, and Vietnamese immigrants all participate in regular social and devotional events. Many participants come for worship; others come for fellowship or in support of their loved ones. A very few others (among them the occasional student) are members of what Paul Numrich has referred to as a parallel congregation—upper-middle-class, Western-educated seekers interested primarily in mediation.[21]

The temple's divisions are manifested in temple activities and in the meanings the temple has for individual members. Ultimately, relations of class and gender prove to be most fractious—particularly between Thai male professionals and the more diverse group of temple founders, many of whom are or were air force wives. Ostensibly over money, these disputes, like those between the monks and laity generally, are actually over control of the temple. Finally, though men—monks and laity—hold temple offices and play active roles in other ways, the temple is, significantly, still, the everyday, ongoing creation of its women.

DIASPORIC ORGANIZATION

In one sense, the diasporic temple is simply the temple whose organization and governance span cultural and national boundaries. As the product of an extensive multistate and transnational organizational effort, Wat Mongkolratanaram is the subject of constant negotiation between the various elements of the diverse membership and the founder. Overseas monks and other members come together not simply as an "imagined community" but as a concatenation of such. Notions of how and what the temple is are constant topics of conversation. Discussions range from quotidian issues of planning a meal or a party to the urgent necessity of having a dream interpreted to long-term debates over building and finance.

At the Tampa temple, there is no self-sustaining Sangha and no hope of one. Everyday authority rests with the monks. *Bhikkhus* are hand-picked in Thailand for positions at all of Venerable Mongkolthepmolin's temples. After arriving at the temple, they tend to remain only a year or two, though some remain for five years or more. Many disrobe and stay in the United States, picking up work as they can. A few return to Thailand. Monastic consultation with Venerable Mongkolthepmolin—usually via phone, although the monks now use e-mail regularly—is close. Final authority in most affairs concerning the temple is, in fact, supposed to remain with the abbot, despite his absence. He visits a couple of times every year, usually around important calendrical celebrations, and may be seen standing to the side of the patio, smoking or talking.

With his visits, the abbot re-imposes his will with his presence. After months of absence, through meetings with his monks and rituals with his temple members, he rededicates the temple to standards of conduct and governance as he sees them from Bangkok. His vision is conservative, especially with regard to monastic rules and lay/monastic interaction. The monks are not supposed to, for instance, drive, touch money (though checks are okay), or have contact with any women, even non-Buddhist or non-Thai women. The original board of directors of monks and laypeople was disbanded after an internal disagreement, and monks retain virtually all decision-making authority, with a senior resident monk representing the head monk. Governance seems, as in Thailand, quite centralized.[22]

Issues of control seem never to be resolved. Some members, both monks and laity, consistently look to Venerable Mongkolthepmolin for leadership. Others look elsewhere—to the local Sangha or certain lay members. While monks live at the temple and have the authority of their positions, it is the laypeople who understand the United States, who are familiar with its economic and political terrain. The laypeople's strategies for negotiating that terrain are occasionally ignored, with near-disastrous results. The original bylaws of the temple set forth a design for leadership with power evenly split between laypeople and monks, but that plan has dissolved. Now all formal authority resides with the monks, the abbot, and the senior monk present. But laypeople, particularly women, must still perform many of the administrative tasks. Arguments between factions of laypeople and the monks are not easily resolved, and often result in arbitrary and autocratic uses of power by members of the board or by influential laypeople. Thus, friction can be high in the everyday life of the temple.[23] Though Venerable Mongkolthepmolin is not universally welcomed, his visits do serve to alleviate that stress.

Martin Baumann has used the terms *recoupment* and *reorientation* to refer to the manner in which diasporic religious groups, such as that of Wat Mongkolratanaram, are reined in ritually and organizationally, brought back from innovation or ambiguity in practice and belief. Baumann notes that through reorientation the "recollection of the supposedly unadulterated and original teaching of one's tradition aims to win a better and more exact understanding of the teaching and intends to restrain certain interpretations and conduct."[24] At the Tampa temple, reorientation is a continual internal process, as well as one that spans continents. I use this word in a different context than Baumann does, but the tension between innovation and reorientation is key to the development of a local form of Buddhist practice.[25] This tension involves an ongoing arbitration with the political realities of the temple's organization and allegiances, as well as with America and with the Thailand of diasporic memory and imagination.

DEVOTIONAL LIFE AND DIASPORIC CONSCIOUSNESS

Despite their diversity and internal divisions, the temple community does possess a sense of itself as separate from those around it, even as it builds a local presence for itself. On the temple grounds, the mix of Thai and local cultural elements is obvious. The Tampa papers are read along with the Thai-language dailies of Bangkok and Los Angeles; Thai food is eaten along with steaks and barbecue from down the road; Thai music is played on the PA system while monks watch the local news. As in Thailand, symbols of the nation are prominent—whether they are pictures of the royal family or a celebration of the king's birthday. But American holidays are celebrated as well.

Life at Wat Mongkolratanaram is self-consciously creative—not dependent upon mimicking Thai-ness. A decade ago, Arjun Appadurai wrote an essay in which he referred to the work of imagination as the hallmark of our global age—cultivated by mass media, exercised by the high speeds of high tech, and powered by the unprecedented swift and violent migrations of the twentieth century.[26] The elements that recall and evoke *Thai*, the things that signify *Thai* in the Thai diaspora, need not have actual referents in Thai practices. The limits of the congregants' creative resources are not formed merely by what seems *Thai*. Being a member of Wat Mongkolratanaram, being involved in this transnational production of consciousness and cultural practice, seems thus to require, above all, imagination.

The ritual and devotional life of Wat Mongkolratanaram does not differ significantly from that of many other Theravāda temples; however, as Penny Van Esterik notes of the Lao Buddhists of Toronto, meanings in diaspora may be radically changed. Ritual practice at Wat Mongkolratanaram turns on merit-making and merit transference—in particular, of course, in giving to the Sangha. As in Thailand, giving sustains the temple while providing the laity with their most efficacious path to salvation. But in America, rites of giving and the tying of the *khwan*, the pouring of water, and other ways of transferring merit have all become metaphors for loss and reverence, or simply remembrance, among the Thai immigrants of the congregation. But for Thai immigrants and the non-Thai alike they solidify, in tangible ways, the internal ties among members of the diverse community.[27]

The ways to give at Wat Mongkolratanaram are nearly endless: by fixing the monks' daily noon meal; by privately offering necessary goods or money on the occasion of a birthday, anniversary, or other special event; as recompense for a special service; or by publicly offering alms on a temple holy day. Monks do not make alms rounds every day, but receive their daily meals at the temple, where temple women prepare the food. Consequently, the offering of food in the traditional manner is only performed on holy days and is made more significant by its rarity. In private giving, a devotee or a family will come before a monk or group of monks and offer a basket of goods, usually domestic necessities—such as toothpaste, aspirin, cotton swabs (in surprisingly large quantities), a meal, or robes. Merit gained from giving is then transferred to the gods, ghosts, parents, or other loved ones. In larger public ceremonies, the range of offerings varies: flowers and envelopes filled with donations, uncooked and cooked food, bottled water, more cotton swabs, and other domestic necessities of modern life. During the Tampa alms-giving, the monks walk slowly around the middle of a U-shaped bank of tables, receiving the goods from the faithful, who crowd in on all sides, standing on tiptoe to reach in and lay down their gifts, bowing carefully. Such large public rites of giving take the place, in an emotionally charged way, of the Buddhist paradigm of daily alms-giving.

Of course, it must be acknowledged that alms-giving in the manner of Wat Mongkolratanaram is not wholly an American innovation. In some

Thai temples, urban and rural, the monks eat much as they do in America, from meals prepared at or brought to the temple.[28] But in the American context, as Penny Van Esterik has noted of the Lao in Toronto, the relationship between *giver* and *given* and *recipient* has changed. On festival days, cooked food, especially cooked sticky rice, is always given in excess, and so the food must be redistributed. Following the chanting and the merit-making, the monks are fed and then a communal meal is shared.

Like these meals, temple social and fund-raising events are important ways in which the people of Wat Mongkolratanaram acknowledge their bonds with each other and with those places from which they have come. The events are also useful products of the community's resourcefulness, raising a large part of the temple's operating budget. Weekly markets, parties in the fellowship hall, dances, and Thai movies are all part of temple life. The social hall is the site of half a dozen parties a year, at the major Thai and Buddhist holidays and at other times. Never do so many central Florida Thai or temple members come together at one place and time as at one of the temple's parties. Large dinners can be cheaply purchased. Beer is served in the hall, though it is not allowed in other buildings. The parties always have two bands—one traditional Thai group and another band consisting of local youths who play Thai or American rock and pop. People dance to both. There are beauty contests for various age groups and Thai fashion shows displaying traditional costumes. At one year's Loi Kratong party, a Vietnamese girl won the beauty contest wearing a Thai dress.

On festival days and on every Sunday, the community comes together in economic unity. The Sunday Market, a weekly bazaar of Thai food and goods, is a simple money-raising venture that has also appealed to everyone as a social event. It has been phenomenally successful. Vendors set up stalls or tables in the driveway and courtyard. The laity socialize as they buy and eat homegrown Thai fruits and vegetables or imported Thai clothing and jewelry. In return for the space, a donation to the temple is handed to the monks at the end of the day. The Sunday Market sustains and reaffirms a model of the temple as both a social and a religious center.[29] Most people come for lunch and some come to worship, but few simply shop, buy, and leave. They stay to visit, to read newspapers, to speak with friends, to eat, and, of course, to make merit. The community gathers for multiple purposes, achieved through multiple activities.

THE SENSE WORLD

The Tampa temple places a high value on the remembrance and re-creation of Thai practices or the invention of practices imagined to be Thai. Much of the collective social and ritual life of the temple aims at traversing the gulf between one metaphorical and religious place and another. Whether members were born in Thailand or not, Thailand is a central (but not exclusive) reference for temple activities. The land itself has, especially for the Thai immigrants and their families, qualities that are both indispensable and irretrievable.[30] At any particular time, at the one place of the temple, through public and private acts of remembrance and reverence, parties, or simple daily acts, the people of the temple reach for other shores and other times. Thai activities, local lives, and Buddhist practices are not intertwined in temple functions. Dance and language are not opposed by meditation and chant, but inextricably related, with each affirming the same ineffable qualities.

In attempting to recapture some aspects of their imagined Thailand, the temple members have constructed a *sense world* that allows them a creative entry into their ancestral culture and binds them communally. Robert Orsi has observed that the creation of a sense world is a means of structuring a "basic point of orientation" for a community.[31] Wat Mongkolratanaram is the forum in which that sense world and that point of orientation are created for the temple members of central Florida.[32] The sense world integrates the members of the community into their own or their parents' own or an adopted culture, place, and time. While the re-integration is only temporary, as is ritual itself, the activities of the temple serve to maintain the integrity of the community and to strengthen the temple's position at its center. As such, it is truly unifying. But the meanings of these imaginative acts may also diverge across the membership. Thai and Thai-Americans certainly attempt to recapture some of the meaningful sacrality of an abandoned or adopted homeland through festival and rite. But for those who are not Thai, these same acts and elements lend both everyday and special events an air of authenticity not reproducible in other contexts. A local Buddhism of smell, sight, and sound is generated. Thus the sense world of Wat Mongkolratanaram defines Buddhism as American or Thai, giving it weight and relevance.

This sense world is made in daily ritual, in large public ceremony, and, perhaps most significantly, in seemingly secular activities—parties, buying and selling, food, and simple conversation. The sounds, sights, tastes, and smells conjure the diasporic consciousness. The scent of incense, the act of chanting, the sounds of music and of monks' voices and of the Thai language all compel in the devotees a sense of themselves as participating in an event bounded and separate from what goes on outside the fence on Palm River Road. Food, in particular, seems uniquely positioned as a central social element in the life of Wat Mongkolratanaram. As in Thailand, food is the primary offering for making merit, but food is also the pivot and focus of the Tampa community, the magnet drawing people into the closest possible contact both with each other and with the members of the Sangha. While food is not what brings people to the temple, it is at the center of their personal ingatherings and conversations.

THE TRANSLATING TEMPLE

The Buddhism practiced at Wat Mongkolratanaram is by no means identical to that of Thailand.[33] And ultimately, it does not attempt to replicate Thai Buddhism.[34] Even when partially transmitted, the institutions and social structures of "home" eventually disintegrate or take on radically altered forms under the pressures of American society. What remains, or is created to fill the social spaces left behind, serves as the moral and spiritual space in which values and ideals are negotiated.[35] This temple is no different. While it is certainly a locus of group cohesion and identity formation (if for multiple identities) the diasporic temple is also, as Rey Chow writes of Asian-American literature, the space in which lived experiences are translated between different peoples.[36] Translation itself is also an act of creation—of transforming old into new: new texts, new expressions, new performances. But what emerges from the fertile matrix of the temple is ultimately representative of neither old nor new, Thai nor American. It manifests the work of the translators themselves.

As control of Wat Mongkolratanaram has ebbed and flowed—between Bangkok and Tampa, between housewife and doctor, between new monk and old layperson—the shapes of the temple and of its activities and aspirations have been molded anew. Life at Wat Mongkolratanaram, and at other explicitly diasporic sites, is lived through its tensions—multiple games of tug-of-war, pulling at the community and its practice. Thus, as Chow also writes, "the very instability of cultural identity" has become a "combative critical base."[37] The temple is, as Lisa Lowe observes of immigrant institutions generally, a place profoundly transforming and transformed by the practices of migration—what she calls "immigrant acts."[38] In this same vein, Lowe has written of the manner in which "local particularisms implicate and are implicated in global movements and forces."[39] The temple people, in their conflict, are operating between multiple sets of complementary and conflicting social imperatives—of Thailand and America, of class, of lay and monk, of doctor and housewife, of Christian and Buddhist. What emerges from the people of Wat Mongkolratanaram is ultimately representative not of an easily comprehended Thai ethnicity, but of the cultural work of the people in this place, referring always to other places. It is an ethnic temple, certainly, if *ethnicity* is understood in Chow's sense of the word as "a social experience which . . . is constituted by a continual, often conflictual working-out of its grounds."[40] In our sense, then, it is also *diasporic*—a place at which the process of reorientation is the only constant.

CONCLUSION

The cover story of a recent issue of the American magazine *National Geographic* explores manifestations of globalization and culture. Inside, a photograph shows a dozen or so Thai Buddhist monks, in orange robes, eating breakfast.[41] Based upon the reactions of some of my colleagues and friends, the picture seems noteworthy because these monks do not live in Thailand. These are the monks of Wat Thai of L.A., the most prominent Thai Buddhist institution in the United States. Furthermore, they are eating scrambled eggs with ketchup and bacon at a Denny's restaurant. Such moments of seeming cultural incongruity, whether personally experienced or captured on film, are of course not unusual in the United States. They never have been. But when this picture appeared, I was asked about it a number of times. Apparently, such scenes remain—to Buddhists, non-Buddhists, and those who observe Buddhism—something of a conundrum.

There are probably good reasons to be puzzled. An episode of this kind, however innocuous, defies our notion of an immutable Asian Buddhism. Often, such a scene might simply cause an observer to marvel at its incongruities. At other times, perhaps on the grounds that authenticity has been compromised, these incongruities provoke challenges: how, after all, can *real* Buddhist monks eat at Denny's? In this case, we might answer: always before noon and usually with a fork.[42] At other times, more lucidly, we might respond that we can no longer afford to presume to know how real monks eat. Whether we refer to *ethnic, convert, culture,* or *diasporic* Buddhists, in the meeting of Buddhisms in the West we should, as a first order of business, be most concerned with understanding the *lived* religion of our subjects and our fellow Buddhists.

There are many such places, many such scenes. Wat Mongkolratanaram is one. At the edge of old Tampa is a Buddhist temple. One rarely hears lengthy conversations in English there. A lunar religious schedule is cut and patched together to fit a five-day work week. A dog named Pepsi understands no English. Monks smoke Winstons and surf the web. Thai women do all the cooking, but a devout European-American man whose son both plays football and takes ordination is depended upon for maintenance. Buddhists of whatever national origin are fixtures of American and European societies now. They should hardly be considered mysterious, even in Denny's. They make homes for themselves in the West (where some have lived all of their lives) and, in the process, remake themselves and their places. It is quite simply the job of observers of Buddhism and of Asian religions in the West to understand how they do that.

NOTES

1. See Paul David Numrich, "How the Swans Came to Lake Michigan: The Social Organization of Buddhist Chicago," *Journal for the Scientific Study of Religion* 39, no. 2 (2000), 189–203.

2. See George E. Pozzetta (ed.), *The Immigrant Religious Experience* (New York: Garland, 1991). This is volume nineteen in a twenty-one-volume series on immigration and ethnicity in the United States.

3. To review the conversation on typologies of Buddhism in North America, see Charles S. Prebish, "Two Buddhisms Reconsidered," *Buddhist Studies Review* 10, no. 2 (1993), 187–206; Jan Nattier, "Buddhism Comes to Main Street," *Wilson Quarterly* 21, no. 2 (Spring 1997), 72–80; Martin Baumann, "Buddhism in the West: Phases, Orders and the Creation of an Integrative Buddhism," *Internationales Asienforum* 27 (1996), 3–4; Martin Baumann, "The Transplantation of Buddhism to Germany: Processive Modes and Strategies of Adaptation," *Method and Theory in the Study of Religion* 6, no. 1 (1994), 35–61; Martin Baumann, "Methodological Smugness and the Transplantation of Symbolic Systems: A Reply to Eva K. Neumaier-Dargyay," *Method and Theory in the Study of Religion* 8, no. 4 (1996), 367–72; Eva K. Neumaier-Dargyay, "Is Buddhism Like a Tomato? Thoughts about the Transplantation of Buddhism to Germany: A Response to Martin Baumann," *Method and Theory in the Study of Religion* 7, no. 2 (1995), 185–94; and Numrich, "How the Swans Came to Lake Michigan."

4. Terms of identity always are tricky, and few more so than *ethnicity* (with the exception of *culture*, perhaps). The primary problem, as scholars of religion will attest, is one of *reification*—that is, the taking of a concept (about a thing) for the thing itself. For a highly theoretical discussion of problems and solutions related to ethnicity, see Thomas Hylland Eriksen, "The Cultural Contexts of Ethnic Differences," *Man* 26, no. 1 (1991), 127–44. For general discussions on the pitfalls of categorizations involving ethnicity, see Gerd Baumann and Thijl Sunier, "Introduction: De-essentializing Ethnicity," in *Post-Migration Ethnicity: Cohesion, Commitments, Comparison*, edited by Gerd Baumann and Thijl Sunier (Amsterdam: Hey Spinhuis, 1995), 1–9. See also Virginia Tilley, "The Terms of the Debate: Untangling Language about Ethnicity and Ethnic Movements," in *Ethnic and Racial Studies* 20, no. 3 (July 1997), 497–522. Terms of identity can be dangerous as well. Often, finally, such terms may be ways in which observers of Buddhism and Buddhists differentiate, as one scholar of identity in America has written, "between people who fit uneasily within the body of the Same"—here, the set of all Buddhists. In using terms of identity without careful qualification, we run the risk of ignoring the manner in which those identities are, in particular ways, both constituted and fragmented in relation with, at least, other Buddhists, other Asians, and

other religions, and, perhaps more importantly, as functions of a specific history. See John Hartigan, Jr., "Name Calling: Objectifying 'Poor Whites' and 'White Trash' in Detroit," in *White Trash: Race and Class in America*, edited by Matt Wray and Annalee Newitz (New York: Routledge, 1997), 53. Also see Sandhya Shukla, "New Immigrants, New Forms of Transnational Community: Post-1965 Indian Migrants," *Amerasia Journal* 25, no. 3 (1999/2000), 19–36.

5. Ulf Hannerz, *Cultural Complexity: Studies in the Social Organization of Meaning* (New York: Columbia University Press, 1992), 267. See also John D. Kelley, "Time and the Global: Against the Homogeneous, Empty Communities in Contemporary Social Theory," in *Globalization and Identity: Dialectics of Flow and Closure*, edited by Birgit Meyer and Peter Geschiere (Oxford: Blackwell, 1999), 239–72.

6. See Ulf Hannerz, "Epilogue: On Some Reports from a Free Space," in Meyer and Geschiere, *Globalization and Identity*, 326. Hannerz writes that the "recognition of global and transnational interconnectedness, in several disciplines . . . has had an emancipatory effect as scholars have allowed themselves to take a more conscious, critical view of the local and 'national' (state) frames within which they have had a habit of placing their research."

7. Ibid., 325.

8. See Thomas A. Tweed, *Our Lady of the Exile: Diasporic Religion at a Cuban Catholic Shrine in Miami* (New York: Oxford, 1997), 138–9. Diasporic populations act on that sense of attachment through broad diasporic financial, professional, social, and religious organizations and activities, all of which the American Thai possess. A great deal of debate remains over how the term *diaspora* should be used. See Martin Baumann, "Conceptualizing Diaspora: The Preservation of Religious Identity in Foreign Parts, Exemplified by Hindu Communities outside India," *Temenos* 31 (1995), 19–35, and "Shangri-La in Exile: Portraying Tibetan Diaspora Studies and Reconsidering Diasporas," *Diaspora* 6, no. 3 (1997), 377–404. See also Frank J. Korom, "South Asian Religions and Diaspora Studies," *Religious Studies Review* 26, no. 1 (January 2000), 21–8.

9. Adam McKeown, "Conceptualizing Chinese Diasporas, 1842 to 1949," *Journal of Asian Studies* 58, no. 2 (May 1999), 306–37.

10. Nancy Abelmann and John Lie, *Blue Dreams: Korean Americans and the Los Angeles Riots* (Cambridge: Harvard University Press, 1995), ix. See also chapter 3, "Diaspora Formation: Modernity and Mobility," 49–84.

11. Paula Richman, "A Diaspora Ramayana in Southall, Greater London," *Journal of the American Academy of Religion* 67, no. 1 (1999), 54.

12. Steven Vertovec, "Three Meanings of 'Diaspora' Exemplified among South Asian Religions," *Diaspora* 6, no. 3 (1997), 277–99. Vertovec actually discusses three ways in which *diaspora* is used, the first of which, diaspora as a social form (as dispersion from a homeland, exile, the process of dispersion, etc.), I will not discuss. Vertovec makes a similar analysis in "Conceiving and Researching Transnationalism," *Ethnic and Racial Studies* 22, no. 2 (March 1999), 447–62.

13. Vertovec, "Three Meanings of 'Diaspora,'" 289. Vertovec cites here in particular a work I will return to later, Arjun Appadurai's "Global Ethnoscapes: Notes and Queries for a Transnational Anthropology," in *Recapturing Anthropology: Working in the Present*, edited by R.G. Fox (Santa Fe, New Mexico: School of American Research, 1991), 191–210. For an influential introduction to the notion of diaspora, see James Clifford, "Diasporas," *Cultural Anthropology* 9, no. 3 (August 1994), 302–38.

14. Abelmann and Lie, *Blue Dreams*, 83.

15. Vertovec, "Three Meanings of 'Diaspora,'" 281. Frederic Jameson has also cited the primary effect of intensifying *binary relations*—nations, regions, and

groups. See Frederic Jameson, "Preface," in *The Cultures of Globalizations*, edited by Frederic Jameson and Masao Miyoshi (Durham, North Carolina: Duke University Press, 1998), xii.

16. Tweed, *Our Lady of the Exile*, 139.

17. One of the effects of transnational experience is a sense of localities as "free spaces" in which the meanings of events and practices become ever more protean. See Peter Geschiere, "Globalization and the Power of Indeterminate Meaning: Witchcraft and Spirit Cults in Africa and East Asia," in Meyer and Geschiere, *Globalization and Identity*, 211–37.

18. Nathan Katz, *Tampa Bay's Asian-Origin Religious Communities* (Tampa, Florida: National Conference of Christians and Jews, 1991), 63. My own research, using U.S. census data and the Immigration and Naturalization Statistical Yearbooks and Annual Reports for the late 1970s, 1980s, and early 1990s, confirms this pattern of immigration. See also Jacqueline Desbarats, "Thai Migration to Los Angeles," *Geographical Review* 69, no. 3 (July 1979), 302–18. See also Paul David Numrich, *Americanization in Immigrant Theravada Buddhist Temples*, (Ph.D. diss., Northwestern University, 1992), 92.

19. Desbarats, "Thai Migration to Los Angeles," 310.

20. This figure is drawn from my own observations over the past seven years and a written, though not scientific, survey conducted in 1994.

21. Paul David Numrich, *Old Wisdom in the New World: Americanization in Two Immigrant Theravada Buddhist Temples* (Knoxville: University of Tennessee Press, 1996), 54–6.

22. According to several authorities, one of the hallmarks of recent decades of reform within the Sangha and Thai religion generally has been increasingly centralized control, especially in urban areas. With centralized authority, lay institutions (such as lay committees) have lost influence, especially in urban *wat*. Richard O'Connor cites the example of the choosing of a new abbot, once a joint monk/lay enterprise, as the decision of a centralized Sangha made with practical deference to the lay community. Richard Allen O'Connor's Ph.D. dissertation, "Urbanism and Religion: Community, Hierarchy and Sanctity in Urban, Thai Buddhist Temples" (Cornell University, 1978), is in large measure concerned with the effects of such reforms on the temple community. See especially pages 271–9. See also Richard Allen O'Connor, "Interpreting Thai Religious Change: Temples, Sangha Reform and Social Change," *Journal of Southeast Asian Studies* 24, no. 2 (1993), 330–9.

23. While people at Wat Mongkolratanaram were understandably reluctant to talk about this matter, and many perhaps knew little about it, this situation was precipitated, according to two informants, in the late 1980s or early 1990s by a struggle between two lay factions over the control of the board. The details are unknown. Venerable Mongkolthepmolin, as chairman of the board of directors, intervened and the bylaws were abrogated or changed. According to some, he happily simplified temple life by eliminating laypeople and their quarrelsome ways from the board. Others maintain that he usurped the power of the board. In any case, only monks now sit on the board of directors, while three lay treasurers continue to control purchases of over five hundred dollars. The senior monk, the monk charged with administrative duties, is simply, as in Thai Buddhism generally, the monk who has been ordained the longest. A secondary factor in seniority is the grade of Pāli exam passed. The senior monk maintains a great deal of control over temple decision-making on a day-to-day basis, but no major decisions are undertaken without earnest and lengthy discussions with a variety of laypeople and the temple president. Many of those most involved with the temple advocate some change. For most, though, this usually benign, somewhat attentive autocracy, so

like those of modern Thailand with its highly centralized religious bureaucracy, works fine.

24. Baumann, "The Transplantation of Buddhism to Germany," 45.

25. Ibid., 44–5.

26. Appadurai, "Global Ethnoscapes."

27. Penny Van Esterik, "Ritual and the Performance of Buddhist Identity among Lao Buddhists in North America," in *American Buddhism: Methods and Findings in Recent Scholarship*, edited by Duncan Ryūken Williams and Christopher S. Queen (Richmond, U.K.: Curzon Press, 1999), 57–68.

28. Sulamith Heins Potter, *Family Life in a Northern Thai Village: A Study in the Structural Significance of Women* (Berkeley: University of California Press, 1977), 92. Even in relatively rural northern Thailand, according to Potter, the "custom of bringing the food to the temple rather than having the monk [*sic*] and novices go out to beg each morning, is a variant in Buddhist practice." The temple in her study was organized into committees that offered prepared food.

29. See O'Connor, "Urbanism and Religion," 228.

30. For a discussion of immigrants and the loss of "sacred geography," see Penny Van Esterik, *Taking Refuge: Lao Buddhists in North America* (Tempe, Arizona: Program for Southeast Asian Studies, Arizona State University, 1992), 132–3.

31. Robert Orsi, *The Madonna of 115th Street: Faith and Community in Italian Harlem, 1880–1950* (New Haven: Yale University Press, 1985), 172–3.

32. Ibid., 173.

33. As Thailand has developed and urbanized, there are, of course, similarities in innovation.

34. What Penny Van Esterik writes of the Lao refugees of Toronto, though their circumstances differ considerably, could also be said of the Thai in Tampa: "Buddhist rituals conducted in new lands cannot reconstitute the religious institutions of Laos, nor do they yet represent a North American hybrid form of religious practice." See Van Esterik, *Taking Refuge*, 133.

35. See Nancy J. Smith-Hefner, *Khmer American: Identity and Moral Education in a Diasporic Community* (Berkeley: University of California Press, 1999).

36. Rey Chow, *Writing Diaspora: Tactics of Intervention in Contemporary Cultural Studies* (Bloomington: Indiana University Press, 1993), 141–2.

37. Ibid., 140.

38. Lisa Lowe, "Work, Immigration, Gender: Asian 'American' Women," in *Immigrant Acts: On Asian American Cultural Politics*, edited by Lisa Lowe (Durham, North Carolina: Duke University Press, 1996), 173. Lowe notes as well that such an institution is also a "regulating site"—a place in which immigrants are shaped into "citizens," or "disciplined" into foreigners and alien subjects.

39. Lisa Lowe, "Immigration Citizenship, Racialization: Asian American Critique," in Lowe, *Immigrant Acts*, 34.

40. Chow, *Writing Diaspora*, 143.

41. Erla Zwingle, "A World Together," *National Geographic* 196, no. 2 (August 1999), 17. Photograph by Joe McNally.

42. Similar questions are frequently thrown about by academics and casual observers alike: how can *real* Buddhist monks—or *real* Buddhists—eat bacon and eggs; smoke; worship spirits; never meditate; perform astrology; support capitalist enterprises; or advocate war? Real Buddhists can and do.

14   Repackaging Zen for the West
David L. McMahan

INTRODUCTION

The embracing of Zen in certain sectors of North American and European societies occurs through an unlikely confluence of histories, ideas, and practices from two starkly different cultural complexes. Observing the routine of a traditional Japanese Zen monastery, especially a Rinzai one, with its strict uniformity, inflexible routine, almost military sense of order and discipline, and the willingness of the monks to subject themselves to blows from a stick, one would think it unlikely that such a form of religious practice would achieve any foothold in Western countries characterized by democratic ideals, reverence for individual freedom, and suspicion of authority and hierarchy. It would seem even less probable that the Americans initially most attracted to Zen would be iconoclastic poets, artists, and refugees from Christianity and Judaism who felt stifled by the strictures of those faiths.

If Zen is paradoxical at its core, with its elegant juxtapositions of candor and conundrum, of spontaneity and discipline, that paradox is only magnified in its presence in the West. Part of this magnification is due to popular culture's odd embrace of the term *Zen*—I will not say the *tradition* of Zen, of which most Westerners remain largely ignorant. A brief perusal of Amazon.com's books containing the word *Zen* reveals titles like *Zen in the Art of Golf* and *Zen Sex*. One also finds the word tossed around casually in more studied culture—a *New York Times* review of an art retrospective by Yoko Ono declares it "very Zen." [1] Whether noun or adjective, *Zen* has, it seems, come to denote a kind of free-floating state of being, both relaxed and disciplined, engaged yet detached. While such a way of understanding the term may have something vaguely to do with the actual practice of this tradition, the use of the term *Zen* to designate a state of mind completely dissociated from the long and complex historical tradition of Chan and Zen in Asia is a unique development of the modern West and the missionary-minded Japanese. Scholars may be tempted to simply dismiss such vagaries, but the manner in which *Zen* has become a household word in many Western countries is worth considering, for this nebulous and disembodied *Zen* to some extent results from the ways in which Zen has been presented to the West by both Asians and Westerners.

I will not in this short essay attempt to clear up the considerable confusion as to what Zen "really is"; my purpose, instead, is to examine a few stretches on the path whereby *Zen* came to be thought of in the West as a free-floating state of being, rather than as a concrete, historical tradition shaped by years of reflection and practice. I shall also mention a few important issues facing Zen in the West and a few individuals and groups who are addressing these issues in ways characteristic of Western Zen.

WESTERN ZEN IN THE MAKING

An important part of Zen's adaptation in the West, and especially in America, has involved an attempt by some of its interpreters, both Asian and Western, to decontextualize it and de-emphasize elements thought to be "too Asian" or "too traditional," or that simply don't work in the West. The re-envisioning of various forms of Buddhism in Western terms—more specifically, in terms influenced by the Western Enlightenment tradition—is an integral part of the story of Buddhism in the West. Europeans encountering Buddhism in the late nineteenth century read many ideas in ancient Buddhist scriptures and philosophical texts that appeared to resonate with the modern, scientific attitude. They saw in textual Buddhism an experimental attitude, a de-emphasis on faith and belief, and a sophisticated philosophy—exquisitely rational, yet soaring beyond ordinary reason. Buddhism as practiced in various Asian countries, however, seemed permeated by things quite counter to the modern, rationalistic attitude—practices and beliefs that appeared superstitious, magical, and ritualistic. A number of early Western admirers and modernizing Asians tried to extract the empirically minded philosophical and practical ingredients of Buddhism from what they considered its idolatrous and superstitious elements.[2] This "demythologized" Buddhism—more accurately, "remythologized" in terms of the dominant European and American attitudes and beliefs—is what most Westerners still know of Buddhism.

The original efforts to bring Zen into a dynamic relationship with modernity and the West were undertaken not by Westerners, but by Japanese Zen Buddhists who understood the ethos of European and American intellectual and religious culture. The adaptation of Zen to the West, therefore, is not simply a Western invention. In the post-Meiji and postwar periods, many Japanese adherents of Zen advocated the modernization and revitalization of the tradition. Some saw the West, especially America, as an arena where such revitalization could flower. Shaku Sōen, the first Zen missionary to America and the first to publish a book on Zen in English, set the stage for how Zen would often be interpreted in the West. Along with Paul Carus, an important promoter of Buddhism in its early life in America, Sōen presented Buddhism in a very modern light, claiming that the Buddha's teachings "are in exact agreement with the doctrines of modern science."[3] Sōen attempted to align Buddhism with the scientific spirit of the times, giving it an intellectual credibility and prestige that were eroding in Christianity among the intellectual elite. Appealing to the ethos of modernity, he displayed an empirical bent and an agnostic indifference about miracles. He presented karma and *Dharmakāya* in terms of both "natural law" and "moral law," concepts that many late-nineteenth-century American and European intellectuals found irresistible. Moreover, he claimed, this moral law leads to enlightenment, in which all great men—including Jesus, George Washington, and Abraham Lincoln—participate to some extent, albeit not to the extent of the Buddha.[4] These themes—an embrace of science combined with the promise of something beyond it, and a universal reality in which different religions and individuals participate, but which Buddhism embodies most perfectly—characterized the tone set for the interpretation of Zen and Buddhism in the West, a tone still present in many writings.

As much as the presentation of Zen by its early emissaries to the West was colored by rationalism and modern science, the *decline* of the rational and the crisis of relativism in the twentieth century may have had a more profound impact on the reception and re-envisioning of Zen in the West. Zen Buddhists came to America at a time when the Enlightenment's combination of rationalism and empiricism was still prominent, even while historical, cultural, and intellectual forces were shaking the foundations of the Enlightenment discourse, and faith in reason waned. Cultural relativism compromised confidence that any one religious form could lay claim to universal truth as diverse cultures became increasingly available to each other. Truths once considered universal now seemed more evidently a product of particular historical, cultural, and geographical factors. William Barrett, in a 1956 introduction to D. T. Suzuki's *Zen Buddhism*, suggested that Zen is a possible answer to the problem of the "meaninglessness" that he considered essential to the experience of modern humanity, as both science and Western metaphysics had failed to provide certainty or meaning in the modern world.[5] Existentialism perhaps best expressed the disaffection with the idea that there is a universal truth; the belief that reason can resolve all problems; and the forms of traditional Judeo-Christian religious institutions. It is no accident that a number of existentialist philosophers were attracted to Zen. Zen appealed to intellectuals and artists insofar as it seemed to acknowledge the limitations of rationality and displayed a suspicion of all words, institutions, authorities, and conventions. While Zen was as iconoclastic as Sartre, it still offered a pure experience of unmediated truth obtainable through one's own effort and insight—a feature that appealed to the individualist tenor of Western, and especially American, society.

Western interpretations of Zen have often remained within the framework of notions of freedom and individualism so deeply rooted in modern Western philosophical and political discourse. The iconoclasm and individualism of Zen appealed to the modern Enlightenment and Protestant mentality, even while those experimenting with Zen attempted to reject and surpass this mentality. Passages in Zen literature that ridicule imitation, empty ritual, rote learning of scripture, and emphasis on the magical and mysterious became the hallmarks of the tradition in Zen literature written for the West.

Another element still important in the interpretation of Zen in the West is the impulse toward universalism and the attempt to find a common spiritual ground for the world religions and their conflicting truth claims. The crisis of cultural relativism in the twentieth century led thinkers such as Aldous Huxley, Carl Jung, and Swami Vivekananda to search for similarities in the world's religions, such that all could be conceived of as leading to or participating in the same ultimate reality. This has been an underlying theme in much of the West's involvement with Asian religions, and is evident in some of the hybrid forms of Zen emerging in the West, such as Christian and Jewish groups that incorporate Zen meditation with their practice.

Perhaps the most important figure in the "repackaging" of Zen for the West is D.T. Suzuki. It is no coincidence that he was the translator for Shaku Sōen's visit to the World Parliament of Religions. More than anyone, Suzuki furthered a process begun by Sōen of attempting to extrapolate the essence of Zen from Zen Buddhism as a religion. Zen, as Suzuki presented it, is the pure experience of unmediated encounter with reality, and the spontaneous living in harmony with that reality. It is not, therefore, a property of Buddhism. The essence of Zen, for Suzuki, was mysticism, which he believed was common to other religious traditions as well. At the heart of the widely variegated forms of historical religions, he claimed, was a common, universal mystical experience—an experience that transcends all cultural trappings.[6] While espousing the universality of mysticism, however, he also claimed that Zen was the purest and most direct form of mysticism, calling it "the ultimate fact of religion."[7] This answered to the need for universalism while removing the meditative aspects of Zen from the rest of the complex tradition of rituals, priesthoods, and hierarchies that held little attraction for many Westerners.

Recent historical and critical study of Zen suggests that Suzuki's presentation of the tradition to the West is, in fact, rather selective and limited.[8] But Zen was proffered to the West not as a historical tradition but as an ahistorical essence of spirituality. What is important to us here is that this image, created during a crisis of intellectual and religious life in Europe and America, was crucial to Zen's enthusiastic reception among those disenchanted with what they saw as the failed promises of Western culture. Such disenchantment entailed a rather idealized vision of Zen, as well as other Asian spiritual paths—an inverse image of the perceived spiritual cul-de-sac of the West. As much as the embracing of Zen was a response to disillusionment with Western cultural, intellectual, and religious forms, Zen was often interpreted in terms of those forms, or in some cases their inverse. Instead of faith, Zen relied on direct experience; rather than relying on culturally limited forms of discourse, it transcended words and made contact with the ineffable; in place of salvation through another being, it offered enlightenment through one's own efforts. Historians of religion can, of course, be suspicious of this picture of Zen because it is tailored too much to Western needs and interpreted too much in Western categories. It would nevertheless be unrealistic to expect otherwise in its short history in the Western hemisphere. Yet the repackaging of Zen in the West has been no more radical and no less inevitable than the cultural transformations Buddhism underwent upon entering China, Tibet, or Japan. This complex process of cultural adaptation will no doubt proceed through continuing reassessment, re-envisioning, and negotiation between novelty and tradition.

WESTERN ZEN: SOME CURRENT ISSUES

Ethnicity and Practice

The overwhelming majority of non-Asian Westerners who practice Zen are white, middle-class, and relatively well educated.[9] Practitioners of Zen meditation in Asia have generally been monastics, and few laypeople take up zazen in earnest. Non-Asian Zen practitioners in the West, however, tend to be interested almost exclusively in meditation, though very few become monastics. This issue is inseparable from the social class of these converts. In Asia, monastics not only have respect and prestige, they have the financial support of the community. In the West, no such support system exists. It takes money and time to go on retreats and to buy books, zafus, and other accoutrements associated with Zen practice. Being of the middle or upper class—that is, having money and leisure time—becomes the surrogate for such support in the West.[10]

These middle- and upper-class Buddhists are unique—even anomalous—in the Buddhist world. Western Zen Buddhists have little connection with the social, liturgical, and ritual aspects of Zen prominent in East Asia. Despite the fact that Zen is the "meditation school," it would surprise Western Zen practitioners to know that most Zen temples in Japan have little to do with meditation. Rather, they function largely as social centers and places for the performance of ancestral death rites. Most Zen temples in the West serve similar functions for those of Japanese ancestry. In contrast to these temples, a small number of monasteries and Zen *centers* offer meditation training, programs, and *sesshins*. In North America, these centers make up a small percentage of the Zen institutions, and the overwhelming majority of those who take advantage of their services are non-Asian Americans.[11]

Therefore, a rather marked separation exists between Asians and non-Asians affiliated with Zen institutions in the West. The former tend to associate with Zen temples as a way to maintain cultural identity. The latter are interested in meditation and de-emphasize distinctively Japanese, Chinese, Korean, or Vietnamese cultural elements as inessential, particularistic, and perhaps even contrary to what they understand as the essence of Zen—the cultivation of the mind through meditation and mindful living. This does not mean that Westerners lack support, training, and guidance from Asian teachers. Asian Zen teachers are the source and continuing support of Western Zen. But the now-substantial number of non-Asian teachers that they have trained and to whom they have given Dharma transmission often head their own Zen centers. This could take Zen in the West in very different directions in future generations. It remains to be seen whether "ethnic Zen" and "Westernized Zen" will continue to follow separate courses or find closer relations in the future.

Social and Political Involvement

Buddhism has always been engaged in its various socio-political contexts, but in Europe and America this engagement tends to take a unique shape. *Engaged Buddhism* is a concept gaining a great deal of attention in a number of modern Buddhist contexts (not all Western), and may become a defining idea in the constitution of a modern, lay-oriented Buddhism in the West. It is an ecumenical approach, including certain practitioners from the Zen, Theravāda, Tibetan Vajrayāna, Jōdo Shinshū, and Sōka Gakkai traditions. *Engaged Buddhism* refers broadly to the application of Buddhism to matters of everyday life, including work, family, politics, and community. Some have refined the term further, designating *socially engaged Buddhism* as a more direct application of Buddhist principles and concepts to the social and political arenas.[12] An example of this application of traditional Buddhist concepts to modern issues is the use of the key concept of the interdependence of all things. In engaged Buddhism, this idea is augmented by contemporary biological and ecological models of the interrelationships between living things. The result implies a modern take on the bodhisattva vow: to save all sentient beings by engaging in environmental activism. This thinking also extends to include the interdependence brought about by the globalization of trade and the part that Western consumers inevitably play—even in the apparently insignificant choices of food, clothing, and other products—in the structural violence and suffering brought about when industry destroys natural resources or exploits labor in developing countries.[13] Another example of the adaptation of classical concepts to contemporary social and political issues is understanding the first precept of Buddhism—*do not kill*—as applying broadly to institutions and governments that perpetrate war and contribute to the killing of endangered species.[14]

It might be tempting to think that this kind of engagement is simply an ad hoc attempt to make Buddhism fit the socio-political concerns of the largely liberal convert community, and it does have connections to 1960s activism and the American spirit of reform-minded Protestantism. The origins of this movement, however, lie in Asia and in worldwide struggles during the late twentieth century with colonialism, war, and social injustice. The Vietnamese Zen monk Thich Nhat Hanh, who coined the term *engaged Buddhism*, is perhaps the most visible figure in the movement. In the 1950s, he and other Vietnamese Buddhists promoted the incorporation of Buddhism in everyday life through mindfulness in activity. During the Vietnam war, this developed into a more overtly social and political movement emphasizing nonviolence, social justice, and freedom from oppression. Influenced by Mohandas K. Gandhi, these Buddhists opposed the war through nonviolent protest, involving demonstrations, strikes, songs, fasting, and non-cooperation with government. Today Nhat Hanh promotes socially engaged Buddhism in a wide variety of formats, including his many publications and a number of communities and organizations in the West. He interprets the bodhisattva ideal and the Mahāyāna concept of interdependence as mandates for action in the world, while maintaining the importance of meditation for cultivating peace and harmony in the individual.[15]

Many Western practitioners of Zen have taken up engaged Buddhism with vigor, and organizations with this orientation have proliferated in the recent decades. The Buddhist Peace Fellowship, which includes in its membership such notable Zen Buddhists as Robert Aitken and Gary Snyder, has actively promoted peace and justice issues. Especially noteworthy is its Buddhist Alliance for Social Engagement (BASE). Modeled on other faith-based volunteer corps movements, such as the Catholic Worker Movement and the Jesuit Volunteer Corps, BASE sends volunteers into the field to mediate conflicts, cook for homeless shelters, care for the dying, and engage in a host of other social service activities.[16] Bernard Glassman Rōshi established the Zen Peacemaker Order, an organization with a distinctively activist agenda. In Yonkers, New York, Glassman has set up drug-abuse treatment clinics, cooperative housing for the poor, AIDS hospices, a bakery, and a construction company that provides training and employment for the homeless and destitute.[17] Other activist Zen teachers have set up prison ministries and care-giving facilities for the dying, like the Zen Hospice Project. Virtually all of these people see social engagement and service not as an alternative to meditation and mindfulness, but as an extension of it. They interpret social service and political action as part of the Buddhist path, taking the peace that can be cultivated in meditation into a wider arena than just the personal.

These projects are obviously innovations in Zen, but they are not just Western adaptations. They are responses by an increasingly global Sangha to suffering not only at the level of the individual, but also at the systemic level. They are another aspect of the contemporary Buddhist reply to the unique problems brought about by modernity: globalization, the dominance of technology, environmental devastation, and large-scale military conflict. Engaged Buddhism is especially important to the lay orientation of the convert community, which sees engagement with life—family, social service, work, political activity—as part of practice. In contrast to this, the monastic model often sets the two in opposition. Engaged Buddhism also tempers the individualistic and personalistic tone set by some early missionaries and interpreters of Zen in the West. The extent to which social engagement will be a formative force in Zen and other forms of Buddhism during the twenty-first century is impossible to determine; but the rapid growth and widespread appeal of engaged Buddhism suggest that it could become an important and enduring development.

Rethinking of Authority and the Roles of Women

In Zen and other Mahāyāna literature, statements abound to the effect that all things are *equal, the same,* or *one* in Buddha nature. Indeed this nullification of distinction at the highest level of truth is part of the appeal of Zen in the West, in part because many have become sensitized to the problems of social inequality and hierarchy. Zen in practice, however, has always maintained strict, formal hierarchies among senior and junior monks, among men and women, and between masters and disciples. The transfer of such a system of authority to the largely lay convert community in the West—with its ideals of equality and democracy, its suspicion of authority, and its valorization of rebellion (the very things that first attracted many to Zen)—was bound to encounter turmoil. Perhaps the most important challenge that Zen communities in the West have faced in this regard involves two intertwined issues: authority and the roles of women. Because of limited space, we can only give a few examples that illustrate the directions Zen communities are taking regarding authority and women's roles.

The first involves the system of leadership at the San Francisco Zen Center (SFZC), one of the earliest centers used primarily by non-Asian American Buddhists. After the sudden flourishing of Zen in America in the 1960s, during the 1980s, scandals involving teachers' abuse of power and sexual relationships with students rocked a number of Zen centers, including SFZC. In the aftermath, the center attempted to democratize the leadership and insure that no one would have too much power. When Richard Baker Rōshi resigned after admitting to an affair with a married student, his Dharma-heir, Reb Anderson, was hired for a four-year term, and a system of electing, rather than appointing, board members was instituted.[18] Another innovation came in the 1990s, with an experiment in shared leadership between Zoketsu Norman Fischer and Zenkai Blanche Hartman, a grandmother and one of Shunryu Suzuki Rōshi's students. The changes were made to discourage a concentration of power and to shift to what Fischer calls a "student-centered," rather than "teacher-centered," organization of the zendō.[19] Such innovations would be highly unlikely in a Japanese temple or monastery.

The incident reveals the tensions that can arise when a system that is traditionally authoritarian, patriarchal, and monastic is taken up by a largely lay population in a more democratic environment. The role of the teacher, the degree of power he or she should hold, and whether it should be taken for granted that the teacher is a moral exemplar are live questions in Zen and other Buddhist traditions in the West. While different communities have responded with different answers, most have been cautioned by such incidents of abuse of power. While the tradition of the teacher as a guide is still strong in Western Zen, many students are reluctant to practice within a system of fixed hierarchy and unquestioned authority.

One striking aspect of Zen in the West is the increasing number and prominence of women and of women teachers. In contrast to Zen in Japan and Korea, where the role of women has been minimal, female converts in the West have emerged as some of the most visible Zen teachers and as some of the boldest innovators. While no one approach characterizes all female teachers, some have been at the forefront of experimenting with less hierarchical Sangha organization, gentler approaches to discipline, and innovation in styles of practice. The large subject of women teachers in Western Buddhism is, fortunately, treated in depth elsewhere.[20] Here I simply mention one teacher worth noting, not because she is typical, but because of the particular way in which she is anomalous.

Toni Packer represents the most striking example of a Western Zen that has virtually ceased to be Zen. Packer was Philip Kapleau Rōshi's successor at the Rochester Zen Center. While Kapleau was an innovator himself, in the *zendō* he nevertheless kept largely to traditional protocol, including bowing, rapid chanting, use of bells, and the *kyōsaku*—the encouragement stick. After becoming disillusioned with traditional forms and hierarchy, Packer left and formed her own Sangha. She now runs the Springwater Center for Meditative Inquiry and Retreats, which holds meditation workshops and retreats influenced by Zen but with no overt affiliation and few of the tradition's standard formalities. She dismisses the value of transmitting a lineage and insuring the transition of teachings from one generation to the next.[21] Instead, she insists on the importance of being present in the moment, openly investigating the network of conditioned thoughts, and allowing the mind to move beyond that network. These themes are, of course, important in traditional Zen; but Packer sees the rest—chanting, bells, bowing, and, most important, the traditional relationship between master and disciple—as inessential and even deleterious to the possibility of awakening.[22]

Toni Packer and her center are not typical of Zen in the West. While nearly all Western Zen centers and teachers have adapted their forms in significant ways to meet the character of their Western practitioners, few have gone as far as Packer in abandoning elements of traditional Zen. Most

Zen centers follow some degree of traditional protocol. They maintain the importance of the teacher, though not in the sense of an absolute authority; they hold to the significance of Dharma transmission and lineage; and they observe some of the rituals and use many of the material implements of traditional Zen. In dismissing most of these elements, Packer admits that she is no longer really practicing Buddhism, while still emphasizing the importance of "meditative inquiry." In this sense, Packer is "post-Zen."

Why, then, mention her in a discussion of Zen in the West? Because Packer's example is instructive in understanding the character of convert Zen insofar as it embodies the extreme, and yet in some ways the logical, conclusion of an important theme in American Zen that can be traced back to Suzuki: the idea that Zen is more an inner process or experience than a historical tradition or institution. Packer, in distancing herself from Zen as the latter, has said that she understands the word *Zen* as "descriptive of a mind that understands itself clearly and wholly from instant to instant" and that it "suggests a way of seeing and responding freely, without the limitations of the self." [23] And it is this idea of Zen—as a condition of mind separable from historical tradition and East Asian cultural forms—that has been one of the prime movers in the development of the unique character of Zen in the West and its adaptation in convert communities.

NOTES

1. Michael Kimmelman, "Yoko Ono: Painter, Sculptor, Musician, Muse," *The New York Times*, 27 Oct. 2000, E35.

2. Martin J. Verhoeven, "Americanizing the Buddha: Paul Carus and the Transformation of Asian Thought," in *The Faces of Buddhism in America*, edited by Charles S. Prebish and Kenneth K. Tanaka (Berkeley: University of California Press, 1998), 207–27.

3. Shaku Sōen's name was first romanized as *Soyen Shaku*, and some of his publications are cited in that form. See Soyen Shaku, "Reply to a Christian Critic (1896)," in *Asian Religions in America: A Documentary History*, edited by Thomas A. Tweed and Stephen Prothero (New York: Oxford University Press, 1999), 139.

4. Ibid., 137–40. See also Soyen Shaku, *Zen for Americans*, translated by D.T. Suzuki (LaSalle, Illinois: Open Court, 1992; original publication, 1906). It is notable, in considering the continuing influence of this general view, that Barnes and Noble Books re-released *Zen for Americans* in 1989, 1993, and 2000.

5. William Barrett, "Zen for the West," introduction to D.T. Suzuki, *Zen Buddhism* (New York: Anchor, 1956).

6. D.T. Suzuki, *Mysticism, Christian and Buddhist* (London: G. Allen and Unwin, 1979).

7. D.T. Suzuki, *Essays in Zen Buddhism* (London: Rider, 1949–53), 270–2.

8. For a critique of Suzuki, see Bernard Faure, *Chan Insights and Oversights: An Epistemological Critique of the Chan Tradition* (Princeton: Princeton University Press, 1993), 53–74.

9. This applies to all meditative traditions of Buddhism in the West. For statistical information on these communities in North America, see James William Coleman, "The New Buddhism: Some Empirical Findings," in *American Buddhism: Methods and Findings in Recent Scholarship,* edited by Duncan Ryūken Williams and Christopher S. Queen (Richmond, U.K.: Curzon Press, 1999), 91–9.

10. Jan Nattier, "Who Is a Buddhist? Charting the Landscape of Buddhist America," in Prebish and Tanaka, *The Faces of Buddhism in America,* 183–95.

11. For further treatment of Zen temples in the United States, see Senryō Asai and Duncan Ryūken Williams, "Japanese American Zen Temples: Cultural Identity and Economics," in Williams and Queen, *American Buddhism: Methods and Findings,* 20–35.

12. Donald Rothberg, "Responding to the Cries of the World: Socially Engaged Buddhism in North America," in Prebish and Tanaka, *The Faces of Buddhism in America,* 266–86.

13. For examples and discussions of this approach, see Stephanie Kaza, "To Save All Beings: Buddhist Environmental Activism," in *Engaged Buddhism in the West,* edited by Christopher S. Queen (Boston: Wisdom, 2000), 159–83; and Mary Evelyn Tucker and Duncan Ryūken Williams (eds.), *Buddhism and Ecology: The Interconnection of Dharma and Deeds* (Cambridge: Harvard University Center for the Study of World Religions Publications, 1997).

14. See Robert Aitken, *The Mind of a Clover: Essays in Zen Buddhist Ethics* (San Francisco: North Point Press, 1984), 19–20.

15. See Thich Nhat Hanh, *Interbeing: Fourteen Guidelines for Engaged Buddhism,* 3rd ed. (Berkeley: Parallax Press, 1998), and *Being Peace* (Berkeley: Parallax Press, 1987); also Patricia Hunt-Perry and Lyn Fine, "All Buddhism Is Engaged: Thich Nhat Hanh and the Order of Interbeing," in Queen, *Engaged Buddhism in the West,* 35–66.

16. See Judith Simmer-Brown, "Speaking Truth to Power: The Buddhist Peace Fellowship," in Queen, *Engaged Buddhism in the West,* 67–94.

17. See Christopher S. Queen, "Glassman Rōshi and the Peacemaker Order: Three Encounters," in Queen, *Engaged Buddhism in the West,* 95–127; Bernard Glassman and Rick Fields, *Instructions to the Cook: A Zen Master's Lessons in Living a Life that Matters* (New York: Bell Tower, 1996); and Bernard Glassman, *Bearing Witness: A Zen Master's Lessons in Making Peace* (New York: Bell Tower, 1998).

18. Rick Fields, *How the Swans Came to the Lake: A Narrative History of Buddhism in America,* 3rd revised and updated ed. (Boston: Shambala, 1992), 362–4.

19. Helen Tworkov, *Zen in America: Five Teachers and the Search for an American Buddhism* (New York: Kodansha America, 1994), 245–6. For a more detailed account of the incident and its aftermath, see Tworkov, 190–252.

20. See Sandy Boucher, *Turning the Wheel: American Women Creating the New Buddhism,* expanded and updated ed. (Boston: Beacon Press, 1993); Lenore Friedman, *Meetings with Remarkable Women: Buddhist Teachers in America* (Boston: Shambhala, 1987); Ellison Banks Findly (ed.), *Women's Buddhism, Buddhism's Women: Tradition, Revision, Renewal* (Boston: Wisdom, 2000).

21. "On Transmission and Teaching," an interview with Toni Packer from the 1997 Buddhism in America Conference in Boston; http://www.servtech.com/public/spwtrctr/bostonQA.html [15 Dec. 2000].

22. These themes are developed in her books, *The Light of Discovery* (Rutland, Vermont: Charles E. Tuttle, 1995) and *The Work of This Moment* (Rutland, Vermont: Charles E. Tuttle, 1995).

23. Friedman, *Meetings with Remarkable Women,* 60. This is Friedman's paraphrase of an uncited quote.

INTRODUCTION

In the spring of 1993, a group of twenty-two Western Dharma teachers from ten different countries in Europe and North America gathered at Dharamsala in north India for a conference with the Dalai Lama. The purpose of the meeting was, in the words of convener Lama Surya Das, to "honestly discuss—in a frank and open forum—the issues and problems involved with transmitting the Buddhadharma from the East to Western lands today."[1] One of the main themes to emerge was "the undeniable importance of the spiritual teacher as a role model—an exemplary one, hopefully—and the ethical responsibilities connected with such a role."[2] The significance that the conference attached to the teacher/student relationship reflects a major feature of Buddhism in the West, where lay Buddhists are most likely to be practicing meditation. The popularity of meditation in the West means that the pedagogical model is a central organizing principle in the formation of Buddhist institutions, for, as Peter Harvey remarks, "any type of meditation" calls for guidance from a teacher.[3] Harvey goes on: meditation requires personal guidance, as it is a subtle skill that cannot be properly conveyed by standardized written teachings. The teacher gets to know his student, guides him or her through difficulties as they occur, and guards against the inappropriate use of the powerful means of self-change that meditation provides. In return, the student must apply himself well to the practice and be open to where it leads."[4]

This description captures vividly the personal qualities and accomplishments both teacher and student need to draw upon for a successful outcome, but it also evokes the potential psychological dangers for both parties. If the teacher or the student fails to measure up to these stringent requirements, the result may be more damaging than a mere sense of disappointment. For teachers to acquire students, they need credibility, which is demonstrated by their possession of certain credentials. A major source of credentials is rooted in the position that a teacher occupies within a spiritual lineage based on the principle of pupillary succession. Traditionally in Buddhism, the teacher (*guru*) claims his, or more rarely her, spiritual legitimacy as the representative of an unbroken lineage that can be traced back through a sequence of distinguished names to a saintly founder, or even to the Buddha himself. The teacher's person and conduct are thereby regarded as an embodiment of the moral and spiritual dimensions of Buddhist teachings (Dharma). It is this ideal that underlies the role of teacher as exemplar and shapes the asymmetrical charismatic relationship between a teacher and his students.

However, the exact nature of exemplary behavior in a teacher can undergo subtle variation, depending on one's choice of Buddhist tradition, lineage, cultural location, and historical period. There is a world of difference between what might be considered acceptable conduct by a follower of the *drubnyon* philosophy in historical Tibet, discussed below, compared, for example, to what is appropriate conduct for ascetic forest monks of the Theravāda tradition of South and Southeast Asia. In contemporary Britain and North America, Buddhists are most likely to be well-educated, white, middle-class folk of liberal persuasion who display permissive attitudes toward their teachers' eccentric behavior and minor indiscretions. But events have shown that tolerance breaks down when teachers make persistent use of the power they wield over their followers to obtain material goods and sexual favors. In this chapter, I will argue that scandals resulting from this kind of conduct by teachers are most likely to occur in organizations that are in transition between the pure forms of charismatic authority that brought them into being and more rational, corporate forms of organization. However, I also propose that despite the constraining effects of the shift to corporate organizational structures, relations between individual meditation teachers and their students continue to retain inherent, and potentially disruptive, charismatic qualities.

By the beginning of the 1990s, several scandals occurred among Buddhist groups in the West. Writing in 1988, the American *vipassanā* teacher Jack Kornfield warned, "Already upheavals over teacher behavior and abuse have occurred at dozens (if not the majority) of the major Buddhist and Hindu centers in America."[5] The reputations of teachers had been compromised and disciples psychologically damaged amid accusations of sexual misconduct, alcohol abuse, financial irregularities, and spiritual waywardness.[6]

The discussion will focus on narrative sketches of two Western Buddhist organizations that have faced such issues, the San Francisco Zen Center and

Shambhala International (previously known as Vajradhatu). These organizations were selected because I had the opportunity to investigate them and not because they represent the worst of what has occurred. Plenty of other examples from Britain and the United States could have been drawn upon. Jack Kornfield is a long-standing teacher and promoter of Buddhism in the West. His preparedness to face up to the scale of the problem, as he saw it twelve years ago, is a strong indicator of its pervasiveness, while subsequent and current reports imply that these difficulties have not evaporated.[7] The two examples are drawn from very different Buddhist traditions.

The San Francisco Zen Center was founded by Shunryu Suzuki Rōshi, a Japanese priest belonging to the Sōtō Zen lineage, who arrived in San Francisco in 1959 to serve as priest to the Japanese Sokoji Sōtō Zen Temple.[8] Suzuki Rōshi acquired students from beyond the Japanese-American community and eventually these students came to occupy a section of the temple that became known as the San Francisco Zen Center. In 1966, this group founded Tassajara, the first residential Zen center in the West. At Tassajara, practitioners could follow the traditions of a Japanese Sōtō monastery in a remote location. In 1969, the original urban San Francisco Zen Center moved to much larger premises, separate from the Japanese Sokoji Sōtō Zen Temple.

Vajradhatu was founded in 1973 in Boulder, Colorado, by an exiled Tibetan *lama* of the Kagyu lineage, Chögyam Trungpa Rinpoche (1939–87). In 1983, a major center was established in Halifax, Nova Scotia, where the movement's international headquarters are currently located.

Despite the differences between these two centers, in spiritual orientation, history, and location, several themes will arise that are common to them both, as well as to other groups not covered here.[9]

VAJRADHATU/SHAMBHALA

Chögyam Trungpa was raised and trained as a religious leader from the age of one, when he was acknowledged as a reincarnate *lama* (Tib. *tulku*) and enthroned as the 11th Trungpa Tulku, supreme *lama* of the Surmang group of monasteries in eastern Tibet. The Surmang monasteries are affiliated to the Karma Kagyupa lineage of Tibetan Buddhism (the Karmapas), and their founding is closely associated with a lineage of famous saints (Skt. *siddha*), including Tilopa, Naropa, Marpa, and Milarepa. Milarepa, a poet, was eulogized by the saintly and erratically behaved *lamas* of the fifteenth and sixteenth centuries (Tib. *drubnyon*). Stories and myths in the Tibetan oral and literary traditions evolved around the paradoxical notion of disruptive holiness, personified by spiritually insightful characters who nevertheless "perpetually engaged in one sort of perverse activity or another—drinking to excess, fornicating, thieving, defying authority, playing magical tricks. . . . " [10] These kinds of religious figures are not all placed in the distant past and examples survive into modern times, among them one of Chögyam Trungpa's teachers, Kenpo Gangshar. [11]

Chögyam Trungpa encouraged his disciples to follow the *drubnyon* philosophy, which traditionally combines exceptional insight and impressive magical power with a flamboyant disregard for conventional behavior. He translated the anarchic ideology of the *drubnyon* into English by use of the term *crazy wisdom,* and that phrase became the hallmark of his charismatic leadership of Vajradhatu. [12] Chögyam Trungpa's appeal to the crazy-wisdom tradition did not in any way detract from the characteristic role of the guru that lies at the heart of Vajrayāna Buddhist practices and that Chögyam Trungpa continued to endorse among his American followers. Practitioners of the higher Tantra believe that its doctrines and practices were taught by the Buddha's Tantric form, Vajradhara, and that it is necessary to see all *lamas,* and in particular one's personal *root lama* (Tib. *tsawe lama*), as the Buddha (Vajradhara). Though a practitioner may have other teachers, the personal *lama,* who is unlikely to be the one who initiated the student into Tantric practices, holds a special place in the student's heart and should inspire fierce loyalty and devotion.

Stephen Butterfield, a former member of Vajradhatu, followed the arduous and lengthy spiritual regime founded on devotion to Chögyam Trungpa as guru known as *ngöndro.* [13] He later wrote, "The single most important quality demanded of the Vajrayāna student is devotion to the guru. . . . The guru is the Buddha. . . . To regard the guru as an ordinary person is a perverted attitude. No matter what the guru does, you must accept it as a teaching." [14]

The large house that Chögyam Trungpa and his English wife occupied in an upper-class district of Boulder was known as the Kalapa Court. Disciples were admitted by invitation only. The residence was sumptuously appointed and organized to reflect a courtly hierarchy, with followers eager to serve as cleaners, attendants, guards, cooks, and so on. Here Chögyam Trungpa was surrounded by an inner circle whose members took a vow not to reveal or discuss his behavior, although it was openly acknowledged that he had sexual relations with a number of his female disciples. [15] The disciples were also unrestrained in their sexual liaisons, believing that sexual jealousy indicated a failure to grasp Chögyam Trungpa's teaching. The resulting tensions led to emotionally charged relationships between individual members of the Vajradhatu community, referred to as the Sangha, and added to the shared intensity of the collective experience.

In 1976, Chögyam Trungpa appointed Thomas Rich, one of his American disciples, as his Vajra Regent and gave him the Tibetan name of Ösel Tendzin. Upon Chögyam Trungpa's death in 1987, Ösel Tendzin inherited his master's spiritual and administrative authority, including the power to override all decisions made by Vajradhatu's board of directors. In December 1988, members of the board of directors revealed that Ösel Tendzin was HIV positive. Furthermore, he had known about his condition for four years and had continued to practice unprotected sex with male, and some female, members of the Sangha. One of the young men with whom Ösel Tendzin had unprotected sex later contracted AIDS and died, after passing the infection on to a girlfriend. It also came to light that members of the board had known about the regent's condition for some time, though they had taken no action.

A period of turmoil followed. Some members left; some called for Ösel Tendzin's resignation as president of Vajradhatu, but stopped short of suggesting he give up his spiritual inheritance; others wanted him stripped of all positions; and others stuck by him. Appeals were made from all sides to eminent Tibetan *lamas* in the Karma Kagyupa lineage and to Dilgo Khyentse, an important *lama* of the Nyingmapa order, who had acted as a teacher to Chögyam Trungpa in Tibet and presided over his cremation ceremony. In the early spring of 1990, Ösel Tendzin accepted Dilgo Khyentse's advice to go into retreat. He died the following August.

After Ösel Tendzin's death, Vajradhatu began a slow period of recovery. Under the urging of Dilgo Khyentse, the now-weakened board of directors agreed to the appointment of Chögyam Trungpa's son, known as the Sawang, as the new leader in 1990. One of his first actions was to disband the board of directors and appoint a new board, to be known as the Kalapa Council. His leadership style was cautious and consultative. A member of the Kalapa Council who had previously served on the old board of directors summarized the major change in organizational style in an interview in 1994: "People no longer depend on a charismatic teacher to be a reference point."

As part of an adaptive strategy intended to revitalize the membership, the new leadership built on groundwork laid by Chögyam Trungpa in the mid-1970s when he introduced "a parallel and supposedly 'secular' form of meditation practice" known as Shambhala Training.[16] The name is drawn from a Tibetan myth that features a kingdom of enlightened beings ruled by sagacious monarchs. The intention of the training is to create people capable of establishing a society in this world that mirrors the Shambhala kingdom. Participants can adhere to their own religious preferences and do not have to think of themselves as Buddhists. Nevertheless, the movement continues to support contemplative centers such as Gampo Abbey in Nova Scotia and conducts weddings and funerals. It promotes education and training programs aimed at business corporations as well as individuals. All of these activities are intended to contribute to Shambhala International's goal of creating what is described as an "enlightened society." For many members, however, their participation remains rooted in their long-standing personal practice based on Chögyam Trungpa's interpretation of Vajrayāna Buddhism.[17]

THE SAN FRANCISCO ZEN CENTER

Richard Baker was a Harvard graduate who studied with Suzuki Rōshi for ten years before being appointed his successor. In 1971, Suzuki Rōshi made Richard Baker abbot with authority over the San Francisco Zen Center's growing community of practitioners and associated centers. Baker possessed a great deal of energy, together with entrepreneurial drive and skills. Under his leadership, the Zen Center established Green Gulch Zen Farm, a practice community in Martin County; the Tassajara Bread Bakery, which became famous through the publication of cook books; and Greens Restaurant, which served up the vegetables grown on the farm. All of these ventures were extremely successful, but Baker seemed to find it hard to delegate authority to other senior practitioners within the expanding organization.

Baker exerted enormous spiritual and institutional authority within the Zen Center's cluster of establishments. The center itself did have a board of directors, consisting of all of the people who had received their ordination as priests from Suzuki Rōshi. But the board met sporadically, and decision-making fell into Baker's hands. However, in spring 1983 a meeting was convened and as a result Baker took an indefinite leave of absence. An item in the winter edition of the center's journal, *Windbell*, explained: "The precipitating event which brought this about was his [Baker's] relationship with a married resident woman student, and the upset which this caused for those principally involved, and for others in the community who knew about it."[18] The item stated that Baker, also married, had been "involved in similar situations before." All this was especially upsetting because Baker had previously told students that although Zen practice did not involve celibacy for priests or laypeople, a person's sexual conduct should not deceive or harm others, while a teacher's behavior should be exemplary. The respected teacher appeared to have broken his own precepts. Disputes remain over what did actually take place. Baker, who has since founded the Dharma Sangha in Europe and the United States, said in an interview published in 1994, "It is as hard to say what I have learned as it is to say what happened." [19]

Senior members recollect that initially Baker did not seem to accept or understand why so many people were so upset. "I think that made things worse," said one. There is some substance for this observation. In the 1994 interview, Baker said, "I had a kind of insecurity and self-importance, which I didn't see for a long time, that was a bad dynamic in the community. . . . I only saw my own motivations and I only trusted my motivations. The problem with that is, I didn't see how that affected others. So I didn't really have sympathy for people. Or empathy." [20]

The *Windbell* item written in the wake of the crisis explained why the event created a "catalyst" leading to an examination of "many fundamental questions concerning our understanding of Buddhism and Buddhist institutions." [21] Many members were completely immersed in the organization; their involvement represented the sum of their everyday lives. "For resident members, especially, whose work, spiritual practice, social life, and, in many cases, financial support are all provided within the institution of Zen Center, these questions, understandably, have become very important and disturbing." [22] It seems clear that the sexual scandal was a spark that ignited a great deal of discontent within the center.

Baker was perceived to have failed to treat other priests, who had also received ordination from Suzuki Rōshi, as equals and peers. Expansion took place at great speed, but little attention was paid to the overall organizational structures of control and decision-making. Baker grew removed from the ebb and flow of community life, and was protected from the complaints and suspicions that surrounded him by an inner circle of "courtiers." [23] The expansion of the center and its associated businesses meant that many students worked within the organization for long hours and low wages, while Baker spent more than two hundred thousand dollars in one year and drove an expensive BMW. There was an unsustainable gulf between the material world inhabited by the abbot and the lifestyles of many of the students, whose labors and financial contributions were sustaining him.

The Zen Center's recovery from its uncomfortable history has been slow but effective. One senior member who was at the center of events in 1983 estimated that it took five or six years for the worst effects to die down and that a "shadow" remains to this day. Nevertheless, the Zen Center is flourishing once more, with a renewal of interest in membership from those under thirty years of age, while there are more applications for residency at the various centers than there are places to fill. There are tentative plans for a new phase of expansion. Actions aimed at reform were initiated by a committee of volunteers soon after the revelations about Baker became known. Counselors were invited in to help individuals deal with their personal feelings. They also ran group sessions, where people were encouraged to think about how the situation had arisen and to develop a collective response toward change.[24]

Blanche Hartman is currently abbess at San Francisco Zen Center. A former student of Suzuki Rōshi, she received ordination as a priest from Baker in 1977. At the time of the crisis, she expressed the view, shared by many others, that experienced practitioners had unwittingly colluded with Baker by allowing him to become so far removed from criticism. She said, "I told him I thought it had been doing him no service to say nothing about my suspicions. It was a mistake to protect him from the consequences of his own consequential actions."[25] Looking back from her position seventeen years later, she told me, "The heat focused on sexual misconduct, but there were lots of other things that we had to face up to, such as the fact that Baker was only thirty-six years old when he became abbot. While in Japan it is unlikely that anyone would find him- or herself in charge of a training monastery until they were around fifty years old. In addition, Baker became isolated from his peers, who should have been encouraged and enabled to provide support and guidance."

During 1984 and 1985, after Baker's departure, careful efforts were made to remodel the organization of Zen Center and its satellites so that power and leadership became more diffuse.[26] This process began with the first edition of *Windbell* published after the crisis broke. Its pages featured photographs and biographies of a dozen individuals—five of them women—who were described as having "taken on many of the teaching and practice responsibilities at Zen Center."[27] These individuals included Harold (Reb) Anderson, who was appointed abbot of the Zen Center by the board of directors in 1986.

Most of the current structure of the Zen Center was conceived in the aftermath of the scandal. Appointees to the board of directors are elected by the Zen Center's membership. The board meets at least six times a year, and one of its most important functions is to appoint the center's president, abbots, and other officers. Nominations for the roles of president and abbot come from a Council of Elders. The Zen Center, which includes Tassajara,

Green Gulch Farm, and the city center, has two abbots. Tassajara and Green Gulch also have boards of directors and at least two abbots. Each location also runs Practice Committees, consisting of senior practitioners, who meet once a week. In 1992, an Ethics Committee and a subsequent Ethics Review Committee were established to produce a statement, "Ethical Principles and Procedures for Grievance and Reconciliation," that was adopted by the board of directors in 1996. The statement provided for a formal grievance procedure to be set in place.

Attempts have also been made to heal the breach with Baker, who accepted an invitation to attend Abbess Hartman's installation ceremony in 1996. In 1997, her co-abbot, Norman Fischer, organized a retreat with Baker and thirty-five students from the 1970s and early 1980s. Fischer later described the retreat as "not an effort to make peace or become friends again" but as part of a longer process "in the direction of forgiveness."[28] He concluded, "If a Buddhist sangha, a group of people dedicated to compassion and understanding, is not willing to try to heal its own wounds and deal with its difficult past with clarity, trying to prevent further harm in the future, does it make sense to hope that others with even more difficult conditions will be able to do their work?"

CONCLUSIONS

Many Buddhist movements in the West, including those described here, were founded during the second half of the twentieth century by charismatic leaders, assisted by an initially small group of devoted followers. It is typical that as a movement expands this group evolves into an inner circle, "a charismatic aristocracy,"[29] that stands between the growing membership and the leader. Increased numbers of students mean that over time certain members of the inner circle also become meditation teachers and candidates for succession to the leadership. The founder, as in the current examples, may nominate a successor who, in adopting the mantle of charismatic authority, becomes remote from the other members of the inner circle who were once his peers. This happened to Richard Baker and to Ösel Tendzin.

Once separated from former peers by being raised above them, a new leader can easily lose the sense of how his power depends on others, for as Weber describes it "the effectiveness of charisma lies in the faith of the ruled."[30] The high-handedness that Richard Baker and Ösel Tendzin displayed toward their critics suggests that they misunderstood the source of their own power. As Lindholm points out, "Charisma is, above all, *a relationship*, a mutual mingling of the inner selves of leader and follower."[31] But, according to his own admission, Baker became blinded to the needs of others by his "self-importance" and lack of "empathy." Ösel Tendzin became so deluded as to believe that he possessed supernatural protection that could prevent HIV from conquering "his body or the extended social body that trusted him."[32] It may be that as Buddhist organizations mature and move away from charismatic leadership toward rationalized and democratically structured models of authority—what Gordon Melton has described as *board leadership*—there will be fewer events like those that occurred at Zen Center and Vajradhatu during the 1980s. Melton has proposed that corporate structures, imposed for tax purposes within new religious movements in the United States, have "given new religious groups an additional stability that no single leader could bequeath."[33] The routinization of charisma into more bureaucratic forms of organization is also mirrored in the management of spiritual hierarchies. For example, resident students at the Zen Center must now have a practice advisor, a senior practitioner whom they have a hand in selecting. Moreover, students can change practice advisors if they wish to do so. Part of Vajradhatu's transformation into Shambhala has involved less focus on devotion to the guru in favor of training workshops, with input from a range of teachers and facilitators.

Nevertheless, in most Buddhist organizations the teacher/student relationship continues to be a central factor, and without careful management there is always a danger of manipulation of the student by the teacher, or that the teacher will succumb to sexually flirtatious students.[34] Devotion to the teacher is encouraged in Buddhism, but devotion readily entails idealization. Such idealization often leads a student to experience strong emotional attachment, with feelings that parallel those associated in Western culture with romantic love and its stress on self-abandonment and glorification of the other.[35]

Mark Epstein, a Buddhist and a psychiatrist, identifies these feelings as stemming from the nature of the spiritual exercise in which the practitioner is engaged:

> The pressure to cast off attachment to one's own ego generates a confusion between the compassion that is supposed to grow out of egolessness, the so-called bodhicitta, with its more primitive over-identification with the glorified other [the teacher]. Meditators with this misunderstanding are vulnerable to a kind of eroticized attachment to teachers, gurus or other intimates, towards whom they direct their desires to be released into "into abandon." More often than not they also remain

masochistically entwined with these figures to whom they are trying to surrender.[36]

Certain characteristics that are inherent in the conduct of the relationship, such as privacy and confidentiality, make it additionally prone to romantic and erotic overtones. For example, in order to discuss the progress of meditation practice with their (usually) male teacher, both male and female students are likely to refer to their closest personal relationships and to unearth their deepest feelings. This is a form of intimacy in which the student is exposed in a way that does not apply to the teacher. Such a confessional relationship is also at risk of falling prey to the processes of psychological transference familiar in psychotherapy, whereby the student may project his or her erotic desires onto the teacher.

People who join Buddhist groups are often seeking communitarian alternatives to what they perceive as egocentric, competitive values that prevail in capitalist market economies. However, competitiveness re-emerges within the group as people try to outdo one another in achieving reputations for spiritual attainment or in currying favor with those whose reputations are already established. Butler describes how senior students at the Zen Center "strove to outdo each other for approval of their insight."[37] She quotes a senior monk as saying that when it came to confronting Baker about his behavior, he felt alone, because "you don't feel like the person you are competing with will support you."[38] New students, too, are unlikely to be critical. Their familiar, commonsense understandings are often in a state of suspension as they try to establish their places within the new milieu by learning unfamiliar ways of thinking and behaving. There is no doubt that despite the rhetoric around the notion of community (Sangha), which is ubiquitous within Buddhist groups, people can feel isolated. This isolation is exaggerated when anxiety about being ostracized causes meditation students to refrain from challenging the behavior of others, particularly members of a charismatic aristocracy. To do so can feel like betraying the idealized notions of Sangha and spiritual friendship that attracted the person to the group in the first place.

Finally, there is the question of whether Buddhist movements that are afflicted with scandals can regain their reputations. The examples suggest that this is indeed possible, if disappointed members have a medium for venting their feelings and listening to one another. At the Zen Center, the formation of affinity groups and the opportunities for counseling constituted such a medium. At Vajradhatu, the creation of a temporary newsletter, entitled *Sangha*, provided an important outlet for disaffected members.[39] In both examples, board leadership steered a course toward more accessible and open institutional forms, based on rationalized forms of organization. Charismatic authority remains, contained in the relationship between students and their meditation teachers. However, with the advent of more teachers and mentors, it is less concentrated and more readily distinguishable from matters of institutional leadership and governance.

NOTES

1. Surya Das, "The Snow Lions Roar: A Report on the Conference of Western Buddhist Meditation Teachers," 1.

2. Ibid., 3.

3. Peter Harvey, *An Introduction to Buddhism* (Cambridge: Cambridge University Press, 1990), 244.

4. Ibid.

5. Jack Kornfield, "Is Buddhism Changing in North America?" in *Buddhist America: Centers, Retreats, Practices,* edited by Don Morreale (Santa Fe, New Mexico: John Muir Publications, 1988), xviii.

6. Rick Fields, *How the Swans Came to the Lake: A Narrative History of Buddhism in America,* 3rd revised and updated ed. (Boston: Shambhala, 1992), 359–69.

7. See for example Franz Metcalf, "We Think Your Behavior is Harming the Buddhadharma, a Zen Intervention" (paper delivered at the annual meeting of the Society for the Scientific Study of Religion and the Religious Research Association, San Diego, 7 Nov. 1997). See also newspaper coverage, including Madeleine Bunting, "The Dark Side of Enlightenment," *The Guardian,* 27 Oct. 1997; Vishvapani, "Buddhism Distorted," *The Guardian,* 8 Nov. 1997; Paul Valley, "I Was a Tantric Sex Slave," *The Independent,* 10 Feb. 1999; Jamie Macaskill, "Monks Dirty Habits," *The Scottish Daily Record,* 17 Apr. 2000; Jamie Macaskill, "Sex Row Monk Admits Fondling Boy Disciple," *The Scottish Daily Record,* 18 Apr. 2000; and "Monk on Girl Assault Charge," *The Scottish Daily Record,* 28 Apr. 2000 (no byline).

8. Fields, *How the Swans Came to the Lake,* 274.

9. See Metcalf, "We Think Your Behavior is Harming the Buddhadharma."

10. John Ardussi and Lawrence Epstein, "The Saintly Madman in Tibet," in *Himalayan Anthropology: The Indo-Tibetan Interface,* edited by James F. Fisher (The Hague: Mouton, 1978), 327.

11. Geoffrey Samuel, *Civilized Shamans: Buddhism in Tibetan Societies* (Washington, D.C.: Smithsonian Institution Press, 1993), 307.

12. Sandra Bell, "'Crazy Wisdom,' Charisma, and the Transmission of Buddhism in the United States," *Nova Religio: The Journal of Alternative and Emergent Religions* 2, no. 1 (1999), 55–75.

13. *Ngöndro* requires the completion of 100,000 full-length prostrations, 100,000 mantra recitations, 100,000 recitations of the vow to become a bodhisattva, 100,000 recitations of a formula for seeking refuge in the Buddha and his teaching, and 100,000 repetitions arranging and rearranging a mandala composed of grains of rice.

14. Stephen Butterfield, *The Double Mirror: A Skeptical Journey into Buddhist Tantra* (Berkeley: North Atlantic Books, 1994), 136.

15. Ibid., 100.

16. Lorne Dawson and Lynn Eldershaw, "Shambhala Warriorship: Investigating the Adaptations of Imported New Religious Movements," in *Croyances et Sociétés: communications présentés au dixième colloque international sur les nouveaux movements religieux*, edited by Bertrand Ouellet and Richard Bergeron (Québec: Editions Fides, 1996), 209.

17. Ibid.

18. See *Windbell* 17, no. 2 (1983), 2.

19. See *Tricycle: The Buddhist Review* 4, no. 2 (Winter 1994), 35.

20. Ibid., 35.

21. *Windbell* 17, no. 2 (1983), 3.

22. Ibid.

23. Katy Butler, "Events are the Teacher: Working through the Crisis at San Francisco Zen Center," *CoEvolution Quarterly* 40 (Winter 1983), 120.

24. The counselors were not Buddhists, but became so through their contact with Zen Center.

25. Butler, "Events are the Teacher," 115.

26. Baker went on to found the Dharma Sangha, with centers in Germany; Austria; and Crestone, Colorado.

27. *Windbell* 17, no. 2 (1983), 12–8.

28. *Windbell* 31, no. 2 (1997).

29. Max Weber, *Economy and Society* (Berkeley: University of California Press, 1978), 1119.

30. Ibid., 1125.

31. Charles Lindholm, *Charisma* (London: Blackwell, 1990), 7.

32. Stephanie Kane, "Sacred Deviance and AIDS in a North American Buddhist Community," *Law and Policy* 16 (1994), 331.

33. J. Gordon Melton, "Introduction: When Prophets Die," in *When Prophets Die: The Postcharismatic Fate of New Religious Movements*, edited by Timothy Miller (Albany: State University of New York Press, 1991), 8.

34. Butler, "Events are the Teacher," 116.

35. Charles Lindholm, "Love as an Experience of Transcendence," in *Romantic Passion*, edited by William Jankoviak (New York: Columbia University Press, 1995), 68.

36. *Tricycle: The Buddhist Review* 1, no. 3 (Spring 1992), 52.

37. Butler, "Events are the Teacher," 120.

38. Ibid., 121.

39. Bell, "Crazy Wisdom."

IV

LIFESTYLE
*Being a Buddhist in Western
Societies*

16 The Challenge of Community

Ajahn Tiradhammo

INTRODUCTION

Disciples of the Thai Forest Tradition master Venerable Ajahn Chah have been resident in the West for nearly twenty-five years.[1] During this time, they have faced a variety of challenges. In the early years, most of these were cultural, that is, learning to adjust to the environment and culture of the West. However, over the last ten years most of the disciples' challenges have related to community and personal dynamics. This essay is a personal perspective on some of these challenges and how they have been dealt with. While this is my own account, it presents a collage of many people's insights, perceptions, and concerns, to which I have been party over the years. I have articulated many of my observations in general terms, because they could apply to any community, while others more specifically concern situations, individuals, or times in our own particular community.

CHALLENGES

Why have most of the challenges over the last ten years related to community and personal dynamics? It seems that challenges of these types are commonly experienced by all organizations undergoing some degree of change. Basically, an organization is set up for a specific purpose, following a particular model, and with certain designated roles. When a certain degree of change occurs, the original model and roles no longer work and crisis ensues. The original model cannot solve new problems effectively, people's roles are threatened, and there is confusion and competition about what new model and roles are suitable. How this crisis is handled depends upon the community dynamics (structures and relationships) and the personal dynamics of the individuals in the organization. If the organization's structures and members are flexible, then the group can easily adapt to change, and perhaps even thrive with it. Difficulties arise because people have different degrees of sensitivity to change and adapt at different rates, depending on their flexibility, understanding, and vested interests.

Over the years, our community grew and diversified. It expanded into eight branch monasteries and took on a wider range of activities. Our traditional Asian form was severely stretched, and the group dynamics considerably altered. This caused changes in relational attitudes, which in turn exposed limitations in personal dynamics. Over time, a number of issues surfaced. Some of us observed that our traditional lifestyle and internalized spiritual practices still left many areas of behavior and attitudes untouched.[2] Most noticeable was the severe limitation in developing awareness of interpersonal processes. This was a special liability in the West, with our increased amount of communal activity. As an example, there was an astonishing lack of awareness of the effects of individual actions and words on other members, causing much misunderstanding, hurt, and resentment. Some people also realized that our inherited Thai cultural and attitudinal forms were not as effective in the West. Particularly unhelpful was the harmony-preserving attitude of nonconfrontation. It is an effective short-term means of maintaining communal harmony, but in the long term it left many issues unresolved and festering. Another difficulty was the inordinate amount of authority invested in senior members, whose decisions could not be questioned. While this seemed to be an easy method of management (and practice of surrender!), it left junior members feeling powerless and manipulated.

Attitudinal tensions began to increase. As the Thai-trained senior monks became older and as younger people entered the community, the generational tension was amplified, in part because most of the senior monks had taken ordination in order to have a supportive environment for meditation practice, while many junior members had taken ordination for the sake of spiritual community. A tension developed about how much of the Thai model to preserve and how much adaptation to the Western context was appropriate. Another tension evolved between the paternalistic/autocratic style of leadership and the oligarchic/democratic style. All these tensions were compounded by the strong reluctance of some members to acknowledge any difficulties. There was also no suitable forum in which to address such issues, and the diversity and wide distribution of community members produced a considerable strain on communication. Some members were comfortable with the old, familiar working model and resisted experimentation with other possibilities, perhaps better suited to the changing situation. This created strains in the community between those who felt threatened by change and those who felt the need to search for a different approach.

Community Dynamics

The Buddha strongly emphasized noble friendship and provided detailed procedures for developing and maintaining a mendicant monastic community. In practice, however, people understand community and spiritual friendship in a number of different ways. For example, the traditional Forest Tradition model is interpreted as emphasizing the ideals of solitude and silence. The ideal community is then seen as a group of solitaries gathered around a teacher, and those who find benefit in a more communal approach to practice are looked down upon. Ajahn Chah saw that solitude and silence can help the refined development of meditation, but they may also be used as escapes from the wisdom-testing difficulties of life. He thought it was most important for each person to assess individual needs for solitude and communal activity.

Another common idea is that community entails homogeneity, rather than a shared commonality. This can result in all manner of presumed appropriate behavior, such as imitation (usually of the leader's behavior and ideas), common jargon, and "group think." Practically, this can produce unconscious taboos that leave whole areas of meaningful relationship (i.e., the enrichment of diversity) untouched. I have observed that many times the unspoken assumptions about what constitutes community membership are destructive to a sense of community. A better approach combines clearly defined boundaries with sufficient allowance for individual expression. The assumption of homogeneity can result in simmering resentments (i.e., toward those who toe the party line and those who don't) or an enforcement of conformity, either by setting a rigid standard or by stifling diversity. All communities are based upon some degree of exclusiveness. If, however, this slips into elitism, a number of other factors come into play. These may include self-congratulatory attitudes and behavior and, in extreme cases, the avoidance of criticism through denial, humiliation, or ostracism. Shutting out criticism or feedback leads to a closed group, causes inflated egos and overconfidence, and may result in manipulation and abuse to silence disagreement.

When a community or organization is growing and exuding an aura of success, its members are at risk of feeling self-satisfaction and arrogance. The headiness of apparent success makes it hard to listen to words of caution or criticism. We then lose touch with the shadow side, the ignored negative consequences of our actions, and only know and exult in our positive side. This inflated imbalance leads to distorted perceptions, misjudgments, and losing touch with our inner directions.

Leadership Dynamics

The position of leader is very complex, mainly because it involves an ongoing, reciprocal relationship between teacher and student, leader and follower, and so on. The leader's degree of influence or power over the community and the degree of power the members give to the leader have important effects upon what kind of community is created. Our relationship to any position of leadership is confusing and complex,[3] and this complexity is compounded where spiritual leadership is concerned. If the relationship between a community and its leader is clouded by a lack of clarity around leadership issues, resistance or refusal to receive feedback, and a lack of humility to learn from problems and mistakes, then the leader's personal limitations may be acted out in community dynamics and will have a wide range of implications. For example, the eccentric behavior of a teacher can have serious consequences for the students. As was acknowledged in regard to one Buddhist teacher's misconduct, "We habitually denied what was in front of our faces, felt powerless and lost touch with our inner experience."[4]

The Forest Tradition model we inherited from Thailand is that of a community of disciples gathered around a teacher (the proverbial *wise elder*), who was usually the most senior member. The teacher was very much the center of the community. Anyone who disagreed with the teacher's instruction or behavior was usually free to find another teacher. With a wise and skillful teacher, this model works exceptionally well. It focuses energy on the practice and realization of the teachings. However, this model is also open to abuse, either through unhealthy community dynamics (sheltering or defending a teacher's excesses) or through conscious or unconscious manipulation by the leader. Even though some people may see what is going on, a conspiracy of silence may prevail, due to fear of rejection, ridicule, or reprisal by the group or teacher. Sometimes voices are silenced through intimidation, under the guise of such virtues as preserving harmony, developing patience and forgiveness, or practicing to be free of negativity.

If the community leader is exceptionally charismatic, the situation is even more complex. First, the charismatic personality attracts particular types of people to the community. Second, if not handled skillfully, the relationship creates dependency and disempowerment in those it is supposed to serve. For the charismatic personality, the situation is equally dangerous. If the leader is unaware of the interactive dynamics, the increased idealization and adoration can lead to self-deluding ego-inflation. Charisma is frequently a fragile commodity: "Charisma may fall on anyone, even on those in whom the ability to lead and to bear authority are woefully absent, thereby deceiving followers who cannot distinguish mastery from magic."[5]

Many people are attracted to the magic of charisma. However, if this is not complemented by a wider range of positive personal qualities, then the attraction may turn to resentment, feelings of betrayal or distrust, and downright aversion. Another complex situation occurs when someone likes the teacher's teachings but not the teacher. At some point, this may result in a crisis of confidence. Shouldn't the teacher embody the teachings he (or she) expounds? If the teacher is an example of the teachings, then maybe the teachings don't actually work, or, at best, perhaps the teacher has not yet fully realized them. Of course, there are several points to consider here. One is the degree of expectation or idealization that the student brings to the situation. Second, and more controversial, is the issue of what degree of psychological integration an "enlightened" person has, can have, or should have.[6]

An especially problematic situation may occur when the community "outgrows" the original leader, because of outmoded or stale teaching or because of teaching style. This creates an extremely awkward situation. Members respect the leader for previous contributions, but feel resentful or frustrated that the leader obstructs a move to a new relationship. At the same time, some members may remain dependent upon the old model, and others may get easily triggered into old attitudes and behaviors. Meanwhile, the leader may be unconsciously working to maintain former glory while cleverly holding students within the gambits of personal, ego-satisfying games. Frequently, the most insightful or exceptional members will have to move away. A truly wise teacher is one who compassionately and generously guides people toward spiritual maturity and freedom, and is genuinely joyful at seeing them blossom in their own right.

In my own experience and observation, I think the centralized leadership model does not work very well in the West.[7] The role of a central authority in Thailand is tempered from most excesses by implicit social standards, the opinions of other senior Sangha members, and Thai laws. I think that a safer and saner approach in the West is to delegate, differentiate, and decentralize the decision-making processes—in other words, to establish a community or Sangha-based model of management. It is noteworthy that the Pāli Canon records that the Buddha refused to appoint a personal successor but left *Dhamma-Vinaya* as the designated teacher.

Personal Dynamics

Communities are comprised of individuals, so eventually many issues devolve to personal dynamics. Every individual brings personal issues to a spiritual community. Ideally, many of these issues can be worked through within the supportive environment and through spiritual exercises. However, the kind of spiritual exercises one does and the approach one has to spiritual practice may also impede resolution. I personally resisted recognizing the negative effects of unprocessed personal issues until one particularly explosive meeting, when their destructiveness on community dynamics was glaringly revealed. More disturbing was the realization that even decades of meditation hadn't dealt with the problems! Gradually I observed that a number of tendencies prevalent among spiritual practitioners could lead to unhealthy results. Probably all of us at some time (and some of us all the time!) are prone to these tendencies.

Personal Spiritual Practice. I think the root cause of many of these tendencies is high-minded idealism. On the positive side, this may be the reason some people are drawn to spiritual practice. However, if idealism is not consciously acknowledged and its effects are not understood, it casts a long shadow into spiritual practice. We come from an attitude of how things *should be* and we find it exceptionally difficult to directly experience how things really are. The shadow of idealism is denial. We conveniently ignore whatever doesn't conform to our self-satisfying ideals. I see this as resulting in a tendency to over-spiritualize, that is, we dismiss problems with high-minded principles, such as "it's all impermanent," or "just let go," or, more seriously, by developing a "disembodied spirituality" that looks down on mundane "worldly" matters and equates spirituality with a higher plane.[8] Thus personal issues are ignored or denied as being "unreal" or unimportant. Practical problems are not given significant attention and are left unprocessed.

At present, an increasing amount of research is being done on the psychology of spiritual practice. For example, there is the phenomenon of *spiritual bypassing*, articulated by the Buddhist psychotherapist John Welwood. He defines this as "using spiritual ideas and practices to sidestep personal, emotional 'unfinished business,' to shore up a shaky sense of self, or to belittle basic needs, feelings, and developmental tasks, all in the name of enlightenment."[9] Eventually, perhaps decades after we begin our practice, some of these habits may catch us up, much to the surprise and bewilderment of an "advanced" practitioner. Another phenomenon which is becoming clearer is *schizoid defense*.[10] In relation to spiritual practice, this means using spiritual exercises as a means of withdrawing or splitting off from reality. This can become especially problematic when meditators become attached to tranquil, blissful, or exceptional experiences. Instead of realizing the true nature of reality, we become obsessed with creating and holding onto special experiences, which block further progress and could lead to psychic disturbances.

Leadership. When someone takes on a leadership or teaching position, many new factors come into play. One monk succinctly remarked that for some people taking on a leadership position "makes them go funny." In our own community, the leadership position was usually determined on the basis of seniority, although sometimes also due to special circumstances, such as being personally chosen. Sometimes leadership responsibility came to people who had no previous experience or not enough versatility to handle its complexities. While the situation was usually perceived as a personal challenge to rise to the occasion, it put stress on the individual and also on the community. Quite a number of senior monks disrobed while in the leadership position. In discussions following the sudden and secretive disrobing of two of these people, the contributing factors of over-identification with the role and over-busy-ness were noted.

Over-identification with the role of teacher means taking it too personally, and thus bringing ego desires and defenses to the forefront. This often leads to an inability to admit to weaknesses, problems, or limitations, because these are seen as personal problems. There is also a strong tendency for unconscious symptoms to be acted out (usually through either abdication or excessive control), because experience comes directly to the ego without the buffer of simply fulfilling a role. In another possible scenario, the leader becomes full of self-importance, thus tending to mania and over-busy-ness, and neglects a personal spiritual practice. This can lead either to burnout (from physical, emotional, or spiritual exhaustion) or to a loss of connection with spiritual practice, the community, or both. A sure sign of over-identification with the role is someone who expounds high-minded values but does not live up to them, and perhaps even denies the hypocrisy. Or the person may get very "high" from the position, due to the ego-massage of praise or of being the center of attention, or, more unsettling, of being in control of students. The two senior monks mentioned above felt isolated or unsupported in their own community. Their greatest source of ego comfort then lay outside the monastic community, and this drew them out of the community.

It is commonly known that a leader receives much projection because of the position of expertise or authority. The receiver of projection is in a very vulnerable position, and may easily succumb to unconscious ego- or shadow-inflation, with their rich litanies of expression.[11] Unfinished psychological issues also get inflated and look for ways of expression. One of the most insidious projections is probably that of teacher-as-parent, which comes from a deep unconscious level. If we observe people who act to please the teacher, or feel fearful in the teacher's presence, or react in a childish way, they are likely caught in this kind of projection. Meanwhile, some teachers give teachings in an authoritarian, parent-like mode, sometimes lapsing into scolding.

SOME RESOLUTIONS

One main strength of our tradition is the continuing commitment to spiritual community. This enables a serious attempt at keeping communication channels open, even when personal issues make communication difficult. I think a lot of our surfacing issues were a result of a process of "growing up." First, we needed to "grow up" into a unique, Asian-based, Western monastic tradition, for which there was no previous precedent. Second, our senior members "grew up" into teachers and leaders with their own particular styles. Third, I think we have faced a need to "grow up" into the discovery of a spiritual practice and tradition that truly work for Westerners.

All this growing up resulted in the development of a greater appreciation of diversity. One of the first practical results of this change was a move to create more individual "space." For example, the original model called for centrally directed *branch monasteries*, in which the senior incumbent was rotated every few years. We shifted instead to a system of *associated monasteries*, where the senior incumbent resided indefinitely and developed a particular style of practice and teaching. More space was also allowed for each individual's unique approach to practice, including the opportunity to request special options, like spending time in Asia, going "wandering," visiting other centers, and so on.

Over the years, mechanisms took shape that provided a basis for further refinement. As the number of branch monasteries increased, we created a committee of "abbots" (later including other senior monks and senior nuns) to discuss community issues. While this committee focused primarily on business, over time it also needed to attend to relational issues.

This required creating a deeper atmosphere of trust, so that issues could be openly addressed without fear of attack or defensive reaction.

Practically speaking, creating an atmosphere of trust required that people learn to empathically listen to others and be more aware of their own personal issues. Experiments were made at creating different kinds of meetings to address a wide variety of issues. At many monasteries, there are now regular meetings, such as listening circles or process meetings, for listening and dialogue about deeper personal issues. Community meetings have also benefited from increased skills in facilitating, and basic education in psychology has helped members recognize and deal with interpersonal and group issues.

Over the years, the leadership issue has been dealt with in a variety of ways. Each monastery has evolved a particular leadership model, ranging from the strong central teacher to shared leadership responsibilities. The Elder's Council, with support and feedback from other senior members and the wider community, is officially responsible for *advisory decision-making* for the larger community. With growing awareness of the influence of unprocessed personal issues, a number of individuals have seriously pursued psychological studies and inner work. Peer groups of various kinds have evolved as a means of providing feedback, support, and assistance, especially for those in leadership roles. This supportive network has made it easier for people in those roles to ask for help, delegate responsibilities, and take time off for personal retreats or sabbaticals.

CONCLUSIONS

One of Ajahn Chah's special methods of teaching was to encourage a considerable degree of communal activity. He saw the communal approach as both supportive of spiritual practice and at the same time challenging, since the individual is frequently pushed outside the comfort zone. While indeed challenging, many of us have found that making the effort to work through issues that arise in community is a priceless opportunity for a deepening of wisdom and for opening the heart of compassion.

NOTES

1. See J. L. Taylor, *Forest Monks and the Nation State* (Singapore: Institute of Southeast Asian Studies, 1993); Kamala Tiyavanich, *Forest Recollections* (Honolulu: University of Hawaii Press, 1997); and Stephen Batchelor, *The Awakening of the West: The Encounter of Buddhism and Western Culture* (Berkeley: Parallax Press, 1994), chapter 4.

2. We are guided by the refined external standards of *Vinaya*, or monastic discipline. For an introduction, see Mohan Wijayaratna, *Buddhist Monastic Life* (Cambridge: Cambridge University Press, 1990).

3. "[C]onfusion of an authoritative voice with an authoritarian one shows how little we grasp this kind of power. It also shows how fearful we are of authority in a democratic society, and one increasingly egalitarian. . . . [W]hat limits our understanding here is not fear of authority but the justified usurpation of it by the ego." See James Hillman, *Kinds of Power: A Guide to Its Intelligent Use* (New York: Currency/Doubleday, 1997), 163.

4. See Katy Butler, in *Meeting the Shadow: The Hidden Power of the Dark Side of Human Nature*, edited by Connie Zweig and Jeremiah Abrams (New York: Tarcher/Putnam, 1991), 140.

5. Hillman, *Kinds of Power*, 172.

6. See Georg Feurstein, "The Shadow of the Enlightened Guru," in Zweig and Abrams, *Meeting the Shadow*, 148–50.

7. For similar views, see Wendy Egyoku Nakao, "Just Trust Yourself," *Turning Wheel*, Spring 1999, 15; and, from a different angle, "Interview with Andrew Harvey," *Common Boundary* (no issue number), Autumn 1994.

8. Ken Wilber, *A Brief History of Everything* (New York: Gill and Macmillan, 1996), 10–1; 234ff.

9. John Welwood, *Toward a Psychology of Awakening* (Boston: Shambhala, 2000), 207.

10. See Donald Kalsched, *The Inner World of Trauma* (London: Routledge, 1996); also Welwood, *Toward a Psychology of Awakening*, 209.

11. See Butler, *Meeting the Shadow*, and also Rick Fields, *How the Swans Came to the Lake: A Narrative History of Buddhism in America*, 2nd ed. (Boston: Shambhala, 1986); James William Coleman, *The New Buddhism* (Oxford: Oxford University Press, 2000), chapter 5; and Peter Rutter, *Sex in the Forbidden Zone* (Los Angeles: J. P. Tarcher, 1989).

17 Buddhist Nuns
Changes and Challenges
Karma Lekshe Tsomo

INTRODUCTION

Many Buddhist temples and Dharma centers in the West are maintained primarily through the efforts of nuns. These nuns serve their temples and centers in a variety of capacities—as organizers, administrators, teachers, translators, accountants, counselors, secretaries, and housekeepers. Although their dedication and hard work are sometimes taken for granted, nuns are having a positive, lasting effect on the future of Buddhist institutions, in both Asia and the West.

The backgrounds and lifestyles of Buddhist nuns in the West vary enormously. Some have no formal schooling, while quite a few hold M.A. and Ph.D. degrees. Some wear monastic robes at all times and spend almost all their time in their temples, while others work at ordinary jobs and wear lay clothes except when attending Dharma activities. Some work full-time, some work part-time, and others are supported by their temples or by family, friends, pensions, or savings. Whether living in community or on their own, these nuns engage in a wide variety of Dharma-related service activities. In addition to the daily tasks required to maintain their temples and centers, nuns teach Buddhism, attend classes, keep up a daily practice, and attend periodic retreats.

Nuns in the West belong to a variety of Buddhist practice traditions: Burmese, Cambodian, Chinese, Japanese, Korean, Laotian, Sri Lankan, Thai, Tibetan, and Vietnamese. This diversity is reflected in the nuns' attire and the precepts (rules of monastic conduct) they observe. Nuns of the Theravāda tradition (Burma, Cambodia, Laos, Sri Lanka, and Thailand) observe 8, 9, or 10 precepts and wear a skirt, blouse, and shawl of white, orange, pink, or brown cloth, depending on the tradition. Nuns in the Tibetan tradition receive the 10 precepts of a *śrāmaṇerikā* (novice nun), plus additional training rules, for a total of 36. These nuns wear maroon robes in the same style as the monks of their tradition, with yellow outer robes for ceremonies. Nuns in the Chinese, Korean, and Vietnamese traditions first receive the 10 *śrāmaṇerikā* (novice) precepts, then the 348 *bhikṣuṇī* (full ordination) precepts; some receive an intermediary *śikṣamānā* (probationary) ordination as well. These nuns generally wear gray robes in the style of a T'ang Dynasty scholar, with brown or dark gold outer robes for ceremonies. At some temples, Chinese nuns wear black, or they alternate black and gray with the seasons. In recent years, some Chinese *bhikṣuṇīs* in positions of authority have begun to wear dark gold or brown robes, with bright gold, yellow, and red robes for special occasions, in the style of high-ranking *bhikṣus*.

The majority of Asian Buddhist nuns living in Western countries were born in Buddhist families and emigrated to Western countries, either as children or as adults. Many became nuns in their home countries (Korea, Taiwan, or Vietnam, for example) before they arrived at Buddhist temples in the West and they have never been married. Most of these nuns received a Buddhist education and were trained in chanting, ritual, and meditation at institutes and temples in Asia. The Chinese nuns at Hsi Lai Temple in Hacienda Heights, California, and at other temples affiliated with the International Buddhist Progress Society, fall into this category.[1] Sometimes Asian women living in Western countries receive ordination as nuns after pursuing studies or other occupations. Because of their educational and professional backgrounds these nuns generally have a higher level of English-language proficiency than immigrant nuns.

Obtaining accurate figures on the number of Asian Buddhist nuns living in Western countries is difficult, not only because they are spread out in several hundred temples in Europe and North America, but also because they frequently travel between temples and to their home countries. Some maintain temples in both Asia and the West, and travel back and forth several times a year. In addition, there are Asian nuns who live singly or in small groups to pursue studies or contemplative practices. Based on personal observations and inquiries, I estimate that several hundred Chinese, several hundred Vietnamese, and perhaps sixty Korean Buddhist nuns live either in temples or independently in North America and Europe at the present time.

It is even more difficult to obtain accurate figures on the number of non-Asian Buddhist nuns living in Western countries. Some live independently and may be only loosely affiliated with a Buddhist temple or center; some stay in city centers or retreat centers; while others move frequently from one temple to another, or from their home country to teachings or retreats in Asia. Many Western nuns have studied with teachers of more than one Buddhist tradition and some have been ordained in more than one tradition.

For example, many Western *bhikṣuṇīs* have received their novice (*śrāmaṇerikā*) ordination in one tradition, but have received their *bhikṣuṇī* ordination in a different tradition, because *bhikṣuṇī* ordination is not available in the tradition in which they were originally ordained. As a result, most Western *bhikṣuṇīs* have been exposed to, have forged links with, and have developed an appreciation for at least one Buddhist tradition other than the one whose robes they wear. *Bhikṣuṇīs* such as Geshin Prabhasa Dharma and Karuna Dharma have been pioneers in ecumenical Buddhist dialogue and have been recognized as teachers in more than one Buddhist tradition.[2]

BUDDHIST MONASTIC COMMUNITIES

In comparison to Asian Buddhist countries and cultures, Western countries are far behind in the establishment of Buddhist monasteries. Whereas Asian monasteries are generally either for nuns or monks, almost all the Western Buddhist monasteries that have been established so far are mixed communities, open to laypeople as well as to nuns and monks. Although it is impossible to mention all the Western monastic communities that have nuns in residence, brief sketches of a few of them will help illustrate the varied circumstances of Buddhist nuns in the West. Included is a sampling of sizable communities of various traditions in North America and Europe, beginning with those that were established earliest.

The earliest Buddhist monastic community in North America was not designed with nuns in mind. Tassajara Zen Mountain Center represents a departure from the traditional model of celibate monasticism, integrating intensive meditation practice and lay activities. Established by the San Francisco Zen Center in 1966 in a remote canyon of Big Sur, California, Tassajara offers intensive Zen training programs from September to April, and in the summer opens its doors to families to enjoy the hot-spring baths, secluded location, and gourmet vegetarian meals. Sexual abstinence is a topic of ongoing concern at Tassajara (and its affiliate centers, the San Francisco Zen Center and Green Gulch Farm), but residents are not required to be celibate. Both women and men may receive ordination as priests and some shave their heads and wear robes, but lifelong monastic precepts entailing celibacy are not currently offered.

Shasta Abbey, by contrast, is an avowedly monastic community. There are thirty-five male and female "monks," many of whom have practiced a celibate lifestyle there for more than twenty years. The abbey, located near Mount Shasta, California, was founded in 1970 by Jiyu Kennett Rōshi

(1924–96), an English *bhikṣuṇī* trained in Malaysia and Japan. In 1983, she established The Order of Buddhist Contemplatives, an international umbrella organization that oversees monasteries, priories (local temples), and meditation groups in Britain, Canada, Germany, the Netherlands, and the United States. Members of the order practice meditation in the Sōtō Zen style, host Dharma talks, and organize a calendar of annual festivals. Shasta Abbey and its affiliate Throssel Hole Priory, established in England in 1972, are examples of stable, harmonious, celibate, Western monastic communities.

The largest community of celibate Buddhist monastics in the United States is at the City of Ten Thousand Buddhas, a vast complex on 488 acres of land in Talmage, California. The monastery is the headquarters of Dharma Realm Buddhist Association, established in 1976 by the Chinese *bhikṣu* Hsüan Hua (1908–96). The organization has a dozen branch temples, monasteries, and institutes in the United States and abroad. The first group of nuns and monks received ordination in Taiwan in 1969. Since then, more than a dozen ordinations have been held in California; twenty-two new *bhikṣuṇīs* were ordained in August 2000. Special events at the City of Ten Thousand Buddhas attract more than a thousand participants, including over one hundred *bhikṣuṇīs* and twenty to thirty *bhikṣus*. The community is unique in its broad ethnic mix. It includes laypeople, nuns, and monks from a variety of backgrounds, primarily Chinese, Vietnamese, Malaysian, American, and Canadian. Residents rise at 4 A.M., take one vegetarian meal per day, follow a demanding program of meditation and study, and sleep sitting up. Periodic intensive meditation sessions feature twenty-one days of meditation from 2:30 A.M. to midnight. Nuns are housed separately from monks and laypeople, maintain the *śikṣamānā* precepts for two years before receiving *bhikṣuṇī* ordination, and follow an extremely strict code of discipline that restricts their movements beyond the monastery and regulates all activities within it.

The International Buddhist Progress Society, a large Chinese Buddhist organization based in Taiwan, primarily serves the overseas Chinese Buddhist community, but attempts to reach out to a wider constituency.[3] It lists four affiliated temples in South America, four in Canada, one in Guam, and seventeen in the United States, the largest of which is Hsi Lai Temple in Hacienda Heights, California. These temples are staffed primarily by *bhikṣuṇīs* who are supported by temple members, most from Taiwan. The nuns receive at least four years of Buddhist studies and training before they are sent out to serve in branch temples. All are proficient in Taiwanese and Mandarin, and may also speak English and Cantonese. Their temples offer classes in Mandarin, English, chanting, *sūtra* studies, and vegetarian cooking, as well as Dharma classes for children. The contributions of nuns are widely recognized and valued, both in the temples and in the wider community.[4]

Gampo Abbey, a monastic community in Nova Scotia, Canada, has three *bhikṣuṇīs* in residence, in addition to several *śrāmaṇerikās*, monks, and laypeople. Founded in 1984 by Chögyam Trungpa Rinpoche, a lineage holder in the Kagyu and Nyingma traditions, Gampo Abbey requires refuge vows and prior experience in meditation for prospective residents. After a period of temporary ordination, a qualified candidate may take a prenovice ordination (*bar ma rab byung*) as a first step to lifelong ordination. It is also possible to take temporary ordination with five precepts, including celibacy. The abbey is directed by *bhikṣuṇī* Pema Chödrön, a well-respected American teacher and author who has been ordained since 1975.[5] Nuns participate in a twice-monthly confession ceremony (*gso sbyong*) and a six-week winter retreat modeled on the traditional rains retreat (*dbyar gnas*), a period of unilocal contemplative practice. Innovative forms of the traditional Karma Kagyu three-year retreat have been developed to accommodate contemporary lifestyles. During retreats, participants maintain a code of ethical discipline, including celibacy, which is regarded as conducive to intensive meditation practice.

One of the largest communities of Vietamese nuns in the United States is Duc Vien Temple in San Jose, California. The temple was founded by the Vietnamese *bhikṣuṇī* Dam Luu (1932–99), who arrived in the United States as a refugee in 1980 and collected cans and newspapers to raise the money for construction costs.[6] Educated in Saigon in the 1950s, Dam Luu instituted many innovations at Duc Vien Temple, including the study of Pāli, the use the vernacular for chanting, and the practice of *vipassanā* meditation. The temple currently has twelve nuns in residence and offers ongoing Buddhist education programs. Several nuns are pursuing university degrees in addition to a busy schedule of temple activities that includes *sūtra* studies, meditation, temple maintenance, and ministering to the needs of the temple's large Vietnamese congregation.

The Bhavana Society, a Theravāda retreat center founded in 1982 in West Virginia by the Sri Lankan *bhikṣu* Henepola Gunaratana, is a conducive practice environment for nuns, monks, and laypeople of various cultural backgrounds. An outspoken advocate of full ordination for women, Bhante Gunaratana encourages nuns to receive the *bhikṣuṇī* precepts, then provides food and lodging for them at the Bhavana Society after their ordination. He feels that the *bhikṣuṇī* lineage will gain acceptance in Asia only after it takes root in the West.[7] Plans for constructing a monastery for women are in process.

One of several well-established communities of nuns in Europe is Kagyu Samyê Ling in Scotland. The first and largest Tibetan Buddhist center in Europe, Samyê Ling includes both ordained Sangha and lay practitioners, and has spearheaded an interfaith retreat center for peace off the Isle of Arran, known as the Holy Island Interfaith Retreat Project. Many nuns in the Samyê Ling community hold academic degrees and have done long-term retreats. Their studies and practice are guided by Lama Yeshe Losal, who has served as abbot since 1995. Eleven nuns received *bhikṣuṇī* ordination at the International Full Ordination Ceremony held in Bodhgaya, India, in February 1998.[8]

Amaravati, a community of Theravāda nuns in Hertfordshire, England, was established in 1984. It is a branch of Chithurst, a monastic community of the Thai Forest Tradition founded by the American monk Sumedho in 1978. A total of seventeen Western nuns of various nationalities now reside at Chithurst and at Amaravati. Although nuns in the Thai tradition generally wear white robes, nuns of the Chithurst and Amaravati communities wear brown. Ajahn Sundara and Ajahn Jindati, both internationally respected meditation teachers, have been leaders in the formation of these communities and pioneers in developing new guidelines for community life.

Plum Village, which was founded in 1982 in the Bordeaux region of France and serves as the headquarters of Thich Nhat Hanh's Order of Interbeing,[9] houses a community of almost fifty Vietnamese, European, and American nuns, as well as a considerable number of monks. The nuns live a simple lifestyle in a number of hamlets that dot the countryside. The order emphasizes mindfulness in daily activities and in personal interactions. An additional thirty *bhikṣuṇīs* and a smaller number of *bhikṣus* live at the affiliated Maple Forest Monastery in Vermont. Sister Chân Không leads the community at Plum Village, Sister Chan Thang Nghiem heads Maple Forest, and other nuns hold similarly important leadership positions in the organization.[10]

PIONEERING WESTERN BUDDHIST NUNS

Buddhist nuns are a relatively new phenomenon in Western society, appearing only as recently as the late 1960s. Although few in number, nuns in the West have accomplished a great deal in their brief history and have also encountered a number of challenges. Many have achieved high levels of both Buddhist and secular education, maintained high standards of contemplative practice and ethical discipline, helped found and maintain a large number of Buddhist temples and centers, and devoted much energy to serving society. Their greatest challenges have been gaining acceptance for their monastic lifestyle, obtaining material support, obtaining Buddhist education and training, establishing suitable monastic communities, and gender discrimination.

In Asian societies, wearing traditional robes and shaving one's head are expected of Buddhist monastics. The robes and shaved head are symbols of renunciation that elicit respect from the lay community. In Western societies, however, Buddhist nuns and monks are still oddities, and robes and a shaved head may elicit curiosity, admiration, scorn, or abuse. An Asian Buddhist nun is more easily accepted, because Buddhism is viewed as a legitimate aspect of Asian culture. By contrast, a Caucasian Buddhist nun represents a rejection of mainstream religious and cultural values, which may arouse resentment or hostility. The issues are somewhat different for nuns than for monks: nuns are considered odd when they shave their heads; monks are considered odd when they wear skirts. When a nun works to support herself, a shaved head greatly limits employment options. At the same time, the robes and shaved head are valuable because they represent a spiritual commitment and an alternative to consumer culture.

Two successful pioneering Buddhist nuns were the English *bhikṣuṇī* Kechog Palmö (1911–77),[11] who was ordained in the Tibetan tradition in 1966, and the German *bhikṣuṇī* Ayya Khema (1923–97),[12] who was ordained in the Theravāda tradition in 1979. Both of these influential nuns trained extensively in Asia before they began teaching internationally. Other Western *bhikṣuṇīs* who have become successful Buddhist teachers are Pema Chödrön of Gampo Abbey in Nova Scotia; Thubten Chodron of Dharma Friendship Foundation in Seattle;[13] Tenzin Palmo of Dongyu Gatsal Ling Nunnery in India;[14] Sangye Khandro of Amitabha Buddhist Centre in Singapore; Chi Kwang Sunim of Unmunsa in Korea, now founding a monastery in Australia;[15] and Mu Jin Sunim of Lotus Lantern International Center in Seoul, now teaching in Switzerland.

The Canadian *bhikṣuṇī* Lobsang Chodron (Ann McNeil) is an example of Western Buddhist nuns' dedication. Ordained in 1970, she is the senior nun in the Foundation for the Preservation of the Mahāyāna Tradition, founded in 1974 by Lama Thubten Yeshe and Lama Thubten Zopa. Its monastic organization, the International Mahāyāna Institute, includes 121 nuns of twenty-two nationalities serving in nearly one hundred centers and related organizations around the world.[16] Lobsang Chodron helped start Kopan Monastery in Kathmandu and Chenresig Institute in Australia in the early 1970s, and later Vajrapani Institute and Land of the Medicine Buddha in California. She has taught weekly at Zuru Ling in Vancouver since 1994 and at many other centers around the world. Since 1996, she has also been teaching in the Canadian federal prisons in British Columbia. Chodron is in the process of establishing another monastic center, Kachoe Zung Juk Ling, outside of Vancouver.

Because nuns receive less financial support than monks, their communities often develop in conjunction with established centers. Chenresig Nuns' Community, in Australia, evolved as nuns helped create Chenresig Institute and began to live together as a group. The twenty nuns currently in this community derive many benefits from living near an established center, including the ability to share its facilities and teachers, but they are responsible for their own expenses. Another monastic community of the Tibetan tradition that accommodates nuns is Rashi Gempil Ling, the First Kalmuk Buddhist Temple of New Jersey. The community, which is affiliated with the Asian Classics Institute established in 1993, includes four nuns (two bhikṣuṇīs and two śrāmaṇerikās). They study with Geshes Lobsang Tharchin and Michael Roach alongside monks and laypeople, many of whom have taken lifelong vows of celibacy. The nuns participate in the twice-monthly confession ceremony on a regular basis and are active in establishing Diamond Mountain, a retreat center in Arizona that will include monasteries for women and men, in addition to schools for children, retirement housing, Buddhist colleges, a translation bureau, and an arts center. Hundreds of other nuns in the West have also taught and served diligently without fanfare for years.

Both in Asian and in Western Buddhist communities, nuns have faced considerable difficulties gaining recognition when they serve as teachers— a traditionally male role. Some still serve in supportive roles as translators, administrators, attendants, and caretakers, leaving the role of teacher to monks and laymen. Many of the challenges they face relate directly to hierarchical gender expectations and assumptions about the subordinate role of nuns that accompany the Buddhist traditions to the West.

STRUGGLES AND SUCCESSES

The wide variety of Buddhist nuns' experiences can be traced to how they begin their ordained life. Most women who seek ordination have similar motivations—a commitment to study and practice the Dharma. Beyond that, however, their goals and expectations vary considerably. Some are interested in joining a community, while others are attracted to the idea of wandering freely. Some receive training in a monastic environment for years before ordination; others have no interest in monastic protocol. Some seek ordination in a well-structured, well-disciplined community; others seek ordination with the intent of living independently. The diverse paths nuns choose yield a host of dividends and deficits.

In contrast to most Catholic nuns, Buddhist nuns in the West lack established orders to provide material support, monastic training, and spiritual guidance. There is no mistress of novices to train aspirants and no systematic program of monastic formations. Some nuns seem content to live independently. Others imagine they are entering a large, supportive community and are rudely awakened to find themselves completely on their own. Without any sense of monastic unity, no guides to train or advise them, and little understanding on the part of the laypeople around them, these nuns grapple with feelings of isolation, abandonment, and rejection.

The Sangha, a broad community of Buddhist monastics spread throughout the world, offers the ordained membership in a broader community. This broad membership does not satisfy the basic needs of a newly ordained nun for food, shelter, and training. It is not uncommon for a Western woman to become ordained as a nun only to discover that the master who ordained her has flown off to his next destination. The fresh novice is left with nothing to eat, nowhere to stay, no training, no arrangements for further education, and sometimes without any knowledge of the precepts she has pledged to uphold for life or how to wear the robes properly. After the first flush of excitement about ordination subsides, she begins to realize her aloneness and lack of a supportive community.[17] As Thubten Chodron relates, "Few monasteries exist in the West and, if we want to stay in one, we generally have to pay to do so because the community has no money. This presents some challenges: how does someone with monastic precepts, which include wearing robes, shaving one's head, not handling money, and not doing business, earn money?"[18]

It is widely assumed that Western Buddhist nuns live in supportive communities and are financially supported by monastic orders. On the contrary, most are on their own when it comes to obtaining food, shelter, education, training, health care, and spiritual guidance. Unlike most Christian nuns' communities, the center where a Western Buddhist nun works may or may not provide her with room and board. Even in Asia, where monks are well respected and cared for, nuns are not always accepted as Sangha and do not receive the same level of material support as monks. In the West, traditional systems of providing monastics with the necessities of life are not yet in place and Western laypeople do not express much interest in developing them. Despite egalitarian ideals and increasing feminist awareness, most nuns are left to fend for themselves, though Western monks generally find sponsorship. Laypeople may even ask nuns, "Why should nuns deserve respect and support?" They may say, "My practice is just as good as yours. Why do you think you are better than I am?" These types of comments reveal a serious lack of understanding of the purpose and principles of monastic life. Often, with Roman Catholicism as the only available model, Western Buddhists themselves are unclear about what ordination means.

Monastic training in Buddhist cultures is traditionally provided by individual monasteries, yet it usually much less formal than the Catholic model. In addition, monasteries for women are generally few in number and poorly supported. The lower status of women in Buddhist societies is reflected in the lower status of nuns. Because nuns often have limited access to Buddhist education, training, and material support, they are less likely to emerge as teachers and role models for the next generation. This self-perpetuating cycle is beginning to change as nuns join forces to encourage each other and improve their circumstances, as has occurred rather dramatically in Korea, Taiwan, and Vietnam.[19]

MONASTICISM IN THE WEST: AN OPEN DIALOGUE

As Buddhism has become more popular in the West, both practitioners and outside observers have begun to notice the lack of female monastics and teachers and the lack of equal opportunities for education and ordination for women. Recognition of the neglect and inequalities Buddhist women have historically experienced has precipitated dialogue among nuns of various Buddhist traditions. This growing awareness has motivated scholars and practitioners to conduct research into Buddhist women's history and current circumstances, particularly the history of the *bhikṣuṇī* lineage and the prospects for instituting or restoring the *bhikṣuṇī* ordination in the various Buddhist traditions. One important achievement has been increased support for Buddhist women's projects in Asia. Another result has been an increased awareness of the need for viable Buddhist monastic institutions for women in the West.

The aim of creating monasteries in the West is not simply to duplicate Asian monastic structures, but to develop a monasticism appropriate for the West. Monastic practice is an attractive option for only a few Western Buddhists at present; far greater numbers prefer lay practice and seek lay teachers, who they think will be better able to understand their problems. Due in part to stereotypes of Christian monasticism, and in part to the tension between the monastic ideal and the secular work ethic, many Western Buddhists are not yet convinced that monastic practice is a meaningful option. Others who agree with the traditional view that monastic institutions are necessary for Buddhism to take root on Western soil are concerned about how monasticism can be profitably adapted in the West.

Another facet of this dialogue is the recognition that women attracted to Buddhism are not always attracted to monastic life. Until suitable monastic environments for women evolve, nuns must live in lay communities, join mixed communities (comprised of monks, nuns, and lay practitioners), train in Asia, or manage on their own. Each option has advantages and limitations. Living in a mixed community of nuns, monks, and laypeople may offer social and educational advantages, but is a very different experience than living in a supportive community of nuns. Training in Asia may be culturally enriching, but may also entail foreign-language acquisition, health risks, visa restrictions, and poverty. Striking out on one's own may offer an independent lifestyle, but provides no systematic study program, training, sense of community, or psychological support. Some Western nuns with independent means are itinerant, taking teachings and doing retreats around the world. Some study with a traditional teacher in Asia for a period of time, but find no suitable community or support when they return to their home countries. Those who find it difficult to be monastic without a monastery generally leave the robes altogether.

The importance of finding a well-qualified teacher cannot be overstated. In traditions that lack qualified female teachers, nuns must rely upon male teachers. As long as both teacher and student carefully observe the precepts, the relationship may be highly beneficial. If open dialogue and gender equality are lacking, however, the relationship may replicate patriarchal patterns and become dysfunctional. Asian nuns who have been raised to accept gender disparities may be willing to accept subservient roles and inequities in the teacher/student relationship, and may even consider them character-building, but few young women in the West are attracted to traditional hierarchical models of monastic life. Those few who do become nuns generally seek a situation with educational opportunities and a measure of independence.

The disparity between the ideal of sentient beings' equal potential for enlightenment and the social reality of gender discrimination can be very discouraging, especially for new nuns raised in the West. Nuns generally play important roles in community organizing, counseling, administration, and communications, but rarely receive training, recognition, or due compensation for their skills. They often encounter biases with regard to their gender and their celibate status. Anxious to implement the Buddhist ideals of compassion and selflessness, they may disregard discrimination or attempt to resolve frustrations by applying appropriate Dharma teachings. Receiving little psychological support or encouragement, nuns in a Western Buddhist environment face high expectations and incessant demands on their time.

When Buddhist institutional structures neglect nuns, whether in Asia or in the West, they have fewer chances to emerge as teachers and role models, and the cycle of subordination becomes self-perpetuating. Without opportunities for systematic education and long-term retreats, the traditional patriarchal assumptions about women's inferiority continue to thwart nuns' advancement. Teachers may affirm the spiritual equality of women, but without gender equity in practice these assurances ring hollow, and may even mask discrimination against women. At international conferences, it is common to hear affirmations of women's equality, but rare to find practical proposals to remove blatant inequalities. Ironically, even in the much-heralded woman-friendly West, nuns may find themselves ignored or rejected until they prove their worth as teachers, translators, authors, fund-raisers, or administrators. By the time a nun has become successful, she has already gained confidence and self-reliance, and the support system she so desperately longed for as a new nun is no longer needed.

Even though many Western nuns are well educated and skilled, they may find themselves marginalized, both in Asian Buddhist environments, due to different languages and customs, and in Western Buddhist environments, where lay Buddhist practice is emphasized. To make matters worse, male teachers may regard nuns who are knowledgeable about Buddhism as a challenge to their authority. Eventually Western nuns find they must balance the benefits of Buddhist practice against their disadvantaged gender status. The eight special rules (*gurudharmas*) that subordinate nuns to monks were clearly designed to prevent nuns from challenging monks' authority in Buddhist institutions. If it can be shown that the eight *gurudharmas* were not spoken by the Buddha, as recent research indicates, this would effectively upset the traditional apple cart and eliminate barriers to women's full and equal participation in Buddhist institutions.[20]

Paradoxically, despite the stark inequalities in opportunities and support, nuns seem to have a much easier time maintaining celibacy. Contrary to the popular myth that women are sexually uncontrollable, the dropout rate among nuns is much lower than among monks. Usually the decision to leave monastic life is more a product of frustration with the lack of a conducive environment for personal growth than the desire for a sexual relationship. Because of their staying power, nuns are likely to exert a strong influence on Buddhist institutions far into the future.

REVISITING THE ORDINATION ISSUE

Western nuns have been leaders in the movement to reinstate full ordination for Buddhist women in traditions where it is not currently available.[21] Because the struggle for equal rights for women has a long history in Western societies, Western nuns are generally more concerned about achieving equal rights within Buddhism than Asian nuns, who either have already achieved a semblance of equality with monks (as in Taiwan and Korea) or do not regard gender equality as an appropriate pursuit for Dharma practitioners (as among many Thai and Tibetan nuns, for example). Proponents of full ordination for women point to the vitality and effectiveness of the *bhikṣuṇī* Sangha in Taiwan and Korea as evidence of the benefits fully ordained nuns can bring to Buddhism. Equally important, the movement to reinstate full ordination is a historical step in intercultural exchange among nuns.

Western nuns generally find *bhikṣuṇī* ordination extremely beneficial for many reasons. First, they receive the karmic benefit in maintaining the full complement of precepts. Second, they appreciate the practical benefits of having a time-tested code to guide their personal conduct and as an aid in developing mindfulness. Third, they gain confidence and benefit psychologically from becoming full-fledged members of the Buddhist Sangha, rather than being relegated to novice status indefinitely. Fourth, whether they receive ordination in Taiwan, Korea, or the West, they gain inspiration from belonging to a community of Buddhist nuns who model the ideals of discipline, dedication, spiritual confidence, and loving-kindness. Finally, as full members of the Sangha community, they become *fields of merit* and therefore worthy of support.

So far, gaining opportunities for full ordination has primarily been a concern of a core of educated Asian laywomen and Western Buddhist nuns. Efforts to educate a larger number of Asian nuns and monks about the issues will require a team of multilingual activists with a strong commitment to these issues. Many Asian nuns are too humble, too poor, or too educationally disadvantaged to take an active interest in receiving full ordination. Some also have been discouraged from seeking full ordination by their teachers, who advise them that novice precepts are sufficient for nuns. By contrast, most Western Buddhist nuns who have received *bhikṣuṇī* ordination feel that all nuns who wish to take full ordination should have the opportunity. These nuns have moved the issue forward simply by taking the ordination themselves and discussing the issue of full ordination wherever they go. This strategy of active commitment and education is designed to gain the support of those who oppose the full ordination of women or are simply unfamiliar with the issues. These efforts have had a number of unforeseen positive results. The full ordination issue has helped nuns find their voice and stimulated research on the *bhikṣuṇī Vinaya*. It has facilitated dialogue, not only among nuns of various traditions, but also among nuns, *bhikṣu* scholars, and male-dominated Buddhist institutions.[22] A tremendous amount of research, community building, and dialogue remains to be done, but awareness of gender-related issues has increased and will surely continue.

Many monks and nuns in the Tibetan and Theravādin traditions are unaware of the large, vital *bhikṣuṇī* Sanghas that exist in Taiwan, Korea, and Vietnam, but anyone who travels to these countries cannot fail to be impressed with the erudition and hard work of these nuns and the benefits they bring to the Dharma and society. Coming into contact with so many well-educated, well-disciplined nuns inevitably causes monks to reevaluate the situations of nuns in their own countries and cultures. Contact with vital *bhikṣuṇī* communities can have the effect of generating a true concern for and commitment to improving conditions for nuns, but it can also be somewhat intimidating. Seeing the excellent conduct and social action programs of nuns in Taiwan, for example, can cause monks to become painfully aware of the inadequacies in their own traditions, not only among the nuns but also among the monks. There is an obvious need for improved monastic training in some traditions, but changes require stable monastic communities and sincere conviction about the benefits of monastic discipline.

Another reason for supporting full ordination for Buddhist nuns is strategic. To ensure the success of Dharma in the West, equality in the Sangha is essential. If Buddhism is to be taken seriously in the long term, women must be granted equal opportunities in Buddhist institutions. Therefore, it is of great historical significance that full ordination for women be made available in all Buddhist traditions, and the sooner the better. Asian monks who lack a *bhikṣuṇī* Sangha in their own traditions hesitate to accept as valid the *bhikṣuṇī* lineages of other traditions for several reasons: (1) doubts about the validity of the extant *bhikṣuṇī* lineages (that is, their purity and unbroken continuity); (2) doubts about the authenticity of the ordination procedures; and (3) doubts about the acceptability of conducting future *bhikṣuṇī* ordinations using *bhikṣus* and *bhikṣuṇīs* of two different *Vinaya* lineages. The prescribed procedures for conducting a dual ordination with ten *bhikṣus* and ten *bhikṣuṇīs* appear to have lapsed periodically in China, Korea, and Vietnam, but there is no evidence that the *bhikṣuṇī* lineage has been interrupted at any time in Chinese history. There are differences of opinion about whether a *bhikṣuṇī* ordination conducted by *bhikṣus* alone is valid or not.

Where *bhikṣuṇīs* do not exist to ordain *śrāmaṇerikās*, novices are selected and ordained by monks, who may not carefully assess their qualifications and may not assume responsibility for their care after ordination. The selection of nuns by monks has resulted in many difficulties, even tragedies, and caused some nuns to recognize the importance of women's participation in the ordination process. *Bhikṣuṇīs* must learn to conduct the *śrāmaṇerikā*, *śikṣamāṇā*, and *bhikṣuṇī* ordinations and assume active responsibility for the training of future generations of Buddhist nuns. Now that sufficient numbers of Western nuns have received *bhikṣuṇī* ordination and have the requisite twelve years of seniority, this has become a possibility. If Western *bhikṣuṇīs* learn to conduct the ordinations for nuns and are willing to serve as mentors, they will be able to ensure that the women who join their order are carefully selected and properly trained. This requires not only that these *bhikṣuṇīs* themselves are thoroughly trained and educated, but also that they are prepared to train and support the nuns they ordain. Monastic communities as conducive environments for the education and training of nuns—and monks—are essential for the authentic transmission of Dharma to the West.

WOMEN, MONASTICISM, AND INTERNATIONAL DIALOGUE

Conferences, seminars, and informal gatherings held around the world in recent years have stimulated research into women's past and present roles in Buddhism and have helped envision an expansion of these roles. Most of these gatherings have been organized informally as a result of private initiatives, without the support of traditional Buddhist institutions. The objectives have been women's empowerment, networking, meditation training, and education on issues relevant to women. In the course of these discussions, the need for an organized, educated, unified, self-sufficient order of nuns has been clearly recognized, but much work remains to make it a reality.

The first international meeting of Buddhist nuns in recorded history occurred in Bodhgaya, India, in 1987. Although the impetus for this first conference was specifically to address the pressing issues facing Buddhist nuns at that time, the consensus at the close of the conference led participants to forge a coalition among nuns and laywomen called Sakyadhita, the first international Buddhist women's organization. Sakyadhita's major objectives include improving education, communications, facilities, and ordination opportunities for Buddhist nuns, and considerable progress has been made on all counts. This organization continues to foster cooperation among nuns and laywomen around the world through local, national, and international gatherings, as well as through publications and other projects.

Nuns have actively promoted dialogue among Western monastics in general. Since 1995, Tenzin Kacho and Thubten Chodron have helped organize an annual Western Monastic Buddhist Conference. Dialogue has centered on such varied topics as friendship, lay/monastic relations, interpersonal communications skills, leadership, counseling, teaching skills, and prison work. Participants sense that ordained teachers have a special role to play in maintaining the authenticity of the Buddhist traditions, whereas lay teachers are more interested in adapting those traditions. If this is the case, then continued dialogue between monastic and lay practitioners is essential for achieving a balance between authenticity and adaptation.

In 1996, a three-week educational program, called "Life as a Western Buddhist Nun," was held in Bodhgaya, attended by eighty nuns (including twenty from Tibet and the Himalayan region) and twenty interested laywomen, several of whom subsequently received ordination. In a message sent to participants in this program, H. H. Dalai Lama observed that, "In the past, in many Buddhist countries, nuns did not have the same educational opportunities as monks, nor access to the same facilities. Due to prevailing social attitudes nuns were often treated or regarded in ways that are no longer acceptable today. . . . It is heartening to observe . . . that Buddhist women are casting off traditional and outmoded restraints." The talks from this program have been compiled by *bhikṣuṇī* Thubten Chodron in *Blossoms of the Dharma: Living as a Buddhist Nun*.[23]

Several conferences on the *bhikṣuṇī* issue have been held in Dharamsala, but Western *bhikṣuṇī* scholars have not been invited to participate in them. Despite the supportive attitude of H. H. Dalai Lama on the matter of higher ordination for women, these discussions clearly indicate that many *bhikṣu* scholars and monastic administrators oppose or are noncommittal on the subject. The issue is complicated by language difficulties, the lack of historical documents to verify the unbroken continuity of the Chinese *bhikṣuṇī*

lineage, age-old attitudes of gender discrimination, and politics, both religious and secular. Hopefully Buddhist institutions will begin to recognize
that equitable dialogue on the *bhikṣuṇī* issue must involve not only
bhikṣuṇī scholars but also those most concerned: the *bhikṣuṇīs* themselves.

ANACHRONISM OR PALLIATIVE?

At a time when vocations are declining drastically in the Catholic monastic
orders, it is reasonable to question the contemporary appeal and value of
Buddhist monastic life. Celibacy is often misinterpreted as repression or as
an unnatural form of self-denial. Women who choose monastic life are assumed to be rejecting the good things in life: men, children, shopping, a lu-
crative career, parties, and fashion. There may be little appreciation in ordinary Western society for the freedoms and advantages that a disciplined
spiritual life can offer. Contemporary societies are currently experimenting with models of family and community. This may be an opportune time
to re-examine monastic life, to discover which aspects are vital and valuable, and which are outdated and expendable.

Many believe that monasticism is anachronistic, hopelessly patriarchal,
and irrelevant to the multiple crises of modern culture. However, the continuing successes of Tassajara, Shasta Abbey, the City of Ten Thousand
Buddhas, Gampo Abbey, and other monastic communities in Western
countries give rise to optimism. They are valuable crucibles for celibate
practitioners, as well as for householders who can practice intensively for a
time and then resume their household responsibilities. The assumption
that Buddhist monastic institutions are inherently patriarchal is largely
based on existing Asian models, but the successful evolution of Western
monastic institutions reveals that nothing is sacred about these models.
Changes these Western institutions have wrought include the inclusion of
householders, women, and non-Buddhists; the decentralization of authority; innovative forms of communication, such as councils; temporary residency; work/study programs; and fluid approaches to monastic rules and
administration.

The traditional rationale behind Buddhist celibacy and circumscribed
sexuality is primarily the assumption that desire, especially sexual desire,
perpetuates patterns of craving and grasping that invariably lead to further
rebirths and sufferings. Sexual desire is treated as a product of the mind,
rather than as a physical need. Buddhist monasticism is therefore based on
the contention that mental and physical discipline will naturally diminish
desires. Though they are not an unbiased sample, contented celibates agree.

It is frequently assumed that the Mahāyāna tradition represents a shift,[24] but, theoretically at least, the value placed on maintaining celibacy remains unchanged. It is when the *Prātimokṣa* precepts are rejected, neglected, or replaced by other values and expectations that lapses of the monastic ideal occur.

Nurturing a generation of fully qualified teachers requires an extended period of intensive education and training. When facilities for this type of education and training are unavailable or too costly, prospective Buddhist teachers will need to study and train in Asia, where facilities, for monks at least, are fully supported by the laity. Women are clearly at a disadvantage in this regard. In many Asian countries, facilities for Buddhist studies for women are sorely lacking. Those Buddhist studies programs that are available to women—in Taiwan and Korea, for example—require near-fluency in the language of instruction and women often lack access to costly language-learning facilities. Few Western women have made the commitment to train in one of these two demanding practice environments, primarily because their teachers belong to other traditions, usually Japanese, Theravādin, or Tibetan. Independent-minded Western nuns generally opt for self-sufficiency, though at considerable cost to traditional monastic orthodoxy.

Asian Buddhist societies have traditionally respected, nurtured, and benefited from having religious specialists who set themselves outside the mainstream, reject family life, and concentrate their energies fully on Dharma study and practice. Although laypeople are also fully capable of intensive practice, monastic life by nature allows more time for this practice. Integrating the teachings into daily life is essential for both monastics and householders, but to achieve the ultimate fruits of practice amidst a family is extraordinarily difficult.

CONCLUSION

As Western Buddhism matures and practitioners experience contemplative practice more deeply, an appreciation for the monastic lifestyle as a conducive context for intensive Dharma practice seems inevitable. Buddhist nuns in the West are hopeful that the value of the lifestyle they have chosen will eventually be acknowledged and appreciated in the West. Hopefully the spirit of tolerance and the celebration of diversity will expand in Western societies to celebrate the practice of celibate monasticism for women. It is often assumed that nuns have chosen monastic celibacy because they lack other opportunities, but the achievements and successes of

Buddhist nuns in the West, as throughout Buddhist history, belie these stereotypes. Though their contributions have often been ignored, Buddhist nuns are emerging as teachers and exemplars of Buddhist values, and preconceptions about their motives and capabilities are beginning to change. Despite practical difficulties and gender discrimination, through their struggle to embody the liberating power of the Dharma, Buddhist nuns living in vastly different circumstances in Western societies are transforming Buddhist religious discourse.

NOTES

1. Bhikṣuṇī Shih I Han, "Chinese Nuns in Los Angeles," in *Sakyadhita: Daughters of the Buddha*, edited by Karma Lekshe Tsomo (Ithaca, New York: Snow Lion, 1988), 304–8.

2. Their stories are included in Lenore Friedman, *Meetings with Remarkable Women: Buddhist Teachers in America* (Boston: Shambhala, 1987).

3. Charles S. Prebish, *Luminous Passage: The Practice and Study of Buddhism in America* (Berkeley: University of California Press, 1999), 146.

4. Yuchen Li, "Ordination, Legitimacy, and Sisterhood: The International Full Ordination Ceremony in Bodhgaya," in *Innovative Buddhist Women: Swimming against the Stream*, edited by Karma Lekshe Tsomo (Richmond, U.K.: Curzon Press, 2000), 168–98.

5. An interview with Pema Chödrön appears in Lenore Friedman, *Meetings with Remarkable Women*.

6. Thich Minh Duc, "Dam Luu: An Eminent Vietnamese Buddhist Nun," in Karma Lekshe Tsomo, *Innovative Buddhist Women*, 104–20.

7. Richard Hughes Seager, *Buddhism in America* (New York: Columbia University Press, 1999), 152.

8. Li, "Ordination, Legitimacy, and Sisterhood," 173.

9. See Bhikṣuṇī Tenzin Namdrol, "Blossoming in Plum Village," in *Blossoms of the Dharma: Living as a Buddhist Nun*, edited by Thubten Chodron (Berkeley: North Atlantic Books, 1999), 75–81.

10. Sister Chân Không tells her story in *Learning True Love: How I Learned and Practiced Social Change in Vietnam* (Berkeley: Parallax Press, 1993).

11. Prebish, *Luminous Passage*, 51–3, 92–3.

12. See Ayya Khema, *I Give You My Life: The Autobiography of a Western Buddhist Nun* (Boston: Shambhala, 1998).

13. Thubten Chodron relates her experience of becoming a nun in "You're Becoming a What? Living as a Western Buddhist Nun," in *Buddhist Women on the Edge: Contemporary Perspectives from the Western Frontier*, edited by Marianne Dresser (Berkeley: North Atlantic Books, 1996), 223–33.

14. Tenzin Palmo's autobiography has been compiled by Vicki Mackenzie, *Cave in the Snow: Tenzin Palmo's Quest for Enlightenment* (New York: Bloomsbury, 1998).

15. Chi Kwang Sunim describes her experiences in "A Strong Tradition Adapting to Change: The Nuns in Korea," in Thubten Chodron, *Blossoms of the Dharma*, 103–18.

16. The nuns are from Australia, Britain, Canada, France, Germany, Italy, Malaysia, Nepal, the Netherlands, New Zealand, Norway, Puerto Rico, Saudi Arabia,

Scotland, Singapore, Spain, Sweden, Switzerland, Taiwan, Tibet, the United States, and Vietnam. Of these nuns, twelve are 20–30 years old, forty-three are 30–50, and thirty-five are 50–70.

17. Bhikṣuṇī Tenzin Palmo, in "The Situation of Western Monastics," records a conversation with H. H. Dalai Lama about the difficulties that face newly ordained Western monastics, which moved His Holiness to tears. In Thubten Chodron, *Blossoms of the Dharma*, 184–7.

18. Thubten Chodron, "Western Buddhist Nuns: A New Phenomenon in an Ancient Tradition," in *Women's Buddhism, Buddhism's Women: Tradition, Revision, Renewal*, edited by Ellison Banks Findly (Boston: Wisdom, 2000).

19. See Samu Sunim, "Eunyeong Sunim and the Founding of Pomun-jon, the First Independent Bhikshuni Order," in "Women and Buddhism," special issue, *Spring Wind Buddhist Cultural Forum* 6, nos. 1, 2, and 3 (1986), 129–62; and Li, "Ordination, Legitimacy, and Sisterhood," 168–98.

20. Bhikkhunī Kusuma, "Inaccuracies in Buddhist Women's History," in Karma Lekshe Tsomo, *Innovative Buddhist Women*, 5–12.

21. "The Bhiksuni Issue," in Tsomo, *Sakyadhita*, 215–76.

22. Li, "Ordination, Legitimacy, and Sisterhood," 188–94.

23. Chodron, *Blossoms of the Dharma*.

24. For example, Bernard Faure states, "With the emergence of Mahāyāna Buddhism, a trend reversal takes place—or perhaps one should speak rather of a progressive shift toward more positive conceptions of desire and passions. Mahāyāna is generally said to have advocated a less ascetic, more tolerant (or laxist, depending on the viewpoint) conception of Buddhist practice." See Bernard Faure, *The Red Thread: Buddhist Approaches to Sexuality* (Princeton: Princeton University Press, 1998).

Western Buddhists as Full-Time Practitioners

Sylvia Wetzel

INTRODUCTION

Buddhism has now come to Western lands, to Europe and North America, where it is undergoing changes and appears differently than in Asia. One striking difference, compared with the East, is the presence of Western lay-women as teachers in non-Buddhist venues. In Sri Lanka, for example, a monk in saffron robes would teach white-clad laypeople in a temple. In India, Tibetan monks in exile, wearing maroon robes, teach Western students in lavishly furnished Tibetan temples. Although robe colors, ritual styles, meditation techniques, and the languages used in recitations may differ from one Asian country to another, many features of Asian Buddhist practice are similar. Thus male monastics or priests with titles, wearing robes, commonly teach in temples.

In the West, as the year 2000 drew to a close, the majority of Buddhist teachers were laypeople and half of them were women. The lay teachers teach mostly in Buddhist lay centers or in secular settings. Who are these lay teachers, and what kind of Buddhism do they teach? Is this still Buddhism? Or is it a Western-style hybridization of psychology and Buddhism?[1] As a laywoman and teacher, I am a natural-born heretic in the traditional Buddhist world of ordained male teachers. But being a lay disciple and being a woman may well be advantages in our times, for these attributes seem to endow a Buddhist teacher with sharp eyes, much humor, an adventurous and playful mind, methodical skills, and great patience . . . all qualities needed to bring the Buddhadharma into a new culture successfully. The foregoing outlook may explain the great hope I place in laywomen who teach Buddhism in the West.

THE NEW TEACHERS

Who are the male and female teachers now active in the West? What are they exactly: laypeople or professional teachers of Buddhism? What is their training? What status do they have in their own Western communities, in the eyes of Asian teachers, and in the ranks of the traditional schools of Buddhism? Are they just hobby Buddhists, just household priests without a temple? Do the changes they evidence reflect something radically new, or are those changes the sort of occurrence that happens whenever Buddhism comes into a new culture? Is the dominant role of teachers who teach without robes, titles, and temples a sign of the degeneration of Buddhism, or is it a specific feature of a slowly emerging, authentically Western style of Buddhism?

In Asia, we find different traditional models for practitioners and teachers. The ordained monks and nuns who constitute the Sangha are considered the "real" professionals.[2] They dedicate their lives, ideally, to the study and practice of Buddhadharma. Laypeople can receive lay ordination; lay practice emphasizes generosity (dāna), ethical behavior (śīla), and supporting the Sangha materially by offering food, money, labor, and organizational skills. The Tibetan traditions include the model of practice by yogis and yoginīs, men and women who are full-time practitioners of Tantric Buddhism and who spend most of their lives in intensive meditative retreat. In Japan, there have been no monks or nuns living and practicing according to the strict code of the Vinaya since the Meiji Restoration in the nineteenth century.[3] The Japanese Shin tradition abandoned the Vinaya from the outset, and its priests are legally married. In the Japanese Rinzai and Sōtō Zen and Shin traditions, future priests are trained in monasteries and live a celibate monastic life through the course of their training. Upon conclusion of the training period, they become householding priests, married for the most part; they manage temples and, with their wives, function as the focal points of the local Buddhist communities. Sons of such men are considered suitable candidates to inherit the paternal temple. The Japanese traditions consider these married priests as monks and "celibates," because they are not legally married but live together with so-called temple wives. Such female priests as there are tend to take care of smaller temples, to remain celibate, and to consider themselves to be nuns. Their lifestyle is closest to the classical Vinaya. Because it would be difficult to find a Japanese husband willing to care for children and household so these women could devote themselves to their religious duties, their view of themselves as nuns is understandable.

Some Western teachers in the Japanese traditions follow the household priest model: they are married, they run small temples in Western cities or bigger centers in the country, they have titles, and they wear robes when they discharge priestly functions. Some of the married Zen priests call themselves *monks*, which leads to debates among some Western students and teachers who suggest that the Western term *monk* should be used strictly for celibates. Some Western teachers in the Tibetan traditions are called *lama* after completion of a three-year retreat. A *lama* may be ordained or lay. The term simply means "my teacher." Some of these Western *lamas* remain celibate monks and nuns after their retreats; most do not. Some non-monastic teachers wear the traditional lay teacher's robes on the occasion of formal teachings and ceremonies. Other Western teachers in the Tibetan traditions teach with the permission of their own teachers, but have no titles and do not wear robes. In the *vipassanā* communities, most Western teachers are lay; a few Westerners who teach in the Theravādin tradition are ordained as monks or nuns and garbed in saffron robes, but the majority are not ordained. To summarize: most Western teachers do not wear robes, do not have temples, do not consider themselves to be priests, and yet are still teachers of Buddhism.

What are these lay teachers? Why do they choose not to take ordination as monks and nuns if they feel drawn to the full-time practice of Buddhism? They are professional Buddhists, in the sense that they are fully dedicated to studying, practicing, and teaching the Buddhadharma, and Dharma is the focal point in their lives. But they live in secular settings, often with partners, with and without children, some married, some unmarried. The *vipassanā* community consists chiefly of lay teachers. Couples exist in which both members teach and lead Buddhist retreats.

Most first-generation lay teachers in the West were trained and authorized by Asian teachers; the second generation was sponsored primarily by Western teachers from the first generation. In general, most male and female lay teachers are well accepted within their Western communities, even though many Asian teachers, and a discernible number of Western students as well, seem to prefer that Westerners who teach be monastic and male. In the Tibetan Gelugpa tradition, an unwritten rule requires that a Western center should first invite an ordained monk to teach, and should invite a lay teacher only if no ordained monk is available.

Once teachings given by non-monastics are allowed, the question of training becomes vital. Western centers began the attempt to establish training courses for older students and for Western teachers in the late 1980s. Programs vary in diversity and depth. Some centers and temples offer traditional training, without much cultural adaptation. Others seek to incorporate Western scientific methods and psychological approaches. For example, since the early 1980s the Kagyu tradition of Tibetan Buddhism has offered a traditional three-year training for Western students. The aim of the training is to qualify Westerners to perform traditional rituals and recitations and to guide Western students in traditional meditation practices. During the training course, the participants live in celibacy. Some receive the title *lama* afterward. The most radical training approach to date (developed by three American teachers, each from a different Buddhist tradition) took place in 1999. This pioneering one-week training was aimed at Buddhist teachers and teacher-aspirants who had already received formal training in one of the major Buddhist schools; its objectives were to help the participants understand and refine their roles as teachers within a context determined by Western cultural conditioning and to focus on intention and how intention leads to content, form, and format.[4]

PROGRAMS AND CHANGES

Most training programs teach students in a single tradition, sometimes in a given subschool of the tradition. These programs offer depth, but often suffer from the failure to provide a broad foundation or to utilize and benefit from Western philological, philosophical, historical, and psychological approaches. A recognizable number of senior students and teachers in Western Buddhism contend that there is great need to establish general study programs for Western students and for future Western teachers that are not confined to one school or tradition and that include and utilize Western methods. The incorporation of Buddhist Studies in Western universities may stimulate Buddhist centers to cooperate in presenting broader general studies. At present, teacher training is a work in progress. In the United States, universities seem more open, fortunately, than universities in Europe to offering courses taught by Buddhist practitioners.

Another, distinctly pragmatic feature of Western Buddhism works to favor lay teachers. As Buddhism is introduced into the secular societies of the West, the people who attend Buddhist courses are not interested just in a religious path. Three groups of people acquire Buddhist books and attend Buddhist courses: one group has a spiritual motivation; the members of the second group are engaged with philosophical questions; the members of the third group want practical help for their daily lives. These three groups correspond to the three levels of aspiration for meditative practice: soteriological (where the aim is liberation or salvation from worldly turmoil), existential, and therapeutic.[5] If it is true that most of the people who attend Buddhist events are interested in advice regarding daily life, Western lay teachers seem especially qualified to serve as advisors. Because women tend to teach more on practical levels and to put less emphasis on traditional and dogmatic aspects of the teachings, women lay teachers may be the best re-sources for these people.

Western teachers, working with Western students, inevitably develop new styles of teaching. To be sure, the preponderance of Buddhist talks and courses are still conducted in the traditional frontal manner, where the teacher talks and the audience, facing the teacher, listens. But question and answer sessions occur more frequently, and so the teacher listens and the audience speaks. Authentic roundtable discussions have begun to take place. Women teachers seem particularly disposed to experiment with a va-riety of teaching methods: sitting in a circle, small discussion groups, painting, writing, even dancing and role-playing. A woman Zen master regularly made walking outings with her students, teaching meditative hiking. A woman Theravāda teacher regularly goes to hot springs with her students and teaches mindful swimming. Other teachers have introduced charts and flip-charts in teaching sessions. E-mail discussion groups exist. The opportunities for introducing innovative teaching methods, in short, are spacious. Women teachers focus both on spoken and on nonverbal com-munication methods, and they work with the senses by means, for ex-ample, of chanting and movement. Male teachers seem more at ease with, and therefore drawn to, intellectual methods and to new media, such as the internet.[6]

Another crucial change underway in Western Buddhism concerns the relationship between teacher and student, which is less hierarchical in the West than in Asia. Granted that a certain hierarchical element inheres in any teacher/student relationship. If a student sincerely wishes to learn something, the student needs to consider the teacher as being more knowl-edgeable. But how this vertical element manifests, and what its conse-quences are for the two individuals involved, depends to a great extent upon social conditioning and upon the genders of the teacher and the stu-dent. In Asia, the model teacher/student relationship resembles the male lord/knight relationship of feudal society. The loyal knight did whatever the lord required.

The early Buddhist *sūtras* suggest that the main refuge is the teaching, not the teacher. As he was dying, the historic Buddha did not appoint a suc-cessor but instead told his disciples to take refuge in the teachings. All Buddhist traditions recommend that a student check out a potential teacher soundly and carefully, and then, once the teacher has been accepted, the student is encouraged to follow the teacher's advice scrupulously and whole-heartedly. The Vajrayāna tradition holds that "the root of the path is proper devotion to a kind and venerable guru," and students of Tantra are taught to regard the teacher who introduces them to a Tantric practice as a Buddha in all his activities.[7] They state that even when a teacher is not enlightened from his side, for the student to regard the teacher as an enlightened being nevertheless is the swiftest path to the purification of the student's heart and mind. The procedure seems psychologically effective if both sides understand that it is a *method*, not a *fact*. But few students understand the critical nuance. They tend to objectify their teacher as authentically enlightened and thereby fall into the traps of idealization and objectification.

Heartfelt devotion to a qualified teacher can greatly speed up the student's maturation process. If a perfect student meets a perfect teacher, the model may yield wonderful spiritual results. We all know the inspiration of learning from a teacher we respect and love deeply. But it seems that such perfect relationships were rare in the past, have been rare in all Asian countries, and are rare today in Asia and the West alike. So it is questionable how useful it is to teach ordinary Western students to orient themselves to such an ideal. If the effects of dysfunctional families in the West are considered, there is a high probability that the *guru* model will lead to serious difficulties. Western students often look for a father figure and try to solve their problems with an idealized *guru*. People with low self-esteem are especially prone to idealizing teachers in an unhealthy way. If Western teachers are aware of problems like these and understand the mechanics of psychological transference, they can work effectively with such formations. At its best, a wholesome teacher/student relationship may help students heal old wounds. In the worst cases, both Asian and Western teachers manipulate and abuse the psychological frailties of their students and exploit the students on psychological and material levels. Women students in particular run the risk of being misused as obedient servants or sex objects if they naively trust a teacher who is psychologically unhealthy.

Thorough education in psychological processes and the professional supervision of teachers in training would help mitigate and avoid abuse of the teacher/student relationship. Some Western teachers have indeed undergone psychotherapeutic training and work with supervisors. In centers founded by Asian teachers with strong personalities, especially in the Japanese and Tibetan traditions, Western teachers (especially the men) tend to reproduce the Asian teacher/student model and assume an authoritarian role in an unwholesome way, particularly where the role is supported by robes, titles, temples, and other trappings of status and power. But there are grounds for hope. A high number of lay and especially women lay teachers are quite aware of these issues. They are open to psychological training and they support the introduction of Western teachers to psychological train-ing. It is right that psychological training should have a high priority in the education of Westerners who teach Buddhism, so that their work can be both clean and more effective. The willingness to name and to deal with psychological issues is a positive development.[8]

SOCIAL AND CULTURAL CONDITIONS

We have considered several aspects of full-time Western Buddhists who function without robes or titles, and several of the effects that they are pro-ducing. Now let us enumerate the main conditions that contribute to the large numbers of lay Buddhist teachers in the West. The following five so-cial and cultural conditions seem particularly salient.

1. *Affluence.*   Life in affluent Western societies allows many members of the (mainly white) middle class to work a relatively few hours for their livelihood and to dedicate the rest of their time to intensive Buddhist stud-ies and practices. Ordination is not a prerequisite to finding time for study and practice. This situation is especially true for women who no longer see the purpose of life as finding a husband and rearing children. Society now widely accepts that women (and men) may live alone, elect not to have chil-dren, and . . . choose to study and to teach Buddhism.

2. *Secularization.*   Monasticism is no longer a pertinent institution in Western societies. It is considered old-fashioned and is associated with the Middle Ages and the feudal society of a pre-industrial, pre-internet agri-cultural economy. In modern Western society, the monastic lifestyle does not attract or appeal much to Buddhist practitioners of either sex.

3. *Criticism of patriarchal structures.*   The celibate lifestyle has existed traditionally in patriarchal societies and patriarchal religions dominated by men and by male values and interests, such as asceticism, renunciation, celibacy, metaphors of the warrior battling against the flesh, purity, per-fection, otherworldliness, dogmas, complex rituals, hierarchies, and so on.

4. *Status of women in society.*   Wherever women obtain and exercise social and economic power, the roles of men and women change and soci-ety as a whole changes. The strong interest in Buddhism on the part of well-educated Western women has led and continues to lead to the training of women as Buddhist teachers. These teachers directly and indirectly in-troduce female values, such as working with feelings, emotions, and rela-tionships; the processes of nurturing and feeding positive qualities; accept-ance of imperfection; emphasis on completeness and connectivity with this world; spontaneous rituals; and networking. In general, women seem less

concerned than men with status; with temples, robes, and titles; and with schools and traditional teachings. This orientation helps to create opportunities and room for new models of teachers and teaching styles to appear.[9]

5. *Individualized lifestyles.* People today live more individualized lifestyles. Social activities and work situations entail more instability and more insecurity, and at the same time offer more choices, than ever before. Westerners who are seriously interested in the study and practice of Buddhism have many options beyond becoming part of a religious structure as a monk, nun, or priest. They can decide to study and practice with pervasive wholeheartedness and also to lead a life in keeping with their individualized Western upbringing. So we find, in the West, people who are neither monks nor nuns, neither priests nor part of a religious structure, and yet are full-time practitioners who teach secular Buddhism in a secular setting. Historically, this seems to be a new phenomenon, for all the societies into which Buddhism has been introduced in the past have been traditional societies, ranging from small Indian republics to societies with feudal or nomadic structures. Asian societies, and the institutions composing them, were organized relatively rigidly. While the option for living as an individual hermit was commonly present, anyone who wished to live inside society as a full-time Buddhist practitioner had to enter a socially determined institution, either a temple or a Buddhist school. The situation is completely different today.

CONCLUSIONS

Several economic, social, and cultural factors contribute to the arising of a new type of Buddhist teacher: the Westerner who leads a secular life and is still a full-time practitioner and teacher. The question of thorough training has been raised. One additional question remains unsettled: how do Western lay teachers earn their livelihood? Tradition prescribes that monastics live from non-monetary donations made by the laity. The monastics give teachings to the lay population, and in return are given donations for their support. The tradition accepts that Tibetan *yogis* and *yoginīs* receive donations from their students, and that Japanese householding priests receive donations from temple-goers or are paid by an institution.

Contemporary Western lay teachers accept money payments from their students for meditation retreats, regular classes, and individual consultations. Some ordained teachers and some laypeople object, and suggest that lay teachers should support themselves with earnings from a secular job. But the objection seems to miss the point. The issue is not whether or not

Buddhist teachers receive money in exchange for teaching, but what the motivation for the teaching is. The traditional argument has been that if teachers receive money for teaching, the payment will spoil their motivation and they will end up selling the Dharma for worldly gain. Of course, the argument is as valid for monastic teachers who receive donations of food and other necessities as it is for lay teachers who receive money. The crux is that any Buddhist teacher, lay or monastic, unordained or ordained, must consciously check his or her motivation for teaching. An argument in favor of paying money in exchange for teaching is that a teacher who has to work in a secular job for support has less time for study and practice.

One solution might be to regard anyone whose main focus in life is studying and practicing Buddhism and who teaches the Buddhadharma as a worthy vessel for receiving donations, whether or not the person is ordained. Today, in fact, the two systems operate side by side quite peacefully. The donation model seems to work for monastics and for many lay teachers in the West, and some monastics receive stipulated monetary honoraria for their work. Many Western teachers offer their services as individual meditation coaches and counselors and charge fees professionally, just as therapists, doctors, and lawyers do, in a number of cases on a sliding-scale basis. Settling the issue and role of money in the context of Buddhist teaching in the West will require more time and experience. As the number of lay teachers increases, so more models of ways to lead a life of Buddhist practice in the West will appear, and time will show what means and ways are useful and supportive for teachers and students alike.

NOTES

1. Some of these questions are discussed in Mark Epstein, *Thoughts without a Thinker* (New York: HarperCollins, 1995); Stephen Batchelor, *Buddhism without Beliefs: A Contemporary Guide to Awakening* (New York: Riverhead, 1997); and Sandy Boucher, *Turning the Wheel: American Women Creating the New Buddhism* (San Francisco: Harper and Row, 1988).

2. The Pāli term *sangha*, literally "community," is traditionally used for the order of ordained men and women. Ordination is given according to the rules of the *Vinaya*, the corpus of ethical guidelines given by the Buddha.

3. For a short survey on the influence of social conditions on the different styles of Buddhism in Asia, see Heinz Bechert and Richard Gombrich (eds.), *The World of Buddhism* (New York: Facts on File, 1984).

4. More information about traditional and Westernized training in the United States is easily found in advertisements in the magazine *Tricycle: The Buddhist Review,* especially in the directory at the end (http://www.tricycle.com [4 Feb. 2002]). For information about the pioneering training course for Western Buddhist teachers, contact Unfettered Mind: Pragmatic Buddhism, 13323 Washington Blvd., Suite 302, Los Angeles, California 90066-5144, (310) 827-7766, www.unfetteredmind.com [4 January 2002], ken@unfetteredmind.org.

5. The three groups were described by an American scholar of Buddhism, Elizabeth Napper, at the Sakyadhita Conference in Frankfurt, Germany, in February 1997. The groups and percentages match my own experience since 1986 in teaching Buddhist courses. The three levels of meditative effects are described by Roger Walsh in Raymond J. Corsini, *Handbook of Innovative Psychotherapies* (New York: Wiley, 1981; German version, 1984), vol. 1, 664.

6. The late Rinzai Zen teacher Prabhasa Dharma Rōshi went hiking with her students in Yosemite Park. The Theravādin teacher Ruth Denison teaches mindful swimming. Sylvia Kolk, also a German Theravādin teacher, and I led a one-week study retreat in spring 2000 at which we asked the students to role-play Buddhist *sūtras* on the five *skandhas*. The students reported uniformly that the role-playing greatly deepened their understanding of texts that are often difficult to comprehend.

7. All Tibetan traditions teach *guru*-devotion at an early stage in training. Thus *guru*-devotion is one of the first topics in the Graduated Path literature (Tib. *Lam-rim*), and many *lamas* love to teach classical texts such as Asvaghosha's *Fifty Verses of Guru Devotion*, even to relatively new students. The Kagyu and Nyingma lineages especially stress *guru*-devotion as the crucial factor for effective practice.

8. For a thorough study of psychological issues for students of Buddhism based on studies in the United States and in Asia, see Ken Wilber, Jack Engler, and Daniel P. Brown, *Transformations of Consciousness: Conventional and Contemplative Respectives on Development* (Boston: New Science Library, 1986). Recommended reading for teachers of all sorts is Peter Rutter, *Sex in the Forbidden Zone* (Los Angeles: Jeremy B. Tarcher, 1986). For psychological training for Western teachers, see note 4, Unfettered Mind: Pragmatic Buddhism.

9. See Epstein, *Thoughts without a Thinker*, and Wilber, Engler, and Brown, *Transformations of Consciousness*. A recent women's guide to Buddhism (mainly in the United States) gives a detailed survey on new topics important for women and lists many women teachers in both the United States and Europe. See Sandy Boucher, *Opening the Lotus: A Woman's Guide to Buddhism* (Boston: Beacon Press, 1997).

Virtues without Rules

*Ethics in the Insight
Meditation Movement*

Gil Fronsdal

INTRODUCTION

Observers have commented that for Buddhism to take firm hold in the West it needs to develop a well-articulated ethic. This chapter is a study of how Buddhist ethics is taught within one rapidly growing movement of Western Buddhism: what I will be calling the Insight Meditation movement. While the movement has so far published no overview of its ethics, enough material is now available for us to discern some general points.

Among Buddhist movements in the West, the Insight Meditation movement is unique in that it is not simply a transplant of an Asian Buddhist tradition. Rather, it can be seen as a new tradition taking shape in the West around particular meditative practices of *vipassanā*, often translated as "insight meditation" or colloquially as "mindfulness practice." *Vipassanā* practice is clearly derived from the Theravāda Buddhism of South and Southeast Asia, where it has a central soteriological role. However, in bringing this meditation practice to the West, the founders of the Insight Meditation movement have consciously downplayed (or even jettisoned) many important elements of the Theravāda tradition, including monasticism, rituals, merit-making, and Buddhist cosmology. Without these and other elements, the Insight Meditation movement has been relatively unencumbered in developing itself into a form of Western Buddhism. In doing so, it has retained only a minimal identification with its Theravāda origins.

Ethics, morality, and virtue have central roles in the Asian Theravāda tradition. All three of these English terms can be used to translate the Pāli word *sīla* that appears in the important three-fold division of the Theravādin Buddhist spiritual path: *sīla, samādhi,* and *paññā* (ethics, meditative absorption, and wisdom). The primary question I ask here is: In what ways has the Theravāda concept of *sīla* been translated in the Western Insight Meditation movement? Other questions asked are: How central is ethics to the Insight Meditation movement? How are Buddhist ethical teachings understood? Are there innovations or developments particular to the movement or to its Western setting? My hope is that addressing these and other issues will contribute to an understanding of the major cross-cultural issue of how ethics and codes of conduct travel from one culture to another.

One of the unique features of this movement is that it consists predominantly of laypeople engaged in meditative practices traditionally associated with monastics. Historically, the Theravāda tradition's teachings on lay ethics were addressed to people who, by and large, did not meditate. Teachings to the laity did not, therefore, emphasize a relationship between ethics and meditation. Lay ethics was advocated by stressing the benefits and merits, or the harm and demerits, that various actions would bring in this or future lives. For the majority of Western lay Insight Meditation practitioners, however, the ideas of merit and rebirth hold little sway. Rather, meditation is the primary Buddhist activity providing the basis for understanding Buddhist teachings. How then, does the movement view the relationship between meditation and ethical behavior?

The next section will give a general introduction to the Insight Meditation movement, including a definition. This is followed by a study of the movement's ethical teachings, including a detailed discussion of the role of the five lay precepts. While these precepts do not always have a prominent role, the way they are handled provides a useful reference for understanding the movement's approach to ethics.

THE INSIGHT MEDITATION MOVEMENT

Currently no clear institutional, doctrinal, or membership boundaries exist for the wide range of Western practitioners of the Theravāda practice of *vipassanā*, that is, the meditative cultivation of undistracted, and at times highly concentrated, attentiveness to what is being experienced in the present. However, the subject of this study and what I am calling the *Insight Meditation movement* are those *vipassanā* practitioners, teachers, institutions, and publications with either formal or close informal affiliation with the Insight Meditation Society (IMS) in Barre, Massachusetts, and Spirit Rock Meditation Center in Marin County, California. This includes the meditation centers and sitting groups led by teachers or practitioners affiliated with these two. IMS and Spirit Rock are the most visible and active *vipassanā* centers in North America. Furthermore, the largest, best organized and most clearly bounded groups of Western *vipassanā* teachers are those associated with these centers.[1] In defining the Insight Meditation movement in this way, it is important to recognize that this definition might obscure some real differences in teachings among the movement's teachers.

It is also important to remember that this Insight Meditation movement is a subset of a much larger movement of *vipassanā* teachers in the West. On one end of a broad spectrum are Theravāda monks and nuns teaching the practice within the religious context of their Theravāda temples. On the other end are people with no personal affiliation with, or even interest in, Buddhism, teaching Theravāda-derived mindfulness practices in such secular applications as pain and stress reduction. In between are many people and centers teaching the practice independent of any affiliation with the Insight Meditation movement. Of particular importance is the influential network of meditation centers operating under the direction of the Indian *vipassanā* teacher S. N. Goenka.

The Insight Meditation movement had its origin in the Theravāda Buddhism of Thailand, Burma, and modern India. During the 1960s, young Westerners traveling in Asia and Americans serving in the Peace Corps encountered Theravāda meditation teachers under whom they trained in *vipassanā* or insight meditation.[2] A few of these Westerners were ordained as monastics; others practiced intensively as laypeople. By the early 1970s, some of them were returning to the West and beginning to teach *vipassanā*. Those who had been ordained while in Asia left the monkhood, so from its inception in North America the Insight Meditation movement was led by lay meditation teachers. The early *vipassanā* teachers primarily taught meditation, consciously choosing to leave out many of the doctrines, practices, rituals, and other elements of traditional Theravāda Buddhism.[3] This choice was not necessarily innovative, but rather was a continuation of the style of practice found in some of the meditation centers in which they trained in Asia. This simplification contributed greatly to the growing popularity of the meditation practice, in part by making the practice accessible to people with little or no interest in Theravāda Buddhism.

The best marker for the beginning of this movement are the meditation courses that Joseph Goldstein and Jack Kornfield taught at Naropa Institute during the summer of 1974.[4] From that start, the movement has grown quickly. Over the years the number of teachers has steadily increased, so that by 2000 the IMS and Spirit Rock network of *vipassanā* teachers consisted of about seventy-five people.[5] In its first issue in 1984, the movement's national journal, *Inquiring Mind*, listed 9 residential retreats around the United States. Its Spring 2000 issue listed about 120. Since the founding of IMS in 1976, there has also been a slow but steady increase in affiliated centers and sitting groups. In 1984, *Inquiring Mind* listed 15 weekly meditation groups around the country; in 1995, it listed 150; and in 2000, 230. A conservative guess is that these numbers represent about half of the actual total.

The growth of the movement is paralleled in the number of books either written or edited by its teachers. The first book, Joseph Goldstein's *The Experience of Insight,* was published in 1976. Jack Kornfield published *Living Buddhist Masters* in 1977. In the 1980s, four books were published, the most significant being Goldstein and Kornfield's *Seeking the Heart of Wisdom.* During the 1990s, the IMS/Spirit Rock network of teachers published twenty-one books—a more than five-fold increase over the previous decade.[6] These books provide evidence for some of the shifts that have occurred over time in the teachings and concerns of some of the major figures in this movement.

Not all these books are specifically or explicitly about insight meditation or even Buddhism. Some discuss meditation without reference to Buddhism and were probably intended for a popular audience broader than the Insight Meditation community. However, all the books are expressions of the spiritual vision and teachings of the movement's teachers. And for some of the teachers, this is a vision of spiritual universalism, that is, they see the teachings as common to a range of spiritual traditions but as also having an existence independent of any specific tradition.[7]

At its inception, the Insight Meditation movement primarily focused on meditation, intensive meditation retreats, and personal discovery. This is seen clearly in Goldstein's first book, *The Experience of Insight,* which is based on transcripts of his talks during the Insight Meditation movement's first residential retreat in 1974. Speaking to these first retreatants on the second evening, Goldstein said, "We have all begun a journey. A journey into our minds. A journey of discovery and exploration of who and what we are." Throughout the book, *vipassanā* practice is presented as a gnostic path, that is, a path of understanding. Goldstein says this explicitly when he says the first and last step is "right understanding" and "wisdom is the culmination of the spiritual path."[8]

However, this gnostic dimension is not confined just to insight meditation or the *vipassanā* retreat journey. Goldstein sees it as the essential aspect of all spiritual practice:

> The elements of mind: thoughts, visions, emotions, consciousness, and the elements of matter, individually are called "dharmas." The task of all spiritual work is to explore and discover these dharmas within us, to uncover and penetrate all the elements of the mind and body, becoming

aware of each of them individually, as well as understanding the laws
governing their process and relationship. This is what we are doing here:
experiencing in every moment the truth of our nature, the truth of who
and what we are.[9]

In this book, we see that in the mid-1970s Goldstein presented spiritual
practice as an individual concern, focusing on personal understanding and
change. While this may be understood as reflecting the particular teaching
focus of an intensive retreat, it is also representative of traditional Theravāda
soteriology, in which the path of liberation is primarily one of personal cultivation (although in the orthodox presentation personal cultivation also includes interpersonal elements of generosity, loving-kindness, and morality).

Several of the movement's teachers have also noted that a focus on personal meditative experience characterized the early years of the Insight
Meditation movement in the West. For example, in *Seeking the Heart of
Wisdom* Jack Kornfield wrote "*vipassanā* in the West has started by placing a great emphasis on inner meditation and individual transformation."[10]

However, Kornfield also clearly believes that there is more to Buddhist
spirituality than the personal transformation. He continues:

> Buddhist teachings have another whole dimension to them, a way of
> connecting our hearts to the world of action. Their first universal
> guidelines teach about the basic moral precepts and the cultivation of
> generosity. These are the foundations for any spiritual life. Beyond this,
> Buddhist practice and the whole ancient Asian tradition is built upon the
> spirit of service. For some, service may seem to be simply an adjunct or
> addition to their inner meditation. But service is more than that; it is an
> expression of the maturity of wisdom in spiritual life.[11]

While making a distinction between a personal and an interpersonal dimension of Buddhist practice, Kornfield also brings them together: ethical guidelines support spiritual practice, and the wisdom of practice is expressed in service. Certain forms of ethical behavior are seen as means to a
goal, and another form, service, is seen as an expression of the goal.

The next section will show that the Insight Meditation movement's
teachings do have a strong emphasis on morality, both as a means for spiritual development and as a goal of the spiritual practice.

THE ROLE OF ETHICS IN THE INSIGHT
MEDITATION MOVEMENT

It is common for books written by the Insight Meditation teachers to have
emphatic statements concerning the importance of both morality and the

precepts. However, among the first of these books this emphasis is not supported with much in the way of explicit teachings on either Buddhist ethics in general or precepts in particular. We begin to find more detailed discussions of these topics in some of the books published in the 1990s.

On the first page of *The Experience of Insight*, Goldstein states that an "indispensable foundation for meditation practice is following certain moral precepts." However, in this book Goldstein provides few overt ethical teachings, except for a brief mention of behavior that supports meditation practice, such as the five precepts and some of the perfections. Rather, he expresses his faith that "if you're mindful, automatically there's right action."[12] The ethical ideal that Goldstein holds up in the book is that of the Taoist sage who, with a mind empty of striving and a sense of self, allows his or her own nature to express itself and is thereby in harmony with the present situation.

In *Living Buddhist Masters*, Kornfield stresses that "[d]iscipline and morality are essential tools in the path of purification." In introducing the five precepts in *Seeking the Heart of Wisdom*, he explains, "For spiritual practice to develop, it is absolutely essential that we establish a basis of moral conduct in our lives." But again, these two books give little explanation or interpretation of Buddhist teachings on either morality or the precepts. The longest discussion is four pages discussing the precepts, found in *Seeking the Heart of Wisdom*. This emphasis on the importance of morality continues in some more recent books. For example, Christopher Titmuss, in his discussion of the precepts in *Light on Enlightenment*, insists that "[m]editation without morality is mental gymnastics."[13]

The importance of ethics is also seen in the descriptions of the goal of insight practice. Most commonly, the ultimate goal is seen to have an ethical component, in that certain moral virtues and behaviors are expected to accompany it. In the quote above, Kornfield states that service "is an expression of the maturity of wisdom in spiritual life." Goldstein points to freedom as the goal of the practice, "because from freedom comes connectedness, compassion, lovingkindness, and peace." Titmuss calls morality a "sure signal of a transformed life," and says "true morality belongs to realization. There is an effortless acknowledgement and appreciation of the five precepts." Salzberg explains: "We cannot create suffering for ourselves without creating suffering for others, nor can we create suffering for others without creating suffering for ourselves. So the model of perfection for the highest development of the human being is someone who has come to a complete end of suffering himself or herself, and therefore will never create suffering for others."[14] The above examples suggest a strong ethical dimension to the Insight Meditation movement. To further understand the movement's general approach to ethics, it is useful to study its teaching on precepts.

THE FIVE LAY PRECEPTS WITHIN THE INSIGHT MEDITATION MOVEMENT

Theravāda Buddhism offers a rich variety of teachings on ethics. Probably no single Western theory of ethics adequately encompasses this range. Within the tradition, we find rule-based approaches that stress strict adherence to precepts. We also find virtue orientations that focus on developing the practitioner's character. In addition, we can find principle-based approaches, involving concepts like *non-harming*. However, within the tradition, the minimum ideal for lay Buddhist conduct is the observation of the five precepts (*pañca-sīla;* more accurately translated as "the five virtues"). These are often referred to as training precepts (*sikkhāpada*). Their formulaic Pāli wording can be translated as follows:

I undertake the training precept to abstain from harming breathing beings.
I undertake the training precept to abstain from taking what is not given.
I undertake the training precept to abstain from sexual misconduct.
I undertake the training precept to abstain from false speech.
I undertake the training precept to abstain from alcohol, liquor, or spirits that are a cause for heedlessness.

In addition to these five precepts, the Asian Theravāda tradition has other sets of ethical guidelines for lay Buddhists. Of particular importance are the eight precepts. These include the five precepts, except that the precept on sexuality is one of celibacy. The additional three involve abstaining from eating between noon and dawn the following day, avoiding various forms of entertainment and the use of adornments, and avoiding the use of high and luxurious beds and seats. The five precepts are said to be applicable to all circumstances, whereas the eight precepts are usually meant for special situations, such as visiting a temple, during the lunar observance days, or during meditation retreats. At most Theravāda ceremonies and during visits to Buddhist monasteries and temples, Theravāda laity will chant a commitment to undertake either the five or the eight precepts for at least the duration of the ceremony or visit.

The eight precepts are rarely mentioned in the Insight Meditation movement. One exception is during the annual three-month retreat at the

Insight Meditation Society in Massachusetts, where some practitioners commit voluntarily to the eight precepts. Another exception is during the occasional retreats taught by Theravāda monastics at Spirit Rock and IMS.

The presence or absence of the five precepts within the Insight Meditation movement varies considerably in different areas of the movement. One of the clearest areas where the precepts do not appear is in the movement's journals, magazines, and newsletters. *Inquiring Mind* is a semiannual magazine that calls itself "a journal of the *vipassanā* community" and contains articles and interviews with teachers on issues that are important and topical for the editors and contributors. From its inaugural issue in 1984 through the Spring 2000 issue, the *Inquiring Mind* has given no indication that the five precepts have an important role in *vipassanā* practitioners' lives. The first reference to precepts was not until the eleventh issue—not in an article about *vipassanā* practice, but in reflections on the role of commitment in author Susan Moon's Zen practice. Even in its Spring 1993 issue on "Buddhist Ethics," the focus was on social engagement, not on the challenges of personal morality. Not until the Fall 1999 issue did an article specifically on Buddhist precepts finally appear. Even here, the discussion was not framed within a *vipassanā* context, but recounted the author's struggles in coming to terms with the five precepts in the context of a Vietnamese Zen community. The only substantial presentation of the five precepts was in the twice-published "Insight Meditation Teacher's Code of Ethics" (Fall 1991 and Spring 2000 issues). Someone learning about *vipassanā* practice only through *Inquiring Mind* could easily conclude that the precepts have no role at all in an average practitioner's life.

Searching through the newsletters and magazines of Spirit Rock and IMS, one finds even fewer references to the precepts than in *Inquiring Mind*. The closest statement by a teacher on this topic comes from an interview with Larry Rosenberg in the Spring 1999 issue of IMS's *Insight* magazine. Here he expresses his preference for having virtue arise from the practices of wisdom and concentration.

The five precepts appear prominently in a few areas of the Insight Meditation movement. They have an important role in virtually all residential *vipassanā* retreats. They are usually introduced and discussed briefly at the opening session, when all participants are expected to commit themselves to adhere to the five precepts for the duration of the retreat. The five precepts are usually modified, in that the third precept is changed to one of celibacy.[15] However, because of the intensive meditation schedule and the almost complete absence of speech on these retreats, for most people it is the retreat format itself, and not the precepts, that delimits their behavior.

The five precepts also have an important role in the recently formulated code of ethics for teachers. In the wake of a series of ethical scandals in American Buddhist communities during the 1980s, Jack Kornfield took the initiative to compose a teachers' code of ethics based on the five precepts.[16] This document explains specific ways in which the IMS and Spirit Rock teachers commit themselves to following the precepts. Some of these commitments are in line with what will be shown below to be the Insight Meditation community's preference to see the precepts as guidelines for reflection and not as rules of restraint. For example, for the precept not to kill, teachers "agree to refine our understanding of not killing and non-harming in all our actions" and to "fulfill this precept in the spirit of reverence for life." However, the precept on refraining from sexual misconduct is unambiguously prohibitive in its specific application to teachers.[17]

Additionally, some *vipassanā* practitioners do take the precepts quite seriously outside of retreat and grapple with trying to live in accordance with them. Furthermore, among teachers there are considerable differences in how the precepts are taught. Some mention them frequently, while others rarely refer to them.

Among the thirty books written or edited by the Insight Meditation teachers as of September 2000, seventeen make some mention of the precepts.[18] Among those books specifically about meditation practice, the rate of mentioning the precepts is considerably higher (approximately seventeen out of twenty-one). In some, the mention is brief, the briefest being a single sentence defining the precepts as "the intention to cultivate clarity that manifests as kindness and compassion."[19] In the seven books published prior to 1993, the longest discussion is four pages long (in Goldstein and Kornfield's *Seeking the Heart of Wisdom*, mentioned earlier). The longer discussions are relatively recent, starting in 1993. These are in five books that have a chapter devoted entirely, or almost entirely, to the precepts.[20]

To place this discussion in a wider context, we can compare this to the books published in English on insight meditation but written by teachers outside of the Insight Meditation movement. A great majority of these books have no mention of the precepts. The books without any reference to the precepts span the range from those written by Theravāda monastics to those composed by lay teachers with minimum affiliation with Buddhism. Among those lacking reference to the precepts are nine of the first ten insight meditation books published in English in the West, all books written by either Theravāda monastics or former monastics.[21] The exception is Sobhana Dhammasudhi's 1965 book, *Insight Meditation*, which briefly mentioned the role of the five precepts in creating personal peace without stating what the five precepts are.[22] In fact, Joseph Goldstein's *The Experience of Insight* (published in 1976) was the first Western *vipassanā* book to provide a list of the precepts and to emphasize their importance. Given that the many books without reference to the precepts are specifically books about meditation practice, it is understandable that they might not cover other areas of traditional Theravāda Buddhist practice.[23] We may note, however, that the practice of insight meditation is presented quite easily without its traditional context of ethics. Furthermore, we see that the Insight Meditation movement's teachers are more likely than *vipassanā* teachers outside the movement to include reference to the precepts in their books.

TEACHINGS ON THE FIVE PRECEPTS

On those occasions when the precepts are discussed, one of the most salient features of the presentation is that they are not to be understood as strict or absolute rules. Goldstein states: "Following these moral precepts as a rule for living keeps us light, and allows the mind to be open and clear. It is a much easier and less complicated way to live. At this level of understanding, the precepts are not taken as commandments but are followed for the effect they have on our quality of life. There is not a sense of imposition at all because they are natural expressions of a clear mind." Kornfield insists that the precepts are "not given as absolute commandments." And Salzberg writes, "In Buddhism morality does not mean a forced or puritanical abiding by rules," and observes that the five precepts "are not intended to be put forth as draconian rules."[24] Christopher Titmuss elaborates on the distinction between Buddhist ethics and "commandments":

> There is a difference between an ethical training and abiding by
> commandments. A major authority will impose commandments upon
> us. We either believe them or we don't, and there is a lack of opportunity
> to enquire into their relevance. Religious baggage also accompanies
> commandments. They cannot be separated from the book, the prophet
> or the saviour. Morality is of a different order. The outcome may be the
> same but the attitude is very different. . . . The Five Precepts, or ethical
> guidelines are a training in inner discipline. The training therefore is not
> a series of *thou shall nots*, but a code of practice.[25]

The teachers' insistence that the precepts are not commandments is also reflected in the seeming reluctance to apply them specifically as rules of restraint with any particularity. For example, in explaining the first precept,

Salzberg never recommends the avoidance of killing. While this may be her implied intent, what she explicitly recommends is using the precept as a reflection on "the oneness of life." In discussing the precept not to lie, she doesn't recommend the avoidance of lying but rather the more vague "attempt not to lie." [26] And in discussing the fifth precept, she writes about the usefulness of temporarily "experimenting" with avoiding intoxicants. Salzberg and other teachers who explain the precepts do so mostly in general terms, focusing on principles behind them, such as non-harming and a sense of interconnection.

Not treating the precepts as rules or commandments goes along with how the observation of the precepts is explained. The most common instruction is to use the precepts as tools for reflection. In the quote above, the "opportunity to enquire" is what Titmuss sees as a defining difference from commandments. For Harrison, the precepts "direct us toward considering our behavior in relationship to the world." Kornfield refers to the "spirit" of the fourth precept as a request to "look at the motivation behind our actions." Salzberg recommends experimenting with the precepts as a way of refining our understanding. Rosenberg sees the precepts as "warning signs" for avoiding trouble. Similarly, for Kornfield the precepts are signals of "when we are about to lose our way, when our fears and delusion entangle us so that we might harm another being." Elsewhere, Kornfield refers to the precepts as guidelines to "become more genuinely conscious." [27]

This avoidance of clear-cut application of the precepts may be, in part, a result of the role of teachers in the Insight Meditation community. The Insight Meditation teachers generally consider themselves "spiritual friends" (*kalayāṇa-mitta*) who give "guidance, instruction, and inspiration" but whose views are not to take precedence over a student's "own inner moral sense." [28] Furthermore, the Insight Meditation community is perhaps too loosely bound for teachers to assume authority for establishing rules for how students are to live.

THE BENEFITS FROM OBSERVING THE PRECEPTS

The reasons given for observing the precepts further illuminate the role of ethics in the Insight Meditation movement. Over the years, there seems to have been a significant shift in what are explained as the benefits and justifications for observing the precepts. Specifically, the early literature of the movement emphasized how the precepts support the practitioner's negotiation of the soteriological path. In the later literature, the emphasis is on how living ethically benefits others. In none of this literature is there any mention of the effect the precepts have on a person's future rebirth. This is a significant contrast with traditional ethical teachings found among Asian Theravāda teachers.[29]

With its focus on personal insight practice, Goldstein's *The Experience of Insight* emphasizes the personal utilitarian benefits of the precepts for one's meditation practice: "Following the precepts will provide a strong base for the development of concentration, and will make the growth of insight possible." More specifically, he discusses the precepts from the perspective of three levels of importance. First, they serve as protections from creating "unwholesome karma." Second, they improve one's "quality of life" by keeping the mind light, open, and clear. Third, they help establish a purity of action and a mind free of remorse and anxiety, which in turn supports tranquility, concentration, and thus insight.[30]

Kornfield says much the same in *Living Buddhist Masters* and *Seeking the Heart of Wisdom*. In addition, he mentions that adhering to the precepts is an important support in the spiritual work of giving up selfishness and desires. In *Seeking the Heart of Wisdom*, Goldstein broadens the scope of the precepts beyond their personal value. He states that observing the precepts is a "gift of trust to everyone we meet, because we are clearly stating in our actions and way of being that no one need fear us" and "[w]e work with the precepts as guidelines for harmonizing our actions in the world. Kornfield also mentions that moral rules are ways of keeping society harmonious and peaceful.[31] However, even with these exceptions, in Goldstein and Kornfield's books published in the 1970s and 1980s, the precepts are primarily justified for the personal spiritual benefit they offer.

In contrast, most of the Insight Meditation movement's books published in the 1990s that mention the precepts stress their interpersonal importance. In *A Path with Heart*, Kornfield writes that the precepts are a means "to expand our circle of understanding and compassion into the world around us." Elsewhere, he stresses that the precepts "actively express a compassionate heart in our life."[32]

Gavin Harrison's *In the Lap of the Buddha* places the precepts almost exclusively in the context of interpersonal relations and caring for the world. Harrison does not mention their role in either meditation practice or traditional Buddhist training. Rather, he sees the precepts as areas of reflection on the question, "Does our action lead to happiness and unity among beings, or toward sorrow and division?" No utilitarian or prohibitive roles for the precepts are given, except as tools for exploring the question of non-harming. Indeed, for Harrison, the basis for *all* Buddhist morality is non-harming and compassionate loving-kindness.[33]

Sharon Salzberg explicitly associates *sīla* with relationships. She writes, "*Sīla* works on all levels of our relationships: our relationships to ourselves, to other people, and to the environment around us," and then defines morality as the manifestation of care and connectedness arising from a "heart full of love and compassion." Furthermore, she emphasizes that "if we truly loved ourselves, we would never harm another, because we are all interconnected." Salzberg's ethical teaching rests firmly on the vision of interconnection and on the idea that the spiritual aspiration for freedom is inseparable from our relationship to all life.[34]

Both Harrison and Salzberg teach that ethical behavior arises as an expression of motivations of non-harming and inner states of compassion and love. In Steven Tipton's typology of styles of ethical evaluation, this is akin to *expressive ethics* that is "mainly oriented toward the agent's feelings, the feelings of others around him, and to the particular situation in which they find themselves."[35] Harrison's and Salzberg's ethics could also be called *relational*, since the behavior is evaluated based on our relationship to others and the world. This expressive and relational framing of the precepts is also found in the writings of Steve Armstrong and Christopher Titmuss.[36] Downplayed or absent in these later writers is any teaching on the personal utilitarian rationale for precepts stressed by Goldstein's and Kornfield's early writings.

The relational dimension of ethics is seen among those teachers who claim that the inner personal developments that give rise to ethical actions include a vision of interconnectedness and sensitivity toward others. Salzberg says, "Moral conduct is the reflection of our deepest love, concern, and care." Closely connected with this is a vision of interconnectedness. So, Titmuss writes, "Morality springs from the awareness of interconnection." And Salzberg writes, "Our deepest insights into happiness and lovingkindness, as well as the perception that we are all interrelated, give rise to a natural inclination that seeks to act according to precepts."[37]

This expressive and relational rationale for the precepts is close to the Western category of *virtue ethics*, in which ethical behavior is seen as the expression of the character of a person.[38] Repeatedly the Insight Meditation teachers explain that as character and virtue are developed, ethical behavior automatically follows. For example, Kornfield writes, "We use the form of rules until virtue becomes natural. Then from the wisdom of the silent mind true spontaneous virtue arises." Elsewhere he writes, "Our actions come out of a spontaneous compassion and our innate wisdom can direct life from our heart." Referring more specifically to the precepts, he

writes, "When our heart is awakened, [the precepts] spontaneously illuminate our way in the world."[39]

The implication of the teaching that a person with spiritually developed character and insight will naturally act ethically is that, for such a
person, the precepts themselves become unnecessary. Harrison says this
most explicitly: "The Buddha said that if we are deeply established in
awareness, the precepts are not necessary." Larry Rosenberg says, "The
wisdom of the practice combines with the mindfulness we develop and
eventually makes the precepts, not exactly unnecessary, just perfectly
obvious."[40]

To summarize up to this point: ethical behavior and the cultivation of
ethical virtue are regarded as important within the Insight Meditation
movement. The movement specifically does not advocate a rule-based approach to observing the precepts, except in the specialized environment
of a retreat. Instead, the teachers encourage a more virtue-based approach
in which the precepts are used to encourage both an increased reflection
on and transformation of one's own motivations and an increased sensitivity to the needs of others. In other words, the precepts are used as ad-
juncts to the movement's central focus on mindfulness and meditative
practices.

THE CULTIVATION OF VIRTUE

The longest and most intensive *vipassanā* training course offered by the
Insight Meditation movement is the three-month retreat held at IMS every
fall. In January 2000, I asked a woman who had just completed the three-
month course how much the precepts were discussed. Without hesitation,
she replied, "All the time." But then, on reflection, she corrected herself,
saying that she could not recall the precepts being discussed at all after the
formal taking of the precepts at the retreat opening. She continued by saying that there was a strong ethical component in the retreat teaching, but
not through the vehicle of the precepts; her initial response came from automatically associating ethics with the precepts.

This anecdote points to the need to look beyond explicit discussions of
the Buddhist precepts to better understand the means of ethical development advocated by the Insight Meditation movement. What we find is that
teachers in this tradition rely primarily on meditation and mindfulness for
cultivating the various virtues that motivate ethical action. These teachers
have a strong conviction that inner spiritual development leads to virtue.
In particular, mindfulness practice is taught with the expectation that it will

have a transformative effect on the practitioner's ethical relationship to the world. This is expressed succinctly by Christina Feldman:

> Meditation is not ethically neutral nor is it solely a path of inner transformation intent upon achieving exotic states of inner experience. It is directed towards not only the cultivation of calm and wisdom, but also compassion, sensitivity, forgiveness, love, and generosity. Meditation is a path not only of inner change, but a path that enables us to touch our relationships and the world around us with compassion, care and peace.[41]

Elsewhere we find claims that mindfulness "leads to compassionate action" and that the practice "brings a caring, loving, and impeccable quality to how we live." Salzberg writes that with the practice of meditation "our lives are transformed . . . [and our] actions flow from a wellspring of genuine caring."[42]

Certainly we find that many of the teachings on insight meditation have ethical implications. In particular, instructions encouraging awareness of, and freedom from, impulses of greed and hate would, if followed, decrease unethical behavior. Furthermore, explicit instructions to be mindful of intentions support the possibility of basing ethical analysis on the nature of one's motivation, rather than on codes of behavior. And indeed, for Salzberg, Buddhist ethics is "a system of morality that is based on awareness of one's intentions having consequences rather than an arbitrary external structure."[43] Also, the Insight Meditation movement's teaching on the role of mindfulness in developing sensitivity and connection with others includes an expectation that this will lead to an increased ethical sensitivity.

In addition, the frequent teachings on and practice of loving-kindness (*mettā*), compassion (*karuṇā*), and the other *brahma-vihāras* aim at cultivating virtuous character and ethical behavior. Kornfield writes that "valuing metta becomes a strong motive for refining our understanding and practice of harmonious action, the non-harming of self and others. . . ."[44]

So, rather than focusing on rules of behavior and restraint, *vipassanā* teachers focus more on the development of insight and virtuous character that provide the motivation for ethical behavior. This is expressed succinctly in Sharon Salzberg's 1997 book, *A Heart as Wide as the World:* "Our deepest insights into happiness and lovingkindness, as well as the perception that we are all interrelated, give rise to a natural inclination that seeks to act according to the precepts."[45]

Jack Kornfield has observed that the primary focus on meditation practice reverses the traditional sequence of training ethics, concentration, and wisdom. Furthermore, he suggests that this is one of the unique features of how Buddhism has been developing in the West. He writes,

> In the East, it is taught that one successively develops morality, concentration, and finally wisdom. . . . In the West in some ways it has been the reverse. Many people here have experienced dissatisfaction with their lives or the society around them. Some have had glimpses of other deeper understandings through psychedelics. Some wisdom has arisen first. They've often gone from that taste of wisdom to learn concentration, to explore various ways of stilling and directing the mind. Finally people are realizing, both in relation to themselves and society, that it is essential to also develop a way of being that is not harmful or injurious to those around them. So in the West we find this reverse development—first of wisdom, then of concentration, then of morality; which is of course cyclical and will develop, in turn, greater concentration and more wisdom.[46]

In other words, interest in ethical sensitivity and training is understood to result from meditation practices. And since insight meditation and mindfulness in daily life are the main avenues for cultivating virtue within the Insight Meditation movement, we would expect this interest to be primarily channeled back into further meditation practice.

CONCLUSIONS

The Insight Meditation movement teachings on ethics are teleological, that is, there is an ideal ethical goal to which the practice leads. The path to this goal is through an inner transformation of the practitioner's motivations and his or her sensitivity to others. Meditation is regarded as the primary vehicle advocated for this transformation. Meditation practice is expected to weaken and perhaps eliminate motivations leading to unethical behavior while strengthening those that lead to ethical behavior.

In relying on meditation as the means to ethical transformation, the Insight Meditation movement can be seen as reversing the traditional Theravāda training sequence of ethics, meditation, and wisdom, which has been normative at least since the time of Buddhaghosa in the fifth century. While this study has not determined the extent to which this is unique to the modern Insight Meditation movement or whether it is a phenomenon received from the Asian Theravāda tradition, it is perhaps interesting to point out that at least some Theravāda monastics strongly oppose this form of change.[47] Michael Carrithers, in his book *The Forest Monks of Sri Lanka*, tells of trying to convince some forest monks that the traditional relationship between ethics and meditation should be reversed. He reports that the monks strongly opposed this idea. He writes, "The impatience and even outrage with which the monks heard it and the unity of view with which it was rejected left no doubt that the monks place moral purity in the central position I had wished to accord to meditative experience."[48] Are there different consequences depending on whether moral purity or meditative experience is given central position in spiritual practice? Can one rely exclusively on meditation when engaged in the Buddhist path? Jack Kornfield has suggested that for most people this does not work. He claims that the "various compartments of our minds and bodies are only semi-permeable to awareness." This raises some question about the viability of such claims as "if you are mindful, automatically there's right action."[49]

It may also be interesting to notice that whereas the Insight Meditation teachers claim that mindfulness practice naturally brings on ethical action, the only Insight Meditation practitioners who are explicitly expected to abide by specific rules of prohibited behavior are the teachers (through the "Teacher Code of Ethics"). In that the teachers are representative of the most developed practitioners within the movement, one would expect that, by the movement's own logic, they would be the ones with the least need for rules.

While the Insight Meditation movement has consistently seen meditation as the basis for transformation, when we compare its earliest books on *vipassanā* to the more recent ones a noteworthy change is seen in the type of transformation envisioned. In the earlier writings, the rationale for ethical behavior was mostly based on the personal benefits of pursuing the goal of liberation, while the later books place an increasing emphasis on the benefits ethical behavior has for others. Further study may reveal whether or not this represents a significant change in both the path and the goal advocated by the movement. Certainly it suggests an increased valuation of interpersonal ethics. It may also represent a shift toward emphasizing this-worldly and humanistic values over traditional Buddhist soteriological ones. In fact, we find Joseph Goldstein concerned that Americans "often practice the dharma in service of human values," in contrast to the goal of transcendental awakening.[50]

NOTES

1. For a fuller introduction to the movement, see my "Insight Meditation in the United States: Life, Liberty, and the Pursuit of Happiness," in *The Faces of Buddhism in America*, edited by Charles S. Prebish and Kenneth K. Tanaka (Berkeley: University of California Press, 1998), 163–80. The reader may wish to keep in mind that I am an Insight Meditation teacher and am a minor participant in shaping the movement I am writing about.

2. An autobiographical account of one Westerner's encounter with *vipassanā* meditation in Asia during the early to mid-1970s is found in Eric Lerner, *Journey of Insight Meditation: A Personal Experience of the Buddha's Way* (New York: Schocken Books, 1977).

3. Discussed more fully in Jack Kornfield, "American Buddhism," in *The Complete Guide to Buddhist America,* edited by Don Morreale (Boston: Shambhala, 1998), xxvi.

4. For a description of this beginning and early history of the insight movement, see Tony Schwartz, *What Really Matters: Searching for Wisdom in America* (New York: Bantam, 1995), 305–37.

5. In preparing for the 2002 teachers' meeting for the movement, Spirit Rock's invitation list has seventy-seven teachers.

6. The following is a bibliography of books authored by the Insight Meditation movement's teachers as of September 2000.

1976 Joseph Goldstein, *The Experience of Insight* (Boston: Shambhala)

1977 Jack Kornfield, *Living Buddhist Masters* (Boston: Shambhala); 1996 as *Living Dharma*

1985 Jack Kornfield and Paul Brieter (eds.), *A Still Forest Pool* (Wheaton, Illinois: Quest Books)

1987 Joseph Goldstein and Jack Kornfield, *Seeking the Heart of Wisdom* (Boston: Shambhala)

1989 Christina Feldman, *Woman Awake* (London: Penguin/Arkana)

1989 Chistopher Titmuss (ed.), *Spirit of Change* (London: Green Print [The Merlin Press])

1991 Christina Feldman and Jack Kornfield, *Stories of the Spirit, Stories of the Heart* (New York: HarperCollins)

1993 Joseph Goldstein, *Insight Meditation* (Boston: Shambhala)

1993 Jack Kornfield, *A Path with Heart* (New York: Bantam)

1993 Jack Kornfield and Gil Fronsdal (eds.), *Teachings of the Buddha* (Boston: Shambhala)

1993 Christopher Titmuss, *The Profound and the Profane* (Totnes, U.K.: Insight)

1994 Christina Feldman, *Quest of the Woman Warrior* (London: Aquarius)

1994 Gavin Harrison, *In the Lap of the Buddha* (Boston: Shambhala)

1995 Sylvia Boorstein, *It's Easier than You Think* (New York: HarperCollins)

1995 Sharon Salzberg, *Lovingkindness* (Boston: Shambhala)

1995 Chistopher Titmuss, *Green Buddha* (Totnes, U.K.: Insight)

1996 Sylvia Boorstein, *Don't Just Do Something, Sit There* (New York: HarperCollins)

1996 Gil Fronsdal and Nancy Van House (eds.), *Voices from Spirit Rock* (Nevada City, California: Clear and Present Graphics)

1997 Sharon Salzberg, *A Heart as Wide as the World* (Boston: Shambhala)

1997 Sylvia Boorstein, *That's Funny, You Don't Look Buddhist* (New York: HarperCollins)

1998 Christina Feldman, *Principles of Meditation* (London: Thorsons)

1998 Wes Nisker, *Buddha's Nature* (New York: Bantam)

1998 Larry Rosenberg, *Breath by Breath* (Boston: Shambhala)

1998 Rodney Smith, *Lessons from the Dying* (Boston: Wisdom)

1998 Christopher Titmuss, *Light on Enlightenment* (Boston: Shambhala)

1999 Christopher Titmuss, *The Power of Meditation* (New York: Sterling)

1999 Sharon Salzberg (ed.), *Voices of Insight* (Boston: Shambhala)

2000 Jack Kornfield, *After the Ecstasy, the Laundry* (New York: Bantam)
2000 Christopher Titmuss, *An Awakened Life* (Boston: Shambhala)
2000 Larry Rosenberg, *Living in the Light of Death* (Boston: Shambhala)

7. See, for example, Feldman, *Woman Awake;* Feldman and Kornfield, *Stories of the Spirit, Stories of the Heart;* Jack Kornfield, *A Path with Heart;* Titmuss, *The Proud and the Profane;* Feldman, *Quest of the Woman Warrior;* Salzberg, *A Heart as Wide as the World.*

8. Goldstein, *The Experience of Insight,* 7, 8, 79.

9. Ibid., 19.

10. Page 165. Also see Salzberg, *Lovingkindness,* 171.

11. Goldstein and Kornfield, *Seeking the Heart of Wisdom,* 165.

12. Goldstein, *The Experience of Insight,* 81.

13. Kornfield, *Living Buddhist Masters,* 8; Kornfield, *Seeking the Heart of Wisdom,* 7, and 7–10; Titmuss, *Light on Enlightenment,* 85.

14. Kornfield's initial quote in this paragraph from Goldstein and Kornfield, *Seeking the Heart of Wisdom,* 165; Goldstein, *Insight Meditation,* 3; Titmuss, *Light on Enlightenment,* 23, 210; Salzberg quoted in Daniel Goleman (ed.), *Healing Emotions* (Boston: Shambhala, 1997), 18.

15. During retreats at IMS, the five precepts are worded as follows:

Not to harm any sentient being; not to kill or intentionally hurt any person or creature, even an insect.

Not to take what is not freely given; not to steal or "borrow" without the consent of the giver; to accept what is offered and not try to change it or get more.

To abstain from sexual activity.

Not to harm by one's speech; not to lie, gossip or use harsh or hurtful language (in the context of the retreat, this also means to observe noble silence).

To abstain from using alcohol, drugs and intoxicants.

Taken from IMS's web site, www.dharma.org/ims/imsinfo.htm [22 Sept. 2000].

16. Printed in Kornfield, *A Path with Heart,* 340–3.

17. "A sexual relationship is never appropriate between teachers and students. During retreats or formal teaching, any intimation of future student-teacher romantic or sexual relationship is inappropriate. If a genuine and committed relationship interest develops over time between an unmarried teacher and a former student, the student must clearly be under the guidance of another teacher. . . . A minimum time period of three months or longer from the last formal teaching between them, and a clear understanding from both parties that the student-teacher relationship has ended must be coupled with a conscious commitment to enter into a relationship that brings no harm to either party." From Kornfield, *A Path with Heart,* 341–2.

18. Those that do not mention the precepts are: Feldman, *Woman Awake, Quest of the Woman Warrior,* and *Principles of Meditation;* Titmuss, *Spirit of Change* and *An Awakened Life;* Feldman and Kornfield, *Stories of the Spirit, Stories of the Heart;* Boorstein, *It's Easier than You Think* and *That's Funny, You Don't Look Buddhist;* Fronsdal and Van House, *Voices from Spirit Rock;* Nisker, *Buddha's Nature;* Smith, *Lessons from the Dying;* Kornfield, *After the Ecstasy, the Laundry;* and Rosenberg, *Living in the Light of Death.* However, while all these books are on spiritual themes, they are not all directly concerned with Insight Meditation or even Buddhism.

19. Boorstein, *Don't Just Do Something, Sit There,* 133.

20. Titmuss, *The Proud and the Profane,* 3–11; Harrison, *In the Lap of the Buddha,* 218–46; Salzberg, *Lovingkindness,* 171–90; Titmuss, *Light on Enlightenment,* 156–73; Salzberg, *Voices of Insight,* 216–30.

21. Nyānaponika Thera, *The Heart of Buddhist Meditation* (London: Rider, 1962); Venerable Sobhana Dhammasudhi (= Dhiravamsa), *Beneficial Factors for Meditation* (Surrey, U.K.: The Vipassana Foundation, n.d.); Venerable Sobhana Dhammasudhi, *The Real Way to Awakening* (London: The Buddhapadipa Temple, 1975); Mahāsi Sayādaw, *The Satipaṭṭāna Vipassanā Meditation* (Santa Cruz, California: Unity Press, 1971); Mahāsi Sayādaw, *Practical Insight Meditation* (Santa Cruz, California: Unity Press, 1972); Nyānaponika Thera, *The Power of Mindfulness* (Santa Cruz, California: Unity Press, 1972); Dhiravamsa (= Venerable Sobhana Dhammasudhi), *The Middle Path of Life* (Nevada City, California: Blue Dolphin, 1974); Dhiravamsa (= Venerable Sobhana Dhammasudhi), *The Way of Non-Attachment* (London: Turnstone, 1975); and A. Sujata, *Beginning to See* (Santa Cruz, California: Unity Press, 1975), although the Celestial Arts edition of this book does list the precepts on page 108 (Berkeley, California: Celestial Arts, 1987).

22. Venerable Sobhana Dhammasudhi (= Dhiravamsa), *Insight Meditation* (London: The Committee for the Advancement of Buddhism, 1965). An expanded edition was published in 1968.

23. Other Insight Meditation books lacking mention of the precepts are:

1979 Stephen Levine, *A Gradual Awakening* (New York: Anchor)
1982 Dhiravamsa, *The Dynamic Way of Meditation* (London: Turnstone Press)
1990 Venerable U Silananda, *The Four Foundations of Mindfulness* (Boston: Wisdom)
1991 Venerable Gunaratana, *Mindfulness in Plain English* (Boston: Wisdom)
1992 Dr. Thynn Thynn, *Living Meditation, Living Insight* (privately published)
1996 Steve and Rosemary Weisman, *Meditation, Compassion and Wisdom* (York Beach, Maine: Samuel Weiser)
1998 S. N. Goenka, *Satipaṭṭhāna Sutta Discourses* (Seattle: Vipassanā Research Publications)
1999 Paul R. Fleischman, *Karma and Chaos* (Seattle: Vipassanā Research Publications)
1999 Steve and Rosemary Weisman, *With Compassionate Understanding* (Saint Paul, Minnesota: Paragon Press)

24. Quotes in this paragraph from Goldstein, *The Experience of Insight,* 77; Kornfield, in Goldstein and Kornfield, *Seeking the Heart of Wisdom,* 7; and Salzberg, *A Heart as Wide as the World,* 23–4, 154.

25. Titmuss, *Light on Enlightenment,* 83.

26. Salzberg, *Lovingkindness,* 174, 176.

27. Harrison, *In the Lap of the Buddha,* 220; Kornfield, in Goldstein and Kornfield, *Seeking the Heart of Wisdom,* 10; Salzberg, *Lovingkindness,* 177; Rosenberg, *Breath by Breath,* 172; Kornfield, *A Path with Heart,* 298; and Jack Kornfield, "Domains of Consciousness," *Tricycle: The Buddhist Review* 6, no. 1 (Fall 1996), 34.

28. Goldstein, *Insight Meditation,* 23.

29. For example, "People observing the precepts can perceive the following benefits. . . . After they die, they are sure to qualify for rebirth on the human plane at the very least," from Ajahn Lee Dhammadharo, *The Craft of the Heart* (private publication), 18. "If a person died in Sakka's kingdom, they never used to be reborn

in a woeful plane of existence because they had observed the Five Precepts. . . . So that we will have a higher birth in the next life, why not keep the Five Virtues?" from Taungpulu Sayādaw, *Blooming in the Desert* (Berkeley: North Atlantic, 1996), 20. For discussions and examples of how Thai and Burmese Buddhists link the precepts with rebirth, see, respectively, Melford Spiro, *Buddhism and Society* (New York: Harper and Row, 1970), 99, and Donald Swearer, *The Buddhist World of Southeast Asia* (Albany: State University of New York Press, 1995), 15.

30. Goldstein, *The Experience of Insight*, 77.

31. For sources of material in this paragraph, see Kornfield on giving up selfishness and desires in *Living Buddhist Masters*, 10, 296; Goldstein, in Goldstein and Kornfield, *Seeking the Heart of Wisdom*, 96, 97; and Kornfield, *Living Buddhist Masters*, 10.

32. Kornfield, *A Path with Heart*, 297, 298.

33. Gavin Harrison, *In the Lap of the Buddha*, 220–1 and 219, respectively.

34. Salzberg, *Lovingkindness*, 172, 72, 72, and 173, respectively.

35. Steven Tipton, *Getting Saved from the Sixties* (Berkeley: University of California Press, 1982), 15–8. While Tipton's *expressive ethics* is not an exact fit for some of the ethical modes of the Insight Meditation movement, his study of counterculture spiritual ethics of the 1960s and 1970s provides a useful reference for further study of the movement.

36. Steve Armstrong, "The Five Precepts: Supporting Our Relationships," in Salzberg (ed.), *Voices of Insight*, 216–30; Titmuss, *Light on Enlightenment*, 83–6.

37. Salzberg, *Lovingkindness*, 172; Titmuss, *Light on Enlightenment*, 86; Salzberg, *A Heart as Wide as the World*, 155.

38. While traditional Theravāda ethics also has a strong virtue orientation, it is interesting that its centrally important virtues of conscience and moral fear (*hiri* and *ottappa*) are virtually absent from the Insight Meditation movement's publications.

39. Kornfield, *Living Buddhist Masters*, 11; Kornfield, in Goldstein and Kornfield, *Seeking the Heart of Wisdom*, 57; Kornfield, *A Path with Heart*, 298.

40. Harrison, *In the Lap of the Buddha*, 221; Rosenberg, *Breath by Breath*, 175.

41. Feldman, *Principles of Meditation*, 7.

42. Goldstein and Kornfield, *Seeking the Heart of Wisdom*, 105, 136–7; Salzberg, *A Heart as Wide as the World*, 13.

43. Sharon Salzberg, "Karma in Daily Life," *Inquiring Mind* 6, no. 1 (Spring 1989), 12.

44. Goldstein and Kornfield, *Seeking the Heart of Wisdom*, 96.

45. Salzberg, *A Heart as Wide as the World*, 155.

46. Kornfield, *Living Buddhist Masters*, 298.

47. It is important to note that some Asian meditation teachers did not explicitly emphasize the precepts when teaching Westerners. The following is from a Summer 1989 *Inquiring Mind* article written anonymously by the Western Theravāda monastics at Amaravati Monastery in England:

When Ajahn Chah started teaching Westerners, Thai people often asked why he just taught meditation, without stressing the first two steps (e.g., generosity and virtuous conduct). He replied that Westerners would in due course find it impossible to make progress without cultivating generosity of heart and a good moral foundation. He was, however, content to let them find this out for themselves.

48. Michael Carrithers, *The Forest Monks of Sri Lanka* (Oxford: Oxford University Press, 1978), 14*ff*.

49. Jack Kornfield, "Even the Best Meditators Have Old Wounds to Heal: Combining Meditation and Psychotherapy," in *Paths beyond Ego*, edited by Roger Walsh (Los Angeles: Tarcher/Perigee Books, 1993), 67; and Goldstein, *The Experience of Insight*, 81.

50. Joseph Goldstein, "Empty Phenomena Rolling On," *Tricycle: The Buddhist Review* 3, no. 2 (Winter 1993), 17.

V

BUDDHISM FACING NEW CHALLENGES

20 The Roar of the Lioness

Women's Dharma in the West

Judith Simmer-Brown

INTRODUCTION

There is perhaps no account which is more appropriately narrative than that of women, and the story of women in Western Buddhism is no exception. And a single article which advances an overview of women in Western Buddhism must be a narrative of limited scope. After all, women have been active players in overwhelming numbers in the globalization of Buddhism, and no single account can appropriately document their importance and contributions. But, given the androcentric record of Buddhism's historical development and the impending patriarchal patterns of Buddhism's institutions in the West, a narrative such as this might suggest the special contributions of women to a global Buddhism.

In a history so recent, so undocumented, so little researched, the sources of this article are often anecdotal, personal, and familial. The magazines, newletters, and web sites of various centers and teachers have been invaluable resources, in addition to the few books on the subject.[1] In addition, I have shared long talks, meditation practice, phone conversations, laughter, tea, tears, or lunch with most of the women mentioned here. I am deeply inspired by the diversity of their perspectives, their passion for practice and liberation, their unselfish work for others, and their commitment to the propagation of a truly Western Buddhism no matter what their views on women's Dharma may be.

Since this volume includes an excellent article on Buddhist nuns, this article focuses upon laywomen; since it is difficult to be comprehensive, the examples here are drawn more often from North America than from Europe; since there is little available research on the subject, ethnic-Asian women are treated only briefly. Much more work must be done in these last two areas to properly survey the subject.

This essay will focus on mainstream convert communities in which women, whether reformers or traditionalists, have made contributions to the development of a genuinely Western Buddhism. There are three considerations which have entered into the narrative. First, the leaders with whom I am most familiar uniquely blend the traditional and reform aspects, and so I will avoid those unhelpful labels. In a Western setting, neither label has meaning, because even teaching Buddhism in the most traditional possible way has required innovation; even the greatest innovation has traditional themes. Second, I am most interested in women who live and practice in community, rather than Buddhists-at-large, for whom a Sangha has been peripheral. This may exclude well-known authors who write from a Buddhist perspective or who have shaped various Buddhist communities. But, for the purposes of this narrative, the contributions of women to their Buddhist communities are of greater personal interest for the future of Western Buddhism. Third, legions of women who are not mentioned here have made significant contributions to Buddhism. This sampling should not be considered authoritative, exclusive, or premeditated in the least.

WOMEN IN ETHNIC-ASIAN BUDDHIST COMMUNITIES

A narrative on women in the globalization of Buddhism in the West must begin with an acknowledgment of the ethnically Asian Buddhist communities, in which women have balanced traditional gender expectations and integration of Western values. There are, of course, tremendous ranges of experience in the disparate Asian Buddhist communities, and so only broad generalizations can be made. But there are certain commonalities in Asian women's experiences that impact their roles in Buddhist institutional life.

Within this context, Asian-American women have played central roles in preserving the culture, traditions, and religion so essential to the identities of their families and communities. The temple is often the center of this activity, and the religious dimensions genuinely mix with the cultural aspects, especially for more recent immigrant populations. Asian-Americans report that unlike convert Buddhists, for whom spirituality is often stripped from religion and culture, for them all three mix together at the temple. Practice is not just sitting meditation as non-Asian Buddhists often imply. Instead, practice is a whole way of life that includes nonverbal communication, relationships with monks and nuns, and social life. And women often play central roles in passing these traditions on to their children. As Jessica Tan heard from her grandmother, "Your (great) grandmother would be so happy that you became a Buddhist." She went on: "So here I am, participating in this practice that has been handed down through the generations—encased in cultural hegemony and oppression, as well as in love, persistence, and trust. I know that to practice deeply, I have to bring in who I am and all of my communities."[2]

Some Asian-American Buddhist women are actively involved also in improving the conditions for women in their ancestral lands. Joanna Sukhoeun Duong is concerned about the victimization of women and children in her native Cambodia. She and her husband have founded NAG-CAPA (National Alliance for the Generation of Cambodian Peoples' Advancement) to systematically improve the lot of orphans and prostitutes through housing, job training, and emotional and spiritual counseling.[3] But Asian-American women are not just concerned about their own peoples. Taiwanese women participate in Tzu Chi, a Buddhist charity founded in Taiwan by the nun Cheng Yen to serve a variety of missions throughout the world, including victims of typhoons in Bangladesh, floods in Nepal, hurricanes in Central America, and natural disasters in mainland China, the mortal enemy of their homeland. In the northern California chapter, the majority of the active members appear to be women who tirelessly serve breakfasts to the homeless in San Jose, and also teach low-income children mathematics and marketable skills. They also teach Mandarin language to Chinese-American children in order to help them preserve their ancestral Buddhist traditions.[4]

While the general segregation of ethnic-Asian and Western convert communities seems also to hold among Buddhist women, there are exceptions.[5] In Sōka Gakkai International (SGI) in the United States, diverse populations of men and women join together in practice, and women are currently stepping into a high percentage of leadership roles.[6] Here, Japanese-American women practice alongside non-Asian Americans who include white, Hispanic, and African-American—in fact, current membership statistics indicate 30 percent of SGI's members are non-white non-Asians. SGI is a rare example of an immigrant Buddhist tradition that has bridged the gap between populations of ethnic and convert women and men.

Generally, however, the patterns of women's participation in ethnic-Asian Buddhist communities in the West are as little known as the general patterns of these communities, and much more must be done to assess these women's contributions, their concerns, and their characteristic styles of practice.

INNOVATION AND TRADITION: THE WOMEN'S DIALOGUE

The recent renaissance of Buddhism among Western converts has coincided with feminist movements that have questioned the privilege associated with patriarchy in Western religious institutions, a coincidence that Rita Gross has called "auspicious."[7] This confluence has produced several contemporary generations of confident women who have turned to Buddhist practice with genuine spiritual appetite, openness to innovation, and aspiration to lead. Current scholars have identified this as a landmark in Western Buddhism, characterizing the development of a "uniquely American form of the *Dharma.*"[8]

But within Western Buddhist communities the issues are more complicated and vary from community to community. Many convert women have pursued Buddhist practice with gusto and inspiration, with little interest in gender issues and institutional structures. They report that meditation practice is transformative and empowering, providing them liberation that political movements could never deliver. In fact, members of the *vipassanā* and Tibetan Buddhist communities with which I am most familiar comment anecdotally that their meditation programs and intensive retreats are populated mostly by women practitioners. Zen communities seem to sustain a more steady balance of male and female practitioners, according to these anecdotal comments.

Yet in established Buddhist communities some feminist concerns about patriarchal patterns have surfaced, especially with reference to broader, more important issues, such as authority and hierarchy. Women and men in Western convert communities are asking vital questions for the future of Buddhism in the West. What is the role of the spiritual teacher in Buddhism, and what social and institutional forms are most appropriate for the teacher/student relationship? To what extent is hierarchy in the spiritual sense a desirable form in Western Buddhism? Do hierarchy and patriarchy go hand in hand?

Asking these questions exposes the central dilemmas of a Buddhism that has not been thoroughly implanted in Western convert environments. Some first- and second-generation convert communities have at times pulled free of their Asian traditions, prematurely rejecting teachers and forms that have nurtured their development. This is especially evident in the writings of certain American women practitioners, whose suspicions regarding patriarchy suggest the culpability of all tradition. The conclusion of one such book that reflects on the importance of personally testing the teachings commented, "We are not being asked to believe anything or accept anything (particularly not to buy something simply because a man said it, however enlightened he may have been). American women, having broken with a patriarchal path, are creating their direction, incorporating wisdom wherever they may find it."[9]

But from the perspectives of many other women, especially those least likely to attend the women's gatherings that produce such books, these women (and men, for that matter) could be depriving themselves of essential cultural nurture from those same Asian fonts of wisdom. The great teachers who brought the Dharma to the West still have a great deal to teach us, and we must be careful not to take a short-term approach regarding what is valuable and what is not valuable in our Buddhist heritages. Recently, a Western Buddhist teacher told the story of his grandmother, who carried an Appalachian herbalist tradition inherited through her mother's line. The grandmother confessed that when she was young, many of the traditional details in the painstaking preparation of herbs seemed superfluous. Only decades later did she come to understand why seemingly useless steps were necessary. In wise and humorous counsel, she advised her grandson to remember that when training with his Buddhist teacher. Now, fifteen years later, this Western Buddhist conceded that he understands and appreciates his Asian teacher's attention to detail in new light, just as his grandmother predicted.

One of the leading American voices for the preservation of close ties with our Asian Buddhist teachers has been Sangye Khandro, a gifted translator and president of Tashi Chöling Meditation Center in Oregon. She laments the democratization of Buddhism, in which the personal teacher is seen only as an ordinary person, since the precious mind-transmission upon which we base our practices stems from devotion to the teacher. This is, of course, especially true in the practice of Vajrayāna Buddhism in the Tibetan tradition. She speaks for hosts of more invisible practitioners, female and male, who feel that feminist and anti-authoritarian impulses counter what is most sacred in Buddhist practice.

These questions also expose the cultural biases of American Buddhist communities, in which hierarchy, tradition, authority, and privilege have been historically charged subjects. It is important to explore these issues with a double-edged sword, critiquing both the cultural trappings of Asian Buddhism and the egalitarian reactiveness of American culture. My European Buddhist friends view these controversies in American Buddhism with a mixture of irony and clarity, recognizing a peculiarly American reactiveness to issues of authority. The European convert Sanghas with which I am familiar, primarily Zen and Tibetan Vajrayāna, have greater appreciation for the spiritual authority of the teacher and for hierarchical patterns of governance. Perhaps in the globalization of Buddhism, American Buddhism will begin to profit from seeing the contours of its own cultural biases in the encounter with Asian traditions.

From this perspective, the confluence of global Buddhism with feminisms and gender-liberation movements may yield a more profound reflection on the issues of transformation of culture. Yet in order to identify what women care about and want, we need to look beyond those who write books, attend conferences, or create alternative communities. An examination of how women's activities are shaping global Buddhism in the West will help us understand issues of cultural transformation. Consequently, this essay will provide a slightly different angle on these difficult and unwieldy questions.

PRACTICE AND COMMUNITY

Women practitioners in Western convert communities have generally found Buddhism's emphasis upon spiritual discipline, personal transformation, cultivation of community, and liberation from inner turmoil to be inspirational. Sandy Boucher has written a women's guide to Buddhism, identifying how the Dharma speaks especially to women.[10] Yet for others the notion of a guidebook especially for women would seem absurd—they view the Dharma as universal, needing no such special packaging.

For many women, it has been personal suffering that has brought them to Buddhist meditation. Sharon Salzberg, a gifted *vipassanā* teacher and one of the founders of the Insight Meditation Society in Barre, Massachusetts, experienced loss and grief early in life. Her father left the family when she was four and a half, and her mother died when she was nine. Her father briefly returned and then abandoned her again when she was eleven. *Vipassanā* meditation, encountered during a junior year in India during college, presented her with her first real opportunity to relate directly to her suffering, and once she began she never stopped her practice.[11]

For others, it is the sheer directness and reliance on personal experience that has drawn them to Buddhism. Pema Chödrön spoke of reaching a certain point in marriage and family life when her domestic tasks seemed to be over. "My real appetite and my real passion were for wanting to go deeper. I felt that I was somehow thick, and that in order to really connect with the truth or with reality or with things as they are—however you want to say it—I needed to put all my energy into it, totally." [12] She became a nun and senior teacher (*ācārya*) in the Shambhala Buddhist tradition of Chögyam Trungpa Rinpoche.

Tenzin Palmo chose retreat. The English-born nun journeyed to the Himalayas to engage in a twelve-year solitary cave retreat under the direction of her Tibetan teacher.[13] After eventual expulsion from India because of visa problems, she took up residence in Italy, where she is raising money for a new nunnery that will re-establish the extinct lineage of *yoginīs (tok-denmas)* within the Drukpa Kagyu lineage of Tibetan Buddhism. Ayya Khema also chose retreat, but alongside her Western nuns of Parappuduwa Nun's Island in Sri Lanka, where she resided until political turmoil expelled her. Born in Germany, she taught also in Australia, South America, and the United States until her death in 1997.[14]

More commonly, Buddhist women have joined practice communities. A number of teachers have developed their own communities after leaving more traditional Sanghas that were patriarchal in structure. In 1981, Toni Packer, the former Zen teacher trained by Philip Kapleau Rōshi, founded the Springwater Center in upstate New York. While her work is informed by Zen and by J. Krishnamurti, she feels that questioning is the heart of the matter and she teaches her students to assume nothing and hold onto nothing, even nothingness itself.[15] Yvonne Rand is a Zen Buddhist priest who teaches at Redwood Creek Dharma Center, drawing from various Buddhist traditions. Her concerns about abuse of authority have spurred her to develop more egalitarian approaches, which she practices in her teaching.[16] Martine Batchelor, a former Korean Zen nun, is the guiding teacher at Gaia House, a nonsectarian Buddhist center in Devon, England, along with her husband, Stephen. Together, they integrate elements of *vipassanā*, Zen, and Tibetan Buddhism in their teachings on meditation and daily life as Western Buddhists.[17] Ruth Denison, who in 1973 founded Dhamma Dena in the Mojave Desert in California, has been teaching *vipassanā* retreats with unorthodox intensity for many years, bringing hippies, dropouts, and the disenchanted to the Dharma.[18]

There are many more communities led by women who have maintained their connections with their Asian or Western Buddhist lineages. Some are just for women, like Taraloka in Shropshire, England, a community and retreat center for laywomen associated with the Friends of the Western Buddhist Order, founded by the Englishman Sangharakshita. This community has a men's counterpart nearby. Community life is "neo-traditional," incorporating Asian elements, like strict refuge vows and precepts, with Western elements, like the cultivation of spiritual friendship and social engagement.[19]

Another innovative community is Tara Mandala, founded in 1993 by Tsultrim Allione, a Tibetan Buddhist teacher of Chöd practice. Tsultrim was authorized to teach Chöd meditation by Namkhai Norbu Rinpoche, and maintains connections with his lineage. Tara Mandala, located on five hundred acres in southern Colorado, is dedicated to Tantric and Dzogchen meditation in a partnership community with equal value for women and men. For Tsultrim personally, one of the aims of the community is "integrating the deep feminine into the fabric of Western Buddhist practice."[20]

Yet there are many other kinds of communities in which Western convert women are practicing, teaching, and leading. Some of these communities are loosely arranged, with gatherings oriented around retreats or meditation programs with little additional community life or design. The prevalent examples of these communities can be found in Western *vipassanā* practice, in which the religious or institutional elements are lacking for laypeople. Other communities, such as many Zen centers, are organized on a residential or semi-residential monastic model around a core of ordained lay priests, both female and male, who lead daily practice and intensive *sesshins*. Still other communities are more structured, with study curricula, social and cultural events, and a variety of meditation programs. In general, these Western convert communities have few gender-based obstacles.

Yet women in Western Buddhist communities have encountered gender bias in the translations of the *sūtras* and ritual, as well as in the iconographic depictions in the *zendō*, shrine room, and meditation hall. For some, this bias has seemed no particular obstacle, for the fundamental connection with the teachings has allowed an immediate translation into personal experience. Pat O'Hara, a Sōtō priest and resident teacher of the Village Zendo in New York, reported that "whenever the gender was vague in a *kōan*, [my teacher] encouraged us to switch it to female."[21] When gender bias has become an obstacle in some communities, the rituals or *kōans* have been retranslated and the icons on the shrine have been changed. Recently, a California Zen center placed a Kuan Yin on the *zendō* shrine, taking the place of Mañjuśrī. For others, care has been taken to re-examine the original texts or iconographic traditions to ensure accurate representation, removing androcentric assumptions about the gender of the deity or the practitioner. Often, searchers have found the Asian-language original ambiguous in gender, and have been able to translate into gender-neutral language.

DISTINCTIVE PATTERNS OF BUDDHIST WOMEN TEACHERS

During the current renaissance of Buddhism in the West, many women teachers have risen to prominence in a variety of convert communities. In fact, it is reported that roughly half of the American *vipassanā* meditation teachers are currently women.[22] It is difficult to generalize about teachers in various communities, because they blend tradition and innovation in unique fashions. For most of these teachers, gender issues are much less important than broad topics of concern for deepening meditation practice, benefiting others, and daily living.

When asked, these teachers often speak of the irrelevance of gender in working with their students. Excessive grasping onto the concept of *man* or *woman* presents obstacles in seeing fully the nature of reality. Barbara Rhodes, the Korean Zen master, spoke of an early encounter with her Korean teacher, Seung Sahn. "I asked him if there were any women Zen masters in Korea, and he said, 'Oh no, of course not. Women can't attain enlightenment.' He said it with a really straight face and then walked into the kitchen. I followed him in and said, 'I've been with you for two years and you've always said just to believe in yourself. How can you say women can't get enlightened?' He just stared at me and pointed his finger and he said, 'So you're a woman?' In other words I had grasped man-woman concept. He was saying that you can't attain enlightenment if you hold on to that self identity. I really liked that approach."[23]

When women teachers meet their students, whether male or female, they report that gender really matters only at first. When mind meets mind, gender is part of the dream of the encounter and the real issues of practice are not gendered ones. On the other hand, in emphasis and delivery of the teachings, women often emphasize elements overlooked by male teachers. Often this is what attracts students, whether male or female, to women teachers. "I asked some men students why my teaching appealed to them, and most of them said they wanted something that was open to the masculine, yet without the martial quality of traditional Zen. They liked the softer approach I offer, particularly in terms of body work—meditating in a position of ease as opposed to a position of tension."[24]

A clear example of "women doing it differently" is the emphasis that certain teachers have placed upon the development of compassion or loving-kindness. Bhikṣuṇī Pema Chödrön, the Shambhala Buddhist *ācārya* and abbess of Gampo Abbey in Nova Scotia, Canada, has devoted her teaching to the bodhisattva practices of mind-training *(lojong)*, developed by the Tibetan master Atīśa. Pema Chödrön has introduced these slogans with her own brand of earthy wisdom and personal experience, demonstrating how one could transform negative experiences into compassion and awakening. She has attracted thousands of students, roughly three-fourths of them women, many of whom had no previous experience of Buddhist meditation.[25]

Vipassanā teacher Sharon Salzberg teaches loving-kindness *(mettā)* meditation, a practice which develops an open heart through contemplating the *four immeasurables.* Sharon was guided by an early teacher, Dipa Ma, to train in this powerful practice as a way to transform suffering into compassion. She is best known for teaching retreats that blend insight practice with *mettā,* and for training other teachers.[26] But, does she teach loving-kindness because she is a woman? "I actually like to think not. I like to think it's more a reflection of something very basic in the teachings of the Buddha. Now, was I drawn to teach about love and compassion because I am a woman? Maybe, but look at the Dalai Lama. Compassion is what he embodies and teaches, and what people seem to long for. So, I'd say no, it's not about my being a woman."[27]

Other women teachers have emphasized the practical quality of meditation practice, bringing Buddhism out of an abstract, conceptual realm into daily living. Joko Beck's book, *Everyday Zen,* expresses her special gifts as a Buddhist teacher.[28] A Dharma heir of Maezumi Rōshi and resident teacher of the San Diego Zen Center, Joko is astonishingly blunt and direct. She has no patience with sentiment or the trappings of religion—"nothing special" is her watchword. She emphasizes real daily practice that includes every aspect of life: emotions, physical sensations, relationships. Her relationships with her students are close and attentive, and include regular phone interviews from her San Diego home. Sylvia Boorstein, a *vipassanā* teacher from the Bay Area in California, brings a different style of teaching to issues of daily life practice. Maternal and funny, Sylvia presents meditation in a delightful stream of earthy examples and anecdotes with a completely contemporary turn of phrase, as exhibited in the titles of her books on meditation: *Don't Just Do Something, Sit There;* and *That's Funny, You Don't Look Buddhist,* a book on the joining of Jewish and Buddhist practice.

Buddhist women have also brought a sense of embodiment to Buddhist practice. Zen practitioners Lenore Friedman and Susan Moon gathered an excellent series of essays composed by women practitioners giving rich variety to embodied practice.[29] Naropa University faculty like Barbara Dilley, Diane Butler, and Susan Aposhyan teach how meditation and movement join in body awareness. They conduct posture workshops with their students, strengthening the mind-body connection. Ruth Denison integrates movement, sensory integration, and rhythm into her *vipassanā* instruction in the Mojave Desert.

African-American Tibetan Buddhist practitioner Janice Dean Willis has devoted her recent work to developing contemplations on diversity and race for Buddhist practitioners, seeing how our concepts and habitual patterns express themselves as prejudice, which inhibits our path to enlightenment.[30] Arinna Weisman, a *vipassanā* teacher affiliated with Spirit Rock in California, has a special interest in working with multicultural and diversity issues, and teaches many retreats for lesbian, gay, and transgendered Buddhists. She was born in Johannesburg, South Africa, and has lived in London, Israel, and Europe.

Other women have brought attention to family practice and how to integrate children into our Buddhist communities, as well as how to bring personal practice into family life. Venerable Diane Van Parijs is a Japanese Pure Land (Jōdo Shinshū) priest with two children. In partnership with her husband, Yuho, she leads the White Lotus Center in Anchorage, Alaska, where she focuses on family practice within her community. The women of the Shambhala Buddhist community have been pivotal in the creation of schools for children of preschool through middle-school age, in both Colorado and Nova Scotia, Canada. Tsultrim Allione's Tara Mandala promotes family practice, with special programs for children.

While spiritual care for the dying is a practice that knows no gender boundary, prominent women teachers have focused their work in this area. Joan Halifax Rōshi, a founding teacher in the Zen Peacemaker Order, does extensive work with death and dying in New Mexico and elsewhere.[31] Judith Lief, an *ācārya* in the Shambhala Buddhist tradition, works with dying patients at Maitri Day Health Center in Yonkers, New York, and has taught widely on death and dying.[32] Christine Longaker, a student of Sogyal Rinpoche,[33] and Reverend Madeline Ko-i Bastis, a Zen priest and founder of the Peaceful Dwelling Project in New York state, are other teachers who have developed expertise in spiritual care for the dying.

RETRIEVING THE ROOTS OF WOMEN'S TRADITIONS

The foremost pioneer in examining the relevance of traditional Buddhist teachings for the lives of contemporary Buddhist women is Shambhala Buddhist Rita Gross, author of *Buddhism after Patriarchy*.[34] Rita is a scholar of the history of religions and of feminist theology who brought years of experience with feminism to her practice of Tibetan Buddhism. Her book, which follows the contours of feminist theology in the Christian and Jewish traditions, brings feminist critique to bear on the central teachings of early Buddhism in order to determine whether they were essentially egalitarian in their message. In finding them to be so, she then traced the sexist or misogynist themes in Buddhist teaching or institutions that contradict the core doctrines, and identified areas of reconstruction necessary in order to align Buddhism with its egalitarian heritage.

Rita's work was groundbreaking for its courage, clarity, and visionary qualities. She brought to bear a perspective on Buddhist teachings that was unprecedented in its scope, structure, and prescriptive program. Her work was controversial from a variety of perspectives. For some Asian Buddhist teachers, it involved an inappropriate questioning of the authority of their traditions, polluting the purity of the Dharma teachings with political considerations. For some American converts, it weighed the arguments of Buddhist teachings against the standard of feminism, giving the latter more ideological weight than the former, a method that seemed dubious in design to those with allegiance to the Dharma. For still others, it took a refreshing systematic look at questions that had been concerning them for a long time, and Rita was lauded as a reformer. Her work has laid the foundation for important additional work in Western Buddhism.

While so much of meditation practice transcends gender, Western women have developed a yearning for female myths and symbols to support their spiritual journeys. Two steps are necessary. To retrieve their Asian forbears, several scholar-practitioner women have endeavored to identify the Asian women's lineages in their respective traditions. Zen student Susan Murcott and *tāntrika* Anne Waldman separately retranslated the *Therīgāthā*, the songs of the nuns in the early Indian Buddhist Sangha, capturing a lyricism expressive of the original Pāli.[35] The Diamond Sangha's journal of women and Zen called *Kahawai* (now out of print) included stories of women in the Japanese and Chinese traditions who were powerful teachers in their time. Tsultrim Allione has recently reissued a revised edition of her groundbreaking collection of hagiographies of Tibetan *yoginīs*, from traditional to contemporary.[36] In her articles and books, Janice Willis has also contributed greatly to the recovery of women's stories and traditions from the Tibetan tradition.[37]

While these hagiographies and myths support spiritual development, it is also important to retrieve the specifically feminine symbols that may enhance the practice of both women and men in the Western Dharma. One such symbol is that of the Tibetan *ḍākinī*, who embodies in female form the dynamic power of inner realization to transform bias, conceptuality, and emotionalism into enlightenment. The *ḍākinī*, a female *buddha*, has been revered in Tibetan meditative traditions for centuries, and yet her tradition has been largely misunderstood, even pathologized, in Western scholarship and practice communities.

According to the Tibetan tradition, the *ḍākinī* may appear in visionary form to male and female practitioners at key points in their spiritual journeys, at times of crisis or intractability. While the meaning of the *ḍākinī* appears to be different in the experiences of women and men, she awakens the inner realization of emptiness and radiant wisdom. Or, without visionary appearance, the term *ḍākinī* is applied to certain yogic experiences, inner transformations, or daily life encounters. In the tradition of the *ḍākinī*, women are deemed to have certain advantages in spiritual practice, because their bodies are emanations of the fundamental wisdom principle. In any case, the careful retrieval of the multifaceted symbol of the *ḍākinī* has the potential to enrich the subjective experiences of women on the path of Dharma, especially in the practice of Tibetan Buddhism in the West.[38]

IS THERE A FUTURE FOR WOMEN'S CONTRIBUTIONS?

While the full participation of women in convert Buddhism in the West at the turn of the millennium is a remarkable phenomenon, it is important to put it into perspective. It is a common observation in the sociology of religion that women often serve in charismatic or leadership roles in marginalized religions or in the first generation of religions being established in new cultural settings.[39] As these traditions enter the mainstream, they most commonly copy the patterns of the cultures in which they reside, and those cultural settings are overwhelmingly patriarchal and androcentric. If the feminist influences on late-twentieth-century Western religion have been insufficient, it is likely that Western Buddhism will return to a patriarchal pattern within the next several generations. If this is the case, the rich contributions of women in Western Buddhism will be forgotten and their accomplishments and insights may be expunged from the historical record. Frankly, it is up to us to make sure that does not happen.

NOTES

1. Sandy Boucher, *Turning the Wheel: American Women Creating the New Buddhism*, updated and expanded ed. (Boston: Beacon, 1993; original edition, San Francisco: Harper and Row, 1988); Lenore Friedman, *Meetings with Remarkable Women: Buddhist Teachers in America* (Boston: Shambhala, 1987). Also see issues of *Shambhala Sun; Tricycle; Inquiring Mind;* and *Turning Wheel*.

2. Jessica Tan, "New Voices of Asian American Buddhism," *Turning Wheel*, Fall 2000, 33.

3. Maia Duerr, "Giving Away the Merit," *Turning Wheel*, Fall 2000, 21.

4. Diana Ames, "Just Do It!" *Turning Wheel*, Fall 2000, 23–5.

5. Kenneth K. Tanaka, "Epilogue: The Colors and Contours of American Buddhism," in *The Faces of Buddhism in America*, edited by Charles S. Prebish and Kenneth K. Tanaka (Berkeley: University of California Press, 1998), 287–98; Alan Senauke and A.J. Kutchins, "The Lion's Roar in America: An Interview with Kenneth Tanaka," *Turning Wheel*, Fall 2000, 12–5.

6. Jane Hurst, "Nichiren Shōshū and Sōka Gakkai in America: The Pioneer Spirit," in Prebish and Tanaka, *The Faces of Buddhism in America*, 79–98. This is

a major change from the previously male-dominated hierarchical approach of the earlier Sōka Gakkai and the current Hokkeko.

7. Rita Gross, *Buddhism after Patriarchy* (Albany: State University of New York Press, 1993), 26.

8. Richard Hughes Seager, *Buddhism in America* (New York: Columbia University Press, 1999), 200; Charles S. Prebish, *Luminous Passage: The Practice and Study of Buddhism in America* (Berkeley: University of California Press, 1999), 75–9.

9. Karma Lekshe Tsomo (ed.), *Buddhism through American Women's Eyes* (Ithaca, New York: Snow Lion, 1995), 158.

10. Sandy Boucher, *Opening the Lotus: A Woman's Guide to Buddhism* (Boston: Beacon, 1997).

11. Friedman, *Meetings with Remarkable Women*, 213–7.

12. Ibid., 99.

13. Vicki Mackenzie, *Cave in the Snow: A Western Woman's Quest for Enlightenment* (London: Bloomsbury, 1999).

14. Ayya Khema, *I Give You My Life: The Autobiography of a Western Buddhist Nun* (Boston: Shambhala, 1998).

15. Friedman, *Meetings with Remarkable Women*, 39–64; Toni Packer, *The Work of This Moment* (Boston: Shambhala, 1990).

16. Friedman, *Meetings with Remarkable Women*, 249–53.

17. Martine Batchelor (ed.), *Walking on Lotus Flowers: Buddhist Women Working, Loving and Meditating* (London: Thorsons/HarperCollins, 1996).

18. Sandy Boucher, "Woman to Woman," *Shambhala Sun* 8, no. 6 (July 2000), 32–7.

19. Dharmacharini Sanghadevi, "A Model for Laywomen in Buddhism: The Western Buddhist Order," in *Buddhist Women across Cultures*, edited by Karma Lekshe Tsomo (Albany: State University of New York Press, 1999), 267–76.

20. Tsultrim Allione, *Women of Wisdom*, rev. ed. (Ithaca, New York: Snow Lion, 2000), 75.

21. Melvin McLeod, "Women's Liberation," *Shambhala Sun* 8, no. 6 (July 2000), 28.

22. Gil Fronsdal, "Insight Meditation in the United States: Life, Liberty, and the Pursuit of Happiness," in *The Faces of Buddhism in America*, edited by Charles S. Prebish and Kenneth K. Tanaka (Berkeley: University of California Press, 1998), 163–82.

23. McLeod, "Women's Liberation," 28.

24. Ibid., 31, quoting Pat O'Hara, Sensei, a Soto priest and resident teacher of the Village Zendo, New York.

25. Pema Chödrön, *When Things Fall Apart: Heart Advice for Difficult Times* (Boston: Shambhala, 1996).

26. Sharon Salzberg, *Lovingkindness: The Revolutionary Art of Happiness* (Boston: Shambhala, 1997).

27. McLeod, "Women's Liberation," 30.

28. Charlotte Joko Beck and Steven Smith (eds.), *Everyday Zen* (San Francisco: Harper and Row, 1989). For more information on Joko Beck's teaching, see also Charlotte Joko Beck and Steven Smith, *Nothing Special: Living Zen* (San Francisco: Harper and Row, 1994).

29. Lenore Friedman and Susan Moon, *Being Bodies: Buddhist Women on the Paradox of Embodiment* (Boston: Shambhala, 1997).

30. Janice Willis, "Buddhism and Race: An African American Baptist-Buddhist Perspective," in *Buddhist Women on the Edge: Contemporary Perspectives from the Western Frontier*, edited by Marianne Dresser (Berkeley: North Atlantic, 1996),

81–92; "Diversity and Race: New Koans for American Buddhism," in *Women's Buddhism, Buddhism's Women: Tradition, Revision, Renewal*, edited by Ellison Banks Findly (Boston: Wisdom, 2000), 303–17.

31. Her book, *Being with Dying*, is forthcoming.

32. Judith Lief, *Making Friends with Death: A Buddhist Guide to Mortality* (Boston: Shambhala, 2001).

33. Christine Longaker, *Facing Death and Finding Hope: A Guide to the Emotional and Spiritual Care of the Dying* (New York: Doubleday, 1997).

34. Gross, *Buddhism after Patriarchy*.

35. Susan Murcott, *The First Buddhist Women* (Berkeley: Parallax, 1991); Andrew Schelling and Anne Waldman, *Songs of the Sons and Daughters of Buddha* (Boston: Shambhala, 1996).

36. Allione, *Women of Wisdom*.

37. Janice Dean Willis (ed.), *Feminine Ground: Essays on Women and Tibet* (Ithaca, New York: Snow Lion, 1987); "Tibetan Buddhist Women Practitioners, Past and Present," in *Buddhist Women across Cultures*, edited by Karma Lekshe Tsomo (Albany: State University of New York Press, 1999), 145–58.

38. See Judith Simmer-Brown, *Dākinī's Warm Breath: The Feminine Principle in Tibetan Buddhism* (Boston: Shambhala, 2001).

39. Catherine Wessinger, "Introduction—Going Beyond and Retaining Charisma: Women's Leadership in Marginal Religions," in *Women's Leadership in Marginal Religions: Explorations Outside the Mainstream*, edited by Catherine Wessinger (Urbana: University of Illinois Press, 1993), 1–4.

21 Engaged Buddhism

Agnosticism, Interdependence,
Globalization

Christopher S. Queen

INTRODUCTION

Over the past half-century, political activism and social service have emerged as salient features of the globalization of the Buddhist tradition. Along with the *democratization* implicit in the new roles that laymen and laywomen are playing in Buddhist institutions, and the *pragmatism* of a tradition that increasingly stresses actions—meditation, chanting, morality, and "the art of happiness"—more than words, doctrines, and philosophies, the *social engagement* of Buddhism may be said to parallel the activism, if not the militancy, of other world religions, notably Judaism, Christianity, Islam, and Hinduism.[1]

In prisons, hospices, refugee camps, and a wide range of social ministries and chaplaincies, engaged Buddhists are often as visible as the Hare Krishnas were a generation ago. But engaged Buddhists are not robed or shaven-headed dropouts, and they do not dance and distribute leaflets at airports and on street corners. In the West, they are more likely to be laymen and laywomen of all ages, often highly educated professionals, committed not to achieving bliss or to levitating themselves or the Pentagon, but to applying the Buddha's teachings to social challenges of the day—human rights, economic justice, ethnic tolerance, racial healing, and environmental protection. In Asia, engaged Buddhists are more likely to be ordained or lay volunteers of the village development movement in Sri Lanka, the Dhamma Yietra peace walk movement in Cambodia, and the Tzu Chi Foundation, offering natural-disaster relief in Taiwan and around the world.[2]

Activists and scholars do not agree on the origins of engaged Buddhism. Did it spring directly from Gautama Buddha's teachings of compassion, interdependence, and morality, or his acceptance of society's marginalized members—particularly untouchables and women—to the Sangha, his religious order? Or did it emerge later, during the reign of Aśoka Maurya in the third century B.C.E., or during a thousand years of cultural assimilation in China, Korea, and Japan, as Buddhist personal ethics encountered the institutional formalities of Confucian civil society? Did it come into being in the nineteenth century, when Buddhist reformers, Western colonialists, and Christian missionaries began to debate the merits of their respective cultures, to compete for the hearts and minds of citizens, and to maneuver for strategic control of Buddhist Asia? Or did engaged Buddhism appear full-blown only in recent times, as the world began to restructure economically, politically, and culturally at the global level—since the middle of the twentieth century?[3]

To be sure, the impact of Buddhist ideas and institutions on Asian societies is an established fact. Yet we must not be too hasty to make the Buddha and his successors into social revolutionaries and utopian reformers of the kind that gave us the modern world. In surveying the range of engaged Buddhism today, we see that its practitioners often think and act differently from their predecessors in Buddhist history and literature. We often encounter attitudes toward suffering—its definition, causes, and remedies—that are fundamentally new in the context of traditional Buddhist discourse and action. Buddhists generally agree, for example, that their path entails an inner transformation in which the painful affects of the three mental poisons—hatred, greed, and delusion—are reduced in the life of the practitioner. And they agree that this change will have beneficial ripple effects in society. But engaged Buddhists, while affirming these teachings, are likely to press on, to seek the harmful *social, institutional,* and *collective* expressions of these mental states in the policies and programs of corporations and governments, and to address them at the social, institutional, and collective levels.[4]

Thus the mass conversion of India's untouchables to Buddhism in 1956 grew out of their struggle to overcome the violence and humiliation of the caste system; the mobilization of Buddhist monks in Vietnam in the 1960s aimed to stop the war and to repair its ravages; in rural Sri Lanka, tens of thousands of students, monks, and laypeople have volunteered to build roads, wells, clinics, and schools in the poorest areas; and the "ecology monks" of northern Thailand and their lay supporters have fought to stop clear-cut logging in the rainforests of their country. In the United States, such organizations as the Buddhist Peace Fellowship in Berkeley, California; the Upaya Foundation in Santa Fe, New Mexico; the Greyston Mandala in Yonkers, New York; and the Peace Pagoda in Leverett, Massachusetts—social service agencies inspired by Buddhist teachings—work to promote peace, serve the poor, comfort the dying, and protect the environment.

COLLECTIVISM AND GLOBALIZATION

These movements and organizations have two things in common, aside from their Buddhist roots and their commitment to relieve suffering. They presume that suffering and its relief have a social dimension that cannot be addressed by private spirituality and morality alone. And they have established themselves as global agencies, inviting participation, membership, and material support from sympathizers throughout the world—by the high visibility, mobility, and collaboration of their leaders, through traditional print and broadcast media, and increasingly by high-speed information systems, the internet, and wireless communication.

These two marks of the new Buddhism—its collectivism and its globalization—are corollary features. For it is not possible to appreciate the social and institutional dimensions of human and environmental suffering in a globalized world without recognizing their transcultural, transnational scope. Thus Dr. B. R. Ambedkar, the leader of the Buddhist conversion of untouchables in India, was trained in Bombay, New York, and London; Thich Nhat Hanh, the Vietnamese Zen master, lobbied in nineteen countries in the 1960s to end the war in his country; and Dr. A. T. Ariyaratne, founder and leader of the Sarvodaya Shramadana rural development movement in Sri Lanka, has raised funds and received humanitarian prizes from international agencies. Likewise, as their names imply, the International Campaign for Tibet, based in the United States, the International Network of Engaged Buddhists, based in Thailand, and Sōka Gakkai International, based in Japan, are global organizations dedicated to addressing the causes and remedies of social suffering.[5]

Like Judaism, Christianity, and Islam, Buddhism has been an international religion from early in its development. Yet the local variations of Buddhism that took root in places like Ceylon, Afghanistan, Tibet, Mongolia, Japan, Cambodia, and Indonesia remained largely isolated from one another following their introduction by itinerant merchants and missionaries. Local assimilations and varieties of Buddhist thought and practice evolved in a branching and coexisting fashion over the centuries, making it unreasonable to speak of *Buddhism* in the singular throughout most of the history of the tradition. Even in countries as small as Ceylon and Tibet, doctrinal and ceremonial differences among the local monastic orders and lineages have engendered intense rivalries over the centuries.[6] Today, these patterns of diffusion and differentiation in Buddhism continue. At the same time, we may begin to see the outlines of a countertendency. As a result of accelerating communication and travel, engaged Buddhism has emerged as a truly global impulse, both growing out of and interacting with all the sectarian and cultural expressions of the ancient tradition. For this reason, and because of the collectivist soteriology at its core, Dr. Ambedkar suggested a new name for socially engaged Buddhism on the eve of his historic conversion in October 1956: "Our Buddhism will follow the tenets of the faith preached by Lord Buddha himself," he told reporters, "without stirring up the old divisions of Hinayana and Mahayana. Our Buddhism will be a New Buddhism—*a Navayana.*" [7]

In this overview of engaged Buddhism in its global manifestations, I shall treat Ambedkar's Navayāna (new vehicle) and its cousins in Asia and the West as a path of belief and practice that incorporates both tradition and innovation. This engaged Buddhism is demonstrably different from the ethics of discipline and virtue of the Hīnayāna (carried on today by the Theravāda *elder tradition* of South and Southeast Asia and the *vipassanā* movement in the West); the altruism of the bodhisattva path in the Mahāyāna, or "great vehicle" (manifested notably by the Zen, Pure Land, and Nichiren-based schools of East Asia and the West); and the monastic ritualism and scholasticism of the Vajrayāna, or "diamond vehicle" (carried on in the four schools of Tibetan Buddhism, now spreading in the global diasporas of forced exile). At the same time, we shall see, the new Buddhism preserves and integrates themes and perspectives from all of its predecessors. Thus I have proposed elsewhere that engaged Buddhism be thought of as a "new vehicle," or "fourth *yāna,*" of Buddhism.[8]

EMERGING THEMES IN THE NEW BUDDHISM

Do not think that the knowledge you presently possess is
changeless, absolute truth. Avoid being narrow-minded and bound
to present views. . . . Find ways to be with those who are suffering
by all means, including personal contact and visits, images, sound.
By such means, awaken yourself and others to the reality of
suffering in the world.

> Thich Nhat Hanh, Tiep Hien Order Precepts, 1987 [9]

I commit myself to not-knowing, the source of all
manifestations. . . . I commit myself to bearing witness fully by
allowing myself to be touched by the joy and pain of the universe.
I invite all hungry spirits into the mandala of my being and

commit my energy and love to my own healing, the healing of the
earth, humanity and all creations.

Bernard Glassman,
Zen Peacemaker Order Tenets, 1998[10]

In order to illustrate both the continuity and the innovation of engaged
Buddhism in its global and collectivist manifestations, let us focus on two
themes—*agnosticism* and *interdependence*—that have emerged in the
teachings and Sanghas of two of the most prominent leaders of the movement: the Vietnamese Zen master Thich Nhat Hanh and the American Zen
rōshi Bernard Tetsugen Glassman. I should like to argue that the precepts
of agnosticism and interdependence that Nhat Hanh and Glassman have
given to their respective religious organizations, the Tiep Hien Order (Order of Interbeing) and the Zen Peacemaker Order, are very old Buddhist
ideas that have been refashioned to resonate with contemporary discourses
on human rights and social justice that derive in turn from the Jewish-
Christian and Roman–Anglo-Saxon traditions of ethics and jurisprudence
we know in the West.[11]

Thich Nhat Hanh, Glassman Rōshi, and other contemporary Buddhists have approached problems of human suffering in two ways: first,
from the perspective of *methodological agnosticism,* "beginner's mind,"
"don't know mind," a radical openness to the novelty and complexity of
each situation; and second, from a perspective of the *oneness and interre-
latedness* of all things, the nonduality or interdependence of factors and
actors in situations, particularly situations involving pain, conflict, and violence, and the necessity of getting close to those who struggle and suffer in order to touch and heal their suffering. These notions, I would
suggest, are at the same time ancient and innovative, traditional and
revolutionary.

Buddhist agnosticism and interdependence are ancient and traditional
when they inform the individual path to spiritual liberation, for this has
been the root perspective of the Dharma from the beginning. They are innovative and revolutionary when they inform a collective response to what
Arthur Kleinman, Veena Das, and Margaret Lock have called *social suffering*—the deprivation and anguish caused by social, economic, political, and
institutional conditions that affect whole communities or populations—a
perspective that has grown in influence with the rise of the social and human sciences over the past century.[12]

My contention is that the old Buddhist virtues of wisdom (*prajñā*) and
compassion (*karuṇā*)—glossed as emptiness (*śūnyatā*) and skillful means
(*upāya kauśalya*) in the Mahāyāna literature—are expressed in new ways

in the engaged Buddhism of Thich Nhat Hanh and Bernard Glassman. In order to shake our attachment to conventional knowledge—as Zen masters have always attempted to do—these teachers insist upon agnosticism, the assertion of our deep ignorance of the way things truly are and how to affect them for good. And in order to break down the sense of ontological and ethical separateness between beings, they teach interdependence, the belief that one's own thinking, being, and behaving have direct and inexorable effects on other human and nonhuman beings, just as one is already constituted by the reality of these other beings.

These Buddhist notions of knowledge and action have significant implications for Western conceptions of human rights and social justice. In light of our ignorance and interdependence, for example, it becomes impossible to say with certainty who are the perpetrators and who are the victims in situations of social suffering. As Thich Nhat Hanh writes in a famous poem, "I am the child in Uganda, all skin and bones. . . and I am the arms merchant, selling deadly weapons to Uganda." Similarly—and this is the promise that gives Buddhism its name, the faith and practice of the *awakeners*—just as it is impossible to evade responsibility for the starving child and the ruthless merchant, however indirect, so it is impossible to identify with them and not to *wake up*, that is, to achieve the spiritual liberation offered in the Dharma: "Please call me by my true names, so I can wake up," Nhat Hanh writes, "so the door of my heart can be left open, the door of compassion." Finally, it is not possible to wake up to the suffering of the child and the arms dealer without *doing something about it*—not merely feeling sorry for them, or meditatively channeling love and compassion to them, or performing intercessory rituals on their behalf, but finding more direct and tangible ways to serve them and to relieve their misery. Thich Nhat Hanh again:

> Once there is seeing, there must be acting . . .
> We must be aware of the real problems of the world.
> Then, with mindfulness, we will know what to do,
> And what not to do, to be of help.[13]

The epistemological and soteriological shifts implicit in these teachings are institutionalized in the social liberation movements of Vietnamese, Tibetan, Burmese, Cambodian, and Sri Lankan Buddhists over the past half-century. Focusing on freedom from war and on economic development, the liberation offered by these Buddhist movements is understood in material as well as spiritual terms—as a "mundane awakening," or *laukodaya*, as the Sarvodaya workers call it. It is a holistic vision encompassing, for example, the "ten basic needs" listed by Sri Lankan villagers: a clean and beautiful environment, an adequate and safe water supply, clothing, a balanced diet, simple housing, basic health care, communication facilities, energy, education, and cultural and spiritual resources.[14] These shifts in Buddhist perception are fundamental, moving away from the highly individual and other-worldly notion of liberation for virtuoso monks in traditional Theravāda culture, toward the collective economic and cultural definitions of liberation among the largely lay communities served by these movements.[15]

Furthermore, many elements of traditional Buddhist culture have evolved in new directions. Ancient conceptions of karma and rebirth; of divine, protective Buddhas and bodhisattvas; of the sanctity and privilege of the Buddhist clergy; and, most important for our discussion, the belief that the ignorance and psychological attachments of sufferers themselves account for their suffering (the Buddha's second Noble Truth) have been overshadowed by highly rationalized reflections on the institutional and political manifestations of ignorance and attachment—that is, on collective greed, hatred, and delusion—and on new organizational strategies for addressing war and injustice, poverty and intolerance, and the prospects for *outer* as well as *inner* peace in the world.

These changes in the Buddhist worldview, resulting from the mutual encounter of Asian and Western cultures over many centuries, form a backdrop to our two themes. Here we may emphasize the contributions that the Buddhist ideas of agnosticism and interdependence can make to Western ethical discourse on human rights and social justice, just as we may note the influence of Western conceptions and values on the evolution of Buddhist thought and practice. For I believe that we are dealing in both cases with a profound mutual assimilation, displaying "hybridity all the way down," as Thomas Tweed has characterized religious evolution.[16]

BUDDHIST AGNOSTICISM

Thich Nhat Hanh's warning against any belief in "changeless, absolute truth" and "narrow-minded[ness] . . . bound to present views" is from the second of his fourteen precepts for members of the Order of Interbeing (Tiep Hien Order), founded during the Vietnam War and now reporting thousands of members in Asia and the West. What is remarkable here is not the existence of such a warning near the top of the list, but the fact that the first and third precepts also deal with what we are calling Buddhist agnosticism. The first one reads, "Do not be idolatrous about or bound to any doctrine, theory, or ideology, even Buddhist ones. All systems of thought are guiding means; they are not absolute truth." And the third one reads, "Do not force others, including children, by any means whatsoever, to adopt your views, whether by authority, threat, money, propaganda, or even education. However, through compassionate dialogue, help others to renounce fanaticism and narrowness." In Nhat Hanh's influential book, *Being Peace,* each precept is followed by a commentary that links it to traditional Buddhist teachings, to the crisis setting of the Vietnam War, and to circumstances faced by readers in less perilous times.[17]

Our second epigram, "I commit myself to not-knowing, the source of all manifestations . . . ," is the first tenet of Rōshi Glassman's Zen Peacemaker Order, founded on the steps of the U.S. Capitol on January 14, 1994, the *rōshi's* fifty-fifth birthday. During a five-day "street retreat" on the Capitol steps and in a homeless shelter near the White House, Glassman and some of his students pondered what they could do about homelessness, AIDS, and violence in the United States. The answer was to start a new, interfaith, activist community, the Zen Peacemaker Order. Tellingly, the first ingredient in Glassman's recipe for social change—he develops his cooking metaphor in his 1996 book with Rick Fields, *Instructions to the Cook*—was doubt: "Doubt is a state of openness and unknowing. It's a willingness to not be in charge, to not know what is going to happen next. The state of doubt allows us to explore things in an open and fresh way."[18] In a similar passage in his latest book, *Bearing Witness,* Glassman asks, "What is peacemaking?" And he answers, "It's about living a questioning life, a life of unknowing. If we're ready to live such a life, without fixed ideas or answers, then we are ready to bear witness to every situation, no matter how difficult, offensive, or painful it is. Out of that process of bearing witness, the right action of making peace, of healing, arises."[19]

Thich Nhat Hanh and Glassman Rōshi are not the only contemporary Buddhist teachers who stress the practice of agnosticism, the renunciation of fixed opinions. Two books that have appeared since the American Zen boom of the 1950s and 1960s reflect this theme in their titles. In *Zen Mind, Beginner's Mind* (1970), the Japanese Sōtō master, Shunryu Suzuki, begins with the aphorism, "In the beginner's mind [Japanese *shoshin*] there are many possibilities, but in the expert's, there are few."[20] Later in the book, he writes, "I discovered that it is necessary, absolutely necessary, to believe in nothing. . . . No matter what god or doctrine you believe in, if you become attached to it, your belief will be based more or less on a self-centered idea."[21] Likewise, the Korean master Seung Sahn titles his book of teaching letters *Only Don't Know* (1982). In the preface, two of his students explain that "*Only Don't Know* means choosing to pay attention. When we choose to just pay attention, confusion is dispelled; just seeing, just hearing, or just perceiving the needs of others is the turning point for clarity and compassion."[22]

Recently, Buddhist agnosticism has surfaced again in the writings of the British teacher, Stephen Batchelor, whose 1992 and 1997 volumes, *The Faith to Doubt: Glimpses of Buddhist Uncertainty* and *Buddhism without Beliefs: A Contemporary Guide to Awakening*, advocate what we might call cognitive renunciation. Batchelor begins the latter book by citing the most often quoted Buddhist text among users of the Buddhist web sites on the internet (according to Richard Hayes of McGill University),[23] namely the Buddha's advice to the Kalamas (*Aṅguttara Nikāya* I:187):

> Do not be satisfied with hearsay or with tradition or with legendary lore or with what has come down in scriptures or with conjecture or with logical inference or with weighing evidence or with someone else's ability or with the thought, "The monk is our teacher." When you know in yourselves, "These things are wholesome, blameless, commended by the wise, and, being adopted and put into effect, they lead to welfare and happiness," then you should practice and abide in them.[24]

In his commentary, Batchelor warns the reader not to confuse Buddhist agnosticism with a refusal to know or to investigate, or with the intellectual passivity that "legitimizes indulgent consumerism and the unreflective conformism dictated by mass media." Instead, he invokes T. H. Huxley, who coined the term *agnosticism* in 1869 to signify the rigorous testing of all propositions by reason and experience. The Dharma, for Batchelor, is thus *something to do*, a consistent, liberating orthopraxy in a world of superficial belief.[25]

When I interviewed Glassman Rōshi in 1996, I wanted to know why a teacher with a doctorate in applied mathematics and recent successes in business management, finance, and community development, would insist on unknowing. "In Zen," he replied, "the words *source* and *essence* are equivalent to unknowing, and they come up again and again. We have the *absolute* and the *relative* perspectives about life, and unknowing is the one source of both of these. At every moment, one starts from unknowing *so that* all the acquired knowledge will arise spontaneously and be used in a new and creative way."[26]

I was reminded of the opening verses of the *Hsin Hsin Ming*, the *sūtra* of Seng-ts'an, the 3rd Zen Patriarch (d. 606), a text from sixth-century China: "The Great Way is not difficult for those who have no preferences. . . . If you wish to see the truth, then hold no opinions for or against anything."[27]

Wishing to pursue the question, I suggested to Glassman that early Buddhism in India abounded in notions of knowledge, wisdom, and technique. Yoga, meditation, and philosophy were all developed by experts, the virtuoso monks. But in China a mistrust of words and concepts and intellectualism came into the early Zen tradition from Taoism, and we hear about book-burning and about Zen masters who do wild, irrational things to break their students' dependency on logic and learning. Is this part of not knowing?

"Yes, and for me it fits in with my Jewish background," Glassman replied. "In contrast to the whole rabbinical tradition of Talmudic learning and scholarship comes the mystical tradition of Kabbalah and Hasidism, where all the earthly qualities and emanations come from the infinite *Ein Sof.* And the Sufis have some of the same ideas. But the important thing is that Not Knowing was emphasized by my teacher Maezumi Rōshi, and it fits my temperament. It just makes so much sense to start from Not Knowing."

But how does this work when you are dealing with people with no educational opportunities, who have a desperate need for knowledge and expertise? Dr. Ambedkar, the untouchable leader, was just as zealous for education as he was for economic opportunities for the untouchables who converted to Buddhism in 1956. Here Glassman agreed, but added, "The other side must be stressed. At every moment one starts from unknowing *so that* all the acquired knowledge will arise spontaneously and be used in a new, creative way. It's like the old monk Hotei's totebag—everything comes out when the time is right." [28]

BUDDHIST INTERDEPENDENCE

The idea of interdependence is widely associated with Buddhism today because of popular perceptions that Buddhism is the religion of ecology and vegetarianism. While neither of these perceptions is completely accurate— most lay Buddhists in China and East Asia have not been vegetarians, for example, and the tradition has not been particularly focused on the natural environment [29]—the metaphysical and soteriological teachings of moral causation (*karma*), dependent co-origination (*pratītya-samutpāda*), nondualism or emptiness (*śūnyatā*), and the interpenetration of all things (*shih shih wu-ai*) have indeed occupied a central place at various stages in the history of Buddhist thought. [30]

Today the aspect of the teaching of interdependence that matters to engaged Buddhist masters is its ethical dimension. Thich Nhat Hahn's third precept invites contact, indeed *intimacy*, with "suffering in the life of the world," meaning both one's own suffering and that of others. He recalls the Buddha's first sermon, focusing on the reality, origin, cessation, and remedy of suffering, and then he reflects on the isolation of Americans:

> America is somehow a closed society. Americans are not very aware of what is going on outside of America. Life here is so busy that even if you watch television and read the newspaper, and the images from outside flash by, there is no real contact. . . . [But] if we get in touch with the suffering in the world and are moved by that suffering, we may come forward to help the people who are suffering, and our own suffering may just vanish.[31]

For Thich Nhat Hanh, the relationship between the suffering of others and one's own suffering is one aspect of their *interbeing*. He coined the expression in English to translate the Vietnamese *tiep hien* (to continuously be in touch [with others] in the present moment) and the notion of cumulative interpenetration found in the *Avataṃsaka Sūtra* (Chinese *Hua-Yen*; Korean *Hwaom*; Japanese *Kegon*). Interbeing represents the co-arising and co-existence of all beings, sentient and nonsentient. "In one sheet of paper," he says, "we see everything else, the cloud, the forest, the logger. I am, therefore you are. You are, therefore I am. This is the meaning of the word 'interbeing.' We inter-are."[32]

In the 1980s, Bernard Glassman moved to the industrial city of Yonkers, north of New York City, because it was the dumping ground for the homeless of affluent Westchester County—an ideal place to develop some of his Zen-based institutions for economic development: a for-profit bakery and a construction company to provide job training and employment, tenant-operated co-op housing in rehabilitated slum buildings, and drug treatment clinics and AIDS hospices, to name only a few.[33] Meeting with him there, amid the abandoned buildings and deafening truck traffic, I asked how Buddhist practices and ideas could make a difference for urban renewal. And, more specifically, how did the meditation retreats he held on the streets each year, among the homeless of Manhattan, benefit the poor?

"The same question could be raised about the Buddha," he replied. "How did he benefit mankind by sitting in meditation? This is a problem with the term 'engaged Buddhism' in a broad sense. Anything anyone is doing to make themselves whole in their own life, or realizing the Way, or becoming enlightened—whatever term you would use—these are all involved in service, because if we realize the oneness of life, then each person is serving every other person and is reducing suffering."

I recalled Thich Nhat Hanh's ethical nondualism in embracing the victims and the oppressors in situations of great social suffering, and Ambedkar's warning that religion not romanticize poverty. Glassman reflected, "I think that the person who has lived with the untouchables can work with the untouchables in a way that others cannot. You can't *become* untouchable in this way, of course. At the same time I believe that those who came out of that experience have a deeper understanding of it, and we should learn from them. I want to figure out how to learn from those who have suffered in a certain way, even though I can't fully enter that realm. So we go on the streets.

"I know we aren't homeless and I make that quite clear," he concluded. "At the same time, those who came will experience something that is closer to that world than those who haven't been there. This is the meaning of 'bearing witness.' It's like entering a church knowing you're not God or the priest. But you will experience something different from someone who stays out of the church or someone who is just hired to fix the roof." [34]

PROFILES IN ENGAGED BUDDHISM

To further illustrate the practice of agnosticism and interdependence in the lives of engaged Buddhists today, let us turn to the experiences of six American Buddhist activists who have been motivated by the Dharma to serve those who are less fortunate.

Rahul Deepankar, a successful medical doctor and community leader in suburban Chicago, recalls the violence and poverty of his childhood in northern India. Born among the 160 million Dalits, or "broken people" (also called untouchables), who make up one-sixth of the Indian population, he speaks with emotion of the Buddhist conversion led by the anti-caste activist, Dr. B.R. Ambedkar, that introduced millions of Dalits to a new faith in the 1950s. He tells of his own ascent from poverty, through government scholarships and employment opportunities established by the same Dr. Ambedkar, who became India's first Law Minister and principal draftsman of the Indian Constitution.

"Growing up as a marginalized person in India has taught me a lesson," Deepankar reflects. "Only by education can the poor survive the ongoing threats to their existence. I am rich now, but I think about my family and my village back home every hour of the day. I go back at least once a year. The school I started for low-caste girls in 1997 now has 350 students from sixth to tenth grades. In two years it will be accredited up to the twelfth grade, and I will start more schools in nearby towns. For me this is a spiritual path—engaging in the lives of others through love, sacrifice and service. This was the Buddhist path taught by Dr. Ambedkar."[35]

Paula Green, founder of the Karuna Center, a Buddhist-inspired peace center in Leverett, Massachusetts, tells of her early encounters with the American women's and peace movements, and the *vipassanā*, or insight, meditation she learned at Buddhist retreats while earning her doctorate in psychology at Boston University. Working now in international conflict resolution, she recalls an incident in 1990, when she joined an observation team from the International Network of Engaged Buddhists to monitor refugee and troop movements on the Thai / Myanmar border. Suddenly the team came under fierce shelling from Myanmar government troops. Her companion, a lifelong Quaker activist in his seventies, commented, "This might not be a bad way to go." But Paula was engaged to marry Jim Perkins, another peace activist who was recently paroled after serving prison time for his participation in the Ploughshares nuclear weapons protests. "Dying now would be a dirty trick on Jim," she reflected, and persuaded her friends to beat a hasty retreat.

Green describes subsequent trips to war-torn central Africa, the former Yugoslavia, the Palestinian settlements on the West Bank in Israel, and the front lines in the Buddhist / Tamil civil war in Sri Lanka. In Zaire, she conducted nonviolence training in a refugee camp on the Rwanda border, among the two hundred thousand Hutus who lived in makeshift shelters supplied by the United Nations. "I looked around, and as far as I could see in all directions there were these little blue plastic tents. And I thought, here I am, with three other trainers, teaching for a few weeks in the world's largest refugee camp, with people whose lives have reached a state of unimaginable misery because they or their kinsmen have recently used machetes to kill their Tutsi neighbors. This task is as absurd as scratching at a mountain with a toothpick. But we taught every day, all day, under our own blue-sheeted tent."

Invited back a year later, Green and her colleagues found to their amazement that participants had translated into French all the materials they had brought the year before. And there were seventeen tents in the camp with a sign in front of each saying, "Center for the Study of Nonviolence."[36]

Claude AnShin Thomas, a Vietnam veteran haunted by memories of the hundreds he has killed in combat, descended into drug addiction and homelessness at the end of the war. In 1995, he joined an international peace walk organized by Japanese Buddhist monks, and traveled from the death-camp grounds in Auschwitz, Poland, through war-torn provinces of the Balkans, the Middle East, South Asia, Vietnam, and into Japan, ending at

Hiroshima, where Americans had dropped the hydrogen bomb exactly fifty years before. Taking ordination as a Zen Peacemaker priest from Bernard Glassman, Claude returned home to start a peace center in New England. He made a solo peace walk from New York to San Francisco in 1998 to raise awareness of homelessness and poverty in the United States and human rights violations throughout the world.

Today Claude Thomas addresses veterans' groups and communities torn by gun violence and domestic abuse, and leads "street retreats," week-long, outdoor meditation retreats in the inner cities of North America and Europe. He often teaches the practice of the Mindfulness Bell, developed and taught in Thich Nhat Hanh's Order of Interbeing. Whenever a bell is heard, whether a temple bell or the doorbell or telephone in one's house, the practitioner stops, listens, breathes, and, before responding, develops a spirit of generosity and acceptance of the circumstances. Once this practice has been mastered, the bell may be heard in situations in which no bell is present, and the same response will follow.

Thomas gives an example. "When it rains, before I can get to the sound of the rain, I have to walk through the sounds of war in Vietnam during the monsoon season. I have to walk through the screams of young men dying. I have to walk through the visions of treelines going up in napalm. I have to listen to seventeen-year-old boys crying for their fathers, for their girl-friends, and their mothers, before I can get to the place where it's just rain. Now I am reaching the place where I hear the bell in the rain." [37]

In 1999, Wangchuk Meston jumped from a third-story window in China to escape his captors. His grave injuries and his personal mission— photographing population movements near the China/Tibet border— prompted the U.S. State Department to pressure the Chinese for his release. Born of American parents, Wangchuk lived in a Nepalese monastery for nine years and speaks fluent English and Tibetan. He and his wife, Phuntsok, a Tibetan exile, are activists in the Free Tibet movement.

The Mestons tell their story. Wangchuk was the son of Caucasian spiritual seekers from California, who placed him in a Tibetan monastery at the age of six for years of religious training. Phuntsok was an ethnic Tibetan girl in the refugee camps at Mundgod in South India. Meeting in Boston in their early twenties, they married and committed themselves to the Tibetan cause. They learned of the World Bank's funding of the Chinese government transfer of ethnic Chinese populations into traditional Tibetan and Mongolian lands. Both the United States government and pro-Tibetan activists like the Mestons opposed this project, but the World Bank was committed. Wangchuk Meston journeyed to Qinghai province to investigate the program and was captured by Chinese police. Only after his failed attempt to escape, when his injuries were reported in the international press, was he released and reunited with his wife. Today, the Mestons continue to work with the International Campaign for Tibet, and with leaders like the Dalai Lama, actor Richard Gere, and Columbia professor Robert Thurman, to restore peace to Tibet.

Dr. Joan Halifax recalls her traumatic childhood, when a virus destroyed her eyesight for two years, and an adult life of restless searching. She participated in anti-war and civil rights protests in the sixties, crossed the Sahara alone in a VW bus, conducted LSD research with her psychologist husband, Stanislav Grof, in the 1970s, and received dual ordination as a Buddhist priest from Thich Nhat Hanh and Bernard Glassman in the 1980s and 1990s.

Joan describes the integration and stability that Buddhist teachings imparted to her broken life. We see images of her work with the dying in San Francisco and the wilderness retreats she leads in the desert near her peace center in Santa Fe. She teaches the techniques of "being with death and dying" to a class of terminally ill patients, doctors, nurses, lovers, family, and friends. She speaks calmly, with authority. In a culture where death is an enemy to be ignored, denied, and hidden away, Joan physically touches the dying. She holds them, listens to them, comforts them, calms them, and eases their suffering by any means possible. She shares their last thoughts and fears; she feels their last shuddering breaths, holding them in her arms. She travels easily from church to synagogue, hospice to hospital, dispensing techniques and training born of Buddhist traditions and beliefs in a culturally and spiritually flexible manner.

Back in Leverett, Massachusetts, Paula Green describes the peace-walk meditation of the monks of the Nipponzan Myohoji Order, who live at the New England Peace Pagoda nearby. In the ritualism of the Buddhist peace walk—very different in atmosphere and purpose from the political marches of Gandhi and of the American civil rights struggle, which were intended to force changes in the political system—the goal is to unite marcher and observer in a feeling of common humanity and aspiration. For example, during the Interfaith Pilgrimage of the Middle Passage, a twelve-month peace walk that retraced the journey of slavery through the United States, the Caribbean, and West Africa, we hear the voice of one of the marchers, the tonsured American nun, Sister Clare:

> When we walk together, our feet touch the same earth, we walk beneath the same sun and soak the same rain. As we journey together with a common purpose, we realize that joys and difficulties need not stop us

walking, we begin to restore the spiritual strength of humanity, the strength to reverse the vicious repercussions of our history and to move onwards toward a genuinely peaceful society nourished by the innate generosity of human beings and the natural world.[38]

THEORETICAL CONSIDERATIONS

The study of engaged Buddhism is still in its infancy. As late as the mid-1980s, volumes like Masao Abe's *Zen and Western Thought* (1985) and Inada and Jacobson's *Buddhism and American Thinkers* (1986) devoted all their attention to comparative metaphysics and epistemology (topics like Emptiness and God, or Nāgārjuna and Nietzsche), with no room left over for spiritual or ritual practice, morality, or social ethics. Meanwhile, scholarly monographs and collections were just beginning to appear on human rights and the world's religions, including Buddhism, such as those of Bradney, Stackhouse, Swidler, and Rouner. For Buddhist Studies, this trend culminated in a 1995 online conference and resulting volume, sponsored by the *Journal of Buddhist Ethics* and titled *Buddhism and Human Rights*.[39]

Studies on engaged Buddhism began to appear during the late 1980s, including Fred Eppsteiner's collection, *The Path of Compassion: Writings on Socially Engaged Buddhism* (1988), Sulak Sivaraksa's *A Socially Engaged Buddhism* (1988), and Ken Jones's *The Social Face of Buddhism: An Approach to Political and Social Activism* (1989). Queen and King's *Engaged Buddhism: Buddhist Liberation Movements in Asia* was published in 1996, and my *Engaged Buddhism in the West* appeared in 2000. The latter volume concludes with a methodological essay, "New Voices in Engaged Buddhist Studies," by Kenneth Kraft, and a bibliography of more than two hundred works. *Action Dharma: New Studies in Engaged Buddhism*, edited by Christopher Queen, Charles Prebish, and Damien Keown, will be published in 2002.

For the purposes of this discussion, let us confine our attention to the relationship between the two themes we have explored in this chapter, the methodological agnosticism and relational ethics propounded by our Zen masters and enacted by the engaged Buddhists in our examples. One might ask, for example, how we can know that beings are deeply interdependent or that our actions have any effect on others, if we approach life with the "don't know mind" advocated by Thich Nhat Hanh and Bernard Glassman. One possibility is that the deep interdependence of things may only be grasped by spiritually realized practitioners, such as the buddhas, *arhats*, *siddhas*, and Zen masters who have achieved awakening to this and related truths, such as no-self, nondualism, and emptiness. For less advanced practitioners or laypersons, *trust* and *faith* are necessary to motivate and sustain the spiritual path. Certainly the role of *śraddhā* (faith) has been a salient feature in both Theravāda and Mahāyāna forms of Buddhism, not to mention the Pure Land and Zen schools that dominated East Asia by the second millennium C.E.

Another approach to understanding the relationship between agnosticism and interdependence is to suggest that the unknowing of beings arises from their status as parts nested in a greater whole, and that their interdependence with other parts and with the whole reinforces the perspectivism inherent in partiality. This interpretation, like the last, must rest on faith in a certain structure of reality, imparted as "right views" handed down by masters of the tradition for investigation and verification by new practitioners, communities, or generations.

Here we may profitably turn to the theoretical analysis of Buddhist epistemology and cosmology formulated by Joanna Rogers Macy, a well-known practitioner and philosopher of engaged Buddhism. In *Mutual Causality in Buddhism and General Systems Theory: The Dharma of Natural Systems* (1991), based on her doctoral thesis, "Interdependence: Mutual Causality in Early Buddhist Teachings and General Systems Theory" (1978), Macy offers a framework for understanding the relationship between unknowing, interdependence, and social ethics, grounded both in the classical Buddhist teaching of *pratītya-samutpāda* (dependent co-origination) and on the work of biological and cybernetic systems theorists Ludwig von Bertalanffy, Irvin Laszlo, Norbert Wiener, and others. After developing the notion of mutual causality in Buddhist philosophy and in Western philosophical and scientific conceptions, Macy devotes the balance of her study to problems related to the self-as-process, the co-arising of knower and known, of body and mind, of doer and deed, and the dialectics of personal and social transformation.[40]

Two references to Macy's study will have to suffice here. On the limits of cognition, she writes,

> If knowing is interactive [as she has shown in a chapter on the cybernetics of perception], it becomes difficult to claim and impossible to prove an ultimate truth. For knowing is not only relative to the perspective of the knower, but conditioned by his past and present experiencing, and colored by the gestalts and constructs he imposes on perceptual data.
>
> In systems thinking these limits to cognition are recognized in a variety of ways. One is implicit in the self-referential character of feedback. By virtue of the causal loops that interconnect the observer with his environment, all percepts and concepts . . . are modified by past

experience and, therefore, interpretive. Furthermore, these circuits are such that only "short arcs," or portions of the factors they link, are discernible by the conscious knower. As [the systems philosopher Gregory] Bateson points out, "life depends upon interlocking *circuits* of contingency, while consciousness can only see such short arcs as human purpose may direct.[41]

In the final chapter, Macy shows how the tree and flame, as examples of open, living systems, are paradigmatic for an ethics of mutual causality:

> Significant to both general systems theory and early Buddhist teachings, these images serve to convey the interdependence of our lives and also the process by which transformation takes place. . . . The holonic structure, reticulating into subsystems and merging in larger branches, is that of a tree, while the process by which it happens in the transformation of energy and information is like that of a flame. . . . As the Buddha's teachings attest, the realization of both transiency and relationship breaks down the walls of ego; freeing us from that anxious cell, it releases the heart to loving-kindness, the will to self-restraint and sharing.[42]

As a major preceptor of engaged Buddhism, Joanna Macy was co-founder, with Robert Aitken Rōshi and Gary Snyder, of the Buddhist Peace Fellowship in the late 1970s and has published on Buddhist liberation movements in Asia, the psychology of activism and social change, and Buddhism and ecology.[43]

In light of these reflections, I would suggest that *agnosticism/interdependence*, as adumbrated by Thich Nhat Hanh and Glassman Rōshi, may be regarded as an indivisible unit in the pedagogy of engaged Buddhism, the same way the *prajñā/karuṇā* (wisdom/compassion) and *śūnyatā/upāya* (emptiness/means) are complex conceptual units in the rationality of Mahāyāna Buddhism. As such, they may be treated as a distinctive contribution to any discussion of Buddhist ethics, human rights, and social justice that offers an alternative rationality to that of the West, which is based on *expertise/entitivity*, the analysis of complex wholes into quasi-autonomous component parts.

CONCLUSION

Engaged Buddhist approaches to social suffering, illustrated by the precepts and tenets of the Tiep Hien and Peacemaker orders and the lives of the activists we have met, promote open-mindedness, creativity, resourcefulness, solidarity, and a search for common ground and consensus among the actors in social conflicts. Such traditional virtues as loving-kindness, compassion, patience, tolerance, impartiality, and the commitment not to harm others are practiced in a context of mutuality and noncompetitiveness, even regarding ideology and cultural values. A famous verse from the Dhammapada acquires new meaning in the context of this agnosticism/interdependence: "'He abused me, he beat me, he defeated me, he robbed me,' the hatred of those who do not harbor such thoughts is appeased. Hatreds never cease by hatred in this world; by love alone do they cease."[44]

Examples of collective strategies based on these precepts in the brief history of engaged Buddhism, from the peace marches of Vietnamese monks between the battle lines of the opposing armies during the American War, to the street retreats and "plunges" of Glassman's Peacemaker Order, would be inconceivable if they were based on the ideological zealotry and zero-sum thinking so characteristic of Western societies. Likewise, the adversarial system of Euro-American jurisprudence would collapse if remodeled on the logic of Nhat Hanh's "Call Me By My True Names." Celebrated attorneys like Johnny Cochran, Alan Dershowitz, and Kenneth Starr would have to take early retirement or to go back to school to learn mediation and peacemaking if engaged Buddhism were to win the heart and mind of the West.

The agnostic-interdependent perspective of engaged Buddhism cannot be maintained by social regulations or willpower; it must be cultivated through spiritual practice in solitude and in community. Thich Nhat Hanh writes:

> Meditation is not to get out of society, to escape from society, but to prepare for a re-entry into society. We call this "engaged Buddhism." When we go to a meditation center, we may have the impression that we leave everything behind—family, society, and all the complications involved in them—and come as an individual in order to practice and to search for peace. This is already an illusion, because in Buddhism there is no such thing as an individual.[45]

In this respect, it is important to remember that engaged Buddhism is a *religion*, "a symbol system that orients us to the ultimate conditions of existence by linking meaning and motivation," in Robert Bellah's still-useful definition.[46] Unlike a mathematical or scientific system, or a system of music, law, or philosophy, religious symbols and rituals return us to the problems of *orientation, meaning,* and *motivation* as ultimate frames of reference. How can we explain and overcome suffering, how can we understand our place in society and the natural world? What would it take to make us whole and happy? What are our obligations to others? Only religions address these issues in a comprehensive way that shapes the personal, social, and political realms.

In Glassman Rōshi's community, group ritual and ceremony play important roles. Often staged with traditional Sōtō robes and vestments and accompanied by gongs, bells, wood blocks, incense, candles, and ritual food offerings before images of the Buddha and Maezumi Rōshi, the late founder of the White Plum sect of Sōtō Zen, Peacemakers chant the *Kanromon,* or "Gate of Sweet Nectar," the words of which have been translated to English and adapted for use by engaged Buddhists:

> Attention! Attention!
> Raising the Bodhi Mind, the supreme meal is offered to all hungry spirits in the ten directions throughout space and time, filling the smallest particle to the largest space. All you hungry spirits in the ten directions, please gather here. Sharing your distress, I offer you this food, hoping it will resolve your thirsts and hungers.[47]

NOTES

1. On religious activism and globalization, see Peter Beyer, *Religion and Globalization* (London: Sage, 1994); Robert Hefner, "Multiple Modernities: Christianity, Islam, and Hinduism in a Globalizing Age," *Annual Review of Anthropology* 27 (1998), 83–104; Mark Juergensmeyer, *A New Cold War: Religious Nationalism Confronts the Secular State* (Berkeley: University of California Press, 1993) and *Terror in the Mind of God: The Global Rise of Religious Violence* (Berkeley: University of California Press, 2000); Bruce B. Lawrence, *Defenders of God: The Fundamentalist Revolt against the Modern Age* (London: I. B. Tauris, 1990); and Phil Marfleet, "Globalization and Religious Activism," in *Globalization and the Third World,* edited by R. Kiely and P. Marfleet (London: Routledge, 1999). On the emergence of democratization, pragmatism, and engagement as marks of contemporary Buddhism, see Christopher S. Queen, "Introduction," in *American Buddhism: Methods and Findings in Recent Scholarship,* edited by Duncan Ryūken Williams and Christopher S. Queen (Richmond, U.K.: Curzon Press, 1999).

2. For the rise and scope of engaged Buddhism in Asia and the West, see Christopher S. Queen and Sallie B. King (eds.), *Engaged Buddhism: Buddhist Liberation Movements in Asia* (Albany: State University of New York Press, 1996); and Christopher S. Queen (ed.), *Engaged Buddhism in the West* (Boston: Wisdom, 2000); for summary accounts, see Donald Rothberg, "Responding to the Cries of the World: Socially Engaged Buddhism in North America," in *The Faces of Buddhism in America,* edited by Charles S. Prebish and Kenneth K. Tanaka (Berkeley: University of California Press, 1998), 253–65; and Richard Hughes Seager, *Buddhism in America* (New York: Columbia University Press, 1999), 201–15. For a concise survey of engaged Buddhist organizations active in Asia and the West, see David W. Chappell (ed.), *Buddhist Peacework: Creating Cultures of Peace* (Boston: Wisdom, 1999).

3. On the origins of engaged Buddhism, see Christopher S. Queen, "Introduction: The Shapes and Sources of Engaged Buddhism," in Queen and King, *Engaged Buddhism,* 1–44; Patricia Hunt-Perry and Lyn Fine, "All Buddhism Is Engaged: Thich

Nhat Hanh and the Order of Interbeing," in Queen, *Engaged Buddhism in the West*, 35–66; and Thomas Freeman Yarnall, "Engaged Buddhism: New and Improved? Made in the USA of Asian Materials," in *Action Dharma: New Studies in Engaged Buddhism*, edited by Christopher S. Queen, Charles S. Prebish, and Damien Keown (Richmond, U.K.: Curzon Press, forthcoming 2002).

4. The notion of a collective source of and remedy for human misery is spelled out in Arthur Kleinman, Veena Das, and Margaret Lock (eds.), *Social Suffering* (Berkeley: University of California Press, 1996), ix: "Social suffering . . . brings into a single space an assemblage of human problems that have their origins and consequences in the devastating injuries that social force can inflict on human experience. Social suffering results from what political, economic, and institutional power does to people and, reciprocally, from how these forms of power themselves influence responses to social problems. Included under the category of social suffering are conditions that are usually divided among separate fields, conditions that simultaneously involve health, welfare, legal, moral, and religious issues. They destabilize established categories. For example, the trauma, pain, and disorders to which atrocity gives rise are health conditions; yet they are also political and cultural matters. Similarly, poverty is the major risk factor for ill health and death; yet this is only another way of saying that health is a social indicator and indeed a social process."

5. For an account of the British support of Ambedkar's movement, see Alan Sponberg, "TBMSG: A Dhamma Revolution in Contemporary India," 73–120; for Thich Nhat Hanh, see Sallie B. King, "Thich Nhat Hanh and the Unified Buddhist Church: Nondualism in Action," 321–64; for Sarvodaya Shramadana, see George D. Bond, "A.T. Ariyaratne and the Sarvodaya Shramadana Movement in Sri Lanka," 121–46; for the International Network of Engaged Buddhists, see Donald K. Swearer, "Sulak Sivaraksa's Buddhist Vision for Renewing Society," 195–236; and for the Sōka Gakkai, see Daniel A. Metraux, "The Sōka Gakkai: Buddhism and the Creation of a Harmonious and Peaceful Society," 365–400; all in Queen and King, *Engaged Buddhism*. For the International Campaign for Tibet, see John Powers, "The Free Tibet Movement: A Selective Narrative," in Queen, *Engaged Buddhism in the West*, 218–45.

6. Some scholars, like the late Professor Masatoshi Nagatomi of Harvard, speak of *Buddhisms* in the plural, to disabuse students of the erroneous impression that a monolithic tradition with universal teachings and practices may be found. Likewise, Professor Jeffrey Hopkins of the University of Virginia describes the way in which abbots of the great Tibetan monastic colleges (now in exile in India) often expectorate before uttering the names of rival schools—recalling behavior found among students at Ivy League universities.

7. This paraphrase of Ambedkar's press conference is based on Dhananjay Keer's account in *Dr. Ambedkar: Life and Mission*, 3rd ed. (Bombay: Popular Prakashan, 1971), 498.

8. For a more detailed argument for the notion of a "fourth *yāna*" in Buddhist history, see Christopher S. Queen, "Introduction: A New Buddhism," in Queen, *Engaged Buddhism in the West*, 17–26.

9. Thich Nhat Hanh, *Being Peace* (Berkeley: Parallax, 1987), 90–1.

10. Bernard Glassman, Zen Peacemaker Order Tenets (undated flyer).

11. In a comparative study, "Judeo-Christian and Buddhist Justice" (*Journal of Buddhist Ethics* 2 [1995], 73), Winston L. King shows that the Biblical concepts of justice and righteousness (Hebrew: *tsedeq, mishpat*), mercy and steadfast love (*hesed*), and truth and fidelity (*'emet*) are not only linked to the holiness (*qadosh*) of God, but also give rise to the notion of the divine rights of kings, and eventually

to universal human rights. He says, "Building upon, but outwardly discarding the Christian doctrine of the immortal soul, fueled by the Renaissance humanist values, modern democrats like to speak of the inalienable right of each individual person to justice—cultural, social, [and] legal." For our purposes, *human-rights/social-justice* may be regarded as a unit of Western ethical thinking, just as we shall propose below that *agnosticism/interdependence* is a conceptual unit in Buddhist ethical thinking.

12. See Kleinman, Das, and Lock, *Social Suffering.*

13. Thich Nhat Hanh, *Peace Is Every Step* (Berkeley: Parallax, 1991), 91.

14. See Queen and King, *Engaged Buddhism,* 9–10.

15. See Queen, *Engaged Buddhism in the West,* 2–11.

16. Thomas A. Tweed, "Night-Stand Buddhists and Other Creatures: Sympathizers, Adherents, and the Study of Religion," in Williams and Queen, *American Buddhism: Methods and Findings,* 73: "[If] we ignore those who affiliate with hybrid traditions, engage in creole practices, or express ambivalent identities, there would be no one left to study. Most of the religions I know emerged in contact and exchange with other traditions, and they continued to change over time—always in interaction. Scholars cannot locate a pristine beginning or precontact essence to use as a norm to define orthodoxy or orthopraxis. There is hybridity all the way down."

17. Nhat Hanh, *Being Peace,* 89–91.

18. Bernard Glassman and Rick Fields, *Instructions to the Cook: A Zen Master's Lessons in Living a Life That Matters* (New York: Bell Tower, 1996), 51.

19. Bernard Glassman, *Bearing Witness: A Zen Master's Lessons in Making Peace* (New York: Bell Tower, 1998), xiv.

20. Shunryu Suzuki, *Zen Mind, Beginner's Mind: Informal Talks on Zen Meditation and Practice* (New York: Weatherhill, 1970), 21.

21. Ibid., 116.

22. Seung Sahn, *Only Don't Know: The Teaching Letters of Zen Master Seung Sahn* (San Francisco: Four Seasons Foundation, 1982), x.

23. Richard P. Hayes, "The Internet as Window onto American Buddhism," in Williams and Queen, *American Buddhism: Methods and Findings,* 170.

24. Stephen Batchelor, *Buddhism without Beliefs: A Contemporary Guide to Awakening* (New York: Riverhead, 1997), xiii.

25. Ibid., 17–18.

26. Christopher S. Queen, "Buddhism, Activism, and Unknowing: A Day with Bernie Glassman," *Tikkun* 13, no. 1 (January/February 1998), 66.

27. Seng-ts'an, *Hsin Hsin Ming: Verses on the Faith-Mind,* translated and edited by Richard B. Clarke (Buffalo, New York: White Pine Press, 1984), 5. These verses further recall the Taoist wisdom of Chuang-tzu (third century B.C.E.): "Tao is obscured when men understand only one of a pair of opposites, or concentrate only on a partial aspect of being. Then clear expression also becomes muddled by mere wordplay, affirming this one aspect and denying all the rest. Hence the wrangling of Confucians and Mohists; each denies what the other affirms and affirms what the other denies. What use is this struggle to set up 'No' against 'Yes,' and 'Yes' against 'No'? Better to abandon this hopeless effort and seek true light!" From Thomas Merton (ed.), *The Way of Chuang Tzu* (New York: New Directions, 1965), 42. And these verses further recall the opening of the *Tao Te Ching* of Lao-tzu (sixth century B.C.E.): "Existence is beyond the power of words to define: terms may be used but are none of them absolute. In the beginning of heaven and earth there were no words. Words came out of the womb of matter; and whether a man dispassionately sees to the core of life or passionately sees the surface, the core and the

surface are essentially the same, words making them seem different only to express appearance. If name be needed, wonder names them both: from wonder to wonder existence opens." From Witter Bynner (tr.), *The Way of Life According to Lao Tzu* (New York: Capricorn, 1942), 25.

28. See Christopher S. Queen, "Glassman Rōshi and the Peacemaker Order: Three Encounters," in Queen, *Engaged Buddhism in the West*, 95–127.

29. For a comprehensive collection of scholarly articles on Buddhism and ecology, see Mary Evelyn Tucker and Duncan Ryūken Williams (eds.), *Buddhism and Ecology: The Interconnection of Dharma and Deeds* (Cambridge: Harvard Center for the Study of World Religions, 1998). On vegetarianism, see Christopher Key Chapple, "Animals and Environment in the Buddhist Birth Stories," in Tucker and Williams, *Buddhism and Ecology*, 137–8; and for a critical review of the arguments on Buddhism and environmentalism, see Ian Harris, "Buddhism and the Discourse of Environmental Concern: Some Methodological Problems Considered," in Tucker and Williams, *Buddhism and Ecology*, 377–402.

30. A succinct presentation of Buddhist philosophy is that of Junjiro Takakusu, *The Essentials of Buddhist Philosophy* (Delhi: Motilal Banarsidass, 1975).

31. Nhat Hanh, *Being Peace*, 92.

32. Ibid., 87. For thorough accounts of the philosophy of Hua-Yen Buddhism, see Garma C. C. Chang, *The Buddhist Teaching of Totality: The Philosophy of Hwa Yen Buddhism* (University Park: Pennsylvania State University Press, 1974); Francis H. Cook, *Hua-yen Buddhism: The Jewel Net of Indra* (University Park: Pennsylvania State University Press, 1977); and Steve Odin, *Process Metaphysics and Hua-yen Buddhism* (Albany: State University of New York Press, 1982).

33. See Glassman and Fields, *Instructions to the Cook*, for the story of the Greyston Mandala for-profit and not-for-profit companies, and their emergence from a Zen-based vision of public/private/social/political/spiritual interdependence.

34. Queen, "A Day with Bernie Glassman," 65.

35. Personal communication, 3 June 2000. For more on Ambedkar and the Dalit movement, see Christopher S. Queen, "Dr. Ambedkar and the Hermeneutics of Buddhist Liberation," in Queen and King, *Engaged Buddhism*, 45–69; and Eleanor Zelliot, *From Untouchable to Dalit: Essays on the Ambedkar Movement* (Delhi: Manohar, 1992).

36. From Susan Moon, "Activist Women in American Buddhism," in Queen, *Engaged Buddhism in the West*, 255–7.

37. See Queen, *Engaged Buddhism in the West*, 56, 109–10, 430, 439, 441, 491.

38. *The Interfaith Pilgrimage of the Middle Passage*, pamphlet of the New England Peace Pagoda, 1998; quoted by Paula Green in "Walking for Peace: Nipponzan Myohoji," in Queen, *Engaged Buddhism in the West*, 155.

39. For a comprehensive bibliography, see Damien V. Keown, Charles S. Prebish, and Wayne R. Husted (eds.), *Buddhism and Human Rights* (Richmond, U.K.: Curzon Press, 1998).

40. Joanna Rogers Macy, *Mutual Causality in Buddhism and General Systems Theory: The Dharma of Natural Systems* (Albany: State University of New York Press, 1991). This book is based on Joanna Rogers Macy, "Interdependence: Mutual Causality in Early Buddhist Teachings and General Systems Theory" (Ph.D. diss., Syracuse University, 1978). See also Christopher S. Queen, "Systems Theory and Religious Studies, a Methodological Critique" (Ph.D. diss., Boston University, 1986).

41. Macy, *Mutual Causality*, 128*ff*.

42. Ibid., 219*ff*.

43. Joanna Rogers Macy, *Despair and Empowerment in the Nuclear Age* (Philadelphia: New Society Publishers, 1983); *Dharma and Development: Religion as Resource in the Sarvodaya Self-Help Movement* (West Hartford, Connecticut: Kumarian, 1983); *World as Lover, World as Self* (Berkeley: Parallax, 1991); and *Coming Back to Life: Practices to Reconnect Our Lives, Our World,* with Molly Young Brown (Gabriola Island, British Columbia: New Society, 1998).

44. Dhammapada 1:4–5; cited by Winston King, "Judeo-Christian and Buddhist Justice," 74.

45. Nhat Hanh, *Being Peace,* 45.

46. Robert N. Bellah, *Beyond Belief: Religion in a Post-Traditional World* (Berkeley: University of California Press, 1970), 3–17.

47. See Queen, *Engaged Buddhism in the West,* 66.

22 The Encounter of Buddhism and Psychology

Franz Aubrey Metcalf

INTRODUCTION

The field of Buddhism and psychology, by its very name, is irredeemably divided. For its first generation, it was a field of battle if it was a field at all. It has since become a field of study, a dialogue evolving in words and, importantly, in practices. As with any sincere dialogue between historically disparate traditions, the discussion involving Buddhism and psychology contains deep divisions, yet the mainstream of this dialogue has been founded on powerful shared assumptions. Both traditions assume that they respond to similar human needs. They assume that they uncover and reshape dynamics inherent in the human mind. Further, they assume that they undermine and possibly eliminate defenses the ego or self creates for its survival. In all this, they share a therapeutic self-image. Both traditions assume that the person or mind develops through life, and is continually being created by experience and by its own reflexive thought. Both assume that the mind is inherently self-corrective when provided with insights into its dysfunctional dynamics. They assume that their practices are able to provide such insights, and an ongoing path on which to integrate them. What is perhaps most remarkable, though, and serves as the impetus for the respectful dialogue between these traditions, is the assumption of each that the *other* follows a similar path and that if it does not provide the same insights it at least provides complementary ones. Such mutual respect provides the ground in which the field of *Buddhism and psychology* has taken root.

One might phrase Buddhist goals many ways, but it is fair to say that Buddhists work to gain insight into the true nature of the person, attaining freedom from illusory ideas of the self that keep us unhappy by chaining us to attachments. Psychologists work to gain insight into the true nature of persons, attaining freedom from illusory ideas of our selves that keep us unhappy by chaining us to earlier attachments. The difference in the connotations of *attachments*, as used in the two traditions, foreshadows the relationship between them. In psychology, attachment is a valuable achievement of the infant and caregiver, and only becomes a hindrance when the attachment is insecure or rigid. In Buddhism, *any* attachment is a hindrance on the path. Psychology has generally expanded its goals in the decades since Sigmund Freud claimed that it was merely trying to turn neurotic suffering into normal human unhappiness. Still, psychology seems to pursue a freedom less expansive than that of Buddhism, which ideally envisions a complete freedom from unhappiness. Nevertheless, despite the historical separation that prevents their goals from being identical, the vocabularies of these two approaches to life show an astounding overlap. Dialogue is almost unavoidable, and unsurprisingly each tradition has assumed that the other has something to offer to it.

These assumptions have begun to reshape both Buddhism and psychology to mirror each other. This is a point I feel compelled to repeat: *assumptions* of those working in the intersection of Buddhism and psychology have, over time, become *fact* as they have influenced the two fields. They have begun to change the courses of both paths. Naturally such change is occurring predominantly in the West, where Buddhism is encountering a psychologized and medicalized culture. Nevertheless, this Western reshaping is acquiring added importance, because it has begun to feed back into Buddhism in Asia, thus providing a growing edge of Buddhism for the entire world.

This reshaping expresses the way Buddhism is being absorbed into Western cultures, generally. Buddhism may be getting psychologized, but psychologists (among others) are also becoming Buddhists. To use a Buddhist metaphor, these two great vehicles are exchanging cargo as well as passengers. This makes examination of this phenomenon integral to an understanding of the development of Buddhism in the West.[1]

Chapters in comprehensive volumes such as this one strive for impartiality (and sometimes give its appearance), but inevitably they present the views of their authors. This chapter seeks to outline the dialogue and practices that constitute Buddhism and psychology. Given the fluidity and variety of this dialogue and these practices, this chapter might justifiably take one of various forms and emphasize several of various subfields, but it cannot do everything. It begins with the history of the dialogue, paying greater attention to the psychological side, which may be less familiar to most readers of this volume. It then looks at the contemporary practices of both Buddhism and psychology, attempting to convey how each side is influencing the other. It concludes with observations on how this contemporary practice calls scholars to play a vital role as Buddhism develops in the West.

HISTORY OF THE DIALOGUE

Psychology began contributing to the dialogue with Buddhism much earlier than Buddhism did, at least in the West. One might argue convincingly that Buddhism *itself* is a psychology and has been in dialogue with other Asian psychological systems for over two thousand years. Unless otherwise stated, when I use the term *psychology* in this chapter it refers to that complex of theories and practices constituting Western psychology over the last century. This chapter sets aside the encounter of Buddhism and traditional psychologies in Asia, and focuses on the West.

To understand the involvement of psychology with Buddhism, we must put psychology in its social context. All of the various forms of modern psychology grew up in response to the waning of the sense of *Gemeinschaft* and the breaking up of the religious identity of the modern person. This includes Freudian psychoanalysis along with its rebellious children—Jungian analytical psychology, Adlerian social psychology, humanistic psychology, existential psychology, object relations psychology, and attachment theory. It even involves, to some extent, cognitive science, neurology, and behaviorism. I cannot here explore the origins of psychology (and other human sciences) as replacements for religion. I refer the reader to the work of Peter Homans,[2] and mention only that we understand psychology best when we see it both as a science and as a secularized technology for achieving a kind of salvation. When we view psychology in the light of its historical rise, we see that despite its early institutional place in opposition to religion, the religious impulse remains close to its heart. It was only a matter of time before the commonalities of psychology and Buddhism captured the attention of practitioners of both.[3]

This attention first began to be paid in the psychoanalytic camp, which demands that therapists and patients look inside and acknowledge the presence of an inner life that the conscious mind does not always appreciate. Freud's research and observation suggested to him that religion functions as a species of wish-fulfilling illusion, able to support cultural systems that force persons to renounce acting on some of their desires. Freud concentrated his attention on Christianity and Judaism; his writing on Buddhism is almost nonexistent. Nevertheless, we can gain an idea of Freud's view of Buddhism in general and meditation in particular from a paper by Franz Alexander, one of his students. Called "Buddhistic Training as an Artificial

Catatonia," it was first delivered in 1922.[4] The title itself reveals a great deal. Classical psychoanalysis sees Buddhism as a renunciative religion, ultimately leading to withdrawal of all desire from the world. In psychoanalytic terms, Buddhism becomes the ultimate defense mechanism and form of regression. Psychoanalysis, on the contrary, views itself as liberating desire from archaic and unhealthy constraints and defenses and devoting this energy to involvement in the world. Seen from Alexander's perspective, Buddhism and psychology share some vital techniques but can have little dialogue, as their aims are so greatly divergent. This view of Buddhism was the consensus until soon after World War II, but remains only among traditional psychoanalysts who have thus retired from the dialogue.[5]

Early on, a contrary view of religion in general, and of Buddhism in particular, came to the fore, promoted by Freud's great acolyte, and later *bête noire*, Carl Jung. Jung's views on Buddhism reflected his tendency to subsume religion and its practices under the banner of individuation. *Individuation* is Jung's name for the process by which the person develops first into relative independence, but later into something less autonomous and more merged into the common heritage of humanity, what Jung called the *collective unconscious*. As this process matures in the latter half of life, the *self* deepens, becoming closer to the *Self*, the whole of human psychic possibility. Jung was open, and his followers have remained open, to religious experience as an entrance to the collective unconscious, a part of the journey toward Self. Jung himself wrote copiously on Asian religions, including Buddhism, and though he cautioned against a too-eager diving into symbols and practices radically different from Western ones, his work became instrumental in the popularization of Yoga, Taoism, and Buddhism in the West.[6]

Since the time of Freud and Jung, three generations of thinkers have profoundly complicated the landscape of Western psychology. The inherently individual focus of Jungian thought has given rise to no organized school, and the comparative rigidity of the Freudian canon has given way to a genuinely bewildering array of theories and therapies. What can be said of this blooming, buzzing confusion with regard to Buddhism is that each school in its own way has embraced Buddhism as a kind of kindred system.

One watershed moment in the rapprochement between Buddhism and psychoanalysis came with the publication of *Zen Buddhism and Psychoanalysis*, by Erich Fromm, D. T. Suzuki, and Richard De Martino.[7] In this work, Fromm, the psychologist, brings both ego psychology and existential psychology into his perspective on Buddhism. He echoes Freud in asserting that the task of psychoanalysis is to make the unconscious fully conscious. He goes beyond Freud in asserting that this means overcoming the division of conscious and unconscious entirely, healing the alienation of the ego from the world. Fromm sees this healing in Zen practice. He evolved this view in dialogue with D. T. Suzuki, and Suzuki's Buddhist influence is felt throughout Fromm's contribution to the book. One can even read Fromm as looking to the prior tradition of Buddhism for validation for psychoanalysis. Fromm sees Zen as contributing a clarifying context for carrying forward psychotherapy, and psychoanalysis as a helpful adjunct for keeping Zen practitioners from delusions of enlightenment. This balanced perspective still carries weight, especially in more Freudian lineages.[8]

The contributions of the Buddhist, Suzuki, make *Zen Buddhism and Psychoanalysis* also an early and still prominent attempt by Buddhism to dialogue with psychology. Suzuki feels that psychology does not and cannot go as far as Zen in carrying forward human development. But Suzuki is free to praise Zen so highly precisely because the Zen he describes is freed from the constraints of actual practice. He idealizes Zen in much the same way that Jung idealizes the process of individuation. From this rarified place, Suzuki's ahistorical Zen can critique all historically situated attempts at insight or awakening (even those of the Zen schools themselves). Though his view of Zen in general has recently come in for sharp critique, Suzuki's presentation of Zen as carrying forward the best threads of the developmental project of Western psychology is, like Fromm's, very much alive today.[9]

More recently, the 14th Dalai Lama, Tenzin Gyatso, has become deeply involved in dialogue with leaders in several Western approaches to the self and consciousness. A review of his voluminous publications reveals an ongoing absorption with questions of the mind and a sophisticated appreciation of Western as well as Buddhist systems of answering these questions. At this writing, he had at least five books in print resulting from conversations and conferences with mental health professionals, neurologists, and cognitive scientists. Rather than focusing on psychodynamics, the Dalai Lama has usually worked with psychologists in the harder-science field of neurology and the more philosophical field of cognitive psychology. These fields overlap strongly with the emphases of his own Gelugpa training in mind, and have moved his understanding and presentation of his own tradition in a psychological direction. To take just one recent example, his *Transforming the Mind: Teachings on Generating Compassion* takes a traditional text and puts it into dialogue with psychologized Western ideas.[10]

If it does not explicitly combine Buddhism and psychology, it surely manifests an encounter between the two. Since the Dalai Lama's message and person will continue to be revered by millions of Buddhists in Asia, here is one example of where American-led Buddhist dialogue with psychology is having an impact on the future of Buddhism around the world.

Despite the importance of publications such as Suzuki's and the Dalai Lama's, most of the Buddhist contributions to the dialogue with psychology have come not in theoretically oriented books but in the actual practice of Buddhism on the ground. Some Buddhist leaders have published books or articles (for example, in *Tricycle: The Buddhist Quarterly* and *The Eastern Buddhist*) that explicitly respond to psychological views, but these have not been the focus of the Buddhist side of the dialogue. Rather, Buddhist leaders in the West have found themselves reorienting their modes of practice in reaction to the ideas and needs of Western Buddhists. This has meant developing more psychologically centered forms of Buddhism and nowhere has this been more pronounced than in the privatized and psychologized religious milieu of America.

THE AMERICANIZATION AND PSYCHOLOGIZATION OF BUDDHISM

As long ago as 1966, Philip Rieff identified the triumph of the therapeutic as America's primary social orientation.[11] Ten years later, Robert Wuthnow's work first identified the individualistic, mystical, and social science–oriented trends in American religion.[12] The most recent generation has accentuated these trends, as Philip Hammond and Wade Clark Roof have illuminated and as recent data supports.[13] Convert Buddhism has taken root in America exactly because it is so well suited to thrive in the laicized and psychologized environment of mainstream American culture.[14] Immigrant Buddhism, in contrast, thrives in the hybrid cultural environment of recent immigrants and has not engaged much in dialogue with psychology. For this reason, most of the discussion below focuses on convert Buddhism.

Buddhism, with its focus on inner experience, was arguably already an "American" religion when it arrived in the nineteenth century. But it was only after World War II that American society and Buddhism began to actually influence each other. Since then, the process of assimilation has emphatically altered the character of American Buddhism. Here I will explore how the psychological dimension of American Buddhism became so important in this assimilation.

With the explosion of interest in Asian religions in the 1960s, a generation of educated and psychologically minded meditators grew up. Prior to the 1960s, the dialogue between Buddhism and psychology was championed by figures in one tradition or the other. With the maturing of the Baby Boomers, the dialogue has been overwhelmingly propelled by people who personally combine both traditions. These people have become not only leading psychologists but also leading Dharma teachers, sometimes at the same time. The impact of this development cannot be overstated; it is the central reality described in this chapter and it is changing the face of Buddhism in America.

We see the phenomenon of the psychologist-as-Dharma-teacher across the board in the spectrum of convert American Buddhism,[15] perhaps most among Americans practicing *vipassanā* (insight meditation) and least in Sōka Gakkai. American practice of insight meditation is dominated by the emphases and values of the Insight Meditation Society (IMS), in Massachusetts, and of the host of other centers growing from that source, including Spirit Rock Meditation Center, in California. The founders and leading teachers of this approach have spread a form of fundamentally psychological Buddhism across America and overseas. Gil Fronsdal's chapter details this form of Buddhism—a form not even called *Buddhism* by many of its practitioners. Further evidence of the remarkably psychologized character of the Insight Meditation movement may be found in that chapter; here, simply consider the astounding concentration of practicing psychologists among teachers in these institutions. Recently at Spirit Rock, nine of the fourteen teachers were trained psychotherapists.[16]

Not only are the numbers of therapists high, but therapeutic assumptions have profoundly shaped the practice and self-definition of this tradition. For example, the Spirit Rock home page does not mention Buddhism,[17] instead speaking of insight into the practitioner's moment-to-moment experience and of lifestyles that reflect these insights. This practice is explicitly nonsectarian, "although the ethics and traditions of Buddhist psychology are included for guidance."[18] Of course this bears more than a passing resemblance to the traditional practice of meditationally oriented Buddhist monks, but at Spirit Rock there is no Buddhist context of a hundred or a thousand nonmeditators for every meditator. This spiritual community (it does not officially call itself a Sangha) operates on some basic assumptions: that each person in it has come to the center by his or her own free choice and to work on his or her own inner issues, and that each person has the psychological capacity and personal autonomy to do this. There is little feeling that this work is the province of the few. The psychological view, that every person can and should gain insight into his or her personal dynamics, has become a consensus in America. In Insight Meditation practice we see this psychological assumption being transferred onto Buddhism, the assumption here becoming that every person can and should gain insight into his or her inner states and mental processes and so gain the freedom the Buddha taught. Just as psychology invites every person into the sacred space of the consulting room, so practitioners of Insight Meditation invite every being into the sacred space of the meditation room.[19] Leaders of the Insight Meditation movement realize that this invitation stands in profound contrast to the traditional directives of Theravāda Buddhism. For this reason, they are careful not to call their centers *Theravāda centers*. Their practices call into question the very dichotomy between Buddhism and psychology. Which are they practicing? But their distinction from Theravāda creates a different split, a split from the elder tradition of Buddhism,[20] and undermines the ability of each to learn from the other. Here the siphoning-off of psychologically minded practitioners may have grave consequences for the future of the root tradition in America.

The Zen analogy to the IMS movement exists in the centers of Toni Packer and Joko Beck Sensei. Packer's center, a breakaway from Philip Kapleau Rōshi's Rinzai lineage, has ceased to refer to itself as Zen, or even Buddhist at all. As in the IMS tradition, much has fallen away in the effort to focus on inner experience on its own terms. Beck Sensei's center, while remaining in Taizan Maezumi Rōshi's dual Sōtō-Rinzai lineage, emphasizes the everyday intimacy of Zen practice, as Beck Sensei has done with great fluidity in her writings. Some American Zen centers also have psychotherapists as their Dharma teachers; this is true in the Korean lineage of Seung Sahn, as well as in several prominent Japanese lineages. In my own research, I have explored with American Zen teachers their efforts at integrating psychodynamic insights into their Dharma teaching. Discussing psychotherapeutic technique, one Dharma holder who is also a psychotherapist told me: "a person who trains with me is going to get a lot of training in that. It's not addressed in the Eastern system. The Western system has mastery in this."[21]

Importantly, the need for such training in transference issues and other dynamics of the therapeutic relationship has come to the fore in the wake of abuses of power by prominent American Zen teachers (and other teachers; see Sandra Bell's chapter in this volume). Several Zen centers turned to psychology to repair the damage caused by psychological naïveté on the part of both teachers and students. They did not bring in *Vinaya* specialists; they brought in abuse counselors and created group sessions organized on therapeutic, not Buddhist, models. At the Zen Center of Los Angeles, such healing circles have become integral to ongoing Dharma practice. These innovations, inspired directly by psychological work, have fundamentally changed the character of these Zen centers and influenced practice around the country.

The varied traditions of Vajrayāna in America display several responses to psychology and psychological thinking. The most traditionalist simply emphasize the psychological acuity of their core texts. They do in practice what some of the Dalai Lama's writings have done in print. But less traditional teachers have gone further. The most celebrated Tibetan teacher in America, Chögyam Trungpa Rinpoche, well educated in Western philosophy and psychology, developed several differing ways of integrating psychology into his teaching. Trungpa and his successors have evolved Shambhala Training to be intentionally nondenominational, even secular. The five introductory levels of the training have a pattern strikingly similar to the development of long-term psychotherapy. Lama Surya Das provides a more recent example of a prominent teacher working to refocus an already psychologically acute Tibetan teaching (in this case, Dzogchen) on its meditative practices. We do well also to see Robert Thurman's recent high-profile call for a new American "cool revolution" in this same light. Thurman's revolution may be Tibetan-inspired, but his advocacy of "inner modernity" is a legacy of Freud as well as Tsongkhapa.[22]

Such innovations reveal how a psychologized American religious public yearns for a spiritual practice responsive to its view of the emotional, developmental, and engaged character of spiritual life. In Zen and Vajrayāna Buddhism, the innovations have not stripped away so many traditions as in *vipassanā* practice; depending on the lineages, they retain a good deal of *sūtra* study, chanting, division of lay and ordained Sanghas, and so on. Nevertheless, like all forms of religion in the American religious marketplace, each school of Buddhism must increasingly orient itself to the needs of individualized lay practitioners.

THE BUDDHICIZATION OF PSYCHOLOGY

The previous section addressed the Americanization of Buddhism, but did not assess the parallel process of the Buddhicization of America. Buddhist assimilation in America includes both of these processes. Other chapters describe other arenas of this assimilation; this chapter will detail just one — the influence of Buddhism on psychological thinking.

A first observation: in contemporary Western psychology, few still cleave to a vision of the self as heroically independent. No contemporary and vital school argues for anything but a provisional and relational self, ultimately composed of its relations with others. One might argue that Western models of an imperial self are going out with Western models of the imperial state.[23] The intellectual debate on the general character of the self is over. Object relations models have triumphed, though no single one has gained widespread acceptance in the way that Freud's model did for a generation.[24] Even Jungian psychologists, carrying the burden of Carl Jung's romantic vision of the self, or Self, have accepted a more relational definition of that self than Jung elaborated. They have become active in the field of Buddhism and psychology, but the most active participants have been object relations psychologists. Here the harmonies between Buddhist relational selves and psychological relational selves ring out most clearly. Here the field is most active and provocative. Here the field is publishing the most and doing the most to influence the theory and practice of psychotherapy.

Scholar and therapist Jack Engler's watershed formulation of the sequence of psychological and spiritual work makes a fit starting place for an examination of the Buddhist influence on psychology. Engler memorably wrote that "you have to be somebody before you can be nobody."[25] Behind this dictum lies the most pervasive model of human development in the conversation on and between Buddhism and psychology.

This model of development accepts as healthy the unitive consciousness of the coherent self, but it goes on to assert—contra classical psychodynamic theories—that this self is not the end of the developmental process. Engler suggests that Buddhist meditation begins to dispel the *illusion of compactness* or the enduring subject.[26] It dispels this illusion through a kind of regression, but this regression "is not a re-living or re-experiencing of past stages of internalized object relations. It is *a controlled retracing of the stages in the representational process itself as this occurs in each present moment.*"[27] Here Engler is drawing on the earlier work of Arthur Deikman, on what Deikman called *deautomatization and the mystic experience.*[28] Deikman described meditation as a way of deconstructing the complex perceptions of our conscious lives into more basic apperceptions or sense data. Twenty years later, Engler was elaborating this position when he wrote that the meditative goal is to *"reverse—retraverse—the key stages in the representational process,* which yields individual self and object representations only as the end-products of a very long and complex reworking of stimulus information."[29] Reversing this process brings the meditator back to a reality existing both before and after the meditator's sense of self. Engler and many others find this reality isomorphic with Buddhist *anatta* (no-self; skt. *anātman*).

From this perspective, Buddhist practice takes human development farther than Western psychotherapies can on their own. This perspective sees both Buddhism and Western psychological development as noble models of human development, but perceives that they focus on different stages of that process. It sees Western psychology as focusing on earlier stages, where the self emerges from an undifferentiated state (though already containing the structures of separateness) and develops into a relational entity, characterized by a sense of independence from and yet relation with other selves. This perspective sees healthy, even optimal, functioning on this level as the limit of human development for Western psychology. In contrast, it sees Buddhist practice as *assuming* a healthy self, then embarking on a journey with the goal of breaking down the processes that have resulted in the experience of coherence and separateness. As these processes reverse, the self is found to be ultimately interdependent, if it exists at all. This perspective then can imagine the goal of Buddhist *bhāvanā* (cultivation, including meditation) as a freedom from the conditioned and negative state of attachment to self and even from the self's positive personal attachments and desires. In all, this provides a Buddhist spectrum model of human development, integrating but relativizing Western models. This model has given rise to a whole new literature of theory and therapy, including the *Journal of Transpersonal Psychology* and several books that have risen to bestseller status.[30]

Importantly, some contributors to the literature feel that the projects of creating and destroying the self go on simultaneously, not sequentially. Jeffrey Rubin is prominent among those who argue for simultaneous self-integration and self-deconstruction, reminding us that the emptying of self and its representations and relationships can lead to an *impoverishment of self* rather than a *liberation from* it.[31] Joseph Bobrow provides a psychological take on the Mahāyāna view of Buddhist goals when he argues that "it *takes* a self to fully *embody* our essential nature." For Bobrow, *no-self* is ironically only fully manifested in the experience of a particular self.[32]

Most influential may be the contributions of Mark Epstein and James Austin. Epstein builds on the work of object-relations pioneer D. W. Winnicott. He moves object relations forward by providing a Buddhist context for some of Winnicott's central values. For Epstein, we can let ourselves go to pieces, as Winnicott suggests, precisely because we are in pieces already, as Buddhist psychology has it. Further, Buddhist experience has given

Epstein the confidence to see that this practice can provide an ongoing holding environment in which persons can balance self-creation and self-disintegration.[33] Such ideas continue the Buddhist influence on dynamic psychology first seen in the work of Erich Fromm and Karen Horney.[34]

Buddhism, especially meditation, has also had an influence on the very different sphere of neurology and experimental psychology, as Austin shows. Studies of meditators have particularly assisted research on brain activity and altered states of consciousness. Some early efforts here were suspect, but recent studies have been increasingly integrated with studies on everyday waking consciousness. Here Charles Tart has done a tremendous amount of work, shaped by his own appreciation of Buddhism. Neurologist James Austin exhaustively reviews this and other literature in his magisterial *Zen and the Brain*. He details Buddhism's influence on his own understanding of developing brain function and suggests where Buddhism can contribute to the growing field of brain research. His most ambitious testable hypothesis is that beneficial shrinkage and fragmentation will be found in specific areas of very advanced meditators' brains.[35] It remains to be seen how Austin's program will foster future research.

The remarkable growth of spiritually oriented psychotherapy in America also speaks for the influence of Buddhism on psychology. This trend is difficult to quantify, but it is supported by the existence of institutions such as the Pacifica Graduate Institute and the Cambridge Institute of Meditation and Psychotherapy, as well as by the remarkable number of recent books written by Buddhist therapists.[36] (This is quite apart from the interactions between psychology and Buddhism in Asia. Morita therapy, a hybrid Japanese-Buddhist/psychological therapy, has even been imported to the West.[37]) Jon Kabat-Zinn's popular work on stress and pain has also arisen from a background in Buddhist practice. In a way, it makes a perfect example of how Buddhism and psychology have blended in America: Kabat-Zinn at times intentionally removes meditation from its Buddhist context and combines it with psychological ideas also divorced from their original academic roots. In doing this, his work has changed the lives of possibly millions of Americans.[38]

SCHOLARS, RESPONSIBILITIES, AND THE PSYCHOLOGIZATION OF BUDDHISM

Charles Prebish has recently documented that the number of Buddhist academics, both in and out of the meditation closet, is rising. He speculates that such scholar-practitioners in the West might fill the role occupied by *gantha-dhura* scholar-monks in the East.[39] Following on the work of Prebish, we might parallel the position of scholar-practitioners to that of psychologist-practitioners. Scholar-practitioners have distorted Buddhism, as Donald Lopez, Jr., has shown in *Curators of the Buddha*.[40] What are the analogous distortions of psychologist-practitioners? This chapter only hints at answers, but I hope conveys the importance of further work in the field.

I have asserted that Western culture is powerfully appropriating Buddhism as psychology. But psychology does not exhaust the richness of the traditions of Buddhism. Many in the West see Buddhism as a form of religious psychotherapy, and this perception is not being corrected by Buddhist psychologists or Buddhist psychology. To take one example, let me turn back to the sincere and valuable work of Epstein. He writes of *Buddhism* and *meditation* without ever giving the reader a sense of what school of Buddhism his meditation comes from, and he gives the impression that meditation is the central fact and focus of Buddhism. In fact, he practices *vipassanā*, a meditative form developed by Theravāda monks. Without the tradition of monks as a pure field for *dāna* (ritual gifting) from the laity, that Theravāda tradition cannot continue. I am not sure Epstein ever even mentions Theravāda monks in his works, yet one must ask, can *vipassanā* survive in America without the traditional institutions that created it— institutions that are threatened now and that convert Buddhists and Buddhist psychologists, such as Epstein, tend to undermine?[41] Conversely, can traditional Theravāda Buddhism itself survive in America without the vital contributions of convert Buddhists and lucid psychologists like Epstein? Can the encounter between psychology and Buddhism avoid diminishing Buddhism in the West?

With or without the contributions of scholars, the answer to these questions may be *no*. But the partial or distorted views of psychologist-practitioners are a clear call for the academy to do its duty and inform the larger public. Such duties are the raison d'être of scholars of religion, and in this case can aid not only society's understanding of Buddhism but Buddhists' understanding of their own traditions. The academy's duty is to see that what passes for Buddhism in the West acknowledges that Buddhism— even each school of Buddhism—goes beyond the practices of any one therapist or Dharma center or teacher. To preserve an authentic Buddhism, perhaps greater than the sum of its parts, individual teachers and promoters must acknowledge their inevitable partialness and the greater tradition's diverse fullness. With this tolerance and, we may hope, a full embracing of the rich diversity of Buddhist traditions along with the gifts that may come from psychology, the separate strands will be free to weave themselves wisely into Buddhism's larger fabric.

NOTES

1. Despite this, only one of the recent major books surveying the field of Buddhism in the West has covered this topic, and that coverage was highly colored and inadequate. I feel a strong sense of responsibility in addressing this need here and wish to thank Nina Ruscio and Aubrey W. Metcalf, M.D., for their close readings of previous drafts of this chapter.

2. Peter Homans, *The Ability to Mourn: Disillusionment and the Social Origins of Psychoanalysis* (Chicago: University of Chicago Press, 1989).

3. We should not be surprised to note that most Western enthusiasts for Buddhism at this same period appropriated just those aspects of it suited to their demythologized, mind-science worldview. Thus the first assimilation of Buddhism in the West, especially in the English-speaking world, was as a form of therapy. In this way, Western Buddhism and modern psychology have been historically analogous from the very first.

4. Franz Alexander, "Buddhistic Training as an Artificial Catatonia: The Biological Meaning of Psychic Occurrences," *Psychoanalytic Review* 18, no. 2 (1931), 129–45.

5. The only early published exception to this consensus in the psychoanalytic camp is Joe Thompson's surprisingly nuanced and neglected article, "Psychology in Primitive Buddhism," *Psychoanalytic Review* 11, no. 1 (1924), 38–47. But this had to be published under the oriental(ist) pseudonym Joe Tom Sun.

6. I am aware, as Jung surely was, that there is a certain irony here. This proceeds directly from Jung's ambivalence about who could benefit from working with culturally foreign symbols. For Jung, most couldn't, but he could. Most of Jung's readers seem to have also given themselves the benefit of the doubt. See the convenient collection, Carl Jung, *Psychology and the East* (Princeton: Princeton University Press, 1978).

7. Erich Fromm, D.T. Suzuki, and Richard De Martino, *Zen Buddhism and Psychoanalysis* (New York: Harper and Brothers, 1960).

8. Lineage, traced through teachers to the source of wisdom (especially Buddha or Freud or Jung), is central to the identity of many teachers in both traditions. This parallel itself would be the foundation for a fascinating study.

9. In some respects, Suzuki's influence is healthy, because it has fostered dialogue. In others, it is unfortunately distorting and misleading, because Suzuki's romanticized picture of Zen is still frequently used as the primary or only source on Zen by authors who then parallel it to the nitty-gritty of psychotherapeutic practice. Such parallels can never be reliable. For more on Suzuki and his historical context, see Bernard Faure, *Chan Insight and Oversights: An Epistemological Critique of the Chan Tradition* (Princeton: Princeton University Press, 1993); James W. Heisig and John C. Maraldo (eds.), *Rude Awakenings: Zen, the Kyoto School, and the Question of Nationalism* (Honolulu: University of Hawaii Press, 1995); and Martin J. Verhoeven, "Americanizing the Buddha: Paul Carus and the Transformation of Asian Thought," in *The Faces of Buddhism in America*, edited by Charles S. Prebish and Kenneth K. Tanaka (Berkeley: University of California Press, 1998), 207–27.

10. Dalai Lama (= Tenzin Gyatso), *Transforming the Mind: Teachings on Generating Compassion* (London: Thorsons, 2000).

11. Philip Rieff, *The Triumph of the Therapeutic: Uses of Faith after Freud* (New York: Harper and Row, 1966).

12. Robert Wuthnow, *The Consciousness Reformation* (Berkeley: University of California Press, 1976).

13. Wade Clark Roof, *A Generation of Seekers: The Spiritual Journeys of the Baby Boom Generation* (San Francisco: HarperCollins, 1993), and *The Spiritual Marketplace: Baby Boomers and the Remaking of American Religion* (Princeton: Princeton University Press, 1999); and Phillip E. Hammond, *Religion and Personal Autonomy: The Third Disestablishment in America* (Columbia: University of South Carolina Press, 1992), and *With Liberty for All: Freedom of Religion in the United States* (Louisville, Kentucky: Westminster John Knox Press, 1998). Recent statistical evidence supports the contentions of Roof and Hammond; see George Gallup, George Gallup, Jr., and D. Michael Lindsay, *Surveying the Religious Landscape: Trends in U.S. Beliefs* (Harrisburg, Pennsylvania: Morehouse, 2000).

14. The debate on the words we shall use to divide American Buddhism into its various camps is by no means ended. I choose here to employ the distinction between *immigrant* and *convert* Buddhism, originally suggested by Paul Numrich, as being reasonably accurate, neutral, and intuitively comprehensible without explanation.

15. For various cultural reasons, this phenomenon has not crossed over to immigrant Buddhism. Such a transition will only occur when either Buddhism or an immigrant community is thoroughly psychologized. Neither development is likely to occur in less than several generations, though the beginnings of it may be seen in the Buddhist Churches of America.

16. Gil Fronsdal, "Insight Meditation in the United States: Life, Liberty, and the Pursuit of Happiness," in Prebish and Tanaka, *The Faces of Buddhism in America*, 170.

17. See http://www.spiritrock.org [21 Sept. 2000].

18. See http://www.spiritrock.org/html/insight.html [21 Sept. 2000].

19. I mean this figuratively, of course, but in fact the parallel is even more detailed. In both practices, there is a small group of persons not ready to enter the charmed circle. Deeply disturbed persons need pharmacological and other medical interventions before they can tolerate the insight of psychotherapy. Seriously neurotic or borderline persons need psychotherapeutic work before they can tolerate the insight of meditation. Thus the IMS views the process of insight as hierarchical, a view I discuss theoretically below.

20. Despite the divisions of Buddhism in America, we can see this as a potential *sanghabheda*, a schism of the Sangha, something the Pāli Canon considers a serious offense in the category of *sanghādisesa*, requiring communal meetings.

21. Franz Aubrey Metcalf, *Why Do Americans Practice Zen Buddhism?* (Ph.D. diss., University of Chicago, 1997), 258. Note that psychotherapists as well often fail to live up to their "mastery."

22. Robert A. F. Thurman, *Inner Revolution: Life, Liberty, and the Pursuit of Real Happiness* (New York: Riverhead, 1999).

23. Changes in political forms both reflect and influence the capacity of citizens for organizing their senses of self and self-awareness, a point first argued by Sigmund Freud in his early cultural works, such as *Totem and Taboo* and *Group Psychology and the Analysis of the Ego*.

24. I acknowledge that anachronists remain who cling to models of the heroic self, eternally striving for some kind of full and virile independence. Many of these are loyal to Freud's topographic model. They also tend to cling to drive theory, which there is good empirical evidence to discredit. Here I ignore them. What can

you say to people for whom neither the support of evidence nor theoretical elegance seem to matter?

25. Jack Engler, "Therapeutic Aims in Psychotherapy and Meditation: Developmental Stages in the Representation of Self," in *Transformations of Consciousness: Conventional and Contemplative Perspectives on Development,* edited by Ken Wilber, Jack Engler, and Daniel P. Brown (Boston: Shambhala/New Science Library, 1986), 24 and 49.

26. Ibid., 41.

27. Ibid., 48–9.

28. Arthur Deikman, "Deautomatization and the Mystic Experience," *Psychiatry* 29 (1966), 324–38.

29. Engler, "Therapeutic Aims," 43.

30. Epstein's books (see note 33) have proven especially popular. For other works, see note 36.

31. This is a major point in Rubin's *Psychotherapy and Buddhism: Toward an Integration* (New York: Plenum Press, 1996).

32. Joseph Bobrow, "The Fertile Mind," in *The Couch and the Tree: Dialogues between Psychoanalysis and Buddhism,* edited by Anthony Molino (San Francisco: North Point, 1998), 319.

33. See Mark Epstein, *Thoughts without a Thinker: Psychotherapy from a Buddhist Perspective* (New York: Basic, 1995) and *Going to Pieces Without Falling Apart: A Buddhist Perspective on Wholeness* (New York: Broadway, 1998), particularly chapters 1 and 2 in the latter. Epstein's upcoming book, *Going on Being: Buddhism and the Way of Change, A Positive Psychology for the West* (New York: Broadway, 2001), again carries a title taken from the work of Winnicott and promises to carry Epstein's and Winnicott's work further forward.

34. My criticism of all the popular work attempting to integrate Buddhist and psychotherapeutic development is that thinkers seldom address the difficult theoretical work of integrating development on an object-relational line and development along a spiritual line into any coherent teleological scheme. For example, it is one thing to claim that Buddhism carries object-relations development beyond the self; it is another thing altogether to show, from the baseline of object relations, *why this should be so.* The burden of proof is on those of us, including myself, who claim that meditative development continues object-relations development.

35. James Austin, *Zen and the Brain: Toward an Understanding of Meditation and Consciousness* (Cambridge: Massachusetts Institute of Technology Press, 1998), 657–9. This shrinkage ought also to be found in the brains of other exceptionally spiritually or psychologically advanced persons.

36. Among these are the works of Epstein and of Rubin, already mentioned. In addition, some notable recent contributions are Paul R. Fleischman, M.D., *Karma and Chaos: New and Collected Essays on Vipassanā Meditation* (Seattle: Vipassanā Research Publications, 1999), and Seymour Boorstein, *Clinical Studies in Transpersonal Psychology* (Albany: State University of New York Press, 1997), both written from a *vipassanā* perspective; John Welwood, *Toward a Psychology of Awakening: Buddhism, Psychotherapy, and the Path of Personal and Spiritual Transformation* (Boston: Shambhala, 2000), a nice compilation integrating *vipassanā* and Tibetan perspectives; the co-edited collection, *The Psychology of Awakening: Buddhism, Science, and Our Day-To-Day Lives* (York Beach, Maine: Samuel Weiser, 2000), edited by Gay Watson, Stephen Batchelor, and Guy Claxton; and perhaps most wide-ranging of all, Anthony Molino (ed.), *The Couch and the Tree: Dialogues between Psychoanalysis and Buddhism* (San Francisco: North Point, 1998), which also offers a good survey of the history of the field.

37. Morita is such an unusually balanced result of the mutual influence of psychology and Buddhism that I hesitate to label it as either. Shoma Morita based his therapy on disciplined attention to action and the exterior world, stemming from his own Zen experience. While Morita gave the therapy Zen values, he also corresponded with Freud and, as a doctor and professor, gave it a psychotherapeutic institutional setting. For more on Morita therapy, see David K. Reynolds, *Flowing Bridges, Quiet Water: Japanese Psychotherapies, Morita and Naikan* (Albany: State University of New York Press, 1989).

38. See Kabat-Zinn's *Full Catastrophe Living: Using the Wisdom of Your Body and Mind to Face Stress, Pain, and Illness* (New York: Delacorte, 1990) and *Wherever You Go, There You Are: Mindfulness in Everyday Life* (New York: Hyperion, 1994).

39. Charles S. Prebish, *Luminous Passage: The Practice and Study of Buddhism in America* (Berkeley: University of California Press, 1999), 197–200.

40. Donald Lopez, Jr., *Curators of the Buddha: The Study of Buddhism under Colonialism* (Chicago: University of Chicago Press, 1995).

41. Both Paul Numrich and Gil Fronsdal ask this question, and neither is sanguine in his answer. See Paul David Numrich, "Theravada Buddhism in America: Prospects for the *Sangha*," in Prebish and Tanaka, *The Faces of Buddhism in America*, 147–61; and Gil Fronsdal, "Insight Meditation in the United States: Life, Liberty, and the Pursuit of Happiness," in Prebish and Tanaka, *The Faces of Buddhism in America*, 163–80.

23 A "Commodius Vicus of Recirculation"

Buddhism, Art, and Modernity

Ian Harris

INTRODUCTORY REMARKS

It is notoriously difficult to trace influences in art without falling into the trap of simplistic and mechanistic theorizing. In art, as in all forms of creative activity, influences interact and unfold in an unpredictable and complex manner, often over considerable periods of time. In addition, how do we know when an artist is merely frolicking on the surface of the subject matter, and how can we distinguish work of this kind from that produced by someone deeply concerned with giving creative form to cherished ideals, symbols, or motifs? When we turn specifically to the work of modern Western artists for whom Buddhism has had special meaning, the problem is further compounded. What aspects of Buddhism has the artist found inspiring? Has the inspiration been philosophical or cultural, or has the artist been attracted to the tradition's emphasis on the cultivation of specific mental states? Of course, the engagement could be with Buddhist art itself. Whatever the initial impetus, an added difficulty will be that a completed work of art can manifest these influences either explicitly or implicitly.

Since such questions cannot be easily resolved in a short space, this survey of approximately one hundred and fifty years of art history is arranged in roughly chronological order. I propose three reasonably distinct phases in the reception of Asian Buddhist influence into Western art. The first, a sort of faddish fascination based on no real knowledge of Asian societies, has its locus in nineteenth-century France. Although exotic in character, it did lead to major and lasting changes, particularly in the fine arts. In the second phase, we find a more significant movement away from Western aesthetic norms, with some artists taking the first steps to understand Buddhism in its Asian contexts. The final phase begins in the late 1960s and continues to the present. It is characterized by a greater involvement of Westerners in almost all aspects of traditional Buddhist activity, and involves a more informed understanding of the function of the arts in such contexts.

A PERIOD OF FASCINATION

Although European familiarity with the arts and manufactures of Buddhist Asia extends back to at least the seventeenth century, as the work of Lach (1970–93) eloquently testifies, Théophile Gautier (1811–72) appears to have been the first true modern to appreciate the literary and artistic potential of these materials. Gautier's particular interest in Chinese Buddhist poetry was made possible by parallel developments in the academic study of East Asia, most elegantly expressed in the publication by Marquis d'Hervey-Saint-Denys of the *Poésies de l'époque des Thang* (1862). The freshness and naturalism of this poetry, combined with its freedom from classical encumberment, fueled Gautier's search for a new, intoxicating, and diversionary art which eschewed familiarity, monotony, and repetition. Gautier even employed a Chinese teacher for his young daughters, one of whom, Judith, later became a significant poet in her own right.[1] This exotic spirit spilled over into the interests of other members of Gautier's circle, which included Hugo, Flaubert, Mallarmé, and Baudelaire. Baudelaire's statement that "the beautiful is always bizarre" perhaps best expresses the outlook of the group. The concept was nicely reinforced by a perceived connection between China, opium, and other varieties of transgression.

The brothers Edmond and Jules de Goncourt (1822–96; 1830–70), also part of the Gautier circle, significantly extended the impact of oriental art influences. In the earlier part of the nineteenth century, Parisian art circles generally considered East Asian culture to be monolithic. This began to change around 1862, when a shop called the Porte Chinoise began dealing in art objects from Japan. The Goncourts, along with Degas, Zola, Baudelaire, Manet, Monet, and Whistler, were among its first customers. Unlike the earlier phase of interest in China, which primarily had an impact on the literary arts, the emerging interest in things Japanese also influenced interior design and painting. Edmond de Goncourt's influential two-volume description of the contents of his villa at Auteuil, *La maison d'un artiste au XIXe siècle* (1880), blazed the way in showing how to adapt Japanese artworks to the structure of a European dwelling. That this new approach to the decorative arts was both deeply fashionable and transgressive can be demonstrated by the fact that the poet Robert de Montesquiou-Fezenac, the model for the arch-decadent Des Esseintes in Huysmans' *À Rebours* (1884), is known to have created just such a sanctuary in his own apartment.

It is generally agreed that the Japanese influence on mid- to late-nineteenth-century French painting worked in two basic modes. In the first of these, *japonaiserie*, oriental items, such as fans or kimonos, are merely included as exotic decorative elements in an otherwise entirely Western painting. The second mode, *japonisme*, is more significant within art history, because it involves the application of Japanese pictorial techniques, particularly those derived from eighteenth-century Ukiyo-e prints. Impressionist painters like Manet (1832–83) and Whistler (1834–1903) were in the vanguard of the new movement, and Zola's essay, "Édouard Manet, l'homme et l'artiste" (1868), is probably the first Western work of art criticism to wrestle with the aesthetic and philosophical demands of Japanese art, particularly as they impinged on the cultural conditions of his time. We have already seen that for members of the earlier Gautier circle oriental motifs were employed for their novel, transgressive, and diversionary value. For Zola, Japanese art pointed in a new direction. Ukiyo-e prints were cheap, mass-produced, and increasingly available. In this sense, they were the epitome of modernity. Not only that, but in subject matter they focused on everyday or vulgar scenes, as opposed to topics hallowed by classical or biblical tradition. They used colors boldly and in any combination, and they eschewed symmetry. Traditional Western concerns with perspective and naturalism no longer seemed to teach anything useful about reality. The new emphasis on transiency, flatness, immediacy, and vividness—so consistent with a Buddhist philosophical outlook—appears then to have been unconsciously assimilated by many artists of the time. This assimilation could be said to have reached its highest pitch in Van Gogh's post-Impressionist, but definitely Ukiyo-e-inspired, *Bedroom at Arles* (1888). We know that Van Gogh had been carefully copying prints by Eisen Kesai and Hiroshige at around this time. Indeed, his painting *Père Tanguy* (1888), which places the central figure in front of a wall covered with Japanese prints, effectively combines the currents of *japonaiserie* and *japonisme*.

The zenith of *japonisme* coincided with the period immediately following the first appearance of Japanese exhibits at the Paris Exposition Universelle of 1867, but by the 1890s the craze was beginning to subside. The European art market was being flooded by Japanese art objects, some of which were decidedly inferior to those that had appeared at the start. In consequence, these objects began to lose their charm in the eyes of the aesthetic elite; the fad was coming to a natural close.

However, some artists of the next generation were keen to become more engaged with the philosophical and religious underpinnings of art from

Buddhist Asia. I am thinking particularly of Odilon Redon (1840–1916) and Paul Gauguin (1848–1903).

In the early 1890s, Redon had been a member of an occult avant-garde circle that included Huysmans, Mallarmé, and Debussy. Seized by religious uncertainty since 1882, when he read Flaubert's *The Temptation of Saint Anthony*, Redon dabbled in Theosophy. But in the early 1900s, he began to read more systematically about Buddhism and Indian philosophy. He appears to have been the first modern artist to depict the Buddha in a manner close to traditional iconographic norms. Two early lithographs (1895) depict the Buddha as a "crazed magus." However, between 1900 and 1906 Redon produced seven paintings that have a recognizable Buddha as the central figure.[2] For instance, *Standing Buddha* (c. 1904, Berger no. 370) is clearly modeled on a Chinese original in which the Buddha wears a robe of multicolored cloth pieces. The centrality of such works to Redon's *oeuvre* is best illustrated by *Buddha's Death* (c. 1905, Berger no. 367), a depiction of the *parinirvāṇa*, which was owned by Matisse (who also acknowledged some debt toward Buddhism in his later life).[3] The most indicative of Redon's "Buddhist" works is a pastel of around 1906 (Berger no. 352), variously titled *Sacred Heart* or *Buddha*. A preparatory sketch makes it clear that Redon meant this to be a figure of Christ. The iconography is quite clear on the point. However, the finished work is a definite fusion of Buddhist and Christian imagery—not surprising, given Redon's earlier involvement in occult and theosophical circles.

Gauguin's interest in Buddhist imagery stems from a visit to the Paris Exposition Universelle of 1889, where he bought photographs of the reliefs at Barabudur, the great Buddhist ceremonial complex in Java. Motivated by a sense of moral and cultural decay, he had originally thought of abandoning Europe for Java before practical difficulties led him to Tahiti instead. Nevertheless, several of his Tahitian works, in which the lessons of the Japanese print have been assimilated, also borrow Buddhist motifs. Indeed, *Where Do We Come From? What Are We? Where Are We Going?* (1897–98), one of his most famous works, seems to have been inspired by the spatial arrangement of figures in a narrative relief from Barabudur.[4] A wooden statuette called *Idol with Pearl* (1894), also made in Tahiti, is more explicit in its influences—a partially hidden and mysterious female figure overshadows a central figure in a niche clearly based on the Buddha in the earth-touching posture (*bhūmisparśamudrā*).

THE BEGINNINGS OF ENGAGEMENT

The artists discussed above were fascinated by the "otherness"—interpreted stylistically, morally, or aesthetically—of the arts and crafts of

Buddhist Asia, but very few felt the need to explore the cultures, and the religions, that animated them *in situ*. Redon and Gauguin can be regarded as transitional figures. Redon stands at the beginning of artistic engagement with oriental "religiosity," while Gauguin chose to physically remove himself from the European art environment.

Japanese art had first penetrated America at the Philadelphia Centennial Exhibition of 1876. Among those impressed was the Boston-based William Sturgis Bigelow, who subsequently moved to Japan. There he amassed a vast collection[5] and inspired Ernest Fenollosa (1853–1908), who arrived in 1878 to serve as a philosophy instructor at Tokyo Imperial University. With his collaborator, Kakuzo Okakura (1862–1913),[6] Fenollosa became a Buddhist[7] and rapidly threw himself into research on the country's artistic heritage. Their work, culminating in the rediscovery of a celebrated eighth-century gilded statue of Kannon at Horyuji in 1884, is of special significance since it persuaded the Japanese for the first time that Buddhist artworks were national assets. Paradoxically, the poor economic condition of Buddhism in the Meiji Period (1868–1912) proved an incentive for monasteries to part with masterpieces, which subsequently entered the international art market.

Fenollosa rejected the preoccupation with the rediscovery of ancient Buddhism that consumed many orientalists of the time. He was especially critical of the exoticism of theosophical and occultist approaches,[8] since he saw Buddhism, particularly in its Japanese forms, as a progressive and hugely relevant cultural force. For him, Buddhism had reached its zenith in China during the Tang and Sung Periods, when artists created living forms by "ordering the materials of their medium in a way harmonious with the root order of the natural world, an order mirrored not by unartistic realism but by artistic 'unrealism.'" This aesthetic persisted among the Japanese, who could still appreciate a picture upside down, for ". . . they admire beauty of line and colour in art, rather than . . . merely depicting nature."[9]

On returning to America, Fenollosa collaborated with Arthur Dow to institute a new and anti-academic form of art education based around linearity, spontaneity, and creativity, rather than on copying work of the past. Georgia O'Keeffe (1887–1986) was one of the more influential students to emerge from the training. Fenollosa had become an important figure in the American cultural and artistic firmament. In his lengthy didactic poem "East and West" (1892), he combined Buddhist, Hegelian, and Emersonian motifs to create the proposition that future culture would be a fusion of the feminine East and masculine West in which the "golden peace" of

Buddhism would mitigate the "sting of the gold" of commercialism. In the final section, the author prophesies the mystical merging of Christ and Buddha: "Into the silence of Nirvana's glory, where there is no more West and no more East."[10] For Fenollosa, the religion of this new age would be the religion of art—a notion that was to have important repercussions.

The influence of oriental and Buddhist elements on twentieth-century American art, particularly Abstract Expressionism, is too great to be ignored. The phenomenon extends to figures as diverse as Carl Andre, Robert Motherwell, and Jackson Pollock. We know this from their reading habits,[11] and from reports of friends and acquaintances, although it is not always easy to read the precise nature of their commitment to Buddhist ideas from the work itself. With Mark Tobey (1890–1976) and Isamu Noguchi (1904–88), we are on firmer ground.

Tobey converted to Bahá'í in 1918 and began a study of Chinese calligraphy five years later. Reflecting in 1946 on his first lesson, he wrote: "The tree is no more a solid in the earth, breaking into lesser solids bathed in chiaroscuro. There is pressure and release."[12] He taught painting at Dartington Hall, England, from 1931 to 1938, where he came into contact with Aldous Huxley, Rabindranath Tagore, and the potter Bernard Leach, with whom[13] he visited the Far East in 1934, deepening his knowledge of calligraphy and staying near Enryakuji, the head monastery of the Tendai sect, on Mount Hiei near Kyoto. Here he meditated on a freehand brush-drawing of a circle and studied elements of traditional landscape painting. Back in England, he developed the technique called *white writing* that ultimately made him famous. Drawing on the Bahá'í emphasis on the cooperation between East and West[14] on oriental calligraphy, and on Buddhism, Tobey's living line opened up " . . . solid form, giving tangibility to empty space . . . breathing life into static Western realism." He once wrote, perhaps thinking of a still-life painter like Chardin, "Why do Western artists only paint a fish after it is dead?"[15] Works like *Broadway* (1936), an evocation of the energy of New York, dissolved received notions of "perspective and illusionism in favor of multiple space and moving focus . . . an historical parallel to the gradual dissolution of barriers between egos, nations, and cultures [taught in Bahá'í]."[16] The long gap between Tobey's first interest in calligraphy and the appearance of this mature work indicates the complexity of the transformation. In fact, his style was not fully realized until the early 1940s, when his disillusionment with America was captured in *The Void Devouring the Gadget Era* (1942). Nevertheless, his debt to Buddhism is explicit. Tobey regarded his *Five Dancers* (1947) as "painted in the spirit of Zen."[17] Ten years later, he returned to Japanese monochrome ink drawings (*sumi-e*) with spontaneous flung ink, as shown in *Space Ritual No. 1* (1957) and the series *Sumi I–IX* (1957), works that show some affiliations to Jackson Pollock. This was followed by a period of intense study of Zen, yielding abstract works that vigorously re-engage with fundamental Buddhist philosophy, such as *Void II* (1960).

Morris Graves (b. 1910) is the American painter most obviously influenced by Tobey. Although not entirely typical, *Hand of the Buddha, Sublime Gesture*, a disembodied hand in an indeterminate mudra, is one of Graves's most explicitly Buddhist works. For Graves, true art represented a "move away from exhibitionism called self-expression, towards the Eastern art's basis of consideration of metaphysical perceptions which produce creative painting as a record . . . of religious experience." [18] This emphasis on ego-lessness, the antithesis of the romantic notion of artist as heroic creator, is also a central theme in the highly influential work of John Cage, whom Tobey first met when he returned to America in 1938. Cage will be examined in more detail shortly. At this point, it is sufficient to note that Cage regarded his work as "a response to Tobey."

Isamu Noguchi (1904–88), the Japanese-American sculptor and garden designer, started his artistic career on a high note, working as Brancusi's studio assistant in Paris. There is some evidence of Buddhist influence in the work of the master; Noguchi's output is generally more explicit.[19] In 1930–31, following his first financial successes as an artist, Noguchi visited the Far East, where he studied brush-drawing, pottery, and Zen garden design. Fine examples of the influence of the latter can be found in his *Sunken Garden for Chase Manhattan Bank Plaza*, New York City (1961–64) and the *Sunken Garden for the Beinecke Rare Book and Manuscript Library*, Yale University (1960–64). The challenge of both is that they simultaneously make reference to traditional Japanese Buddhism and to twentieth-century abstraction. Later sculptures include works like *Ojizousama* (1985), a roughly worked stone reminiscent of traditional Japanese Daruma figures, partly punctured by a cleanly cut disk recalling the brush-drawn circle. Noguchi's preference for largely unworked stone underlined his belief in the necessity of noninterference. He came to regard the desire to produce art as a hindrance to creativity. For him, the true artist should be an "innocent," not a "specialist."

The significance of American composer John Cage (1912–92) has already been mentioned. Through his friendships, writings, and interviews, Cage acted as a major fellow interpreter of oriental and Buddhist ideas to fellow avant-garde artists. Having studied counterpoint with Schoenberg in the early 1930s, by the late 1940s he was turning to Eastern models, as exemplified by his ballet *Seasons* (1947), a work produced by the New York Ballet Society, choreographed by Merce Cunningham, and with sets by Noguchi. An early influence had been the writings of Ananda Coomaraswamy (1877–1947), who held Fenollosa's old post of Curator of Oriental Art at the Museum of Fine Arts, Boston. In fact, Coomaraswamy was a convinced traditionalist, strongly hostile to abstraction. However, he also held that the responsibility of the artist is "to imitate nature in her manner of operation." This does not imply that the artist should represent things as they are in themselves, but should present them "as they are in God." In short, art is a kind of spiritual discipline that leads to the contemplation of the Absolute. This was the notion that inspired Cage, who wrote in the late 1940s that the purpose of music is "[t]o sober and quiet the mind thus rendering it susceptible to divine influences," for "our culture has its faith not in the peaceful center of the spirit, but in an ever-hopeful projection on to things of our own desire for completion." [20] The twenty short pieces contained in *Sonatas and Interludes* (1949), his first masterwork for the prepared piano, were designed to express the eight permanent emotions of Indian aesthetics (Skt. *rasa*) "and their common tendency to tranquility," which Cage had first found described in Coomaraswamy's book *The Dance of Shiva*.

Cage claims to have heard a highly stimulating lecture on Dada and Zen by Nancy Wilson Ross, an acquaintance of Morris Graves, some time in the 1930s. I think that this must have been somewhat later, but by the early 1950s he had certainly begun a more informed study of Buddhism with D. T. Suzuki at Columbia University.[21] He also visited Suzuki in Japan on two separate occasions, although he claims never to have practiced meditation. In a letter to Pierre Boulez in 1950, he describes his new phase of Zen-influenced composition as "throwing sounds into silence." He began to feel that he had broken free from the requirements of expressive continuity. Sounds cast into unbounded time would now find their "own unimpeded and interpenetrating expressiveness." Cage maintained that he had always been taught that a composer has to have something to say. Exposure to these new ideas convinced him that self-expression actually hindered the true functioning of music.

Such notions are quite consistent with the "no-mindedness" of the *Zen Teaching of Huang Po*, the only Buddhist work Cage specifically refers to in his writings. The chance techniques or *experimental actions* used by Cage around this time emerge from a similar source. He argued that, by short-circuiting the logical and abstractive activities of the mind, it might be possible to apprehend unmediated sound. Thus, use of the *I Ching* began to influence (or undermine through chance operations) his compositional technique, as in the piano piece *Music of Changes* (1951). The static and expressive quality of *Seasons* was giving way to a form of music in which musicians were urged to adapt themselves to the world, rather than impose artificial structures upon it. Although Cage's tour of Europe in 1954 generated a largely hostile reaction, it did succeed in influencing the thinking of Karlheinz Stockhausen (b. 1928). Even in his late career Cage still drew inspiration from Zen, in this case the stone garden of Ryoanji, in Kyoto, which he had first visited in the 1950s. A piece for oboe, voice, flute, contrabass, and trombone, *Ryoanji* (1983–85), contrasts the raked sand, as expressed in percussive effects, with the stones, described by the oboe. In this work, Cage has moved beyond a concern for "pure sound" alone. This is "program music" that does not describe but rather attempts to embody the garden.

We should not suppose that this deeper engagement with the religio-philosophical aspects of Asian Buddhist culture was the sole preserve of American artists. The principle holds good for Europe as well. As a student in Saint Petersburg, Nicholas Roerich (1874–1947) became part of the "decadent" World of Art (*Mir Iskusstva*) circle associated with Serge Diaghilev. Today Roerich is principally known for his stage designs, including sets for *Prince Igor* (1909) and *Le Sacre du printemps* (1913) for the Ballet Russe. As a painter of atmospheric and monumental landscapes, he blended a variety of Western, Russian, and oriental styles. However, Indian motifs began to appear in his work from around 1905[22] and Rabindranath Tagore, who first saw these paintings in London in 1920, invited Roerich to India. Traveling via America, he founded the Roerich Museum in New York in 1923, as a permanent home for his work. The specially designed twenty-four-story building incorporated a Tibetan library, exhibition spaces, a theater, and apartments for rent. Harvey Wiley Corbett, its architect, originally planned to top off the structure with a Buddhist *stūpa*, although this was never actually realized. Even had he been so inclined, Roerich's arrival in America was probably too early for him to be touched by the developments in abstract art put in train by Fenollosa.

From his arrival in India, mighty mountains that provided backgrounds for, and somewhat dwarfed, scenes of spiritual life began to dominate Roerich's work.[23] Many of his concepts derive from traditional Tibetan Buddhist iconography. *Treasure of the World — Chintamani* (1924), in which a windhorse *(rlung rta)* carrying the flaming jewel of the universal monarch *(cakravartin)* is foregrounded, is typical. The paintings in the series entitled *Banners of the East* (begun 1924) are all similarly set. This group consists of nineteen Tibetan-style *thangkas* depicting "great teachers, including Jesus, Moses, Buddha, Padmasambhava, Milarepa, and a wrathful deity (entitled *Dorje the Daring One*, from 1925). Despite the catholicity of his religious tastes, Buddhist imagery recurs again and again. Indeed, while traveling in Central Asia in the mid-1920s Roerich had already executed a series of seven works on the theme of Maitreya. Many of his later works also reflect a specifically Himalayan Buddhist environment. In *Tibet* (1933), *stūpas* and monastery buildings are placed before a highly atmospheric mountain landscape, and *Castle of Ladakh* (1933) shows a dramatic rendering of the sTog Palace in Leh.

Although not a great painter, Roerich powerfully conveys the highly romantic atmosphere in which the spiritual life might be lived. He also appears to have been the first important European painter to carefully study and creatively manipulate elements of traditional Buddhist iconography.

Lama Anagārika Govinda (born Ernst Lothar Hoffman [1898–1985]) seems to have been made from the same mold. Originally a member of a small group of German monks based in Sri Lanka under the direction of Nyānatiloka Thera, Govinda experienced visions of various Mahāyānist deities some time after attending an international Buddhist conference in the Darjeeling in 1931. This led to a rather unorthodox adoption of Tibetan Buddhism combined with a conviction that creative visualization is the true purpose of sacred art. Govinda specialized in sacred landscapes (perhaps influenced by Roerich), most of which are housed at Govinda Hall, Allahabad, created in 1938.[24] In 1935, Govinda delivered a series of lectures on the symbolism of the Buddhist *stūpa* at Santiniketan, Tagore's academy for East-West cooperation in south Bengal. These subsequently became a book, *Some Aspects of Stupa Symbolism*.[25]

Govinda's theories on the connection between meditation (he prefers the term *inner vision*) and art are expounded in an essay called "Art and Meditation," first published in the 1940s. Here he argues that art and meditation are both creative mental states, but that their directionality is different. Meditation is oriented to the internal world while art is concerned with externality. Art, then, is the measure of a living religion, and the most perfect combination of art and meditation is to be found in medieval Buddhism. Contra-Roerich but pro-Fenollosa, Govinda maintains that the true artist must break free from the external forms of nature and embrace abstraction; painting should be primarily concerned with form and color. The essay concludes with a discussion of the symbolism of three basic forms (cube, cylinder, and sphere) and the three primary colors, which seems to owe something to Jung, and a series of eight paintings illustrating the theory.[26]

Our discussion of this group of very disparate artists, bound together merely by their firsthand experience of Buddhist culture, began with

Fenollosa's modernist pronouncement that art would become the religion of the new age. This prophecy finds partial fulfillment in the work of Tobey and of Noguchi, who declared: "If religion dies as a dogma, it is reborn as a direct personal expression in the arts. I do not refer to work done in churches ... but to the almost religious quality of ecstacy and anguish to be found emerging here and there in so-called abstract art." [27] Abstract artists who seek to transcend the limitations of form are almost bound to feel restricted by the requirements of institutional religion, for their faith is in art itself. While they may look for inspiration here and there, and this may include Buddhist Asia, they cannot be regarded as "Buddhist artists." Govinda, although more clearly connected with institutional Buddhism, draws close to this position with his insistence on the priority of creative visualization. The artist whose inner vision is turned on is no longer required to express himself in the formal manner authorized by tradition. Although it is difficult to gauge the precise nature of Roerich's involvement with Tibetan Buddhism, his life and work are signs of a more romantic motivation. From his theosophical beginnings to his artistic concern with depicting the mountain fastnesses in which great masters of wisdom lay concealed, we can trace an antiquarian desire for contact with a lost age—a quest for Shangrila. For Roerich, the forms of institutional religion, as expressed for example in iconography and iconology, are the keys to this hidden realm. The artist's role, then, is one of accurate reproduction, not creative manipulation. He or she could be regarded as a kind of priest or *lama*. The term *Buddhist artist* may not be inappropriate in these circumstances. As we shall see, this tension between modernism and romanticism carries through into the artistic preoccupations of Western Buddhists of the most recent period.

A NEW AGE?

The opportunities for Western access to Buddhist cultures grew exponentially as the twentieth century unfolded. Nonetheless, the numbers of Europeans and Americans prepared to commit themselves wholeheartedly to a Buddhist way of life in Asia remained small until the 1970s, and the vast majority of these were more interested in meditation and philosophy than in the Buddhist arts. Characters like Fenollosa, Roerich, and Govinda were rare. The situation changed dramatically in the 1960s, with the arrival of Tibetan refugees in northern Indian and the subsequent development of a worldwide diaspora. As time progressed, Dharamsala established itself both as the seat of the Dalai Lama and as a center for the preservation of Tibetan arts and culture. From the late 1960s, it began to act as a powerful magnet to Westerners, a number of whom took advantage of newly emerging facilities to train in traditional painting techniques. Early figures in this movement include the English monk Kevin Rigby (d. 1979), the Japanese painter Kenji Babasaki (who, after his teacher Jampa died in 1987, took on the role of tutoring a number of Tibetan students), and Andy Weber. The most prominent of these Western Tibetan artists is Robert Beer, whose main teacher was the 8th Khamtrul Rinpoche from Tashijong (d. 1980). Beer claims to have "developed an understanding of Eastern and Western esoteric traditions" in 1969 following a "full-blown Kundalini crisis [which] catapulted [him] into another reality." [28] It was this experience that led him to Dharamsala, where, bar one innovation—the introduction of the airbrush—he came to be recognized as an authentic exponent of the normative New Menri (sMan-ris) style of painting. [29]

The phenomenon of non-ethnic Tibetan artists has created some intriguing paradoxes, as the case of Gonkar Gyatso (b. 1962) illustrates. A Tibetan born in Lhasa as the son of government employees, Gonkar Gyatso studied art according to the social-realist canon then considered de rigueur by the Chinese authorities. As a good citizen of the People's Republic of China (PRC), he accepted the official view that Tibet was wild and backward and he shared the official hostility toward the Dalai Lama and toward the Buddhist religion itself. This meant that he had no knowledge of traditional styles of Tibetan painting. Nevertheless, some of his teachers did expose him to Western modernism, particularly the Cubist work of Braque and Picasso, something that underwent considerable reinforcement following his enrollment in the Minority School in Beijing in 1979. In reality, his dependence on social realism had already received a severe knock following an official visit to Chamdo to depict the lifestyle of the Kham peasants. He was stunned by the conditions in which they were living. In 1984, he returned to the Tibetan Autonomous Region (TAR) and enrolled in the Fine Art Department of Lhasa University. During this period, coincidentally a time of liberalization in the PRC's attitude toward Tibetan culture, he first attempted to engage with specifically Tibetan themes. His fascination with the Tibetan landscape, which seems to have been occasioned by his airplane flights to Beijing, led to the creation of a series of highly anti-realist landscapes, culminating in Lhamo Latso (1980s)—a portrayal of the sacred lake south of Lhasa associated with Palden Lhamo, the wrathful protector-deity of the traditional Tibetan state. Dissatisfied with the official attitude toward the arts in Tibet, in 1985 he and some fellow students established the first independent artists' group, the Sweet Tea Painting Association. A number of small exhibitions of this new art were exhibited in the tea houses close to Lhasa University. At this time, Gonkar Gyatso was experimenting with the concept of "modern *thangkas*," that is, religious paintings not dependent on traditional stylistics, iconography, and iconology. In 1987, the Sweet Tea Painting Association disbanded against a background of official harassment of the newly emerging Tibetan cultural forces. Soon after, Gonkar Gyatso escaped to Dharamsala, but not before he produced two exceptional works, *Buddha and the White Lotus* and *Red Buddha*. The first of these is divided into three horizontal sections. To the left, the roots of a lotus grow sideways into a mass of red and black and flowering in the central section of black that itself half-obscures a seated Buddha-image that occupies the left side of the final section. According to Harris, the partial absence of the Buddha represents the Dalai Lama's absence from Tibet.[30] The artist has added that, given present circumstances, the Buddha "could not look the Tibetans in the eyes." In both coloring and form, the work is highly reminiscent of late Rothko.

One would have expected that Gonkar Gyatso's arrival in the bosom of the Tibetan exile community would have acted as a further impetus to his artistic development. Quite the contrary; his work has been received with a mixture of incomprehension and antagonism. To the traditionalists who dominate this world, both Tibetan and Western, Gonkar Gyatso's work is untutored and sacrilegious. He seems unable or unwilling to produce *thangkas* in the accepted style. While a non-ethnic traditionalist—Robert Beer—has been accepted by the exile community, the way is barred to a Tibetan modernist.

Another obvious feature of the post-1960 Buddhist context is the emergence of distinctive forms of Western Buddhism. One of the more successful groups, at least in Britain, is the Friends of the Western Buddhist Order (FWBO), founded in 1967 by Venerable Sangharakshita (born Dennis Lingwood, 1925). Sangharakshita appears to have been intrigued by the spiritual potential of artistic creation for many years, and his *The Religion of Art*, originally written in Kalimpong during the 1950s, discusses the topic clearly and in considerable detail. For Sangharakshita, art has nothing to do with egoistical pleasure or enjoyment. On the contrary, it is "primarily a means of liberation from the egoistic life."[31] True art, then, must be distinguished from that which masquerades as art. The general territory may be discerned under four headings:[32]

1. Work that is religious in subject but non-religious in sentiment. Included here is much "mushy" Christian art that "positively strengthens the ego-sense."

2. Naturally or essentially religious art that is religious in sentiment but non-religious in subject, such as Shelley's poetry or a Chinese landscape painting.

3. Work that is religious in subject as well as sentiment, for example, a Buddha image.

4. Art that is religious neither in sentiment nor in subject. This refers to almost all contemporary art, which he dismisses in an Olympian manner as "pseudo-artistic rubbish."

In Sangharakshita's opinion, true art, being "natural art," falls into category 2. As such, it has neither a ritual nor a didactic function. Like Govinda, he stresses its creative and transformative qualities: "The Religion of Art may . . . be defined as conscious surrender to the Beautiful, especially as manifested in poetry, music and the visual arts, as a means of breaking up established egocentric patterns of behavior and protracting one's experience along the line of egolessness into the starry depths of Reality." [33] However, unlike Govinda, he subscribes to a romantic, almost gnostic, vision of the artist as a fearless explorer of the interior world. Nodding approvingly in the direction of Rilke, Sangharakshita argues that, while the ordinary person squanders love on inappropriate and transient objects, the ego-lessness of the true artist enables him to sublimate, intensify, and discharge these lower emotions in an act of creativity. The true artist is clearly a rather exalted figure!

A curious feature of the essay, given that its author is the founder of a modern Buddhist movement, is that it hardly engages with Buddhist ideas at all and contains no substantive treatment of Buddhist art. Indeed, a consequence of Sangharakshita's insistence on naturalism is that work created within a specifically Buddhist context tends to be relegated to a lower level, an impression reinforced by the strongly protestant tone of the conclusion: "The Religion of Art has no temple and no church; wherever men feel the touch of Beauty, there is holy ground. It possesses no scriptures; the whole of nature is its sacred book. It has no priests, for those who enjoy and those who create works of art behold Beauty face to face, and have no need of any mediator or intercessor." [34] Brief discussion cannot do justice to the richness of the text. Its significance lies in the fact that it pulls together, not always in a fully coherent manner, many of the elements touched upon in our preceding treatment of individual artists. It is strong on abstraction and naturalism, yet romanticism and a hint of the transgressive also find their place. A Hegelian might be tempted to interpret the essay as a synthesis of some of the tensions manifested at earlier stages in the Western response to the art of Buddhist Asia.

The fact that the text is still regarded as relevant in the FWBO is underlined by the organization of a seminar on *The Religion of Art,* led by Sangharakshita, in spring 1999. More generally, the centrality of the arts to the movement seems to have had a significant impact on recruitment. A London Buddhist Arts Centre has been in existence for many years, since January 1999 subsumed under the auspices of the FWBO's London Buddhist Centre. Similar centers operate in the provinces. Members also publish a magazine, *Urthona,* specifically focused on Buddhism and the arts. Founded in 1992, it is partially funded by Sangharakshita.

Chintamani is an artist associated with the London Buddhist Centre. For a number of years, he has created fairly traditional Buddha *rūpas* with distinctly Western facial features. In 1999, he designed a five-foot-high *stūpa* based on a simplified Indian model, with this type of Buddha in the niche. His significant innovation involves the incorporation of floral motifs, including Green Man masks, into the base of the structure. Chintamani explains that he "wanted to make a connection with indigenous sensibilities and evoke a very ancient, pre-Christian image for the forces of the land and nature as a supporting protector for the higher life (as symbolized by the rest of the *stūpa*). The masks are intended to be a reminder of the sort of necessary foundation that we need to live the higher life." [35] The Green Man motif appears to have been quite popular in FWBO circles several years ago, when the movement was keen on exploring links with indigenous features of the British religious landscape, an adaptation strategy linked with the movement's desire to break free from an "orientalist" approach to the practice of Buddhism. Additionally, the motif fed nicely into the emerging currents of EcoBuddhism. [36] In one sense, the piece displays some of the naturalistic concerns expressed by Sangharakshita, even though these are displayed in a highly concrete manner. Chintamani's work represents a constructive engagement with traditional Buddhist forms, yet displays little enthusiasm for abstraction. Although Chintamani has seriously engaged with Sangharakshita's thinking on the nature of art, it is clear that there is no party line.

CONCLUSION

Many of the queries about the precise nature of the Western artistic engagement with Buddhism, first raised in the introduction, remain unresolved. Indeed, no overarching consensus has emerged, nor is it likely to in the foreseeable future. Having said that, the basic tension between romanticism and modernism will ensure that a vigorous current is maintained, though further developments in mass communication, globalization, and the postmodern condition are likely to contribute to an even greater fracturing than has been the case until now. The growth of Buddhism in the West has drawn more and more artists into the arena of its influence. The list has become bewildering, including figures as diverse as the Spanish painter Antoni Tàpies, the English sculptor Anthony Gormley, American minimalist composers like Philip Glass and Terry Riley,[37] and even hard-nosed movie directors like Martin Scorsese, for Hollywood now has the bug in a big way.[38] However, as the example of the FWBO makes clear, this is not a movement confined to the ranks of professional artists. As historic Buddhism made its lengthy pilgrimage across Asia, it adapted to the cultural and aesthetic character of each new host culture. It is probable that this pattern will continue in territories beyond the ancient Buddhist heartlands as the new millennium progresses.

NOTES

1. Judith played a minor role in Wagner's attempt to write an opera based on scenes from the life of the Buddha, by supplying him with copies of various Indic texts in translation. Wagner started drafting *The Victor (Die Sieger)* in May 1856. It was never completed, largely because of the difficulties involved in giving it dramatic form. Nonetheless, its central theme of sensual renunciation was eventually transposed into *Parsifal*. Raymond Schwab, *The Oriental Renaissance: Europe's Rediscovery of India and the East, 1680–1880* (New York: Columbia University Press, 1984), 438, observes that Wagner's concern with oriental subjects was part of a larger plan to destroy the legacy of "routine Italian-French opera."

2. See Klaus Berger's catalogue, *Odilon Redon: Fantasy and Colour* (London: Weidenfeld and Nicolson, 1964): nos. 198, *Head of Buddha with Flowers* (1905); 198a, *Young Buddha* (no date); 366, *Buddha's Enlightenment* (around 1900); 367, *Buddha's Death* (c. 1905); 368, *Living Buddha* (1903–04); 369, *Buddha Wandering among Flowers* (1905); and 370, *Standing Buddha* (c. 1904).

3. When Matisse was working on the commission to design and decorate the interior of the Vence Chapel near Nice (1948–51), he made the following statement on his religious beliefs: "I meditate and let myself be penetrated by what I'm undertaking. I do not know if I have faith or not. Perhaps I'm somewhat Buddhist. The essential thing is to work in a state of mind that approaches prayer." He is quoted in Roger Lipsey, *An Art of Our Own: The Spiritual in Twentieth-Century Art* (Boston: Shambhala, 1988), 256. One does not have to dig far to find similar statements from other notable French modernists. André Breton, in *Surrealism and Painting* (London: Macdonald, 1972), 224, for instance, claimed that Dada was "a flake of Zen."

4. Michael Sullivan, *The Meeting of Eastern and Western Art* (Berkeley: University of California Press, 1989).

5. Bequeathed in 1890 to the Museum of Fine Arts, Boston.

6. Many American artists were impressed with Okakura's *The Book of Tea* (1906). One of these, Frank Lloyd Wright, also claimed to have been influenced by Okakura's Japanese Pavilion at the Chicago Exhibition of 1893.

7. Not everyone relished Fenollosa's Buddhist zeal. After visiting him in Japan, Henry Adams complained: "He has joined a Buddhist sect; I was myself a Buddhist when I left America, but he has converted me to Calvinism." Quoted by Christopher Benfey in "Tea with Okakura," *New York Times Review of Books* 47, no. 9 (2000), 44.

8. See Lawrence W. Chisholm, *Fenollosa: The Far East and American Culture* (New Haven: Yale University Press, 1963), 104.

9. Ibid., 217 and 94.

10. Ernest Fenollosa, *East and West: The Discovery of America, and Other Poems* (New York, 1893), 55.

11. We know that when Eugen Herrigel's *Zen in the Art of Archery* (New York: Pantheon) appeared in its first American edition in 1953, it was devoured eagerly by Tobey, Motherwell, and Pollock, among others. See David James Clarke, *The Influence of Oriental Thought on Postwar American Painting and Sculpture* (New York: Garland, 1988), 48.

12. See Arthur L. Dahl, et al. *Mark Tobey: Art and Belief* (Oxford: George Ronald, 1984), 5.

13. Leach's account of the journey is given in his autobiography, *Beyond East and West: Memoirs, Portraits, and Essays* (London: Faber, 1978).

14. Tobey wrote of an art future in which ". . . East and West will embrace as long-lost lovers." There are shades of Fenollosa here!

15. See Dahl, *Mark Tobey,* 5 and 22.

16. See William C. Seitz, *Mark Tobey* (New York: Museum of Modern Art, 1962), 40.

17. Clarke, *The Influence of Oriental Thought,* 199.

18. Ibid., 94.

19. During his early years in Paris (he arrived in 1904 after an eighteen-month journey on foot from his native Romania), Constantin Brancusi (1876–1957) was a frequent visitor at the Musée Guimet. Emile Guimet, accompanied by Kuki Ryuichi, a close friend of Kakuzo Okakura, had began to reconnoiter Japanese temples and shrines in 1876, eight years before Fenellosa. Brancusi was fascinated by the eyes of some sleeping Buddha (= *parinirvāṇa*) images in the museum—a possible influence on his many heads, as, for example, *Sleeping Muse* (1910). See Anna Chave, *Constantin Brancusi: Shifting the Bases of Art* (New Haven: Yale University Press, 1993), 169. Brancusi's interest in Buddhism can definitely be traced to 1925, when Bacot's French translation of *The Life of Milarepa* was first published. The sculptor used it as a kind of "bedside Bible," although Mircea Eliade maintains that the primitivity embodied in Romanian peasant culture was the dominant force in Brancusi's artistic output. See "Brancusi and Mythology," in Mircea Eliade, *Symbolism, the Sacred, and the Arts,* edited by Diane Apostolos-Cappadona (New York: Crossroad, 1986), 93–101. Nevertheless, Brancusi is reported as saying, "Buddhism isn't a religion, it is a morality and a technique through which one can come closer to the gods. Buddhism is my morality. I have neglected the technique." Quoted in Lipsey, *An Art of Our Own,* 237).

20. James Pritchett, *The Music of John Cage* (Cambridge: Cambridge University Press, 1993), 37.

21. Cage's memory of the timing of these sessions is muddled. For a detailed discussion, see Clarke, *The Influence of Oriental Thought,* 81 ff. Noguchi also attended Suzuki's seminars at Columbia around the same time. Given the collaboration that had already taken place, he may have accompanied Cage. It is worth noting that Suzuki's writings on Zen naturalism are themselves highly contentious artefacts in an attempt to resuscitate and rework Japanese Buddhism after a period of official persecution. For a more detailed discussion, see my "Buddhism and

Ecology," in *Contemporary Buddhist Ethics*, edited by Damien Keown (Richmond, U.K.: Curzon Press, 2000), 113–35, particularly 129*ff*. See also Robert H. Sharf's "The Zen of Japanese Nationalism," in *Curators of the Buddha: The Study of Buddhism under Colonialism*, edited by Donald S. Lopez, Jr. (Chicago: University of Chicago Press, 1995), 107–60.

22. With his wife, Elena, who translated Blavatsky's *Secret Doctrine* into Russian, he is associated with the teachings of Agni Yoga (founded 1920). Roerich's theosophical background explains the fact that, while in America, he persuaded Henry Morgenthau, Secretary of the Treasury, that the Great Pyramid should be engraved on the dollar bill. Marc Chagall, one of his students at the School of Drawing, Saint Petersburg (1907–08), was no great admirer. In *My Life*, he commented that Roerich wrote and recited "unreadable poems."

23. Arriving in 1923, by 1929 Roerich finally settled near Naggar in the Kulu Valley, where he established the Himalayan Research Institute.

24. Tandart's 1940 catalogue of Govinda's work was published as part of a series of the Roerich Centre of Art and Culture, Allahabad. Although I have not been able to confirm this fact, it looks likely that Govinda Hall and the Roerich Centre were closely connected.

25. Published in 1940, and republished in 1976 as *The Psycho-Cosmic Symbolism of the Buddhist Stupa*.

26. They are titled *Becoming, Being, Dissolving, Turning Inwards, Unification, Birth of Happiness, Samadhi,* and *Mandala*. See Lama Anagārika Govinda, "Art and Meditation," in *Creative Meditation and Multi-Dimensional Consciousness* (London: Allen and Unwin, 1977), 182*ff*.

27. From a lecture Noguchi gave in 1949, quoted in Lipsey, *An Art of Our Own*, 356.

28. Robert Beer, *The Encyclopedia of Tibetan Symbols and Motifs* (London: Serindia, 1999), xiii.

29. For a detailed discussion of Tibetan painting styles, see David Jackson, *A History of Tibetan Painting* (Vienna: Verlag der Österreichischen Akademie der Wissenschaften, 1996).

30. See Clare Harris, *In the Image of Tibet: Tibetan Painting after 1959* (London: Reaktion Books, 1999), 189.

31. Maha Sthavira Sangharakshita, *The Religion of Art* (London: Windhorse, 1980), 4.

32. Ibid., 22*ff*.

33. Ibid., 35.

34. Ibid., 65.

35. "Stupa at Order Conference," *Urthona* 12 (Winter 1999), 53.

36. On this topic, see my "Getting to Grips with Buddhist Environmentalism: A Provisional Typology," *Journal of Buddhist Ethics* 2 (1995), 173–90.

37. A visit to Riley's official web site gives a fairly immediate flavor of the influence: http://www.terryriley.com [22 Feb. 2002].

38. Glass composed the music for Scorsese's *Kundun* (1997), a fictionalized account of the life of the Dalai Lama. Glass began Buddhist study and meditation practice around 1966 after reading Cage's *Silence*. Prior to that date he transcribed Ravi Shankar's music for Conrad Rooks's film *Chappaqua* (1966). Rooks's subsequent work, *Siddhartha* (1972), based on the Hesse story, stands at the beginning of the cinema's recent obsession with things Buddhist. For an enjoyably romantic account of the influence at its most glitzy, see Orville Schell's recent *Virtual Tibet: Searching for Shangri-la from the Himalayas to Hollywood* (New York: Metropolitan Books, 2000).

Selected Bibliography

BUDDHISM BEYOND ASIA, GENERAL ACCOUNTS

Batchelor, Stephen. *The Awakening of the West: The Encounter of Buddhism and Western Culture.* Berkeley: Parallax, 1994.

Baumann, Martin. "The Dharma Has Come West: A Survey of Recent Studies and Sources." *Journal of Buddhist Ethics* 4 (1997), 194–211. Reprinted in *Critical Review of Books in Religion* 10 (1997), 1–14; http://jbe.la/psu/edu/4/baum2.html [8 Jan. 2002].

—. "Global Buddhism: Developmental Periods, Regional Histories and a New Analytical Perspective." *Journal of Global Buddhism* 2 (2001), 1–43.

Bechert, Heinz. "Buddhist Revival in East and West." In *The World of Buddhism,* edited by Heinz Bechert and Richard Gombrich, 273–85. London: Thames and Hudson, 1984.

Bishop, Peter. *Dreams of Power: Tibetan Buddhism and the Western Imagination.* London: Athlone, 1993.

Coleman, Graham (ed.). *A Handbook of Tibetan Culture: A Guide to Tibetan Centres and Resources throughout the World.* London: Rider, 1993.

Prebish, Charles S. "Selected Bibliography on Buddhism in the West." In *Luminous Passage: The Practice and Study of Buddhism in America,* by Charles S. Prebish, 301–10. Berkeley: University of California Press, 1999.

Rawlinson, Andrew. *The Book of Enlightened Masters: Western Teachers in Eastern Traditions.* Chicago: Open Court, 1997.

Rommeluere, Eric. *Le Guide du Zen.* Paris: Editions de Livre de Poche, 1997.

EUROPE

General Overviews and Surveys

Batchelor, Stephen. "Buddhism and European Culture in Europe." In *Religion in Europe: Contemporary Perspectives,* edited by Sean Gill, Gavin D'Costa, and Ursula King, 86–104. Kampen, Netherlands: Pharos, 1994.

Baumann, Martin. "Buddhism in Europe: An Annotated Bibliography" (2001). http://www.globalbuddhism.org/bib-bud.html [19 June 2002].

—. "Creating a European Path to Nirvana: Historical and Contemporary Developments of Buddhism in Europe." *Journal of Contemporary Religion* 10, no. 1 (1995), 55–70.

Bell, Sandra. "Practice Makes Perfect: Symbolic Behaviour and Experience in Western Buddhism." *Diskus* 2, no. 2 (1994). http://www.uni-marburg.de/religionswissenschaft/journal/diskus/bell.html [3 Mar. 2002].

de Lubac, Henri. *La rencontre du bouddhisme et de l'Occident.* Paris: Aubier-Montaigne, 1952.

Freiberger, Oliver. "The Meeting of Traditions: Inter-Buddhist and Inter-Religious Relations in the West." *Journal of Global Buddhism* 2 (2001), 59–71.

Hahlbohm-Helmus, Elke. "Buddhism as Philosophy and Psychology: Performance Aspects of Tibetan Buddhism 'in the West' between 1959 and 1990." *Recherches Sociologiques: Le bouddhisme en Occident* 31, no. 3 (2000), 49–66.

Hutter, Manfred (ed.). *Buddhisten und Hindus im deutschsprachigen Raum.* Frankfurt: Peter Lang, 2001.

Peiris, William. *The Western Contribution to Buddhism.* Delhi: Motilal Banarsidass, 1973.

Snelling, John. *The Buddhist Handbook: A Complete Guide to Buddhist Teaching and Practise.* London: Century Hutchinson, 1987.

Welbon, Guy Richard. The *Buddhist Nirvāṇa and Its Western Interpreters.* Chicago: University of Chicago Press, 1968.

Geographical Studies

AUSTRIA

"Buddhisten in Österreich." *Ursache und Wirkung: Zeitschrift für Buddhismus,* special issue (1998).

Hecker, Hellmuth. "Buddhisten im alten Österreich." *Bodhi Baum* 18, no. 2 (1993), 16–19.

Hutter, Manfred. "Österreichische Buddhisten: Geschichte und Organisation." In *Buddhisten und Hindus im deutschsprachigen Raum,* edited by Manfred Hutter, 99–110. Frankfurt: Peter Lang, 2001.

Ritter, Franz. "Austro-Buddhismus: eine kleine Geschichte des Buddhismus in Österreich." *Bodhi Baum* 18, no. 2 (1993), 4–10.

FRANCE

Chelli, Norbert, and Louis Hourmant. "Orientations axiologiques dans le bouddhisme du mouvement Soka Gakkaï France." *Recherches Sociologiques: Le bouddhisme en Occident* 31, no. 3 (2000), 89–102.

Choron-Baix, Catherine. *Bouddhisme et migration: la reconstitution d'une paroisse bouddhiste Lao en banlieue parisienne.* Paris: Ministère de la culture, conseil du patrimoine ethnologique, 1986.

—. "De forêts en banlieues: la transplantation du bouddhisme Lao en France." *Archives de sciences sociales des religions* 36, no. 73 (1991), 17–33.

Gira, Dennis. "La présence bouddhiste en France (1991)." *Documents Episcopat: Bulletin du secrétariat de La conférence des évègues de France* 13 (Sept. 1991), 16-page special issue.

Hourmant, Louis. "La Soka Gakkai: un bouddhisme 'paria' en France?" In *Sectes et Démocratie*, edited by Françoise Champion and Martine Cohen, 182–204. Paris: Le Seuil, 1999.

Kalab, Milada. "Cambodian Buddhist Monasteries in Paris: Continuing Tradition and Changing Patterns." In *Cambodian Culture since 1975: Homeland and Exile*, edited by May M. Ebihara, Carol A. Mortland, and Judy Ledgerwood, 57–71. Ithaca, New York: Cornell University Press, 1994.

Lenoir, Frédéric. *Le bouddhisme en France*. Paris: Fayard, 1999.

Obadia, Lionel. *Bouddhisme et Occident: la diffusion du bouddhisme tibétain en France*. Paris: L'Harmattan, 1999.

—. "Tibetan Buddhism in France: Implantation Strategies of a Missionary Religion." *Journal of Global Buddhism* 2 (2001), 92–109.

—. "Une tradition au delà de la modernité: l'institutionnalisation du bouddhisme tibétain en France." *Recherches Sociologiques: Le bouddhisme en Occident* 31, no. 3 (2000), 67–88.

Raphael, Liogier, and Bruno Etienne. *Etre bouddhiste en France aujourd'hui*. Paris: Hachette Littératures, 1997.

Ronce, Philippe. *Guide des centres bouddhistes en France*. Paris: Noesis, 1998.

GERMANY

Baumann, Martin. "Culture Contact and Valuation: Early German Buddhists and the Creation of a 'Buddhism in Protestant Shape.'" *Numen* 44, no. 3 (1997), 270–95.

—. *Deutsche Buddhisten: Geschichte und Gemeinschaften*. 2nd enlarged ed. Marburg, Germany: Diagonal-Verlag, 1995. Original edition, Marburg, Germany: Diagonal-Verlag, 1993.

—. "Entsagung und Entselbstung: eine Neuinterpretation des Lebens und Werkes des Buddhisten Paul Dahlke." In *Living Faith: Lebendige religiöse Wirklichkeit*, edited by Reiner Mahlke, Renate Pitzer-Reyl, and Joachim Süss, 263–82. Frankfurt: Peter Lang, 1997.

—. *Migration, Religion, Integration: Buddhistische Vietnamesen und Hinduistische Tamilen in Deutschland*. Marburg, Germany: Diagonal-Verlag, 2000.

—. "The Transplantation of Buddhism to Germany: Processive Modes and Strategies of Adaptation." *Method and Theory in the Study of Religion* 6, no. 1 (1994), 35–61.

Bitter, Klaus. *Konversionen zum tibetischen Buddhismus: eine Analyse religiöser Biographien*. Göttingen, Germany: E. Oberdieck Verlag, 1988.

Hecker, Hellmuth. *Lebensbilder deutscher Buddhisten: ein bio-bibliographisches Handbuch*. 2nd enlarged ed. 2 vols. Konstanz, Germany: University of Konstanz, 1996, 1997. Original ed., Konstanz, Germany: University of Konstanz, 1990, 1992.

Ho, Loc. *Vietnamesischer Buddhismus in Deutschland: Darstellung der Geschichte und Institutionalisierung.* Hannover, Germany: Pagode Vien Giac, 1999.

Kantowsky, Detlef. *Wegzeichen: Gespräche über buddhistische Praxis.* 2nd enlarged ed. Ulm: UKAS, 1994. Original ed., Konstanz, Germany: University of Konstanz, 1991.

Litsch, Franz-Johannes. "Engaged Buddhism in German-Speaking Europe." In *Engaged Buddhism in the West,* edited by Christopher S. Queen, 423–45. Boston: Wisdom, 2000.

Saalfrank, Eva Sabine. *Geistige Heimat im Buddhismus aus Tibet: eine empirische Studie am Beispiel der Kagyuepas in Deutschland.* Ulm, Germany: Fabri, 1997.

Usarski, Frank (ed.). "The Perception of Christianity among Early German Buddhists." *Hightech and Macumba: Bulletin of the Goethe-Institute São Paulo, Brazil* (2000). http://www.goethe.de/br/sap/macumba/usarski_long.htm [8 Dec. 2001].

GREAT BRITAIN

Almond, Philip C. *The British Discovery of Buddhism.* Cambridge: Cambridge University Press, 1988.

Bell, Sandra. "Being Creative with Tradition: Rooting Theravāda Buddhism in Britain." *Journal of Global Buddhism* 1 (2000), 1–30.

—. "British Theravāda Buddhism: Otherworldly Theories, and the Theory of Exchange." *Journal of Contemporary Religion* 13, no. 2 (1998), 149–70.

—. "Change and Identity in the Friends of the Western Buddhist Order." *Scottish Journal of Religious Studies* 17, no. 1 (1996), 87–107.

Buddhist Society, The. *The Buddhist Directory.* 8th edition. London: Buddhist Society, 2000.

Cousins, Lance S. "Theravāda Buddhism in England." In *Buddhism into the Year 2000: International Conference Proceedings,* edited by the Dhammakaya Foundation, 141–50. Bangkok: Dhammakaya Foundation, 1994.

Cush, Denise. "British Buddhism and the New Age." *Journal of Contemporary Religion* 11, no. 2 (1996), 195–208.

Humphreys, Christmas. *The Development of Buddhism in England.* London: The Buddhist Society, 1937.

—. *Sixty Years of Buddhism in England, 1907–1967: A History and a Survey.* London: The Buddhist Society, 1968.

Kay, David. "The New Kadampa Tradition and the Continuity of Tibetan Buddhism in Transition." *Journal of Contemporary Religion* 12, no. 3 (1997), 277–93.

Mellor, Philip A. "Protestant Buddhism? The Cultural Translation of Buddhism in England." *Religion* 21, no. 2 (1991), 73–92.

Morgan, Daishin. "Soto Zen Buddhism in Britain." In *Japanese New Religions in the West*, edited by Peter B. Clarke and Jeffrey Somers, 132–48. Folkestone, U.K.: Curzon Press, 1994.

Oliver, Ian. *Buddhism in Britain*. London: Rider, 1979.

Waterhouse, Helen. *Buddhism in Bath: Adaptation and Authority*. Leeds, U.K.: Community Religions Project, University of Leeds, 1997.

——. "Who Says So? Legitimacy and Authenticity in British Buddhism." *Scottish Journal of Religious Studies* 20, no. 1 (1999), 19–36.

Wilson, Bryan, and Karel Dobbelaere. *A Time to Chant: The Sōka Gakkai Buddhists in Britain*. Oxford: Clarendon Press, 1994.

HUNGARY

Baumann, Martin. "Gegenwärtige Entwicklungen des Buddhismus in Ungarn." *Zeitschrift für Missionswissenschaft und Religionswissenschaft* 78, no. 1 (1994), 38–46.

Duka, Theodore. *Life and Writings of Alexander Csoma de Koeroes*. London: 1885.

Webb, Russell. "Buddhism in Hungary." *Buddhist Quarterly* 2, no. 2 (1969), 7–10.

ITALY

Benavides, Gustavo. "Guiseppe Tucci, or Buddhism in the Age of Fascism." In *Curators of the Buddha*, edited by Donald S. Lopez, Jr., 161–96. Chicago: University of Chicago Press, 1995.

Dobbelaere, Karel. *La Soka Gakkai: Un movimento di laici diventa una religione*. Torino: Elle Di Ci, Leumann, 1998.

Falà, Maria Angela. "Italy, Buddhism in." In *Encyclopaedia of Buddhism*, edited by G. P. Weeraratne, vol. 5, 600–4. Colombo, Sri Lanka: Government of Sri Lanka, 1993.

NETHERLANDS AND BELGIUM

Gemert, Victor van. *Boeddhisme in Nederland: overzicht van boeddhistische stromingen in Nederland en Belgi*. Nijmegen, Netherlands: Zen-uitgeverij Theresiahoeve, 1990.

Janssen, R. H. C. "Buddhism in the Netherlands: History and Present Status." In *Buddhism into the Year 2000: International Conference Proceedings*, edited by the Dhammakaya Foundation, 151–6. Bangkok: Dhammakaya Foundation, 1994.

POLAND AND CZECH REPUBLIC

Doktór, Tadeusz. "Buddhism in Poland." In *New Religions and New Religiosity*, edited by Eileen Barker and Margit Warburg, 83–94. Aarhus, Denmark: Aarhus University Press, 1998.

Luszny, Dusan. "The Influence of Asian Religions in Czechoslovakia after 1989." In *Religion and Modernization in China*, edited by Kangsheng Dai, Xinying Zhang, and Michael Pye, 161–6. Cambridge: Roots and Branches, 1995.

RUSSIAN FEDERATION AND BALTIC STATES

Andreev, Aleksandr Ivanovich. "Soviet Russia and Tibet: A Debacle of Secret Diplomacy." *The Tibet Journal* 3 (1996), 4–34.

Batchelor, Stephen. "Bidiya Dandaron: Russian Connections." In *The Awakening of the West*, by Stephen Batchelor, 283–302. Berkeley: Parallax, 1994.

Belka, Lubos. "Buddhism in Estonia." *Religion, State and Society* 17, no. 2 (1999), 245–8.

—. "Oriental and Buddhist Studies in Estonia." *Archiv Orientalni* 64 (1996), 399–404.

—. "The Restoration of Buddhism in Buryatia: The Current State." In *Religions in Contact*, edited by Iva Dolezalová, Bretislav Horyna, and Dalibor Papousek, 163–77. Brno, Czech Republic: DaTaPrint, 1996.

Snelling, John. *Buddhism in Russia: The Story of Agvan Dorzhiev, Lhasa's Emissary to the Tsar.* Rockport, Massachusetts: Element, 1993.

Talts, Mait. "Friedrich Voldemar Lustig (Ashin Ananda), 26.04.1912–04.04.1989." http://gaia.gi.ee/~talts/lustig/ [23 Feb. 2002].

Terentyev, Andrey. "Tibetan Buddhism in Russia." *The Tibet Journal* 3 (1996), 60–70.

SWITZERLAND

Baumann, Martin. "Buddhism in Switzerland." *Journal of Global Buddhism* 1 (2000), 154–9.

Brauen, Martin, and Detlef Kantowsky (eds.). *Junge Tibeter in der Schweiz: Studien zum Prozess kultureller Identifikation.* Diessenhofen, Germany: Ruegger, 1982.

Ott-Marti, Anna-Elisabeth. "Problems of Tibetan Integration in Switzerland." *Ethnologia Europaea* 9, no. 1 (1976), 43–52.

Périer-Chappuis, Marianne (ed.). *Répertoire des centres bouddhistes en Suisse.* Yverdon, Switzerland: Fleury, 1993.

Van Dyke, Mary. "Grids and Serpents: A Tibetan Foundation Ritual in Switzerland." In *Constructing Tibetan Culture: Contemporary Perspectives*, edited by Frank J. Korom, 178–227. Montréal: World Heritage Press, 1997.

YUGOSLAVIA (FORMER)

Klar, Helmut. "Kalmucks and the Wheel." *Middle Way* 29, no. 3 (1954), 136–7.

[Pekic, Mile.] Kalmyk Buddhist Temple in Belgrade, 1929–1944: An Exhibition. http://members.tripod.com/kakono/ [8 Dec. 2001].

NORTH AMERICA

United States: General Overviews and Surveys

Coleman, James William. *The New Buddhism: The Western Transformation of an Ancient Tradition.* Oxford: Oxford University Press, 2000.

Fields, Rick. "The Future of American Buddhism." *The Vajradhatu Sun* 9, no. 1 (1987), 1, 22, 24–6.

——. *How the Swans Came to the Lake: A Narrative History of Buddhism in America.* 3rd revised and updated ed. Boston: Shambhala, 1992. Original ed., Boulder, Colorado: Shambhala, 1981.

Goldberg, Ellen. "The Re-Orientation of Buddhism in North America." *Method and Theory in the Study of Religion* 11, no. 4 (1999), 340–56.

Hunter, Louise. *Buddhism in Hawaii.* Honolulu: University of Hawaii Press, 1971.

Jackson, Carl T. "The Influence of Asian upon American Thought: A Bibliographical Essay." *American Studies International* 22, no. 1 (1984), 3–31.

——. *The Oriental Religions and American Thought.* Westport, Connecticut: Greenwood Press, 1981.

Kornfield, Jack. "Is Buddhism Changing North America?" In *Buddhist America: Centers, Retreats, Practices,* edited by Don Morreale, xi–xxviii. Santa Fe, New Mexico: John Muir Publications, 1988. Reprinted as "American Buddhism." In *The Complete Guide to Buddhist America,* edited by Don Morreale, xxi–xxx. Boston: Shambhala, 1998.

Layman, Emma McCloy. *Buddhism in America.* Chicago: Nelson-Hall, 1976.

Lorie, Peter, and Hillary Foakes (eds.). *The Buddhist Directory: United States of America and Canada.* Boston: Charles E. Tuttle, 1997.

Morreale, Don (ed.). *Buddhist America: Centers, Retreats, Practices.* Santa Fe, N.M.: John Muir Publications, 1988.

——. *The Complete Guide to Buddhist America.* Boston: Shambhala, 1998.

Numrich, Paul David. "How the Swans Came to Lake Michigan: The Social Organization of Buddhist Chicago." *Journal for the Scientific Study of Religion* 39, no. 2 (2000), 189–203.

——. "Local Inter-Buddhist Associations in North America." In *American Buddhism: Methods and Findings in Recent Scholarship,* edited by Duncan Ryūken Williams and Christopher S. Queen, 117–42. Richmond, U.K.: Curzon Press, 1999.

Padgett, Douglas M. "'Americans Need Something to Sit On,' or Zen Meditation Materials and Buddhist Diversity in North America." *Journal of Global Buddhism* 1 (2000), 61–81.

Prebish, Charles S. *American Buddhism.* North Scituate, Massachusetts: Duxbury Press, 1979.

—. "Ethics and Integration in American Buddhism." *Journal of Buddhist Ethics* 2 (1995), 125–39.

—. *Luminous Passage: The Practice and Study of Buddhism in America.* Berkeley: University of California Press, 1999.

—. "Reflections of the Transmission of Buddhism to America." In *Understanding the New Religions,* edited by Jacob Needleman and George Baker, 153–72. New York: Seabury, 1978.

Prebish, Charles S., and Kenneth K. Tanaka (eds.). *The Faces of Buddhism in America.* Berkeley: University of California Press, 1998.

Prothero, Stephen. *The White Buddhist: The Asian Odyssey of Henry Steel Olcott.* Bloomington: Indiana University Press, 1996.

Rapaport, Al, and Brian D. Hotchkiss (eds.). *Buddhism in America: The Official Record of the Landmark Conference on the Future of Buddhist Meditative Practices in the West.* Rutland, Vermont: Charles E. Tuttle, 1997.

Seager, Richard Hughes. *Buddhism in America.* New York: Columbia University Press, 2000.

Tamney, Joseph B. *American Society in the Buddhist Mirror.* New York: Garland, 1992.

Tweed, Thomas A. *The American Encounter with Buddhism, 1844–1912: Victorian Culture and the Limits of Dissent.* Bloomington: Indiana University Press, 1992.

Tweed, Thomas A., and Stephen Prothero (eds.). *Asian Religions in America: A Documentary History.* New York: Oxford University Press, 1999.

Williams, Duncan Ryūken, and Christopher S. Queen (eds.). *American Buddhism: Methods and Findings in Recent Scholarship.* Richmond, U.K.: Curzon Press, 1999.

Canada: General Overviews and Surveys

McLellan, Janet. "Buddhist Identities in Toronto: The Interplay of Local, National and Global Contexts." *Social Compass* 45, no. 2 (1998), 227–45.

—. *Many Petals of the Lotus: Five Asian Buddhist Communities in Toronto.* Toronto: University of Toronto Press, 1999.

Mullins, Mark R. "The Organizational Dilemmas of Ethnic Churches: A Case Study of Japanese Buddhism in Canada." *Sociological Analysis* 49, no. 3 (1988), 217–33.

Sugunasiri, Suwanda H. J. "Buddhism in Metropolitan Toronto: A Preliminary Overview." *Canadian Ethnic Studies* 21, no. 2 (1989), 83–103.

North America: Buddhist Traditions and Schools

CHINESE BUDDHISM

Chandler, Stuart. "Chinese Buddhism in America: Identity and Practice." In *The Faces of Buddhism in America,* edited by Charles S. Prebish and Kenneth K. Tanaka, 13–30. Berkeley: University of California Press, 1998.

—. "Placing Palms Together: Religious and Cultural Dimensions of the Hsi Lai Temple Political Donations Controversy." In *American Buddhism: Methods and Findings in Recent Scholarship*, edited by Duncan Ryūken Williams and Christopher S. Queen, 36–56. Richmond, U.K.: Curzon Press, 1999.

Lin, Irene. "Journey to the Far West: Chinese Buddhism in America." *Amerasia Journal* 22, no. 1 (1996), 107–32.

Wells, Marianne Kaye. *Chinese Temples in California*. San Francisco: R and E Research Associates Reprints, 1971. Original publication, Berkeley: University of California Press, 1962.

JAPANESE BUDDHISM: PURE LAND, OR JŌDO SHINSHŪ

Becker, Carl. "Japanese Pure Land Buddhism in Christian America." *Buddhist-Christian Studies* 10 (1990), 143–56.

Bloom, Alfred. "Shin Buddhism in America: A Social Perspective." In *The Faces of Buddhism in America*, edited by Charles S. Prebish and Kenneth K. Tanaka, 31–47. Berkeley: University of California Press, 1998.

Kashima, Tetsuden. *Buddhism in America: The Social Organization of an Ethnic Religious Organization*. Westport, Connecticut: Greenwood Press, 1977.

—. "The Buddhist Churches of America: Challenges for a Change in the Twenty-First Century." *Pacific World*, 2nd ser., 6 (Fall 1990), 28–40.

Tanaka, Kenneth K. "Issues of Ethnicity in the Buddhist Churches of America." In *American Buddhism: Methods and Findings in Recent Scholarship*, edited by Duncan Ryūken Williams and Christopher S. Queen, 3–19. Richmond, U.K.: Curzon Press, 1999.

—. *Ocean: An Introduction to Jodo-Shinshu Buddhism in America, A Dialogue with Buddhists and Others*. Berkeley: WisdomOcean, 1997.

Tuck, Donald R. *Buddhist Churches of America: Jodo Shinshu*. Lewiston, New York: E. Mellen Press, 1987.

Yanagawa, Keiichi (ed.). *Japanese Religions in California*. Tokyo: University of Tokyo, 1983.

JAPANESE BUDDHISM: ZEN

Aitken, Robert. *Original Dwelling Place: Zen Buddhist Essays*. Washington, D.C.: Counterpoint, 1997.

—. *Taking the Path of* Zen. San Francisco: North Point, 1982.

Asai, Senryō, and Duncan Ryūken Williams. "Japanese American Zen Temples: Cultural Identity and Economics." In *American Buddhism: Methods and Findings in Recent Scholarship*, edited by Duncan Ryūken Williams and Christopher S. Queen, 20–35. Richmond, U.K.: Curzon Press, 1999.

Finney, Henry C. "American Zen's 'Japan Connection': A Critical Case Study of Zen Buddhism's Diffusion to the West." *Sociological Analysis* 52, no. 4 (1991), 379–96.

Furlong, Monica. *Zen Effects: The Life of Alan Watts.* Boston: Houghton Mifflin, 1986.

Glassman, Bernard, and Rick Fields. *Instructions to the Cook: A Zen Master's Lessons in Living a Life That Matters.* New York: Bell Tower, 1996.

Hori, C. Victor Sōgen. "Japanese Zen in America: Americanizing the Face in the Mirror." In *The Faces of Buddhism in America,* edited by Charles S. Prebish and Kenneth K. Tanaka, 50–78. Berkeley: University of California Press, 1998.

—. "Sweet-and-Sour Buddhism." *Tricycle: The Buddhist Review* 4, no. 1 (1994), 48–52.

Hoshino, Eiki. "The Birth of an American Sangha: An Analysis of a Zen Center in America." In *Japanese Religions in California,* edited by Keiichi Yanagawa, 29–72. Tokyo: University of Tokyo Department of Religious Studies, 1983.

Kapleau, Philip. *The Three Pillars of Zen: Teaching, Practice, and Enlightenment.* 25th anniversary ed. New York: Anchor, 1989. Original publication, Tokyo: Weatherhill, 1965.

Kraft, Kenneth. "Recent Developments in North American Zen." In *Zen: Tradition and Transition,* edited by Kenneth Kraft, 178–98. New York: Grove, 1988.

Loori, John Daido. *The Eight Gates of Zen: Spiritual Training in an American Zen Monastery.* Mount Tremper, New York: Dharma Communications, 1992.

—. *The Heart of Being: Moral and Ethical Teachings of Zen Buddhism.* Boston: Charles E. Tuttle, 1996.

Preston, David L. *The Social Organization of Zen Practice: Constructing Transcultural Reality.* Cambridge: Cambridge University Press, 1988.

Schneider, David. *Street Zen: The Life and Work of Issan Dorsey.* Boston: Shambhala, 1993.

Senzaki, Nyogen, Soen Nakagawa, and Eido Shimano. *Namu Dai Bosa: A Transmission of Zen Buddhism to America,* edited by Louis Nordstrom. New York: Theatre Arts Books, 1976.

Sharf, Robert H. "Sanbokyodan: Zen and the Way of the New Religions." *Japanese Journal of Religious Studies* 22, nos. 3–4 (1995), 417–58.

Storlie, Erik Fraser. *Nothing on My Mind: Berkeley, LSD, Two Zen Masters, and a Life on the Dharma Trail.* Boston: Shambhala, 1996.

Tworkov, Helen. *Zen in America: Profiles of Five Teachers.* New York: Kodansha America, 1994. Original publication, San Francisco: North Point Press, 1989.

Watts, Alan. *Beat Zen, Square Zen, and Zen.* Rev. ed. San Francisco: City Lights Books, 1959.

JAPANESE BUDDHISM: NICHIREN SHŌSHŪ AND SŌKA GAKKAI

Hammond, Phillip E., and David W. Machacek. *Soka Gakkai in America: Accommodation and Conversion.* Oxford: Oxford University Press, 1999.

Hurst, Jane. "Nichiren Shoshu and Soka Gakkai in America: The Pioneer Spirit." In *The Faces of Buddhism in America,* edited by Charles S. Prebish and Kenneth K. Tanaka, 79–97. Berkeley: University of California Press, 1998.

—. *Nichiren Shoshu Buddhism and the Soka Gakkai in America: The Ethos of a New Religious Movement.* New York: Garland, 1992.

Metraux, Daniel. *The Lotus and the Maple Leaf: The Soka Gakkai Buddhist Movement in Canada.* Lewiston, New York: University Press of America, 1996.

Snow, David A. *Shakubuku: A Study of the Nichiren Shoshu Buddhist Movement in America, 1960–1975.* New York: Garland, 1993.

VIETNAMESE AND KOREAN BUDDHISM

Barber, A. W., and Cuong T. Nguyen. "Vietnamese Buddhism in North America: Tradition and Acculturation." In *The Faces of Buddhism in America,* edited by Charles S. Prebish and Kenneth K. Tanaka, 129–46. Berkeley: University of California Press, 1998.

Breyer, Chloe Anne. "Religious Liberty in Law and Practice: Vietnamese Home Temples and the First Amendment." *Journal of Church and State* 35 (1993), 368–401.

Eui-Young Yu. "The Growth of Korean Buddhism in the United States, with Special Reference to Southern California." *Pacific World: Journal of the Institute of Buddhist Studies,* NS, 4 (1988), 82–93.

Farber, Don, and Rick Fields. *Taking Refuge in L.A.: Life in a Vietnamese Buddhist Temple.* New York: Aperture Foundation, 1987.

Hein, Jeremy. *From Vietnam, Laos and Cambodia: Refugee Experience in the United States.* New York: Twayne, 1995.

Rutledge, Paul James. *The Vietnamese Experience in America.* Bloomington: Indiana University Press, 1992.

Soeng, Mu. "Korean Buddhism in America: A New Style of Zen." In *The Faces of Buddhism in America,* edited by Charles S. Prebish and Kenneth K. Tanaka, 117–28. Berkeley: University of California Press, 1998.

LAOTIAN AND CAMBODIAN BUDDHISM

Canda, Edward R., and Thitiya Phaobtong. "Buddhism as a Support System for Southeast Asian Refugees." *Social Work* 37, no. 1 (1992), 61–7.

Hein, Jeremy. *From Vietnam, Laos and Cambodia: Refugee Experience in the United States.* New York: Twayne, 1995.

Smith-Hefner, Nancy J. *Khmer American: Identity and Moral Education in a Diasporic Community.* Berkeley: University of California Press, 1999.

Van Esterik, Penny. "Ritual and the Performance of Buddhist Identity among Lao Buddhists in North America." In *American Buddhism: Methods and*

Findings in Recent Scholarship, edited by Duncan Ryūken Williams and Christopher S. Queen, 57–68. Richmond, U.K.: Curzon Press, 1999.

—. *Taking Refuge: Lao Buddhists in North America*. Tempe, Arizona: Program for Southeast Asian Studies, Arizona State University, 1992.

THERAVĀDA TRADITION AND VIPASSANĀ MEDITATION

Fronsdal, Gil. "Insight Meditation in the United States: Life, Liberty, and the Pursuit of Happiness." In *The Faces of Buddhism in America*, edited by Charles S. Prebish and Kenneth K. Tanaka, 164–80. Berkeley: University of California Press, 1998.

Numrich, Paul David. *Old Wisdom in the New World: Americanization in Two Immigrant Theravada Buddhist Temples*. Knoxville: University of Tennessee Press, 1996.

—. "Theravada Buddhism in America: Prospect for the Sangha." In *The Faces of Buddhism in America*, edited by Charles S. Prebish and Kenneth K. Tanaka, 147–61. Berkeley: University of California Press, 1998.

—. "Vinaya in Theravada Temples in the United States." *Journal of Buddhist Ethics* 1 (1994), 23–32.

TIBETAN BUDDHISM

Bell, Sandra. "'Crazy Wisdom,' Charisma, and the Transmission of Buddhism in the United States." *Nova Religio: The Journal of Alternative and Emergent Religions* 2, no. 1 (1998), 55–75.

Butterfield, Stephen. *The Double Mirror: A Skeptical Journey into Buddhist Tantra*. Berkeley: North Atlantic, 1994.

Goss, Robert E. "Buddhist Studies at Naropa: Sectarian or Academic?" In *American Buddhism: Methods and Findings in Recent Scholarship*, edited by Duncan Ryūken Williams and Christopher S. Queen, 215–37. Richmond, U.K.: Curzon Press, 1999.

Kane, Stephanie. "Sacred Deviance and AIDS in a North American Buddhist Community." *Law and Policy* 16 (1994), 323–39.

Korom, Frank J. "Old Age Tibet in New Age America." In *Constructing Tibetan Culture: Contemporary Perspectives*, edited by Frank Korom, 73–97. Saint-Hyacinthe, Québec: World Heritage Press, 1997.

—. "Tibetans in Exile: A Euro-American Perspective." *Passages: Journal of Transnational and Transcultural Studies* 1, no. 1 (1999), 1–23.

Lavine, Amy. "Tibetan Buddhism in America: The Development of American Vajrayāna." In *The Faces of Buddhism in America*, edited by Charles S. Prebish and Kenneth K. Tanaka, 99–115. Berkeley: University of California Press, 1998.

Surya Das, Lama. *Awakening the Buddha Within: Tibetan Wisdom for the Western World*. New York: Broadway, 1997.

Swick, David. *Thunder and Ocean: Shambhala and Buddhism in Nova Scotia*. Lawrencetown Beach, Nova Scotia: Pottersfield Press, 1996.

Thurmann, Robert A. F. *Inner Revolution: Life, Liberty, and the Pursuit of Real Happiness.* Edited by Amy Hertz. New York: Riverhead, 1999.

SOUTH AMERICA

Clarke, Peter B. "The Cultural Impact of New Religions in Latin and Central America and the Caribbean with Special Reference to Japanese New Religions." *Journal of Latin American Cultural Studies* 4, no. 1 (1995), 117–26.
—. "Japanese New Religious Movements in Brazil: From Ethnic to 'Universal' Religions." In *New Religious Movements: Challenge and Response*, edited by Bryan Wilson and Jamie Cresswell, 197–210. London: Routledge, 1999.
Ozaki, André Masao, S. J. *As Religiõs Japonesas no Brasil* (Japanese Religions in Brazil). São Paulo: Loyola, 1990.
Paranhos, Wilson. *Nuvens Cristalinas em Luar de Prata* (Clear Clouds over a Silver Moon). Porto Alegre, Brazil: Fundação Educational Editorial Universalista (FEEU), 1994.
Pereira, Ronan Alves. "Japanese Religions and Religious Diversity in Brazil." *Japan Studies Review* 3 (1999), 87–100.
Rocha, Cristina Moreira. "The Appropriation of Zen Buddhism in Brazil," *Japan Studies Review* 4 (2000), 33–52.
—. "Buddhism in Brazil: A Bibliography" (2000). http://sites.uol.com.br/cmrocha/ [8 Dec. 2001].
—. "Zen Buddhism in Brazil: Japanese or Brazilian?" *Journal of Global Buddhism* 1 (2000), 31–55.
Usarski, Frank (ed.). *Budismo no Brasil: Uma religião entre tradição e adaptação.* São Paulo: Verbo Humano, 2002.

AUSTRALIA AND NEW ZEALAND

Adam, Enid. "Buddhist Women in Australia." *Journal of Global Buddhism* 1 (2000), 138–53.
Adam, Enid, and Philip J. Hughes. *The Buddhists in Australia.* Canberra: Australian Government Publishing Service, 1996.
Bentley, Peter. "Religious Community Profiles." *Australian Religious Studies Review* 10 (1997), 47–65.
Bouma, Gary D. (ed.). *Many Religions, All Australian.* Melbourne: Christian Research Association, 1996.
Bucknell, Roderick S. "The Buddhist Experience in Australia." In *Religion and Multiculturalism in Australia: Essays in Honour of Victor Hayes*, edited by Norman Habel, 214–24. Adelaide: Australian Association for the Study of Religions, 1992.
—. "Engaged Buddhism in Australia." In *Engaged Buddhism in the West*, edited by Christopher S. Queen, 468–81. Boston: Wisdom, 2000.
Croucher, Paul. *Buddhism in Australia: 1848–1988.* Kensington: New South Wales University Press, 1989.

de Jong, Klaas. "Buddhism in Queensland." *Buddhism Today: Journal of the Buddhist Federation of Australia* 1 (1986), 8–16.

Lyall, Graeme. "Buddhism: Australia's Reaction to a New Phenomenon." *Without Prejudice* 7 (1994), 30–5.

Spuler, Michelle. "Buddhism in Australia: A Bibliography" (2001). http://www.spuler.org/ms/biblio.htm [8 Dec. 2001].

—. "Characteristics of Buddhism in Australia." *Journal of Contemporary Religion* 15, no. 1 (2000), 29–44.

—. *Facets of the Diamond: Developments in Australian Buddhism.* Richmond, U.K.: Curzon Press, 2002.

AFRICA

Batchelor, Stephen. "No Man's Land: A Letter from South Africa." *Tricycle: The Buddhist Review* 11, no. 4 (1993), 68–9.

Clasquin, Michel. "Transplanting Buddhism: An Investigation into the Spread of Buddhism, with Reference to Buddhism in South Africa." Ph.D. diss., University of South Africa, Pretoria, 1999.

Clasquin, Michel, and Jacobus S. Krüger (eds.). *Buddhism and Africa.* Pretoria: University of South Africa Press, 1999.

Krüger, Jacobus S. *Along the Edges: Religion in South Africa—Bushman, Christian, Buddhist.* Pretoria: University of South Africa, 1995.

Nash, J. "Tip of the Tiger's Tail: Buddhism in South Africa." *Middle Way* 65 (May 1990), 35–9.

Van Loon, Louis H. "Buddhism in South Africa." In *Living Faiths in South Africa,* edited by John W. de Gruchy and Martin Prozesky, 209–16. Cape Town: David Philip, 1995.

—. "The Indian Buddhist Community in South Africa: Its Historical Origins and Socio-Religious Attitudes and Practices." *Religion in Southern Africa* 1, no. 1 (1980), 3–18.

Wratten, Darrel. "Buddhism in South Africa: From Textual Imagination to Contextual Innovation." Ph.D. diss., University of Cape Town, Cape Town, 1995.

—. "Engaged Buddhism in South Africa." In *Engaged Buddhism in the West,* edited by Christopher S. Queen, 446–67. Boston: Wisdom, 2000.

TOPICAL ISSUES IN BUDDHISM BEYOND ASIA

Academic and Disciplinary Issues

Brear, Douglas. "Early Assumptions in Western Buddhist Studies." *Religion* 7, no. 2 (1977), 136–59.

Cabezón, José. "Buddhist Studies as a Discipline and the Role of Theory." *Journal of the International Association of Buddhist Studies* 18, no. 2 (Winter 1995), 231–68.

de Jong, J. W. *A Brief History of Buddhist Studies in Europe and America.* 2nd ed. Delhi: Sri Satguru Publications, 1987.

Hayes, Richard P. "The Internet as Window onto American Buddhism." In *American Buddhism: Methods and Findings in Recent Scholarship*, edited by Duncan Ryūken Williams and Christopher S. Queen, 168–79. Richmond, U.K.: Curzon Press, 1999.

Hubbard, Jamie. "Upping the Ante: budstud@millenium.end.edu." *Journal of the International Association of Buddhist Studies* 18, no. 2 (1995), 309–22.

Lopez, Donald S., Jr. *Prisoners of Shangri-La: Tibetan Buddhism and the West.* Chicago: University of Chicago Press, 1998.

Lopez, Donald S., Jr. (ed.). *Curators of the Buddha: The Study of Buddhism under Colonialism.* Chicago: University of Chicago Press, 1995.

Nattier, Jan. "Buddhist Studies in the Post-Colonial Age." *Journal of the American Academy of Religion* 65, no. 2 (1997), 469–85.

Prebish, Charles S. "The Academic Study of Buddhism in America: A Silent Sangha." In *American Buddhism: Methods and Findings in Recent Scholarship*, edited by Duncan Ryūken Williams and Christopher S. Queen, 183–214. Richmond, U.K.: Curzon Press, 1999.

——. "The Academic Study of Buddhism in the United States: A Current Analysis." *Religion* 24, no. 3 (1994), 271–8.

Webb, Russell. "Buddhist Studies in the West." *Buddhist Quarterly* (London Buddhist Vihāra) 6, no. 4 (1974), 10–7.

Williams, Duncan Ryūken. "Where to Study?" *Tricycle: The Buddhist Review* 6, no. 3 (1997), 68–9, 115–7.

Ethnicity Issues

Fields, Rick. "Divided Dharma: White Buddhists, Ethnic Buddhists and Racism." In *The Faces of Buddhism in America*, edited by Charles S. Prebish and Kenneth K. Tanaka, 196–206. Berkeley: University of California Press, 1998.

hooks, bell. "Waking Up to Racism." *Tricycle: The Buddhist Review*, no. 13 (Fall 1994), 42–5.

Mullins, Mark R. "The Transplantation of Religion in Comparative Sociological Perspective." *Japanese Religion* 16, no. 2 (1990), 43–62.

Nattier, Jan. "Buddhism Comes to Main Street." *Wilson Quarterly* 21, no. 2 (Spring 1997), 72–80.

——. "Visible and Invisible: The Politics of Representation in Buddhist America." *Tricycle: The Buddhist Review*, no. 17 (1995), 42–9.

——. "Who is a Buddhist? Charting the Landscape of Buddhist America." In *The Faces of Buddhist America*, edited by Charles S. Prebish and Kenneth K. Tanaka, 183–95. Berkeley: University of California Press, 1998.

Prebish, Charles S. "Two Buddhisms Reconsidered." *Buddhist Studies Review* 10, no. 2 (1993), 187–206.

Tweed, Thomas A. "Asian Religions in America: Reflections on an Emerging Subfield." In *Religious Diversity and American Religious History: Studies in Traditions and Cultures,* edited by Walter Conser and Sumner Twiss, 189–217. Athens: University of Georgia Press, 1998.

—. "Night-Stand Buddhists and Other Creatures: Sympathizers, Adherents, and the Study of Religion." In *American Buddhism: Methods and Findings in Recent Scholarship,* edited by Duncan Ryūken Williams and Christopher S. Queen, 71–90. Richmond, U.K.: Curzon Press, 1999.

Socially Engaged Buddhism

Badiner, Allan Hunt (ed.). *Dharma Gaia: A Harvest of Essays in Buddhism and Ecology.* Berkeley: Parallax, 1990.

Eppsteiner, Fred (ed.). *The Path of Compassion: Writings on Socially Engaged Buddhism.* Berkeley: Parallax, 1988.

Jones, Ken. *The Social Face of Buddhism: An Approach to Political and Social Activism.* London: Wisdom, 1989.

Kraft, Kenneth. *The Wheel of Engaged Buddhism: A New Map of the Path.* New York: Weatherhill, 1999.

Kraft, Kenneth (ed.). *Inner Peace, World Peace: Essays on Buddhism and Nonviolence.* Albany: State University of New York Press, 1992.

Kotler, Arnold (ed.). *Engaged Buddhist Reader: Ten Years of Engaged Buddhist Publishing.* Berkeley: Parallax, 1996.

Nhat Hanh, Thich. *Interbeing: Fourteen Guidelines for Engaged Buddhism.* Rev. ed. Edited by Fred Eppsteiner. Berkeley: Parallax, 1993.

Queen, Christopher S. (ed.). *Engaged Buddhism in the West.* Boston: Wisdom, 2000.

Sponberg, Alan. "Green Buddhism and the Hierarchy of Compassion." *The Western Buddhist Review* 1 (December 1994), 131–55.

Victoria, Brian Daizen. "Engaged Buddhism: A Skeleton in the Closet?" *Journal of Global Buddhism* 2 (2001), 72–91.

Women's Roles, Gender, and Lifestyle Issues in Western Buddhism

Austin, James H. *Zen and the Brain: Toward an Understanding of Meditation and Consciousness.* Cambridge: Massachusetts Institute of Technology Press, 1998.

Boucher, Sandy. *Opening the Lotus: A Woman's Guide to Buddhism.* Boston: Beacon, 1997.

—. *Turning the Wheel: American Women Creating the New Buddhism.* Updated and expanded ed. Boston: Beacon, 1993. Original ed., San Francisco: Harper and Row, 1988.

Butler, Katy. "Encountering the Shadow in Buddhist America." *Common Boundary* 83 (May/June 1990), 14–22.

—. "Events are the Teacher: Working through the Crisis at San Francisco Zen Center." *CoEvolution Quarterly* 40 (Winter 1983), 112–23.

Corless, Roger. "Coming Out in the Sangha: Queer Community in American Buddhism." In *The Faces of Buddhism in America,* edited by Charles S. Prebish and Kenneth K. Tanaka, 253–65. Berkeley: University of California Press, 1998.

Dresser, Marianne (ed.). *Buddhist Women on the Edge: Contemporary Perspectives from the Western Frontier.* Berkeley: North Atlantic, 1996.

Epstein, Mark. *Going on Being: Buddhism and the Way of Change, A Positive Psychology for the West.* New York: Broadway, 2001.

Fox, Stephen. "Boomer Dharma: The Evolution of Alternative Spiritual Communities in Modern New Mexico." In *Religion in Modern New Mexico,* edited by Ferenc Szasz and Richard Etalain, 145–70. Albuquerque: University of New Mexico Press, 1997.

Friedman, Lenore. *Meetings with Remarkable Women: Buddhist Teachers in America.* Boston: Shambhala, 1987.

Gross, Rita. *Buddhism after Patriarchy: A Feminist History, Analysis, and Reconstruction of Buddhism.* Albany: State University of New York Press, 1993.

—. "Helping the Iron Bird Fly: Western Buddhist Women and Issues of Authority in the Late 1990s." In *The Faces of Buddhism in America,* edited by Charles S. Prebish and Kenneth K. Tanaka, 238–52. Berkeley: University of California Press, 1998.

Klein, Anne C. *Meeting the Great Bliss Queen: Buddhists, Feminists, and the Art of Self.* Boston: Beacon, 1995.

Sidor, Ellen S. (ed.). *A Gathering of Spirit: Women Teaching in American Buddhism.* Cumberland, Rhode Island: Primary Point Press, 1987.

Tsomo, Karma Lekshe (ed.). *Buddhism through American Women's Eyes.* Ithaca, New York: Snow Lion, 1995.

Wellwood, John. *Toward a Psychology of Awakening: Buddhism, Psychotherapy, and a Path of Personal and Spiritual Transformation.* Boston: Shambhala, 2000.

Contributors

MARTIN BAUMANN is Professor of the History of Religions at the University of Lucerne, Switzerland, and research fellow in the Department of Religious Studies at Hannover University, Germany. His fields of interest are the spread and adaptation of Buddhist and Hindu traditions outside of Asia, diaspora and migrant studies, and theory and method in the history of religions. He has published extensively on these topics, in both German and English, and is editor of the online *Journal of Global Buddhism* (http://www.globalbuddhism.org).

SANDRA BELL is a Lecturer in the Department of Anthropology at the University of Durham, U.K. She has published papers on the expansion and development of Buddhism in the West in the *Journal of Contemporary Religion, Novo Religio: The Journal of Alternative and Emergent Religions,* and other academic journals dealing with religion. She has also written on gender and sexuality in Theravāda Buddhism. She is coeditor, with Simon Coleman, of *The Anthropology of Friendship: Community beyond Kinship* (1999) and, with Elisa Sobo, of *Celibacy, Culture and Society: The Anthropology of Sexual Abstinence* (2001).

MICHEL CLASQUIN lectures in the Department of Religious Studies at the University of South Africa. A practicing Buddhist since 1984, he is currently not affiliated with any Buddhist group.

GIL FRONSDAL teaches at the Sati Center for Buddhist Studies in Palo Alto, California. He has a doctorate in Buddhist Studies from Stanford University. He is a Buddhist meditation teacher at the Insight Meditation

Center of the Mid-Peninsula, also in Palo Alto, and at Spirit Rock Meditation Center in Marin County, California.

IAN HARRIS was educated at the Universities of Cambridge and Lancaster. He is a Reader in Religious Studies at St. Martin's College, Lancaster, and cofounder, with Peter Harvey, of the U.K. Association for Buddhist Studies. The author of *The Continuity of Madhyamaka and Yogacara in Early Mahayana Buddhism* (1991) and editor of *Buddhism and Politics in Twentieth Century Asia* (2001), he has written widely on Buddhism in the modern world, with particular reference to environmental ethics. He is currently working on a study of Buddhism in Cambodia, to be published by the University of Hawaii Press.

BRUCE MATTHEWS is the C.B. Lumsden Professor of Comparative Religion at Acadia University, Nova Scotia. A former Commonwealth Fellow in Pāli and Buddhist Civilization at the University of Ceylon, Peradeniya, he completed his graduate studies at McMaster University, Ontario. The author of *Craving and Salvation: A Study of Buddhist Soteriology* (1983) and many articles, his research now focuses on Buddhism and politics in Sri Lanka and Myanmar.

DAVID L. MCMAHAN is an Assistant Professor in the Department of Religious Studies at Franklin and Marshall College. He has also taught at the University of California, Santa Barbara, and the University of Vermont. He is the author of *Empty Vision: Metaphor and Visionary Imagery in Mahāyāna Buddhism* (2002), "New Frontiers in Buddhism: Three Recent Works on Buddhism in America" in *Journal of Global Buddhism*, "Orality, Writing and Authority in South Asian Buddhism: Visionary Literature and the Struggle for Legitimacy in the Mahayana" in *History of Religions*, and "A Long Awaited Call: A Buddhist Response," in *Ethics and World Religions: Cross-Cultural Case Studies*, edited by Regina Wentzel Wolfe and Christine E. Gudorf (1999).

FRANZ AUBREY METCALF received his Ph.D. from the Divinity School at the University of Chicago, where he wrote his dissertation on American Zen practice. He has published scholarly work on both contemporary Buddhism and the psychology of religion and is book review editor for the *Journal of Global Buddhism*. He co-chairs the Person, Culture, and Religion Group of the American Academy of Religion and teaches Comparative Religion at California State University, Los Angeles. Franz is a founding member of the Forge Institute for Spirituality and Social Change and author of two books applying Buddhist teachings to contemporary life.

LIONEL OBADIA is lecturer in Anthropology in the Charles-de-Gaulle University of Arts and Social Sciences at Lille, France. He is the author of *Bouddhisme et Occident: La diffusion du bouddhisme tibétain en France* (1999) and the forthcoming *Le bouddhisme en Occident*. He has published articles and reviews and edited a special issue, *Le bouddhisme en Occident: approches sociologiques et anthropologiques*, for the Belgian journal, *Recherches Sociologiques*.

DOUGLAS M. PADGETT is a Ph.D. candidate in the Study of Religion at Indiana University, where he has concentrated on East Asian Buddhism and issues relating to identity, migration, and religion. He is currently working on a dissertation on Buddhism in both Vietnam and overseas Vietnamese communities.

CHARLES S. PREBISH is Professor of Religious Studies at Pennsylvania State University. He is the author of eleven books, including *Luminous Passage: The Practice and Study of Buddhism in America* (1999). He is a founding coeditor of two online publications, *Journal of Buddhist Ethics* and *Journal of Global Buddhism*. He is a former officer and member of the board of directors of the International Association of Buddhist Studies and has held the Numata Chair of Buddhist Studies at the University of Calgary, as well as a Rockefeller Foundation National Humanities Fellowship at the Centre for the Study of Religion at the University of Toronto.

CHRISTOPHER S. QUEEN is the Dean of Students for Continuing Education and lecturer on the Study of Religion in the Faculty of Arts and Sciences, Harvard University. He has edited and contributed to *Engaged Buddhism in the West* (2000), *American Buddhism: Methods and Findings in Recent Scholarship* (1999, with Duncan Ryūken Williams), and *Engaged Buddhism: Buddhist Liberation Movements in Asia* (1996, with Sallie B. King). He is currently working on a monograph on the life and teachings of B.R. Ambedkar and the rise of engaged Buddhism.

RICHARD HUGHES SEAGER holds a Ph.D. in the Study of Religion from Harvard University. He has written *The World's Parliament of Religions: The East / West Encounter, Chicago 1893* (1995) and *Buddhism in America*

(1999). He is currently Associate Professor of Religion at Hamilton College in Clinton, New York.

JUDITH SIMMER-BROWN, Ph.D., is chair of the Religious Studies Department at Naropa University, where she has been a faculty member since 1978. She is also an *ācārya* (senior teacher) in the Shambhala Buddhist lineage of Chögyam Trungpa Rinpoche of the Tibetan Kagyu and Nyingma Buddhism traditions. In 1981, she organized the first symposium that launched conversations on women in Western Buddhism, and she has been part of the conversation between communities ever since. She writes on American Buddhism, Buddhist-Christian dialogue, and women and Buddhism. She is author of *Dākinī's Warm Breath: The Feminine Principle in Tibetan Buddhism* (2001).

MICHELLE SPULER formerly taught in the Department of Religious Studies at the Victoria University of Wellington, New Zealand, and at Colorado College. She received her Ph.D., on the development of Zen Buddhism in Australia, from the University of Queensland in Brisbane, Australia. She recently completed a book, to be published in 2002, based on her doctoral thesis.

AJAHN TIRADHAMMO was born in Canada in 1949. He was introduced to Buddhism during his university studies and learned meditation in Sri Lanka during a trip to South Asia in 1971. He then traveled to Thailand in 1973 for further meditation practice. There he undertook ordination as a novice and, in 1974, as a *bhikkhu*. Seeking further meditation guidance, he studied with Ajahn Chah for six years before moving to the Western Branch Monastery in Britain under Ajahn Sumedho. He spent six years as one of the senior monks in several of the branches in Britain, then helped establish a new monastery in Switzerland, where he has been resident for the last twelve years.

KARMA LEKSHE TSOMO is Assistant Professor of Theology and Religious Studies at the University of San Diego. An American nun practicing in the Tibetan tradition, she is secretary of Sakyadhita: International Association of Buddhist Women and has been active in the international Buddhist women's movement. She completed her doctorate in philosophy at the University of Hawaii, with a dissertation on death and identity in China and Tibet, and has edited a number of books on women in Buddhism, including *Sakyadhita: Daughters of the Buddha* (1988), *Buddhism through*

American Women's Eyes (1995), *Innovative Buddhist Women: Swimming against the Stream* (2000), *Sisters in Solitude: Two Traditions of Monastic Ethics for Women* (1996), and *Buddhist Women Across Cultures: Realizations* (1999).

THOMAS A. TWEED is Professor of Religious Studies at the University of North Carolina at Chapel Hill, where he also serves as Associate Dean for Undergraduate Curricula. He edited *Retelling U.S. Religious History* (1997) and coedited, with Stephen Prothero, *Asian Religions in America: A Documentary History* (1999). He also wrote *The American Encounter with Buddhism, 1844–1912: Victorian Culture and the Limits of Dissent*, which was originally published in 1992 and recently reissued in a revised edition with a new preface (2000). His ethnographic study, *Our Lady of the Exile: Diasporic Religion at a Cuban Catholic Shrine in Miami* (1997), won the American Academy of Religion's Award for Excellence.

FRANK USARSKI, Ph.D., lectured between 1988 and 1997 at German universities in Hannover, Oldenburg, Bremen, Erfurt, Chemnitz, and Leipzig. Since 1998, he has held an appointment as a long-term Visiting Professor at the Pontifical Catholic University (PUC) of São Paulo, Brazil. Among the projects he has undertaken at the PUC has been the founding of a research group on Buddhism in Latin America, which is currently focusing its investigations on the history and contemporary situation of Buddhism in Brazil.

B. ALAN WALLACE began his formal studies of Tibetan Buddhism and language in Germany in 1970, and he has been teaching Tibetan Buddhist philosophy and meditation in Europe and America since 1976. Ordained as a Buddhist monk for fourteen years, he has trained under and served as interpreter for many eminent Tibetan scholars and contemplatives, including His Holiness the Dalai Lama. He completed his undergraduate education at Amherst College, where he studied Physics and the Philosophy of Science, and he earned his doctorate in Religious Studies at Stanford University, where he pursued interdisciplinary research into ways of exploring the nature of consciousness. He has written, translated, edited, or contributed to over thirty books on many facets of Tibetan Buddhism and culture, as well as the interface between religion and science. He presently teaches courses on Tibetan Buddhism and the interface between science and religion in the Department of Religious Studies at the University of California, Santa Barbara.

SYLVIA WETZEL, born in 1949, is a high school teacher of politics and language and, since 1977, of the study of Buddhism. She worked for twenty years in Buddhist institutions—at centers, at publishing companies, as a board member of the German Buddhist Union (DBU), as editor of the Buddhist quarterly *Lotusblätter*, as a full-time lay teacher of relaxation, meditation, and Buddhism in Europe, as a founding member of Sakyadhita (Bodhgaya, 1987), with the Network of Western Buddhist Teachers (Dharamsala, 1993), and with Women Awake (Köln, 1999). She is currently initiating a nonprofit International Buddhist Academy (Berlin, 2000).

DUNCAN RYŪKEN WILLIAMS received his Ph.D. in the study of Buddhism at Harvard University and is currently Assistant Professor of East Asian Buddhism at the University of California, Irvine. His research interests include medieval and early modern Japanese Zen Buddhism, the relationship between Buddhism and hot springs, and the history of Japanese-American Buddhism. His recent publications include two coedited volumes, *American Buddhism: Methods and Findings in Recent Scholarship* (1998) and *Buddhism and Ecology* (1997).

Index

Compositor: G&S Typesetters, Inc.
Text: 10/13 Aldus
Display: Aldus
Printer and binder: Maple-Vail Manufacturing Group